Adamant:
The Life and Pursuits of Dorothy McGuire

by Giancarlo Stampalia

BearManor Media

Orlando, Florida

Adamant: The Life and Pursuits of Dorothy McGuire
© 2020 Giancarlo Stampalia. All Rights Reserved.

No portion of this publication may be reproduced, stored, and/or copied electronically (except for academic use as a source), nor transmitted in any form or by any means without the prior written permission of the publisher and/or author.

The stills illustrating this volume were issued by the original copyright owners; unless noted otherwise, they are reproduced courtesy of the author's collection (no copyright ownership implied or intended). The same applies to the news passages quoted herein.

[Front cover illustration: an early studio portrait of Dorothy McGuire, circa 1945, one that reveals both her vivaciousness and her positive outlook.]

Published in the USA by
BearManor Media
1317 Edgewater Dr. #110
Orlando, FL 32804
www.BearManorMedia.com

Softcover Edition
ISBN-10: 1-62933-554-1
ISBN-13: 978-1-62933-554-4

Printed in the United States of America

Adamant:
The Life and Pursuits of Dorothy McGuire

Table of Contents

Acknowledgments — xi
Caveats — xv

Part I: *Solve*

1. Exordium — 1
2. What's in a Name I — 11
3. What's in a Name II: Δωροθεα — 15
4. Omaha and the Wagon of Thespis — 21
5. A Claudia Is Born — 35
6. To Selznick or Not to Selznick — 67
7. Swopes — 83
8. 20th Century-Fox, 1943–1959 — 129
9. La Jolla Playhouse, 1947–1959 — 205
10. RKO Radio Pictures, 1945–1951 — 249
11. Radio Days, 1938–1955 — 285
12. Tantamount, Adamant, and Others — 367
13. Other Studios, 1951–1973 — 389
14. Other Theater, 1945–1971 — 459
15. *Iguana* — 491
16. Theater after *Iguana*, 1976–1987 — 511
17. Television, 1938–1990 — 525
18. Olympian Jamborees — 555

Part II: *Coagula*

1. Mysteries and Un-Definitions — 595
2. *Turangalila* I: A Streak of Bravery — 601
3. *Turangalila* II: Apollonian — 613
4. The Conundrums of Commerce — 633
5. *Turangalila* III: In the Eye of the Beholder — 651

6.	*Turangalîla* IV: Positivity	673
7.	*Turangalîla* V: Tapping the World Source	697
8.	*Turangalîla* VI: Shinings	709
9.	*Turangalîla* VII: Adamant	713

Afterword: What's in a Name III   727
Selected Bibliography   741
Index   755

Consider ye the seed from which you sprang;
Ye were not made to live like unto brutes,

But for pursuit of virtue and of knowledge.[1]

Dante Alighieri, *The Divine Comedy*

Solve et coagula

Alchemical motto

---

[1] Dante Alighieri, *The Divine Comedy*, translated by Henry Wadsworth Longfellow, Ticknor and Fields, 1867. Inferno, Canto XXVI, tercet 40, vv. 118–120. The original Italian text is: "*Considerate la vostra semenza: fatti non foste a viver come bruti, ma per seguir virtute e canoscenza.*"

Acknowledgments

It is a pleasant state of things that grants us the opportunity to feel gratitude towards other human beings, for it means that those beings' lives and our own have intersected fruitfully. In the case of the creation of a biography, its author finds himself in a position to disrupt people's routines and intrude in their lives in order to ask them for help. Reactions to this kind of disruption may range from indifference (I reached out to several famous people who knew or worked with Dorothy, and the result was silence) to joyful participation. I am happy to report that a sizable number of the individuals I contacted fell into the latter category. To them, I am very grateful.

First of all, I would not have been able to advance as well as I did in drafting Dorothy's biography without the help of her family and friends, who happily shared their memories with me. Briefly, I was in touch with Dorothy's son Mark Swope shortly before his passing; although he was happy about the project and supportive of my work, unfortunately he was not able to contribute. His sister, Topo Swope, did, enthusiastically. I am indebted to both of them, and feel great sorrow that Mark was not able to be part of the team. My heartfelt thanks also go to family friends Jim Fernald, Dwight Holing, and Dan "Peter" Levin, who were willing to evoke vivid recollections of someone they loved.

To my dear friend Maria Bulian, indefatigable in her willingness to keep the fire of my writing burning and to offer opinions and suggestions about the work in progress I presented to her, my thanks and love.

To Tovah Feldshuh, my thanks for her enthusiastic participation in the book, and for her testimony. Enthusiastic thanks also go to actor Daniel J. Travanti, brilliantly argumentative as always, and to film historian Dan Van Neste. My gratitude also goes to portrait artist Don Bachardy, for sharing his memories about Dorothy and contributing some of his portraits of her.

To my ever-gracious friend, C. Robert Rotter of the website "Glamour Girls of the Silver Screen" (www.glamourgirlsofthesilverscreen.com), my most sincere thanks for his urbane savviness, his knowledge of Hollywood glamour and his lasting help and support.

To Roma Kail, Head, Reader Services (Research and Instruction Librarian) of the Victoria University Library in the University of Toronto, for being a cheerful and generous purveyor of information, beyond the call of duty.

My warmest, most enthusiastic thanks to Peggy Reall, Director of Marketing and Public Relations at the Omaha Community Playhouse, for her surprising speed and friendliness in helping me with photographic material from the Omaha, Nebraska, theater where it all started for Dorothy. Similarly warm thanks are due to Gvido Trepsa, Director of the Nicholas Roerich Museum in New York, and to Don Bachardy's longtime assistant, artist Phyllis Green, for digging up photographs of Mr. Machardy's work to be included in the book. A big thank you also to photographer Robert Yasinsac, for providing a lovely photograph of the famed Hudson Valley mansion The Croft.

To Rocco Romano and Lorenzo Slama of Legatoria Romano Cartabianca, Trieste, my very friendly thanks for being practical, generous companions to my writings, and for helping me make physical what begins in my head.

Caveats

Upon returning home, I found [my friend] Quantorzo deep in conversation with my wife Dida. [...] They must have been talking about me, for, when they saw me come in, they both exclaimed in unison:

—Oh, there he is!—

And since there were two of them seeing me come in, I was suddenly tempted to turn around and look for *the other* who was entering with me, though I knew full well that not only were the "dear Vitangelo" of my fatherly Quantorzo and my wife Dida's "Gengè" both in me, but that the whole of me was none other than "dear Vitangelo" for Quantorzo and none other than "Gengè" for Dida. Two, then, not in their eyes, but only for me, who knew that, for those two, I was *one* and *one*; which for me did not make a *plus* but a *minus*, as it meant that, in their eyes, I—as myself—was no-one.[2]

Luigi Pirandello, *Uno, nessuno e centomila*

---

2 Luigi Pirandello, *Uno, nessuno e centomila*, Bemporad, 1926, 149–150. From the chapter entitled "Multiplication and Subtraction." The translation is mine. Here is the original Italian text: "*Rientrando a casa, vi trovai Quantorzo in seria confabulazione con mia moglie Dida. [...] Parlavano certo di me, perché, come mi videro entrare, esclamarono a un tempo: 'Oh, eccolo qua!' E poiché erano due a vedermi entrare, mi venne la tentazione di voltarmi a cercare l'altro che entrava con me, pur sapendo bene che il 'caro Vitangelo' del mio paterno Quantorzo non solo era anch'esso in me come il 'Gengè' di mia moglie Dida, ma che io tutto quanto, per Quantorzo, altri non ero che il suo 'caro Vitangelo', proprio come per Dida altri che il suo 'Gengè'. Due, dunque, non agli occhi loro, ma soltanto per me che mi sapevo per quei due uno e uno; il che per me, non faceva un più ma un meno, in quanto voleva dire che ai loro occhi, io come io, non ero nessuno.*"

There may come a time in our lives when we find ourselves experiencing a feeling quite similar to the one expressed in the above quotation: the feeling that each man or woman around us sees us as a different person, or that our real inner self is not known to the people closest to us, perhaps even to ourselves. That our sister, for example, sees us as one entity, while our father, brother, mother, wife, employer, colleagues, and friends see us as something else entirely. The dilemma implicit in such feeling is more real than one might think, and not at all an intellectual issue. That dilemma is in some ways the theme of this biography. It could be the theme of all biographies.

I like to think of a biography as an essay, in the oldest and purest sense of the word: an attempt. It can hardly be anything else, for what we can really know about a person's life is little indeed. We can know the "facts," certainly. We can know the external "events," if they have been witnessed and recorded. We can know other people's impressions and opinions about the subject, if those people have known the subject personally. And we can know the subject's opinions from his or her statements.

Those external events, however, when witnessed and reported, are filtered through the subjective views of their witnesses, whose versions must by definition throw into question the truthfulness of each of those accounts. People "see" differently, remember differently, and judge differently, through their own "baggage" of experience and thought—and this without taking into account that people can also lie. In cinema, this unstable relativity of inter-personal truths was expressed searingly by Japanese director Akira Kurosawa in his very Pirandellian film *Rashomon* (1950), where four eyewitnesses to a crime offer four contrasting accounts of it, each account contradicting the previous one.

From these facts, events, impressions, opinions, and statements, we can construe or hypothesize some kind of partial truth about the subject. Not much else.

Then there are facts and events that are not visible to anyone; these facts and events belong to a realm—the inner world of the subject—

that cannot be witnessed externally, except in special circumstances and through special processes. Those facts, those events, are as real to the subject as they are unknowable to witnesses. It matters not whether those witnesses are family members, friends, or strangers: those events are not visible to the naked eye.

It also matters little whether the subject is living or dead. One would think that, if one could ask the right questions, one could glean many precious insights from the living subject of a biography, and that those insights would be unassailable, and true. They might, or they might not. A lot depends on the level of self-knowledge, and self-investigation, that the subject has essayed on him/herself. From a living subject, one might get splendid insights into his/her human nature, and into his/her inner world. Or, one might get, again, the external facts and events of a life, and the subject's feelings and opinions about those facts and events. Even the subject might not be able—or willing—to interpret his or her life exhaustively, beyond offering a fleshed-out version of his or her CV. Likewise, the journalists reporting on that life might be incapable of probing any deeper. I myself was perfectly content with the most superficial of anecdotes when I knew Dorothy; today I would probably know what to ask her, but she is no longer available to be interviewed.

How many Dorothy McGuires were there? One, probably, from her own point of view, or at the most two (we are all divided to some extent). From the point of view of external observers, at least eleven, if not ten million and ninety-seven. At a minimum, then:

1) Dorothy, as she was according to herself;
2) Dorothy, as she was according to her husband John;
3) Dorothy, as she was according to her son Mark;
4) Dorothy, as she was according to her daughter Topo;
5) Dorothy, as she was according to her close friends (let's say twenty);
6) Dorothy, as she was according to each member of her public (let's say ten million);
7) Dorothy, as she was according to David O. Selznick;

8) Dorothy, as she was according to Darryl Zanuck;
9) Dorothy, as she was according to Henry Fonda;
10) Dorothy, as she was according to her colleagues of stage and screen (let's say fifty);
11) Dorothy, as she was according to her critics and interviewers (let's say twenty).

And one could go on.

"Know thyself," "γνῶθι σαυτόν," screamed the Oracle of the Temple of Apollo at Delphi many centuries ago. Few listened, and fewer still followed the advice. Centuries later, that same phrase, inscribed in the temple's stones, still screams its advice to humanity, silent and unheeded. People all over the Earth still believe, in good faith, that they already know themselves well enough, and that no special research is necessary to complete that knowledge. Alas, the unhappiness of human beings everywhere seems to suggest otherwise.

With the same ease and superficiality, people often believe, in good faith, that they know their parents, wives, husbands, siblings, friends, and colleagues well enough (or very well), and that no special research is necessary to know them any better.

This author believes, not that a biography is a futile effort, for a first biography of a subject, such as this one, indubitably fills the gap where no biography previously existed, but that a biography, even the most earnest and thoroughly researched, must be considered incomplete, and must leave both reader and author wishing for more, as if something essential about its subject, like a Kantian "thing-in-itself," inexorably slipped farther away from their grasp every step of the way.

Gathering and laying down the external facts of the subject's life, as thoroughly and correctly as possible, is of course a dutiful step in creating a biography. In fact, the eager, sometimes obsessive search for even the smallest minutiae of the subject's life may be the biographer's *horror-vacui*[3] attempt to counteract that sense of unknowability hovering over

---

3 *Horror vacui* is a Latin phrase used to describe the "horror of emptiness" or of empty spaces

his or her endeavor. Like many of its brethren, this biography too gathers as many data about its subject's life and work as possible, using as varied a collection of sources as possible: the press, the World-Wide Web, living eyewitnesses, other biographies and texts, quotations from the subject itself, the author's own experience of the subject, etc.

Since most facts and events of the subject's life are reconstructed through reports, and since one can safely state that those reports, whatever the source, are at least once removed from the original facts and events (even when they quote the subject's words), I have deemed it wiser to distinguish clearly between the reports and the reported facts. However authoritative those sources might seem to be, they are still outside sources, and therefore subjective, or second-hand. Therefore, I have seldom incorporated the sources' reports into the biography's narrative, as is the prevailing convention in biographies, or have done so only prudently, lest the result be as unreliable as a round of the telephone game. This preservation of the original quote as something separate from the main text represents one of the ways in which the present piece of writing resembles an essay: it borrows tropes not so much from memoirs as from scientific or academic studies.

That gathering of data, at any rate, is only one of many steps in a ladder that somehow seems to keep moving downward just as the biographer has the illusion of ascending; the undertaking cannot but remain unfinished. Dig as one may, much of the truth about the subject remains buried deep: it remains unknowable.

The observation of the inner workings of a simple machine—say a clock—does not yield knowledge of the clock unless one can grasp the concept that governs its parts, their movement, their interconnected functions, etc. A clock, however, is man-made, so that concept can be gained through study: the thought that went into conceiving and building that

---

(also known as kenophobia) and the compulsion to fill those spaces in the visual arts. The first use of the term in art criticism is often attributed to Italian literary critic and historian Mario Praz (1896–1982).

machine is within our reach, and can be retraced. A person, on the other hand, is not man-made, and the concept of his or her inner workings is more complex and elusive, and remains incomplete even after extensive observation.

Ultimately, not the gathering of facts and figures, not the accumulation of names and dates constitutes the aim of a biography in this author's view, but the gaining of even a little insight from those data, and the making of a convincing argument for such insight. Though the ultimate "whole truth" may perforce remain unknowable, a convincing interpretation able to synthesize, illuminate, and penetrate those facts of the subject's life must be made: a plausible hypothesis about what set them in motion. A larger question, in other words, looms large over the project of a biography, a question that can be crudely synthesized as "What is the meaning of all this as far as the person is concerned?" For some, the factual information about a subject's life—the annotated CV—might be enough; for others, those external facts and events might feel hollow without the concepts that should fill them and explain them.

No biography, not even one written by its subject, should be called definitive.

*   *   *

In the case of biographies of artists, musicians, or actors, the enumeration of facts and events must focus heavily on the subject's artistic accomplishments, which is perfectly logical. That is what the subject's profession suggests, and that is what most readers expect.

The question of whether an artist's output is more or less important than his or her humanity—for the biographer and for the reader—is a complex one; the answer one gives to it, and the proportion one adopts in applying such answer, may slant the biographical examination in one direction or the other. A fluid mixture of both aspects is possible, but that fluidity, if strictly chronological, may often bring with it a lack of detail, an alternate subtraction of depth from both introspections. Depending on the chosen emphasis, one of the two examinations, the human or the artistic, may seem an alternate interruption to the flow of the other, a flaw that is often remedied by brevity in one or the other of the two examinations.

While, on the one hand, this biography is concerned with ascertaining the facts, and is prepared to delve microscopically into their investigation (as much as possible, at any rate), on the other hand it is also concerned with engaging its sense of peripheral vision to examine the context, and roots, of those facts. If this means occasionally going off on tangents, so be it: the detour is intentional, for more things are connected to those facts than their obvious immediate explanation.

Separating the investigations seemed to me the wisest course, for it allowed independent studies of Dorothy's various aspects. The first part of this book therefore examines each element of the life and career of Dorothy McGuire, artist and person, separately, going into considerable detail in each discreet search. The second part pulls together what has been separated, centripetally, to try to build a concept of the person from those disparate pieces, from a higher vantage point. Hence, at least four intertwined investigations are carried out: (a) an exo-investigation, expanding from the center of Dorothy's person centrifugally to the immediate periphery of her family, her friends, her environment, and the times in which she lived; (b) an endo-investigation, examining Dorothy's inner world centripetally, from other people's points of view and from her own. These two investigations are in turn developed on two fronts, (c) the artistic and (d) the personal, cross-referencing (a) and (b).

In the manner of an essay, this biography is arranged thematically, in order to try to study the "pieces" of Dorothy's life and artistry before putting them back together again—before pulling back to observe the whole rather than the parts and drawing a conclusion by grasping some sort of concept of Dorothy. Part I separates in order to discern and distinguish, to make visible and clear; Part II then re-unites to create a holistic synthesis of what has been taken apart. The two parts express the two complementary impulses that animate this investigation: the impulse to gather data, and the impulse to interpret them.

Part I: *Solve*[4]

---

[4] Present imperative of the Latin transitive verb '*solvere*' (sólvere): to loosen, to release, to separate or discern, to melt, to unbind, to free, to thin out, to make fluid, to divide, to make visible and open, to make clear.

1. Exordium

> One of the rewarding things about this columnist wing-ding is watching the young stars of the industry grow. Dorothy McGuire has changed more and has lost less of her original values in the process than most. [...] The girl who came to tea with me on the first rainy day of [this] season had the poise of well-schooled royalty [...].
> Hedda Hopper, February 1950

Any actor working in film during the golden age of Hollywood would naturally be exposed to, and learn to coexist with, certain facts of life. One of these facts was the influence wielded by the gossip columnists of the time. Among these columnists, two names towered over the others, ominously: those of the two "Queens of Hollywood," Hedda Hopper and Louella Parsons.

Both Hopper and Parsons could make or break careers in extreme cases, and Hopper especially could out-Winchell the lethal Walter Winchell as a smear artist. Apart from those extreme cases, Hopper's seemingly casual items about stars big and small could range from insouciant to glowing, and her affections from fickle to fickler. When careers were not actually ruined by her, they could be dismissed or made redundant.

In terms of dates, Dorothy McGuire (1916–2001) outlived Hedda Hopper (1885–1966), as did her career. What is truly curious about this particular columnist's treatment of Dorothy during their mutual acquaintance is that Hopper never spent a cross, or even tepid, word about the actress from Omaha, Nebraska. Between 1943 and circa 1960, Hopper wrote about Dorothy with admiration and respect, one could even say with devotion: she never forgot to say something nice about her. It is as if the graciousness for which Dorothy was justly famous as a person had rubbed off indelibly on the journalist. Also, there seems to have been little or no fabrication on the part of the Hollywood press where Dorothy was concerned: most items were simple and credible, and can be verified by cross-referencing other sources.

Fearsome Hollywood gossip queen Hedda Hopper showing off one of her famous hats. Press photo, 1960.

Exordium

A variety of reasons, and a multitude of strategies (by Dorothy and by her agents/studios/producers, by the press), may have been responsible for such devotion, and, after the fact, it is difficult to determine in what exact proportion. But, at the very least, Hopper's attitude towards Dorothy can be seen, from a wider perspective, as a symbol of the attitude of the press as a whole. Virtually without exception, the press—through the pens of columnists such as Walter Ames, Brooks Atkinson, Marilyn Beck, Charles Champlin, Bosley Crowther, Sheilah Graham, Geoffrey T. Hellman, Erskine Johnson, Lydia Lane, Virginia MacPherson, Louella Parsons, Rex Reed, Paul Rosenfield, Edwin Schallert, Wood Soanes, Dan Sullivan, Bob Thomas, and Katherine Von Blon—loved, even adored, Dorothy McGuire. Even the reviewers of *Variety*, seldom prone to excessive enthusiasm, lavished superlative after superlative on most of Dorothy's performances, sometimes regardless of their opinions about the particular films in which she starred.

The generous attitude of the press towards Dorothy was reflected not only in the quality of the items written about her, but also in the quantity. During the two main decades of her film career, and before she switched to television, say between 1943 and 1965, coverage of both her work and her personal life was extensive. Even after 1965, the press was far from silent about her: aside from covering her periodic forays in the theater or on the small screen, it produced affectionate profiles of her and happy reminiscences of her past successes. As late as 1976, the *Los Angeles Times* chose Dorothy for its Woman of the Year Award.

Such consistent, undiluted warmth on the part of both the press and the *hoi polloi* was not the norm in Hollywood, and was reserved for a relatively small number of performers; in Dorothy's case, one can reasonably infer that the reasons for such treatment had to do with a number of interconnected factors. Here are a few.

(1) In Hollywood terms, Dorothy's artistic provenance was exalted: she hailed from the theater, and from a huge Broadway hit, *Claudia* (1941), which translated into an equally big hit in its film incarnation

(1943); Dorothy's inventive, fresh characterization in both play and film virtually seduced the nation, and transformed her overnight into America's sweetheart.

(2) Dorothy married "well." Her non-Hollywood husband, John Swope, was not a film actor, director, or producer. He had friends in Hollywood (for example, Henry Fonda, another Nebraskan, and James Stewart, who was best man at John's wedding), but was not a Hollywood type. The gracious scion of a well-to-do family from the East Coast, John was a renowned photographer (for example for *LIFE* magazine) and aviation instructor/manager. Over the years, the Swopes were well-respected and well-loved, and came to be regarded as Los Angeles aristocracy.

(3) Both Dorothy and John were very much involved in the social life of Los Angeles, particularly in charities and in the artistic development of the city. One never got the sense that the two, together or separately, participated in social events merely to "appear": rather, one sensed that they were sincerely interested in furthering the cause of their adopted city.

(4) Both Dorothy and John were instrumental in founding and running the celebrated non-profit theatrical venue the La Jolla Playhouse and the Actors' Company that went with it,[5] bringing into its fold some of the best performers, designers and directors of stage and film operating in Southern California.

(5) But, above all, those other reasons had to do with Dorothy's personal warmth and graciousness. Wherever Dorothy went, she made and kept friends, easily;[6] whatever the environment, she gained the trust, respect and affection of her interlocutors.

---

5 The Actors' Company was often referred to as "the Actors Company," without the apostrophe. One finds both spellings in the press of the time. See part I, Chapter 9.

6 This was partially contradicted by Hedda Hopper in one of her early interviews with Dorothy ("She doesn't make friends easily, but when she does she keeps those she's made." See Hedda Hopper, "Independence Pays for Dorothy McGuire," *Pittsburgh (PA) Press*, September 21, 1947. My experience with Dorothy was different, and Hopper's statement does not seem plausible when applied to the Dorothy I knew. The Dorothy I knew made friends very easily. It may have applied somewhat in the early phases of her life.

When I first met Dorothy on December 4, 1976,[7] I was a bushy-tailed freshman at Columbia University and she, at sixty, was performing on Broadway in Tennessee Williams' *The Night of the Iguana*, co-starring Richard Chamberlain and Sylvia Miles. A star-struck American kid from the Italian provinces I certainly was, and my first personal exposure to a *bona-fide* world celebrity during that first semester in New York City certainly dazzled me; but only the warmth of Dorothy's personality could transform that superficial meeting into a real, and long-lasting, epiphany. Bright, funny, vivacious and welcoming, Dorothy was willing, not only to chat with a perfect stranger, but also to socialize in the warmest, most disarming of manners, and to let the acquaintanceship grow with virtually no barriers. In the ensuing months, she and I corresponded, and I saw the show two more times. I was introduced both to her husband and to her co-star. On closing night, I sent a large bouquet of yellow roses to her dressing room before attending the show, and received an invitation to visit the Swopes in Los Angeles. In December of 1977, I took my first trip to the West Coast, and the Swopes picked me up at the airport in their inconspicuous—and tiny—Renault car. A friendship developed, which I was able—most clumsily and superficially—to keep alive fitfully for the next decade and a half.

That frequentation was the purveyor of much wonder, and the reader will forgive me if I occasionally put in my two cents, even though I definitely cannot consider myself an "insider." I promise I will do so only insofar as it helps the thoroughness of the endeavor. During my friendship with Dorothy, I was certainly attracted to the allure of her fame, and of her artistry; but something more personal, and more evanescent, was occurring during that frequentation of ours, something that left a trace.

---

[7] I remember the date well, for it was on that Saturday morning that my Columbia University dormitory, Livingston Hall, at Amsterdam Avenue and West 115th Street, caught fire, and I almost did not make it to the theater in time to see Dorothy's matinee performance. When I did, it was with smoky house clothes, which was quite a conversation starter when I met her backstage.

Decades hence, what remains indelibly significant for me about those human contacts is their emotional substance, and the ineffable meanings behind the physical events that gave it form. It is to that substance and to those meanings that I try to pay homage through this biography.

The point of all this is, there was something special about Dorothy as a person, aside from her often Oscar-worthy acting (Dorothy was only nominated for the accolade once, and never won).[8] It is not an irrelevant coincidence that her colleagues of both stage and celluloid regarded her as a very genteel creature. Her theatrical co-star John Barrymore, in a rather slurred 1939 interview for an Omaha radio station,[9] described his young stage colleague as "one of the most enchanting people" he had ever encountered.[10] In 1948, film star Melvyn Douglas, known in Hollywood as a "suave gentleman of the screen," named Dorothy one of Hollywood's most sophisticated women, saying:

> McGuire [...] gives you the feeling she's worldly without being bored. She's the new pattern in sophistication.[11]

---

[8] Neither did such classy colleagues as Jean Arthur, Lauren Bacall, Joan Blondell, Doris Day, Marlene Dietrich, Irene Dunne, Greta Garbo, Judy Garland, Julie Harris, Miriam Hopkins, Madeline Kahn, Deborah Kerr, Veronica Lake, Carole Lombard, Myrna Loy, Marilyn Monroe, Thelma Ritter, Rosalind Russell, Ann Sheridan, Sylvia Sidney, Jean Simmons, or Gloria Swanson.

[9] The April 1939 interview was conducted on the occasion of the pre-Broadway run/tour of the play *My Dear Children*, written by Catherine Turney and Jerry Horwin and starring John Barrymore.

[10] According to a 1982 interview with McGuire, on her closing night Barrymore went off script to deliver a sonnet he had written in her honor. See: Paul Rosenfield, "Fate Takes a Hand Again for McGuire," *Los Angeles Times*, February 7, 1982.

[11] Bob Thomas, "Douglas Has Four Examples of Stars Sophisticated," *Canandaigua (NY) Daily Messenger*, June 24, 1948. Douglas's other three examples of sophistication were Greta Garbo, Myrna Loy, and Katharine Hepburn.

And Gene Tierney, a nervous Hollywood beauty, was quoted in 1951 as saying about Dorothy, "She has a real flair, an innate chic."[12]

These commentators were pointing to a real phenomenon, and to an impression that most people shared upon meeting Dorothy.

This was true from her very first years in Hollywood. Syndicated columnist Bob Thomas, who met the actress on the set of *The Spiral Staircase*, had this impression of Dorothy:

> I would conclude upon our short acquaintance that Dorothy is a very nice person. She appears unimpressed with her own fame, but is still very intent upon being a good actress. She is considerate. She provides five gallons of lemonade every day for the whole crew on the pictures she works in.
>
> [...] She keeps her dressing room door open, and anyone with or without business can readily talk to her.[13]

As we will see in the following chapters, those qualities of Dorothy's were no mere sporadic accidents of nature.

If there was a downside to those positive qualities, it had to do with Hollywood's love for repetition. The film industry could not resist typecasting its stars, and, to a large extent, its treatment of Dorothy was no exception. The Internet Movie Database (IMDb) describes her as "a genuine model of sincerity, practicality and dignity in most of the roles she inhabited," which puts the accent on the tender, sincere, girlish, or nurturing colors of her spectrum as an actress. By focusing on those "nice" colors, the Hollywood industry mostly made and remade Dorothy into variations of the same figure: the girlish fiancée, the wounded, vulnerable doe, the loving mother, the sensitive spinster, etc. Wonderful as they are,

---

[12] Erskine Johnson, "In Hollywood," *Bakersfield (CA) Californian*, July 12, 1951.

[13] Bob Thomas, "Roles of Dorothy McGuire In Movies Now Questioned," *St. Cloud (MN) Times*, October 27, 1945.

many of her iconic successes—*The Enchanted Cottage* (1945), *The Spiral Staircase* (1946), *Three Coins in the Fountain* (1954), *The Dark at the Top of the Stairs* (1960), *Swiss Family Robinson* (1960), *The Greatest Story Ever Told* (1965)—conform perfectly to such stereotype.

In its glowing obituary of Dorothy, the *Guardian* had this to say:

> The producer Darryl F Zanuck called her an "angel", which, according to Elia Kazan, robbed her of her sexuality. She certainly had little chance to exude either sexuality or be malicious, like Bette Davis or Joan Crawford, but there was always room for an actor who was so good at being good.[14]

Nice Dorothy certainly was, and an excellent actress; but her Hollywood career, built around what could be seen as an excess of niceness, yielded results that were sometimes a bit syrupy, and occasionally bland, thus depriving the audience of the joy of discovering Dorothy's true versatility. In hindsight, it is the exceptions to that rule that prove particularly interesting: exceptions in which other qualities of hers were allowed to come to the surface, qualities such as intelligence, self-reliance, a sense of irony and a touch of mischief. These qualities—which could also be found in Dorothy as an off-screen person—were best showcased in the comedies (*Claudia*, 1943; *Mister 880*, 1950; *Callaway Went Thataway*, 1951; *The Remarkable Mr. Pennypacker*, 1959), and in dramas where Dorothy's character was eccentric or slightly negative (*A Tree Grows in Brooklyn*, 1945; *Till the End of Time*, 1946; *Gentleman's Agreement*, 1947). In many of those cases, maturity helped Dorothy, by allowing her to develop her persona into a well-rounded entity. Also, in several of her 1950s and 1960s roles, she was often able to strip her characters of the excess treacle, making them resplendently intelligent while retaining their loveliness (*Callaway*

---

14 Ronald Bergan, "Dorothy McGuire: Actor of intelligence, integrity and charm on and off the screen," *Guardian* (UK), September 17, 2001.

Went Thataway, 1951; *Friendly Persuasion*, 1956; *Old Yeller*, 1957; *A Summer Place*, 1959).

Dorothy was undoubtedly a film star, and is justly remembered as such; but perhaps the theatrical stage (together with live radio) was the medium in which all of Dorothy's qualities were best allowed to surface, and where her true versatility expressed itself most interestingly. Her intelligent, organic character construction and her ability to sustain a performance in a lively, multi-faceted manner could only partially be captured even by her best Hollywood vehicles. At heart, Dorothy remained a stage actress to the last.

But it was as a human being that Dorothy, through both nature and nurture, achieved her greatest success, by molding her inner raw material—her character—into a truly enlightened incarnation of sterling moral ideals and virtues: into a paragon of adamantine consistency.

2. What's in a Name I

One of the first comments that were made by Hollywood journalists upon Dorothy's arrival in Filmland, fresh off the Broadway boards, concerned her name. It may seem now (it may have seemed then) a silly topic for discussion, but the subject of Dorothy's name was, simply, a way for those Hollywood scribes to get a handle on this new, atypical creature that had landed on their plates. Dorothy did not conform to the usual canons of glamour and stardom, but her talent, her personality, and her provenance from one of the biggest Broadway hits to date could hardly be ignored. As one *Oakland Tribune* columnist (probably Wood Soanes) put it, Dorothy was "somehow Ingrid Bergman, Shirley Temple, Claudia and herself, all enchantingly packaged in tweeds, with pale blue eyes, ash blond hair, [and] scrubbed face [. . .]."[15] Many years later, hindsight allowed Charles Champlin of the *Los Angeles Times* to write: "The truth is that her gift to Hollywood was freshness and originality, [. . .] and her combination of spontaneity and intelligence had no precise match among the established stars."[16]

---

[15] "Dorothy McGuire Escaped from Claudia Long Enough to Do Two Pictures," *Oakland (CA) Tribune*, November 26, 1944.

[16] Charles Champlin, "Woman of the Year: An Endearing Sensitivity," *Los Angeles Times*, April 29, 1976.

In 1943, those columnists had to find something to say about the new star, and they chose to start with semantics. Syndicated Hollywood columnist Robbin Coons wrote one of the first valentines to the actress in June 1943:

> Names are funny things. You take one like "Dorothy McGuire." There's no special ring to it. There must be millions of Dorothys, and certainly no shortage of McGuires. The combination isn't startling. It doesn't attract attention, it doesn't sound like the name of an actress. It's all wrong—there ought to be a Tanya or a Mona or a Cherille hooked on to that McGuire to make it authentically theatrical.
>
> There isn't, and there won't be. It's the little lady herself who makes "Dorothy McGuire" an unusual, distinctive, wonderful name.
>
> A lot of stage stars arrive with fancy names, with stage mammas, pet leopards, gold toenails and tons of luggage, all items warranted to gain attention. Dorothy McGuire came to town without a single pair of high-heeled shoes. But she's different in other ways too.[17]

This charming opening, meant to introduce not only the ways in which Dorothy was "different" but the ways in which she was "authentic" and "simple," led to a more conventional discussion about her talent and achievements.

There was, however, something interesting about that name issue; just how interesting, and in what way, would not become apparent until much later down the timeline of Dorothy's career. That common, unadorned name would come to symbolize not only something special—stardom,

---

[17] Robbin Coons, "Dorothy McGuire to Keep Her Name," *Lancing (MI) State Journal*, June 1, 1943.

talent, achievements—but also something warm and reassuring, something homey and genuine emanating from Dorothy McGuire, star and woman.

More than thirty years after Coons's piece, another columnist, film critic Rex Reed, mirrored Coons's opening when introducing his affectionate tribute to Dorothy, written on the occasion of her celebrated performance in Tennessee Williams' *The Night of the Iguana* at New York's Circle in the Square Theater. Here is Reed's opening, published in January 1977:

> Dorothy McGuire. The simple act of repeating the name aloud is an act of reassurance: there's something solid and comfortable in the sound. For 20 years, she radiated kindness, warmth and understanding from the movie screen as one of Hollywood's most appealing leading ladies.
>
> With a voice like creamy melted cocoa, bordering on the soft whisper, and a gentle, unselfish femininity that spilled over into the floodlight and illuminated the dark corners of the screen around her, she was the living embodiment of Currier and Ives Christmases and plenty of tea and sympathy. She could never have been a Rita or a Lana. No, she had to be a Dorothy.[18]

Reed's opening is only apparently similar to Coons's. It is, in fact, quite different, for it contains, implicitly, all that had intervened between 1943 and 1977: it contains the accomplishments of maturity. Reed's touching statements about Dorothy's name are as different from Coons's as, for example, the rave reviews Dorothy received for her performance in *The Night of the Iguana* in 1975 and 1976 are different from the rave reviews

---

18 Rex Reed, "Lack of competitive spirit helped her survive," *Long Beach (CA) Independent Press-Telegram*, January 16, 1977.

she received for her performance in *Claudia* in 1941. Those 1941 raves had been the recognition of a young talent, and of a promise; the 1975–76 raves were the recognition of the fulfillment of that promise.

The name "Dorothy McGuire" may have been cute and homey, and unusual for a star, in 1943, but, symbolically, it contained nothing but great potential. In 1977, that same name contained a lifetime (Dorothy's theatrical career was far from finished in 1977, but a peak had definitely been reached with *The Night of the Iguana*, one that would never be equaled). Metaphorically if not literally, those two name discussions were both similar and opposite: loving bookends to the splendor of an actress's world, and to her life's work.

An early Hollywood portrait of Dorothy, circa 1945. The photographer may have been Ernest A. Bachrach (1899–1973), a celebrated portrait photographer who, from 1929 to circa 1959, worked at RKO Radio Pictures as head of the studio's camera department.

3. What's in a Name II: Δωροθεα

The name Dorothy is an English variant of the original Greek Δωροθεα (Dorothea), which literally means "gift of God," being the union of δωρον (*doron*, gift) and θεος (*theos*, god).

The name has been used in most Indo-European languages. Here are some of the equivalents or variants: Dorota (Czech), Dorotea, Doroteja (Croatian), Dorte, Dorthe, Dorete (Danish), Dorothea (Dutch), Dorothy, Dortha, Dorthy (English), Dorotea, Tea, Teja, Tiia (Finnish), Dorothée (French), Dorothea (German), Dorottya, Dóra, Dorina, Dorka (Hungarian), Dorotea, Tea (Italian), Dorothea (Latin), Doroteja (Macedonian), Dorothea (Norwegian), Dorota, Dosia (Polish), Doroteia (Portuguese), Dorotija, Dora (Serbian), Dorota (Slovak), Tea, Teja (Slovenian), Dorotea, Dora, Dorita (Spanish), Dorotea, Tea, Ea, Thea (Swedish).

Originally, because of its etymology, the name was given to children who had been tardy in coming to a family.

The name resonates with the memory of several Saints venerated by the Roman Catholic and Orthodox churches, as well as of other religious or esoteric figures. Here are some:

Dorothea of Caesarea (died c. 311 or 284) was a 4th-century martyr executed at Caesarea Mazaca (Kayseri) in Central Anatolia during the persecution by Emperor Diocletian (after his abdication in 305). The fifth-century *Martyrologium Hieronymianum* describes her as "charitable, pure, and wise." The legend of her martyrdom narrates that, on her way to her decapitation, Dorothea met a jurisconsult by the name of Theophilus, who mockingly asked her to bring him some flowers and apples from the blessed garden where she was headed. The saint replied that she would. Along the way, an angel appeared to her in the form of a young boy, bearing a basket of roses and apples; instructed by Dorothea, the youth offered the basket to Theophilus. Also according to the *passio* of the saint, so stunned was Theophilus by her gesture, that he converted to Christianity and was executed himself. Dorothea is the patron saint of florists, gardeners, and farmers, as well as the patron of the town of Pescia, in Tuscany. Several Italian convents, for example in Rome and Venice, are named after her, and their nuns are called Dorotheas (*Dorotee*). Several artists have depicted the saint, usually bearing a basket of flowers and fruit; among them, Andrea della Robbia (1435–1525), Lucas Cranach the Elder (1472–1553), and Sebastiano del Piombo (1485–1547). According to some sources, the Saint's remains are kept in an urn under the main altar of the church of Santa Dorotea, in the Roman neighborhood of Trastevere.[19]

Dorothea of Alexandria (died c. 320) was a virgin martyr; the legend states that she was beheaded at the request of Emperor Maximinus, whose suit she had rejected. Sources, such as Eusebius Pamphilus, are vague as to the history of this Dorothea, who is not recognized by Roman Martyrology.[20]

---

[19] See the church's website, parrocchiasantadorotea.com.

[20] See: Eusebius Pamphilus, *An Ecclesiastical History*, Translated by Rev. C.F. Cruse, Samuel Bagster and Sons, 1847, VIII, 14.

One of the artists who painted Saint Dorothea was the Spanish Francisco de Zurbaràn (1598–1664). This work (c. 1640) is kept in the Museo Provincial de Bellas Artes in Seville, Spain. Oil on canvas. Wikimedia Commons.

Dorothea of Montau (1347–1394) was a hermitess and visionary in 14th-century Germany. She was canonized by Pope Paul VI in 1976.

Dorotheus of Sidon (first century) was a Hellenistic astrologer, who wrote the Pentateuch, a seminal source of information about the Hellenistic practice of astrology. Believed to have been born in the city of Sidon (Lebanon), Dorotheus probably worked and lived in Alexandria, a vibrant center for all scientific, literary, astrological and esoteric studies.[21]

---

21 See: Dorotheus Sidonius, *Dorothei Sidonii carmen astrologicum*, B.G. Taubner, 1976. See also: Dorotheus of Sidon, *Carmen Astrologicum: The 'Umar-al-Tabari Translation*, Translated and edited by Benjamin N. Dykes, PhD, The Cazimi Press, 2017.

Dorotheus (died c. 304) was a Christian eunuch in the Roman Imperial Palace at Nicomedia (Izmit) and a martyr under Emperor Diocletian (244–312), during the sovereign's "Great Persecution"; according to legend, he was tortured to death together with martyrs Peter Cubicularius and Gorgonius (the latter also a palace eunuch).

Saint Dorotheus, priest of Antioch and Bishop of Tyre, Lebanon (255–362), traditionally credited with the *Acts of the Seventy Apostles*, was martyred under Julian the Apostate in the city where he had been exiled, Odyssopolis (Varna, Bulgaria).[22]

Dorotheus of Gaza or Abba Dorotheus (c. 505–565), Christian monk and abbot, was the author of a series of instructions to the monks of his monastery (ἀσκητικά, "ascetics"), later compiled by his followers as *Directions on Spiritual Training*.[23] Like the "Golden Verses" of Pythagoras, these rules for spiritual advancement dealt with the issue of dominating one's passions and thoughts and cultivating certain seminal virtues, for example humility. Like Pythagoras, Dorotheus instituted a veritable "school of the soul," or "school of life." Like Pythagoras, he advocated the Delphic "knowing oneself" as a necessary first step (through humility) towards the understanding of the human obstacles to grace.[24]

On the profane side, the name Dorothea boasts an exalted lineage of royalty and aristocracy, mostly of Central-European descent. Among the many noblewomen who were thus named: Dorothea "Doroslava" of Bul-

---

22 See: Meredith Hanmer, transl., *The Aunciente Ecclesiasticall Histories of the First Six Hundred Yeares after Christ, written in the Greeke tongue by Three Learned Historiographers, Eusebius, Socrates, and Euagrius*, Relnk Books, 2017 [1577].

23 See: Dorotheos of Gaza, *Discourses and Sayings*, translated by E. P. Wheeler, Cistercian Publications, 1977.

24 See: E. Kadloubovsky and G. E. H. Palmer, *Early Fathers from the Philokalia*, Faber and Faber, 1981, 154–163. See also: "Dorotheus of Gaza," *The Oxford Dictionary of Byzantium*, Oxford University Press, 1991, 654. See also: Sr. Pascale-Dominique Nau, Les instructions de Dorothée de Gaza, Lulu.com, 2014. See also: De Rossi, J.B. and Duchesne, L., eds., *Martyrologium Hieronymianum ad fidem codicum adiectis prolegomenis*, Societé des bollandistes, 1971.

garia, Queen of Bosnia from 1377 to c. 1390; Dorotea Gonzaga (1449–1467), daughter of Ludovico III Gonzaga and Queen Consort of Milan; Dorothea of Saxe-Lauenburg (1511–1571), Queen Consort of Christian III of Denmark; Dorothea Maria of Anhalt, Duchess of Saxe-Weimar (1574–1617); Dorothea Hedwig of Brunswick-Wolfenbüttel, Princess of Brunswick-Wolfenbüttel and Princess of Anhalt-Zerbst (1587–1609); Dorothea of Anhalt-Herbst, Princess of Anhalt-Herbst (1607–1634); Dorothea Sophie of Neuburg, Duchess of Parma (1670–1748); Dorothea Friederike of Brandenburg-Ansbach (1676–1731), last Duchess of Hanau and half-sister of Queen Caroline of Great Britain (1683–1737), wife of King George II; Dorothea Maria Henriette Auguste Louise of Saxe-Coburg and Gotha, Princess of Saxe-Coburg and Gotha and *Herzogin zu Sachsen* (1881–1967); and Princess Dorothea of Bavaria, member of the House of Habsburg and Grand Duchess of Tuscany (1920–2015).

And, of course, the name Dorothy cannot fail to remind many of us of the most famous Dorothy of all: the protagonist of L. Frank Baum's *The Wonderful Wizard of Oz* (1900), and her incarnation in Hollywood's 1939 rendition, *The Wizard of Oz*.

4. Omaha and the Wagon of Thespis

> From the time I was a little girl in Omaha, I knew I would be a movie star. There was no question in my mind.
> Dorothy McGuire, 1975.[25]

Dorothy Hackett McGuire—social security number 131-03-1373—was born in the Heartland of America, in the city of Omaha, Nebraska,[26] on June 14, 1916, the only child of Thomas Johnson McGuire (1882–1932) and Isabelle Flaherty Trapp McGuire (1893–1968). Louisiana-born Thomas[27] was a successful general-practice lawyer who worked in the firm

---

25 Marilyn Beck, "Dorothy McGuire . . . A name from the past reappears for a TV special," *Chicago Tribune TV Week*, Section 10, March 30–April 5, 1975.

26 Many famous people hailed from Omaha: among them, dancer-actor Fred Astaire (1896–1981), actor Marlon Brando (1924–2004), actor Montgomery Clift (1920–1966), American President Gerald Ford (1913–2006), actress Swoosie Kurtz (1944–), actor Nick Nolte (1941–), director Alexander Payne (1961–), author Nicholas Sparks (1965–), singer Paul Williams (1940–), and activist Malcolm X (1925–1965).

27 According to the 1930 Federal Census, Thomas's birthplace was Louisiana; the 1920 Census lists him as having been born in Missouri.

of McGuire and More with his partner Walter T. More, out of offices located in the State Bank Building in Omaha.[28] He would eventually be Commander of Post No. 1 of the American Legion in Omaha. Nebraska-born Isabelle was a sometime stenographer with the National Far Co., and subsequently a full-time mother.

Many sources, such as the *New York Times*, the *Guardian* and the *Telegraph*, offer an alternative birth year for Dorothy: 1918. I am inclined to consider ancestry.com, the Internet Movie Database, and Dorothy's family more reliable.[29] Curiously, the Omaha Community Playhouse and the Omaha, Nebraska, press of the 1920s and '30s seemed to prefer 1918 as well, but even so were prone to citing slightly inaccurate ages in covering Dorothy's home-town performances; for example, age twelve in October 1929, when Dorothy would have been thirteen. Throughout Dorothy's career, the ages mentioned for her in news reports oscillated between those birthdates, with the majority of reporters flatteringly opting for the later one.[30]

At least until 1920, the McGuires lived with Isabelle's family at their home at 1122 S. 35th Avenue, Omaha. The other members of the household were Dorothy's maternal grandfather, Andrew J. Trapp (1877–1953),[31] a well-known detective with the Omaha Police Department, noted "for his work in smashing narcotics rings and recipient of a commendation for bravery";[32] Mary A. Lavelle Trapp (1870–1958), Dorothy's

---

[28] 1915 Omaha Nebraska City Directory.

[29] Topo Swope, Dorothy's daughter, is categorical: Dorothy's birth date was June 14, 1916. Correspondence with the author, March 2018.

[30] The *New York Times* obituary stated that Dorothy had died at the age of 83; the *Washington Post* and *Los Angeles Times* obituaries, at the age of 85.

[31] Dorothy did not attend her grandfather's funeral services in Omaha on February 18, 1953: she was pregnant with her son Mark, and was in her last trimester (Mark was born on May 14). See: "A.J. Trapp Dies, Grandfather of Dorothy McGuire," *Lincoln (NE) Star*, February 17, 1953.

[32] "A.J. Trapp Dies" (1953), op. cit.

maternal grandmother; and Nellie Lavelle, Mary's unmarried sister, who worked as a high school teacher.

By 1930, the year Dorothy appeared at the Omaha Community Playhouse with a pre-Hollywood Henry Fonda, her parents owned their own home at 602 S. 38th Avenue, Omaha (the house was valued at $12,000 in the 1930 Federal Census), but were already divorced.

Dorothy seldom spoke about her family of origin, except in passing; when she did, she usually expressed affection for her father. According to her daughter Topo Swope, Dorothy did not get along with her mother.[33] Throughout her career, at any rate, she was tight-lipped about her early family life. Her only hint: in a 1976 interview, Dorothy's cryptic description of her family nucleus, while not saying anything explicit, reverberated with eloquent undertones:

My father was a lawyer. My mother was—my mother.[34]

Just by glancing at the facts, one can make certain reasonable assumptions. One can infer, for example, that Dorothy's mother Isabelle was something of a nervous or restless type. Compared to Dorothy's own marriage, for example, Isabelle's marriage to Thomas J. was brief and unstable. The couple married circa 1915, and divorced in 1930. Thomas died in 1932; in January of that year, Isabelle married Harry V. Burkley, Jr., an officer of the Burkley Envelope and Printing Company.[35] The couple divorced in 1939. There is no trace of any further marriages.

---

33 Topo Swope, conversation with the author, February 2017.

34 Champlin, "Sensitivity," (1976), op. cit.

35 Burkley—and the alternative Burkeley—is the spelling that the contemporary press offered of Isabelle's second husband; according to other sources, such as Dorothy's daughter Topo, the man's last name was Berkley. The Burkley Envelope and Printing Company was founded in 1891 and is still in business, after moving its headquarters from Omaha to Wahoo, Nebraska.

Thomas J. McGuire died by his own hand, something that left Dorothy, aged sixteen, devastated. At the time, Dorothy's parents were already divorced, and Dorothy was living with her father, whom she adored, rather than with her remarried mother. Thus, it fell upon her to discover her father's dead body when she came home from school one afternoon.[36] As Dorothy commented years later:

> It was a terrible blow emotionally, but finally it led me to a better understanding of myself, of him, of the emotional struggles within us all.[37]

Exactly what kind of soul-searching took place, and exactly what Dorothy discovered that led her to that "better understanding," we do not know. At any rate, that tragic event, which she only mentioned once or twice in her career, was, in fact, a seminal event, one that injected a darker color in an otherwise sunny life; or, better, one that led to a resolute confirmation of Dorothy's sunny, *positive* disposition.[38] Her initial reaction to that event may have been emotional, but her processing of it was not. It is evident from her conduct throughout her life that Dorothy found a way to deal with her negative experiences not only constructively, but also transformatively. This transformation—from lead to gold, one might say—would determine many of her choices, in her private life, in her sociality, and in her acting. Her selection of projects and characters, too, was ultimately the expression of her determination not to be her parents, or not to feel that pain again except to learn from it.

---

[36] Geoffrey T. Hellman, "Dorothy McGuire: Actress Fits Her Part So Well It Is Hard to Tell Where McGuire Ends and 'Claudia' Begins, *LIFE* magazine, November 17, 1941, 122

[37] Champlin, "Sensitivity" (1976), op. cit.

[38] See Part II, Chapters 3 and 6.

Tovah Feldshuh, Dorothy's co-star in the 1982 Ahmanson Theatre production of Lillian Hellman's play *Another Part of the Forest*, has expressed this with some degree of insight:

> The suicide of Dorothy's father changed her entire life. Happiness is a choice, and, boy, did she make it. Niceness became a value for her. If you're nice, you get to be loved, and you get to be connected with people; you get to feel valued. How can a person who is so loved want to kill themselves? They don't. This would have consequences in her acting, as well: it was more important for her to be nice than to portray *a full slice of life*.[39]

There may be some truth to Feldshuh's last assessment of the consequences of Dorothy's processing of grief on her acting; as we will see, however, there is also a flip side—a positive side—to be found in those consequences.[40]

Even at an early age, Dorothy had always wanted to act; the dream future she imagined for herself took place on the boards of a stage, or on a film set. As she put it in an interview, "All children play-act, and I never grew up."[41] The quotation from Dorothy that opens this chapter seems to indicate that this imagined Hollywood future had the certainty of a premonition for her; her statement having been uttered in 1975, though, such certainty could have been the result of hindsight.

---

[39] Tovah Feldshuh, conversation with the author, March 2017. The italics are mine.

[40] See Part II, Chapter 4.

[41] Nancy Anderson (Copley News Service), "Dorothy McGuire hated first role," *Green Bay (WI) Press-Gazette*, March 26, 1972.

The Richardsonian Romanesque building that housed the Columbian School was built in 1892, to celebrate the anniversary of Columbus' discovery of America. It is located at 3819 Jones Street in Omaha. In 1990, after the school closed, the building was added to the National Registry of Historic Places and declared an Omaha Landmark. Photo: Wikimedia Commons; user: Ammodramus.

While still in grade school (Dorothy attended the Columbian Elementary School at 3819 Jones Street),[42] she was already writing and performing in plays. The potency of her innate talent must have been apparent to her "observant principal,"[43] who urged Dorothy to join the Omaha Community Playhouse, a wise piece of advice that, down the line, would yield results neither he nor Dorothy could have anticipated.

[42] The original two-story Columbian School building, designed by Liechtenstein-born American architect John Latenser, Sr. (1858–1936) in the Richardsonian Romanesque style and inaugurated in 1892, was listed in the National Registry of Historic Places in 1990 and has been converted to residential apartments.

[43] Champlin, "Sensitivity" (1976), op. cit.

The Omaha Community Playhouse began as a small venue promoted by a group of business leaders, academics and theater lovers. These patrons of the arts gathered in September 1924 with the objective of founding a community theater in Omaha. Initially part of the "Little Theater" national movement,[44] the venue assumed different names before settling on its current appellative: Community Playhouse, Omaha Playhouse, and finally Omaha Community Playhouse. It was the first non-professional community theater in town.

The inauguration took place on March 4, 1925, with a variety show starring, among others, Dorothy "Dodie" Brando, mother of future celebrity Marlon Brando. The first actual play to be performed was *The Enchanted Cottage*, in April 1925, Dodie Brando again starring. Henry Fonda, a native of Grand Island, Nebraska, began acting at the playhouse at age twenty, starring in the theater's third show (his father was house manager).

The "new temporary" Omaha Community Playhouse building, erected in 1928. Courtesy of the Omaha Community Playhouse.

---

44 For further reading, see: Dorothy Chansky, *Composing Ourselves: The Little Theatre Movement and the American Audience*, Southern Illinois University Press, 2004.

In 1928, the "temporary" theater of those first years was replaced by another temporary venue designed by Alan McDonald, the architect who would be responsible, with his father John, for the imposing Art Deco home of the Joslyn Art Museum (or Joslyn Memorial) in 1931. In 1963, this museum would mount an exhibit of John Swope's photography (see Part I, Chapter 7).

A rendering of the exterior of the Joslyn Memorial, Omaha, Nebraska, designed by architects John and Alan McDonald and inaugurated in 1931. From a postcard, Eric Nelson News Co., Omaha, circa 1940.

Erected in a record-breaking two weeks and four days, the "new temporary" 252-seat playhouse was located at 40th and Davenport and was endowed with an intimate stage measuring fifty feet wide by twenty-four feet deep, with a proscenium arch thirty by thirteen feet. It was inaugurated on October 30, 1928.[45] This "new temporary" playhouse would in turn be supplanted by a larger 520-seat theater which had its grand opening in 1959, with performances of the play *Say, Darling* by Abe Burrows and Richard and Marian Bissell. The opening was covered by a live television

---

45 Warren Francke, *The Omaha Community Playhouse Story*, Omaha Community Playhouse, 2014, 64–66.

special showing the theater facilities and welcoming first-nighters. Dorothy and Fonda appeared on the show, introducing the special. The Playhouse would eventually establish itself as the largest community theater in the United States, a distinction it still held at the time of writing this.

According to drama critic Robert Francis of the *Brooklyn Eagle*, who wrote an early profile of Dorothy on the occasion of her Broadway performance in Thornton Wilder's *Our Town* (1938), Dorothy's Omaha debut occurred when, aged eleven, she appeared in an adaptation of Frances Hodgson Burnett's *A Little Princess*.[46] The Omaha Community Playhouse history confirms that such debut occurred on October 12, 1929.[47] Dorothy played Ermengarde, to good local reviews. Just months later, in January 1930, Dorothy performed a dual role (as the Fairy and as Madame Berlingot) in Maeterlinck's *The Blue Bird*.[48] According to Kevin Sweeney's biography of Henry Fonda, Dorothy also played the part of Snow White before her famous turn in *A Kiss for Cinderella*, though no such role or play is referenced in Francke's in-house history of the Playhouse.[49]

The star-making turn that Dorothy would unfailingly mention for the rest of her life when talking about her beginnings (often referring to it as her real "stage debut")[50] occurred in 1930. A thirteen-year-old Dorothy, whom just about everyone even marginally involved in the production later claimed to have discovered, played in the Playhouse's fifth-season production of James M. Barrie's 1916 play *A Kiss for Cinderella*. Her co-star was Henry Fonda, who, having cut his teeth with the University Players of Cape Cod and in some pre-Broadway shows, returned to his hometown to make a guest appearance at the theater where he had first treaded the

46 Robert Francis, "It Can Happen Here," *Brooklyn Eagle*, September 11, 1938.

47 Francke (2014), op. cit., 73.

48 Ibid., 75

49 See Kevin Sweeney, *Henry Fonda: A Bio-Bibliography*, Greenwood Press, 1992, 8.

50 For example in Anderson, "First Role" (1972), op. cit.

boards. Fonda, touted as a "celebrity" in the Playhouse's publicity, played the Policeman-Prince. The set was designed by Fonda, the lighting was by Ernest Zschau, and the play was directed by Bernard Szold.[51]

In his autobiography, Fonda himself claims he "discovered" young Dorothy and selected her to play Cinderella opposite him. For two reasons: (1) she looked "awful pretty," and (2) she was the only woman performing her audition without a script. Here is Fonda relating this version of a story he told (and embellished) often during his lifetime:

> She came center stage and we did the scene together, neither of us using scripts. And that was it. There was no more contest. Her name was Dorothy McGuire and she was wonderful.[52]

So popular was the show that one of its performances had to be moved to a larger venue, the auditorium at Tech High School, seating 1,500. Seven performances were given to packed houses, from April 28 to May 3, 1930.[53] That summer, Fonda also performed and directed the play for the University Players in West Falmouth, Massachusetts, and on tour, future wife Margaret Sullavan[54] co-starring.[55]

---

51 According to Sweeney's biography of Fonda, however, Director Greg Foley was also involved, and cast Dorothy in the part of Cinderella together with Fonda, even though, according to Francke, by 1928 Foley had already left the Playhouse as its director, to be replaced by Bernard Szold (Francke [2014], op. cit., 59–60). See: Sweeney (1992), op. cit., 8.

52 Howard Teichmann, *Fonda: My Life, As Told to Howard Teichmann*, New American Library, 1981, 57.

53 Ibid., 78–80.

54 Sullavan was married to Fonda from 1931 to 1933.

55 See: Sweeney (1992), op. cit., 8. See also: Bob Fischbach, "As the Omaha Community Playhouse turns 90, we look back at its rich history," *Omaha (NE) World-Herald*, March 30, 2015.

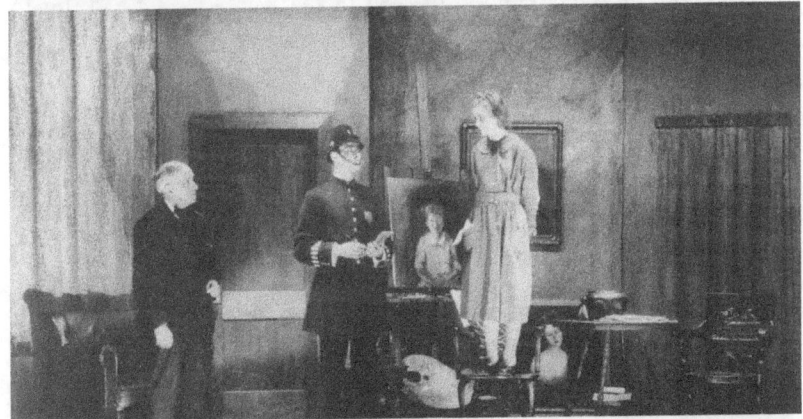

Three moments from *A Kiss for Cinderella*, starring Dorothy McGuire and Henry Fonda, April 1930. Courtesy of the Omaha Community Playhouse, Omaha, Nebraska.

The cast of *A Kiss for Cinderella* was the following: Dorothy McGuire (Cinderella), William Higgins (Man in the Penny Shop), Mrs. J. Dick Anderson (Mrs. Maloney), Agnes Cragin Krell (Marion), Daniel F. Greenhouse (Man with the Shirt), Patty Ann Farber (Marie Therese), Betty Porter (Gladys), Betty Moore (Gretchen), Harold Thom (Lord Mayor), H. M. Baldridge (Lord Times), William Higgins (The King), Mrs. J. Dick Anderson (The Queen), Henry Fonda (The Prince), Cecil Erickson (The Censor), Mildred Cody and Nellie Ann Cody (Two Ugly Sisters), and others.

Drama critic Keene Abbott of the Omaha *World-Herald* had this to say about Dorothy in *Cinderella*:

> Only now and then, and that very rarely, it is given to a child of 13 to have a perception of emotions far beyond its years while it still retains the artless innocence of childhood. Such a gift has Dorothy McGuire. She may do something unusual with her gifts as the years go on, but Omaha will remember her as Barrie's adorable Cinderella.[56]

The following two seasons would see Dorothy appearing at the Playhouse as her mentor Bernard Szold's leading lady, first in Alberto Casella/Walter Ferris's *Death Takes a Holiday*[57] (playing Grazia Lamberti to

---

[56] Quoted in Francke (2014), op. cit., 79.

[57] The play was a 1929 English-language adaptation by Walter Ferris of a 1924 play by Italian playwright Alberto Casella, originally entitled *La morte in vacanza*. The play was the inspiration for several official and unofficial remakes, such as the 1934 film *Death Takes a Holiday*, starring Fredric March and directed by Mitchell Leisen, and *Meet Joe Black* (1998) starring Brad Pitt and Anthony Hopkins. Poet, drama critic, short-story writer, playwright, screenwriter and theater director Alberto Casella (1891–1957) wrote for all dramatic media, including radio. *La morte in vacanza* was his biggest success. The play's Broadway production at the Ethel Barrymore Theatre ran for 180 performances (December 1929–June 1930); it starred Rose Hobart in the part of Grazia and Philip Merivale as Death. In 2011, the Roundabout Theatre Company produced a musical based on the play, with a book by Peter Stone and Thomas Meehan and music and lyrics by Maury Yeston. It ran at the Laura Pels Theatre in New York from July 14 to September 4, 2011, to mixed

Szold's Death) in April 1931, then in Booth Tarkington's *Mister Antonio* in the 1931–32 season. Keene Abbott of the local *World-Herald* defined her performance in *Death* as "unforgettable," interestingly remarking that Dorothy brought "an ethereal quality which is exquisite."[58] That exquisite, ethereal quality would remain a signature trait of Dorothy's.

A headshot of actor-director Bernard Szold, 1941. Photo: Johan Hagemeyer.

Young Dorothy was still almost incurably shy and just as incurably insecure at this stage of her career, but something clicked within her during *A Kiss for Cinderella*, as she reported to columnist Virginia Irwin in 1942:

> I didn't lose my shyness, but I did lose that awful feeling that I was no good. And it was then that I knew suddenly that

but generally favorable reviews. Julian Ovenden played Death, Jill Paice Grazia.

58 Quoted in Francke (2014), op. cit., 87.

I would never want to be anything but an actress. Up until that time I had toyed with the idea of either becoming an opera singer, an artist or a dancer. But after 'A Kiss for Cinderella,' I was positively on fire with the ambition to become an actress.[59]

The "definitive" Omaha Community Playhouse building under construction, captured by a September 1958 snapshot. The venue would be inaugurated in 1959. Courtesy of the Omaha Community Playhouse.

---

59 Virginia Irwin, "Cinderella Girl of the Stage," *St. Louis (MO) Post-Dispatch*, December 21, 1942.

5. A Claudia Is Born

> *Bennett Cerf: You say you were on the Broadway stage briefly?*
> *Dorothy McGuire: In several plays, yes. Several flops and a couple of successes, yes.*
> Blindfolded panelist Bennett Cerf[60] questioning mystery guest Dorothy McGuire to try to guess her identity on the television program *What's My Line?* (July 25, 1954)

The story of Dorothy's rise to Broadway success reads like a Cinderella fable, and that is exactly the way the American press told it to its readers once such success had been achieved.

After Dorothy's starring role in *A Kiss for Cinderella* in Omaha, her mother re-established order in her daughter's priorities by shipping her

---

60 Columbia University alumnus Bennett Alfred Cerf (1898–1971) was an American author, joke and anecdote collector, humorist, radio host, television panelist, lecturer and publisher. In 1925, together with Donald Klopfer, he founded Random House. Cerf was a regular panelist on *What's My Line?* from 1951 until the show's demise in 1967. He was briefly (1935–1936) married to actress Sylvia Sidney. Already an acquaintance of Herbert Bayard Swope in the 1920s, he later became friends with Dorothy and John Swope, and published John's first photography book.

off to the Ladywood Convent School outside Indianapolis for two years; Dorothy comported herself well at the school, receiving an average of 91 ½ in her courses.[61] In 1941, the *Indianapolis Star*, having researched Dorothy's school years after her rise to Broadway fame, commented on her personality:

> [Dorothy] was a vivacious and effervescent schoolgirl, and had the happy faculty of giving and taking gracefully.[62]

After Indianapolis, Dorothy was whisked off to Pine Manor College in Wellesley, Massachusetts, which had an excellent drama department and coach.[63] Occasionally, Dorothy told a different version of events, in which she attended Junior College in Omaha before traveling to Wellesley.[64] Perhaps the slight uncertainty in Dorothy's tales of her late teenage years was due to her antipathy to higher education; as she put it in an interview with Virginia Irwin in 1942:

> I wasn't the slightest bit interested in being educated. All I wanted to do was act. [At Pine Manor] I was president of the dramatic club and kept so busy acting that I finally flunked French. Of course, that kept me out of the next play, and I got long lectures on how every bit of knowledge would some day come in handy if I were on the stage. I thought my teachers were just a lot of old poohs, and so I hauled myself off to New York to get started in the theater.[65]

---

61 Hellman, "McGuire" (1941), op. cit., 126.

62 Quoted by Hellman, "McGuire" (1941), op. cit., 126.

63 Champlin, "Sensitivity" (1976), op. cit.

64 For example in her bio in the program for the Actors' Company production of *Summer and Smoke*, 1950.

65 Irwin, "Cinderella" (1942), op. cit.

A Claudia is Born

Pine Manor, Dana Hall School, Wellesley, Massachusetts. From a postcard, circa 1940.

After graduation, Dorothy took a trip to New York with her mother to see the sights and take in some shows. She then decided to further her instruction and search for theatrical employment, and settled in New York, sharing "an apartment with a slightly older Omaha girl."[66] The year was 1937. Her late father had left her just enough money to live on modestly, and this took the edge off Dorothy's lean New York years. She studied singing and dancing, and began to knock on the doors of producers' offices. One of these producers was Jed Harris. Here is the anecdote about her first meeting with him, as recounted by Hellman:

> Somehow, Dorothy got in to see him, and he asked her what experience she had had. "I directed and acted in plays at Pine Manor Junior College," she said, with the confidence of

---

66 Hellman, "McGuire" (1941), op. cit., 126.

a girl who had never heard of Jed Harris until the day before. "What plays?" asked Harris, with the indifference of a man who had never heard of Pine Manor Junior College. "Well, we did a pirate play," Dorothy replied. "Oh," said Harris. He gave her a part to read, listened irritably for a few moments, said, "Don't scream it," and the interview was over.[67]

Harris would play an important part in Dorothy's nascent Broadway career about a year later, but neither he nor Dorothy knew it yet. Her Omaha and Wellesley curricula impressed no one, so Dorothy decided she must gain experience. She performed in summer stock theater in Harrison, Maine (or, according to one source, in Deetress, Maine), living "at the undertaker's parlor"[68] and appearing with stars such as Joe E. Brown and Mildred Natwick (in George Kelly's *The Show-Off*).[69] She then went back to New York to knock on more doors. Dorothy described those New York rounds in a 1941 interview:

> [...] I played understudies and I played bits and I walked from benches in one manager's office to another. And I lived in Broadway hotels and argued with Chinese landrymen about when I could pay my bill.[70]

One of those "bits," according to an interview Dorothy gave in 1972, was in the play *Bachelor Born* written by Ian Hay. According to that interview, this had been Dorothy's "first New York role," in a play that

[67] Ibid.

[68] Reed, "Competitive Spirit" (1977), op. cit.

[69] See Burns Mantle, "Jai Alai Again Shows Its Face to Americans," *Chicago Tribune*, September 18, 1938. See also: Champlin, "Sensitivity" (1976), op. cit.

[70] Mark Barron, "Girl's Persistence Leads to Broadway Success," *Rochester (NY) Democrat and Chronicle*, February 24, 1941.

Dorothy termed "a flop."[71] No corroboration, however, could be found for Dorothy's presence in the cast of the play, which was not so big a flop as Dorothy reported: it opened at the Morosco Theatre[72] in January 1938 and, having transferred to the Lyceum Theatre,[73] ended up running for 400 performances. Not a bad number, considering that Thornton Wilder's Pulitzer Prize-winning play *Our Town* ran for 336. She may have been an understudy. It would appear that, though there are plenty of solid points in Dorothy's reports to triangulate her early New York career, many of the details are a bit blurry, and only come into focus when recounting her most successful roles. This is only natural: her early experiences in the New York theater were fraught with disappointment and heartache, and she must have been eager to forget them; only the persistence of journalists forced her to remember those events, reluctantly. One thing is certain: those early disappointments were no boost to Dorothy's ego, nor to her confidence:

> [. . .] I walked into a job because I happened to look just right, but on the third day I got bounced out. Of course, I was so heartbroken I was sure I'd never recover. All my confidence was gone. Finally I mustered enough courage to go on and get

---

71 Anderson, "First Role" (1972), op. cit.

72 The Morosco Theatre was designed by architect Herbert J. Krapp and opened in 1917. It seated 955. The venue closed in 1981 and was demolished in 1982, along with the Helen Hayes, Bijou, Astor, and Gaiety Theaters, to make place for the Marriott Marquis Hotel and Marquis Theatre. This five-theater demolition has been popularly referred to as "The Great Theater Massacre of 1982."

73 The Lyceum Theatre still stands at 149 W. 45th Street in New York City's theater district. Designed in the *Beaux-Arts* style by architects Henry Beaumont Herts and Hugh Tallant of Herts & Tallant, the theater, which seats 922, opened in 1903. The firm of Herts and Tallant was responsible for the design of several famous Broadway theaters, such as the New Amsterdam Theatre (214 W. 42nd Street), the Fulton (later the Helen Hayes, destroyed in 1982, see previous note), the Gaiety (1547 Broadway, also razed in 1982), and the Brooklyn Academy of Music (BAM's Peter Jay Sharpe building, at 30 Lafayette Avenue, Brooklyn), designed in 1908.

a job as understudy, but the play was a flop and ran only two weeks.⁷⁴ Then I really did give up and it was then I turned to radio. I was the 'little sister' on the 'Big Sister' program⁷⁵ and after every performance I'd have what practically amounted to a nervous breakdown.⁷⁶

A significant break came Dorothy's way when she was chosen as Martha Scott's understudy in the Broadway production of Thornton Wilder's *Our Town*. Producer Jed Harris had been interviewing dozens of applicants and his mind was almost made up, when Dorothy walked in. This time, he saw something special in the young actress, and hired her on the spot, offering her an uncharacteristic contract to play the role of Emily for the remainder of the play's run. The standard procedure would have been to hire her only until another "name" could be cast in the part.⁷⁷

Martha Scott enjoyed exceptionally good health during the first six months of the play's run (February–July 1938), but then signed for the film version and decided to leave the play to go to Hollywood. Dorothy took over. Audiences, and a few isolated late-hour reviewers, liked what they saw. However, as Dorothy explained:

> Critics, agents, producers and scouts usually attend only opening nights or performances during the early weeks of a play's run, and so I escaped their notice.⁷⁸

---

74 The play was entitled *Stop-over,* and played at the Lyceum Theatre in New York (January 11–January 29, 1938) for twenty-three performances. See *Decatur (IL) Daily Review,* September 28, 1938. See also: IBDB (Internet Broadway Database).

75 Replacing Haila Stoddard, who had previously played the part.

76 Irwin, "Cinderella" (1942), op. cit.

77 Actress Teresa Wright was Dorothy's understudy. See: Paul Rosenfield, "Teresa Wright: Enter Teacher, Stage Left," *Los Angeles Times,* January 18, 1982. See also: Erskine Johnson (NEA), "In Hollywood," *Dunkirk (NY) Evening Observer,* April 14, 1947.

78 Irwin, "Cinderella" (1942), op. cit. See also: Robert Francis, "It Can Happen Here,"

A Claudia is Born

Partially contradicting this early tale of the events surrounding *Our Town* is a version that Dorothy told in later years. As *Los Angeles Times* Arts Editor and critic Charles Champlin explained in his lovely profile of Dorothy in 1976:

> The break [of playing Emily] carried another break with it. The night she replaced Martha Scott was also the night Thornton Wilder, the author, took over for Frank Craven as the play's narrator, and all the critics came by to review Wilder, reviewing her, too, and pleasantly.[79]

Here is one of those critics, Robert Francis of the *Brooklyn Eagle*, commenting on the new casting:

> [. . .] I stopped in one night last week at the Morosco to see what it was all about. It hardly seemed possible that a young woman with such slight professional background could step into and adequately fill a difficult Broadway role. Strange as it seems, the play has lost nothing by the change. In fact, I liked Miss McGuire in the last act better than her predecessor, who I thought in her last scenes had somewhat of a tendency to be fluttery and to overact.[80]

Brooklyn Eagle, September 11, 1938.

79 Champlin, "Sensitivity" (1976), op. cit.

80 Robert Francis, "It Can Happen Here," *Brooklyn Eagle*, September 11, 1938. One can have an inkling of the quality of Dorothy's acting in the last act of *Our Town* by listening to her rendition in the radio adaptation she performed, with Wilder himself in the role of the narrator/stage manager, for the *Theatre Guild on the Air* in 1946 (see Part I, Chapter 11).

Burns Mantle, special New York correspondent for the *Chicago Tribune*, introduced the young Nebraskan newcomer in his Broadway report on September 18, 1938:

> Incidentally "Our Town" has a new bride in the person of a young woman from Omaha, Neb., named Dorothy McGuire. Dorothy is one of those sensitive, eager, and talented ingénues who arrive periodically to confound the prophets and disturb the parents of pretty daughters with stage ambitions. [. . . Dorothy] walked smack into this chance to play one of the most sought after parts on Broadway. Plays it very nicely, too.[81]

Young Dorothy did not escape the notice of Thornton Wilder himself, who would choose to co-star with her in a radio version of his play eight years later. Bewildered Dorothy certainly was at being chosen to play Emily in *Our Town*, as she readily admitted in interviews; but a telegram from her beloved father, one that she had kept with her and would keep for some years, helped her remain centered. The wire, which Mr. McGuire had sent to her from New York when Dorothy had played her role in *A Kiss for Cinderella* in Omaha, recited, "Head in the clouds but toes on the ground. Two kisses for Cinderella, Father."[82]

Playing a leading role in such a grand project as *Our Town*, and on Broadway, gave Dorothy artistic prestige but little help in making her famous. Therefore, she started making the rounds again. Finally, she landed a job playing the role of Portia Trent, one of John Barrymore's daughters, in the pre-Broadway tour of the play *My Dear Children* (1938), written

---

[81] Mantle, "Jai Alai" (1938), op. cit.

[82] William F. Frank, "The Man About Town," *Wilmington (DE) News Journal*, March 23, 1939. In another interview some forty years later, Dorothy remembered the text of that telegram differently: "Touch the stars with your head. Keep your feet on the ground. Twenty-one stars for Cinderella." (See: Champlin, "Sensitivity" [1976], op. cit.)

by Catherine Turney and Jerry Horwin. Lois Hall and Barrymore's wife Elaine Barrie co-starred. The play toured the nation, running in cities such as Washington, Detroit, and Chicago for some eight months with Dorothy,[83] before opening on Broadway *sans* Dorothy at the Belasco Theatre[84] and running for three and a half months the following year (January 31–May 18, 1940).

According to contemporary newspaper coverage of the out-of-town tour of *My Dear Children*, the production was something of a middling affair: the play was only mildly amusing, and John Barrymore, in his last stage role, was an erratic mess. Discreet, oblique reports of Barrymore's anti-social behavior and drunken stupors made it abundantly clear just how difficult it must have been to work or socialize with him. Audience reports were not much more positive, denouncing an inconsistent, startling, occasionally embarrassing stage performance. In one article covering the play's run in Omaha, Dorothy's mother, interviewed about the production, refused to comment on Barrymore's acting.[85] Dorothy herself commented on Barrymore's shenanigans two years later: "I'd come blissful and starry-eyed from Our Town into this roughhouse. I really and truly was shocked."[86]

Unhappy with the production's roughhouse atmosphere and scheduled to begin rehearsals for a show in New York, Dorothy left the cast of *My Dear Children* during the pre-Broadway tour, at Chicago's Selwyn Theatre, around the time when Elaine Barrie separated from husband Bar-

---

[83] "Claudia Was Truly Hard to Find but Dorothy McGuire Walked In One Day and She Was It," *Brooklyn Eagle*, February 9, 1941.

[84] Originally the Stuyvesant Theatre, the Belasco was designed by architect George Keister for impresario David Belasco and inaugurated in October 1907. It is located at 111 W. 44th Street in the New York theater district.

[85] "Omaha Upset By Barrymore," *Des Moines (IA) Register*, May 3, 1939.

[86] Hellman, "McGuire" (1941), op. cit., 129.

rymore. Dorothy was replaced by Patricia Waters.[87] Another cast member, Lloyd Gough, also withdrew, and was supplanted by Kenneth Treseder.[88]

Her golden ticket still about two years away, Dorothy joined the cast of William Saroyan's Pulitzer Prize-winning play *The Time of Your Life* (1939) as general understudy for the female roles[89] while rehearsing for the role of Helena in *Swingin' the Dream*, a "Musical Variation of Shakespeare's *A Midsummer Night's Dream*"[90] set in 19th-century Louisiana.

This particular *Dream*, in which white performers played the members of Theseus' court (Theodore in this version) and African-American performers the "mechanicals" and fairies, was created by Gilbert Seldes and Erik Charell; the sets were designed by Herbert Andrews and Walter Jagemann "after cartoons by Walt Disney" (and with special permission from Walt Disney Productions); the dances were choreographed by none other than Agnes de Mille;[91] the dialogue was directed by Philip Loeb; and the jitterbugs were created by Herbert White. Musical direction was by Don Voorhees, with music by Louis Armstrong, Count Basie, Benny Goodman, Jimmy Van Heusen, and others.[92] The cast included

---

[87] Ms. Waters' father, Captain Pierce Powers-Waters, was the manager of John Barrymore's company. (See *Chicago Tribune*, October 1, 1939.)

[88] Cecil Smith, "Looking Back Over 1939–40 Theater Fare," *Chicago Tribune*, June 9, 1940.

[89] See Harold W. Cohen, "The Drama Desk," Pittsburgh (PA) Post-Gazette, October 24, 1940. This was the play's third run in two years, which took place at the Guild Theatre in New York. The play went on tour following the Guild Theatre closing date, October 19. According to other sources (e.g. Hellman, "McGuire" [1941], op. cit., 129), Dorothy's job was understudy to protagonist Julie Haydon.

[90] From the Center Theatre playbill for *Swingin' the Dream*, November 1939.

[91] Celebrated dancer and choreographer Agnes de Mille (1905–1993) is best remembered for her ballet *Rodeo*, with a score by Aaron Copland, and for her work in some famous Broadway musicals of the 1940s, such as *Oklahoma!* (1943), *Carousel* (1945), *Brigadoon* (1947), and *Gentlemen Prefer Blondes* (1949). A lifelong friend of legendary choreographer and dancer Martha Graham (1894–1991), de Mille was Cecil B. DeMille's niece.

[92] *Chicago Tribune*, October 1, 1939.

Louis Armstrong as Bottom/Pyramus, Maxine Sullivan as Titania, Juan Hernandez[93] as Oberon, Butterfly McQueen as Puck, and the Dandridge Sisters as three Pixies.[94]

Unfortunately for Dorothy, nothing came of her understudy job in the former project, and the latter musical flopped miserably after a thirteen-performance stint at New York's Center Theatre (November 29–December 9, 1939). In the case of *Swingin' the Dream*, this is a shame, for the show was probably a joyous, riotous mess.

Dream was plagued by trouble even before being snubbed by critics and audiences alike. One anecdote connected to the show concerns celebrated cartoonist Al Hirschfeld, who drew the artwork for programs and window displays. Here is a version of it from the website of the Al Hirschfeld Foundation:

> And how does Al Hirschfeld figure into all of this? He created the artwork [...] for the prints [sic] ads and program cover, and he subsequently drew a wild drawing of the show for the *New York Times*. Alas he was not paid for the former (although we are quite sure he was renumerated [sic] for the latter, as he continued to work for the publication for another sixty-three years). A lawyer friend suggested Hirschfeld sue the producers Erik Charell and Jean Rodney, and indeed the lawyer got an injunction against the production, which resulted in an impounding of all the musicians' instruments from kettle drums on down, including Armstrong's trumpet. All of

---

[93] Juan Hernandez also performed under the name Juano Hernandez; he was the actor who would co-star with Dorothy in the film *Trial* (1955). See Frances Teague, *Shakespeare and the American Popular Stage*, Cambridge University Press, 2006, 127.

[94] Information from several sources, including the original Center Theatre playbill. For an interesting academic take on the production, see Alan Corrigan's paper "Jazz, Shakespeare and Hybridity: A Script Excerpt from 'Swingin' the Dream,'" published in the online Shakespeare periodical *Borrowers and Lenders: the Journal of Shakespeare and Appropriation* (www.borrowers.uga.edu/781411/show).

which were hauled to Hirschfeld's studio, then located atop the Osborne apartment building on 57th Street. Hirschfeld was paid, the insttruments [sic] returned, and the drawings filed away in the Hirschfeld studio for more than a half century before entering public collections.[95]

Louis Armstrong as Bottom and the Dandridge Sisters as Pixies, from a period publicity postcard for *Swingin' the Dream*, 1939.

Brooks Atkinson of the *New York Times* recognized the potential greatness of the talents involved in the eccentric show, but sentenced:

> It would have been better to throw Shakespeare out the window. The pedestrian jest cracked in his name merely stands in the way of a lively raree-show. Every now and then a flare of dancing breaks through the professional patter, and the Benny Goodman boys perform brilliantly on a piece of music. But

---

95 Al Hirschfeld Foundation (www.alhirschfeldfoundation.org), News, "Musical Monday: Swingin' the Dream," posted on April 23, 2012.

the going is heavy through long stretches of the evening. "The Boys from Syracuse" did better by forgetting Shakespeare altogether.[96]

Here is scholar Alan Corrigan commenting on the reviewers' stance towards the show:

> Most reviewers of *Swingin' the Dream* focused on the production through the discursive lens of either swing or Shakespeare. One reviewer writes, for example, that "the show which was meant to be a mammoth orgy of swing missed its objective.» He makes no mention of Shakespeare, but describes the "dreadful distance" that "separated the audience from dancers and music alike" and complains that the elements of the production did not "reach out to the spectator and make him take part, even vicariously, in the festivities" (*Theatre Arts* 1940 review). For the reviewer, the production should have capitalized on the conception of jazz as an interactive art form, one in which the distance between performer and audience is minimized. This was, after all, dance music. [...]
>
> A few reviewers complained that the play should have focused more on Shakespeare; one called it "more Cotton Club than bard," and a "hybrid Shakespearean shageroo"; but by far the consensus was that the production should have stuck to what its players knew best: swing (*Variety*, review, December 5, 1939). This bias resulted in part because fewer of the kinds of reviewers who would have wanted more Shakespeare would have seen the play. In a survey of the most recent spate

---

[96] Brooks Atkinson, "Swingin' the Dream," *New York Times*, November 30, 1939; quoted by Frances Teague, *Shakespeare and the American Popular Stage*, Cambridge University Press, 2006, 129.

of Shakespearean productions, for example, the theater critic from *Time* acknowledged *Swingin' the Dream* only in a disparaging footnote: "Swingin' the Dream, a jitterbug version of *A Midsummer Night's Dream*, opened a week earlier; but no self-respecting Bard-hunter would stalk such mongrel prey" (*Time*, review, December 18, 1939). The reviewer's dismissive comment, especially his use of the term "mongrel," betrays an anxiety about intermixing cultures, and suggests that the text itself has been miscegenated. "At one moment you hear genuine pentameters in the style and sometimes the original wording of the bard," said a reviewer, "at another you hear anticlimactic lines like 'go fly a kite' that are appropriate neither to Shakespeare nor to the New Orleans 1890 setting into which the story has been dumped" (Laurence Bergreen, 1997, 396).[97]

Dorothy then went into a play called *Medicine Show*, which was termed a "Living Newspaper." Living Newspapers (originally part of the New Deal program called the Federal Theater Project, 1935–1939) were plays written by teams of researchers/playwrights, usually addressing social and political themes, often from a left-wing perspective. The play opened at the New Yorker Theater[98] in New York on April 12, 1940, "at good democratic prices."[99] A descendant of similar projects produced by the defunct Federal Theater, the show was a socially informative, dramatized treatise on the topic of socialized medicine. Here is some information about the production from Arthur Pollock's *Brooklyn Eagle* review:

---

97 Corrigan, "Jazz, Shakespeare" (2004), op. cit.

98 The New Yorker Theatre, 254 W. 54th Street, New York, would later close as a theater and become a performance/radio space for CBS, and eventually the world-famous disco Studio 54.

99 *Brooklyn Eagle*, April 7, 1940.

Oscar Saul and H.R. Hays wrote "Medicine Show," making it, first, a show, then filling it with exciting statistics, the while knotting it together into a tight loop for the neck of the American Medical Association, villain of the piece. Two hundred and fifty thousand who need not die, die, nevertheless, in this country every year. So says "Medicine Show," citing facts, drawing sharp pictures to make it clear. They die because doctors and patients cannot get together, being kept apart by money.

[...] Perhaps all this sounds as if "Medicine Show" were a shade dry. Don't be so sure. The Living Newspaper has never been dry. They dramatize statements of fact at the New Yorker, and when the play came to an end last night its merits were rewarded with a lively display of enthusiasm from the audience. In fact, it was interrupted a number of times by such displays as it went along. They are deserved, for everything is well done in all respects—acted with simple force, directed in natural fashion by Jules Dassin, whose actors seldom act like actors; aptly set and lighted by Samuel Leve.

[...] Martin Gabel, always natural without affectations of weak casualness, plays a statistician explaining to laymen who come on the stage from the audience just why and how men, women and children die when death could be avoided. They pass through a vast door in their willingness to learn, only to discover that they cannot leave the world they enter, remaining locked in with the problem. Coburn Goodwin, Dorothy McGuire, Norman Lloyd, Olive Deering, Alfred Ryder—no use to mention names, for they are all sound, carefully directed actors.

So here is "Medicine Show." It is a show. It has even a pair of chorus girls with legs (pretty) and a song to sing. A show not precisely frivolous, but one that takes hold of you, startles you with its machine-gun fire of facts. A vital play, in short.[100]

---

[100] Arthur Pollock, "'Medicine Show' Puts Drama Into Doctoring," *Brooklyn Daily Eagle*,

Medicine Show was a noble project but, after 35 performances, proved an artistic/commercial flop. Dorothy also played a small role (Ada the lunatic girl) in the 1940 Broadway revival of Edward Chodorov's *Kind Lady*, starring Grace George (September–November 1940); the play was described by one contemporary critic as "a smooth and entertaining drama of genteel horror."[101] The original 1935 production at the Longacre Theatre[102] had only survived for twenty performances; the revival at the Playhouse Theatre[103] fared much better, lasting 107 performances.

It was during her understudy job for *The Time of Your Life* (October 1939–April 1940) in Chicago that, uncharacteristically, Dorothy was briefly targeted by a particular beast that would seldom stalk her during her successful Hollywood years except in the nicest of ways: the gossip column, or, more precisely, the smear item. The offending columnist was Harold W. Cohen, drama critic of the *Pittsburgh Post-Gazette*, who would eventually have complimentary things to say about Dorothy after her breakthrough role in *Claudia* just months later. Here, in October 1940, Cohen mentions the actress in his column "The Drama Desk," which often gave a Winchellian flavor to its society innuendos:

> That Jerry Freshman, of Chicago's Hotel Ambassador, certainly gets around—and with the nicest people. He was in town for only a few hours on Tuesday and had dinner at the William Penn's Italian Room with Julie Haydon and supper at the Chatterbox with Dorothy McGuire.[104]

April 13, 1940.

[101] Jack Gaver (UP), "Up and Down Broadway," *Bradford (PA) Evening Star*, September 6, 1940.

[102] The Longacre Theatre is located at 220 W. 48th Street, New York. It was designed by architect Henry B. Herts and inaugurated on May 1, 1913.

[103] The Playhouse Theatre, designed by architect Charles A. Rich and inaugurated on April 15, 1911, was located at 137 W. 48th Street. It closed in 1926 and was demolished in 1969.

[104] Cohen, "Drama" (1940), op. cit.

Which would seem innocuous enough, except for the fact that thirty-two-year-old Jerry Freshman was a notorious man-about-town and womanizer.[105] The profligate assistant manager of the Ambassador East Hotel in Chicago had extravagant tastes and was known to cultivate every vice known to man, particularly in the sexual arena. Thus, the whiff of spoiled innocence that wafts through Cohen's item seems odd when applied to Dorothy, even if it was intended as a benevolent plug for her budding acting career.

But, again, fame eluded Dorothy. Radio provided some relief, as in 1940 Dorothy briefly joined the cast of the medical soap *Joyce Jordan, M.D.* But her life as an actress was still precarious. Here is Dorothy commenting on her understudying job in *The Time of Your Life*:

> When I left the play in Chicago to go back to New York, I promised myself that it would be my last try at Broadway. And then the impossible happened.[106]

The impossible, in this case, was her being chosen for the title role in the Broadway production of Rose Franken's *Claudia* (1941), an event that would change Dorothy's life. Even this achievement, however, came at a price for her, and was accompanied by its share of heartache and suffering.

As the story goes, playwright/director Rose Franken and producer John Golden had already seen more than two hundred candidates for the role,[107] practically exhausting all the new talent that was circulating

---

105 See: Alexander H. Hadden, *Not Me! The World War II Memoir of a Reluctant Rifleman*, Merriam Press, 2007, 24–25.

106 Irwin, "Cinderella" (1942), op. cit.

107 According to Dorothy, 209 or 208, depending on the interview. Other sources, such as Akron *Beacon Journal* Theater Editor Betty French, quoted even larger numbers. See Betty French, "U.S. Favorite Bride On Screen," *Akron (OH) Beacon Journal*, July 28, 1943.

in New York City. Their search had gone on for ninety-six days.[108] Franken despaired of ever finding an actress who could embody Claudia, the unspoiled, eccentric, immature-wise nineteen-year-old protagonist of her play, as she had envisaged her.

> Then at last [Franken] was rewarded for her toilsome auditions by discovering Dorothy McGuire, aged only 22[109] and yet possessed of considerable professional stage experience since graduating from Little Theater performances in Omaha.
>
> "The moment I saw her," says Miss Franken, "walking through the door of John Golden's office, I knew she was Claudia. I could only pray she would be able to read the lines as well as she looked the part. And she did that—even better."
>
> The part, of course, is the kind young actresses dream of. It requires Miss McGuire to be on the stage for all except three minutes of the entire play, and her part consists of 142 sides, or sheets of cues and speeches. The usual leading or star part is only about 90 or 100 sides.[110]

A less romantic version of Franken and Golden's epiphany in discovering Dorothy was printed about a decade later, in Leonard Lyons's syndicated column, "The Lyons Den":

> [Miss McGuire] went to the officer [sic] of Producer John Golden, who told her: "Drop your hair. Yes, you're Claudia.". . . He later explained his quick decision: "She was the first girl who didn't apply in mink coat and nail polish."[111]

108 See Alice Hughes, "A Woman's New York," *Indianapolis (IN) Star*, March 11, 1941.

109 She was actually 24.

110 "Hard to Find" (1941), op. cit.

111 Leonard Lyons, "The Lyons Den: Social Note," *Long Beach Independent*, August 2, 1955.

Which, given the number of candidates that had been seen before Dorothy (209) and Dorothy's talent, seems an unlikely reason for Golden and Franken's choice.

Dorothy told a variation of this story in 1976, the same variation that Hellman had told in his 1941 profile. In this version, Dorothy very much wanted to be in another play, Philip Barry's allegorical fable *Liberty Jones*, produced by the Theatre Guild. She auditioned for the titular part and did not get it. Someone suggested she read for the role of Claudia; Dorothy's heart was not in it, but she went anyway. She "breezed in in sweater and skirt and no makeup, and that was it."[112] Actually, that was not it, as the drama desk of the *Brooklyn Eagle* reported after the fact:

> For weeks she practically talked her head off trying to convince the producer [of *Liberty Jones*] she was the only girl who could do justice to the character. At the same time Nancy Coleman was haunting Rose Franken. Nancy had an obsession that she was the actual incarnation of the impulsive, scatterbrained "Claudia."
>
> Dorothy McGuire lost the "Liberty Jones" role. Then and there she was sure her theatrical career was beyond redemption. When she heard that Nancy Coleman got the part she wanted so badly her gloom deepened. She could scarcely pull herself together a few days later when Rose Franken sent for her to discuss the lead in "Claudia."
>
> At the time Dorothy wasn't even interested in accepting the part. She still felt that "Liberty Jones" was the sort of play that had been definitely written for her. She felt it would bring her immediate success. But, having no alternative and

---

[112] Champlin, "Sensitivity" (1976), op. cit.

under pressure from Miss Franken, she reluctantly accepted the "Claudia" role.

Three weeks later "Liberty Jones" folded.[113] "Claudia" ran for three years on the stage before being filmed by 20th Century-Fox, with Dorothy in her original role [...].[114]

In yet another version of the story that Dorothy told again and again over the years, Ms. Franken and her producer had already given up on the project when Dorothy came into Mr. Golden's office to read for the part of Claudia, as correspondent Nancy Anderson reported:

> Actually, Miss Franken wasn't casting "Claudia," though she'd tried. She and John Golden had interviewed 209 unsuccessful applicants for the part and had almost decided against producing the play at all because no proper lead was in sight when Dorothy walked in.
>
> An hour later, the girl from Omaha had the part which would make her a star.[115]

During that first audition in Golden's office, Franken had Dorothy read some pages of the script and was intrigued. She then told Dorothy to change her hairdo and visit her at her country home to read the part again over the weekend. Apparently, Dorothy was still smitten, or disappointed, with *Liberty Jones*. Here is a mention of that weekend from *LIFE*'s 1941 profile of Dorothy:

---

[113] After twenty-one performances. See: Albert Wertheim, *Staging the War: American Drama and World War II*, Indiana University Press, 2003, 40–41.

[114] "Dorothy McGuire Zooms Up From Frustration to Success," *Brooklyn Eagle*, October 31, 1943.

[115] Anderson, "First Role" (1972), op. cit.

[For] an actress to do her best in a play she must be in love with it. When Dorothy tried out for Claudia, she was still in love with *Liberty Jones*. Rose Franken, who saw in her 210th candidate a natural Claudia, perceived this fact, and proceeded, on behalf of her play, to woo Dorothy. She took Dorothy to her Connecticut farm for the weekend, introduced her to her three sons with "This is Claudia," made her swallow huge draughts of milk, and called in the cook to listen as she read the part. The cook pronounced her O.K. Dorothy was softened but not entirely won over.[116]

Dorothy was signed for the role, but her troubles were not over.

At Miss Franken's country home Miss McGuire recovered from some of her shyness, but when she was signed for the role she became so frightened that they decided to fire her.
Then they decided to let her go on for the first two performances in Wilmington and there they discovered: A: That Miss McGuire is an awkward actress in a producer's office; B: She is, as the critical reviewers said, one of the best new actresses on stage Broadway has seen in seasons.[117]

Producer Golden, who was still skeptical of Dorothy's talent, presented her with a "straight Equity" contract, terminable on two weeks' notice. Dorothy's acting during the Washington, DC, try-outs, however, was so excellent that Golden decided to supersede that agreement with a run-of-the-play contract.[118]

---

[116] Hellman, "McGuire" (1941), op. cit., 130.

[117] Barron, "Girl's Persistence..." (1941), op. cit.

[118] Hellman, "McGuire" (1941), op. cit., 130.

Success had finally smiled upon young Dorothy. *Claudia* opened at the Booth Theatre in New York City[119] on February 12, 1941. The other actors in the cast were Donald Cook (David Naughton), Frances Starr (Mrs. Brown), Olga Baklanova (Madame Daruschka), Audrey Ridgewell (Julia Naughton), Adrienne Gessner (Bertha), Frank Tweddell (Fritz), and John Williams (Jerry Seymour).[120] Scenic design was by Donald Oenslager; direction was by Rose Franken. The play was an instant, and thundering, success. It closed temporarily on March 7, 1942, only to be moved to the St. James Theatre[121] on May 24, 1942. It ran at the St. James until November 8, 1942, then moved immediately to the Forrest Theatre,[122] where it finally closed on January 9, 1943, after a total of 722 performances.[123]

Here is how columnist Virginia Irwin reported Dorothy's reaction to that opening-night success:

---

119 The Booth Theatre is a Broadway theater situated at 222 W. 45th Street (George Abbott Way). Designed by architect Henry Beaumont Herts (1871–1933) and named after American Shakespearean actor Edwin Booth (brother of the infamous John Wilkes Booth), it was inaugurated on October 16, 1913.

120 John Williams created the role of Jerry Seymour, the philandering English novelist, but left the show in June 1941 for Army service in his native England. He was replaced, successively, by Arthur Margetson and Wilton Graff. See Harold W. Cohen, "The Drama Desk," *Pittsburgh (PA) Post-Gazette*, March 12, 1942. Olga Baklanova and Frank Tweddell would reprise their respective roles in the 1943 film.

121 Designed by the architecture firm of Warren and Wetmore (designers of the original Grand Central Terminal, 1913), built on the site of the original Sardi's restaurant and inaugurated in 1927 as the Erlanger, the St. James Theatre is located at 246 W. 44th Street in New York City.

122 Designed by prolific theater architect Herbert J. Krapp (1887–1973) and inaugurated in 1925, the Forrest Theatre was renamed the Coronet Theatre in 1945, and subsequently the Eugene O'Neill Theatre in 1959. It is located at 230 W. 49th Street, New York. Among the other New York theaters that Krapp designed there were the Ambassador Theatre, the Brooks Atkinson Theatre, the Ethel Barrymore Theatre, the Biltmore Theatre, the Imperial Theatre, the Majestic Theatre, and the Neil Simon Theatre.

123 One source cites 453 performances, but that may be the number of performances at the Booth Theatre only. See Gerald Bordman, *American Theatre: A Chronicle of Comedy and Drama, 1930–1969*, Oxford University Press, 1996, 200.

When the curtain fell on the opening night of "Claudia" on February 12, 1941, Dorothy had her first taste of triumph. As the cast took curtain call after curtain call, the audience yelled for Dorothy McGuire.

"Excited and bewildered, I stumbled forward to take my

Donald Cook and Dorothy McGuire in a scene from Rose Franken's *Claudia*. Booth Theatre, 1941. Photo: Lucas & Monroe Studio, New York.

Claudia was very successful, and threatened to branch out into quite a franchise, as Hellman explained in his 1941 profile:

A second *Claudia* opened [in September 1941] in Chi-

---
124 Irwin, "Cinderella," op. cit.

cago and is selling to capacity every night. A Number Three *Claudia* company, to tour the country in one-week stands, opens Nov. 14 [1941] in Upper New York. A Number Four *Claudia* company for one-night stands is being seriously considered. A Negro *Claudia* company is being discussed by Miss Franken and John Golden, the play's producer; Miss Franken has already begun tentative casting for this. A radio version of Claudia, sponsored by Grape-Nuts, was a tremendous success last summer, but Miss Franken is now too busy to write it. A television *Claudia* and a comic-strip *Claudia* are under consideration. A Hollywood *Claudia* is a sure bet for 1942, movie rights to the play having been sold to David Selznick for $187,500. Claudia stories are still running strong in *Redbook*. Two Claudia novels—*Claudia* and *Claudia and David*—have been published; a few weeks ago Farrar & Rinehart issued both of these in one volume, entitled, with Biblical simplicity, *The Book of Claudia*. The only reason there isn't a Claudia Skirt in department stores all over the country is that Miss Franken vetoed this as undignified.

In addition to her domestic fame, Claudia is manifesting signs of universality. She has snowballed onto the stages of Sweden and South America and only the war has prevented her foreign vogue from spreading further. Miss Franken, for example, has refused to sell Italian and German rights to the play, for both of which she has refused offers. If the war were to stop tomorrow, Claudia would probably double her momentum abroad. As a character of cosmic appeal, students of trends are beginning to compare her with Penrod and Mickey Mouse.[125]

---

[125] Hellman, "McGuire" (1941), op. cit., 119. Phyllis Thaxter was the Chicago Claudia and replaced Dorothy in the original company when Dorothy left for Hollywood (see also: Patricia Bosworth, *Montgomery Clift: A Biography*, Harcourt Brace Jovanovich, 1978, 80). Pamela Brown was the London Claudia. American actress Terry Walker was the

Dorothy was ranked at a par with Ethel Barrymore for her performance by a *Variety* poll of Broadway critics.[126] Even the usually severe Walter Winchell was quite taken with her performance in the play, writing, with typical pithiness, "She is grand in it [...]."[127] *Claudia*, the crowning success of Dorothy's early theatrical career, was, however, only the beginning of the rest of her professional life. Around the corner, Hollywood was watching.

Once such theatrical success was achieved, many came forward, laying claim to discovering the actress when she was still an unknown, or to prophesying her success before the fact. An amusing syndicated article by columnist Wood Soanes of the *Oakland Tribune* listed the people who had laid such claims, and commented with skepticism on the alleged clairvoyance of all those discoverers. Those prophesies were reported to Soanes by theater manager Al Spink, interviewed for the occasion. Here are some excerpts:

> "Several discoverers have valid evidence of their prior discovery of Miss McGuire as a comer," Spink has discovered. "Harold Cohen, critic of the Pittsburgh Post-Gazette, has resuscitated his review of the touring company of 'Our Town' to prove that he hailed her as a certain star-to-be as early as December, 1938.
>
> "Jay Carmody of the Washington Star has a similar vindication of his early judgments and all of the Chicago critics have early claims in the form of their acclaims bestowed on the then obscure youngster when she appeared in their city

Australian Claudia. Helga Lundberg was the Swedish Claudia.

[126] "Dorothy McGuire Acclaimed By the Hard-Boiled Critics," *Pittsburgh (PA) Press*, March 8, 1942.

[127] Walter Winchell, "On Broadway," *High Point (NC) Enterprise*, April 6, 1941.

with John Barrymore in 'My Dear Children.'

"But far and away the earliest claim is that of Violet Heming, who has not made the claim herself. Her sound prophecy is on record as having been made so long ago that she has probably forgotten it herself.

"The record consists of a newspaper clipping in Miss McGuire's childhood scrap-book which her mother has sent on from her home in Omaha. Many of its leaves are filled with clippings from Omaha newspapers concerning her first hit in her home town, a community theater production of Barrie's 'A Kiss for Cinderella,' in which Henry Fonda, another Omaha thespian, played the romantic policeman.

"That was in 1931 [sic], when Dorothy was just 13 and in the eighth grade of the Columbian School."

[. . .] Omaha made a great deal of [McGuire's performance in the play] and business at the Community began to cut into that of the neighboring stock company where Miss Heming was appearing [as star].

Finally, out of curiosity I presume, Miss Heming decided to take a look at her youthful rival [. . .] and promptly made a statement about her.

"The gal is a born actress," Miss Heming said. "She reads lines with natural intention, not as a child who's been coached. She is like a breath of spring. I hope her parents will let her continue her training and go on the professional stage. I wouldn't have missed seeing her performance for anything."[128]

Soanes, of course, knew how harrowing the road to success was, and was rightly skeptical of those clairvoyant recipes for sure fame:

---

[128] Wood Soanes, "Many Lay Claim to Discovery of 'Claudia' Star, Dorothy McGuire," *Oakland Tribune*, August 21, 1942.

The interesting part of all this, it seems to me, is that three years of work elapsed before Miss McGuire reached Broadway [after her replacing Martha Scott in *Our Town*] and that was called "overnight success." It proves, if nothing more, that there is no such animal as overnight success.[129]

And here are the statements Harold V. Cohen, one of Dorothy's early "discoverers," had made about Dorothy in his review of *Claudia* some five months earlier:

> Miss McGuire is acting the title role with a touch of pure magic. [...] Probably the most talented young actress to come into the theater in a lot of seasons, she is so very right in the title part, so very, very right, that the role and she were apparently made for each other. It would be entirely possible to talk about Miss McGuire as Claudia for columns but time and space forbid, so let it be enough for you to know that the young lady is giving one of the truly memorable performances of the year.[130]

Dorothy's relatively humble origins and her painful rise to theatrical fame were not the only two factors that would help her cope with the monstrous Hollywood machine and with her new career in film. Dorothy's relatively unglamorous lifestyle (even after her "aristocratic" wedding to John Swope), her levelheaded pragmatism, her sense of irony, and other things such as the lack of any addiction or desperation helped as well. So did her soul-searching investigation into her emotional life, and her

---

[129] Ibid.

[130] Harold V. Cohen, "Nixon Gets Smash Hit In 'Claudia,'" *Pittsburgh (PA) Post-Gazette*, March 10, 1942.

cultivation of a positive, unselfish openness towards people and the world. Those two first factors, however, were essential, as Dorothy would explain in her interview with Rex Reed in 1977. Reed started off with a significant psychological diagnosis after their discussion of her happy marriage to John:

> It isn't surprising that [McGuire] turned out more gentle and less neurotic than other stars her age. "I was never very competitive. If you were suddenly discovered and very beautiful and got paid fabulous sums of money, there's no reason why you should not be mixed-up in a business all exaggerated and out of proportion with reality to begin with.
> "It's different when you come from the theater, where you lived in small dressing rooms and studied your craft and learned a humbling experience through hard work."[131]

Just how much technical theatrical training Dorothy had gained during her early studies is unclear. Dorothy never talked about acting from a technical standpoint, and rarely talked about it at all, except cryptically. She must have done some studying at Pine Manor Junior College, and in the classes she took in New York in the 1930s. Also, in her personal library there was an English copy of Constantin Stanislavski's *An Actor Prepares*, published in 1936, which she had probably purchased in New York and had signed as belonging to "Dorothy Hackett McGuire."[132] In fact, a hint that Henry Fonda drops in his autobiography seems to suggest that Dorothy was quite familiar not only with Stanislavski but also with Lee Strasberg's Actors Studio. In discussing his daughter Jane's early lessons at Strasberg's studio, Fonda reminisces about his first visit to the hallowed acting school: "I had visited the Studio once. Dorothy McGuire

---

131 Reed, "Competitive Spirit" (1977), op. cit.

132 Constantin Stanislavski, *An Actor Prepares*, Theatre Arts, Inc., 1936.

told me it was not only interesting but instructive."¹³³

When Dorothy broached the subject of acting at all, she usually spoke of the *experience* of acting rather than of the preparation for such experience. It is from experience—and what experience—that she must have learned most of what she knew and used in her profession, and it is from experience that her innate talent was able to develop and unfold as it did. She suggested as much, obliquely, in her 1977 interview with Rex Reed:

> I love young actors and their passion, and I don't know how they ever make it today. In those days, it was simple. There wasn't the competition [. . .] or the demand that you had the right training.¹³⁴

What Dorothy was suggesting in the above statement was that, in pre-Actors Studio Hollywood, an actor was not required to have "the right training" to be considered viable, or to become a star. If by "the right training" one means extensive and accredited schooling in the various aspects of the craft, both technical and emotional, then many film stars of the Golden Age of Hollywood did not have it. To this day, many brilliant thespians shine on stage and screen not out of rigorous schooling, but out of talent and practice; even not all British Shakespeareans are RADA-trained. Two examples: the wonderful Dame Emma Thompson and Sir Ian McKellen.

Though, technically, Dorothy was not a Method actress, or even a fully schooled actress, one could argue that, by vesting her characters with intelligence, truthfulness, and full empathy, she often incarnated the central tenets of many revered naturalistic dramatic doctrines, but without the certificates that came with their schools.

Dorothy's longtime friend Dan Levin, who—as Peter Levin—direct-

---

133 Teichmann (1981), op. cit., 265.

134 Reed, "Competitive Spirit" (1977), op. cit.

ed Dorothy in a 1985 TV movie,[135] thinks likewise:

> Oscar Wilde once said, "Only the mediocre improve."[136] Some of these people that are talented, they are talented right off the bat. Henry Fonda, for example, was extraordinary; so was Dorothy; and I don't know if they ever took an acting lesson. It's a gift.[137]

Dorothy's acting talent was a gift; this was expressed by two early appraisers of her talent, actress Violet Heming and producer David O. Selznick, who referred to her on separate occasions as "a born actress."[138] Producer William Perlberg echoed that assessment when he declared about Dorothy in May 1943: "The greatest actress I've seen in years."[139] That such a gift was surprisingly mature for Dorothy's age found confirmation in Heming's statement that, during her early community theater efforts, the inexperienced actress "[read] lines with natural intention, not as a child who's been coached." At the tender age of thirteen, Dorothy already had an intuitive understanding of human nature, and an uncommon capacity to express it "with natural intention." The talent she demonstrated was more observation and feeling than technique, more insight than schooling. Later in life, Dorothy would refer to acting as "mysterious" and

---

[135] See Part I, Chapter 17.

[136] The full quote is, "Only mediocrities progress. An artist revolves in a cycle of masterpieces, the first of which is no less perfect than the last." From a letter by Wilde to the editor of the *Pall Mall Gazette*, September 22, 1894. See: Dr. R. S. Pathak, *Profiles in Literary Courage: Studies in English Literature*, Academic Foundation, 1992, 74.

[137] Dan "Peter" Levin, conversation with the author, February 2017.

[138] Heming in Soanes, "Discovery" (1942), op. cit.; Selznick in "It's All In Hollywood," *Arizona Republic* (Phoenix, Arizona), May 22, 1943.

[139] "It's All in Hollywood," *Arizona Republic* (Phoenix, AZ), May 22, 1943.

as a "life experience,"[140] for that is fundamentally what it was for her: the flowing of the tributary of her study of the human being (starting with herself) into the river of intuitive artistic expression.

"Typically, McGuire understates," Paul Rosenfield of the *Los Angeles Times* would wisely observe in his 1982 profile.[141] In life as in art, Dorothy was never one to boast, or to go into any detail about the amount of study or fatigue that contributed to the glowing results she obtained, as a human being and as a thespian. This real-life Claudia was feather-light and modest, lithe and luminous, with hardly any trace of vanity or selfishness. All this without ever becoming somber or gloomy, and without denying herself the joys of success and achievement.

These personal and artistic traits of Dorothy's point to a virtue that she would demonstrate—and hone—throughout her life: humility.

And not false humility, either, but a true virtue that counteracts and dissipates the damaging influence of pride, haughtiness, self-satisfaction, conceit, arrogance and hubris: a virtue that looks lovingly to a scheme broader than the concerns of one's ego.

A touching syndicated piece of journalism concerning Dorothy appeared in the *Oakland Tribune* in June 1941, four months after her debut in *Claudia*. It was written by New York theater critic Richard Watts, Jr. (1898–1981), who, presciently, foresaw Dorothy's imminent fate as a prisoner of Hollywood, and virtually begged her to resist the movie industry's siren call:

> For the next portrayal [of the last theater season] which I remember most vividly we must turn from the veterans to the younger actresses. In fact, one of the most pleasant phenomena of the season was the number and the excellence of the feminine newcomers to the stage. Of course, all of them are

---

140 Champlin, "Sensitivity" (1976), op. cit.

141 Rosenfield, "Fate" (1982), op. cit.

almost inevitably destined to be snatched from Broadway by Hollywood before they get started and are doomed to become extremely profitable puppets of the celluloid, but it was nice to have them around for a while, anyway.

    The most triumphant of the comparatively new girls was, as I need hardly remind you, Miss Dorothy McGuire, whose characterization of the charming young wife in Miss Rose Franken's "Claudia" was tender and beautiful and gently moving. I think that Miss McGuire, above all the other youthful actresses, should think three or four times before setting off for Hollywood, because she is a player of unusual potentialities, and there is every reason to believe that she is in a position to achieve a distinguished position in the theater. Somehow I do not think it is entirely selfishness on my part which makes me feel that she should stick to the old-fashioned drama.[142]

Anti-cinema prejudice aside, Watts was perhaps suggesting that Hollywood, profit-making mass industry that it was, would not be able to appreciate and exploit those "unusual potentialities" of Dorothy's without spoiling them to some extent, or without pigeonholing her to fit a cliché.

---

[142] Richard Watts, Jr., "Best Women's Acting of Season by Ethel Barrymore and Gertrude Lawrence," *Oakland Tribune*, June 29, 1941.

6. To Selznick or Not to Selznick

Of all the studio heads and producers in Hollywood, David O. Selznick was the quickest out of the gate when the time came to sign up the Broadway star of *Claudia*, namely the toast of New York, Dorothy McGuire.

He was also the quickest to buy the rights to Rose Franken's play, which he did at the considerable price of $187,500.[143] Selznick originally wanted his then-favorite star, Jennifer Jones (who was not his wife yet), to play the part, but Ms. Franken would not hear of it, and had a clause put into her contract ensuring that Dorothy would be signed for the role.

At any rate, Selznick, often prone to changing his mind, had originally chosen Dorothy for another project altogether. News of his intentions appeared in November 1941 through the pen of Edwin Schallert of the *Los Angeles Times*:

> From New York by phone comes word that David O. Sel-

---

[143] See "Rose Franken, 92, Author of the 'Claudia' Stories," *New York Times*, June 24, 1988.

znick has picked his Nora for "Keys of the Kingdom." She's Dorothy McGuire, who plays Claudia Naughton in the play "Claudia," one of the outstanding hits of the past several semesters on the stage in Manhattan.

Choosing her represents the fulfillment of a quest, not as broad nor as long, by any means, as the one for Scarlett in "Gone with the Wind," but still a search of proportions.

[...] In "Keys of the Kingdom," Miss McGuire will portray the childhood sweetheart of the boy who grows up to become a priest, remaining in love with him throughout her life. The priestly role is all but set for Maurice Evans, but Spencer Tracy may yet play it. Ingrid Bergman has already been cast as the nun, Maria Veronica.[144]

Selznick eventually scrapped the entire deal; *The Keys of the Kingdom* was released by 20th Century-Fox in 1944. The part of the priest went to Gregory Peck; Nora was played by Jane Ball, Maria Veronica by Rosa [Rose] Stradner.

By December 1941, International News Service (INS) correspondent Edwin C. Stein was reporting that Dorothy would star in Selznick's film version of *Claudia*.[145]

The prospects were rosy, and Dorothy was feted royally upon landing in Tinseltown. The day after her arrival, she was invited to a dinner party at the home of her boss, David O. Selznick, and suddenly she felt the star-struck kid from the Heartland of America, as she explained in an interview:

---

[144] Edwin Schallert, "Selznick Selects Nora; 'Tales' Cast Colossal," *Los Angeles Times*, November 6, 1941.

[145] Edwin C. Stein, "Selznick Plans Active 1942 Film Schedule After Long Inactivity," *Lansing (MI) State Journal*, December 13, 1941.

> Honestly, I didn't know what to say. You see, I'm a movie fan and I just stood there and gawked when I recognized Kay Francis and some other stars. It was like a movie. You know, Kay Francis always in a drawing room. Anyway, the guests gawked at me, too. I guess they expected me to rush up and ask for their autographs.[146]

The fate of *Claudia* in Selznick's hands appears today to be a symbol of his professional relationship with Dorothy and several other contract players of his: once in Selznick's possession, Franken's property was promptly sold to 20th Century-Fox after negotiations with Paramount Pictures had failed; thus *Claudia* never became a Selznick film. The same could be said of Dorothy, who, having signed a seven-year contract with the producer, never officially made a Selznick International Pictures film, a David O. Selznick Productions film, a Vanguard Films, Inc. film, or a Selznick Releasing Organization film in that period. By 1948, shortly before the expiration of her contract, Dorothy was ready to buy out the remainder of her commitment and sign with 20th Century-Fox, which she did in 1949.

Between the novelty of signing with a major Hollywood studio and the discovery of how intricate the machinations of the film industry could be, Dorothy was in a daze soon after arriving in Los Angeles. Never a fighter, Dorothy wisely thought she should at least seek external advice about those confusing wheelings and dealings. Here is Edwin Schallert of the *Los Angeles Times* recounting this early transition from Broadway to Hollywood:

> The tide just swept along then, and ultimately Miss McGuire was signed by David O. Selznick for the picture version [of *Claudia*]. However, he changed his mind about making it

---
[146] "Hollywood," *Arizona Republic* (1943), op. cit.

himself. And next thing Dorothy heard was that Paramount was going to produce the film. Then after that she learned it wasn't Paramount, but 20th Century.

The tide was by that time indulging in such whirligigs, according to her way of thinking, that she felt she should do something about it. She went to see her lawyer to discover whether she could be bounced about in the film contractual seas in this fashion. The answer from her lawyer was "Yes," and so she let fate have its way.[147]

Dorothy, though new to the Hollywood game, was no dumbbell; a hint to this effect had been planted as early as 1941, while Dorothy was weighing studio offers, by columnist Walter Winchell:

> Dorothy McGuire [...] got offers from nearly every flicker company, but Fox is a bit miffed with her ... Because of the things she demanded before signing, Dorothy got the right to approve all scripts, pick her own leading men, six months off a year for theatre jobs and all the other things good actors and actresses rate. Clap hands for her, huh? ...[148]

Given how things turned out with Selznick, it is reasonable to guess that Dorothy did not succeed in negotiating all the above perks.

Ultimately, her arrangement with Selznick was a compromise, as demonstrated by the fact that Dorothy's entire career under him consisted of loan-outs to other studios, and that most of the films she made between 1943 and 1950 were for Zanuck's 20th Century-Fox. In 1947, columnist Louella O. Parsons even stated that Dorothy was "under joint contract to

---

[147] Edwin Schallert, "While the Films Reel By," *Los Angeles Times*, July 4, 1943.

[148] Winchell (1941), op. cit.

David Selznick and Twentieth Century-Fox.")[149] It is, therefore, difficult to establish definitively the extent to which there was a "Selznick period" where Dorothy is concerned. Certainly, Selznick was involved in the projects he "sold" for his loan-out stars, and in many of those outside projects one may still detect a "Selznick touch." For example, both *The Spiral Staircase* and *Till the End of Time* (1946), while released by RKO, were actually co-produced by Selznick's Vanguard Films, but such involvement was uncredited. In any event, whether due to financial troubles or to personal indecision, Selznick's investment in Dorothy's early career ended up seeming half-hearted. Corroborating evidence of this may be found in the number of "aborted" Selznick-McGuire projects that popped up in the Hollywood press during that period.

False starts are not uncommon in Hollywood, and deals are made, broken, mended and rescinded every day; nonetheless, Dorothy's Selznick period, which was filled with good films made under other studios, was also crowded with near misses, cancellations and false hopes, to a degree that defies credulity.

The earliest of these sailor's promises was reported by columnist Hedda Hopper in June 1943:

> Look for Dorothy McGuire in "The Eve of St. Mark," Maxwell Anderson's Broadway success, for which Twentieth Century paid $300,000 and which Bill Perlberg will produce. She's the only one set so far, and this before finishing her first picture, "Claudia"....[150]

The film was indeed made by 20th Century-Fox in 1944, starring

---

[149] Louella O. Parsons, "Parsons Sees Wanda Hendrix, Newcomer, as Future Luminary," *Rochester (NY) Democrat and Chronicle*, November 25, 1947.

[150] Hedda Hopper, "Barrymore's Leading Man Possible Choice for Screen's Gershwin Role," *Salt Lake Tribune*, June 1, 1943.

Anne Baxter.

On March 2, 1944, another possible project for Dorothy was announced by Edwin Schallert of the *Los Angeles Times*:

> Dorothy McGuire is practically set now for her next film at 20th Century-Fox. Producer Otto Preminger will probably have her as the star of "All Out Arline," by H. I. Phillips, which is a story of the Wacs. It has been in preparation for eight months and will go before the cameras May 1, according to present plans. Miss McGuire, who established herself in "Claudia" at the same studio, is to portray a secretary who gives up her position to join the service.[151]

Next up was a possible starring role at RKO, which caused a rebellion on Dorothy's part, as reported by the other "Queen of Hollywood," Louella O. Parsons:

> Dorothy McGuire said "No," and so she is not reporting to RKO for Norman Crasna's [sic] coming movie, That Hunter Girl. She had been loaned by David Selznick, but she did not feel the story was right for her. Selznick's other player, Alan Marshall [sic], who is one of the most attractive actors on the screen, keeps his job. He will have Laraine Day as his co star, instead of the little McGuire girl, who apparently has ideas of her own about her movies. The minute Selznick heard of Dottie's rebellion, he suspended her—and then put her to work immediately on a Red Cross short—so he could not have been too mad.[152]

---

[151] Edwin Schallert, "Unusual War Tale Set; McGuire to Play Wac," *Los Angeles Times*, March 2, 1944.

[152] Louella O. Parsons, George Cukor Will Direct Screen Version of Wartime Epic Show, Winged Victory," *Fresno (CA) Bee*, March 17, 1944.

The film, retitled *Bride by Mistake* and produced by Bert Granet, was released in 1944, with a screenplay by Henry and Phoebe Ephron based on Krasna's story and starring Alan Marshal and Laraine Day. Otto Preminger was replaced by Richard Wallace as director.

The wartime short in which Dorothy acted as "punishment" for her rebellion was *Reward Unlimited*, written by Mary C. McCall, Jr. and directed by Jacques Tourneur. The other cast members were James Brown, Aline MacMahon, Spring Byington, Tom Tully, Robert Forest, Vanessie Clark, Beatrice Gray, Fay Holden and Jackie "Butch" Jenkins. The film promoted the work of volunteer military nurses for the US Cadet Nurse Corps during World War II. On the eve of her fiancé's (Brown) departure for active duty, protagonist Peggy Adams (McGuire) chooses to become a nurse; the ten-minute film narrates her training and early work as a health care volunteer. Selznick was listed as a producer on the project for Van-

Instruction in the bacteriology laboratory is undertaken by Dorothy as

Peggy Adams (second from right, sitting) and by her fellow students, in *Reward Unlimited*, Vanguard's US Cadet Nurse Corps short subject produced for the US Public Health Service, 1944. Production still.

According to several sources, including Wikipedia and the IndieWire website, Selznick wanted Joseph Cotten and Dorothy McGuire to play the roles that would eventually go to Gregory Peck and Ingrid Bergman in Hitchcock's *Spellbound* (1945, a pet Selznick project). Bergman had also been offered the part of Helen in *The Spiral Staircase*, but had refused.[153] It is fascinating to speculate how both films would have turned out with that casting swap, and how both Dorothy's and Bergman's careers would have been reshaped.

Yet another project that was being considered for Dorothy was reported by International News Service (INS) correspondent Dorothy Manners in October 1944:

> Dorothy McGuire, who never has made a picture for David Selznick in the two years she's been under contract, heads back to the home base for one of the most important stories ever purchased by David.
>
> The first Henry James novel to see the movies, The Wings of the Dove, has been acquired by Selznick, who loves fiction like a blood relative. Dorothy will play the American girl in colorful period drama that deals with the social scene in America, England and Italy at the turn of the century.
>
> She will be one of the three stars for this movie, and two other top names from the Selznick boxoffice bonfires get equally important roles. Miss McGuire is certainly the original lend-lease girl of the Selznick contract players.[154]

---

[153] J. Greco, *The File on Robert Siodmak in Hollywood, 1941–1951*, Dissertation.com, 1999, 74.

[154] Dorothy Manners (INS), "Dorothy McGuire, Under Contract Two Years, Will Make Picture For Selznick," *Fresno (CA) Bee*, October 25, 1944.

At one point, Ingrid Bergman was also to be attached to Selznick's project, which seems to have evaporated completely.[155] After World War II, Selznick briefly entertained the idea of a remake of *Little Women* (1933), with Jennifer Jones as Jo and Dorothy as Meg. He lost interest in this project too, or else was discouraged by postwar problems and a craft workers' strike, and sold it to MGM, who released their version of Louisa May Alcott's story, *sans* Dorothy, in 1949.[156]

On July 22, 1946, Hedda Hopper reported a new starring role for Dorothy, and an interesting co-star for her: "Dorothy McGuire will co-star with Rex Harrison in 'The Ghost and Mrs. Muir.'" Instead, Harrison's female partner in the 1947 20th Century-Fox film turned out to be Gene Tierney. In the same period, Dorothy reportedly turned down 20th Century-Fox's *Anna and the King of Siam*, in order to be able to travel to the Far East with her husband.[157] The film, starring Irene Dunne, Rex Harrison and Linda Darnell and directed by John Cromwell, was released in 1946.

More interesting still was Hopper's following announcement, in August 1946:

> Rex Harrison will costar with Dorothy McGuire in "The Snake Pit." His role, that of the weird psychiatrist, Dr. Kik, will be built up. Anatole Litvak directs. I don't know how romance will be woven into the story but in movies miracles are

---

155 See also: Laurence Raw, *Adapting Henry James to the Screen: Gender, Fiction, and Film*, Scarecrow Press, Inc., 2006, 30.

156 See *The Louisa May Alcott Encyclopedia*, edited by Gregory Eiselein and Anne K. Phillips, Greenwood Publishing Group, 2001, 183. See also: Neil Doyle, "Quiet Serenity," Classic Images (classicimages.com), posted September 5, 2007. See also: the March 2011 post about David O. Selznick by Allan R. Ellenberger, on the website Hollywoodland: A Site about Hollywood and its History.

157 Rosenfield, "Fate" (1982), op. cit.

performed.[158]

The Snake Pit was eventually released by 20th Century-Fox in 1948, directed by Litvak but starring neither McGuire nor Harrison. Olivia de Havilland played psychiatric patient Virginia Stuart Cunningham, while Leo Genn played Dr. Kik.

Laconic and mysterious, the following announcement was made in the *Los Angeles Times* on November 15, 1946: "Joe Cotten costars with Dorothy McGuire in 'The Dark Medallion' before he does 'Portrait of Jenny' with Jennifer Jones."[159]

Another interesting project and co-star were announced a few months later, in vain:

> Dorothy McGuire, who doesn't want to leave New York, will likely do a picture on the Maine Coast this summer. She's approved the script "Spoon Handle," for which 20th Century is paging Henry Fonda to costar. The film will be produced by Sam Engel, and shot in Technicolor. It's the story of an island whose inhabitants are poor but happy until the rich move in and take over the place as a summer resort.[160]

That summer, Dorothy acted in 20th Century-Fox's *Gentleman's Agreement* instead.

Next up, Dorothy was briefly slated to participate in the film *Act of Violence*, which was to be produced by the Mark Hellinger Production Company and released by David Selznick's organization. The cast was to include Gregory Peck, Robert Mitchum, and Alida Valli.[161] The film was

---

[158] Hedda Hopper, "Looking at Hollywood," *Los Angeles Times*, August 24, 1946. This was McGuire's third botched chance to co-star with Rex Harrison.

[159] *Los Angeles Times*, November 15, 1946.

[160] Hedda Hopper, "Looking at Hollywood," *Los Angeles Times*, March 1, 1947.

[161] Sheilah Graham, "In Hollywood Today," *Indianapolis Star*, January 5, 1948.

instead released by MGM the following year, starring Robert Ryan, Van Heflin, Mary Astor, Phyllis Thaxter, and Janet Leigh.

Perhaps the most prestigious, and most persistent, of the Selznick-McGuire projects that never materialized was the film version of Henrik Ibsen's *A Doll's House*. According to Dorothy (as reported by Hopper),[162] Darryl Zanuck had conceived the idea of casting her in *Gentleman's Agreement* (1947) after hearing her perform Ibsen's play on the radio in January 1947 (see Part I, Chapter 11). Starting in October 1947, another idea—probably connected to that same radio broadcast—began to circulate, this time originating with David O. Selznick himself: filming *A Doll's House* with Dorothy McGuire as Nora Helmer. On October 30, 1947, Edwin Schallert of the *Los Angeles Times* reported:

> With Dorothy McGuire already slated to acquire the acting plum of the Nora role, "A Doll's House" is moving toward realization, because John Rodell has been assigned to the screen play. Even more interesting is the fact that Christian Kelleen is now named as the top candidate for the part of the husband in this picture, most recently played here on the stage in a rather stylized version by Francis Lederer. Kelleen should be very right for the part considering his Scandinavian background.
>
> Henrik Ibsen's famous play was done once before as a silent picture in Hollywood with Alla Nazimova and, incidentally, it was one of her finest efforts.[163]

For the following seven months or so, the press was teeming with in-

---

[162] Hedda Hopper, "Battle Won by Dorothy McGuire," *Los Angeles Times*, September 21, 1947.

[163] Edwin Schallert, "Kelleen Top Prospect for 'Doll's House' Lead," *Los Angeles Times*, October 30, 1947.

teresting but contradictory news items about the film. Hedda Hopper, for example, on February 7, 1948, announced that Robert Montgomery had been "asked to play Dorothy McGuire's husband in 'A Doll's House.'"[164] There were also reports of changes in the behind-the-camera team: an unsigned (but possibly by film staffer Lew Sheaffer) announcement was made in the *Brooklyn Eagle* on January 28, 1948:

> The David O. Selznick version of Ibsen's "A Doll's House," starring Dorothy McGuire, will have a screenplay by Ingmar Bergman. Alf Sjöberg, who directed "Torment," will do the theme for the Selznick production. The entire movie will be made overseas in England with an All-American cast.[165]

Curiously, in April 1948, the possibility of another war in Europe—this time due to the threat of Soviet invasions—was blamed for a delay in laying the groundwork for the film. Edwin Schallert made the report:

> War clouds over Europe are disturbing Hollywood production plans. "A Doll's House," scheduled to start by mid-May in Sweden, will be delayed, and Dorothy McGuire, who went to Italy,[166] may return home before beginning the picture, even if it is finally made abroad.
>
> Alf Jorgensen, the Swedish producer, and Harold Molander, vice-president of the Svensk Film Industrie, left over the week end after a discussion of arrangements with Daniel T. O'Shea, but it has been pretty well decided that "Doll's House"

---

164 Hedda Hopper, "Story of Associated Press Should Be Fabulous Film," *Sioux Falls (SD) Argus-Leader*, February 7, 1948.

165 "Selznick Set to Film 'A Doll's House' Abroad," *Brooklyn Eagle*, January 28, 1948.

166 Dorothy took this particular trip to Italy with her husband while pregnant with her first child, Topo Swope. See next chapter.

plans will have to be held in abeyance until the European situation clears up.[167]

Also in April, Louella Parsons wrote another version of the status of *A Doll's House*:

> Rumors have been flying fast and thick that Dorothy McGuire will not play Nora in "The Doll's House" [sic] because she can't wait until it's ready. Although the Selznick Co. admits the Ibsen play has been postponed and up to now they have no script, they say Dorothy McGuire has not backed out.
> Lillian Hellman has been handed the script. Alf Sjoberg, Swedish director, is directing, and there will not be a whole galaxy of big stars, as Selznick usually uses. There will be the two principal characters, and the rest of the players will be selected from Swedish talent—if and when the picture reaches the screen.[168]

Finally, the passing of *A Doll's House* was reported in May 1948:

> Dorothy McGuire, impatiently tapping her foot, no doubt, is marking time in Sweden until her boss, David O. Selznick, makes up his mind. Seems that his plans to film Ibsen's "A Doll's House" in the original Scandinavian locale, with Miss McGuire starring have been temporarily shelved by script trouble.

---

[167] Edwin Schallert, "European War Clouds Force Cinema Delays," *Los Angeles Times*, April 6, 1948.

[168] Louella O. Parsons, "Hollywood," *Philadelphia (PA) Inquirer*, April 29, 1948.

In the meantime, Mr. Selznick is already bound by commitments for studio space in Stockholm and for various personnel. He hopes to find another story immediately that could replace "A Doll's House" and allow the Swedish project to go into action.[169]

Another project announced and then shelved before Dorothy bought her way out of her commitment with David O. Selznick was reported by Louella Parsons in March 1949:

> Dorothy McGuire who hasn't made a movie since the prize-winning Gentleman's Agreement returns to 20th and Darryl Zanuck for Three Came Back. Dorothy, as one of three who returns from a concentration camp, has a real tear-jerker in this heavy drama by Nunnally Johnson.
> This should kill all those rumors that Dorothy had retired in favor of matrimony and her new baby. There is no reason why she cannot have her home and her career, too.
> Jean Negulesco, whose direction of Jane Wyman in Johnny Belinda has been so highly praised, will direct Dorothy.[170]

The film, renamed *Three Came Home*, directed by Negulesco and starring Claudette Colbert, was released in 1950.

The last aborted project of Dorothy's Selznick period was announced by Hedda Hopper in September 1948:

> [Producer] Jesse Lasky tells me that if he can pry Dorothy

---

[169] Lew Sheaffer, "Dorothy McGuire Marks Time; Other News of Screen Projects," *Brooklyn Eagle*, May 1, 1948.

[170] Louella O. Parsons, "Dorothy McGuire To Play Three Came Back," *Arizona Republic* (Phoenix, AZ), March 7, 1949.

McGuire away from David Selznick, James Mason will play in "Trilby."[171]

By April 1949, Dorothy had ended her professional relationship with Selznick and signed with the competition, namely 20th Century-Fox, the studio with which she had made four films during her nominal Selznick contract (1943–1949). The remaining three films she had made with RKO Radio Pictures. In June 1949, columnist Hedda Hopper gave a slap in the face, not to Dorothy but to David O. Selznick, by reporting:

> Dorothy McGuire is on her last picture for David Selznick in "Oh, Doctor!"[172] She's signed a new contract at 20th at a big up in pay for Dorothy—not Selznick.[173]

If nothing else, the above panorama of canceled projects shows that the road to Hollywood hell was paved with excellent intentions, for most of the properties that never came to be for Dorothy were quite interesting. The ifs and ands of never-made deals also demonstrate that even the sturdiest of Hollywood careers are not solid things, but fragile, evanescent mental constructs.

---

171 Hedda Hopper, "In Hollywood," *Elmira (NY) Star-Gazette*, September 14, 1948.

172 *Oh, Doctor!* was an early working title for *Mother Didn't Tell Me* (1950).

173 Hedda Hopper, "Glenn Ford Would Assist Leigh Deal," *Los Angeles Times*, June 24, 1949.

7. Swopes

> Survival to me was two words: John Swope.
> Dorothy McGuire, 1982

On July 18, 1943, Dorothy married John Swope, then vice-president of Southwest Airways, in a private ceremony held before intimate friends and relatives in the garden of the Brentwood home of Mr. and Mrs. Leland Hayward,[174] friends of the bride and bridegroom. The nuptial rites were performed by Rev. Gilbert P. Prince of St. Alban's Episcopal Church.[175] James Stewart, Captain of the Army Air Forces and Hollywood star, on leave from an instructor's assignment in Idaho, was best man; actress Frances Starr was maid of honor. The bride and groom, who

---

[174] Leland Hayward, aside from being friends with John Swope, James Stewart and Henry Fonda, had also been Dorothy's theatrical agent at the time of her success in *Claudia*. Mrs. Hayward was film actress Margaret Sullavan.

[175] St. Alban's Episcopal Church, 580 Hilgard Avenue, Los Angeles, is located on the east side of the UCLA campus at the intersection of Hilgard and Westholme in the Westwood neighborhood of Los Angeles.

had met in Los Angeles[176] early in 1942 during Dorothy's tour with the play *Claudia* and had fallen in love "right away,"[177] obtained their license in secret on the day of the wedding. Mrs. Isabelle Burkley of New York (formerly Isabelle Flaherty Trapp McGuire), mother of the bride, and Mrs. Gerard Swope, mother of the groom, both attended the ceremony. The bride was attired in a white silk pique dress.[178]

This Associated Press photo of Dorothy's wedding made the rounds of American newspapers the day after the ceremony. Left to right: Best man James Stewart, bridegroom John Swope, bride Dorothy McGuire, and maid of honor Frances Starr.

176 Champlin, "Sensitivity," op. cit.

177 Ibid. According to other sources (see Part II, Chapter 6), they had met in 1940, well before Dorothy's star-making turn in Claudia, through mutual friend Leland Hayward.

178 See: "Dorothy McGuire Weds John Swope," *Corpus Christi (TX) Caller-Times*, July 19, 1943; see also: "Captain James Stewart Best Man at Hollywood Wedding," *Indiana (PA) Gazette*, July 19, 1943; "Actress Dorothy McGuire Wed to Industrialist's Son," *Los Angeles Times*, July 19, 1943.

At the time of the wedding, the plan was for the bride and groom to take up residence in Phoenix, Arizona, near the location of Thunderbird Field where John was serving as field manager and flight instructor, upon their return from a brief honeymoon.

According to some sources, this honeymoon took place in Mexico City, Mexico.[179] According to daughter Topo Swope,[180] on the other hand, the couple honeymooned by taking a motorcycle trip to Arizona. While on their way to Thunderbird Field, the couple would camp out in the wild, for a (probably uncharacteristic for Dorothy) communion with nature. This communion apparently turned into a minor nightmare for Dorothy one night when she withdrew to answer the call of nature, only to be promptly "attacked" by a "jumping cholla" cactus as she was squatting over it. The duty of plucking the offending barbed spines out of the actress for the next couple of days fell on husband John; as Topo states, "that's true love, right there." On that same trip, the couple set camp for the night in an apparently isolated spot, unaware that active railroad tracks ran beside it. At the arrival of the first nighttime train, husband and wife awakened to what sounded like the end of the world.

The simple elegance of the Swopes' small but star-studded wedding was an apt symbolic image of the unadorned, disarming elegance that characterized their stable, loving marriage: the couple remained together until John's death in 1979, and Dorothy never remarried. In 1947, four years into their marriage, Dorothy briefly dealt with the theme of her marriage during an interview with Hedda Hopper. The passing reference is interesting, obviously, for the fact that she states how happy she is with her husband, but also for two adjectives she uses (emphasis mine):

[John and I] are *intrigued* and *interested* after almost

---

[179] Associated Press syndicated press release, "Swope Weds Dorothy McGuire," *Des Moines (IA) Register*, July 20, 1943.

[180] Topo Swope, conversation with the author, March 2017.

five years of marriage, and that's a fairly good test, don't you think?[181]

January 1932: President Gerard Swope (peeking out the cockpit window) takes a ride in the new General Electric airplane, a Stinson Detroiter purchased for experimental purposes in demonstrating new aeronautical equipment developed by G.E.'s engineers. With Mr. Swope is A.H. French, pilot and manager of the aeronautical department of the company. Photo and press release by General Electric, Schenectady, New York.

---

181 Dorothy McGuire, quoted in Hopper, "Battle" (1947), op. cit.

That "test" would remain successful for thirty-two more years. An example from the other end of the timeline: in a 1976 interview, Dorothy called her husband "miraculous."

Star-struck Swope: Henrietta Swope, John's only sister, poses with a device used to measure the light from the stars at a laboratory of the California Institute of Technology in Pasadena, California, December 1, 1962. At the time this photograph was taken, Henrietta was a research fellow in astronomy at the Mt. Wilson and Palomar observatories. Photo: Associated Press Wirephoto.

John Swope—social security number 563-16-9953—was born in New Brunswick, New Jersey, on August 23, 1908, to Gerard Swope (1872–1957) and Mary Dayton Hill Swope. Gerard, an engineer, soon graduated to preeminent executive positions, becoming vice president of the Western Electric Company (1913–1918) and president of the General Electric Company (1922–1939; 1942–1944). In different periods, he was also director of the National Broadcasting Company, director of the

RCA Victor Company, director of the RCA Radiotron Company, and chairman of the New York City Housing Authority (1939–1942). [182]

Gerard Swope graduated from a mortgaged apartment in New Brunswick to an apartment at 1040 Park Avenue, Manhattan, which he owned outright, and later to a vast estate, The Croft, near Ossining, New York. He sired five children: Henrietta (1902–1980, a renowned astronomer in her day), Isaac, David, Gerard Jr., all born in St. Louis, Missouri (Gerard's place of birth), and John, the youngest, born in New Brunswick, Mary's home town. Gerard Sr. died in 1957 at the age of 84.[183] His equally famous younger brother Herbert Bayard Swope (1882–1958) was an editor, Pulitzer Prize-winning reporter, legendary poker player, *bon vivant*, and friend of the Algonquin Round Table.[184]

Future founder of Random House Bennett Cerf, who worked for Boni & Liveright publishers in New York (later Liveright, Inc.) in the 1920s, penned a quick sketch of Herbert B. Swope in his autobiography, published posthumously in 1977:

> One of Liveright's intimates was Herbert Bayard Swope, who was then the young editor of the *New York World*. [. . .] Swope was a great man. *Swoping* became a word. When anybody went around acting the big shot, they'd say, "He's Swoping." He did throw his weight around quite a bit all his life, and he had a booming voice: "Swope talking!" But I admired him. And he was a great newspaper editor, until he began to

---

[182] For further reading, see: David Loth, *Swope of G.E.: The Story of Gerard Swope and General Electric in American Business*, Simon & Schuster, 1958.

[183] See: "Gerard Swope, 84, Ex-G.E. Head, Dies," *New York Times*, November 21, 1957.

[184] See: E. J. Kahn, *The World of Swope: A Biography of Herbert Bayard Swope*, Simon & Schuster, 1965.

get interested in too many other things and then the whole *World* collapsed—I mean the paper, not the world itself.[185]

It would seem that Herbert's brother Gerard possessed the same voice genes. According to Gerard's secretary at G.E.,

> [The] only man I've ever seen who can talk louder and faster than Mr. Swope is his brother, Herbert.[186]

Gerard's son John inherited none of his uncle's high-society swagger and little of his father's monumental business ambition; but he was a remarkable person nonetheless. Though he became known mainly as a photographer, he was a man of several skills. As the *Los Angeles Times* put it in 1967:

> As a man with the name of Swope, and the money and position that goes with it, he had a pleasant enough life. Married to a vivacious, talented wife, Dorothy McGuire, and possessed of uncommon skills (he's been a flight instructor, author, La Jolla playhouse producer, magazine photographer), it has been a full life.[187]

John was always interested in theater. While attending Harvard University, he joined an inter-collegiate theatrical group called University Players, based in West Falmouth on Cape Cod, whose members included future theater and film director Joshua Logan and future film stars Henry

---

[185] Phyllis Cerf Wagner and Albert Erskine, eds., *At Random: The Reminiscences of Bennett Cerf*, Random House, 1977, 33.

[186] Loth (1958), op. cit., 16.

[187] Maggie Savoy, "John Swope: a Light, Shadow Artist," *Los Angeles Times*, September 25, 1967.

Fonda, Margaret Sullavan and James Stewart. These artists would remain his friends after John, having graduated from Harvard with a B.A. in English Literature, moved to Los Angeles. On and off, John also roomed with Stewart and Hayward in a Brentwood house during the 1930s.

Before his move to the West Coast, however, and before embarking on his career as a freelance photographer, between 1931 and 1936 John also worked as a "Washington bureaucrat." According to his *New York Times* obituary, he served "the Administration of President Franklin D. Roosevelt for several years as director of national code compliance of the Depression-born National Recovery Administration."[188] Swope, in fact, worked as mass compliance officer in Washington, D.C., and, in 1934, as head field officer (and photographer) in the Management Division for Resettlement Administration in Los Angeles.[189]

John was also an accomplished sailor; according to some sources,[190] it was during a 1936 yacht race from Los Angeles to Honolulu—which he joined with camera—that his interest in the medium blossomed. Once on dry land, Swope used his position as production assistant to producer, production manager and talent agent Leland Hayward to gain access to the film world and capture behind-the-scenes images of Hollywood. These images were included in his first photography book, *Camera Over Hollywood* (1939),[191] commissioned and published by Bennett Cerf of Random House.[192] Here are some impressions of that book from a March 1939 review:

---

[188] Adam Clymer, "John Swope, Noted Photographer," *New York Times*, May 15, 1979.

[189] See Swope's life chronology in Carolyn Peter, *A Letter from Japan: The Photographs of John Swope*, Grunwald Center for the Graphic Arts/Hammer Museum/Steidl, 2006, 250. See also "N.R.A. Officers Get New Posts," *Los Angeles Times*, April 13, 1934.

[190] See: John Swope biography, © 2011, Craig Krull Gallery, Santa Monica, CA.

[191] John Swope, *Camera Over Hollywood*, Random House, 1939.

[192] "Memorial Services Held for Producer John Swope," *Los Angeles Times*, May 19, 1979.

The book, as figurative and graphic a collection of photographs as has been published in some time, abounds in the color of Hollywood as photographed by John Swope, an earnest, determined young man with a refreshing viewpoint.

Swope, who is described as a "paid slave in the galley pits" of a Hollywood photographing agency, determined to portray Hollywood merely as it is. This he does, with unusually brief notations.

Few people, subjects and situations eluded the range of Swope's camera [...]. And, while he traveled some oft beaten paths consumed since the candid camera rage, and while there is occasionally too much white contrasting with the black, Swope's effort is a sincere characterization of the film capitol's [sic] population.

Outstanding are the cinema city's extras. You observe them endeavoring to be natural while off the set, playing cards, trekking to find work, expressionless in disappointment, gay in a land not always gay. And their kind and the more noted are scattered throughout a panorama of streets, homes, night scenes, beaches and gentle hideaways.

While it is a succession of pictures, "Camera Over Hollywood" actually tells a story, brief and expressive. Camera devotees, in particular, will at once perceive its value. The close-up of Norma Shearer, nameless in the caption, is superb and typical of Swope's art.[193]

Archival sources, and Carolyn Peter's excellent essay about John's life in the 2006 exhibition catalogue *A Letter from Japan*, have revealed that John's *Camera Over Hollywood* "may actually have been a collaboration: the captions may have been written by Claude Binyon, a man who as-

---

[193] "Hollywood Inside Out," *Brooklyn Eagle*, March 7, 1939.

sisted John in the preparation of the book."[194] In 1950, Binyon would direct Dorothy in the 20th Century-Fox film *Mother Didn't Tell Me*, whose screenplay he also wrote.

Charles Champlin of the *Los Angeles Times*, commenting on *Camera Over Hollywood* many years later, wrote: "The wit and bite of [Swope's] photographs could have illustrated 'Day of the Locust.'"[195]

In 1938, Henry Street Settlement House commissioned John to document the work of nurses in Harlem and the Lower East Side of New York; in 1940, he and Joshua Logan received an assignment from *Harper's Bazaar* to travel to South America, as photographer and writer respectively.[196] It was also in 1940 that John began his freelance work for *LIFE* magazine.[197]

John was also an accomplished pilot, and at the onset of World War II, he enlisted as a U.S. Army Flight Instructor. This led to an assignment from the Army Air Forces to work on a book with writer John Steinbeck, no less. The book, entitled *Bombs Away*, was published by Viking in 1943. Here is a description from an ad in the *Los Angeles Times*:

> Bombs Away: the Story of a Bomber Team.
> At the request of the Army Air Forces, John Steinbeck tells how American youths from every walk of life are being welded into perfect bomber teams. From home town, through their training period, to the brink of combat, he follows the pilot, navigator, bombardier, radio man, crew chief, and gun-

---

[194] Peter, *Japan* (2006), op. cit., 34. See also: John Swope to Josh Logan, May 16, 1938, pp. 1–2, and Bennett Cerf to John Swope, July 11, 1938, p. 2, John Swope Trust Archive.

[195] Champlin, "Sensitivity" (1976), op. cit. The reference is to Nathanael West's biting, despairing portrayal of Los Angeles society and of the shattering of American dreams in his 1939 novel *The Day of the Locust* (Random House, 1939)

[196] See: Peter, *Japan* (2006), op. cit., 34.

[197] Ibid., 250.

ner. The world has marveled at America's swift creation of bomber personnel. Steinbeck tells how that miracle is being performed.

60 photographs by John Swope.[198]

Speaking of flying, as early as 1941 John was involved in the planning, building and running of an Air Training Center called Thunderbird Field, part of a multi-million-dollar government training scheme in Arizona's Salt River Valley, near Phoenix. Many prominent figures in Hollywood pumped money and effort into the project, which was duly noted by the press of the time:

A rare (and fuzzy) photo of the Thunderbird Field training site in action during World War II.

---

[198] Book ad, *Los Angeles Times*, January 17, 1943.

How Hollywood money jumped the barrier of California's Sierra Nevada and crossed the desert to this winter resort has to do with Leland Hayward, the effervescent actors' agent and husband of Actress Margaret Sullavan, and John H. Connelly, who used to fly over here from the west coast to see his girl.

With a group of movie figures—James Stewart (now in the army), Brian Aherne, Henry Fonda and Cary Grant among them—Hayward adopted Connelly's plan to establish a school [in the Salt River Valley] near Phoenix to give Uncle Sam's flying cadets primary instruction.

[...] Today the valley has two vast training fields. A third is under construction. A fourth is projected. A fifth, an older one, is used both by airliners and for the instruction of non-military students under the C.A.A. civilian pilots training program.

A sixth, for that matter, is already in use. Students at Thunderbird Field, the one established with movie money, use it as an auxiliary to the home port.

In addition to Hayward, Stewart, Aherne, Fonda and Grant, Gilbert Miller, the New York producer; John Swope, son of Gerard Swope, former president of the General Electric Co. and nephew of Herbert Bayard Swope, editor of the old New York World; Kenneth McKenna, movie producer; and Hoagy Carmichael, the song writer, are interested financially in Thunderbird Field.

Everything on the field except the place where the planes take off and land is airconditioned.

Hayward called in Millard Sheets of Claremont, California, famed in art circles for his water colors, to make the place presentable. Even the hangars where the airplanes are housed are painted in pastel colors. The barracks have furniture after the Cecil B. De Mille manner.

The training system, in sequence, is primary-basic-advanced. The 30-odd primary schools in the United States, like Thunderbird, are civilian-run under army supervision.

Now at the field are 100 British students, brought here under the plan for training 8,000 a year in the United States.[199]

John would end up running the airfield as director and superintendent of operations.

Inducted into U.S. Navy Reserve as a lieutenant and assigned to Edward Steichen's special U.S. Navy photographic unit in May 1945, John found himself, first in Europe, then in Japan to cover the signing of the Declaration of Surrender and the release of Allied POWs in August–September 1945. After the war, he continued his freelance work for *LIFE* magazine (until 1959) and produced a substantial body of work over the years, especially in the fields of theater and film; John was especially adept at natural or candid portraits of celebrities, sometimes taken from unusual angles. "Swope had the unique ability to juxtapose his subjects with specific elements from their environment which revealed intimate aspects of their lives."[200] Always an enthusiastic traveler, over the years John roamed the world with his camera (and often with his wife) and captured many treasures. In 1975, his images of the domains of the Maharajas of India were featured in James Ivory's book *Autobiography of a Princess*, published by Harper & Row.

There was something truly special, and luminous, about many of John's photographs. According to the Craig Krull Gallery of Santa Monica:

> [Swope] created deceptively simple but well-thought-out pictures that are intricate in composition and infused with

---

[199] Devon Francis (AP), "Phoenix Area Becomes Air Training Center," *San Bernardino (CA) Sun*, July 31, 1941.

[200] Craig Krull Gallery biography, op. cit.

emotion. Hallmarks of his work are the use of available light; shooting scenes from unusual angles; and informal portraits of people made possible by Swope's easy, often humorous rapport with people. His unvarying advice to neophyte photographers was to "keep it simple." Swope was a master practitioner of this most difficult of arts.[201]

Keeping it simple was also the advice that John gave himself. On the occasion of an exhibition of his photographs (*Jacques Lipchitz, Sculptor and Collector—a Photographic Study*) held at UCLA's Dickson Art Center in September 1967, the *Los Angeles Times* profiled both the photographer and his art:

> It is hard to know when a hobby stops being an interest and becomes a part of the man himself. And so becomes an art.
>
> John Swope [...] thinks it may have happened when he got rid of 40 of his 42 cameras, put away his tripod, extra lenses, strobes, light meters and flash bulbs, and began to feel the exultation of light and shadows and emotion. Swope shot all the [...] panels in the Lipchitz show with a common garden-variety Rolleiflex[202] and whatever light there was.
>
> [...] You will see Lipchitz as Swope sensed him, a genius of course, but also an "animated man, intense, religious, articulate, with a fey humor and with a happiness that is his own."
>
> [...] The "Ah" instant is pure accident, sometimes surprising Swope himself. If it comes, "click. click. click." If he gets it, fine. If not, he keeps moving around, talking, waiting.

---

201 Ibid.

202 The Rolleiflex cameras were high-end, twin-lens reflex cameras originally made by the German company Franke & Heidecke, and later by Rollei-Werk.

"I don't set stage, don't maneuver, never say 'Hold' or 'Can you get that expression again.'

"It just has to happen. And I have to catch it," he explains.

The Swopes' home in Beverly Hills, overlooking a panorama of green hills and trees, is filled with blow-ups of his black and white recordings of emotion, caught on these split-seconds when life stood still for a man with a simple camera and a sensitive eye.

In the closet are 300 rolls of film yet undeveloped. Each roll has a notation of the light, and he does all his own developing because only he knows exactly what the light was.

This sixth sense for light-and-shadows is part of his art, and he can't analyze how he does it. "Light passes *through* John; it is a part of him," says Dorothy. "It is the way he sees things."[203]

Though slightly more withdrawn than his wife, and slightly less accustomed to the direct scrutiny of fame, John was a warm, humorous, sociable man who made friends easily. He enjoyed sociality and even the rarified atmosphere of Hollywood, but was able to observe—and how he observed—the hustle and bustle of humanity from the relaxed vantage point of someone standing just outside the limelight. He was possessed of an inquisitive, positive gaze that, with or without a camera, unfailingly captured some essence of what was happening around him moment after moment: his was a photographer's eye even before picking up the technical instrument that made him a photographer. John's portraits of people were elegant, apparently simple accidental glimpses into what the surface of those people might be revealing in that particular moment; choosing the moment when such glimpses could be caught was John's talent. As John explained:

---

[203] Savoy, "Artist" (1967), op. cit.

Camera-seeing can make everything you do or see more exciting. It sharpens your eyes when you travel—you see more. When you get back, it helps you remember all over again the emotion you felt, the beauty you saw. [. . .] Life's surprises. Beauty captured.[204]

John was fortunate enough to be a well-regarded photographer during his lifetime (in 1967, the *Los Angeles Times* called him "photographer par excellence" in one article).[205] As early as 1938, he had the first of his many exhibitions when the Carroll Carstairs Gallery on 57th Street in New York displayed fifty-four of his pictures, mostly of beach and sea scenes taken on the West Coast (February–March 1938). Over the years, John's work was showcased at galleries and museums across the United States, including the Albright Art Gallery in Buffalo (1952), the Joslyn Art Museum in Omaha (1963), and the Los Angeles County Museum of Art (LACMA). Aside from the above-mentioned Jacques Lipchitz exhibition he did for the University of California at Los Angeles, John was also commissioned to photograph Henry Moore's sculptures for LACMA (October 1–November 18, 1973).

Occasionally, these exhibitions occurred in conjunction with larger events, and in unlikely locations. Such was the case of his one-person exhibition correlated to an installation of Far Eastern artifacts and furniture mounted at the May Co. Wilshire department store in Los Angeles. "Four rooms of a model home on the store's fourth floor [were] outfitted in Far Eastern style. Photographs of John Swope [were] added to the décor."[206] The exhibit ran between September 8 and September 30, 1959.

204 Ibid.

205 Henry J. Seldis, "Lipchitz Hewn by the Camera Eye," *Los Angeles Times*, October 1, 1967.

206 "May Co. Wilshire Opens Far Eastern Art Exhibit," *Los Angeles Times*, September 9, 1959.

John was also "re-discovered" after his death, mostly through the efforts of his son Mark, himself an artist and a photographer. As family friend, writer Dwight Holing, explains:

> Mark was the Trustee of the John Swope Photo Trust until his death; early on he embarked on a very intensive campaign to promote John's work posthumously. He went through the entire collection, catalogued it, and digitized handpicked images. He found and contracted with Graham Howe of Curatorial Assistance and worked closely with him to re-publish *Camera Over Hollywood* and have the show placed at various galleries. Mark traveled to Japan for the exhibition of John's work that wound up in both print and shows. Gallerist Craig Krull, who also spoke at Mark's memorial, was a personal friend of Mark's and represented both John's work and Mark's.[207]

Several group exhibitions featured John's work after his passing, for example at the Los Angeles County Museum of Art (1987–1990), the Art Center College of Design in Pasadena (1992), and the G. Ray Hawkins Gallery, Los Angeles (1994–1996). Five solo exhibitions of John's work were mounted by the Craig Krull Gallery in Santa Monica: "A View from Above" in 1996, "Camera Over Hollywood" in 2001, "Photographs" in 2003, "New York" in 2005, and "Trees" in 2006. The book *Camera Over Hollywood* was re-published by Art Publishers in 1999, and the event was commemorated by a tour of sixty-three vintage photographs featured in the book. The exhibition, organized by Curatorial Assistance, Pasadena, California, toured North America between 2000 and 2001. It appeared at the Santa Barbara Museum of Art, Santa Barbara, CA (June–August 2000), at the Presentation House Gallery in Vancouver, Canada (Septem-

---

[207] Dwight Holing, correspondence with the author, 2016.

ber–October 2000), at the Walter Greer Gallery on Hilton Head Island, SC (June–July 2001), at the Public Library of Charlotte and Mecklenburg County, Charlotte, SC (July–September 2001), and at the Fresno Metropolitan Museum, Fresno, CA (October–November 2001).

In 2006, the Armand Hammer Museum of Art at UCLA mounted the exhibition "A Letter from Japan: The Photographs of John Swope," curated by Carolyn Peter. The show combined nearly eighty vintage prints detailing John's coverage of the 1945 liberation of Allied POW camps in Japan with excerpts from an interesting 144-page letter John had written to his wife during his stay in the country (reproduced in full in the exhibition's catalog). The letter began with the words: "My dearest far-away darling wife [...]."[208]

The exhibition opened on March 5, 2006, and closed on June 4, 2006. It then traveled on loan to the Block Museum of Art at Northwestern University, Illinois (September–October 2008), and to the Canadian War Museum of Ontario, Canada (December 2008–March 2009).

John was a born traveler, and did not limit himself to carrying out his assignment on that 1945 wartime trip. Here is the *Los Angeles Times*:

> [Swope's] job was to document the POWs, and he did so with all the patriotic flair that would have been expected. In his off time, however, he ventured beyond the camps and into the country, quietly flouting orders against fraternization to document the faces on the other side of the divide.
>
> The curiosity stemmed in part from his having visited Japan 15 years earlier on a post-college, round-the-world trip, staying for a month with a friend and business associate of his father. Given that this friend was the founder of Nippon Electric (Swope's father was the president of General Electric), this early visit was no doubt far more luxurious than the later

---

[208] Peter, *Japan* (2006), op. cit., 214.

one and his experience of the Japanese far more amicable. But it left him with a perhaps greater-than-average sensitivity to the Japanese perspective and an appreciation for the cultural value beneath the devastation.

[...] This awareness and the relative humility with which Swope struggles with his impressions of the Japanese Other make the letter a profoundly illuminating document.[209]

As the journalist admits, John was "a product of his time" and his view of the "Japanese Other" came complete with a degree of Western distrust and even a degree of default racism; yet whenever he looked at the faces of those "Other" individuals, the photographer was willing to question his own point of view and was "not only ready but eager to be proved wrong." John wanted to know, and to explore.

Photography was not John Swope's only love. For several years, he served as executive producer at the La Jolla Playhouse in La Jolla, California. He may have been a silent partner to the more famous co-founders of the Playhouse (Gregory Peck, Mel Ferrer, and Dorothy), and he may have found himself omitted from photographs and newspaper articles depicting the above triumvirate, or only mentioned in his role as Dorothy's husband, but, according to witnesses,[210] he was a major driving force of the venue during at least part of its initial lifespan (1952–1959), and sometimes the most practical-minded of the four (see Part I, Chapter 9). Occasionally, John co-produced Broadway shows, which provided good revenue in at least one instance: he and Dorothy owned "a piece" of Rodgers and Hammerstein's *South Pacific*, which ran for 1,925 performances.[211]

John's love for the theater pre-dated his marriage to Dorothy, but was

---

209 Holly Myers, "Life after wartime," *Los Angeles Times*, March 22, 2006.

210 Levin (2017), op. cit.

211 Hedda Hopper, "Dorothy McGuire Retains Ideals While Maturing in Film Parts," *Los Angeles Times*, February 5, 1950.

boosted by it, and it was in loving support of his wife's La Jolla enterprise that he lent his involvement to the project. Whether through photography, producing or fundraising, John skirted in and out of show business most of his life, and was obviously fascinated by it, while often keeping himself at a safe distance as an observer. At once an outsider and an insider, he was nonetheless a benevolent, bemused independent participant in the world of theater and film.

John's photography was in some ways a symbol of the man himself. When he reported throwing away forty of his forty-two cameras and shedding his complicated equipment to whittle down the art to its essentials, he was really talking about simplifying himself, about being unencumbered by unessential things. John's advice to his fellow photographers, quoted by the 1967 *Los Angeles Times* interview at the time of John's Lipchitz exhibition, is revealing:

> Learn the technique, until it becomes a reflex part of you. Know exactly what your camera can do.
> Then throw away all the gadgets. When you're all tangled up with equipment, you hamstring yourself, and the moment of beauty will flick by while you're juggling lenses or lights. Even the weight burdens you. There should be nothing in the way of your eyes.[212]

In other words, shed all the weight and become light as a feather; shed the pretense and try to get to the truth. Use your eyes to perceive the world as it happens and becomes; if you are lucky and attentive, you might witness its happening and becoming and be able to bring back a souvenir of the event through your camera.

When thinking of John Swope, the word "unpretentious" may come to mind. There was little vanity to the man, and little excess weight. A

---

[212] Savoy, "Artist" (1967), op. cit.

gracious, friendly man with a gentle, impish sense of humor, John was a talented darling with a piercing but benevolent gaze. Levelheaded and perceptive, he saw what was around him with enough clarity and simplicity to be able to size up almost anything, and anybody, with little or no judgment impeding his vision.

Above all, throughout his marriage, his love for his wife was immense, and immensely reciprocated. To say that the marriage of Dorothy McGuire and John Swope was a stable one is to understate the issue grossly. To this day, their daughter, for example, expresses wonder at their continued, undiluted love for each other;[213] those who knew the couple even a little, myself included, know that this is no exaggeration. During my conversations with the Swopes at their beautiful Beverly Hills home, I remember them holding hands virtually without interruption, and this after thirty-four years of marriage. Jim Fernald, a friend of the family, puts it this way:

> Dorothy's marriage was unusual by Hollywood standards. She was married to the same man for thirty-six years, and was still in love with him when I moved into the house, twelve years after John's death. So much so that, for example, in the television room, where she spent the majority of her time when she was not out and about, she still kept all the magazines and books in the exact same position they had been when he died. She had not moved a thing. The same goes for all the photographs that were hanging on the walls, all taken by John. All through the house were these huge four-foot-wide blow-ups of his photographs, with subjects ranging from a view of the city of Rome to Marlon Brando on the set of *Julius Caesar* (the latter was in the front hallway).[214]

---

[213] Topo Swope, conversation with the author, February 2017.

[214] Jim Fernald, conversation with the author, April 2017.

Dorothy commented on her marriage often. During his 1977 interview with her, for example, Rex Reed noticed Dorothy smiling "meltingly at her husband of 33 years, the famous photographer who sits nearby." A question about her career prompted Dorothy to muse about John's role in her life:

> If you knew my husband better, you'd know how lucky I've been. I love my career, but I never really thought much about how to nurture it. I had a strong marriage, a secure home to go home to, and we traveled a great deal. All of those things were terribly important.[215]

John and Dorothy provided reciprocal inspiration and support to each other; just as John became a loving advisor for Dorothy, she counselled John, sometimes simply by being there. In an unpublished interview, John mentioned her role in his photography:

> Dorothy is my first critic. When we travel she has another viewpoint and another set of eyes. I like it.[216]

Throughout their life together, Dorothy's positive gaze reinforced John's and John's did likewise to hers, in a mutual process of discovery and openness.

It is only logical that photography, John's main passion and skill, would spill over into the Swope household. John's darkroom and photograph storage/archive space was one of the pulsating hearts of the Swopes' house on Copley Place, Beverly Hills, and John was meticulous in

---

[215] Reed, "Competitive Spirit" (1977), op. cit.

[216] John Swope, interview by Alicia Wille, transcript (John Swope Trust Archive), quoted by Peter, *Japan* (2006), op. cit., 17.

cataloguing negatives and photographs and in keeping detailed journals of his photo shoots and of his *oeuvre*.[217]

Apparently, John's passion was contagious. In 1952, on the occasion of the release of Dorothy's film *Invitation*, several articles (for example an unsigned one in the *Brooklyn Eagle*, or one by Marjorie Turner in the *Syracuse Herald-Journal*) shrewdly focused on her relationship with photography rather than on the film itself. Dorothy participated in the game, tongue in cheek, and offered her opinions on the problems of living in a photographic household. This particular promotional take may or may not have been a studio-assisted ploy to focus on a "friendly," human aspect of its star; at any rate, it included examples of photography-mania on the film set as well. Here are some excerpts:

> Camera shy?
>
> The term has now joined company with "23 Skidoo," "Oh You Kid" and "Ishkabibble"—and no self-respecting dictionary would give it page room.
>
> Take the word of Dorothy McGuire, an outstanding star of both the stage and screen. And Miss McGuire is not speaking from a motion picture actress' point of view. She's speaking as Mrs. John Swope, wife of photographer John Swope whose profession started as a hobby.
>
> "More money in America is spent on cameras and photographic material than on golf, tennis or any other so-called hobby," she said. "The camera is now a regulation bit of household equipment, no more mysterious than vacuum cleaners or pop-up toasters. Being shy of cameras today would be on a par with bolting at the sight of the family automobile. As a result, camera-wise rather than camera-shy wives and children are a dime a dozen. The camera-bug, you see, is a democratic

---

[217] Topo Swope, conversation (2017), op. cit.

soul and can bite in any household. And in any household the problems it creates are the same."

These problems, as listed by the star, include the business of becoming wary at unwary moments lest a shutter click from some unexpected corner; steeling oneself to look at one's own portrait, unretouched, and with an appreciative eye to realism; figuring out ways and means to store negatives and prints that threaten to take over all available closet room ... and at last, in self-defense, stalking one's own prey with tripod and camera and letting the flashbulbs fall where they may.

Miss McGuire [...] recently did triple duty as a camera subject. Professionally she appeared in the dramatic Metro-Goldwyn-Mayer film, "Invitation" [...]. When official cameraman Ray June was not focusing on her winsome profile, unofficial camera-fan Van Johnson was. And at home? It was here that Mr. Swope took over, using her as a human guinea-pig to try out a new light arrangement which paid no heed to the good or bad side of her face. [...]

As far as her own ability along these lines is concerned, the star admits that she has never developed a system.

"Every camera addict is alike in one respect," [Miss McGuire] smiled. "He or she is never satisfied until husband or wife, as the case may be, also adopts photography as a hobby. John is no exception. In self-defense I agreed to learn the mysteries of lens stops, apertures, light meter readings and all the rest. And I took some fairly good pictures. The best is one of Topo at the Japanese Tea House in San Francisco's Golden Gate Park. I did take the picture. It hardly seems necessary to explain that John took the meter reading, set the lens, measured the distance and then passed the camera over to me. But I tripped the shutter!"[218]

---

[218] "Dorothy McGuire's Hobby Now Family Photography," *Brooklyn Eagle*, February 24,

A similar publicity angle was featured in the pressbook for the film *Friendly Persuasion* (1956), where a large, frivolous page was devoted to the various hobbies that kept the talent occupied during their idle hours on the set. William Wyler was pictured relaxing at the piano, Gary Cooper painting at an easel; Dorothy was depicted in costume as she took photographs with a camera, and was described as an "ardent camera fan."[219]

John's camera was ready to assail any subject, willing or unwilling; including his daughter, as Dorothy explained:

> "Topo has no feeling whatsoever where cameras are concerned," the two-and-one-half-year-old's mother beamed. "She accepts them along with her spinach, milk and afternoon nap. Of course Topo started early. She faced a camera for the first time at the age of 45 minutes and has been facing one every hour on the hour since.[220] We have books on Topo. "Topo at the Age of One Year,"—"Topo in San Francisco"—"Topo in New York"—it sounds like a set of juvenile fiction.
>
> "One wonderful thing about photography," she said, "one never takes a picture of anything he doesn't want to remember."[221]

John Swope passed away on May 11, 1979. Informal memorial services were held by Dorothy in the Swopes' Beverly Hills home at 121 Copley Place. About one hundred friends and relatives were in attendance. John's daughter and son, his sister Henrietta and his brother Gerard were joined

1952.

219 *Friendly Persuasion*, Allied Artists Campaign Book, 1956.

220 According to *LIFE* magazine and the John Swope photo that graced its March 14, 1949, issue, Topo was 176 minutes (two hours and fifty-six minutes) old when she faced the camera for the first time.

221 "Dorothy McGuire's Hobby" (1952), op. cit.

by Mr. and Mrs. Henry Fonda and Mr. and Mrs. James Stewart. Also attending were Mr. and Mrs. Gregory Peck, Mr. and Mrs. Norton Simon (Jennifer Jones), John's goddaughter Brooke Hayward and Mr. and Mrs. Harry Horner, Mr. and Mrs. Randolph Scott, Mr. and Mrs. William Wyler, Mr. and Mrs. Samuel Goldwyn Jr., Mr. and Mrs. Edgar Ward (Jane Wyatt), Mr. and Mrs. Daniel Selznick, Mr. and Mrs. Edwin Knopf and others.[222]

John had left instructions to be cremated, and an intimate private ceremony occurred on a rented launch on the Pacific Ocean, a few nautical miles off the shore of Marina Del Rey. James Stewart and Shirlee and Henry Fonda were the only people outside the family who were invited to attend. The members of the family who were present were Dorothy, her children Topo and Mark, and John's sister Henrietta. Here is Fonda's recollection of that event, as told to his biographer Howard Teichmann:

> We went pretty far out to sea, maybe ten, fifteen minutes, and then Dorothy told them to make a big, wide circle, about two hundred feet. She signaled Mark, John's son, that it was time. He'd been holding on tight to the box with his father's ashes since we left the house. Dorothy said, "Now," and Mark and Dorothy opened the box over the end of the boat.
> [...] Oh, my God, [...] the ashes came out in their hands, and the breeze carried the ashes down into the water. The boat was going very slowly, and Dorothy had brought a long wicker tray of flowers from their home, bougainvillea fresh from the vines, gardenias, other colorful flowers. Dorothy gave all of us some to toss into the ocean. I knew it was tough on the family, so afterward I went under a little protective area, away from the others, to pull myself together.[223]

---

[222] See "Services" *Los Angeles Times* (1979), op. cit.

[223] Teichmann (1981), op. cit., 339.

Naturally, John's death was a big blow for Dorothy, and a great loss for his closest friends. Dorothy withdrew temporarily into sorrowful solitude, even refusing to see anyone or answer the telephone. This prompted Fonda to try to express in writing what he could not in person, by penning a touching letter to Dorothy:

> Dearest Dorothy,
>
> Although we talk to you almost every day and see you frequently and think of you constantly, I never feel that I have expressed my great feeling about John. But then, that's the story of my life. For reasons that are too deeply buried for me to understand I have never been able to articulate my emotions. [...]
>
> I loved John. I truly did. I was just 23 when we first became friends and I don't think I originally appreciated how much his outgoing, giving, resounding personality affected me in a positive way.
>
> But it wasn't long before I recognized that he was truly unique. And what an experience. What a pleasure it was for me to be in his company. I have never known a man to so thoroughly enjoy life as John did and to live it as fully. His enthusiasms were contagious. You always felt better for having been with John.
>
> Today, it is hard for me to accept the fact that he isn't available any more. There isn't a day that I don't think to myself . . . I have to talk to John about this and ask his advice about something.
>
> Just last night, he was with me in the most realistic dream, surrealistic, really. A rowboat, a beautiful rocky coastline, a majestic, pounding surf. We were both young and strong and unafraid. I think it will always be like that. I'll miss the hell out

of him. But I'll always see him in dreams and my wonderful memories.

I don't know how well I've said it but I wanted to say it to you because you completed John's life. And it was beautiful and inspirational to watch. I count one of the blessings of my life that it so often touched yours.

All my warmest and dearest love,
Henry[224]

I am sure Dorothy received many such letters. I myself sent her one from Italy, where I was living during the summer of 1979; she never responded to it. Though in time Dorothy recovered from the trauma of John's passing, she would never be quite the same after it. The Dorothy I frequented in the 1980s, near the end of her career, was not quite the Dorothy I had known in the 1970s. A touch of insecurity had crept into her character, and both her detachment and her aging had accelerated slightly after that event. I even remember detecting some slight lapses in her memory, but I believe they were minor, isolated incidents.

Dorothy's first pregnancy was announced by the ubiquitous Hedda Hopper in April 1946:

> Claudia is having a baby. She told me so.
>
> When I asked Dorothy McGuire why she was asking for a 10-month vacation from pictures, she disclosed her secret—that she and her husband, John Swope, are expecting the stork in November.
>
> At 20th Century-Fox, where she is playing in "Claudia and David" on loan-out from David O. Selznick, she denied to studio acquaintances that there would soon be three in her family.

---

[224] Quoted in Teichmann (1981), op. cit., 339–340.

But later she called me to tell me that the rumor is true and that she is so happy.

"I'd hoped to finish the picture," she said, "before telling anybody. But—well, Hedda, it's just too wonderful for me to deny it any longer."[225]

Almost exactly a month later, it was Hopper again who announced that Dorothy had suffered a miscarriage:

> It's such a pity that Dorothy McGuire lost her baby. During her illness her husband, John Swope, has been cooking the most wonderful dinners and serving them at Dottie's bedside. As soon as she's well enough they'll go east to visit his family.[226]

In October 1948, Hopper reported Dorothy's second pregnancy. The news, Hopper announced following a UP press release,[227] had come from Naples, Italy, where the Swopes were vacationing. John and Dorothy had actually been on an extended tour of Italy and Southern Europe (Hopper mentioned "the Swiss Alps") for some five months. The couple announced they were leaving immediately from Naples for New York.[228]

Renowned for their ability to travel light, the Swopes had conducted this tour in a tiny Italian coupe, the FIAT 500 nicknamed "FIAT Topolino." The word "*topolino*," a diminutive of *topo* (mouse), had been chosen

---

[225] Hedda Hopper, "Film Claudia Expecting to Have Baby," *Los Angeles Times*, April 11, 1946.

[226] Hedda Hopper, "Looking at Hollywood," *Los Angeles Times*, May 17, 1946.

[227] "Dorothy McGuire, to Become Mother" (UP), October 6, 1948.

[228] Hedda Hopper, "Dorothy McGuire Awaits February Visit of Stork," *Los Angeles Times*, October 6, 1948. See also: "Dorothy McGuire to Become Mother" (UP), *San Bernardino (CA) Sun*, October 7, 1948.

by the Italian car manufacturer in honor of the vehicle's diminutive size and of its resemblance to Mickey Mouse's car (*Topolino* is also the Italian name of Disney's character). The measurements of the car, which was in production from 1936 to 1955, were: length, 10 ft. 6 inches; width, 4 ft. 2 inches; height, 4 ft. 6 inches. Hopper commented on this pregnancy style:

> She's still very McGuire about lots of things. Most girls, expecting a baby, join the ranks of semi-invalidism. Dorothy chose this time to take a tour of Europe with her husband, John Swope, in a tiny motorcar piled high with camera equipment and all her wardrobe stuffed into a musette bag.[229]

The FIAT 500 nicknamed *Topolino*, in a period photograph, circa 1939.

---

229 Hopper, "Ideals" (1950), op. cit.

That car, and its name, would be the reason for the nickname given to Dorothy's first child, a daughter by the name of Mary Hackett Swope, who was born via C-section in Ossining, New York, on February 14, 1949. That nickname was Topo, the name Ms. Swope used in her own movie career and uses to this day. In a conversation with Hopper, Dorothy expressed some slight misgivings about the nickname: "I dread the day when I'll have to tell my daughter she was nicknamed for an automobile."[230]

Dorothy and Mary Hackett (Topo), circa 1951. Courtesy of Topo Swope's private collection.

---

[230] Hedda Hopper, "Jane Russell, Mitchum Will Costar in 'Macao,'" *Los Angeles Times*, April 18, 1950.

It is only logical that a child born to a celebrity family would feel some pressure from her environment. It did not make things any easier that, 176 minutes into her life, Topo found herself something of a celebrity, captured in all her early glory by her father's camera and placed on the cover of *LIFE* magazine.[231]

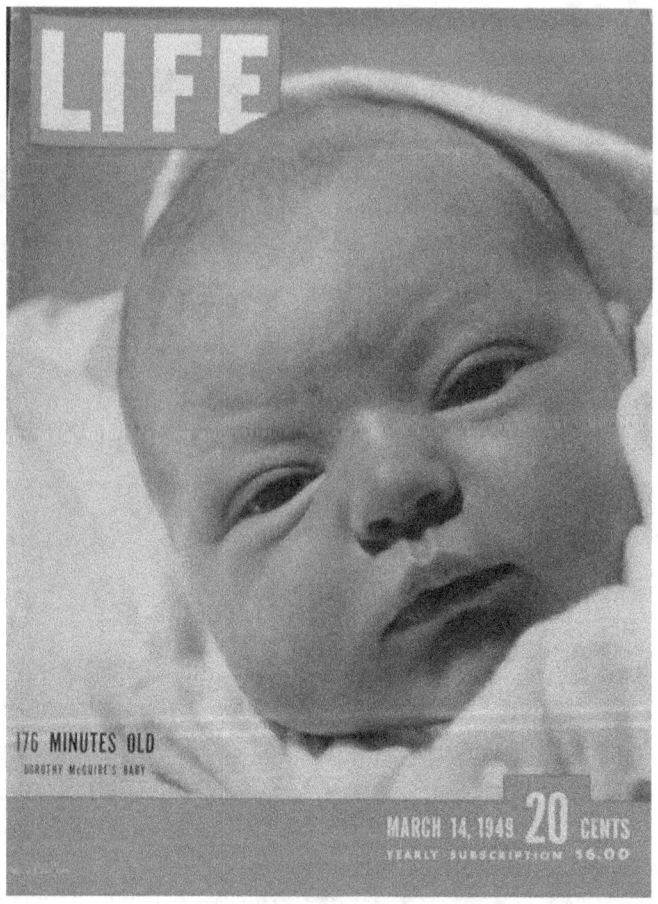

176 minutes old: Mary Hackett, aka Topo, Swope captured by her father's camera for *LIFE* magazine, March 1949. Scan of magazine cover.

---

231 *LIFE*, March 14, 1949 issue.

In her early years, Topo did not immediately realize that the air at home was "rarified," but she did in due time.[232]

The Swopes at home, 1954. Left to right: Dorothy, Mark, Topo, and John. Courtesy of Topo Swope's private collection.

I will let Topo tell this part of her story:

> The wonderful black woman named Ruby who worked as a nanny for my family for many, many years was more of a mother to me than my own mom, because mom was such a movie star. I think she wasn't really into parenting, first of all. Also, she loved traveling. She would get a movie, say *Three Coins in the Fountain*, and book a trip for the shoot; my father would go with her, and then they would extend their trip and go on long tours after the movie was finished. They were gone for long stretches, sometimes four to six months out of the year. Then either one or both of them would come back home,

---

[232] Topo Swope, conversation with the author, March 2017.

and my father would retreat into the darkroom. My parents weren't around a lot.

I had a good relationship with my father; but even he wasn't always available. When he was home, he was usually in the darkroom. I would be knocking on that door hoping he would come out. If I were to write a book about my relationship with my father, it would be called 'The Other Side of the Darkroom Door.'[233]

Mary Hackett (Topo) Swope ice-skating with her mother, circa 1955. Courtesy of Topo Swope's private collection.

---

233 Ibid.

At least initially, Dorothy must have been aware of the problem of her absences, which she acknowledged partially in a 1950 interview:

> The baby has changed me tremendously. When John and I were at Thunderbird Field in the first months of our marriage we flew all the time. Now we won't get on a plane together because we're conscious of Mary Hackett's safety and her future. Besides we've had some narrow squeaks lately, and it's taken some of the joy out of flying.
>
> I was gone from the baby and when I came back she'd grown more hair and had four teeth. I gave the nurse three days off and then spoiled my baby completely. She was a good child but now she screams bloody murder if she's left alone a minute. But it was fun having her all to myself.[234]

**Topo and Dorothy in St. Mark's Square, Venice, Italy, circa 1959.
Courtesy of Topo Swope's private collection.**

---
[234] Hopper, "Ideals" (1950), op. cit.

When the time came to choose a high school for young Topo, John handpicked a small school in Arizona, a rather unique, progressive school. Freshmen and juniors would go live in Indian reservations for a month, while sophomores and seniors would travel down to Mexico and stay with different families to get the feel of the culture. John had been on a photography trip in Arizona and taken one of those school trips prior to choosing the school; he had liked what the school stood for.

Arguably, this progressive, eccentric (and far from home) academic retreat fostered the progressive, eccentric ideas that would make Topo Swope into an even freer spirit than her parents. Not only that, it forced her to be away from family life for long stretches of time, ironically mirroring what she felt had been her parents' absences from *her* childhood life: in the years that her mother liked to call "the tunnel years" (the teenage years), she returned home only during the summers.

The atmosphere at the school was relaxed and informal, perhaps too informal for Dorothy: apparently, she was not a big fan of the institution, for she felt that its students for the most part had no manners. Despite her progressive views, Dorothy liked manners and politeness, and she found that, during her visits to the campus, she was not treated with sufficient respect, especially by the male students (who for example would not get up for her).

Topo admits she might have been a rebellious kid. At any rate, her stint at the Arizona high school was not the end of her peripatetic travels away from home. Her first attempt at college took place at Millbrook, New York; the attempt was unsuccessful, for Topo hated the place. After one year, she transferred to the University of Southern California in Los Angeles, where she studied acting and writing. Acting more than writing, actually: this is where the seed was planted for what would turn out to be a relatively successful but short-lived career as a film actress.

Topo makes no secret about her inclination to be "a hippie":

> I was a hippie (still am, kind of), and lived in a commune

out in Topanga Beach. I was an original Flower Child. I lived in all the canyons: Laurel Canyon, Benedict Canyon, Beverly Glen.... I was a Canyon Girl.[235]

Though Topo's "hippieness" might appear to be a break from family tradition, it is, in fact, only a transformation, or metamorphic development, of family traits that she shared with both her parents, who were, in their own way, eccentric free spirits themselves.

In the background of this development, there was, perhaps, a degree of restlessness, or of rebellion. Topo had neither the stable career nor the stable marriage that her mother had had. She has married three times (the first in a photographer's studio, seventy-two hours after the couple's first meeting) and divorced three times. Over the years, she has also held a colorful variety of different jobs.

Topo started working at the age of fifteen, not out of necessity but out of enthusiasm. She liked working then, and still does today. She says of herself that she has "a good work ethic." Among the various jobs: working for "A Moveable Feast" (delivering sandwiches to office buildings); selling plants for a shop in Hollywood named "The Plant Pusher"; doing plant maintenance; painting and selling furniture; running an art gallery located on S. La Brea Avenue, where an exhibition of Henry Fonda paintings and lithographs took place in 1981;[236] and selling cat-themed artwork and objects in her own shop in Santa Monica, called "Montana Paws" after the street where it was located.[237]

While it lasted, Topo's acting career in film and television (from 1970 to 1979) was fairly successful. Her most famous film remains *The Hot Rock* (1972), an ingenious caper movie written with witty virtuosity by screen-

---

[235] Topo Swope (2017), op. cit.

[236] Roderick Mann, "Fonda Turns a Hat Trick," *Los Angeles Times*, September 13, 1981.

[237] Mother and daughter certainly shared one thing: they were both animal lovers.

writer William Goldman and directed by Peter Yates, in which she played sister to Robert Redford's character.

But it was not in the cards that such career should develop further, and Topo's aversion for the audition process was so strong that she decided to put an end to that particular aspect of her professional life. She remained firmly committed to the arts, however, and to acting. Today Topo runs her own talent agency, Topo Swope Talent, based in Seattle, a city she loves better than her native Los Angeles (whose constant sunshine and hot weather she cannot abide—another symbolic rebellion?).

Christmas at home with the Swope family unit, circa 1957. Courtesy of Topo Swope's private collection.

Like her younger brother Mark, Topo has been blessed with good looks, talent, and a quirky, free-spirited eccentricity. She was always very close to her brother, whom she loved dearly. The following episode in their relationship is ample proof of this:

> The year was 1978. I was in New York, pursuing my acting career. My parents had been out of the country, and were coming back to the States. My brother was supposed to come to New York too, from San Francisco where he was studying at the Art Institute.[238] We were all going to go out to Cape Cod, where many of the Swopes had houses. Mark, however, had testicular cancer at the time, and had decided not to share that particular piece of news with anyone except me. He underwent all the treatments for it without saying a word to anybody. (Those treatments, which at that time consisted of Cobalt radiation sessions, may be what gave him the lung cancer that eventually killed him.) So, Mark did not come out to New York, and I was the one who had to tell our parents that their son had cancer. It was horrible. So, we all flew to San Francisco to be with Mark.
>
> On that occasion, I moved back into my parents' house, occupying the pool room downstairs. I had my two cats with me, Chaplin and Steve Martin. I lived there for a while, then moved out and continued my acting career.

Dorothy gave birth to her second and last child, Mark, on May 14, 1953. At birth, he weighed 8 pounds, 2 ounces, and was delivered by Caesarean section by Drs. Robert Fagan and James Davis.[239]

---

[238] While Mark was studying at the Art Institute, Dorothy was quite smitten with San Francisco. During the time of my initial frequentation of the Swopes, while I was studying at Columbia University, Dorothy even sent me an illustrated guidebook to the city, writing that I *had to* see San Francisco!

[239] "Son Born to Dorothy McGuire," *Los Angeles Times*, May 15, 1953.

Strolling in the park: From left to right, Topo, Mark, and Dorothy, circa 1958. Courtesy of Topo Swope's private collection.

A handsome, athletic, talented charmer that his longtime friend, writer Dwight Holing,[240] describes as "the quintessential beautiful son," Mark Swope was devoted to his parents, and very close to his mother until the end of her days. On the desk of his studio were photographs of both Dorothy and John.

---

240 Dwight Holing and Mark Swope were best friends, and best men at each other's weddings. Dwight Holing's took place on March 20, 1982; Mark Swope's on April 14, 2007.

Mark lived his formative years in a household steeped in film, theater, and art, and frequented film stars and theater actors from an early age; good looking and athletic that he was, it would have been perfectly natural for him to become an actor. He certainly developed an artistic sense, and loved both theater and film. At the age of twenty-two, he even played a bit part in a James Ivory film, the ill-fated *The Wild Party*, 1975; but acting was not his passion, and was not to be his destiny. After studying at Immaculate Heart College in Los Angeles and earning a Master of Fine Arts from the San Francisco Art Institute, Mark began his artistic output as a painter and sculptor with a penchant for formal exactness, but soon graduated to photography, and it is as a photographer that he became especially known. In this respect, he definitely followed his father's example. As Dorothy phrased it, "He inherits from John a liking for precision."[241]

Quintessential beautiful son: Mark Swope in 1978. Photo: Dwight Holing. Courtesy of the photographer.

---

[241] Champlin, "Sensitivity" (1976), op. cit.

Dorothy admired Mark's artistic ambition during and after his study at the Art Institute, and his early efforts in the visual arts found her ecstatic. In our correspondence in 1977 and 1978, she mentioned her son often; in a postcard, for example, she fawned, "Marco—actually Mark—is an artist, and a brilliant one, though his *'parenti'* must confess they do not always understand his creations."

Mark's favorite photographic subject was his home city, and its surrounding county. His portrayals ranged from depictions of the Los Angeles River to views of the rooftops of Downtown Los Angeles or of suburban neighborhoods.

According to his longtime gallerist, Craig Krull, Mark's photographs were "grounded in the aesthetic and theoretical approach of the New Topographic photographers, such as Henry Wessel Jr., Joe Deal and especially Robert Adams." In other words, his work was often akin to that of photographers whose watchful depictions of man-altered landscapes constituted sociological or ecological commentaries—often camouflaged as plain, innocent portrayals.

That Mark Swope should somehow inherit traits of his father's approach to photography is not surprising. Reviewing Mark's exhibition of Los Angeles River photographs, art critic Leah Ollman wrote in the *Los Angeles Times*:

> Mark Swope's photographs of the Los Angeles River are documents in the truest sense—not just evidence, but (using the Compact Edition of the Oxford English Dictionary's definition) lessons, warnings. In the large, black and white pictures at Craig Krull, Swope assumes a straightforward stance. Each view is crisp, neatly organized, dense with information. There are no theatrics at work in terms of lighting or composition, but that doesn't make the images neutral, only less overt in their revelation of tragedy.[242]

---

[242] Leah Ollman, "Mark Swope at Craig Krull Gallery," *Los Angeles Times*, February 5,

Another critic, Sharon Mizota, wrote in the same newspaper about Mark's exhibition entitled "Foliage":

> Swope's series "Foliage" provides a humorous, sometimes startling glimpse into the hidden life of domestic shrubbery. Or perhaps not so hidden. In image after image, Swope finds moments of fantasy embedded in everyday suburban landscapes: geometric topiary gone rogue, hulking ivy monsters gingerly spreading their skirts across the sidewalk or tangles of branches as blustery as a Turner landscape.[243]

Mark's photographs from that exhibition often seem magical or disquieting in a way not warranted by either their innocuous subjects (shrubberies, trees, and topiaries) or their parts. Despite their unfussy, straightforward views and balanced compositions, the photographs somehow appear subtly surreal, like stopped frames from a René Clair silent film or establishing shots from a Carl Theodor Dreyer vampire story. That there were occasionally subtle points of contact between Mark's way of viewing the world around him and his father's can be verified by examining some of John's photographs of similarly innocuous subjects. Some of his 1945 photographs of Japanese landscapes or scenes suggest feelings of loss and uncertainty despite the simplicity of their compositions and the detached eye of the photographer observing the subjects. Similarly, Mark's views of man-altered plant life could be interpreted in either the tragic or comic vein; whatever the feelings suggested, Mark's approach is understated and unobtrusive.

Other exhibitions of Mark's work included a group exhibition at the Los Angeles County Museum of Art in 2013 ("Little Boxes: Photogra-

---

2010.

[243] Sharon Mizota, "Mark Swope Spies Drama Along the Sidewalk," *Los Angeles Times*, December 18, 2012.

phy and the Suburbs"), and exhibits at the Craig Krull Gallery in Santa Monica "(Between"), the South Pasadena Arts Council ("Stand Alone"), the Fresno Art Museum ("Urban California"), and Paris Photo Los Angeles ("Both Sides of Sunset: Photographing Los Angeles").

From both his mother and his father, Mark inherited recognizable personality traits, such as a sense of humor and an artist's touch. As Holing explains:

> Mark was a lot like his father in many ways, and beyond his photographic talent. But he was also a lot like his mother. He had that artistic sense, that artistic "eye," and that sense of the theatrical. He was artistic in his tastes before being artistic in his expression. While we were roommates at Robert Louis Stevenson High School in Pebble Beach, California, he introduced me to the things he liked, such as foreign films by Godard and others. I am sure he got that artistic sense from being exposed to it from an early age, from having a mother who was an actress and a father who produced plays. Mark too in some way was part of that Hollywood world that routinely streamed through his parents' house in Beverly Hills, and he had a deep appreciation of film, theater, drama and comedy.
>
> Speaking of comedy, the first word that always comes to my mind when I think of Mark is "humorous." Mark had an open, curious attitude towards the world, and an almost childish, joyous glee about things. He could be fascinated by just about anything, and had this great, ironic sense of humor. He could see funny aspects in any place, setting or situation. His humor and irony never stooped down to the level of cynicism or sarcasm, and seldom expressed themselves at the expense of other people.
>
> He also had a way of speaking that could sound almost like Esperanto: you really had to make an effort to try and

understand what he was getting at through an eccentric kind of shorthand that used synthetic, quirky phrases. When you "got it," it was hilarious. He also had nicknames for everyone. His cousin Mary Swope, who was also a photographer, was "Big Girlie." He had at least three different names for his sister, such as "The Topester" and "Topato." He called Dorothy "Mummo." I had a couple of nicknames, one of them being "Dwightbulb." That was the way he showed his affection for people.[244] Mark kept his sense of humor until the end. Even when he was dying of cancer, he would say, "My prescription is hope and humor."

Mark Swope was diagnosed with cancer in 2015 and died on December 19, 2016. Like his father and mother before him, he chose to have his ashes dispersed in the Pacific Ocean, some three nautical miles off the shore of Marina Del Rey.

---

[244] Holing (2017), op. cit.

8. 20th Century-Fox, 1943–1959

Though Dorothy would eventually sign an exclusive two-year contract with Darryl Zanuck's 20th Century-Fox sometime in 1949, she actually started making films with the studio well before becoming an exclusive player for them, and continued to do so after the expiration of her contract. In fact, she started working for Zanuck immediately after setting foot in Hollywood: her very first film, *Claudia*, was made by 20th Century-Fox with Dorothy as a loan-out from David O. Selznick, who ended up being a theoretical boss for her as far as cinema history is concerned.

Claudia (1943)
In 1941, aged twenty-four, Dorothy took Broadway and the theatergoing public by storm when she played the titular character in Rose Franken's play *Claudia*. In 1943, she did likewise to the moviegoing public with the film version of that play. The film too was a resounding success and grossed $2,500,000 in US rentals (eighth position in 20th Century-Fox's top-grossing films).[245]

---

245 "Top Grossers of the Season," *Variety*, January 5, 1944.

A 20th Century-Fox publicity portrait of their contract player, Dorothy McGuire, circa 1950. This particular still was not associated with any particular film.

Dorothy's transition from playing the character on Broadway to playing it on screen was a logical one—for everyone except Dorothy. According to some reports, she was as unhappy about getting the role of Claudia in the film as she had been two years earlier about not getting the role of Liberty Jones in Philip Barry's eponymous play, a failure that had allowed her to get the role of Claudia in Franken's play instead. Here is one report of such Hollywood first-night jitters from the *Brooklyn Eagle*:

> Miss McGuire is unhappy because she doesn't feel that she's the right person for the screen role—which is probably the first time in Hollywood history that an actress felt she wasn't good enough for her part!
> "I really wish they had gotten someone else for the role,"

Miss McGuire said, her blue eyes mirroring the seriousness of her voice; "someone who was really a screen star. Why, I've never even appeared in a short subject!"

Producer William Perlberg and Director Edmund Goulding [...] have felt no uncertainty on this score. After all, Dorothy McGuire played "Claudia" for years on Broadway and on the road, with critics and public alike going overboard on her performance wherever she played. Furthermore, to millions of Americans who had read and loved Rose Franken's "Claudia" stories in Red Book Magazine, Miss McGuire is "Claudia." She looks like Arthur William Brown's famous illustrations for the story, and also the tremendous amount of publicity she has received in newspapers and magazines throughout the country has made her name synonymous with the character.

Everyone is sold on Dorothy McGuire but Dorothy McGuire.

"Joan Fontaine would be wonderful in the part," she murmured. "She's got so much feeling and beauty—I can just imagine her in the scene when Claudia learns that her mother is terribly sick. Joan [...] would reveal all her emotion in one look—without a word!"

Miss McGuire paused a moment, obviously deep in thought. "Now, why can't I be like her?"[246]

With all due respect for Dorothy's feelings at the time (if they were true), Joan Fontaine would have been quite wrong for the role, and probably too mawkish. At any rate, Fontaine screen-tested for the part, as did Loretta Young and Margaret Sullavan.[247]

---

[246] "Dorothy McGuire Is Scared," *Brooklyn Eagle*, August 23, 1943.

[247] Rosenfield, "Fate" (1982), op. cit.

Claudia examining an egg and philosophizing: *"Life does become complicated the minute you're born, doesn't it? An egg doesn't know how lucky it is."* Left to right, Robert Young and Dorothy McGuire. Production still for *Claudia*.

Like the play on which it is based, this beautiful film is a strange creature; even stranger is its protagonist, the teenage bride who goes to live on a Connecticut farm, away from the bustle of nearby New York City, with her architect husband, David (Robert Young). The title character is an original blend of contradictions. Part child, part curious monkey, part leading lady, part flirt, part lover, part fool, part wise old soul, part egotist, and part incurable Pollyanna (and I could go on), young Claudia is an eccentric, mercurial figure. The story that is built around her inherits most of her qualities: it is breezy and mellow, comic and tragic, flippant and romantic alternatively. As Brooks Atkinson of the *New York Times* wrote about the play, "It is an admirable amalgamation of gayety and seriousness."[248]

[248] Brooks Atkinson, "Claudia," as quoted by the Booth Theater Souvenir Program for *Claudia*, 1941.

David (Robert Young) meditates on Claudia's (Dorothy McGuire) latest outlandish assertion. Production still for *Claudia*.

Rose Franken's dialogue, adapted by Morrie Ryskind, may not always have the razzle-dazzle virtuosity of Philip Barry's, but it crackles and pops nonetheless: there is just no extinguishing the fire burning inside this play, even during its more tragic moments. The news of her mother's terminal illness sobers Claudia up temporarily, but she faces the new experience of grief with the same irrepressible verve—and above all with the same openhearted curiosity—with which she faces the frivolous, joyous moments in life. Like a wondrous toy with a magical battery in her, Claudia just keeps going, and going, and going.

Three years after this film, Franken's screenplay for *Claudia*'s sequel, *Claudia and David* (1946), co-written with Vera Caspary, William Brown Meloney, and uncredited Writers Frank Davis and Tess Slesinger, would punch the contradictory traits developed here into overdrive, losing some of the amazing equilibrium of this film. Here, the many balls that screenwriter Morrie Ryskind and director Edmund Goulding juggle all stay up in the air, in a surprising gravity-defying act. There is a crystalline balance to this story, and to its main character, which rarely makes you feel the fatigue of what is being accomplished. The credit for this tightrope act goes in no small part to Dorothy.

Claudia (Dorothy McGuire) practices some of her contradictions on her husband David (Robert Young) in *Claudia*. Production still.

So deft is Dorothy in rapidly slaloming through the various facets of her character, and in changing emotional direction in mid-air like an expert dancer, that each contradictory element evaporates and vanishes as soon as the next one appears, in a weightless, fluid continuum. As in a piece of elaborately constructed music, each emotional phrase modulates to the next, and the spectator is irresistibly pulled forward into the flow, with no apparent memory of what has come before, as the musical discourse is articulated. Dorothy's performance is so light, so fast, so agile, and so athletic (literally as well as figuratively) that she hardly leaves a trace as she moves through the text.

In *Claudia and David*, the relationship between the two titular characters, too, would change. In the later film, the weight is visible, and the scale is tipped in David's direction: Claudia's antics are so extreme that

David appears condescending, when not irritated (the audience might feel the same), towards his wise-foolish wife. Here, in *Claudia*, the two pans of the scale achieve a perfect zero: there is no weight. David's annoyance, when it exists, liquefies almost before it has had time to manifest. The give-and-take between the two characters hides no judgment, just momentary feelings that pass and give way to new feelings. It is a testament to the quality of Franken's text, certainly, but also to the lightness of touch of the two lead players and to the comedic wisdom of director Goulding, that this experiment is as successful as it is.

Robert Young is excellent in the part that was initially supposed to go to none other than Cary Grant. Some scheduling conflicts stood in the way, courtesy of the U.S. Air Force. Here is Louella Parsons's 1942 report of that original casting intention:

> Who would be more perfect for the role of David in "Claudia" than Cary Grant? And that, my friends, is the deal that is sizzling now between Cary and 20th Century-Fox. The only thing that stands in the way is the exact date Cary checks into the Air Force and if it stays Jan. 15, which seems likely, the picture will roll immediately. The script, as turned over by David Selznick, is completed and okayed. In fact, Cary read it from cover to cover over the week-end and he is crazy about the role of the young husband who helps the lovable but dizzy "Claudia" keep her feet on the ground.
>
> Dorothy McGuire, who is set for "Claudia," is still touring with the New York hit. But she may get a wire any minute that will bring her back to Hollywood. What a build-up this long tour will mean for the picture.[249]

---

[249] Louella O. Parsons, "Cary Grant Slated For Role in 'Claudia,'" *Philadelphia Inquirer*, November 24, 1942.

In hindsight, it is not difficult to see that, though the idea of snagging Cary Grant for the picture might have had its allure, his presence alongside Dorothy would probably have thrown the piece off-balance. Grant was a lithe, ironic, but relatively cold performer, and a bulky star. *Claudia* is not David's film, but Claudia's, all the way through. Dorothy's character requires the support of a "sidekick" who is warm and self-effacing. Robert Young is ideal for the job, and there is undeniable chemistry between him and Dorothy. The two actors would end up making three films together.

New to the world, Claudia processes grief for the first time as her husband watches, amazed. Production still for *Claudia*.

Though the serious life lessons that David and Ms. Franken's story try to teach Claudia, to "hold [those you love] close with open hands" and to "make friends with pain," may be important for the character's rite of passage from adolescence to adulthood, for us they may seem like little more than patronizing platitudes (and the reason why *Variety* termed this film "a happily sentimental tearjerker").[250] In fact, they are not important. It is

---
250 "Claudia," *Variety*, August 18, 1943.

the quality of the journey that counts, and the sound and pace of Franken's words in Dorothy's rendering. In dramatic terms, this is still a comedy, though a delicate one, and it is as a comedy that it is memorable. However, a beautifully conceived somber finale, full of goodbyes and hellos, separations and reunions, endings and new beginnings, is very well done indeed.

Athletic, I said. One of the first stage directions in Franken's play describes Claudia as "young and full of voltage." It is not only in the delivery of the dialogue that Dorothy is exceptional in this piece, but also in the hormonal energy she injects into her character. This play is a physical as well as verbal race for her: it could have been called *Run, Claudia, Run!* Whether she is rushing down a country road to check the results of a small car accident, moving from one part of the house to the other, kneeling on the floor to gather the bank statements she has dropped, bumping her head on a window frame as she lies back on a window seat, reacting to a comical threat from her husband, or falling into his arms, Claudia's (and Dorothy's) pace is, more often than not, a breathless one. A fidgety, restless, but joyous human puppy, Claudia is always "doing" something, either verbally or physically. Even when she is silent and motionless (rarely), her inner clock is ticking up a storm. In her dialogue with David or with her neighbor Jerry (Reginald Gardiner, who would become a regular player at the La Jolla Playhouse), and especially in a wonderful early threesome with David and her mother (Ina Claire), the contrast between Claudia's energy and rhythm and the slower rhythms of the other characters/players provides most of the "musical" and dramatic pleasure in this play.

Like the puppy that she is, Claudia enthusiastically explores her new adult world, testing every phenomenon she encounters with breathless abandon. She tests herself that way, too. When she flirts with her British neighbor—womanizing playwright Jerry Seymour—she does so without a trace of malice, and only to prod the mystery of her own sexual attractiveness. That flirt is not so much a seduction as a scientific experiment (her term for it, not mine), and the two characters' dialogue not so much a sexy exchange as a philosophical discussion. Whatever she essays, Claudia remains an innocent, guileless explorer of life's secrets. Prejudice, negativity, nervousness, and passivity have not had time to get hold of her yet.

Like a human puppy: Claudia (Dorothy) flirts innocently with her womanizing neighbor, playwright Jerry Seymour (Reginald Gardiner), in order to learn about the world of adults. Production still for *Claudia*, © 1943, 20th Century-Fox.

Variety was positive about the film, but quibbled endlessly about its minor flaws. Arguably, some of these flaws do exist. It is true, for example, that a minor subplot involving the criminal background of the housekeepers' son and some missing money, "which was a trifle obscure in the stage version, is badly muddled in the picture." It is also true that the outdoor settings "look palpably faked" and that "the interior scenes suggest a labyrinth rather than a quaint Connecticut farmhouse." One may even concede that Dorothy "is handicapped by unbecoming makeup, costuming and murky lighting." These objections aside, *Variety* liked the film, and believed it would "draw hefty business and satisfy audiences—especially femmes." About Dorothy, it opined: "She has a captivating personality and her playing is believable and expressive, particularly in the emotional scenes later in the picture [...]."

The *New York Times* was much more positive, and free of objections, both about the film as a whole:

> A morality play, [Claudia] treats its moral lightly; a comedy, it conceals a smooth and feminine wisdom behind a mask of frivolity, and for its highly personal issues it provides the easy solvent of tears. In short, it is a film both sophisticated and emotionally luxurious. Wittily written, deftly directed and handsomely acted by Dorothy McGuire and Robert Young in the central roles, "Claudia" is one of the more engaging comedies of the season.[251]

and about Dorothy specifically:

> Under Mr. Goulding's sensitive direction Miss McGuire has easily carried into another medium the astonishing performance she originally gave in Claudia's transition from girlhood to maturity. In the film's earlier scenes her tomboyish gaucheries sometimes are a little too flamboyant and like a precocious youngster trying to show off, but in the latter scenes her tortured transition is entirely believable and touching.

Edwin Schallert of the *Los Angeles Times* gave a glowing appraisal of the proceedings in his review:

> "Claudia" arrives on the screen practically intact. Spice of the stage play necessarily is somewhat missing, but Dorothy

---

[251] T.S., "At the Music Hall," *New York Times*, November 5, 1943.

McGuire not only preserves—she also develops her sprightly, amusing and irrepressible character.

Moreover, she is a pleasant addition to the ensemble of stars. With the right subjects she will probably have an interesting, and possibly even provocative, career. [...]

[Director Edmund Goulding and screenwriter Morrie Ryskind] permit Miss McGuire's unique talents to be plentifully highlighted.[252]

Back from an evening out, Claudia reflects on the little conundrums that life always seems to be throwing her way. Her husband David waits for the punchline that inevitably his wife will throw *his* way. Production still for *Claudia*.

Dorothy got tired of Claudia quite early in her career. Here is an anecdote about her reaction to a 1940s screening of the film from a 1972 Hollywood-written syndicated article:

---

[252] Edwin Schallert, "Dorothy McGuire Sparkles as Cinematized Claudia," *Los Angeles Times*, September 3, 1943.

20TH CENTURY-FOX, 1943–1959

> Dorothy McGuire was sitting in a theater balcony in Phoenix, Ariz., watching herself in her first motion picture, "Claudia," when the man sitting in front of her exploded, "How could any man stand a woman like that!"
>
> "He's right," Miss McGuire announced. And with that she got up and walked out.[253]

A Tree Grows in Brooklyn (1945)
If one had any doubts about Dorothy's versatility as an actress, or about her ability to learn how to act in the new medium of film, one would only have to compare her performance in *Claudia* (1943) with her performance in this, her second film. Dorothy turns her previous characterization (sweet, chipper and eventually melancholy) inside out like a glove—or, better, like a gutted squid—and exposes the raw, vulnerable underbelly of those feelings. Surrounded by good actors and directed by a young, talented Elia Kazan in his feature-film debut, Dorothy gives a spectacularly good performance in a spectacularly good film.

The film was based on Betty Smith's bestselling novel of the same title, first published in 1943. Ms. Smith had no interest in taking over as screenwriter, and declined the offer to adapt the novel for the screen. She sold the rights and believed that this meant severing the umbilical cord with her story forever. She did, nonetheless, take an interest in what was being done with her work, and kept a watchful eye on the casting and filming process from a safe distance.

In March 1945, just after the film's premiere, Smith wrote a syndicated piece about the process she had witnessed from afar and about the film itself in the *New York Herald-Tribune*:

> I heard that Elia Kazan would direct. I was pleased. 'Gad-

---
[253] "Dorothy McGuire critical of work," *New Castle (PA) News*, April 3, 1972.

get' Kazan and I had been classmates for three years at the Yale Drama School. I had intimate knowledge of and the utmost trust in his directing genius. I slept pretty well nights after I knew he had taken over.

I began to get news about the actors. Joan Blondell as Aunt Sissie was inspired casting. I had once seen Jimmy Dunn give a tender portrayal in a long-ago picture—"Bad Girl" I think it was. When his name came up as a possibility, I kept my fingers crossed. When I saw the first stills of him in the role, my hands got ice cold. He was the original Johnny Nolan come back to life.

I had been much moved when I saw a young actress portray the child Jane Eyre in the picture of that name. Her untricked simplicity was sensational. I had never thought of any one else than Peggy Ann Garner playing Francie. I'm a Lloyd Nolan fan and naturally was pleased when he drew the McShane assignment.

Frankly I was a bit thoughtful about Dorothy McGuire as Katie. I had seen her in nothing but the Claudia play and picture, and I'm one of the few people, I suppose, who are allergic to the bright sweetness of the Claudia type. We'll see how she handles it, I thought.[254]

Thus, it would appear that Ms. Smith's only doubt concerned the casting of Dorothy. Here is her reaction upon seeing the finished film at an industry preview in New York:

> A word about Dorothy McGuire. The other actors fitted their parts. Miss McGuire had to stretch to become Katie.

---

[254] Betty Smith, "Author's Word for 'Brooklyn': 'Good,'" *Minneapolis (MN) Star Tribune*, March 18, 1945.

And she did it! It is utterly unbelievable, unless seen, that this "cute" young woman is transformed into practical, worried Katie Nolan, disillusioned without bitterness. It's a remarkable performance.[255]

And here is Smith's wise conclusion:

> Hollywood has kicked around such words as sensational, super, colossal, until they have no meaning any more. I think a new word will have to be dug up to describe the picture, a word that has more meaning than colossal. I offer the word: good. I feel that I am qualified to call it good. I had no hand in the making of the picture and I am in the position of being its coldest critic.
> Therefore, as a cold critic and as a person prejudiced in many ways against the screen, I pronounce that the picture made from my 'A Tree Grows in Brooklyn' is a good picture.[256]

The film is, indeed, as good as they come. The touching story of life in the impoverished tenements of Brooklyn, New York, in the early years of the twentieth century, *A Tree Grows in Brooklyn* focuses on the members of the Nolan family, and tells its story from the point of view of eleven-year-old Francie (Peggy Ann Garner), a sensitive, intelligent girl with a knack for writing, and, to a lesser extent, from that of her younger brother Neeley (Ted Donaldson). Their mother, Katie (Dorothy McGuire), has to support her family all by herself as a cleaner, for her alcoholic, hopeless dreamer of a husband, Johnny (James Dunn), is not capable of keeping his feet on the ground. Katie is a practical person, as Smith noted, constantly worried about making ends meet. Through hardship and sac-

---

255 Ibid.

256 Ibid.

rifice, she has lost the ability to dream, and apparently the ability to be happy. The things she used to love about her husband—his cheerfulness, his courtesy, his imagination and his loving, positive outlook on just about anything and anybody—no longer charm her. They still charm Francie, who adores him no matter what. Katie's sister, Sissie, a strong-willed free spirit (Joan Blondell), tries to shake Katie out of her gloom, but barely makes a dent in the tin armor that Katie has built around herself. The neighborhood police officer, McShane (Lloyd Nolan), likes the family and keeps an affectionate eye on them, discreetly.

Officer McShane (Lloyd Nolan) and Katie Nolan (Dorothy) in their final scene together. Production still for *A Tree Grows in Brooklyn*, 20th Century-Fox, 1945.

When Katie becomes pregnant, she braces herself for tragedy. She has an earnest talk with her husband, and plans are made to yank Francie out of school so that she can take over working in her mother's stead. Realizing that this drastic measure might ruin the life of his talented, intelligent daughter irreparably, Johnny resolves to disappear; he is found dead in the wintry street the following day. The gray cloud of gloom that was hovering over the family turns black. Francie, who resents her mother's coldness towards Johnny and has probably learned from her mother to keep her feelings bottled up, does not cry. Nor does Katie. After the funeral, the owner of the bar where Johnny used to get drunk (James Gleason) pays a call to Katie, telling her the improbable story of some money that he was keeping for her husband and offering to hire the children for some part-time, after-school work. The insurance that Katie was faithfully paying helps too. Things are looking up for the family, but still those feelings are bottled up safely.

Katie goes into labor, and Francie is at her side. In a memorable scene, Katie launches into a delirious dialogue/monologue with her daughter; she asks to hear one of Francie's compositions, which Katie has never read. Francie chooses one about her father, and all the guilt that Katie has been feeling comes out into the open. Francie's feelings stay inside.

A healthy baby girl is born. At school, both Francie and her brother Neeley get their diplomas. In another beautiful scene, Aunt Sissie corners Francie in an empty classroom and presents her with a bunch of flowers. The card that comes with the flowers is from Francie's father, Johnny. He had given Sissie the money for those flowers well before Christmas, or so she claims. Francie's feelings are fighting to come out, and Sissie takes her to the ladies' room, telling her to "*Let it go*." Francie finally does.

The family (with Aunt Sissie) goes out to the ice cream parlor to celebrate. Back home, the Nolans are alone with Officer McShane, who was holding the baby for Katie. In an expertly acted scene, McShane asks Katie's permission to "keep company" with her and eventually, if the time comes, to marry her and give a name to the newborn child. Katie consents; the children approve. A new chapter begins for the Nolans; and the chopped-down, burnt tree that used to grace the tenement's yard lives and blossoms again, against all odds.

One of the film's most enlightened qualities is its determination not to let any of its characters become "types." Katie never becomes "the embittered poor woman with a useless husband"; Francie never becomes "the sensitive child crushed by poverty"; Johnny never becomes "the foolish good-for-nothing"; Sissie never becomes "the coquettish free spirit," etc. Everything is beautifully balanced, and at every turn, a new facet is revealed for each character, adding dimension after dimension and surprise after surprise.

Sissie, for example, clings to her carefree, chintzy persona to cheer people up, but she is ready to let it go the moment she has to come to the rescue of her glum sister. In her heart-to-heart talk with Katie, Sissie is more than willing to express real feelings and volunteer all the wisdom of which she is capable. She too can be practical, but never in a tragic mode.

Dorothy is splendid throughout the film, and most audiences readily remember her "tragic" scenes (such as her sickbed repentance). But her performance is just as astonishing—if not more so—in the ensemble scenes, and in her quick exchanges with her family or with characters such as McGarrity the bar owner or McShane the police officer. A dinner scene with her two children is a masterpiece of timing, the fast dialogue constantly counterpointed by asides and deft physical actions.

The Nolan family listens to the gossip of their insurance salesman in a transitional scene. Left to right: Peggy Ann Garner, Dorothy, Ted Donaldson, and an uncredited Charles Halton. Production still, 20th Century-Fox, 1945.

Archaic courtship: Katie Nolan (Dorothy) listens to Officer McShane's awkward marriage proposal in *A Tree Grows in Brooklyn*. Production still, 20th Century-Fox, 1945.

James Dunn is very good as Johnny the frivolous husband, and won an Oscar for his performance. The remarkable Peggy Ann Garner also won a special "Juvenile" Academy Award. Garner is certainly a revelation, but, in my opinion, it is Dorothy McGuire, Joan Blondell and Lloyd Nolan who quietly steal the show. Nolan, in what must be one of the best performances of his career, is adorable as the shy, dignified police officer. His big scene, where McShane makes his honorable intentions clear to the Nolan family, is a delightful tour de force of hesitations, subtext, emotional confusion and charm. McShane's proposal and Katie's response, which in the novel become a somewhat wordy negotiation, are realized economically and subtextually in the film: it is all in the acting, in the pauses, in the body language, and in what is *not* said. Lloyd Nolan modulates his sonorous *basso* voice to a solemn *pianissimo*, his eyes expressing the embarrassment, respect, affection, and joy of his character with understated but crystal-clear—and moving—intensity. The language itself, through its reticence and its ritualistic formality, becomes a homage to archaic formulas of courtship, and a marvelous expression of ceremonious respect.

Variety loved the film, and had this to say about Dorothy's performance:

> To Dorothy McGuire, who has appeared in only one other film, in the title role of "Claudia," also for 20th-Fox, went the prize part of Katie Nolan. For the first reel or so it's difficult to associate the girl wife of "Claudia" with the almost-calloused character of Katie, but soon Miss McGuire develops with the part, and the part with her. It is a role that she makes distinctive by underplaying.[257]

Bosley Crowther of the *New York Times*, who also liked the film, wrote thus of its lead actress:

> [The] film transmits a deeply affecting conception of the mother, Katie Nolan, whose life was a constant struggle against the family's only adversary, poverty. As Dorothy McGuire plays her, she gains strength and clarity through the film until a beautiful and rewarding understanding of her troubled, noble nature is revealed.[258]

George L. David of the Rochester *Democrat and Chronicle* piled yet more praise on Dorothy:

---

257 "A Tree Grows in B'klyn," *Variety*, January 24, 1945.

258 Bosley Crowther, "At the Paramount at the Fifty-fifth Street 'A Tree Grows in Brooklyn,' Film Version of Betty Smith's Novel, With a Uniformly Fine Cast, Opens at the Roxy," *New York Times*, March 1, 1945.

[The character of] Katie is acted with fine perception and beautiful clarity by Dorothy McGuire. It is an outstanding portrayal in its restraint and delicate shading and suggestion.[259]

In her column "Looking at Hollywood" in early 1946, Hedda Hopper made this comment about Dorothy and *Tree*: "Dorothy really deserves an award for 'A Tree Grows in Brooklyn,' but I doubt her getting it."[260] She did not receive an Oscar then, nor in years to come.

In 2010, the film was selected by the Library of Congress for inclusion in the United States National Film Registry as being "culturally, historically, or aesthetically significant."

Claudia and David (1946)
Claudia and David, the first and only sequel to Dorothy's successful film debut, starts with a cliché. Young Claudia, the lovable scatterbrain who three years earlier had been the protagonist of *Claudia* (1943), is driving down a city street on her way to pick up her husband, David, from work. She has just bought presents for their three-year-old son at a toy store, and received a parking ticket. She slams on her brakes, gets rear-ended by the car behind her, and, after telling the driver that everything is all right, cheerfully does an illegal U-turn to park in front of the construction site where David is supervising one of his architectural creations. "*What makes men think women are bad drivers?*" she asks her husband as he is getting in the car. "*Women drivers*," answers David. During the drive to Connecticut, she lets go of the steering wheel to examine her parking ticket and almost causes a frontal collision with a truck when she daringly overtakes a car.

---

259 George L. David, "'Tree Grows in Brooklyn' Fine, Absorbing Film at Palace," *Rochester (NY) Democrat and Chronicle*, March 16, 1945.

260 Hedda Hopper, "Looking at Hollywood," *Los Angeles Times*, January 26, 1946.

Her husband is accustomed to such incidents, and is amusedly tolerant—and only slightly apprehensive.

Dorothy in her dressing room while shooting *Claudia and David*. Press photo by Clifton Maupin, 1946.

This particular cliché—women are such lovable featherheads—to some extent is carried over through the entire film, in an exaggerated comic form that has little to do with the tone of the original *Claudia*.

Three years earlier, Claudia the immature girl bride was new to life, and her erratic behavior and virtually bipolar mood swings had a tender, childish quality that made her tolerable: the audience, while guiltily enjoying her antics, expected her character to mature and develop, and life to teach her a lesson or two. Now, three years later, her immaturity is less understandable. She is a young woman, and a mother, yet she is just as unschooled. The persistence of the child in her is beginning to be irksome rather than funny.

That bipolar oscillation of moods is the whole character in a nutshell, even though occasionally Claudia's uncharacteristic insights into people, as in a confrontation with a jealous woman whose husband she has innocently befriended, are as truly surprising in this film as they had been in *Claudia*. The logic of this character is that she has no particular logic.

It is a tribute to Dorothy's skill and likability that, notwithstanding this heightened hodgepodge of contrasting traits, the character remains mostly sympathetic. As Bosley Crowther of the *New York Times* put it, "Dorothy McGuire, as previously, plays Claudia with such candid tenderness that she overcomes all the discomfort that such a character might inspire."[261] She also plays the character, and the story, with irrepressible energy, bounding from set to set and from situation to situation with nary a pause, spouting Claudia's mostly inane lines with vertiginous speed.

Regardless of the limitations of Claudia as a character, Dorothy's confidence as a player and her ability to navigate the meanders of her character's mind through body and feeling are extraordinary. Her skill in changing expressions rapidly—as rapidly as Claudia changes moods and thoughts—is especially uncanny. A phone call she makes (with no audible interlocutor), for example, is a little jewel of timing, realism, and comic color.

This time around, a potential double romantic triangle provides the pep to the husband-wife relationship, with Claudia guilelessly accepting, or not discouraging, the attentions of a smooth sophisticate (John Sutton) and David cultivating a professional relationship with a rich client

---

[261] Bosley Crowther, "'Claudia and David,' Sequel to Rose Franken's Film of Three Years Ago, Opens of Roxy-- Dorothy McGuire Again Star," *New York Times*, August 15, 1946.

(Mary Astor) with excessive relish. But nothing comes of those subplots; instead, the plot is turned at the climax by a car accident that sends David to the hospital with serious injuries. Like the illness of Claudia's mother in the first *Claudia* picture, this event is supposed to sober Claudia up and mature her. Sure, she cries and is very worried while David is in the hospital, and very relieved when he recovers without problems. Whether this event has done the trick for her in the end or whether she is ready to revert once more to her immature self for the next Claudia installment (which thankfully never materialized) is another matter.

David (Robert Young) and Claudia (Dorothy, middle) discuss architecture in their barn with David's attractive, rich client (Mary Astor). Production still for *Claudia and David*, 20th Century-Fox, 1946.

The plots of both *Claudia* and *Claudia and David* were adapted from a series of short stories written by Rose Franken and originally published in the *New Yorker*. A sequel to *Claudia* was envisaged as early as 1943, and for years thereafter there was talk of a whole series of films based on Franken's characters in the gossip columns. Wisely, Dorothy held off on the first sequel for three years and most likely refused any further participation in the franchise. For a stretch of time after the release of *Claudia*, it looked as if she would never get another important role unless it resembled her first success. In the eyes of many, she *was* Claudia. And when she learned that the first sequel was finally slated for shooting, her resigned shrug was, "Oh well, got to do a pal a favor now and then!"[262] Here is Hedda Hopper discussing the issue in 1947:

> Dorothy McGuire arrived in Hollywood to play "Claudia" on the screen just five short years ago, but when the picture was made Claudia became a full time career, and threatened to become a menace. The picture was so good people started to identify Dorothy in private life as Claudia, the zany bride, and movie men began talking about doing a series of those pictures like "The Hardy Family," "The Thin Man," and so on. This so terrified individualistic McGuire that she'd have nothing to do with another Claudia picture. No one loathes regimentation so much as Dorothy. At the first, the powers that be took her "no" good naturedly and said, "O well, give her a few months and she'll change her mind." But she didn't, she hasn't, and she won't. [...]
>
> Today, after a long siege of battling Claudia down, Dorothy McGuire is tops in her profession by reason of a unique list of characterizations, none of which even faintly resembles Claudia. For the varied field she has covered in both theater and movies this Irish-Scotch-English girl from Omaha, Neb., can thank her integrity, independence, and intelligence.[263]

---

262 "Dorothy McGuire Escaped from Claudia Long Enough to Do Two Pictures," *Oakland (CA) Tribune*, November 26, 1944.

263 Hopper, "Independence" (1947), op. cit.

David (Robert Young) tries to teach his child bride some age-appropriate lessons. Production still, 20th Century-Fox, 1946.

According to Hopper, Dorothy and her co-star Robert Young gave a farewell party for their stand-ins, and most likely for other members of cast and crew, once shooting was completed. John Swope flew to Los Angeles to pick up his wife as soon as retakes were out of the way, and they flew to the East Coast together.[264]

Gentleman's Agreement (1947)
There can be little doubt that *Gentleman's Agreement* represented an important moment in Dorothy's career, and for various reasons. Aside from being an excellent product that showcased Dorothy's talents to great advantage, the film created quite a few ripples, directly or indirectly, in the lives of its stars and in Hollywood. For her performance in *Gentleman's Agreement*, Dorothy received her only nomination for an Academy

---
[264] Hedda Hopper, "Looking at Hollywood," *Los Angeles Times*, April 20, 1946

Award;[265] the film won three Oscars: for Best Picture (Darryl F. Zanuck, producer), Best Supporting Actress (Celeste Holm), and Directing (Elia Kazan). The other nominations were for Best Actor (Gregory Peck), Best Supporting Actress (Anne Revere), Film Editing (Harmon Jones), and Best Writing, Screenplay (Moss Hart). The film also paired Dorothy—for the first and only time in her career—with Selznick player Gregory Peck, who would become a lifelong friend.

A publicity portrait of the three leads of *Gentleman's Agreement*. Left to right: Dorothy, Gregory Peck, and John Garfield. 20th Century-Fox, 1947.

---

265 One way or another, the Academy of Motion Picture Arts and Sciences succeeded in snubbing Dorothy not only during her lifetime but also beyond it. At its 2002 Academy Award ceremony, the Academy managed to omit the actress from its yearly "in memoriam" compilation. Queried by Dorothy's family, the organization added insult to injury by citing time constraints as the cause for the omission.

Philip Green (Gregory Peck) relaxes on the couch of his new apartment (with shoes) as his mother (Anne Revere) unpacks. Production still for *Gentleman's Agreement*, 20th Century-Fox, 1947.

It was during the filming of *Gentleman's Agreement* (May–August 1947) that the triumvirate of Dorothy, Peck and Mel Ferrer concluded their search for a venue for their ambitious theatrical project, the La Jolla Playhouse, and it was during such filming that the playhouse was inaugurated, on July 8, 1947 (see Part I, Chapter 9).

Because of its liberal, left-wing proclivities, the film naturally displeased the House Un-American Activities Committee; in the following two years or so, several people involved in the film were called to testify, Kazan most notoriously.[266] Anne Revere, who played Gregory Peck's mother in the film, refused to appear and was blacklisted in 1951;[267] John

---

266 See for example: Wendy Smith, "The Director Who Named Names," in the quarterly magazine *The American Scholar*, December 10, 2014 (Winter 2015 issue).

267 See for example: Peter B. Flint, "Anne Revere, 87, Actress, Dies; Was Movie Mother of Many Stars," *New York Times*, December 19, 1990.

Garfield appeared, and was blacklisted anyway (then taken off the list, then put back on it again); he died of a heart attack in 1952 at the age of thirty-nine.[268] Both actors had been put on the infamous Red Channels list in 1950.[269]

Blossoming romance: Cathy (Dorothy) has found a match in Philip Green (Gregory Peck). Production still for *Gentleman's Agreement*, **20th Century-Fox, 1947.**

---

268 See for example: Bernard Weinraub, "Recalling John Garfield, Rugged Star KO'd by Fate," *New York Times*, January 30, 2003.

269 See: Wikipedia, "Hollywood Blacklist." See also: Ellen Schrecker, *The Age of McCarthyism: A Brief History with Documents*, Palgrave, 2002. One of Dorothy's best friends, Jane Wyatt, who had a small part in the film, was not called before the Committee but was put on something called the "graylist": although not officially blacklisted, she was not able to get any film roles for a year or two and temporarily moved to New York. See also Wyatt's 1999 two-hour interview for the Archive of American Television (emmytvlegends.org) conducted by Gary Rutkowski.

Speaking of blacklists and Red Channels lists, in March 1951 acidulous syndicated columnist Leonard Lyons reported a curious, and possibly false, anecdote involving José Ferrer and a rather uncharacteristic Dorothy:

> Dorothy McGuire lunched at Sardi's yesterday, and saw José Ferrer, the producer-star-radio commentator Academy Award nominee. Ferrer soon will testify before the House un-American Activities Committee. Miss McGuire mentioned the matter of his appearing in Washington, and said: "But you're not a Communist, Joe. You couldn't be." . . . "Of course I'm not," Ferrer assured her. . . "No, you couldn't be a Communist," said Miss McGuire. "You're too much of an egotist."[270]

The above quote takes on a slightly more credible hue if we keep in mind that Dorothy, like her colleague John Garfield, had political ideas, and was often outspoken about them. Exhibit A: On November 2, 1947, Dorothy spoke the impassioned closing remarks in a radio special produced by the Committee for the First Amendment and entitled *Hollywood Fights Back*. The thirty-minute special, the second of two broadcast in the space of eight days, aimed at expressing outrage at the House Un-American Activities Committee, aired on ABC. Among the artists who joined Dorothy in offering brief comments on the issue at hand were Dana Andrews, Lauren Bacall, Humphrey Bogart, Bennett Cerf, Moss Hart, Hurd Hatfield, June Havoc, Rita Hayworth, Paul Henreid, John Huston, George S. Kaufman, Danny Kaye, Gene Kelly, Burt Lancaster, Peter Lorre, Myrna Loy, Gregory Peck, Anne Revere, Richard Rodgers, and Jane Wyatt.[271]

---

270 Leonard Lyons, "Einstein's Haircut Shocks Guests at Birthday Party," *Philadelphia Inquirer*, March 17, 1951.

271 Ronald L. Smith, *Horror Stars on Radio*, McFarland and Company, Inc., Publishers, 2010, 168.

Thoughtful intimacy: Dorothy and Gregory Peck explore their characters' relationship in *Gentleman's Agreement*. Production still, 20th Century-Fox, 1947.

The topic of *Gentleman's Agreement* is not anti-Communism but anti-Semitism. Schuyler, or Philip, Green (Gregory Peck), a young, widowed journalist, moves to New York with his son and mother to work for magazine editor John Minify (Albert Dekker), who proposes a series of articles on anti-Semitism. Green is not satisfied with the usual facts and figures, and searches for an interesting "angle" to make the series unique; finally, a light bulb goes on over his head after his mother suffers a heart attack: he will pretend to be Jewish for six months and gather first-hand evidence. Along the way, he romances Minify's niece, Cathy Lacey (Dorothy McGuire), and receives moral support from his Jewish best friend, Dave Goldman (John Garfield). He also learns more than he bargained for about his topic, as he faces not only overt but covert prejudice, for example from his secretary, Elaine Wales (June Havoc), who is secretly Jewish herself, or from his girlfriend Cathy, who is uncomfortable with anything that might shake the foundations of her affluent status quo. The title of the series of articles: "I Was Jewish for Six Months."

Today, a vocal majority seems to believe that the film's handling of the subject is tame.[272] This may well be the case from our distant vantage point more than seventy years down the line, but the film was groundbreaking in 1947 and remains a sensitive, intelligent treatment of the theme. The picture moves at a leisurely pace, but contains sparkling, thoughtful performances from its leads.

According to Hedda Hopper, Dorothy was sold on the project as soon as she read the novel, which was not until she learned about the project in Hopper's column (!):

> When Darryl Zanuck bought "Gentleman's Agreement," he sent a copy of the book to Dorothy McGuire with a note saying he wanted her for the role of Kathy. But he didn't hear from her until two days ago, when Dorothy telephoned to say, "After I read what Hedda Hopper had to say about the story in her column and how you planned to film it, I grabbed the book and couldn't put it down until I finished it. I'd love to play Kathy."
>
> The thing that "got" Dorothy in the story was the little daily terrors—not the big ones—that it depicted.[273]

For once, Dorothy had the chance to play a shaded, intelligent, ambivalent character—something she had started to do to a certain extent the year before in *Till the End of Time*—rather than a demure virgin or a

---

[272] For example critic and historian Leonard Maltin, in his *Leonard Maltin's Movie Guide*, Signet, 2009.

[273] Hedda Hopper, "Looking at Hollywood," *Los Angeles Times*, March 5, 1947.

tragic victim. When Cathy and Philip first meet at a dinner party, they have a short exchange before dinner is served, where her character deftly and wittily gives voice to one of the film's themes, namely prejudice. After Philip is informed that it was Cathy who first suggested the anti-Semitism articles to her uncle, he expresses surprise:

Philip: Funny your suggesting the series.
Cathy: Is it? Why?
Philip: Oh... Lots of reasons.
Cathy: You make up your mind too quickly about people, Mr. Green. Women, anyway. I saw you do it when you sat down.
Philip: Hmm. As apparent as all that.
Cathy: Cross-filed and indexed me. Uh... a little too well-bred, self-confident, artificial, trifle absurd. Typical New York.
Philip: Now, I didn't have time for all that!
Cathy: Oh, yes you did. I even left out a few things: faintly irritating upper-class manner, over-bright voice...
Philip: All right, all right. You win.
Cathy (laughing): I'm sorry, I couldn't resist it. Because it's only partly true.

Even Philip Green classifies people when he first meets them, Cathy is saying; but the accusation could work both ways: it is *she* who attributes the prejudice to Philip, so she is also making up her mind about him rather quickly, or at least about his opinion of her. The dialogue intelligently gets the theme off the ground, and the double-mirror ricochet of the mutual sizing up by the two characters already reveals an important fact: prejudice has many faces, not necessarily visible.

Dorothy's performance is fast, confident, funny, and nuanced. In this film, she demonstrates just how quick on her feet she could be as an actress, moving subtly and gracefully in and out of Cathy's minute emotional changes. She also demonstrates how attractive and interesting she could be as a romantic lead, but as an intelligently seductive one rather than a languid or childish one. There are few moments of sentimentality in the film, and Dorothy handles them quickly and with conviction.

Philip Green (Gregory Peck, right) tries to explain anti-Semitic prejudice to his son Tommy (Dean Stockwell). Production still for *Gentleman's Agreement*, **20th Century-Fox, 1947.**

Ambivalent, I said. As a result of Philip's gimmick, and of his hands-on research, all the relationships are transformed in this story, though not necessarily spoiled: the mature story allows each individual, and each relationship, to come to terms with the ideas on hand. To put it with Cathy's opening statements, anyone who has made up his or her mind too quickly about people or ideas is given a chance to revise his or her opinions and to learn to deal with those ideas like an adult. Thus, the central romantic relationship between Cathy and Philip seems irreparably ruined after their violent disagreement, only to be saved through the intervention of providential Jew-*ex-machina* Dave Goldman, who gives Cathy a chance to mull things over and see the light.

Reparatory hug: Cathy (Dorothy) and Philip (Gregory Peck) make peace after an argument in *Gentleman's Agreement*. Production still, 20th Century-Fox, 1947.

The film, a top grosser for 20th Century-Fox in 1947, was extremely popular upon its release, and was the object of much positive criticism. It won Academy Awards for Best Picture, Best Director, and Best Supporting Actress (Celeste Holm). It also won the New York Critics' Circle Award for Best Picture and Best Director.

Variety gave the film a rave, calling it "brilliant and powerful" and adding that it was "one of the most vital and stirring and impressive in Hollywood history." In fact, *Variety* went so far as to write that the film was "an improvement over the novel"[274] and, elaborating on that last concept, added:

> This is not merely because the story has been better fo-

---

[274] "Gentleman's Agreement," *Variety*, November 12, 1947.

cused and somewhat condensed, without softening the treatment. It is also more graphic and atmospheric than the book and, more importantly, because it has greater dramatic depth and force, and more personal, emotional impact.

[. . .] The basic elements of the [Laura Z.] Hobson work are not only retained, but in some cases given greater dimension and plausibility. This is true of the adaptation, direction and performances. Thus, the first meeting between Phil Green and Kathy is more understandable on the screen than it was on the printed page. Similarly, the couple's other scenes, especially the initial love scene, dramatize their irresistible mutual physical attraction, which overcomes their violent philosophic disagreements.[275]

About Dorothy, *Variety* concluded:

Dorothy McGuire [. . .] is dramatically and emotionally compelling as Kathy, adding considerable scope and depth to anything she has done heretofore. The range from her somewhat flippant opening scene to the searing final one with John Garfield is impressive.[276]

Bosley Crowther of the *New York Times* made similar points in his review, which appeared on the same day as *Variety*'s, the day after the New York premiere on November 11; he noted that novelist Hobson's story had been "[s]haped by Moss Hart into a screenplay of notable nimbleness and drive" and that the result was "a sizzling film."[277]

275 Ibid.

276 Ibid.

277 Bosley Crowther, "'Gentleman's Agreement,' Study of Anti-Semitism, Is Feature at Mayfair -- Gregory Peck Plays Writer Acting as Jew," *New York Times*, November 12, 1947.

Dave Goldman (John Garfield, center, grabbing man's lapel) fights against prejudice at a restaurant, while friend Philip Green (Gregory Peck, standing left) and Philip's sympathetic colleague Anne Dettrey (Celeste Holm, sitting at table) look on. Production still for *Gentleman's Agreement*, 20th Century-Fox, 1947.

Crowther was pleased with the leads' performances, but had some minor reservations about the characters themselves. About Dorothy's Cathy, he opined:

> Also the role of his young lady, which Dorothy McGuire affectingly plays, is written to link in a disquieting little touch of "snob appeal." Maybe the image of the actress in conjunction with the "station-wagon set" is a bit reminiscent of "Claudia" and her juvenile attitudes. But the suggestion of social

aspiration—and accomplishment—confuses the issues very much.[278]

Cozy new love: Philip Green (Gregory Peck) and Cathy Lacy (Dorothy) cuddle in this production still for *Gentleman's Agreement*. 20th Century-Fox, 1947.

Mother Didn't Tell Me (1950)
This bland, flawed comedy, based on a novel by Mary Bard entitled *The Doctor Wears Three Faces* (1949) and scripted by director Claude Binyon, is not entirely without charm.

The film narrates the vicissitudes of a young woman who decides to marry a physician, heedless of the warnings that other doctors' wives throw her way. She soon finds out that being married to a doctor entails a certain amount of loneliness, and learns to adjust. That is the plot in a nutshell. The film is really a collection of vignettes detailing the courtship, wedding and long period of adjustment of Jane Morgan, radio jingle writer, and Dr. William Wright.

The opening credits are promising: British composer Cyril Mock-

---
278 Ibid.

ridge's delightful music seems to usher us into the world of screwball comedy, as black titles written in a gracefully kooky italic font flash on a shaded white background. Alas, Mockridge, who had also written the music for *Claudia and David* (1946), is excessively optimistic, for the film fails to live up to the tuneful promise of those titles. It almost does, but not quite.

Jane Morgan (Dorothy) goes a-courtin' to try to snag charmless doctor Wright (William Lundigan), who, she will discover, is actually not wright for her at all. Production still for *Mother Didn't Tell Me*. 20th Century-Fox, 1950.

One of the film's problems is William Lundigan, who plays William Wright, M.D., Jane's intended (and then actual) husband. Dr. Wright is a likable square of a man, and his comedy, like the comedy of most of the characters in this film, is situational. He is also one of the most shortsighted, socially awkward, gullible, and thickheaded fuddy-duddies to walk on this earth. He is rather good-looking, though. Dr. Wright is a difficult straight role to pull off, and would have required a different type of actor. Lundigan is appealing enough, but he is just too mild—and technically guileless—for the part. He has neither the ironic snap of a William

Holden (or of a Cary Grant!) nor the screwy puzzlement or comic timing of a Joel McCrea. He plays everything straight and flat, and neglects to endow his character with a distinctive characterization, other than the obvious empty likability of a conventional "nice guy." As a result, he makes his character appear charmless for most of the story.

The bulk of the comedy in this film comes from Jane Morgan's actions and reactions rather than from an equal interplay between the two leads; thus, the comedic responsibility in this family rests on Dorothy's shoulders. Dorothy was no Jean Arthur, but she had a delicate comedic touch that worked well in scripts that provided a graceful comedy-of-manners environment. Binyon's script, like Bard's novel, cannot provide such environment. It seems to aspire to be a screwball comedy, *I Love Lucy*-style, but, without the farce, all it can be is a middling romantic comedy. There are no great disasters in this particular *I Love Lucy* episode, just minor mishaps and embarrassments. The one "gag" of the film—a doctor is always on call, and all his wife can do is wait for him—is repeated *ad nauseam* reel after reel: just about every event in Jane and Bill's relationship is interrupted by a phone call from some needy patient or other, even their wedding ceremony. Perhaps under a different director, such as, say, Preston Sturges or Edmund Goulding, the tone of the film could have been made off-color enough to fit into the screwball canon. Or, with a judicious push from the writers, this story of loneliness could have fallen within the drama mode; yet the writers desperately try to keep it comedic, succeeding only sporadically.

That this story might have been more effective as a delicate human drama than as a conventional comedy is suggested by its main theme, which can be synthesized as follows: one should not take one's romantic expectations too seriously when it comes to relationships, but be willing to know one's companion fully before deciding to accept him or reject him. Once Jane Morgan-Wright resigns herself to the fact that her husband is a doctor through and through and stops trying to change him to her ends, serenity reigns once again in her world. She learns to love him rather than her idea of him.

The joys to be had from this film are mostly small, and subtle. Dorothy's graceful, intelligent playing is pleasant; June Havoc as the wisecracking wife of Bill's best friend, another doctor, is amusingly world-weary; Leif Erickson is almost surreal as a predatory, womanizing psychiatrist; and the Wrights' eccentric Asian maid (played by Reiko Sato) speaks an amusing variation of the English language ("*I fix. Many times I work at cocktail parties, making sandwich with the open face*").

Four years after this film was released, Dorothy co-starred with Frank Lovejoy in a *Lux Radio Theatre* adaptation of the same story, with unexciting results; a few of the differences between the two versions may help us point out ways in which the film is, at least, the funnier of the two.

The first scene is a perfect example. In the film, Jane Morgan, walking in from the rain, enters the waiting room of Dr. William Wright, very ladylike. As soon as she has closed the door behind her, she lets out one single cough, a cough that sounds like something a large animal might utter; the walls of the office positively shake. Graceful lady that she is, Jane covers her mouth with her clutch purse, then resumes her walk to the nurse's desk, wearing the most innocent, ladylike expression on her face. She sits down by the nurse's desk, tells her about her appointment, and proceeds to give out her new-patient information. She does so with perfect grace, except when her last sentence is again punctuated by that single cough, which echoes around the room; again, she covers her mouth with her clutch. The nurse points to a far corner of the room and responds with a diffident "*Wait over there, please.*" Once Jane gains admission to the doctor's office (after all the other patients have been seen) and realizes how young and handsome he is, her voice becomes girlish and delicate: when he sticks a depressor on her tongue, she knows the drill and says "*Aah.*" Dorothy, her voice the softest, most angelic instrument, puts a question mark after the word ("*Aah?*"), which is quite funny. Soon thereafter, as the doctor is standing close to her, that single cough pops out again, startling the doctor. He says, "*You caught me off guard. Have you thought of selling that cough to a bull moose?*" The actual payoff of the gag comes when Jane's cough pops out again while Dr. Wright is auscultating her lungs with a stethoscope, rattling him completely.

That cough is so loud, so inhuman, and so brief—and it so contrasts with Dorothy's elegant look and demeanor—that it shocks; by itself, it might not be funny; but Jane Morgan's determination not to break the flow of her elegant manner makes it so incongruous a sound that it becomes humorous.

By contrast, in the radio adaptation, where a single, isolated cough might not have registered at all, Dorothy fills her entire first scene with persistent, continuous coughing, which is much more naturalistic from a clinical point of view (that is what bronchitis usually sounds like) but not funny. Her entire performance in the radio version is constellated by different choices. For example, during his visit, Dr. Wright asks her to "*Say Aah*," and Dorothy responds by giving him a sensual "*Ooh*." When the doctor protests, "*No no no; 'Aaah*,'" she replies, "*That's what I said: 'Ooh*.'" The change in vowel might be funny if it were not an unlikely sound for someone to make under medical scrutiny (impossible if a depressor is used), and if the gag did not cheapen the tone of the comedy significantly. The audience present at the radio taping seemed to enjoy it, however.

While it is true that Dr. Wright is not a particularly fascinating, nor bright, man, it is also true, unfortunately, that the character Dorothy is stuck with is irrational and silly. As Bosley Crowther rightly noted in his *New York Times* review, she comes off as a "Claudia" type, reacting to situations with impulsiveness and concocting utterly moronic schemes. For example, her plan to fit in with her husband's doctor pals at a dinner party entails memorizing entire paragraphs about peptic ulcers from an old textbook and repeating them verbatim to her guests at cocktails or at dinner, much to the embarrassment of everyone around her.

Moronic scheme: newlywed Jane Morgan (Dorothy, right) ponders her misguided social strategies, as new friend Maggie Roberts (June Havoc) looks on skeptically, in *Mother Didn't Tell Me*. Production still, 20th Century-Fox, 1950.

The irrational streak that Crowther noted manifests itself, for example, when Jane, neglected by her husband due to his many house calls, falls for the preposterous advances of an eccentric psychiatrist at a house party with the light-headed abandon of a teenager. The immaturity of Dorothy's character hurts the film, especially when coupled with the blandness of Lundigan's. Crowther concurred with me that Dr. Wright was an uninteresting creation:

> And what's more, the husband set up for her in Claude Binyon's hot-air script is not a lot brighter than she is. He is hooked, in the first place, by no more than a fake call for bedside attention, a flimsy lace nightgown and a smile. He goes around buying houses without even looking at them. And his attitude towards his giddy helpmate is that of a tolerant father

towards a child. As William Lundigan plays him, he is a pretty lame specimen of a man, and, in this corner's unamused opinion, he gets just about what he deserves.[279]

Crowther's conclusion took the form of an attack on writer-director Claude Binyon: "[Binyon] has not elevated the reputations of doctors, Miss McGuire nor Twentieth Century-Fox."[280]

Edwin Schallert of the *Los Angeles Times* was apparently smitten with the film, just as he was with Dorothy. Entitling his review of the film "Mother Didn't Tell Me' Bright, Clever Comedy," Schallert proceeded to wax positive about the finished product and about its lead actress:

> Leave it to Dorothy McGuire to proceed through all the typical feminine routines if she gets a chance in a picture. And she can always manage to accomplish this successfully as she has proved in such widely divergent exploits as "Claudia" and "Gentleman's Agreement."
>
> "Mother Didn't Tell Me" installs her in a new spoiled darling role which more closely approximates the "Claudia" venture [. . .]. Miss McGuire achieves a type which shines at its brightest in comedy. [. . .] "Mother Didn't Tell Me" is a good high comedy.[281]

Dorothy enjoyed making the film, as she told Hedda Hopper in a 1950 interview:

---

279 Bosley Crowther, "'Mother Didn't Tell Me,' Comedy Starring Dorothy McGuire, Arrives of the Roxy," *New York Times*, March 4, 1950.

280 Ibid.

281 Edwin Schallert, "'Mother Didn't Tell Me' Bright, Clever Comedy," *Los Angeles Times*, February 25, 1950.

20th Century-Fox, 1943–1959

I had fun making "Mother Didn't Tell Me" with Bill Lundigan. It was quite an experience working with a director who had also written the script. I am certain Claude Binyon didn't remember every word of the script but he'd know when we missed by the change in the rhythm. And, of course, he knew the characters so thoroughly it made it very easy for us to know them too.[282]

* * *

It is certain that Dorothy, or 20th Century-Fox on her behalf, bought out the remainder of her contract with David O. Selznick at some point before its expiration, but the actual dates oscillate between 1948 and 1949 in printed reports. Nineteen forty-nine seems more likely, since the press reported the details of the arrangement in September 1949, mentioning that *Mother Didn't Tell Me* was Dorothy's last picture under Selznick. Her new two-year contract[283] called for one picture a year, with an option for another.[284]

Darryl Zanuck's 20th Century-Fox had already established a good relationship with Dorothy as early as *Claudia* (1943), her first loan-out film with Selznick, and had continued to cultivate such relationship in three more films during the actress's Selznick years.

Aside from the constant loan-outs, Dorothy's years with Selznick had been constellated by near misses, aborted projects and false alarms (the most prestigious of these aborted projects being *A Doll's House*). Her years under 20th Century-Fox were undoubtedly more stable, but there too a

---

282 Hopper, "Ideals" (1950), op. cit.

283 Ibid.

284 Hedda Hopper, "Betty Hutton Aglow Over Latest Picture," *Los Angeles Times*, September 9, 1949. See also: Hedda Hopper, "'Three Little Words' Yields Role for Dahl," *Los Angeles Times*, September 30, 1949.

number of projects did not quite get off the ground for her. The first of these, in 1949, was reported by Louella Parsons:

> Dorothy McGuire tells me she has read the script of "Cost of Living," sent to her by Sam Spiegel and John Huston. She is crazy about it.
>
> "I think it is one of the most exciting scripts I read," said Dorothy, "but some arrangement has to be made with 20th Century-Fox before I can agree to do it."
>
> I was wondering if possibly the picture might be released by 20th? Huston won't direct it since he won't be finished with "Asphalt Jungle," but it is to be part of their independent set-up.[285]

The film, reshaped and renamed *The Prowler*, was eventually made by Horizon Pictures and Eagle Pictures in 1951, co-written by Dalton Trumbo and with United Artists as theatrical distributor. The leading lady was Evelyn Keyes and the director was Joseph Losey. Spiegel and Huston were credited as producers but not as writers.

Next up, again in 1949, was a suspense yarn entitled *Mischief*, based on an unpublished novel by Charlotte Armstrong (it would be published by Coward-McCann in 1950). Zanuck bought the rights for Dorothy, whose role was to be that of a psychopathic babysitter.[286] Her co-star was to be William Lundigan, and the film was to be directed by Jules Dassin.[287] The film, retitled *Don't Bother to Knock*, was made by 20th in 1952.

---

[285] Louella Parsons (INS), "Story Built Up on 'Disk' Pictures," *Cedar Rapids Gazette*, September 21, 1949.

[286] Hedda Hopper, "Berman to Produce 'Ivanhoe' in England," *Los Angeles Times*, November 7, 1949.

[287] Hedda Hopper, "Dot McGuire Makes 'Mischief,'" *Salt Lake Tribune*, December 23, 1949.

It starred Richard Widmark, Anne Bancroft, and Marilyn Monroe, and was directed by Roy Ward Baker

Another crushed hope, this time involving director King Vidor, was reported by Hedda Hopper in June 1950:

> King Vidor's next will be "The Bright Scarf," with Dorothy McGuire, he hopes. The story has a great spiritual message. The heroine, instead of being a remote kind of girl like we used to put on the screen, is a modern Joan of Arc in blue jeans, with her shirt tail flying. She not only goes to school with her husband, but is his guiding spirit. Vidor may make it for Darryl Zanuck at 20th Century as an independent.[288]

Then the news items about the project ceased. Next, in October 1950, columnist Erskine Johnson reported the following:

> The deal is cold for Shelley Winters to co-star with John Garfield in "He Ran All The Way." Now Garfield wants Dorothy McGuire, who's on tour in the Actors Company roadshow of "Summer and Smoke."[289]

He Ran All the Way was released in 1951, Winters and Garfield co-starring.

Another interesting project saw Dorothy briefly involved in the possible filming of *Main Street to Broadway*, a backstage drama. Edwin Schallert of the *Los Angeles Times* reported:

> [Lester Cowan] is the film producer in charge of the

---

[288] Hedda Hopper, "Ferrer Considered for Painter Role," *San Antonio (TX) Express*, June 14, 1950.

[289] Erskine Johnson, "Hollywood Report," *Athens (OH) Messenger*, October 2, 1950.

Council of the Living Theater project to bring "Main Street to Broadway" to fulfillment as a film.

He expects to start the picture in July in New York, and will have nine top Broadway stars in special scenes, plus Gregory Peck from Hollywood.

Cowan was here to arrange details of the Peck deal and to seek a director. The story has been written by Robert E. Sherwood, national chairman of the Council of the Living Theater, his immediate associate being Katharine Cornell as cochairman.

Such stars as Miss Cornell, Olivia de Havilland, Dorothy McGuire, Jose Ferrer, Betty Field and John Garfield are already set for the picture, while the names of Ethel Merman, Tallulah Bankhead and Jimmy Durante also were mentioned. In the majority of cases they are to enact scenes from their more notable stage plays.

Peck is to have a special sequence touching on his experiences as a student at the Neighborhood Playhouse in New York. He was chosen because he has been aligned with stage activities here through the La Jolla Playhouse, Inc., and the Actors Company. He is a moving spirit in both these organizations, as is Miss McGuire.[290]

The film, with Sherwood's story more or less intact, was instead released in 1953 by Metro-Goldwyn-Mayer, with a large cast of thespians that included Tallulah Bankhead, the Barrymores, and many others, but no trace of Peck or Dorothy.

Also in 1951, Hedda Hopper reported that Dorothy was slated to play opposite Spencer Tracy in *The Plymouth Adventure*.[291] The role in the

---

[290] Edwin Schallert, "Hollywood in Review," *Los Angeles Times*, April 22, 1951.

[291] Hedda Hopper, "Nina Foch to Wear Famous Costumes," *Sioux Falls (SD) Argus-Leader*, September 3, 1951.

1952 film went to Gene Tierney. Again in 1951, Edwin Schallert of the *Los Angeles Times* reported that Dorothy was being sought by Fidelity Pictures for a role in "Gardenia," based on a story by Vera Caspary. Scheduling conflicts with Dorothy's film *Invitation* (1952) and her Broadway role in Jean Anouilh's play *Legend of Lovers* (1951) impeded the project.[292] Anne Baxter took Dorothy's place in the film, which was directed by Fritz Lang and released as *The Blue Gardenia* in 1953.

Other projects intended for Dorothy were reported in 1957, during her "freelance" period. One was the film *Year of Danger*, written by Andre De Toth and Jack [John] Hawkins. The film was to be made by Rexford Productions, with Tage Nielsen of the Palladium Studios in Copenhagen as producer and possibly Dana Andrews as male star.[293] The renamed film was released in 1958 as *Hidden Fear*, with John Payne as male lead. The other project was a biopic on Sinclair Lewis' life, or at least on the latter half of his life. Dorothy was to play a fictional female character. The project was still in treatment form (no finished screenplay yet), penned by writer Stuart Jerome. The name of actor Fredric March was bandied about, as was that of director Michael Curtiz.[294]

Mister 880 (1950)

One of Dorothy's best projects with 20th Century-Fox, and one of the best of her film career, was this underrated, practically forgotten comedy-thriller about the Treasury Department's hunt for an amateur counterfeiter in New York. Based on a true story as it had appeared in *The New*

---

[292] Edwin Schallert, "Dorothy McGuire Rated Desirable for 'Gardenia,'" *Los Angeles Times*, October 8, 1951.

[293] Edwin Schallert, "Drama," *Los Angeles Times*, January 8, 1957.

[294] Edwin Schallert, "Lewis Life Aimed at Curtiz," *Los Angeles Times*, May 18, 1957.

Yorker in August 1949,[295] it is a pleasant surprise all round, and contains one of Dorothy's most relaxed and confident comic performances. It also pairs her with an interesting leading man, Burt Lancaster,[296] and with one of Hollywood's most lovable character actors, Edmund Gwenn, who was nominated for an Academy Award and won a Golden Globe for his scene-stealing performance in the film.

20th Century-Fox publicity still depicting Dorothy McGuire on the *Mister 880* set. 1950.

295 St. Clair McKelway, "Annals of Crime: Old Eight-Eighty," the *New Yorker*, August 27, 1949.

296 According to Burt Lancaster biographer Kate Buford, Lancaster had originally wanted this property for his production company, Norma Productions. See: Kate Buford, *Burt Lancaster: An American Life*, Alfred A. Knopf, 2000, 383.

Never in a million years would Ann Winslow (Dorothy McGuire) dream that Steve Buchanan (Burt Lancaster), the nice, handsome young man who has rescued her from the unwanted attentions of a lecher on the street, had ulterior motives for doing so, and that he is a Secret Services agent in pursuit of a counterfeiter.

Ann, you see, has unknowingly passed a false bill, and the Secret Services, who have been after this particular forger unsuccessfully for ten years, are on their guard after the arrival in New York of one of their top men from Washington (Steve), who takes over the case. Being the smart, funny woman that she is, Ann soon begins to suspect something is afoot when a colleague of hers at the United Nations, where she works as an interpreter, tells her that Steve has been following her. She does some investigating of her own, and discovers Steve's place of work. Assuming that he suspects her of being a counterfeiter, she reads up on counterfeiting lingo in some books to bait him playfully with the right phrases. The phrases are hopelessly outdated, and Steve knows he has been found out. From the romantic point of view, he is not discouraged one jot. From the investigative point of view, he fesses up and tells Ann the whole story.

Ann Winslow (Dorothy), teases Steve Buchanan after secretly finding out he is a Federal agent. Notice the "fake-counterfeit" dollar bills in her purse. Production still for *Mister 880*, 20th Century-Fox, 1950.

At this point, the audience already knows that the culprit Steve is looking for is a lovable, indigent elderly man, William "Skipper" Miller (Edmund Gwenn), who lives in Ann's apartment building and has slipped her a false bill by mistake. He forges one-dollar banknotes occasionally (printed with a blatant spelling mistake), only to cover the barest of his needs, and rigorously spends them one at a time in different places in the city in order not to damage any one shopkeeper too severely.

The film describes the cat-and-mouse chase that gradually closes in on the adorable coot, and his eventual arrest. It also describes the love story between Ann and Steve, and their friendly relationship to "Skipper."

Adorable codger: William "Skipper" Miller, indigent counterfeiter (Edmund Gwenn, right), elicits love wherever he goes. Here he is with friend Ann Winslow (Dorothy) and her new boyfriend, Federal Agent Steve Buchanan (Burt Lancaster, left). Production still for *Mister 880*, 20th Century-Fox, 1950.

By the time Steve has to arrest "Skipper," both he and Ann have developed great affection, even respect, for the fundamentally honest, generous geezer. In a touching courtroom scene, the abbreviated trial has "Skipper" candidly admitting his guilt, and making a rather disarming argument for his actions. Steve, who has been won over to the old man's plight, has done some legal research of his own and makes an impassioned plea for a minimum sentence. By the end of the trial, the judge himself has been charmed, and comes up with a solution to shorten the old man's punishment even further, but not before ordering the payment of a fine—one dollar.

The film has a warm heart but is seldom sentimental and never melodramatic. It is, rather, endowed with a comedic breeziness in both its dialogue and action. Director Goulding and his cast keep the tone light and the characterizations real. An expert, unsensational director, Goulding (*Grand Hotel*, 1932; *Dark Victory*, 1939; *Claudia*, 1943; *The Razor's Edge*, 1946) knows how to move the story along without any unneeded hurry, and endows it with a relaxed pace and a cheerful, feather-light realistic tone.

In one scene, Goulding amusingly turns one particular cinematic trope on its head, which results in an incongruous—and delightful—stylization.

The way the trope normally unfolds is this: dialogue taking place inside a room is shot through a window, with the camera positioned in the street; thus, all we hear is the traffic noise outside while the dialogue is mimed silently inside.

In this particular scene, Ann stops in front of the window of an art store to look at some paintings. Agent McIntire (Millard Mitchell), who has been shadowing her, pretends to be a "masher" intent on harassing her; she tries to ignore him, but he is persistent, and unpleasant. The fake molestation, however, is merely a ruse to allow Agent Buchanan to witness the event and "rescue" Ann by confronting the molester and punching him in the jaw, in order to pull Ann away from danger and be alone with her. A vociferous crowd gathers; a police officer is called. After Ann and Steve have left and the crowd has dispersed, the fake molester flashes his FBI badge to the policeman and avoids arrest.

Window view, René Clair-style: in the street, Dorothy (fourth from left) watches as "good Samaritan" Steve Buchanan (Burt Lancaster, middle, his back partially turned towards the camera) protects her from the unwanted advances of a "masher" (Millard Mitchell, facing Lancaster). But all we can hear is traffic noise. Production still for *Mister 880*, 20th Century-Fox, 1950.

Nothing extraordinary from the point of view of plot and story, certainly. But here is what is special about the scene: Goulding shoots this entire vignette from the point of view of the shopkeeper inside the art store, through the large display window. We clearly see the actions of the actors outside, yet we never hear the dialogue at all, nor any voices, but only traffic noise! An illogical, surreal absurdity worthy of directors like Ernst Lubitsch, Jacques Tati, or René Clair. Two years after this film, Clair would give a similarly surrealist twist to street noises in his amiable fantasy *Les belles de nuit* (1952), starring Gérard Philipe and Gina Lollobrigida. In one scene, the dialogue between the protagonist and another character, taking place in the protagonist's room, is intermittently rendered inaudible by the loud clatter of a jackhammer in the street; when the characters move into the building hallway and close the door to the room, their exchange is still—incongruously—made mute by those street noises. Those same noises then become the sounds of the protagonist's debut opera (he is a composer) in one of his nightmares.

Brief as the *Mister 880* scene is (one minute and fifty seconds), it does much more than twist the conventions of realistic sound: it is also a moment of meta-theatrical self-reflexiveness. The store's window acts as a frame to the pantomime outside, like a proscenium arch; the storekeeper even opens the window-display curtain at the beginning of the action as if it were a theater curtain, and acts as spectator (or stand-in for us, the audience) of the silent puppet show that is being acted out in the street.

Just how deftly offbeat Goulding could be in his use of characterization is demonstrated by several vignettes in the film. In one of these, old Skipper's encounter with a street kid (Skipper loves children, and always carries candy with him) who looks and sounds like a rebel Munchkin turns into a duet of grotesque animal cries. Goulding steadfastly avoids the syrupy cliché of the cute child, and colors both the character of the kid and the scene as a whole with a comical monstrousness that is both unexpected and vaguely disquieting.

It is a pleasure to see Dorothy play smart and funny; her interactions with all the other characters in the story, but especially those with Lancaster and Gwenn, are limber and amusing. Even the most transitional of secondary dialogues seem written to endear her character to us through her elegant irony. Here is a short example: After questioning the art store owner the following day about the outcome of her molestation, Ann begins to be suspicious. As she arrives at work, she questions her supervisor at the United Nations, Mr. Beddington (played by an uncredited Frank Wilcox):

Ann: Mr. Beddington, when I applied for this job, wasn't I thoroughly checked?
Beddington: Of course you were, why?
Ann: Can you think of any reason why the United States Secret Service would be after me?
Beddington: Oh, it'd have nothing to do with your job here.
Ann: I met a man yesterday, and I just found out he's a Secret Service agent.
Beddington: The two chief functions of the Secret Service are to guard the president and catch counterfeiters. I'm safe in assuming you're not the president.
Ann: I'm suspected of being a counterfeiter?
Beddington: Oh, chances are a counterfeit bill fell into your hands, you passed it on to someone who reported you. It happened to a friend of mine once. They watched him for a few days, decided he was innocent, and suddenly dropped him. Never heard from them again. You'll probably have the same experience.
Ann: Thank you.
(Ann walks away from her boss and towards the booth where she is to work. She turns back to face him for one last line.)
Ann (cont'd): He's a very attractive man, I don't think I'd like to be dropped so suddenly.

Lancaster plays a comedic variation of his *noir* characters, with only a hint of that iconic acrobatic nimbleness from his pirate movies. Both he and Dorothy underplay confidently and calmly, reserving speed for their dialogue, which crackles along lithely. Edmund Gwenn seems to take everything with turtle-like aplomb, but his inner rhythm is expertly comedic. He sinks his actor's teeth into his lovable character and makes him both eccentric and interesting.

Bosley Crowther of the *New York Times* was pleased, almost enthusiastic, and his few reservations were won over (much like the authority figures in the film itself) by Gwenn and by the film's comedic tenderness. Of Dorothy and Lancaster, he noted:

Mixing business and pleasure: Steve Buchanan's (Burt Lancaster) investigation brings him to Coney Island; just for fun, he brings his new squeeze Ann (Dorothy) with him. Press photo for *Mister 880*, 20th Century-Fox, 1950.

It so happens that Mr. [Robert] Riskin and Twentieth Century-Fox, which made the film, saw fit to devote most of it to the side-line pursuit of a romance—a romance between the Treasury agent and a young lady who translates for the United Nations. (How the U. N. gets into it is a matter of no concern.) But fortunately Mr. Riskin has made this romance spin, too, with some clever and easy situations and some saucy and fluent dialogue. And Edmund Goulding has deftly directed Burt Lancaster and Dorothy McGuire in the roles of the incidental romancers so that they are beguiling, too.[297]

Beguiling romancers: Agent Steve Buchanan (Burt Lancaster) receives a phone call from his office while cultivating his romance with Ann Winslow (Dorothy) in *Mister 880*. Production still, 20th Century-Fox, 1950.

---

[297] Bosley Crowther, "Edmund Gwenn Plays Lovable Counterfeiter in 'Mister 880' at the Roxy Theatre," *New York Times*, September 30, 1950.

Variety also liked the film:

> St. Clair McKelway's New Yorker mag stories, about the counterfeiter of $1 bills who eluded the Secret Service for 10 years, has [sic] been given an absorbing screen treatment in "Mister 880." Here is a film of gentle humor, pathos—and entertainment. It has excellent narrative values, fine cast and production, plus superb direction. It can't miss at the box office.
>
> [...] Direction by Edmund Goulding has captured all the human elements so vital to a story of this type, and there are special evidences of his craft.

About Dorothy, *Variety* sentenced laconically, "[...] McGuire lends an able assist."[298]

Three Coins in the Fountain (1954)

The successful *Three Coins in the Fountain*, directed mostly on location in Rome (and, briefly, Venice) by Jean Negulesco in 1953 from a screenplay by John Patrick based on a novel by John H. Secondari,[299] was well regarded upon its release, and received two Academy Awards (Best Cinematography and Best Song) and a nomination for Best Picture. Truth be told, the CinemaScope, Eastmancolor, 4-track stereo rom-com, while pleasant, is a mixed bag of goods, especially in hindsight, and its uneven acting talents are matched by the erratic, contrived quality of its cliché-ridden script.

---

[298] "Mister 880," *Variety*, August 23, 1950.

[299] John H. Secondari, *Coins in the Fountain*, J.B. Lippincott & Co., 1952.

Dorothy's Miss Frances strikes a wistful pose in this 20th Century-Fox production still, issued when the film was still entitled *We Believe in Love*.

The three women protagonists, Americans Miss Frances (Dorothy), Anita Hutchins (Jean Peters), and Maria Williams (Maggie McNamara), have comfortable jobs in Rome, Anita and Maria's paid in American dollars under a favorable rate of exchange with the Italian Lira. Thus, the three are able to share a palatial penthouse apartment in a villa located in the historical center of one of the most breathtakingly beautiful cities in the world.[300] Yet, this being 1954, at least two of the women seem to have one purpose in life, and one purpose only, obsessively: to ensnare an eligible bachelor.

Maria is the new arrival, and the youngest. After she gets settled in

---

[300] The villa is called "Villa Eden" in the film. In real life, it is called Villa Lante and is situated at number 10 of the lovely Passeggiata del Gianicolo. At the time of writing, the villa was the site of the Finnish Embassy at the Vatican.

her new apartment and goes through her office orientation at the "United States Distribution Agency,"[301] where Anita also works, she is invited to a party with her two roommates and meets a handsome Roman prince by the name of Dino Dessi,[302] played by Louis Jourdan. Prince Dino is a handsome, snobbish bore with a citywide reputation as a sexual predator, so, of course, Maria cannot resist pursuing him. Not being very intelligent (in many of the film's scenes, her reactions to just about anything make her seem positively retarded), she takes Miss Frances's misguided advice too literally and begins to collect evidence as to Dino's tastes, in order to be able to lie about her own. When with him, she pretends to like everything he does, gauchely spouting all the empty platitudes she has memorized about art, music, and fine cuisine; she even pretends to take up the piccolo, the instrument Dino plays as a hobby. (A phallic symbol? Maybe, but a tiny one.)

Maria accepts Dino's invitation to fly to Venice in his private airplane (everyone in town knows what that trip implies, and the women who accept to take it are thereafter called his "Venice girls"), but only on condition that Miss Frances chaperone her. Dino is chagrined, but goes through with the trip. The wooing persists after this disappointment, and Dino even introduces Maria to his forbidding mother, the *Principessa* (Cathleen Nesbitt). If she were one of the three little pigs, Maria would

---

301 The Agency is depicted as being located in the *Foro Italico*, the monumental Fascist-Art Deco-styled complex that today houses, among other things, the Italian National Olympic Committee (CONI), an Olympic Pool, the 1937 *Palestra del Duce* (The *Duce's* Gym), and the Physical Education department of the Rome University circuit. An unforgettable landmark within the *Foro Italico* is the so-called *Stadio dei Marmi* (Stadium of Marble Statues), an imposing outdoor sports arena surrounded by sixty-four thirteen-foot-tall elevated marble statues of male athletes, each representing a different sport. Each statue was executed by a different artist and offered to Rome by a different Italian city/county. *Foro Italico* was designed by architect Enrico Del Debbio and inaugurated in 1932 as *Foro Mussolini*.

302 The Internet Movie Database (IMDb) erroneously lists the character's name as Dino di Cessi, which, if translated from the Italian, would be something like "Dino of the Toilets."

be the one who builds his house out of straw: her lies soon catch up with her, her house topples, and she must confess and repent. Prince Dino is absolutely furious, and stops seeing her.

Venice Girls: Prince Dino Dessi (Louis Jourdan), Maria Williams (Maggie McNamara) and Miss Frances (Dorothy) savor the beauties of Venice, Italy, in this production transparency for *Three Coins in the Fountain*.

The middle woman is Anita Hutchins, who is tired of not finding a suitable husband in Rome and wants to go back to America. She appears to be the coolest of the three, and colors her every remark with a touch of cynicism. Anita is blind to the doe-eyed attentions of handsome office interpreter Giorgio Bianchi (Rossano Brazzi), but young Maria's nudging soon opens her eyes. Giorgio is played by the same unctuous wolf who a year later would gobble up Katharine Hepburn's spinster in David Lean's *Summertime* (1955), set in Venice. Anita has never been to an Italian *festa*—like many Hollywood Americans living in Rome, these characters are oddly insulated from their environment: they only frequent other Americans, and, with the exception of Miss Frances, barely know the basics of the Italian language—and, when Giorgio invites her to attend his sister's weekend engagement party in the country, she accepts. While traveling with a colorful truckload of stereotypical Italian *festaioli*, she is accidentally seen by her American boss. Come Monday, said boss interrogates naïve Maria, who spills the beans readily. Giorgio is fired, Anita disgraced.

Notwithstanding her obsession with matrimony, until this point Anita has been a levelheaded girl, and Jean Peters manages that aspect of her role with considerable charm. Now, Anita's wooden imperviousness is shattered, and she falls to pieces. She reacts to the negative event, not with combativeness but with overacting: like a character in a 19th-century melodrama, she packs her things, moves out of her apartment and marches to Giorgio's door, suitcase in hand, offering to throw herself tearfully on the sword of his tragedy. He is slightly more rational than she is, and thinks it might be more practical if they fell in bed together. They do, for a whole weekend.

Neither Rossano Brazzi nor Louis Jourdan can act much. All they seem capable of doing is be suave, i.e. inexpressive, or go through the emptiest of motions mimicking the feelings their characters are supposed to be feeling; in other words, they simplify and reduce their characters' emotional lives to a child's view of them, making them uncomplicated—or, rather, truncated. Much the same can be said of Ms. McNamara, who gives a monotonous rendition of an infelicitous character; hers is a one-note-at-a-time interpretation: for each scene, she picks the one feeling or emotion she thinks is needed, and clings to it stolidly, perhaps for fear of losing it forever.

Dorothy strikes a conversation with co-star Louis Jourdan at Rome's Grand Hotel (today the St. Regis Rome, via Vittorio Emanuele Orlando 3) during a pause in the filming of *Three Coins in the Fountain*, August 3, 1953. Photo: Associated Press/Walter Attenni.

Thank God for Dorothy (who looks lovely, and very sophisticated, in the film), and for Clifton Webb. Rome aside, the two stars are the best thing in the film. Dorothy plays Miss Frances, the eldest of the three women (but not by much: in 1954, Dorothy was only thirty-eight, and only ten years older than Jean Peters). A worldly, intelligent woman, Frances works as secretary to famous novelist John Frederick Shadwell (Webb), who has not written a novel in some fifteen years and lives in a sumptuous Roman palazzo.[303] Shadwell writes newspaper articles, living on the laurels of his past fame. He may be declining in terms of his writ-

---

303 Shadwell's home is actually Villa Vaini Giraud Ruspoli, situated in Via di Porta San Pancrazio (though the film only shows its entrance in Via Garibaldi). Like the villa where the three women protagonists live, this house too is located in the Gianicolo, opposite the famous Fountain of the Gianicolo, known to Romans as "*il fontanone*." The villa houses the Spanish Embassy for Italy.

ing, but he is financially secure and is an *éminence grise* in Rome, which means that he travels in the best social circles.

The relationship between Frances and Shadwell is the only marginally adult one in the film, and the acting of Dorothy and Webb is the only adult acting. The two actors know how to inhabit a character, and how to be economical without being empty. They eke out just enough of their characters—with finesse and confidence—while indicating that there are enough secrets lurking in their breasts to make them interesting. These secrets they gradually reveal. Of the three little pigs, Miss Frances would be the one who builds his house out of solid bricks, which is what she has used to erect an emotional wall around the love she has felt for her curmudgeonly employer these fifteen years. She has not revealed her secret to anyone, including Shadwell, though, as Prince Dino reports to Shadwell towards the end of the film, "*For years all of Rome has known how Miss Frances felt*"; both Frances and Shadwell mask their affections carefully with the veneer of irony and professionalism. Notwithstanding this reciprocal guardedness, the warmth and esteem between the two are palpable, even though, at sixty-five, Webb is not exactly in Dorothy's age range. No matter: marrying older men was not uncommon in the 1950s, and Frances and Shadwell's love appears to be platonic anyway: they never even kiss during the film.

In fact, Frances is more nurse than lover to Shadwell, even before her accidental discovery of her employer's terminal illness, which he is trying to keep secret. This discovery prompts her to lose her inhibitions. After following her employer to a Roman café where he intends to get drunk on six double scotches, she confronts him about his condition. When she starts to get weepy, his response is, "*Your greatest asset, Miss Frances, has always been your detachment, your freedom from sentimentality.*" Exasperated, Frances moves to an adjoining table and abandons that detachment altogether by ordering six double scotches herself. Once drunk, she makes a scene at a fountain, wading waist-deep, then neck-deep in water. It is Shadwell's turn to play nurse now, which he does after he has brought her to his home and given her dry clothes. As he coaxes her to sleep, his realization that he loves her, lit with glowing warm colors by cinematographer Milton Krasner, is predictable and perfunctory, but quite touching.

Curmudgeonly employer and doting secretary: Clifton Webb and Dorothy sit in a car as the rear projection behind them transports them to a street that could be Via del Corso in Rome, Italy. Production photo for *Three Coins in the Fountain*, 1954.

Variety had this to say about Dorothy and Webb in its review:

> Outstanding performances—perhaps because they are the only believable ones—are given by Miss McGuire and Webb. [...] Miss McGuire, playing a not-so-young American, is excellent in every respect. Her final scene with Webb, in which she gets drunk and wades into a pool, has pathos and great appeal. Webb is seen in a familiar role and makes the most of it without being as brash as usual in his defiance of convention and his biting witticisms.[304]

[304] "Three Coins in Fountain," *Variety*, May 12, 1954.

The fairy tale comes to a close with a vacuous and arbitrary "happy" ending despite the preceding complications: the three couples are all united successfully by the Fountain of Trevi, God help them. But all of the huffing and puffing that has gone on before does not change the fact that the real star of the picture remains Rome (and, in one sequence, Venice). Bosley Crowther of the *New York Times*, who scoffed at the film, called *Three Coins* "a nice way to take the movie audience on a sightseeing tour of Rome, with a flying side trip to Venice, through the courtesy of Cinema-Scope [...]."[305] And a wonderful tour it is, too.

The film opens with a pre-credit "Overture" featuring the Jule Styne-Sammy Cahn title song, crooned by an unbilled Frank Sinatra, and a stunning montage of the many fountains of Rome and environs. The bulk of *Three Coins* was shot on location, and offers audiences a rare opportunity to see Rome as it was in 1954, much as William Wyler's charming *Roman Holiday* had done in Academy ratio and black and white two years earlier. Some liberties are taken with location continuity (people drive from one location, and appear in a different location altogether when they turn the corner), but, for the most part, the geography is correct. For anyone who knows Rome today, seeing Jean Peters park her car in an empty Piazza dei Cinquecento in front of Termini Station when she picks up Maggie McNamara is a real treat: having been turned into an outdoor city bus terminal, the Piazza is today an ugly example of urban chaos.

Many significant landmarks of the Eternal City are featured in the course of the film: the Spanish Steps, the Coliseum, St. Peter's, the Fountain of Trevi, Piazza del Popolo, Piazza Esedra (officially Piazza della Repubblica, but many native Romans still call it by its original name), the Passeggiata del Gianicolo, the Colle Aventino, Piazza Venezia, Piazza del Quirinale, etc. *Three Coins* was an early example of 20th Century-Fox's proprietary CinemaScope widescreen technique, and director Negulesco

---

[305] Bosley Crowther, "Screen: 'Three Coins in the Fountain'; Eternal City Glows in Film at the Roxy CinemaScope and Stars Offset Light Story," *New York Times*, May 21, 1954.

and cinematographer Krasner's enthusiasm is evident. *Variety* was enthusiastic, too:

> Here, in the first CinemaScoper to be lensed abroad, the wide screen really comes into its own, capturing the charms of Rome and Venice as an unforgettable backdrop for this pleasant but insignificant story. It ought to earn 20th a mint at the b.o. and chances are it'll win CinemaScope a host of new friends.
>
> [...] Negulesco and cameraman Milton Krasner couldn't resist the fascination of their setting. "Coin" is introed by some absolutely magnificent lensing of Roman fountains and, later, of the Fountain of Trevi [...]. Throughout the film, occasionally slowing up its action, the camera takes a leisurely look at Roman landmarks [...].[306]

Crowther's conclusion says it well: "The jokes are limpid, the plot is entirely contrived and the logic is minus zero. The whole thing is as slick as Cellophane. But the city of Rome looks mighty handsome in all the aspects in which it is viewed."[307]

In other words, the film's stars and their acting are overshadowed by the city of Rome; which, in the grand scheme of things, and given the quality of the film's screenplay, is probably as it should be.

The Remarkable Mr. Pennypacker (1959)
Fundamentalist Catholic groups were not the only ones objecting to this film and to its awkward humor, outwardly on moral grounds;[308] most of

---

306 *Variety* (1954), op. cit.

307 Crowther, "Coins" (1954), op. cit.

308 "The Remarkable Mr. Pennypacker," *Variety*, February 11, 1959.

the major critics were condescending towards *The Remarkable Mr. Pennypacker*, when not downright hostile.

The story of a prissy early-20th-century sausage manufacturer who finds confirmation for his bigamy in the progressive ideas he espouses (Darwinism, female emancipation and free thinking), the film takes the outer form of a comedy, but incompletely. Mr. Horace Pennypacker Jr. (Clifton Webb) shuttles between two cities, Philadelphia and Harrisburg, for his sausage business (!), and thus finds it convenient to have a wife in each, with kids to boot, seventeen in all. Except, he has kept this a secret from both families. The film describes what happens when the truth is accidentally exposed.

It is a sign of the changing times that the theme of bigamy could be considered suitable for comedy, let alone for farce, in 1959, while in today's entertainment world one is most likely to find it associated with murder and tragedy in television shows such as *Law & Order: Special Victims Unit*[309] or *The Closer*.[310] The UK pressbook for *Pennypacker* had this to say about the comic possibilities of the film's theme: "Imagine the riotous laughter-making possibilities with a man who has two wives, leads a double life, and has 17 kids calling him 'Pop.'"[311]

Personally, I do not find the Pennypackers' predicament very funny at all, nor, for that matter, does the poor first Mrs. Pennypacker (Dorothy). Be that as it may, Liam O'Brien, the author of the 1953 Broadway play on which the film is based, decided that bigamy was to be hilarious. Given this decision, it is a pity that the film never seems to find the right tone to make its premise interesting, and that its intended comedy never really gets off the ground. It is also a pity that the brittle, icy manner of Mr. Webb, here paired with Dorothy for the second time, gives the story

---

309 "Snitch," Season 9, Episode 10, 2007.

310 "Homewrecker," Season 3, Episode 1, 2007.

311 *The Remarkable Mr. Pennypacker*, UK Pressbook, page 2.

all the wrong colors. Both Dorothy and Webb, great pros of stage and screen, are ultimately miscast and misdirected in this film, and deserved better. With, say, Rock Hudson and Doris Day, and music by De Vol, *Pennypacker* might have been more amusing, *Pillow Talk*-style, though the casting of more "carnal" players would have raised the issue of sexuality, which barely registers here. For example, the fact that Mr. Pennypacker has bred like a rabbit these past twenty years is barely touched upon in the body of the film's text: Mrs. Pennypacker makes a pointed but discreet reference to "glands" in her climactic confrontation with her husband, and Mr. Pennypacker Sr. (Charles Coburn) makes a passing remark about his son not having been "idle." But sex is a minor, almost incidental issue in the film, as proven by Webb's aged frigidity (he was 70 when this film was released) and Dorothy's iciness.

Despite its positive resolution, the film is a fitting, though insufficient, illustration of the Pirandellian theme of the unknowability of those closest to us, the theme discussed in the caveat that opens this biography and in the book's afterword. When the Harrisburg Mrs. Pennypacker, having learned of her husband's "dirty" secret, travels to Philadelphia to confront the second Mrs. Pennypacker, she finds a houseful of nine children but no mother: Mr. Pennypacker's other wife died eight years earlier. Mrs. Pennypacker sits with the children at the breakfast table, and has the eldest child of this second family, Horace Pennypacker III (whom she has met before: he was the unwitting instrument of her discovery), introduce her to his siblings:

Mrs. Pennypacker: Well, Horace, why don't you introduce me.
(Horace hesitates.)
Mrs. Pennypacker (cont'd): Please, Horace. Tell them who I am.
Horace: This is Dad's . . . . This is Mrs. Pennypacker, kids.
Child I: Our mom's name was Mrs. Pennypacker, too!
Child II: Does she know our pa?

Child III: I think she does.
Mrs. Pennypacker: Vaguely.

Vaguely. If that is not an exact example of Pirandello's theme of the tragic distance between humans, and of the fact that humans ultimately know neither themselves nor those around them very well, I do not know what is. Appropriately, Dorothy does not deliver that line for laughs but with bitter irony, as if seriously explaining an incontrovertible fact about her relationship with her husband.

The film's main problems are related to tone and pace, and extend to many aspects of the production: the casting, the writing, the acting, and the directing. This uncertainty of tone is perfectly embodied by the film's opening and by its musical accompaniment. A cutesy pre-credit intro has all seventeen of Mr. Pennypacker's children appearing, one after the other, on the horizontal expanse of the CinemaScope screen, as if in a proscenium line-up, and introducing themselves by name and surname, as composer Leigh Harline Mickey Mouses cutely to comment on the introduction. Then Mr. Pennypacker himself appears, in medium close-up, saying: "*Well, do you wonder that I'm called the remarkable Mr. Pennypacker?*" The "funny" tone of this prologue is then promptly negated by Harline, who immediately switches styles and segues into a credit-sequence tune that is unfunny and lushly romantic, as if he were writing a score for *Kings Row* (1942) or *A Tree Grows in Brooklyn* (1945).

A thorough re-write I believe would have helped. Despite the glib philosophizing that Mr. Pennypacker does, throwing in big ideas such as Darwinism, religion, the law, and free thinking, no issue is thoroughly discussed or properly dramatized: this is a comedy, you see, so it would be out of place to gain too much insight. A scene between Pennypacker and the neighborhood vicar (Larry Gates) comes the closest to delving into those issues, but is ruined by some facile comedic shortcuts.

Eliminating all children in both cities, and concentrating on the two wives, might have simplified the story and made the argument about honesty, fidelity and the institution of marriage clearer and more cogent. No matter: despite the highbrow ideas he borrows, Mr. Pennypacker is no philosopher, and is culpable of one capital sin above all: intellectual dishonesty. He may use those progressive philosophies as a defense for his actions, but ultimately he does not live by them consistently. He does not live by the rules he has made for himself.

His family is quick to expose him for the selfish, self-aggrandizing liar he is. In a wonderful scene, a jury composed of his Harrisburg children dismantles his arguments one by one and concludes that what he did was wrong; not because he broke the rules (rules are made to be broken, he has taught them), but because he did not do it openly; not because he married two women, but because he was not open about it. This self-contradiction, rather than his illegal or immoral actions, is Mr. Pennypacker's undoing in the eyes of his family.

Had those issues been properly articulated, for example by writing this piece as an argument, in the manner of, say, George Bernard Shaw (*Pygmalion*, *Candida*), Henrik Ibsen (*A Doll's House*), or Jerome Lawrence and Robert E. Lee (*Inherit the Wind*, another Darwinian play about inconsistent philosophies), *The Remarkable Mr. Pennypacker* might have turned out to be an interesting investigation into the mysteries of human relationships, personal identity, and societal, religious, and philosophical lies. But the film cannot make up its mind whether it is a comedy of errors, a farce, a romantic comedy, or a comedy of ideas. It insists on placing gags where gags do not fit and therefore fall flat, and on shortchanging its romance, its ideas, and its comedy at alternate turns.

The film's happy ending is both hasty and contrived. As the young lovers (Pennypacker's eldest daughter and the vicar's son) celebrate their wedding, Emily Pennypacker accepts to renew her vows to her husband, and to celebrate their second wedding. This conclusion is probably intended to be romantic, yet it seems more like an insult added to Emily's injury, in a spirit reminiscent of Lorenzo Da Ponte's cynical libretto for Wolfgang Amadeus Mozart's opera *Così Fan Tutte* (1790). At the closing of that *opera buffa*, as the two male protagonists are trying to think of an exemplary punishment for their fiancées, who have both proven utterly unfaithful in a fiancée-swapping seduction intrigue suggested by a wager, their philosopher friend Don Alfonso suggests: "*I know what [that punishment] is: marry them.*"

Tightening the pace of the performances and giving these characters a little more frenzied urgency would have helped make this into a funnier—possibly farcical, in the manner of Georges Feydeau or Michael Frayn—ensemble piece. But director Henry Levin[312] seems lost when it comes to comedy and pace (one could drive trucks through the gaps between characters' lines) and, sinfully, allows his actors to overact shrilly at a lethargic pace; this sounds like an oxymoron, but you have to see it to believe it. Also, the casting is all wrong for a comedy. Webb is too cold and poised, Dorothy too earnest and noble. Of the other players, Ron Ely and Jill St. John as the young romantic couple are the most inept, while the children are average. Only Dorothy Stickney (who had starred in Rose Franken's first Broadway play, *Another Language*, in 1932) as Mr. Pennypacker's sister Jane seems to have a solid comedic instinct—which is surprising, given that the great Charles Coburn is in the cast.

Some pruning of the text would also have been advisable. For example, the film does not give the proper weight to its various subplots, and tends to linger on the wrong scenes too long. The romantic subplot involving Mr. Pennypacker's eldest daughter Catherine and the young vicar's son is an illustration of this flaw. Rather than treating their uninteresting engagement as the mere inciting incident that it is (the event that forces Mr. Pennypacker to return to Harrisburg ahead of his customary monthly schedule and sets all the complications in motion) and getting on with it, the film devotes too much time to the banalities of the young-

---

[312] Director Henry Levin was the uncle of Dan (Peter) Levin, a friend of the Swope family who worked as apprentice at Dorothy's La Jolla Playhouse in the early 1950s before becoming a director in his own right.

sters' romance, to the point that the two lovers almost become elevated to the status of co-protagonists, undeservedly.

Dorothy plays Emily Pennypacker with perfect Victorian haughtiness and aplomb. She is not particularly funny, but fares well in the more dramatic exchanges. Her best scene, probably the best scene in the movie, is her climactic confrontation with Webb at the end of the film's second act. Here, Dorothy's consummate theatrical experience and dramatic instincts come together beautifully, and with great naturalness. Incongruously, this serious confrontation opens with one of the film's few funny moments. As Emily returns to her room after her trip to Philadelphia, Mr. Pennypacker approaches her. He takes her hand and kisses it. She pulls her hand away, looks at it, and uses it to slap her husband in the face. Then she walks away from him, leaving him befuddled. The comedic timing of these actions is perfect. The *Oakland Tribune*'s drama editor, Theresa Loeb Cone, who detested the film, had this to say about Dorothy's performance:

> Somehow managing to be appealing, dignified and attractive in the midst of all this as the first Mrs. P. is Dorothy McGuire, an actress of such accomplishment that she manages to rise above any of the leaden qualities of her role.[313]

Ultimately, the fact that Mr. Pennypacker's Philadelphia wife is dead helps slant the moral argument in his favor: the Philadelphia children need a mother, and Aunt Jane gladly volunteers to step in for the duty. In the end, the Harrisburg Mrs. Pennypacker accepts her husband warts and all and makes peace with him; which is arguably what all of us might have to do with the "others" in our lives, barring (a) an endless string of divorces, breakups and grudges or (b) the ability to transform those others and ourselves. Again, what hurts the film most is its failure to investigate

---

[313] Theresa Loeb Cone, "Comedies Seem to Be Misfiring," *Oakland Tribune*, February 27, 1959.

and articulate its interesting issues, which would make them more dramatic, and/or to twist its characters' reactions to those issues explosively, which would make them funnier.

Variety's objections were for the most part technical rather than moral or philosophical. The magazine expressed disappointment rather than hostility, calling the film amiable but adding that "amiable is about the strongest word that can be used."[314] Accusing director Henry Levin of not setting up the jokes properly, or not at all, and therefore of killing the potential comedy of the film, *Variety* concluded bitterly that "even such experts as Clifton Webb and Charles Coburn are defeated. Webb seems too casual and Coburn too broad." About Dorothy, it wrote only: "Dorothy McGuire manages credibility because her role is straight anyway [...]."[315]

Bosley Crowther of the *New York Times* was contemptuous of the film, finding all sorts of faults big and small with the players, the writing and the direction, and finding the main character cold, unappealing, pompous, dogmatic, unconvincing, and sterile. Unfortunately for the film, Crowther was correct on all counts. About the other players, he lamented:

> Under these circumstances, the remaining members of the cast seem like so many energetic actors pretending something is there that is not. Miss McGuire gives a sweet pretense of being idolatrous and then shocked toward a travesty of a husband who has no more consistency than air. Charles Coburn grumbles loudly and vainly as the father of this shadow of a man, and Jill St. John plays at being prettily outraged as his daughter who wants to wed the vicar's son. Ron Ely as the latter and Larry Gates as the prudish papa give fair imitations of romantic and comical parsons, respectively.[316]

---

314 *Variety* (February 11, 1959), op. cit.

315 Ibid.

316 Bosley Crowther, "'Pennypacker'; Clifton Webb Seen in Film at Paramount," *New York*

Theresa Loeb Cone of the *Oakland Tribune* eagerly joined the chorus of naysayers and sentenced:

> "The Remarkable Mr. Pennypacker" is most remarkable for its total pointlessness. [. . .] Never really coming to grips with the proposition of how to accept calmly the fact that a seemingly respectable citizen of both Harrisburg and Philadelphia, Pa., has indulged in prolonged bigamy, the Paramount's feature meanders all over the plot and ends up by saying precious little during its 87 drawn-out minutes.[317]

After which, Ms. Loeb Cone concluded that the one redeeming feature of the film (aside from Dorothy) was the quality of the lavish sets and costumes.

Mr. and Mrs. Pennypacker confront each other with perfect Victorian hauteur in *The Remarkable Mr. Pennypacker*. From a British lobby card ("front-of-house card"), 1959, 20th Century-Fox.

Times, February 21, 1959.

317 Loeb Cone, "Misfiring" (1959), op. cit.

9. La Jolla Playhouse, 1947–1959

Years of Hope and Promise: 1947–1952

In 1947, a small piece of Hollywood detached itself from its Los Angeles mainland headquarters and generated an exalted island of theatrical talent called the La Jolla Playhouse, situated in the coastal town of La Jolla, California, on the northern outskirts of San Diego County.

The birth of this unusual, and unusually enlightened, project was initially due to the impetus of Gregory Peck, a native La Jollan. Peck, however, was not alone in his yearning for good theater, and in the realization that, in the 1940s, the Los Angeles theatrical offer was woefully inadequate compared to that of the East Coast (this was before the creation of the Music Center, and before the proliferation of "equity-waiver" venues in the 1970s and 1980s). He found like-minded fellow travelers that shared his appetite, namely David O. Selznick, Mel Ferrer, Dorothy, and others, such as Joseph Cotten and Jennifer Jones. Selznick, probably as an incentive to keep his contract players happy, acted as godfather of the enterprise and even contributed $15,000 of seed money.[318] The play-

---

[318] See: the website Life of an Actor (lifeofanactor.com/lajolla.htm); see also: Gary Fishgall, *Gregory Peck: A Biography*, Scribner, 2002; see also: "Unpaid Film Stars Love La Jolla Playhouse Jobs," *Albert Lea (MN) Sunday Tribune,* October 15, 1950, and Edwin Schallert, "Rogers, Guizar Stellar Partners in Big Western," *Los Angeles Times*, April 18, 1947.

ers acknowledged Selznick's initial involvement by naming the company "Selznick's Actors' Company," but the producer's name was eventually dropped. The list of actors willing to go the distance for the project and become out-and-out producers soon became a very short one, in the form of a triumvirate: Peck, Ferrer, and Dorothy. These three became the founders of the La Jolla Playhouse.

Goldfish Point, a cape just northeast of La Jolla, California, from a period postcard, circa 1950. Frasher's, Inc., Pomona, California.

Peck was certainly instrumental in finding and securing the venue, and an improbable one at that: the auditorium of the La Jolla High School. A small, simple proscenium theater with a long, rectangular auditorium equipped with plain folding chairs, the place was, at any rate, functional. And available, once pressure was applied to the school board by Peck's friend Frank Harmon, president of the Kiwanis Club. Social clubs such as the Kiwanis, and the volunteers that came with them, became essential to the enterprise, given the project's shoestring possibilities. As Gary Fishgall explains in his biography of Peck:

Triumvirate: the three co-founders of the La Jolla Playhouse, circa 1947.

[The three founders] derived considerable help from La Jolla volunteers. In addition to the men on the Kiwanis Club's Sponsoring Committee, dozens of socially prominent women from the San Diego area served on the Women's Committee, headed by Mrs. Walter M. Trevor, and later by Marian Longstreth, who became the company's foremost advocate. "The actors and actresses took care of the plays," noted San Diego reporter William Sullivan years later, "but the committee handled all the details, such as selling tickets, publicity, selling Coca-Cola and acquiring properties and costumes. Some locals even took small roles in the productions."[319]

---

[319] Fishgall (2002), op. cit., 127.

The advance publicity—and Peck's impassioned speech to present the first summer season (before knowing what plays or stars would be featured)—was so effective that the company sold something like eighty percent of the season on subscription, and on faith.

According to several sources, including the cited Peck biographer, Dorothy was not very good at organizing things, and admitted as much readily to her co-founders. Peck and Ferrer therefore took care of the production aspects, while Dorothy read and submitted scripts, made casting suggestions, and acted in several productions. However, Peck and Ferrer also hired an increasingly sizable staff to aid in the running of the playhouse, and eventually rented a full-time production office on Canon Drive in Beverly Hills. Both actors were represented by MCA, a talent agency that helpfully provided several of its clients for the playhouse's shows.

The company briefly entertained the thought of moving the enterprise from La Jolla to Beverly Hills. Dorothy was probably referring to this second venue in 1950 when she said to Hedda Hopper:

> Those La Jolla people expect good theater from us, not just a stock performance. That's our problem with the new Actors Theater in Beverly Hills. We hope to do top-draw productions which we cannot do without money and lots of time. We must have more than one-week rehearsals. If we take a tiny theater now and rush into things without correct preparation it will hurt the Actors Company when we do get it going. [You] can't make half-way attempts at the theater.[320]

It was around this time that the enlarged group of actors gravitating around the three founders officially incorporated as a company—the Actors' Company—and made their ambitions known to the public. Here is

---

[320] Hopper, "Ideals" (1950), op. cit.

one version of the events leading up to those expansion plans, as penned by the group itself, or someone close to it, in one of their 1950 souvenir programs:

> In April 1947, three top-flight motion picture stars sat in a New York hotel discussing their favorite subject—the theater—and bemoaning the lack of opportunity for actors to appear on the legitimate stage on the west coast. Before they separated they decided to do something about it. They were not swept away by their enthusiasm as others have been, but prudently started in a small way with a summer theater far enough away from Hollywood so that if it had merit it could grow naturally. For their purpose they chose the high school auditorium at La Jolla, California, a hundred miles south of Los Angeles.
>
> These three stars: Mel Ferrer, Dorothy McGuire and Gregory Peck, called their theater The La Jolla Playhouse, and from the start it was a success. The community must have been dubious of such a venture, but the complete sincerity of the group quickly won them over and the Playhouse became the center of civic pride and is now a thoroughly established community project. It is also the most star-studded summer theater in the country, and a listing of its four years of productions and star casts would take several pages.
>
> At the end of their first season they plunged into the second phase of their project: to take plays to audiences of the entire west coast, and toured with "Angel Street" starring Laraine Day and Gregory Peck.
>
> About this same time the well-known architect William Pereira[321] was having consultations with the theater owner-

---

[321] Famed architect William Leonard Pereira (1909–1985) remains one of the most celebrated (or controversial) mid-twentieth-century architects. Among his most iconic

managers Fanchon and Marco for a new theater building in Beverly Hills. Mr. Pereira recognized a similarity of purpose and brought the actors and managers together. The result was an enlarged group with the express purpose of presenting fine plays with members of The Actors' Company and other leading players of stage and screen in the theater in Beverly Hills, with West Coast tours of plays, and, in the case of new productions, national tours.

The enlarged group incorporated as The Actors' Company, and includes: Charles Boyer, Fanchon Simon, Mel Ferrer, Henry Fonda, John Garfield, Gene Kelly, Deborah Kerr, Dorothy McGuire, Gregory Peck, William Pereira, N. Peter Rathvon, Rosalind Russell, and Jerry Wald.[322]

For the purpose of establishing a building fund for the new theater they produced three national radio broadcasts over CBS. The first, on Christmas Day, 1949, was "The Man Who Came to Dinner" directed by Mel Ferrer, and included in the cast Charles Boyer, John Garfield, Jack Benny, Henry Fonda, Gene Kelly, Dorothy McGuire, Gregory Peck and Rosalind Russell. The second, on Easter Sunday [1950], was "Dinner at Eight" and included Charles Boyer, Paul Douglas, John Garfield, Otto Kruger, Dorothy McGuire, Rosalind Russell and Jan Sterling; and the third was "The Philadelphia Story"

California buildings: the Los Angeles International Airport (1958), the Los Angeles County Museum of Art (1965), the astonishing Geisel Library at the University of California, San Diego (1970, an example of "brutalist architecture" in quaint La Jolla), the Pepperdine University campus at Malibu (1972), and the Transamerica Pyramid in San Francisco (1972).

322 The respective roles of the Actors' Company members were the following, according to Edwin Schallert of the *Los Angeles Times*: Gregory Peck, president; Rosalind Russell and Gene Kelly, vice-presidents; Charles Boyer, secretary; Mel Ferrer, treasurer; and Henry Fonda, John Garfield, Deborah Kerr, Dorothy McGuire, William Pereira, N. Peter Rathvon, and Fanchon Simon, members. (see Edwin Schallert, "Hollywood in Review: Actors' Company Makes Brilliant Plans for Fall," *Los Angeles Times*, May 14, 1950.)

on Mother's Day [1950], with Jane Cowl, Robert Cummings, John Garfield, Otto Kruger, Burt Lancaster, John Lund, Margaret O'Brien, Dorothy McGuire and Rosalind Russell.

The theater building is the long-range project of The Actors' Company, but their immediate objective is to present actors in plays before audiences. With this in mind, they chose as the first production under the banner of The Actors' Company, the play "Summer and Smoke" by the distinguished American playwright, Tennessee Williams.[323]

The Beverly Hills venue never came to fruition, and the company settled at La Jolla stably; eventually, the dream of a larger venue, this time in the La Jolla area, would resurface.

Theatrical producer Shepard Traube became involved with the La Jolla Playhouse and with the Actors' Company for their inaugural production of Patrick Hamilton's *Angel Street* (*Gaslight*, for those who know the film or the English title of the play), whose successful Broadway premiere (1,295 performances) he had produced and directed in 1941, and whose 1947 La Jolla revival he directed. Gregory Peck and Laraine Day co-starred.[324]

It was during the West Coast tour of *Angel Street* that Traube became entangled in a controversy with *Oakland Tribune* syndicated drama critic Wood Soanes. Traube's indignant reaction to Soanes' negative review of the production when it played in San Francisco took the form of an enraged letter to the critic, a letter that Soanes then printed in his column with Traube's permission. The letter was no mere defense of the produc-

---

323 "The Actors' Company," Program for the Actors' Company tour of Tennessee Williams' *Summer and Smoke*, summer 1950.

324 Originally, Peck was to co-star with Jennifer Jones and Eve Arden in John Van Druten's *The Voice of the Turtle*. But Jones backed out, and *Angel Street* was chosen instead. (See Hedda Hopper, "Looking at Hollywood," *Portland [ME] Press Herald*, August 21, 1947.) Van Druten's play would be performed at the playhouse in 1951, Mel Ferrer starring.

tion; it was an impassioned peroration of the cause of the Actors' Company, and of the fate of theater on the American West Coast. First, here is the first paragraph of Soanes' review, which gives you some indication of his sarcastic tone:

> Glamor and melodrama came to the Geary last evening and from all indications a perfectly wonderful time was had by all—by all, that is, except those captious characters who feel that there should be a little talent mixed in with good looks.[325]

And here are some excerpts from Traube's peroration:

> [...] Unless I am mistaken, you have been advised by my press correspondent that the chief reason in sending out this touring production of "Angel Street" is to initiate professional theater for the West Coast on a continuing basis. Since I happen to be completely professional in my theater standards, I know that the current production of "Angel Street" is as good as anything the American theater can provide. It's top flight in every department, a subject that you manage to ignore in your notice.
> Lemuel Ayer's designing, Feder's lighting, the staging, the appointments, every aspect of the venture are completely skillful, a rare occurrence for theatrical effort in this neck of the woods. It is our hope that the West Coast, with the wealth of talent that exists in Los Angeles, may prove to be a real theater-producing center in years to come. The members of the Actors' Company—Mel Ferrer, Joseph Cotten, Dorothy

---

325 Wood Soanes, "Movie Stars Fail to Shine on S.F. Stage," Oakland Tribune, October 22, 1947.

McGuire, Gregory Peck, Jennifer Jones—and I are dedicated to this proposition.

It seems to me you are remarkably obtuse not to recognize the potentials of this. As for your comment on the acting talents of Gregory Peck and Laraine Day, you simply don't know what you're talking about when you refer to them as giving off "a flavor of high-school actors." Judging actors is my profession. Both Mr. Peck and Miss Day are extremely fine actors, and their performances in "Angel Street" are cunningly conceived and executed with extraordinary variety and style.

I have further news for you: Gregory Peck hails from the New York theater, where he gave several brilliant performances before he was brought to Hollywood by the film studios. If you had seen him in Emlyn Williams' "Morning Star," for instance, you would know that he is a trained stage actor. Miss Day, too, has done a great deal of work in the legitimate theater, principally on the West Coast, before becoming a film star. Your bland notion that these two people are "movie personalities" and not actors just doesn't happen to have any foundation. There are such stars in the movie industry, certainly, but not these two people.

You declare: "Nevertheless, 'Angel Street' remained good entertainment." How this is possible, if the two principal players are as deficient as you declare, completely eludes me.

Finally, you should be told that Gregory Peck, after four years of steady picture making, took his first free time to appear in this play, first at La Jolla and then on tour. Do you think he is doing this because he needs money? Or does it occur to you that he is a conscientious artist who wants to make direct contribution to a vital theater?

Your abuse does you little credit. [...] This is an academic discussion, you will appreciate, since our box-office business is thumping at the Geary [in San Francisco] and everywhere else in our bookings. We don't happen to be interested in the subject of money-making, however, but in establishing top-flight theater. All of us do very nicely out of our film employment. Sincerely yours, Shepard Traube.[326]

On November 29, Theresa Loeb of the *Oakland Tribune* wrote a second review of *Angel Street*, this time commenting on its Oakland Auditorium performances, and she was just as negative as Soanes had been, if not more so:

> For a play which is supposed to be chock full of suspense, melodrama at its best, and the sustained mood of a good thriller, "Angel Street" was decidedly slow-paced [...]. [The] three acts [...] dragged along in fearful monotony.
>
> Audience applause was extremely generous, it seemed to this reviewer, since it cannot in all honesty be said that the performance of Laraine Day or Gregory Peck merited any special praise. [...]
>
> Peck [...] almost bounced in and out of scenes like the villain in a century-old production, vied with Miss Day in achieving poses and never once made his role anything but the most incredible caricature.
>
> [...] We had been informed that Shepard Traube's original production of "Angel Street," recently performed in San Francisco with the same cast, had received some overhauling and that an outstanding director had been hired to go over the rough spots of the play. There was no evidence of such improvement, however, in last night's presentation.[327]

---

[326] Wood Soanes, "Curtain Calls: That Man with Shiner May Be Critic," *Oakland (CA) Tribune*, November 4, 1947.

[327] Theresa Loeb, "'Angel Street' Slow-Paced," *Oakland Tribune*, November 29, 1947.

In all fairness, Gregory Peck himself was convinced he was not right for the villainous role in *Angel Street*, and held a self-deprecatory view of his acting in the play. Despite generally tepid or poor notices,[328] the California tour was relatively successful, and helped rake in some much-needed cash for the company, which had ended its first season $5,000 in debt.[329]

A bearded Gregory Peck plays the sinister villain in the La Jolla Playhouse tour of *Angel Street*, 1947.

---

[328] A notable exception was the *Billboard* magazine review, which, notwithstanding some mild criticism of Peck, was rather glowing. Some excerpts: *"Angel Street* proves to be an exciting, suspenseful piece of stagecraft. Play is nearly actor-proof and can't help score, despite some unevenness in acting and a heavy directorial hand."; "[. . .] special nod to Miss Day, who emerges as a full-fledged emotional actress, exceptionally convincing in the play's tenser moments [. . .]"; "Supporting cast is excellent." See Alan Fischler, "Angel Street," *Billboard*, December 13, 1947.

[329] See: Fishgall (2002), op. cit., 128.

Aside from the three founders, the list of actors who appeared in productions at the playhouse during its first twelve years of existence (the playhouse would close in 1959, only to reopen in 1983 under different management) was indeed impressive. It included: Eve Arden, Tallulah Bankhead, Ann Blyth, Leo G. Carroll, Wendell Corey, Joseph Cotten, Jane Cowl, Ray Danton, Olivia de Havilland, José Ferrer, Hurd Hatfield, Charlton Heston, Patricia Hitchcock, Miriam Hopkins, Ruth Hussey, John Ireland, Jennifer Jones, Louis Jourdan, June Lockhart, Guy Madison, Groucho Marx, James Mason, Raymond Massey, Roddy McDowall, Mildred Natwick, David Niven, Vincent Price, Ginger Rogers, Robert Ryan, Sylvia Sidney, Robert Walker, Dame May Whitty, John Williams, Teresa Wright, and Jane Wyatt.

Among the directors who worked at the venue were Jane Cowl, José Ferrer, Mel Ferrer, Norman Lloyd (thirteen times), James Neilson (sixteen times), Otto Preminger, and Bernard Szold.

All these artists, including the lead actors, were paid close to nothing (virtually room, board and gas money), and did the work for a variety of reasons that had nothing to do with pay. Among those reasons were the desire to work in the theater and to test themselves, the desire to keep working during hiatuses, and the desire to be paired with unconventional co-stars and in plays outside their normal film repertories.

Each play was rehearsed for a week in one of the rooms at the high school, and ran for a week, from Tuesday to Sunday, with matinees on Wednesday and Saturday (by 1950, only on Saturday). Dress rehearsals took place on dark night, Monday. With or without Dorothy's loose organizational skills, things tended to be done quickly at the playhouse, and summer seasons were organized at a frenzied pace, or at the last minute. Probably because of the lack of financial incentives, actors backed out of productions or made other commitments, scripts were chosen or switched just weeks before curtain time, casts were announced and then retracted. As late as June 25, 1947, the property for Dorothy McGuire's first-season debut in August had not been officially chosen yet,[330] and this state of affairs would continue during the following seasons.

Emmy-nominated art director, designer and producer Robert Tyler Lee (1910–1987) designed twenty-six productions at La Jolla between 1949 and 1951. This is how he reminisced about the venue in 1981:

> With me, even though I sort of hooted for years about needing a break, I was having a good time, so when it came, it was really unexpected. I was asked to become executive art director for CBS Television as a result of the summers I spent with the La Jolla Theater.
>
> That was really a wonderful explosion of talent—Gregory Peck, Dorothy McGuire, Mel Ferrer. Everybody let their hair down and the productions were stunning.[331]

Between 1947 and 1954, Dorothy starred in six productions at the La Jolla Playhouse.

The first, in 1947, was a triptych of one-act plays by Noël Coward under the umbrella title of *Tonight at 8:30*; this program replaced the originally announced production of Ibsen's *A Doll's House*, a play that Dorothy had performed for *Theatre Guild on the Air* the previous January with Basil Rathbone. The idea was apparently discarded due to "the difficulty of securing a suitable director for the Ibsen drama."[332] The three plays in the triptych were *The Astonished Heart*, *Fumed Oak*, and *Still Life*. Originally produced in 1935, Coward's cycle initially comprised not three but ten short plays. The play *Still Life* was later expanded by Coward to become *Brief Encounter*. The supporting cast at La Jolla included Heather Angel,

---

[330] Hedda Hopper, "Looking at Hollywood," *Portland (ME) Press Herald*, June 25, 1947.

[331] Stacey Peck, "Robert Tyler Lee," *Los Angeles Times*, June 7, 1981.

[332] Edwin Schallert, "Flynn Alpinist Soon," *Los Angeles Times*, August 4, 1947.

Richard Haydn, John Hoyt, Una O'Connor, Ann Richards, John Williams, Thomas L. Brooks, Constance Cavendish, Elisabeth Fraser, George Pelling, and Ben H. Wright.[333] The production was designed by Robert Davison and directed by Edna Best and Harry Ellerbe, and played from August 12 through August 17, 1947. The review that follows appeared in the *Los Angeles Times* on August 14, 1947.

>Dorothy McGuire displays her astonishing versatility in Noel Coward's "Tonight at 8:30" series of three one-act plays, the Actors Company's sixth offering.
>
>In succession, she is a designing woman who ensnares a psychiatrist in spite of himself, a black-stockinged, sniveling girl and a dignified, charming mother who indulges in a clandestine affair.
>
>Miss McGuire is supported by a capable cast, notably Ann Richards and John Hoyt in the tragedy of the psychiatrist, "The Astonished Heart," Richard Haydn, Heather Angel and Una O'Connor in the hilarious story of a man's rebellion against his drab middle-class English family life, "Fumed Oak," and John Williams, her earnest lover in "Still Life."
>
>Coward's moral, if there be one, is that love outside the family circle is doomed to a tragic end. To prove it, he goes to theatric extremes in "The Astonished Heart," including violently passionate scenes between Hoyt and Miss McGuire, and the culminating suicide of Hoyt by leaping through a window.
>
>On the other hand, the escape of Richard Haydn from the tyranny of his vixenish wife, Heather Angel, and his petulant mother-in-law, Una O'Connor, in "Fumed Oak" is a clarion call for freedom of repressed husbands.

---

333 Cast information available at the La Jolla Playhouse website (lajollaplayhouse.org).

"The Astonished Heart" was directed by Harry Ellerbe, and "Fumed Oak" and "Still Life" by Edna Best. Settings by Robert Davison are exquisite.[334]

The other plays of the 1947 season were *Night Must Fall* by Emlyn Williams, starring Dame May Whitty and Patricia Hitchcock;[335] *Dear Ruth* by Norman Krasna, starring Diana Lynn and Guy Madison; *The Hasty Heart* by John Patrick, starring Richard Basehart and John Williams; *The Guardsman* by Ferenc Molnár, starring Ruth Hussey and Kent Smith; *Biography* by S.N. Behrman, starring Eve Arden and Barry Sullivan; *The Shining Hour* by Keith Winter, starring Robert Walker and Beatrice Pearson; and *Angel Street* by Patrick Hamilton, starring Laraine Day and Gregory Peck (the subject of the first Actors' Company West Coast tour and of the controversy between Traube and Soanes).

Dorothy did not perform at La Jolla during the 1948 season. The plays for 1948 were *Kind Lady* by Edward Chodorov, starring Sylvia Sidney and Tom Helmore; *The Road to Rome* by Robert E. Sherwood, starring Eve Arden and Wendell Corey; *The First Mrs. Fraser* by St. John Ervine, starring Jane Cowl and Reginald Mason; *For Love Or Money* by F. Hugh Herbert, starring June Lockhart and Leon Ames; *The Glass Menagerie* by Tennessee Williams, starring Ann Harding and Richard Basehart; *Ultramarine* by Peter Blackmore, starring Diana Lynn and Reginald Gardiner; *Serena Blandish* by S.N. Behrman, starring Jennifer Jones and Louis Jourdan; *Rope* by Patrick Hamilton, starring Roland Culver and Hurd Hatfield; and *The Male Animal* by James Thurber and Elliott Nugent, starring Gregory Peck and Martha Scott.

The premiere production especially, *Kind Lady*, starring Sylvia Sidney,

---

334 "Star Scores in Playlets," *Los Angeles Times*, August 14, 1947.

335 In the triumvirate's intention, the inaugural show was to be Patrick Hamilton's *Rope's End* (1929), soon to be filmed by Alfred Hitchcock as *Rope* (1948). Peck's commitments with 20th Century-Fox, however, prevented him from considering this option, and *Rope's End* was replaced by *Night Must Fall*. See Fishgall (2002), op. cit., 128.

Tom Helmore, Dennis Hoey, Sig Ruman, Doris Lloyd and John Newland, with set design by John Boyt and direction by William Spier, was a veritable triumph, and an indication of the consistent caliber of the playhouse's output, despite the company's tradition of financial debt. Here is Katherine Von Blon of the *Los Angeles Times* reporting:

> It was an evening of triumph both for the Actors Company and for Sylvia Sidney, whose superb performance in "Kind Lady," Edward Chodorov's adaptation of the Hugh Walpole novel, won her a deserved ovation at the La Jolla Playhouse Tuesday night.
>
> If it is true art to conceal art, Sylvia Sidney certainly accomplished this. She created a sort of feeling of superb though pathetic isolation in later scenes when, though gently reared, she revealed the courage of a thoroughbred.[336]

Those early years were years of sweet promise and high hopes for the players of the La Jolla Playhouse and of the Actors' Company. This promise and these hopes yielded a happy generosity on the part of the three co-founders that was sometimes truly surprising. Gossip Columnist Louella Parsons was the recipient of such generosity on one occasion, and was certainly surprised. Here she is telling the story in her column in August 1948:

> In all my years of being a critic—and I ain't tellin' how many—I've never been so flattered as I am by a gesture from the La Jolla playhouse, the star Gregory Peck and the cast and crew.
>
> I wanted very much to see Greg and his actor's [sic] com-

---

[336] Katherine Von Blon, "'Kind Lady' Wins Praise at La Jolla," *Los Angeles Times*, July 1, 1948.

pany in "The Male Animal," but duties in Hollywood made it impossible for me to see the show before Monday night. What I didn't know is that it was supposed to close on Sunday. Greg said:

"But if you will really promise to show up, we will extend the run another night just for you."[337]

The Actors' Company's desire to extend its reach into mainstream Los Angeles, and to present viable theater in the founding triumvirate's adopted city, was evidenced by a production that surfaced at the 267-seat Coronet Theatre at 366 N. La Cienega Boulevard, two blocks north of Beverly Boulevard, in October 1948.[338] Curiously enough, the play was Jean Anouilh's *Eurydice*, translated into English for the first time by director Mel Ferrer. The play is a modern-dress, symbolist/existentialist retelling of the myth of Orpheus and Eurydice. The text, in a second translation by South African-born British writer Kitty Black, would enjoy its more resounding "English-language premiere" in London two years later, and, more unhappily, on Broadway the year after that; the officially acknowledged "West Coast premiere" occurred in Los Angeles in 1961. Dorothy would star in the Broadway production (for more about both the play and its Broadway incarnation, see Part I, Chapter 14). A peculiar intersection of events if ever there was one.

In this particular case, Dorothy, Ferrer, and Peck produced the play's actual American premiere, which evidently went unnoticed by theatrical historians. Christian Kelleen played Orpheus, Viveca Lindfors Eurydice,

---

[337] Louella O. Parsons (INS), "Radio Show to be Filmed," *San Antonio (TX) Light*, August 31, 1948.

[338] The Coronet Theatre opened in 1947 under the sponsorship of Freida Berkoff, a member of a famous Russian dancing family, with a production of Bertolt Brecht's *Galileo* starring Charles Laughton. Since 2008 the theater has become the new venue for Club Largo; it is now called Largo at the Coronet. Information from the website Los Angeles Theatres.

John Beal Monsieur Henri (Death) and Melville Cooper Orpheus's father; Ferrer directed. David Raskin provided the music; George Jenkins designed the sets and costumes.[339] *Billboard* magazine gave the show a positive, almost glowing review, which ended with this paragraph:

> Mel Ferrer seems to have successfully caught the subtlety of the drama, and as a result, Eurydice loses little of its original merit in the process of translation. Ferrer, as director, reveals thoro [sic] understanding of the playwright's purpose. Viveca Lindfors, Hollywood's recent Swedish importation, delivers a highly sensitive performance as Eurydice in this, her American stage debut. Christian Kelleen, also a product of Sweden and also making an American stage bow, fashions an Orpheus to match Miss Lindfors' Eurydice. John Beal's Henri is rich and vibrant, giving death a warm and kindly look. Ferrer capably balances the wealth of talent afforded by these three and aided by a competent supporting cast delivers a taste of good theater that will linger long in local memories.[340]

Edwin Schallert of the *Los Angeles Times* appreciated the courage of the Actors' Company, but was pessimistic about the commercial possibilities of such an "esoteric" project as *Eurydice*:

> The Actors Company, which has had an impressive record during two summers at La Jolla, did themselves proud in their

---

[339] Production designer and art director George Jenkins (1908–2007) worked in film (and occasionally television) from 1946 until 1990. He won an Oscar for the film *All the President's Men* (1976). At the time of this theater production, he was working for producer Samuel Goldwyn, for whom he had been art director on *The Best Years of Our Lives* (1946), *The Secret Life of Walter Mitty* (1947), *The Bishop's Wife* (1947), *A Song Is Born* (1948), and *Enchantment* (1948).

[340] Lee Zhito, "Eurydice," *Billboard*, October 30, 1948.

effort to bring a new theatrical piece before the public. They will find it a very limited public, I fear.

While "Eurydice" may be intriguing in plan and design, it simultaneously falls considerably short of being really good theater.

When it finds its place at all in this country it will be in the experimental centers of drama rather than those which are commercial if for no other reason than it practically talks itself to death.

[...]

Kelleen and Miss Lindfors played the young enamored pair with remarkable intensity and earnestness so that you were inclined to be enchanted by this. Cool criticism must regard the fact that while Kelleen's reading of his role was clear most of the way Miss Lindfors' rendition was often cloudy, partly because of the very fervor which distinguished it.

It was a relief to have such a thoroughing trouper as Melville Cooper on the stage to bring the action down to earth, even when he was out of key with the play's esoteric mood.

John Beal, as the figure who emerges from background mystery to great prominence as the action goes on, ably threaded his way through long and difficult orations.[341]

By 1949, there must have been some unrest among the managing trio of the playhouse, or else the triumvirate felt that help was needed to keep the playhouse project running properly, for two additional managing directors were brought in to aid in the planning of the following season and in development. Possibly, this addition to the management related to the dreams of expansion that would haunt the La Jolla Players for the

---

[341] Edwin Schallert, "Ably Staged 'Eurydice' Loquacious, Undramatic," *Los Angeles Times*, October 18, 1948.

next years and would ultimately be crushed during the lifespan of the first playhouse. Or, the management's unrest had something to do with Gregory Peck's slackening commitment and with his eventual disappearance from the venture; this same unrest would lead to Dorothy and John Swope's taking over the playhouse management in 1953.

At any rate, in February 1949, the announcement was made of the hiring of producer Al Johnson and his wife, Bertha French Johnson. Here is a comment from the *Bakersfield Californian*:

> The Johnsons were chosen by La Jollans to assure a continuance of the high standard of stage plays set by Gregory Peck and Mel Ferrer and their Actors' Company, which has operated in La Jolla during the past two summers.
>
> Since coming to La Jolla the Johnsons have tripled the La Jolla Playhouse patronage, and have drawn distinguished talent into their casts.
>
> Before coming to La Jolla the Johnsons won academic recognition on the faculty at Cornell College, where for 15 years they were directors of the now famous Cornell Theatre which they were instrumental in establishing.
>
> As a corporate member of the American National Theatre and Academy, Al Johnson is influential in the current move to decentralize the theater of Broadway and bring about the development of excellent regional theaters.[342]

John Garfield, an enthusiastic member of the Actors' Company, referred to this unrest obliquely in a 1950 interview:

> So far, no fights, just healthy discussions [...]. We invited

---

342 "Al Johnson, Wife, Are Chosen Directors of La Jolla Group," *Bakersfield (CA) Californian*, February 21, 1949.

a big actor to join our board recently and he walked in just as we were having a hot argument. The next day he sent in his resignation and explained that he couldn't take discussions like that. We said, "That's just too bad."[343]

A stellar cast performed a classic British gem of a text between August 2 and August 7, 1949. The play was Oscar Wilde's *The Importance of Being Earnest*, and the cast was the following: Dorothy (Cecily Cardew), Jane Wyatt (Gwendolen Fairfax), Mildred Natwick (Lady Bracknell), Mel Ferrer (Algernon Moncrieff), Hurd Hatfield (Jack Worthing), Lillian Bronson (Miss Prism), and Whit Bissell (the Reverend Canon Chasuble). Bob Lee designed the sets and La Jolla Playhouse regular James Neilson directed the production.

Front cover of the La Jolla Playhouse playbill for *The Importance of Being Earnest*, 1949.

---

343 Erskine Johnson (NEA), "In Hollywood: Garfield Isn't Ashamed of Using 'Man-Makers,'" *Gastonia (NC) Gazette*, October 6, 1950.

The *Los Angeles Times* was fairly satisfied with the results:

> The upper classes get quite a tanning in La Jolla Playhouse's version of "The Importance of Being Earnest." Oscar Wilde himself might have felt that the actors fall a little short of conveying the sharp nonsense that overlays a probing satire, but the atmosphere of British snobbery is withal admirably reproduced.
>
> Mildred Natwick has a definite flair for British types. On top of her success as the medium in La Jolla's opening summer play, "Blithe Spirit," she scores again as the monumental epitome of unflinching, self-assured aristocracy, Lady Bracknell.
>
> Hurd Hatfield and Jane Wyatt bring a vivid elegance to their roles as one pair of lovers. Mel Ferrer and Dorothy McGuire, the other couple constantly jousting over the microcosmic importance of a man's name, aren't as overweening with pride. For that reason, they may appear less in the Wildean tradition.
>
> Whit Bissell provides chuckles as the parson with an amorous eye for Lillian Bronson, a prim, squeaky governess. Gordon Nelson and Colin Campbell are definitely correct butlers.
>
> James Neilson's direction strives for an authentic Wilde atmosphere of fanciful arrogance. Bob Lee's three sets, a garden and two interiors, are exquisitely done.[344]

Petticoat Fever (subtitled *A Non-Tropical Farce*) by Mark Reed[345] was

---

344 "Wilde Play Well Done," *Los Angeles Times*, August 4, 1949.

345 The play opened at the Ritz Theatre on Broadway on March 4, 1935, and closed in July of the same year after 137 performances. The setting: a wireless station on the coast of Labrador. The film adaptation, released by MGM in March 1936 and starring Myrna Loy, Robert Montgomery, Reginald Owen and Winifred Shotter, changed the setting to Alaska.

the next play in which Dorothy appeared that same summer, between August 30 and September 4, 1949. This had not been her original plan, as Dorothy explained to Hedda Hopper the following year:

> [I stayed in La Jolla much] longer than I originally intended. I went down for "The Importance of Being Earnest" which was fine because we all knew one another so well which took some of the handicap off the short rehearsal time. Then when they couldn't get a girl for "Petticoat Fever" I played that too. It's really a small routine part but when you're a stockholder in an enterprise you want to see it come off, so I offered to do it.[346]

The cast of *Petticoat Fever* included Robert Ryan, Ruth Warrick, Dan Tobin, and Clifford Brooke. The sets were designed by Bob Lee and the production was directed by James Neilson.

The other plays of the 1949 summer season were *Blithe Spirit* by Noël Coward, starring Mildred Natwick and John Emery; *Here Today* by George Oppenheimer, starring Eve Arden and Robert Alda; *Arrangement for Strings* by Michael Clayton Hutton and Samuel Rosen, starring Anne Revere and Tom Helmore; *Light Up the Sky* by Moss Hart, starring Jean Parker and Gregory Peck;[347] *Art and Mrs. Bottle* by Benn Levy, starring Jane Cowl and Roland Winters; *Arms and the Man* by George Bernard Shaw, starring Richard Basehart and John Ireland; and *Command Decision* by William Wister Haines, starring John Lund and Ward Bond.

There was great anticipation in the theatrical community of Southern California for the production that premiered at the La Jolla Playhouse

---

346 Hopper, "Ideals" (1950), op. cit.

347 According to Peck biographer Gerard Molyneaux, Peck actually played "a bit part" in *Light Up the Sky*. See Gerard Molyneaux, *Gregory Peck: A Bio-Bibliography*, Greenwood Publishing Group, 1995, 64.

on July 18, 1950, and ran through July 23. *Summer and Smoke*, under the aegis of the Actors' Company, had the enthusiastic imprimatur of author Tennessee Williams.

La Jolla Playhouse co-producer Mel Ferrer, quoted by Barry Paris in his biography of Ferrer's one-time wife Audrey Hepburn, had this to say about the production:

> Dorothy McGuire gave a moving performance and Tennessee came all the way from Florida to see it. He hugged me with tears in his eyes when the curtain went down and told me it was "the best production of mah play I ever had."[348]

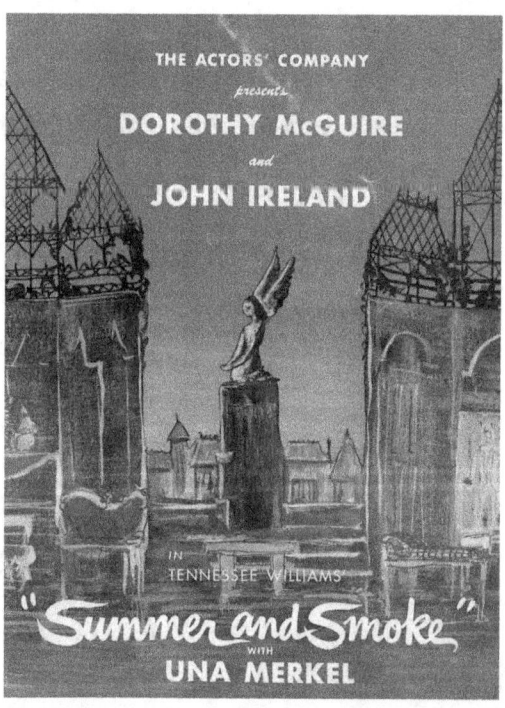

Front cover of the Actors' Company souvenir program for Tennessee Williams' *Summer and Smoke*, 1950.

---

[348] Barry Paris, *Audrey Hepburn*, Berkley Books, 1996, 87.

The playhouse triumvirate, however, was quivering with its own anticipations. Most of their attention seems to have been devoted to the resuscitated dream of expansion. Originally, the Actors' Company's dream had only included the building of a more appropriate venue; now, it included something else: freedom from the fetters of community theater status. That this last hope for the playhouse had something to do with money was made clear by United Press correspondent Bob Thomas in a slightly tongue-in-cheek syndicated article he wrote about Gregory Peck and the La Jolla project, which centered almost entirely on the issue of remuneration. Here are some excerpts:

> The man seated behind the desk and looking like a theatrical producer was Gregory Peck. He gave a convincing performance. He handed letters to a couple of secretaries, interviewed an actor for a role, weighed the billing on forthcoming plays, tossed scripts around and talked to his theatre on the phone.
>
> This is a real-life role for the long-limbed actor. It is the result of his long romance with the theatre.
>
> [...]
>
> [This summer] Peck went to work for the playhouse the day after he returned from England where he made "Capt. Horatio Hornblower." He puts in a full afternoon at the office. Normally, he earns several thousand dollars a week in movies. I asked him how much he made on his theatrical venture.
>
> He held up his finger and thumb joined in a zero.
>
> Peck and his partners are also members of the actors' company, which plans a Hollywood theatre some day.
>
> "We have put on all-star holiday radio shows to start raising a fund," he said. "We had plans to build our own theatre here, but that has been put off for a while. Now we would like

to find a new play, stage it here and elsewhere on the coast and perhaps take it to New York."

This would be a full-fledged, paying enterprise, he said, adding: "You can carry this non-profit idea too far."[349]

One might even hypothesize that the triumvirate's decision not to try to go the "public theater" route with their playhouse (the way Robert Porterfield had done with his Barter Theatre in 1933 and Joseph Papp would do with his Public Theater in 1967) indicated that "non-profit" was never really a priority.

The above article was written in July 1950, just as the summer season's second play, Rose Franken's *Claudia* (starring Joan Caulfield) was in progress. Another fact one might infer from the various pieces of news concerning the Actors' Company in early 1950 is that the dream of Broadway recognition was also high on their priority list. Here is one such news item from syndicated Hollywood columnist Sheilah Graham:

> Rosalind Russell will star in a play for the Actor's [sic] Company in New York. With their theatre in Beverly Hills still in the dream stage—I doubt it will ever be built—the stars, Roz, Dorothy McGuire and John Garfield, are going to Broadway instead.[350]

Except they did not. The dreams of the Actors' Company would have to remain slightly more local. The third play of the 1950 La Jolla season was to be Tennessee Williams' *Summer and Smoke*, starring Dorothy, John Ireland, and Una Merkel, a production that would represent a special peak both for the playhouse's progress and for Dorothy's career.

---

[349] Bob Thomas, "Life in Hollywood," *San Mateo (CA) Times,* July 15, 1950.

[350] Sheilah Graham, "Lookers, No Buyers for Rita's Hollywood Home," *Bluefield (WV) Daily Telegraph,* May 25, 1950.

John Ireland and Dorothy in the La Jolla Playhouse production of *Summer and Smoke*, 1950. Press photo, photographer undetermined.

The cast of *Summer and Smoke* was the following: Dorothy McGuire (Alma Winemiller), John Ireland (John Buchanan, Jr.), and Una Merkel (Mrs. Winemiller) in the leading roles; Michelle Farmer (Pearl), Fred Ferris (Dusty), Paula Morgan (Rosa Gonzales), Hunter Gardner (Dr. Buchanan), Peggy O'Connor (Nellie Ewell), John Mantley (Roger Doremus), Bradford Hatton (Reverend Winemiller), Lilian Hamilton (Mrs. Bassett), Hugh Simpson (Vernon), Beverly Churchill (Rosemary), Anthony Roux (Papa Gonzales) and Bill Erwin (Mr. Kramer) in supporting roles. Robert H. Barrat, Adrienne Marden, Dolores Mann and Naomi Stevens were also in the company by the time the production returned to

Los Angeles from its tour. The production was designed by Robert Tyler Lee; lighting design and direction were by James Neilson. According to Hedda Hopper, Dorothy had tried to convince Robert Mitchum to star in the play before casting John Ireland.[351]

On September 24, 1950, the company of *Summer and Smoke* departed for an extended US tour of the production. This tour included locations up the West Coast with a stop in Vancouver, then back to the Southwest. It then traveled to Texas (El Paso, Austin, Houston, San Antonio, Ft. Worth, Dallas, Wichita Falls, and Amarillo). Then, Albuquerque, Pueblo, Colorado Springs, Cheyenne, Denver, and Laramie; then on to Oklahoma and Utah, and back to Los Angeles for a one-week run at the historic Biltmore Theater on October 23.[352]

Tom Mathews of the *Salt Lake Tribune* reviewed the play when it landed at the Capitol Theater in Salt Lake City on October 16, 1950, and his reaction was resoundingly positive:

> [...] The performances of Dorothy McGuire, John Ireland and Una Merkel were a delight and an excitement—they are so obviously good and sure at what they are doing. Miss McGuire and Mr. Ireland played Williams' themes and tensions with precision and feeling.
>
> [...]
>
> With the critically sharp portraits achieved by Miss McGuire and Mr. Ireland are a whole gallery of smaller but still perfect characters. The polish of the troupe is brilliant.[353]

---

[351] Hedda Hopper, "Sorority Story Put on Jeanne Crain Slate," *Los Angeles Times*, June 10, 1950.

[352] The Biltmore Theater was a historic venue in Los Angeles. Designed by New York architects Leonard Schultze and S. Fullerton Weaver, who also designed the adjacent (and still extant) Biltmore Hotel, the theater was built at 520 W. 5th Street in Downtown Los Angeles and inaugurated in 1924. Run under Erlanger circuit management, it seated 1,654 people. The Biltmore Theater was demolished in 1964.

[353] Tom Mathews, "Experts Heighten Conflict of 'Summer and Smoke,'" *Salt Lake (UT)*

Edwin Schallert, drama critic of the *Los Angeles Times*, reviewed the Biltmore Theater post-tour performance:

> "Summer and Smoke" arrived last night at the Biltmore Theater as an event of quality, following its tour sponsored by the Actors' Company through the Western States. It is preeminently Dorothy McGuire's play, and as such is worthy of much popular interest. It is a credit to the organization, which has set a high standard in its aims and purposes, headed as it is by Miss McGuire, Gregory Peck, Mel Ferrer and their associates.
>
> The occasion was a gala one in the theater. More stars probably joined in welcoming the company than for any stage attraction of this type in several seasons. Six or seven final calls rewarded the company, with particular applause for Miss McGuire and John Ireland as the stars of the production, and for Una Merkel as the featured member of the cast.
>
> The Actors' Company originally presented "Summer and Smoke" at La Jolla during the summer. It was one of the most successful attractions during the season. It was reshaped for the tour, and its advent here has the benefit of much playing before varied audiences.
>
> Audibility is a problem in the current environment for the Actors' Company. Miss McGuire in her delicately shaded performance is bound to suffer somewhat from this handicap. It was difficult at times to understand her rapid speeches even toward the front of the theater.
>
> But in view of the rare sensitiveness and feeling that she brings to the entire characterization, the intelligence of her approach, this is not such a great matter in the long run. She

---

Tribune, October 17, 1950.

made the character a gem of purest ray in the majority of the scenes.

Many new hopes were entertained by the three executive producers of the Actors' Company following *Summer and Smoke*. Here is the ever-watchful Hedda Hopper reporting them:

> When I talked with Peck, he was highly pleased with the reception that "Summer and Smoke" got on tour with Dorothy McGuire. One week it did $23,000 worth of business. So the Actors' Company plans to send another play, this time a comedy, out on the road as soon as a cast can be assembled. Greg says the theater managers, who want movie names, think they can successfully handle three or four plays a year.
>
> Incidentally, Dorothy McGuire tells me she'd love doing a film version of "Summer and Smoke," but so far no studio has bought it. She thinks it would be even better as a picture, since much that has to happen off-stage in the play could be shown in the film.[354]

No film version was forthcoming, however. *Summer and Smoke* would eventually be made as a film by Peter Glenville in 1961 for Paramount Pictures, starring Geraldine Page and Laurence Harvey.

The success of play and tour, however, definitely a peak in the La Jolla Playhouse's early history, encouraged the birth of new ideas and new possibilities for the venue. The Actors' Company was touted as a paragon of a new kind of hybrid theatrical creature that received blood from both the theatrical community and the film industry. On September 17, 1950,

---

[354] Hedda Hopper, Lou Costello Plans Film Autobiography," *Los Angeles Times*, October 25, 1950.

Katherine Von Blon wrote a glowing article about both venue and company for the *Los Angeles Times*, and her praise was high indeed:

> Not since the grandiose days of those great ladies of the theater, Duse, Sarah Bernhardt and Modjeska, has the "road" received such a shot in the arm as is being administered by the Actors Company, headed by Gregory Peck, Mel Ferrer and Dorothy McGuire.
>
> These young actors have executed a brilliant coup in negotiating a tie-up with one of the largest exhibitors in the motion picture industry, Bob O'Donnell, who owns Inter-State and controls all the theaters of the great Southwest.
>
> This is the first time in history that such a connection between the theater and pictures has been affected. This is almost revolutionary, but it may be a starting point from which these two entertainment fields may get together.
>
> Most ironical, also, is the fact that the very industry that has been blamed most for the fading theatrical road is now so clearly instrumental in reviving it.
>
> [...] The Actors Company, in hitching its wagon to [movie] stars, has found the rainbow's gold.
>
> "After all," said Mel Ferrer, "we did not have to revive the theater or the road. The people were there, eager and wondering why the theater had deserted them. Just think, in Laramie, Wyo., there hadn't been a theatrical performance since the last tour of the great Duse. Those people are just as anxious and thrilled as they were then to see the great people of the stage."
>
> The Actors Company numbers 13, and its members prefer to believe this a lucky number.
>
> Besides Greg, Mel and Dorothy, others on the roster are Charles Boyer, Peter Rathvon, Jerry Wald, William Pereira, set designer, just signed to do the television studio sets on

Gilmore Island; Rosalind Russell, Henry Fonda, Gene Kelly, John Garfield, Deborah Kerr and Fanchon of Fanchon and Marco.[355]

Von Blon rightly noted—with considerable wonder—that these film stars' devoting so much time and effort to the enterprise, virtually without pay, was something of a miracle. She concluded that their genuine love for the theater was only one of the factors motivating them. The other was "a deep urgency within themselves, a determination not to stagnate, but to grow in their art rather than to snatch at mere straws of prominence, profit and pleasure."[356]

Dorothy herself, interviewed shortly before the opening of her (unfortunately unsuccessful) Broadway stint in Jean Anouilh's *Legend of Lovers* in December 1951, commented on the tour with joyful frivolity:

> In the fall we [of the Actors' Company] decided to try our wings as actor-managers and take the show on tour. We hoped to get some practical managing experience with the tour.
>
> And it was wonderful. We went to Portland and Seattle and Tacoma; we went up to Vancouver and went cashmere-crazy: bought sweaters and socks and mittens and stuffed them inside our blouses because we weren't sure the authorities would let us take them out of the country. And the men broke out in a rash of Scotch knitted caps and loud mufflers. We did the long jump from Vancouver to El Paso and got in at seven in the morning and nothing was open so we went over to Juarez and did some sightseeing and came back to El Paso in time for the matinee. We went all over Texas—to Dal-

---

[355] Katherine Von Blon, "Plan Links Theater With Picture Houses, *Los Angeles Times*, September 17, 1950.

[356] Ibid.

las and Houston and Austin, where the people jammed the theater and cheered us until they were hoarse, and to a place called Pueblo where nobody came.[357]

The other plays of the 1950 summer season were *Born Yesterday* by Garson Kanin, starring Marie McDonald and Robert Ryan; *Claudia* by Rose Franken, starring Joan Caulfield and Don DeFore; *Arsenic and Old Lace* by Joseph Kesselring, starring Richard Carlson and Florence Bates; *The Front Page* by Ben Hecht and Charles MacArthur, starring Pat O'Brien and Michael O'Shea; *Our Town* by Thornton Wilder, starring Ann Blyth and Millard Mitchell; *The Silver Whistle* by Robert E. McEnroe, starring Jose Ferrer and Teresa Wright; *Clutterbuck* by Benn Levy, starring Arthur Treacher and Claire Carleton; and *Goodbye Again* by Alan Scott and George Haight, starring Wendell Corey and Audrey Totter.

Dorothy did not perform at the playhouse in 1951 and 1952. The plays for 1951 were *Ring Around the Moon* by Jean Anouilh, starring Diana Lynn and Mel Ferrer; *Second Threshold* by Philip Barry, starring Raymond Massey and Adele Longmire; *Susan and God* by Rachel Crothers, starring Joan Bennett and Walter Coy; *The Voice of the Turtle* by John Van Druten, starring Diana Lynn and Mel Ferrer; *Come Back, Little Sheba* by William Inge, starring Una Merkel and Philip Ober; *Room Service* by John Murray and Allen Boretz, starring Barry Sullivan and Harry Carey, Jr.; *The Petrified Forest* by Robert E. Sherwood, starring Jan Sterling and Charlton Heston; and *On Borrowed Time* by Paul Osborn, starring Victor Moore and Beulah Bondi.

The plays offered in 1952 were *The Moon Is Blue* by F. Hugh Herbert, starring Diana Lynn and David Niven; *Remains To Be Seen* by Howard Lindsay and Russel Crouse, starring Monica Lewis and Carleton Carpenter; *Time for Elizabeth* by Groucho Marx and Norman Krasna, starring

---

357 "Miss McGuire Felt Homesick and Headed for Broadway," *Brooklyn Eagle*, December 23, 1951.

Groucho Marx and Peggie Castle; *Season in the Sun* by Wolcott Gibbs, starring Terry Moore and Howard Duff; *Affairs of State* by Louis Verneuil, starring Marsha Hunt and Tom Powers; *The Happy Time* by Samuel Taylor, starring Fay Wray and Onslow Stevens; *The Corn Is Green* by Emlyn Williams, starring Ann Harding and Diana Barrymore; *Strike a Match* by Robert Smith, starring Eva Gabor and Richard Egan; and *The Lady's Not for Burning* by Christopher Fry, starring Vincent Price and Marsha Hunt.

The Swopes Take Over: 1953

In 1953, Dorothy and John Swope took over the La Jolla theater as executive producers; drama critic Edwin Schallert reported this in his *Los Angeles Times* column on March 19, 1953:

> While Gregory Peck and Mel Ferrer are in Europe for pictures, Dorothy McGuire and John Swope, to whom she is married, will keep La Jolla Playhouse going this summer. This is good news for many theater followers throughout Southern California because this institution has established a fine record for its productions. Miss McGuire was a co-founder of the theater with Peck and Ferrer and also a co-producer. Swope has been identified with theatrical activities in New York and has just returned from the East where he has been negotiating for current Broadway hits.
>
> La Jolla Playhouse season will start June 30 and run through Aug. 30, with a different play presented each week. The enterprise will be sponsored by the San Diego County Committee, headed by Harper Olinstead as chairman, with Millard Smith as treasurer and Martin T. Steinkamp as auditor. They hope to set up the La Jolla Playhouse continuance fund, which will eventually be used to build a theater.
>
> This will be the seventh season conducted by the Peck-Ferrer-Miss McGuire group. For a time it was doubted

whether the project would continue this summer, because among other things, Miss McGuire is anticipating the birth of a child in May. However, she expects to join her husband in carrying on the work by the end of June.[358]

Gregory Peck had actually started shooting films in Europe in 1950 (*Captain Horatio Hornblower R.N.*) and would continue to do so the following year (*Moby Dick*, *Roman Holiday*); thus, his activities for the playhouse had slackened even before 1953 (possibly for financial reasons as well; perhaps, for him, "this non-profit idea" had been carried "too far" already).[359] Ferrer, in turn, had also been filming on location and at foreign studios (in Italy, England and Morocco, for example); in September 1954, he then married Audrey Hepburn before diving headlong into the lengthy filming of King Vidor's *War and Peace* (1956) at Cinecittà Studios and other Italian locations. Thus, his presence in La Jolla was sporadic too.

In the summer of 1953, just over a month after giving birth to her son Mark, Dorothy appeared in John Van Druten's play *I Am a Camera*, inaugurating the playhouse's seventh season. In the cast with her were Don Taylor, Lee Patrick, Alan Hale, Jr., Edit Angold, Ruth Hill, and Lamont Johnson. The production was designed by Bill Martin and directed by Norman Lloyd. The play ran from June 30 to July 5, 1953. Edwin Schallert of the *Los Angeles Times* was relatively pleased:

> "I Am a Camera" was seen during the past 12 months in Los Angeles with Julie Harris playing the feminine starring role, a role that she made a very special and personal triumph.

---

358 Edwin Schallert, "McGuire, Swope Will Guide La Jolla," *Los Angeles Times*, March 19, 1953.

359 Actor/director Dan "Peter" Levin, who served as apprentice at the La Jolla Playhouse in the early 1950s, does not remember ever seeing Peck at the venue during the five years of his apprenticeship.

She gave a stylistically perfect interpretation and one that would be a great temptation to follow.

However, Miss McGuire in the La Jolla rendition definitely avoided that lure and made her portrayal individual. She humanized the character notably in the important scenes.

If a fault was to be charged against her this would pertain to the clarity of her dialogue reading in the opening performance. Her comedy in the role was exceptional but it might have been better had all the lines carried their full impact. It is to be assumed that her enactment of the part will have attained a full-fledged quality in the next night or two at the latest. She proves herself a competent actress as always in her delineation of the young woman tossed about in a period of emotional turbulence after World War I in a European environment.

It was the work of Don Taylor particularly that gave distinction to the performance. He has a sensitiveness that is exceptionally fitting to the part of the author (Christopher Isherwood) and maintained a balance in the production that was not typical of the company that visited Los Angeles during the past winter. The combination of Miss McGuire and Taylor in this play was therefor [sic] an especially happy one [. . .].[360]

The other plays of 1953 were *Jane* by S.N. Behrman, starring Edna Best and Howard St. John; *My Three Angels* by Sam and Bella Spewack, starring Kurt Kasznar and Wilton Graff; *The Dazzling Hour* by Anna Bonacci, starring Olivia de Havilland and Kent Smith;[361] *Stalag 17* by Don-

---

[360] Edwin Schallert, "McGuire, Taylor Score in 'Camera' at La Jolla," *Los Angeles Times*, July 1, 1953.

[361] It was during the rehearsal and performance period for this play that de Havilland was courted by the Frenchman who would become her second husband, Pierre Galante. And it was shortly following the play's run that she accepted his proposal of marriage. (See Olivia de Havilland, *Every Frenchman Has One*, Random House, 1962, 16–17.)

ald Bevan and Edmund Trzcinski, starring Aldo Ray and Robert Strauss; *You Never Can Tell* by George Bernard Shaw, starring Allyn McLerie and Ron Randell; *Dial M for Murder* by Frederick Knott, starring Leora Dana and Douglass Montgomery; and *Don Juan in Hell* by George Bernard Shaw, starring Jan Sterling and John Emery.

The 1953 summer season was a successful one, with one exception. The *Los Angeles Times* commented on both the season and the exception, and on John Swope's management, in an August 1953 blurb:

> Something should be said for the courage of John Swope in giving latitude to this tryout in his program [the play *The Dazzling Hour* starring Olivia de Havilland], because such tryouts are essentially risky. He and the other sponsors of "The Dazzling Hour" apparently bet on the wrong horse,[362] but it can be said for Swope, and Dorothy McGuire, too, as the heads of La Jolla's destiny this season, that they have done splendid duty in their productions, and have thoroughly proved that they can carry on even when their partners Gregory Peck and Mel Ferrer are long sojourning in Europe.
>
> Swope can be credited with casting Kurt Kasznar brilliantly in "My Three Angels," as well as presenting the play. He did well also in trying to reinstate James M. Cain's "The Postman Always Rings Twice" on the stage and in giving Don Taylor opportunities not only in this play but also in the opening event, "I Am a Camera," with Miss McGuire. He is evidently also going to do well through the balance of the season beginning this week with "Stalag 17."[363]

---

[362] A new play by Anna Bonacci, *The Dazzling Hour* premiered at the La Jolla Playhouse on July 28, 1953; neither the play nor Ms. de Havilland's performance was well received.

[363] "Miss De Havilland Put Up a Battle; Swope Praised," *Los Angeles Times*, August 9, 1953.

The popular and critical success of the season as a whole emboldened both the theater's founders and the community forces around them to rekindle hopes of an expansion. Between December 1953 and January 1954, the La Jolla-San Diego County Theater and Arts Foundation was formed and incorporated, with support from the sponsoring committee for the La Jolla Playhouse. The foundation brought together thirty incorporators, with representatives from all over San Diego County. Its primary objective was "to conduct a center for theater, music, lectures and other similar arts." On January 27, 1954, the *Los Angeles Times* reported the event:

> Mrs. Edward Longstreth of La Jolla, executive vice-chairman, started collecting signatures, Nov. 21, 1953. "With corporation members scattered all over this country and in Europe, it took less time than we anticipated. At last we've taken the first important step toward realizing our eight-year dream to build a beautiful theater and related buildings for the Playhouse."
>
> Gregory Peck signed the articles of incorporation in Paris in the United States Embassy before a Vice-Consul on Dec. 4.
>
> Other key La Jolla Playhouse members, Mel Ferrer, president, Dorothy McGuire and John Swope signed in Hollywood.[364]

Those dreams for the future of the playhouse were articulated more exactly by *Los Angeles Times* drama critic Edwin Schallert later that year:

> Four film festivals annually will be the aim of La Jolla-San Diego Theater and Arts Foundation, in addition to an elaborate program of musical events and the summer season of plays. Mel Ferrer as board president yesterday announced

---

[364] "La Jolla Plans New Theater," *Los Angeles Times*, January 27, 1954.

from New York the remarkable project now in the making. Immediate construction of a 1200-seat theater is forecast. Favored films will be of art theater and prestige type.

Ferrer, Gregory Peck, Dorothy McGuire and John Swope will continue the theater operation each summer, while musical events, with the film festivals, are to fill out the rest of the year. A special symphony orchestra will eventually be organized, with guest conductors and soloists. An effort will simultaneously be made to have the Los Angeles Philharmonic and San Diego Symphony take part in musical fetes.

Temporary chairman of the La Jolla-San Diego Theater and Arts Foundation is Harold B. Starkey and other officers besides him and Ferrer include Dr. Roger Revelle, head of the building committee; Mrs. Edward Longstreth, vice-president; Mayor John Butler, Mrs. H.S. Darlington and Mrs. Kathryn T. Hosmer, board members; Frank J. Kockritz Jr., board counsel; Armistead Carter, chairman of the finance committee.[365]

Winding Down: 1954–1959

In 1954, the Kiwanis Club withdrew its support to the La Jolla Playhouse, and producer John Swope cut the number of summer plays from its previously standard number of eight–nine to a maximum of five (then four in 1955 and three in 1958). By the latter half of the decade, a series of interconnected factors was impinging on the venue's health: economics, the inadequacy of the high school auditorium, short rehearsal times, the crumbling of the traditional contract-player covenant at the Hollywood studios, television, poor reviews, and so on.

That some of the initial enthusiasm had evaporated from the La Jolla enterprise can also be evinced from the following facts: (a) Gregory Peck was conspicuously absent from the playhouse after circa 1950; (b) the star

---

[365] Edwin Schallert, "La Jolla Film Festival Plans Expand," *Los Angeles Times*, June 19, 1954.

power of the featured actors decreased somewhat, particularly during the last two seasons, despite the persistence of some faithful players such as Reginald Gardiner and Howard Duff; and (c) Dorothy aided her husband as executive producer of the venue starting in 1953, but did not act in any productions after 1954.

In the summer of 1954, Dorothy co-starred with Vincent Price in her last play at the venue, Terence Rattigan's play *The Winslow Boy* (which she had performed on the air with Ray Milland five months earlier as a *Lux Radio Theatre* play). In the cast with Dorothy and Price were Eduard Franz, Sean McClory, Hilda Plowright, Richard Lupino, and Christopher Cook. The production was designed and lit by Robert Corrigan and directed by Norman Lloyd. The play ran from June 29 through July 11, 1954.

The other plays of 1954 were *Anniversary Waltz* by Jerome Chodorov and Joseph Fields, starring Howard Duff and Marjorie Lord; *Sabrina Fair* by Samuel Taylor, starring Joseph Cotten and Arleen Whelan; *The Seven Year Itch* by George Axelrod, starring Don Taylor and Kathleen Hughes; and *The Vacant Lot* by Paul Streger and Berrilla Kerr, starring Alan Dinehart III and Brett Halsey.

With John Swope acting as executive producer and scouring his many acquaintances in New York for viable properties to be negotiated for purchase by the playhouse, Dorothy spent a large portion of her summers at La Jolla, acting commitments and travel permitting. Here is a comment from the *Los Angeles Times*:

> Her husband, John Swope, is executive producer of the Playhouse and he likes to have Dorothy around to advise him. Of course she receives no money for her work but it gives her a chance to help other young actors and actresses over the rough spots.

"I want to help young people," she says, "but don't make me out to be a Lady Bountiful."[366]

The plays for 1955 were *The Rainmaker* by N. Richard Nash, starring Teresa Wright and James Whitmore; *Native Uprising* by D.N. Roman, starring Howard Duff and Marjorie Lord; *The Time of the Cuckoo* by Arthur Laurents, starring Claire Trevor and Stephen Bekassy; and *Oh, Men! Oh, Women!* By Edward Chodorov, starring John Sutton and Steve Forrest.

In 1956, the offerings were the following: *Bus Stop* by William Inge, starring Sally Forrest and Lee Marvin; *King of Hearts* by Jean Kerr and Eleanor Brooke, starring Jackie Cooper and Patricia Breslin; *Miss Julie/ The Stronger* by August Strindberg, starring Viveca Lindfors and Stephen Bekassy; *Pal Joey* by John O'Hara, Lorenz Hart and Richard Rodgers, starring Gene Nelson and Benay Venuta; and *The Little Hut* by Andre Roussin, starring Marsha Hunt and Leon Ames.

The 1957 offerings consisted of *The Reluctant Debutante* by William Douglas Home, starring Reginald Gardiner and Brenda Forbes; *Paul and Constantine* by Dario Bellini, starring James and Pamela Mason; *The Potting Shed* by Graham Greene, starring Gladys Cooper and Leo G. Carroll; *Career* by James Lee, starring Don Taylor and Una Merkel; *Androcles and the Lion/The Proposal*, by George Bernard Shaw/Anton Chekhov, starring Leon Ames and Marilyn Erskine.

A "stellar junket," as the *Los Angeles Times* called it, was organized in La Jolla on September 15, 1957, for a telecast intended to promote the playhouse and ensure its future. By that point, the estimated pricing of the intended new theater was also clear: the venue, to be situated on a Torrey Pines promontory overlooking the Pacific Ocean between La Jolla and Del Mar (San Diego), would cost $1,500,000.[367] Among the personali-

---

366 Walter Ames, "Miss McGuire Full of TV Fire," *Los Angeles Times*, August 22, 1954.

367 This estimate, reported in the press at the time, was probably conservative, for seven years earlier *Oakland Tribune* drama critic Wood Soanes, commenting on the La Jolla

ties who flew in via Convair either to attend the event at the playhouse or to take part in the television program were Leon Ames (new head of the Screen Actors Guild), Beulah Bondi, Gladys Cooper, Taina Elg, Mel Ferrer, Audrey Hepburn, Charlton Heston and wife, Susan Kohner, Mrs. Edward Longstreth, Norman Lloyd, Don Taylor, producer Jerry Wald, and Vincent Price, who acted as master of ceremonies for much of the show. Gregory Peck was absent.[368]

Then, the news items ceased; in all likelihood, the noble dream of a large multi-art La Jolla festival ceased too, even though the name La Jolla Playhouse would re-surface occasionally in the press with a glimmer of hope.

In 1958, the season offered *Bell, Book and Candle* by John Van Druten, starring Felicia Farr and Scott Forbes; *A View from the Bridge* by Arthur Miller, starring Martin Balsam and Rita Moreno; and *Visit to a Small Planet* by Gore Vidal, starring Reginald Gardiner and Alan Reed.

The final season of the playhouse's first incarnation, before the dark years (1959–1983), took place in June–August 1959 with the following program: *Look Homeward, Angel* by Ketti Frings, starring Roy Roberts and Andrew Prine; *Who Was That Lady I Saw You With?* by Norman Krasna, starring Wendell Corey and Phyllis Avery; *Two for the Seesaw* by William Gibson, starring Barry Sullivan and Patricia Huston; *Once More, With Feeling* by Harry Kurnitz, starring Fernando Lamas and Helen Walker; and *Too Many Husbands* by W. Somerset Maugham, starring Estelle Winwood and Byron Palmer.

The first La Jolla Playhouse, a noble theatrical enterprise if ever there was one, went dark on September 5, 1959, at the end of the last performance of its 1959 summer season. The play in question was Maugham's

---

Playhouse's fundraising aim during its tour of *Summer and Smoke*, had quoted the sum of $2,500,000. (Wood Soanes, "Curtain Calls," *Oakland Tribune*, August 7, 1950.)

368 See: Edwin Schallert, "Novelist Gann Writes Screen Original," *Los Angeles Times*, September 17, 1957.

Too Many Husbands, starring Byron Palmer, Ann Lee, Oliver Lee and special guest stars Estelle Winwood and Gale Gordon.

The rebirth of the playhouse would have to wait—eighteen more years, to be exact.

A decisive step forward was made towards the realization of the ambitious dream, or at least towards the building of a larger venue, through the Theater and Arts Foundation of San Diego County, in 1980. This step found Dorothy still involved.

Mel Ferrer and Dorothy were present (Peck, again, was not) at the groundbreaking ceremony that was held on June 27, 1980, after construction had finally started on the theater. Others present at the champagne "christening" included casting director Ruth Burch, attorney Frank Kockritz; Susan, Roger and Ellen Bevelle, Foundation president Ewart Goodwin Jr., board members Eric Bass and Betty, David Thompson and Mackie, Walter S. J. Swanson and Rusty, actor Eric Christmas, and departing chancellor William McElroy. The theater's opening was expected to occur in the summer of 1981.[369] It occurred in 1983. The 492-seat theater was named the Mandell Weiss Theatre and was the first La Jolla Playhouse dedicated venue. On that occasion, the La Jolla Playhouse was revived under the leadership of Des McAnuff, who served as artistic director from 1983 to 1994. McAnuff was succeeded by Michael Greif, who served as artistic director from 1995 to 1999. At the time of writing, the theater was being led by artistic director Christopher Ashley and managing director Debby Buchholz.

---

369 "San Diego on View: Groundbreaking Turns Corner," *Los Angeles Times*, June 29, 1980.

A Katharine Hepburnish portrait of Dorothy, most likely taken by RKO photographer Ernest A. Bachrach, circa 1946.

10. RKO Radio Pictures, 1945–1951

Dorothy made a total of four films with RKO Radio Pictures, three of them while under contract to David O. Selznick, between 1945 and 1946. The first two have forever become associated with her, iconically.

The Enchanted Cottage (1945)
Based on a 1921 play by Sir Arthur Wing Pinero, *The Enchanted Cottage* is a sentimental, talky melodrama whose poignant punchline is so predictable, and whose premise is in some ways so unsavory (viz., plain or disfigured people are ashamed of their ugliness until they can be viewed as beautiful by someone who loves them) that most of its dramatic power might today be lost for the average viewer. Produced by Harriet Parsons (Louella's daughter) and directed by John Cromwell, the film was successful with audiences, and remains to this day indelibly associated with Dorothy's fame, beyond proportion. Even after the end of her film career, most of the fan mail Dorothy received was about this film, with *The Spiral Staircase* a close second.[370]

---

[370] Dan Van Neste, correspondence with the author, April 2018. Van Neste acquired the information directly from Dorothy during his correspondence with her.

Laura Pennington (Dorothy McGuire) is a homely young woman who works as a maid in a cottage run by disenchanted widow Abigail Minnett (Mildred Natwick), who knows the magical power of the house but does not reveal it readily. New tenants are on their way: dashing Army Air Force officer Oliver Bradford (Robert Young) and his fiancée Beatrice (Hillary Brooke), who plan on moving in after their wedding. Oliver's plans are upended by his being called into wartime service. When he is badly disfigured in a plane accident, he calls off his wedding and hides his secret shame from his family and fiancée, by retreating to a life of seclusion in the cottage.

Initially, Laura and Oliver are wary of each other, but her shy demeanor and tender outlook are beneficial to Oliver, who gradually overcomes his depression and begins to enjoy her company. As love develops between them, a transformation takes place: they become beautiful. At first, they believe this metamorphosis to be real, an effect of the magical power of the "enchanted" cottage. A blind composer who befriends them (Herbert Marshall) knows the truth, but cannot find the right moment to tell them. When Oliver's parents come for a surprise visit, the couple has to face facts: they are beautiful only to each other, through the power of their love; everybody else still sees them as plain (Laura) or disfigured (Oliver). After the initial shock, the couple accepts this state of things, and learns that a love such as theirs is a thing to be cherished.

There is, of course, something quite lovely about the idea that love can make you see things in your loved one that others are blind to; but the story's insistence on the distinction between "ugly" and "beautiful" is quite unpleasant. The final "revelation," which does carry some poetry with it, takes so long to come, and is accompanied by so much unnecessary exposition, that any minimally attentive viewer gets the point long before the film's climax. Also, the optical trickery involved in that climax slants the argument away from any meaningful conclusion. The point, as visualized in the film, is not that the power of love makes the usual standards of physical beauty irrelevant and meaningless, but rather that it makes you see the beloved person as something they are not: conventionally beautiful.

That repulsive point is driven home with the subtlety of a hammer driving a nail through wood in the film's final shot. The two protagonists brace themselves for a society evening at the composer's house—and walk up the steps of his front door hand in hand, as if walking to the guillotine (for they know that other people cannot possibly see them as they see each other). Incongruously, this finale, which contrasts with the treacly tenderness of Laura and Oliver's previous scene in the cottage, has all the chiaroscuro ominousness of another famous final shot, in which Nazi collaborator Claude Rains walks up the steps to the front door of his Brazilian home—and to certain death—at the end of Alfred Hitchcock's *Notorious* (1946).

That Oliver Bradford should suffer from some depression, and from some PTSD anxiety, after his wartime misadventures is understandable; but the psychological help he needs has nothing to do with beauty. The film is wise enough to acknowledge this, by dramatizing the fact that his recovery is helped by his long dialogues with the serene Laura and by his long walks with her. Yet, when the time comes to make the final argument, we are presented with the blunt fact that worries the protagonists, the other players, and the film's writers: Oliver and Laura are ugly to look at.

Dorothy is very sweet in the film, and plays her bland, underwritten character with honesty; she is also made appropriately homely through most of the story via an unflattering hairdo and some judicious make-up and lighting. Robert Young remains handsome despite the disfigurement of half his face.

Bosley Crowther of the *New York Times* made more or less the same argument I have made, rather wittily:

> [The] current film version of the wistful drama, which came to the Astor yesterday, contemporizes the subject in

peculiarly obsolete terms. Despite all the marvelous advances in plastic surgery, it assumes that a shattered Air Force pilot would be returned to society with a face very badly disfigured and frightening to behold. It forgets that a casualty quite as bitter as the American hero in this case would be studiously rehabilitated through modern treatment before being dismissed. And it violates an obvious tenet of feminine beauty culture today—which is that a girl of moderate features (and fair intelligence) can make herself look very sweet.

As a consequence, the deep and studied poignance of this elaborately heart-torturing film appears not only unreasonable but very plainly contrived. It is hard to believe that a depressed veteran's entire recuperation would be allowed to devolve upon a frustrated girl, an intuitive blind man and a honeymoon cottage possessing charm. And it is fair to insist that no young lady with a face and figure such as that of Dorothy McGuire would permit herself to look so dingy and woebegone as she does in this film.[371]

Variety was less polemical in its positive review. About Dorothy, it stated the following: "Miss McGuire turns in an outstanding performance [. . .]."[372]

Edwin Schallert of the *Los Angeles Times* had his own reservations about the film, some in tune with Crowther's, but was ultimately charmed by its *schmaltz*, and especially by Dorothy:

> Actually it is Dorothy McGuire and Robert Young, especially Miss

[371] Bosley Crowther, "'Enchanted Cottage,' Remake of Play by Sir Arthur Pinero, With Dorothy McGuire, Robert Young, New Film at the Astor," *New York Times*, April 28, 1945. Columnist Mildred Martin of the *Philadelphia Inquirer* made much the same point as Crowther in her review of May 20, 1945.

[372] "The Enchanted Cottage," *Variety*, February 14, 1945.

McGuire, through the deep, rich feeling of their performances in the fantasy portion of "The Enchanted Cottage" who give it the values that belong.

It is Miss McGuire's rare talent and adaptability in a seemingly unending variety of roles which stand out the most shiningly.[373]

Left to right: Dorothy McGuire, Robert Young, and Herbert Marshall in RKO's *The Enchanted Cottage*. Publicity still.

A curious Oscar-nomination poll was reported by Edwin Schallert of the *Los Angeles Times* after the film's release:

> The G.I. contingent at Ft. Lewis, Wash., challenged my choice of probable Academy winners of a couple of weeks ago in some aspects, and carried out a poll of their own at this, one of the largest Army installations.

---

[373] Edwin Schallert, "Basic Values Transfigure Love Story," *Los Angeles Times*, May 28, 1945.

[. . .] They thought Dorothy McGuire of "Enchanted Cottage" is the No. 1 actress.[374]

In 1973, there was talk of a remake. Here is actor Robert Young announcing the project to A.H. Weiler of the *New York Times* News Service:

> This time, the setting will not be World War II, of course, and Dorothy and I will not be playing the leads. We'll play the parts of the housekeeper and the blind pianist, done by Mildred Natwick and Herbert Marshall in the original.[375]

One can be thankful, I think, that the project never took off.

The Spiral Staircase (1946)

An iconic Dorothy McGuire film, perhaps *the* most iconic of her early career, this sinister little thriller, beautifully directed by *noir* master Robert Siodmak (*Phantom Lady*, 1944; *The Killers*, 1946; *Criss Cross*, 1949), contains a splendid performance by Dorothy for which both *Leonard Maltin's Movie Guide*[376] and *Variety*[377] have used the adjective "unforgettable."

I say "little," not because *The Spiral Staircase* is an unimportant film, but because, with the exception of some early scenes, its entire story takes place in one set (or several sets functioning as one location), an "old dark house" where a serial killer might be lurking under the guise of one of its apparently harmless dwellers. I also use the term "little" because, this being an RKO film of the 1940s, its dark atmospheres, limited size and

---

[374] Edwin Schallert, "New York Stage Takes Rap on Movie 'Names,'" *Los Angeles Times*, January 22, 1946.

[375] A.H. Weiler (*New York Times* News Service), "Dr. Welby in a movie," *Mattoon (IL) Journal Gazette*, February 5, 1973.

[376] Maltin (2009), op. cit.

[377] "The Spiral Staircase," *Variety*, January 9, 1946.

elliptic treatment of violence might put one in mind of the low-budget work of another *noir*, or horror, master who worked for that studio, namely producer Val Lewton.

An atmospheric publicity still for *The Spiral Staircase*, showing Dorothy on the titular staircase lit by Nicholas Musuraca's masterly chiaroscuro lighting. RKO Radio Pictures, 1946.

The story in brief: In the early days of the twentieth century, a small New England town is plagued by a series of murders, whose victims are disabled young women. The police fear for the safety of young Helen (Dorothy McGuire), who works in the above-mentioned house as live-in lady-in-waiting for a wealthy dowager, the bedridden Mrs. Warren (Ethel Barrymore). Helen is mute, having lost her voice as a child due to the trauma of losing her parents in a fire. Widowed Mrs. Warren has a son (Steve, played by Gordon Oliver) and a stepson (Professor Albert Warren, played by George Brent). The story (and Siodmak) does everything it can to make us believe that handsome, flippant Steve is the culprit, but it is all a game of misdirection. Soon, we realize that it is the gloomy stepson, respectable Professor Albert Warren, who is harboring a secret grudge against the deformities of the world. In the film's climactic sequence, Helen finds herself virtually alone in the house with the killer: the housekeeper, wonderfully played by Elsa Lanchester, is drunk and unconscious; the family doctor has gone to see a patient; Helen herself has locked Steve in a room in the cellar thinking that he has killed Albert's secretary; and Mrs. Warren is theoretically bedridden. Thus, Helen is about to be killed by the deranged professor after a chase up and down that titular staircase, when Mrs. Warren, who has managed to drag herself out of bed and has always been an excellent shot, executes her stepson. As a result of this last shock, Helen regains the use of her voice. With that new, lovely voice (Dorothy's), she tearfully telephones the town doctor for help, and the moment is indeed touching.

For once, contrary to perceived Hollywood wisdom, we can safely say that the story is *not* the thing in this thriller. There is little depth to the conventional old-dark-house plot, to the dull characters, and to the lackluster dialogue. The greatness of this film lies in the director's visual/aural handling of the raw material, in the film's pace, in the protagonist's silence, and in a few of the performances.

Director Siodmak avails himself of one of the most brilliant cinematographers of the time, Italian-born Nicholas Musuraca (born in Riace, the town in the Italian region of Calabria where the famous Greek bronze figures, the "*Bronzi di Riace,*" were discovered in 1972), whose chiaroscuro lighting contributed greatly to such films as *Cat People* (1942), *Out of the Past* (1947) and *The Blue Gardenia* (1953). For his work on Robert Wise's *I Remember Mama* (1948), Musuraca was nominated for an Academy Award.

Musuraca's lighting and photography, in conjunction with Siodmak's compositions and camera angles, Roy Webb's spooky score, and Albert S. D'Agostino and Jack Okey's art direction, creates a vertiginous, distorted pictorial world, worthy of the best efforts of German directors of the 1920s such as Fritz Lang, F. W. Murnau and Robert Wiene. That house may be one location, but that location is a marvel of elegant expressionism, full of staircases (not one, but many), banisters, dark corners, drapes, levels and sub-levels, rhythmic wrought-iron fences, mirrors, and dark cellars, all of which Siodmak's camera explores broodingly.

This expressionistic exploration is also aural. One of the most disquieting moments comes early in the film, as Helen, hurrying home as darkness follows dusk and a thunderstorm breaks out, takes the time to rattle a stick across a wrought-iron fence as she runs to the garden gate, and Musuraca's camera runs with her. This playful detail does more than establish Helen's childish, frightened innocence; it creates an unsettling sonic counterpoint to the sounds of the wind and of the approaching thunder, like a dissonant musical omen of dangers to come.

The main conceit of the film, the fact that its protagonist is a mute, did not come from Ethel Lina White's novel *Some Must Watch* (1933),[378] nor did the central image of the film, the staircase. Those were all changes made in Mel Dinelli's screen adaptation. Some sources have stated that director Siodmak was responsible for that central image, and that it was this visual change that prompted Dinelli to retitle the film;[379] be that as it may, the director makes that image his own and turns it into the overriding expressionistic sign of the film. The spiral, the vortex, the whirlpool, the descent into darker and darker levels of consciousness (the "house," as a place of the mind or as family identity, hides secrets down below) become the real themes. It is in the subconscious strata of the mind that Helen herself hides the secret cause of her loss of speech, a secret that

---

[378] Ethel Lina White, *Some Must Watch*, Ward, Lock & Co., 1933.

[379] For example: Greco (1999), op. cit.

Doctor Perry (a dull Kent Smith), who loves Helen, clumsily tries to unlock. She too, like the killer, harbors a secret, and must descend into fear and despair through a metaphorical spiral movement until that secret can be "shocked" into the open.

Italian film critic Andrea Cardosi, in a brief review of the classic film, took the Freudian idea mentioned above even further:

> The house is perhaps the real protagonist of The Spiral Staircase, with its three distinct floors (cellar, first floor and second floor). If one wished to venture a not-so-farfetched parallel—using Freud's theories as a basis—between the structure of our psyche and the structure of the house, one might point out that the cellar corresponds to the *id*, which constitutes the unconscious mind, [all that has been] removed or repressed from consciousness: a plane devoid of logic and rationality where the basest impulses take shape. It is here that Blanche is killed, and that is no coincidence.
>
> The first floor, on the other hand, represents the *ego*, governed by the principle of reality, and it is the most superficial stratum of the psyche's apparatus; it presents itself as a mediation between the impulses of the id and the external world. The second floor (where Helen will be saved) is the *superego*, the moral conscience that, via the person of Mrs. Warren, takes on the role of moral censor who judges (and punishes) the evildoer's actions and instincts.
>
> The function of the staircase is to connect the three floors of the house, and hence the three levels of consciousness.[380]

On a plane more strictly germane to cinematic style, a similar Victori-

---

[380] Andrea Cardosi, "Films on TV: The Spiral Staircase, by Robert Siodmak," *Sentieri selvaggi* (www.sentieriselvaggi.it), October 19, 2014.

an-era suspenser, George Cukor's 1944 film version of Patrick Hamilton's *Gaslight*, had also exploited the architectural structure of a house—but inverted, with the utmost tension originating from an attic instead of a cellar—to induce terror in its female protagonist, with striking points of similarity to this film: the house as theater of the mind, murder, staircases, a murderer hiding in plain sight, a deaf housekeeper, etc. Here is film historian Carlos Clarens commenting on the "expressionist/psychological" use of that 1944 location:

> The house is no mere element of décor but a third protagonist, upholstered, stifling, a closed world. Cukor's master touch is in the way he assigns various charges of tension to each level, and the vertical suspense this generates is uniquely filmic and disturbing. The attic bears down on the rest of the house: it holds the missing diamonds the husband seeks, and with them the obsessions and guilt of the past, pervading the place with a musty odour of murder and madness. The various levels always seem to define the characters, shape their states of mind. As she grows uncertain of her own sanity, the wife retreats into her bedroom, situated directly beneath the attic, the locus of madness. At one point, she screams hysterically from the top of the stairs and is reassured by the unconcerned drone of the deaf housekeeper making her way up from the lower floors, which now seem as out of reach as sanity itself.[381]

The "vortex" theme of descent is further developed in *The Spiral Staircase* by the other distinctive visual sign of the film: the close-up of the killer's eye. This close-up, repeated as a leitmotif throughout the film whenever the killer is about to strike, is a variation of the round spiral motif. About a decade later, starting with *Vertigo* (1958) and continuing

---

[381] Carlos Clarens, *George Cukor*, Secker & Warburg/The British Film Institute, 1976, 77.

with *Psycho* (1960), Alfred Hitchcock would appropriate this image, and its association with the spiral, indelibly.[382] Here, Siodmak indulges in both expressionism and personal vanity by using his own eye as a subject for those disquieting shots of the killer lurking and watching. Roy Webb's eerie theremin[383] motif does the rest.

In some ways, Helen is the killer's parallel figure. Both are "abnormal," he because of his psychosis, she because of her speech impairment and childhood trauma. His eye and her mouth both become symbols of that shared abnormality. Both he and Helen are being followed by Mrs. Warren's watchful gaze. The killer is "cured" of his derangement by being killed; his death in turn cures Helen of her impairment.

One must not take this film's plot, or its gauche attempts at psychology, too seriously. That plot and those attempts are just a pretext to indulge in images and atmospheres. The weakest scenes of the film are those in which any kind of serious discussion is essayed, whether psychological or otherwise. In one of those scenes, Dr. Perry, who is a real troglodyte when it comes to psychological healing, vividly describes Helen's childhood trauma for her (and for the audience), trying to traumatize her into speaking. When that fails, he grabs her by the arms and shakes her, yelling: "*Try to talk! Try it! Try it!*"

With uncouth writing such as that, one can easily see why Siodmak

---

[382] The eye motif had already appeared the year before *The Spiral Staircase* in the Salvador Dali-inspired dream sequences of Hitchcock's *Spellbound*.

[383] The earliest widely used electronic musical instrument, the theremin was patented by Soviet inventor Léon Theremin in 1928. (Its more aristocratic keyboard sibling, the Ondes Martenot, was invented by Maurice Martenot the same year, but is mostly known for its use in symphonic music, for example by French composer Olivier Messiaen. In film, it was used by composers such as Maurice Jarre in *Lawrence of Arabia*, 1962, and Elmer Bernstein in *Ghostbusters*, 1984.) The monophonic theremin uses two antennas as sensors for the player's hands (the hands never touch the instrument), allowing the thereminist to control volume with one hand and pitch with the other. Its eerie sonorities were used by film composers such as Miklós Rózsa (*Spellbound*, *The Lost Weekend*, both 1945), Bernard Herrmann (*The Day the Earth Stood Still*, 1951), Dimitri Tiomkin (*The Thing from Another World*, 1951), and Danny Elfman (*Mars Attacks!*, 1996).

decided to concentrate so forcefully on the visual atmosphere. Dorothy, who never speaks until the closing shots of the movie, is spared the affront of mediocre dialogue and can concentrate on the visuals too. Her performance is a jewel of speed, flexibility and warmth: like a pantomime of Claudia without the bipolarity. While she never says a word in the film until the final scene, her character is constantly dialoguing with the rest of the cast (and with herself in her mirror scene), wordlessly. Every expression, every feeling, is perfectly clear without the need for words.

Helen (Dorothy McGuire) on the titular staircase, checking if there are any serial killers around. Production still for *The Spiral Staircase*, RKO Radio Pictures, 1946.

Reportedly, Dorothy experienced some trouble, initially, in playing the part of a mute. According to a 1945 interview with Bob Thomas, she only learned that she would be playing a non-speaking part shortly before starting work on the film:

> Dorothy didn't even know that she was going to play a mute until shortly before she began the picture. While she was vacationing in the east, she received a hurry call to report for work. So she drove across the country.[384]

Which would seem to indicate that Dorothy had not read the script before that time, or that the script had been altered drastically after she read it. In any event, the problem of how to play a speech-impaired character was technical. United Press correspondent Virginia MacPherson visited the set of *The Spiral Staircase* (still entitled *Some Must Watch* at that time) the day after Dorothy, after six weeks of silent acting, had finally uttered that final scream and spoken those final words:

> "It was pretty hard at first," [Dorothy] said. "I started holding my mouth very stiff and prim."
>
> She looked just like a persimmon-faced school teacher, and that, decided Director Robert Siodmak, would never do.
>
> "So he told me to relax," she added. "I did, and found my mouth was hanging open. I was mouthing the words I was trying to get across without saying them."
>
> That was worse. So to keep Siodmak from tearing out what hair he has left, Miss McGuire did a little research on mute people—how they expressed themselves without talking, etc.
>
> That did the trick. After that she did her talking without

---

[384] Bob Thomas, "Roles," (1945), op. cit.

saying anything. And Siodmak could get on with his directing, a happy man.

Yesterday was [the day Miss McGuire finally got to scream, and to say five words]. But she almost didn't get to say 'em, after all.

According to the script, Miss McGuire was supposed to dash up a flight of winding steps—just a few feet ahead of [the] murderer—and do her screaming on the landing.

Director Siodmak had the camera perched on the stairway. And it turned out to be a tough job keeping Miss McGuire in focus. Time after time she pounded up the stairs, got her mouth open ready to scream—heard the cameraman's, "We haven't got her yet."

Seems the steps weren't high enough. So the carpenters got busy hoisting 'em up an inch or two, and Miss McGuire got ready to scream again. This time she tripped on her long skirts. The next time she went too far upstairs.

After two hours of this, she hit it just right and got out her screams. Next came those five precious words. Because she had spoken 'em perfectly the first time, there weren't even any re-takes.

So that washed up Miss McGuire's dialogue in this picture.[385]

Dorothy is indeed unforgettable in this picture, and her role so unique that it allows her to try out a whole range of expressions, silently and with a minimum of sentimentality. Of the other actors, George Brent, Gordon Oliver, and Rhonda Fleming are serviceable, Kent Smith stolid, Elsa Lanchester delightful. The great Ethel Barrymore, though arguably

---

[385] Virginia MacPherson, "Dorothy McGuire Finds It's Hard For Woman to Remain Silent," *Rochester (NY) Democrat and Chronicle*, October 8, 1945.

wasted in her small role, is mesmerizing as Mrs. Warren the former big-game hunter. Even immobilized in her bed, Barrymore dominates the few scenes she is in, with no visible effort. With the raising of an eyebrow and a voice that hardly ever rises above a whisper, she radiates strength and wisdom with every underplayed word, her gaze so piercing that it is a wonder it does not burn the celluloid.[386]

Helen's character benefits from no real empowerment, but this is par for the course in a 1946 Hollywood film. Though she is a resilient creature, Helen can do little but run fast in her climactic scenes, and is ultimately saved by Mrs. Warren's *deus ex machina*. The script does not allow her to be combative, relegating her to the role of pathetic victim. In later years, things would gradually change for disabled damsels in distress: even the demure, abused deaf-mute Belinda McDonald of Jean Negulesco's *Johnny Belinda* (1948) has the strength to resort to murder to protect her baby from the violence of her rapist. Seth Holt's 1961 *Scream of Fear* exploits the disability trope through its intelligent protagonist Penny Appleby (Susan Strasberg), but it is all a ruse to expose the killer: Penny is not disabled after all, and in her climactic scene, having solved the murder mystery, she rises triumphantly from her wheelchair. In 1967, in Terence Young's *Wait Until Dark*, it is a blind woman's (Audrey Hepburn) turn to be resourceful in exploiting her very disability to defend herself from a psychotic killer, by using darkness to her advantage. Finally, in Guillermo del Toro's Oscar-winning *The Shape of Water* (2017), a mute cleaner, Elisa Esposito, strikes a blow for disabled victims everywhere by falling in love with a regal "Amphibian Man," defeating her abuser, and enacting an

---

[386] In a story Dorothy told the cast members of the play *I Never Sang for My Father* in 1987 (see Part I, Chapter 16), she mentioned working with Ms. Barrymore. Here is colleague Daniel J. Travanti recounting that episode: "She talked about the time when she worked with Ethel Barrymore in *The Spiral Staircase*. She said that she was in awe of the actress, and when she met her, she was so nervous, she was on edge through the whole film. She said about Barrymore, 'Those *eyes!*'" (Daniel J. Travanti, conversation with the author, March 2018.)

extraordinary metamorphosis with her lover that enables her to live in a medium where speech does not matter: water.

Ethel Barrymore and Dorothy McGuire in a production still for *The Spiral Staircase*. RKO Radio Pictures, 1946.

Thomas M. Pryor of the *New York Times* thought that *The Spiral Staircase*'s subject was unsubtle and obvious, but loved the acting, as well as Siodmak's work:

> That Mr. Siodmak and his players, notably Dorothy McGuire, had a packed early-morning house under their spell most of the time was evident by the frequent spasms of nervous giggling and the audible, breathless sighs.[387]

Of Dorothy's performance, he wrote:

---

[387] Thomas M. Pryor, "The Spiral Staircase," *New York Times*, February 7, 1946.

As a mute serving-girl in a sinister household, where family hatreds are deep and searing, Miss McGuire gives a remarkably lucid performance in pantomime. Her characterization of one who senses a dread shadow hovering over her but is incapable of communicating her fears, is restrained and effectively pathetic. In this day of much talk on the screen few actresses would dare to undertake a role which only permitted six words of speech. Miss McGuire is to be heartily commended for her adventurousness and the high degree of resourcefulness with which she has tackled the demanding and little used art of pantomime.[388]

Dorothy with Kent Smith in *The Spiral Staircase*. Production still, detail. 1946, RKO Radio Pictures.

---

[388] Ibid.

The folks at *Variety* liked the film and called it "a smooth production [...], ably acted and directed." They were enthusiastic about Dorothy:

> Dorothy McGuire's stature as actress will be increased by her performance as a maidservant bereft of speech by a shock since childhood [...]. Miss McGuire's portrayal of a tongue-tied girl in love; the pathos of her dream wedding-scene; her terror when pursued by the murderer—are all etched sharply for unforgettable moments.[389]

An impish Helen teases the formidable Mrs. Warren (who is pretending to be asleep) in this scene from *The Spiral Staircase*. Production still, © 1946, RKO Radio Pictures.

---

389 *Variety*, "Spiral" (1946), op. cit.

The London *Telegraph*, in Dorothy's obituary, commented about *The Spiral Staircase* (which it called "her best film"):

> [McGuire] might, just, have become a precursor of Meryl Streep. Her early film, *The Spiral Staircase* (1946), in which she played a mute servant girl menaced by a serial killer whose identity and presence she could not verbally reveal, was a small triumph of visual signals and changing facial expressions.[390]

Wood Soanes of the *Oakland Tribune* was pleased with the film, and glowing about Dorothy's performance:

> [The film] provides Miss McGuire, who came into fame in "Claudia," on stage and screen, and who won further laurels in "A Tree Grows in Brooklyn," with an opportunity to give one of the really fine performances to reach the screen [...].
> [...] Miss McGuire's performance is as close to perfection as one could ask [...].[391]

Perhaps the most enthusiastic appraisal of Dorothy's performance came from Dorothy's staunch supporter since her Broadway days, Harold V. Cohen of the *Pittsburgh Post-Gazette*:

> Being speechless, of course, has natural advantages. For the eyes [of the spectator] never leave Miss McGuire as they look at the dread that's written in her face. But that also places quite a burden on the actress; a false emotion and caricature is liable to set in. Miss McGuire, however, never falters; her

---

[390] *Telegraph*, Dorothy McGuire obituary, September 18, 2001.

[391] Wood Soanes, "Curtain Calls: Dwarf Steals 'Saratoga Trunk,'" *Oakland Tribune*, March 29, 1946.

make-believe is quick and sure-footed, and she puts an extra little bulge on the goose-pimples "The Spiral Staircase" produces.

[. . .] But most of all, it is Miss McGuire's stunning performance that pushes "The Spiral Staircase" beyond the boundaries of the simple shocker. Her timing is superb and her movements are flawless. With only her frightened eyes and expressive hands, she is able to illustrate the terror at being in a home where family hatreds are deep and brooding and where she may be the next victim of a murderous fiend. And the daylights which are constantly being scared out of Miss McGuire, with no voice to defend her, she keeps transferring to the audience.[392]

The first remake of *The Spiral Staircase* was produced for television's NBC in 1961, starring Elizabeth Montgomery as Helen, Eddie Albert as Albert Warren, and Lillian Gish as Mrs. Warren. The second remake, for film this time, was made in 1975, starring Christopher Plummer in the George Brent role and Jacqueline Bisset in the Dorothy McGuire role, with middling results. In 2000, another television remake, told with an excess of broad daylight and a dearth of dramatic logic, was broadcast by the Fox Family network. It starred Nicollette Sheridan, Judd Nelson, and Holland Taylor as the bedridden Mrs. Warren. Here, the Warren family is altogether spared the indignity of harboring a killer: for a tawdry motive of financial gain, the culprits are revealed to be the Warrens' housekeeper (Christina Jastrzembska), biological mother to one of the Warren sons, and the young family handyman (David Storch).

---

[392] Harold V. Cohen, "New Film: Dorothy McGuire At the Stanley In 'Spiral Staircase,'" *Pittsburgh (PA) Post-Gazette*, March 15, 1946.

Dorothy was featured on the cover of *LIFE* magazine on February 18, 1946, shortly after the New York premiere of *The Spiral Staircase* on February 6, 1946.

Till the End of Time (1946)
All the arguments are out in the open, and everybody's heart is worn on a sleeve, in *Till the End of Time*, a sensitive post-war drama based on Niven Busch's novel of the same title, scripted by Allen Rivkin and directed by Edward Dmytryk.

The film contains a series of vignettes in the lives of three young soldiers re-adjusting to civilian life after serving in World War II: Marines Cliff Harper (Guy Madison) and William Tabeshaw (Robert Mitchum), and Tabeshaw's hospital friend Perry (Bill Williams), who has lost both his legs. Tabeshaw had a silver plate implanted in his head after he was injured in Iwo Jima; and Cliff may not have been injured physically, but he is pretty confused and disturbed psychologically. Thus, all the interactions between these young people are interactions between damaged souls.

Despite its on-the-nose dramatics, its tendency to explain rather than to dramatize, and Edward Dmytryk's tepid direction, the film offers nonetheless tender, compassionate portraits of the lead characters' plights.

A behind-the-scenes still for RKO Radio Pictures' *Till the End of Time* (1946). Sitting in the car, Dorothy (Pat Ruscomb) and Loren Tindall (Pinky).

Most effective, and most interesting, is Cliff Harper's relationship with Pat Ruscomb (Dorothy), a young war widow who is fairly confused herself. Pat has reacted to the loss of her husband by hiding behind a levelheaded, easy-going, cynical façade. She is introduced as a casual flirt and an easy conquest for young Cliff. As the truth about her family loss emerges, Cliff reacts with childish moralism. Their entire relationship, in fact, is a series of love-me-and-leave-me conflicts, eventually tempered by cool rationalizations, frank confessions and unrealistic personal ambitions.

Robert Mitchum (left) and Guy Madison as WWII soldiers returning home in RKO Radio Pictures' *Till the End of Time* **(1946). Production still.**

Pat is an adult character, and her relationship with Cliff an adult relationship, despite their young ages. She seems twenty years his senior in some ways, and his confused child in need of fatherly advice in others. Their discussions about their lives, their desires, and their dreams and torments are as frank and uninhibited as the times permitted. Delicate those discussions might be, but the writer, the director and the players never intentionally hide anything of themselves. Dorothy, more overtly sensual and flirtatious than ever before (or since), is surprisingly realistic as a conflicted woman, despite some of the necessary 1940s soft-pedaling. Cliff and Pat are ready to admit that they are confused, which is a healthy, honest character trait in the long run. An example of this well-written honesty occurs during their first lovemaking scene at Pat's apartment:

Cliff: I've got to tell you something. It's true. I saw you, funny things happened. Couldn't wait to put my arms around you.
Pat: Don't be frightened. It isn't love.
Cliff: I don't think so. What is it?
Pat: Lots of things. Growing up, six-eight-ten months in the Pacific, uh . . . juke-box joint, and in a room that's not too crowded. All those things.
Cliff: Half of them's enough.
(They kiss.)
Pat: You're pretty grown up. For a kid your age.
Cliff: If you're laughing at me, I don't like it.
Pat: I'm sorry.

It is unfortunate that Guy Madison, a likable player, is such a naive, childish actor. Who knows what the relationship between these two characters could have become with a more expert male lead. But, at twenty-four, Madison is stunning, and looks the part; and it is refreshing to see Dorothy paired romantically with such a fine physical specimen.

The *New York Times* reviewer was quite annoyed by the characters' "immaturity":

> They find love, or something resembling the same, at first sight, have a misunderstanding and make up, quarrel again and find bliss in each other's arms until finally one is quite exasperated with their juvenile behavior.[393]

But in fact, that very immaturity, that confusion, makes them healthier: they are honest about their confusion, a confusion that many "normal" people share with them, in love as in life. It is true that Pat and Cliff's spats display a substantial amount of childishness; on the other hand, to

---

393 "Post-War Film, 'Till the End of Time,' Offered at Rivoli," *New York Times*, July 24, 1946.

expect two youngsters to be mature would be to expect them to be conventional movie characters rather than human beings. About the performances, the *New York Times* had this to say:

> With the exception of Dorothy McGuire's characterization of the moody girl and Robert Mitchum's portrayal of the breezy cowboy, there is nothing exceptional about the performances. Guy Madison, who plays Cliff Harper, is a personable youngster, but he has much to learn about the art of acting.[394]

Guy Madison and Dorothy in a production still for *Till the End of Time*. © 1946, RKO Radio Pictures.

Variety liked the film well enough, but suggested that it was "earnest but overlong," and might have benefited from "a well-oiled shears and some generous snipping." About Madison, it opined:

---

[394] Ibid.

Dorothy with Guy Madison in a promotional still for *Till the End of Time*, probably one of a series taken by famed photographer Ernest A. Bachrach for the film.

As the central figure, [Madison] doesn't dig deep enough into his part to explain convincingly the source of his discontent. Superficial performance deprives his characterization of the psychiatric overtones, which the script apparently marked out.[395]

And about Dorothy:

Miss McGuire, armed with her usual charm and elfin appeal, does a bangup job as the war widow. She does manage to

---

[395] "Till the End of Time," *Variety*, June 12, 1946.

get across the sense of loss which blocks her return to normal emotional responses.[396]

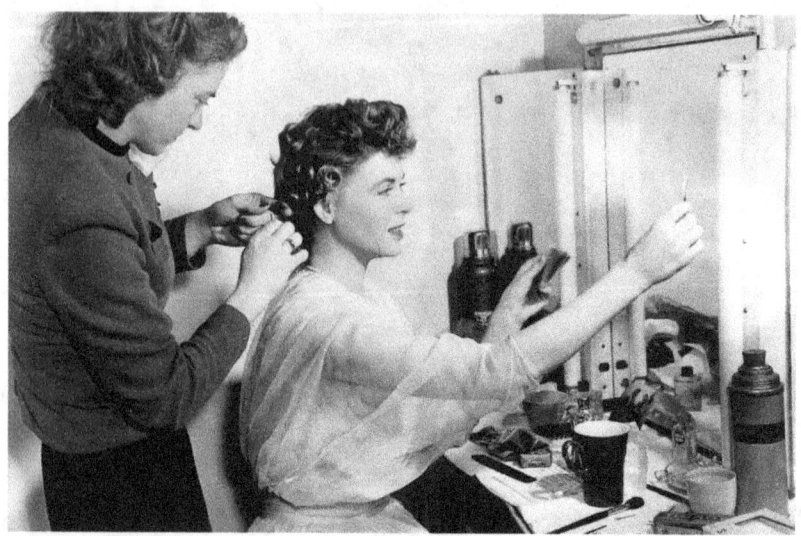

Dorothy (right) with studio hairdresser Kay Shay, preparing for a test for the film *Till the End of Time*. Incidentally, this preliminary, unfinished hairdo looks better on Dorothy than the definitive one she wore in the film (see photo on page 274).

Herbert Kohn of the *Brooklyn Eagle* gave a balanced, moderately positive appraisal of the film. Here is an excerpt:

> "Till the End of Time" moves at a leisurely pace in small circles, very much like 23-year-old ex-Marine Cliff Harper, who also runs in circles looking for a place to anchor himself. It sets its scene slowly, watching Harper come home, catching the sentiment of his return to his family, noting how he tried to pick up the threads of his life only to find that he didn't "fit" with the jitterbug crowd, that he was far behind the men his

---

[396] Ibid.

own age who had moved on in civilian war jobs, that there was no one around who understood the futility he felt except a career sergeant in the Marines who could do nothing but help him with jobs that put him on edge. "Till the End of Time" is only episodically dramatic, but it is straight out of life, as true as a news reel. And it never ceases to be honest, sincere and full of heart.[397]

Harold V. Cohen of the *Pittsburgh Post-Gazette* expressed his absolute disdain of the film rather irately, but his admittedly negative appraisal of Dorothy was mitigated by his pitiless (and justifiably so) critique of her co-star:

> If the writing in "Till the End of Time" is stringy and laborious, the direction of Mr. Edward Dymtryk [sic] and the acting are probably more so. The usually able Miss Dorothy McGuire is at her least effective as the wistful widow of a bomber pilot who doesn't quite know in what direction to head, but that may be partly due to her leading man. Miss McGuire has a good case of non-support here against Mr. Guy Madison, for the inexperienced lad is hopelessly inadequate and stumbles through the role without the slightest idea of what it's all about.[398]

I Want You (Samuel Goldwyn/RKO, 1951)
This film was not well received upon its release, and has been largely forgotten since. It was reviewed ambivalently by *Variety*, and negatively by

---

[397] Herbert Kohn, "Dorothy McGuire in a Touching Drama at the Rivoli; Mason at Winter Garden," *Brooklyn Eagle*, July 24, 1946.

[398] Harold V. Cohen, "The New Film: Dorothy McGuire At The Stanley in "Till The End of Time," *Pittsburgh (PA) Post-Gazette*, October 12, 1946.

the *New York Times*; it was also called "dull" and "tepid" by one of its stars, Farley Granger.[399] In all honesty, *I Want You* is not as bad as the above opinions might suggest, and benefits from two things at least: a classy old-Hollywood look and feel, and the earnest underplaying of its lead players. *Variety* also thought that the film was "devoid of any real dramatic highpoints." I beg to differ.

The story, initially narrated in voice-over by its nominal protagonist in an amiable tone reminiscent of the opening narration of Orson Welles' *The Magnificent Ambersons* (1942), reveals its choral nature fairly soon. The real protagonist of the film is an entire family: the Greers. Martin Greer (Dana Andrews) is the protagonist/narrator, but is surrounded by characters that are no less important than he is: his father Thomas (Robert Keith), his mother Sarah (Mildred Dunnock), his wife Nancy (Dorothy McGuire), and his younger brother Jack (Farley Granger). This Greer microcosm intersects the lives of two other microcosms: the Turner family, in the persons of young Carrie Turner (Jack's main squeeze, played by Peggy Dow) and her parents Judge Turner (Ray Collins) and his wife (Marjorie Crossland); and the Kress family, in the persons of George Kress Jr. (Martin Milner) and his father George Sr. (Walter Baldwin). The film observes these families' reactions to the beginning of the Korean War, and to the drafting of American men within each of those family units.

I believe *Variety*, the *New York Times* and Farley Granger were excessively stern in their judgments. The film is not so much "dull" or "tepid" as conversational: it introduces itself—through Martin Greer's relaxed narration—as a delicate drama bordering on comedy (or vice versa), *Our Town*-style, and allows its family vignettes to unfold softly and without hurry. Many of these vignettes seem unimportant, almost inconsequential; the gloomy angel of war and patriotism is left hovering over the story,

---

[399] Farley Granger with Robert Calhoun, *Include Me Out: My Life from Goldwyn to Broadway*," St Martin's Press, 2007, 116.

but is allowed to flap its wings and create ripples in the story's tone only sporadically.

Despite *Variety*'s statements to the contrary, there *are* dramatic "highpoints." The most surprising of these is a splendid scene which occurs about two thirds into the film, powerfully and unexpectedly, momentarily shattering both the pace and the balance of the relaxed storytelling around it. Oddly, the scene involves a character that has heretofore been a peripheral one: Martin's mother Sarah, the quiet, long-suffering family matriarch. Her character has been simmering with unspoken reproach until this point. After seeing Jack off at the train station as he leaves for his Army training, she returns home (to the living room that her husband Thomas has proudly decorated with war relics) and finally explodes, interrupting one of Thomas's military boasts:

(Thomas and Sarah Greer enter their living room. He is cheerful; she is numb.)
Thomas: I'll bet that boy'll go far in the army. He's like I was when I was his age! I'm gonna write him to have his picture taken in uniform right away.
(Sarah approaches the fireplace mantel, filled with war bric-a-brac.)
Thomas (cont'd): And we'll put it here beside Riley and Martin–
(Suddenly, Sarah sweeps all the bric-a-brac off the mantel with a violent gesture; it clatters noisily to the floor. As Thomas rushes to pick up some pieces, she proceeds to one of the walls,, and takes down some swords that were hanging on it.)
Thomas (cont'd): What on earth . . . What are you doing!
Sarah: I hate this room. I've hated it for twenty years. I've had enough. No more.
Thomas: Sarah, you can't do that!
Sarah: Oh, can't I. You just watch me.
(Sarah keeps taking war memorabilia off walls, tables, etc.)
Sarah (cont'd): Guns, bayonets, flags . . . and another thing: you, the hero, the veteran of Luneville and Baccarat!

(Bewildered, Thomas has been putting objects back up on the mantel; Sarah now throws them down again.)

Sarah (cont'd): *If I ever hear you mention one of those places again, I'm going to tell everybody what I know about you.*

Thomas: *Sarah, what's come over you?*

Sarah: *Liar. You crazy, crazy liar! You never were in any one of those places and you know it. You never heard a shot fired! You were in Paris all through the war, shining up a general's boots, bringing him bicarbonate of soda in the morning when he'd drunk too much the night before. I went along with you. I thought it was childish, foolish, but I didn't think it did any harm. I thought if it made you feel any better to pretend you'd won the war alone, who did it hurt? Then I saw something. When your son Riley was killed, you were proud. When Martin was missing for four days in France, it made you feel important. You were a big man in Iverson's Bar for an evening.*

(Thomas sinks down in an armchair, devastated.)

Sarah (cont'd): *Well, that's all over. You can take all this junk right back where you captured it with your own two hands: back to the pawn shops on Sixth Avenue in New York. As of this evening, there are no more professional heroes in this house!*

It is a credit to actress Mildred Dunnock, to writer Irwin Shaw and to director Mark Robson that the above scene is as effective as it is. So effective, in fact, that Dunnock's character suddenly becomes a powerful, and powerfully ambivalent, moral pivot in the whole issue of war or no war, patriotism or no patriotism. That credit must be renewed when, in a later scene, as Sarah is bidding farewell to her elder son Martin, who has decided to enlist voluntarily, Sarah remarks, with devastating resignation, "*Goodbye, Son. [. . .] Seems all my life I've been saying goodbye to my sons.*" Here, Dunnock's mother figure becomes elevated to the status of a true tragic character.

No such honor is reserved for Dorothy's character. Nancy, the protagonist's wife, is badly underwritten. She seems to stand on the patriotic side of the fence, but her big scene halfway through the movie, where she disrupts a dinner by pointing an accusing finger at young Jack and calling him selfish and cowardly for wanting to avoid the draft, comes out of nowhere, and feels arbitrary and contrived. For the rest, Nancy's dialogue is so inane that, as a character, she virtually fades into the *faux* Americana wallpaper that coats the film.

I Want You was called "a lugubrious story" by the *New York Times*' Bosley Crowther, who admired much of the acting in the picture but concluded as follows:

> With all due regard for Mr. Goldwyn and the facile pen of Mr. Shaw, it must be said that the quality of their persuasion does not match the intensity of their concern. The home lives created for all these people are pretty mawkish and artificial affairs, looking more like the ones in the advertisements than in actual American homes. And the romance of Mr. Granger with a college girl, played by Peggy Dow, is so stilted and overstuffed with whimsey that it seems a caricature. Mark Robson, who directed the effort, might have been dressing a window for a department store.
>
> All in all the running crisis of the "cold war" has been absorbed in the cotton padding of sentiment. A straight recruiting poster would be more convincing and pack more dramatic appeal.[400]

Variety liked the acting, and wrote: "Dorothy McGuire convinces in a toned-down part."[401] Its reservations were about the dramatic power of

---

[400] Bosley Crowther, "Samuel Goldwyn's 'I Want You' Opens Run at Criterion-- Script by Irwin Shaw," *New York Times*, December 24, 1951.

[401] "I Want You," *Variety*, October 31, 1951.

the story and screenplay. *Variety* opined that the film never really got "off the ground with any real fireworks." According to the magazine, the "tone of the dramatics is quiet. The point of the entire treatise is obscure, for the pic offers no solution of its characters' problems, nor does it come to a close with any clear-cut finality."

Farley Granger thought "that the screenplay was not only dull, but felt dated." When the film was released, he did not revise his opinion: the film, he felt, was "as tepid and old-fashioned" as he had feared. On the plus side, Granger was happy to have the chance to work with the good actors in the cast, and with a personal favorite of his, Dorothy. In his autobiography, Granger recalls having a champagne lunch with Dorothy at her home during a break in rehearsals, and enjoying her company immensely. This is how he recounts what happened when they returned to the studio to resume rehearsals, "slightly giddy and light-headed":

> The reading went smoothly, except that Dorothy and I got the giggles during a confrontation scene around the dinner table. We could never get through that scene without losing it. Neither of us wanted to; in fact, we were ashamed of ourselves and tried desperately not to let it happen, but the harder we tried, the harder we laughed.
>
> The day we filmed it was hell. Remote, taciturn Dana [Andrews] finally blew his top, turning to Dottie, and yelled, "For God's sake, Dorothy, pull yourself together! Farley is just a Hollywood kid, but you're from the theater! You should know better!"
>
> She looked at me and up we went again . . . helpless. Somehow we finally got that scene in the can and the rest of the film went smoothly.[402]

---

[402] Granger/Calhoun (2007), op. cit., 117.

Columnist Hedda Hopper, always happy to say something nice about Dorothy, commented on her acting when the film (which Hopper liked) was released: "Dorothy McGuire proves again that she's our modern Helen Hayes. Her acting is great."[403]

Dorothy with Dana Andrews in a publicity still for *I Want You*. RKO Radio Pictures, 1951.

---

403 Hedda Hopper, "Carolina Cotton Due to Costar With Autry," *Los Angeles Times*, November 8, 1951.

11. Radio Days, 1938–1955

It may be true that many dramas presented by the "Playhouses" crowding the American radio airwaves between the 1920s and the 1950s were little more than "reader's digest" versions of better originals, whether novels, plays or films. It is also true, however, that the "theater of the mind" being showcased on network radio in those years was a rare opportunity for audiences to enjoy the work of the stars of film and stage, and for those stars to ply their trade and demonstrate their talent between larger projects.

It was also an opportunity for unusual castings: pairings that did not happen on the silver screen could happen on the radio waves. In her extensive career as a radio star between 1941 and 1955, Dorothy was able to work opposite several interesting leading men, such as Jack Benny ("The Man Who Came to Dinner," 1949), Humphrey Bogart ("The Valiant," 1945), Charles Boyer ("Cluny Brown," 1950), Joseph Cotten ("I'll Be Seeing You," 1945), Maurice Evans ("Romeo and Juliet," 1948), John Gielgud ("Hamlet," 1951), James Mason ("Wuthering Heights," 1951), Ray Milland ("The Winslow Boy," 1954, "Gentleman's Agreement," 1955), David Niven ("The Thief," 1952), Basil Rathbone ("A Doll's House," 1947) and Thornton Wilder ("Our Town," 1946).

Radio was performed live in front of a theater audience, without retakes, and was therefore the closest thing to an actual theatrical presentation for home listeners and for the live audience members. Not counting occasional star-studded specials (for example, "The Man Who Came to Dinner," 1949), in most instances only one or two major stars were showcased; in the majority of programs, the audience's attention could focus resolutely on the star protagonist(s), while lesser-known character actors dutifully filled the surrounding roles.

These radio programs may appear as second-rate cousins to Dorothy's film and theater career output; like the television programs she participated in two decades later, however, they were also an opportunity for Dorothy to be visible (so to speak), to keep in practice, and to essay texts she might otherwise not have tackled. They were, in other words, a glorified (and paid) form of theatrical workshop. If a negative side existed to such an interesting "theatrical presence," it had to do with three factors: (a) the occasionally inferior or derivative quality of the scripts, (b) the short rehearsal time available, and (c) the fact that Dorothy was often required to "plug" the products of the featured sponsors in place of, or together with, the program announcers.

One of the side effects of Dorothy's constant presence on the radio was that her voice—a distinctive instrument to begin with—became something of a household item. For any audience member even marginally familiar with the entertainment industry, Dorothy's fluted *mezzosoprano* was instantly recognizable. Thus, it is probably only because of the exigencies of comedic banter that, of the panel of blindfolded showbiz experts on the 1954 episode of the quiz program *What's My Line?*—columnist Dorothy Kilgallen, showman Steve Allen, actress Arlene Francis and publisher/columnist Bennett Cerf—only Swope family friend Cerf professed to guess the name attached to the voice he heard. Even when affecting a languid Southern accent, at the peak of Dorothy's fame that voice was unmistakable.

Radio Days, 1938–1955

An early photograph of Dorothy in front of the radio microphones of NBC.

Dorothy's career in radio began in 1938, well before her rise to fame in theater and in film, when she joined the cast of the soap opera *The Big Sister*, playing the character of Sue Ellen. On that occasion, one anonymous newspaper commentator wrote about the new star: "She is regarded as one of the most promising young dramatic actresses in the radio world."[404] Dorothy also made a few guest appearances to discuss her early theatrical successes (such as her guest visit to WGN's[405] weekday show

---

[404] "Around the Dial...," *Altoona (PA) Tribune*, July 18, 1938.

[405] WGN ("The World's Greatest Newspaper") was the *Chicago Tribune*'s radio station, broadcasting news, talk, and music of various kinds beginning in 1924.

"Tom, Dick, and Harry" on December 1, 1942)[406] and supporting character appearances in the "medical" soap *Joyce Jordan, M.D.* as well as in a drama broadcast by *The Free Company* ("One More Free Man," 1941).

To the best of my knowledge, Dorothy made over fifty radio appearances as a protagonist or co-protagonist between 1941 and 1955; I was able to listen to a good number of those programs, and found at least half of them excellent in terms of both the material and the performances. All of them were professional and accomplished; a few were quite extraordinary. The following are my notes on some of those productions.

Armstrong Theater of Today, December 20, 1941
Newspapers carried the following announcement (or one just like it) on December 20, 1941:

> Dorothy McGuire and James Dunn have the top roles in "Armstrong's Theater of Today," at 11 a.m., KRNT-WMT-WNAX.
>
> Dorothy McGuire appeared last season in the leading ingénue role in the still-running hit, "Claudia," and immediately shot to theatrical fame.
>
> [...] On "Armstrong's Theater of Today" Dunn and McGuire appear in a romantic drama specially written for them, and directed by Kenneth Webb.[407]

This Is My Best: "Miracle in the Rain," December 12, 1944
On December 12, 1944, Dorothy co-starred with Robert Bailey in *This Is My Best*'s radio adaptation of Ben Hecht's novella *Miracle in the Rain* (1943).

---

406 See the *Chicago Tribune*'s radio listings, December 1, 1942.

407 Radio listings, *Des Moines (IA) Register*, December 20, 1941.

Lux Radio Theatre: "The Enchanted Cottage," September 3, 1945
Dorothy would perform in eight dramas (or nine, counting one drama for the *Lux Summer Theatre*) for the anthology program *Lux Radio Theatre* between 1945 and 1955.

On September 3, 1945, *Lux Radio Theatre* produced a version of the film *The Enchanted Cottage*, which had premiered a mere seven months earlier. The two stars of the film, Dorothy McGuire and Robert Young, reprised their leading roles. The film is discussed in the previous chapter; here, I will only mention a few thoughts about the radio adaptation.

The main conceit of the film *The Enchanted Cottage* is a visual one: two lonely, unattractive people (she is homely, he is disfigured after fighting in the war) live together (as tenant and maid, initially) in a cottage that is believed to be magical in some way. As their love blossoms, it becomes so potent and genuine that they appear beautiful to each other, but to no one else. (At first, they believe that theirs is a physical transformation, but are disillusioned when the first guests intrude on their idyllic seclusion.)

Obviously, the central "gag" of the film (the disparity of visions) could not be transferred to an aural medium without losing some of its magic (such as it was). Granted, the talky, over-expository dialogue of the film also contains redundant explanations; nonetheless, there is something missing from the radio play. Ultimately, the radio transposition is an incomplete duplicate of the film, and can only serve as a pleasant way for the audience to have the illusion of keeping company with the two charming featured stars for an hour through a live rather than filmed performance. In this respect, and in terms of the two players' performances, it is a modest success.

The Lady Esther Screen Guild Theater: "The Valiant," September 17, 1945
Actor/writer Robert Middlemass wrote the radio adaptation of the play he had co-written with Holworthy Hall in 1921, entitled *The Valiant*. The *Screen Guild Theater*, or the *Lady Esther Screen Guild Theater*, as the anthology program became known after Lady Esther cosmetics assumed its

sponsorship in 1942, presented this adaptation on September 17, 1945. The cast of four included Humphrey Bogart as the prisoner, Dorothy as the girl, Pedro de Cordoba as the chaplain and author Robert Middlemass as the warden.

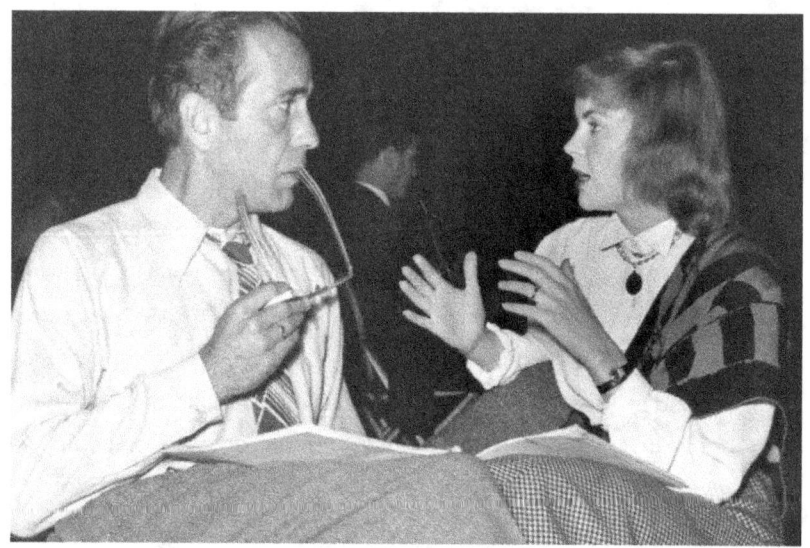

Dorothy discusses the radio play "The Valiant" with co-star Humphrey Bogart. Photo: Bob Beerman, 1945.

The story: James Dyke is a prisoner at the Connecticut State Penitentiary. He has pleaded guilty to a murder, and is an hour away from being executed. "Dyke" may be his real name, but the prison's warden and chaplain have their doubts; they have been trying to convince the prisoner to reveal his identity, so that out there some family, some mother, or some sweetheart may have closure. Dyke has always refused, and refuses still. He shows no repentance for the crime he has committed: the man he killed was a bad man, who deserved to be killed. Almost literally at the last minute, a young woman presents herself at the prison, sent by the governor; she comes from Ohio and claims that Dyke might be her vanished brother Joe. She herself was only a little girl when her brother disappeared, but she claims there are details of their childhood habits only she and her brother would know, such as their ritual of wishing each other good night by quoting Shakespeare's Romeo and Juliet's parting words at dawn. The warden allows her to speak to Dyke alone, in the hope that she might learn the truth. Dyke consents.

Josie Paris's quest for the truth is disappointing: Dyke insists that the name he is using is his own, and that he has never had a sister. He does not read books and knows nothing about poetry or Shakespeare.

Suddenly, the name of the woman's brother, Joseph Paris, rings a bell with Dyke, and he tells Josie a convincing story of how he was present at a young officer's death during the war; the officer's name was Joseph Anthony Paris, and he died a hero; Dyke is glad that Josie and her mother can finally learn the truth about what happened to their Joe.

Josie's presence has melted Dyke's stoic hardness somewhat, and he expresses the desire to receive a proper goodbye from someone, even if that someone (Josie) is nothing to him. She says he can kiss her if he likes. They kiss. She leaves with tears in her eyes, warmly bidding Dyke farewell by quoting *Romeo and Juliet*. As the door closes and she is out of hearing range, Dyke suddenly launches into another quotation from *Romeo and Juliet*: "*Sleep dwell upon thine eyes, peace in thy breast. Would I were sleep and peace, so sweet to rest.*" The warden comes in, and tells Dyke it is time. But Dyke does not stop and, ignoring the warden, continues to declaim, switching to Act II of Shakespeare's *Julius Caesar*: "*Of all the wonders that I yet have heard, It seems to me most strange that men should fear, Seeing that death, a necessary end, Will come when it will come.*" As the warden insists, calling his name, Dyke continues: "*Cowards die many times before their deaths. The valiant never taste of death but once.*"

The warden calls his name again. This time, Dyke answers, "*All right. Let's go,*" getting up to follow the warden and the chaplain. And now, in a wonderful *coup de theatre*, the chaplain starts declaiming the Bible as Dyke continues to repeat the line "*The valiant never taste of death but once,*" again and again, alternating with each line of the chaplain's prayer. The music swells, and the play comes to an end.

Thus, the doubt is planted in the listeners' minds that Dyke might be the girl's brother after all, and that he might be lying to spare her the sorrow of (a) having a criminal in the family and (b) witnessing his execution. Maybe. But maybe not.

The play, built on a series of interlocked reticences on Dyke's part, is quite intriguing, and the possible revelation/surprise in the final scene quite moving. Much of the play's focus is on the character of Dyke, and Bogart is magnificent in the part. Always a specialist in playing gruff, disillusioned men with hearts of gold, Bogart unravels the first section of Dyke's story with his customary bitter dryness; in the final act, however, he pulls off a series of vocal transformations to his character, one more startling than the other.

Yet everything is subtle enough to make each of those transformations as ambiguous as it is stirring. A complex crisscrossing of subtextual undercurrents runs below the reticent text of this denouement, pulling the characters forward with the impetus of some mysterious riptide, almost despite themselves. I spoke of subtlety; most surprising of all is Bogart's use of his voice to indicate, with extreme delicacy, those subtextual currents. Bogart reveals himself a sophisticated, sensitive voice artist here, and the result is golden.

Some Internet bloggers dealing with old-time radio have declared themselves disturbed by the supposed erotic/romantic charge of the relationship between Dyke and the young woman, and by their kiss.[408] I believe they are worrying over nothing, and prudishly so. Even assuming that the character of Dyke is indeed the girl's sibling (despite his protestations to the contrary), one gets the sense that their brief encounter is never romantic, and certainly never erotic. There is tenderness between them, of course; both the prisoner's desire to kiss the girl and her willingness to submit seem to point to the loneliness, sadness and repressed warmth of both the characters. But the kiss they exchange is chaste; it is sorrowful,

---

408 For example, The Bogie Film Blog (bogiefilmblog.wordpress.com).

desperate and full of desire (desire for human contact, for closeness, for affection), but it is not sexual. The above is all the more true if Dyke is not the girl's brother.

Those undercurrents below the surface of the text—the themes of the play, which, felicitously, are not stated explicitly—have to do with longing, loneliness, loss, death, self-sacrifice and honor. This play is not a romance, so there is no danger in that kiss.

Dorothy is fine in her part, which is linear and rather simple; all the complexity of the play is reserved for Dyke, so Dorothy can only deliver a tender, heartfelt portrayal of an uncomplicated character (playing younger than her age), while knowing that Bogart will probably steal the show from under her feet. He does.

Lux Radio Theatre: "I'll Be Seeing You," December 24, 1945
On Christmas Eve, 1945, Joseph Cotten reprised his role from the 1944 film *I'll Be Seeing You* for *Lux Radio Theatre*, while Dorothy took on Ginger Rogers' part. Sentimental the story certainly was, but it was conducted with conviction and sensitivity by both actors.

Mary Marshall (McGuire) and Sergeant Zach Morgan (Cotten) have secrets they would rather keep to themselves. Zach has just been released from the military hospital where he is being treated for shell shock, and Mary has been generously let out of prison for the holidays so that she can spend Christmas and New Year's with her aunt and uncle. They meet on the train that is taking Mary to Pinehill, and lie about their conditions: she introduces herself as a traveling salesperson, he as a sergeant on a furlough. When she gets off the train, he does too, pretending that he is visiting his sister. Mary tells him how he can reach her. He checks into the local YMCA.

While chatting with her aunt, uncle and niece, Mary receives a phone call from Zach, who tells her his sister is away and invites her to join him for dinner. Mary's aunt suggests inviting him to dinner at their place instead.

The romance begins. Both characters are attracted to each other, both are uncomfortable in their lies. The secret of Zach's mental imbalance after being shell shocked in the war and the secret of Mary's conviction for involuntary manslaughter are gradually revealed to the audience (through inner monologues in Zach's case, through dialogue with her family in Mary's case) but not to each other. Thus, as the story progresses the two young outcasts sink deeper both in their affection for each other and in their hiding the truth from each other (or mixing truth with fiction).

Zach and Mary's frequentation of each other is as idyllic as it can be, given the circumstances, and their flawed love blooms between Christmas and New Year's. By then, it is time for both of them to return to their respective prisons. It is while Mary is getting ready to accompany Zach to the train station that Zach finds himself alone at the dining table with Mary's young niece Barbara, who, glib, foolish girl that she is, inadvertently blurts out information about Mary's prison sentence. Zach falls silent, and is gloomy all the way to the station. He boards the train, and Mary guesses what must have happened. Resigned that their love must be shattered, Mary returns to her aunt's home to pack for prison.

She arrives at the prison gate and rings the bell to be let in. The guard tells her she still has some time left, and informs her that there is a man waiting for her at the corner. It is Zach, who has come to declare his love for Mary, who reciprocates joyfully. These two lonely, flawed people need each other.

Both stars acquit themselves admirably. The real surprise here is Cotten. The star of Orson Welles's Mercury Theatre both on Broadway and on the air, and Katharine Hepburn's Broadway co-star in the original *The Philadelphia Story*, Cotten had a low-pitched, raspy voice that could often make him sound inexpressive. Here, as in some of his best film roles, he reveals a sensitive, poetic use of his vocal instrument, keeping his croakiness in check and modulating his performance almost musically. Thus, both his character's inner turmoil and his love scenes with Dorothy's Mary are quite believable and touching.

Theatre Guild on the Air: "Our Town," September 29, 1946
Theatre Guild on the Air was arguably the most prestigious, and ambitious, radio drama program gracing the American airwaves. Here is some background information from the radio logs of the excellent website the Digital Deli Too: Preserving the Golden Age of Radio for a Digital Future:

> United States Steel Corporation, for decades by then one of the Blue Chip stocks and corporations of the 20th Century, found an opportunity to mount one of Radio's most prestigious drama anthologies near the waning years of The Golden Age of Radio. The relatively young ABC network was just making a name for itself in 1945 and 1946. It was a great coup for ABC and it was a relative bargain for U.S. Steel. And so it was that U.S. Steel and ABC brought *Theatre Guild On the Air* to Radio for the first time on September 9, 1945, the first of over eight years of broadcasts over two major networks.
>
> During a run that would span eight seasons, *Theatre Guild On the Air*'s per show budget averaged between $10,000 and $15,000 per 60-minute program. First airing for four seasons on ABC, the program premiered over NBC in the fall of 1949 for another four successful seasons. The talent costs over the run of the series can be borne out by reviewing the starring talent that U.S. Steel brought to the series. The greatest names from Stage and Screen gave the entire run it's [sic] well-earned patina of quality and polish. With Hooper Ratings over the years varying from an 8.3 share to a 12.1 share, and given the program's late night timeslot on the east coast and it's [sic] 60-minute length, the ratings supported the popularity of the series.
>
> The headline performers for every *Theatre Guild On the Air* program throughout its entire run comprised the greatest names from Stage and Screen, generally two featured big

name actors for every production, and as many as three to five for some productions. Most of the competing drama anthologies of the late 1940s featured one major stage or screen star to headline their productions. But with a no holds barred budget U.S. Steel's productions combined the greatest talents of the era, irrespective of the cost.

Acting couples were also prominently featured, often two to three times during a season. Frederic [sic] March and Florence Eldridge appeared in five productions together. Burgess Meredith, in addition to appearing in the premiere presentation over ABC and numerous subsequent performances also appeared with wife Paulette Goddard twice. Charles Laughton and Elsa Lanchester appeared together twice. Alfred Lunt and Lynn Fontaine [sic] appeared together in eight performances over the series' run. Jessica Tandy and Hume Cronyn appeared together during both the ABC run and the NBC run. Great character actor Walter Huston appeared in numerous performances over the first two seasons of *Theatre Guild On the Air*. Helen Hayes appeared in twelve programs over the run. David Niven appeared in five presentations.

If the above name stars are giving you an impression of the caliber of talent, you can understand the almost unprecedented cost of these productions over their eight seasons. With an estimated $15,000 budget for name talent alone, the weekly cost of each production would have been in the neighborhood of $18,000 to $20,000 per production, or a seasonal cost of approximately $750,000. Over all eight seasons, U.S. Steel poured an estimated $6M into their landmark production.[409]

Taking the directorial helm of the *Theatre Guild*'s productions for

---

409 *Digital Deli Too* website radio logs, "The Theatre Guild On The Air."

much of its run was Homer Fickett (1898–1953), a colorful character with little or no theater training but a healthy ambition and an impetuous temperament. Here is a sketch of the man from a 1948 Associated Press profile written shortly after Dorothy's performance in the *Guild*'s *Romeo and Juliet*:

> A wide-waisted, heavy-shouldered man who looks like Winston Churchill bosses more stars than any other director in the despotic, temperamental, complicated state of confusion called show business.
>
> As director of the Theatre Guild on the Air for three seasons, Homer Fickett hires a different brace of stage or motion picture stars every week, 42 weeks a year. In the course of a month he will work with, fuss over and rule such diverse talents as Maurice Evans, Dorothy McGuire, Florence Reed, Ray Milland, Marlene Dietrich, Burgess Meredith, Judy Holliday, Eddie Albert and Paul Douglas.
>
> Alfred Lunt and Lynn Fontanne appear on the air only under his direction. Miss Fontanne says simply, "He understands our foibles."
>
> [. . .] He is a magnet for the creative force in actors. His strength probably lies in knowing his stars, relying on their thespic judgment, and keeping order in the house.
>
> During rehearsals of "Romeo and Juliet" he said several times to Dorothy McGuire: "That isn't quite what I want." Finally she said, "Here, you read it!" But he couldn't. Unlike most of his colleagues Fickett was never an actor. He was a newspaperman in his home town of Rochester and Buffalo.
>
> Years ago, Fickett fostered such stunts as Ted Husing broadcasting from an airplane or Dewolf Hopper speaking from the top of the Empire State Building. He was exploring

the possibilities of the new medium for an advertising agency in Philadelphia.

Since then he has been director of "March of Time," "Cavalcade of America," "The Inside Story" and "This is My Best,"

His direction is almost invisible, but effective. [. . .][410]

Dorothy appeared in eleven *Theatre Guild on the Air* presentations between 1946 and 1953.

On September 29, 1946, the *Theatre Guild on the Air* broadcast a one-hour adaptation of Thornton Wilder's play *Our Town* (1938), starring Thornton Wilder himself in the role of the Narrator/Stage Manager and Dorothy as Emily. The relationship of young George Gibbs and Emily Webb constitutes the spine of Wilder's story, but the play is really a meta-theatrical ensemble piece, pointing as it does a spotlight on many moments in the lives of the inhabitants of the Appalachian town of Grover's Corners between 1901 and 1913. Just as, on the stage, the play does so virtually without scenery and props, in this radio adaptation it can put its points across without bodies, faces, and physical space.

The narrator (played here by playwright Wilder) addresses the audience directly, and the play is performed as a theatrical work in progress, on an empty stage. The touching story is both very specific (the small town, the milkman, the minister, the lovers, the mother, the father, etc.) and very universal (all the characters are Everyman and Everywoman), and the characters' relationships are small parables of the foibles humans must undergo while on this earth.

Though both the theatrical device and the commentary on human life are interesting, the play's insights are not intellectual: they never reach the intricacy of kindred meta-theatrical authors such as Pirandello or Beckett. Pirandello articulated human topics such as personal identity and truthfulness by delving deep into the human psyche and intellect, and

---

[410] Jean Meegan (AP), "Mr. Fickett Bosses Stars," *Cincinnati (OH) Enquirer*, May 2, 1948.

delving, and delving, with a rational ferocity that had few equals in the theatrical world of the twentieth century.[411] Wilder's investigation, on the other hand, is poetic rather than intellectual. Within the realm of poetic observation, his play is chock-full of examples of an illuminating, intuitive understanding of human nature, such as the brilliant wedding act—where, in this adaptation, the playwright lets all the characters speak their innermost thoughts out loud (and not to each other), thus revealing their inner conflicts explicitly. Wilder's play is endowed with a lilting lyricism that, paired with its human observation, is often quite sublime.

The play's theatrical abstraction—its universality—points to a fundamentally metaphysical intent, which becomes explicit in the last act, where the dead are allowed to speak, and to comment on the living, and on life. Through the Stage Manager, who acts as a link between the two groups, the play takes on an omniscient, high vantage point to tell its story. Cold and warm, impersonal and friendly, the Stage Manager is simultaneously a theatrical prop, an omniscient narrator, and a character who acts as a tuning fork for the instruments of the play. In the extraordinary third act, he and the departed souls of Grover's Corners take the liberty of making matter-of-fact pronouncements about immortality, about the imperfect experience of life, about death, about Purgatory and the Afterlife, and—very discreetly, between the lines—about reincarnation, or at least incarnation, and about the soul being "weaned away from earth" to continue its voyage.

Dorothy was not the original Emily in the 1938 Broadway production of *Our Town*; she was, however, Martha Scott's understudy. When Scott was signed for the film version (1940), Dorothy took over for the remainder of the run (on her first night, notably, with Wilder as Stage Manager). So, she was the *second* Broadway Emily. In this radio produc-

---

411 For example in his complex dramas *Il giuoco delle parti* (1918), *Sei personaggi in cerca d'autore* (1921), *Enrico IV* (1922), and *Così è (se vi pare)* (1925). It is a pity that Dorothy never essayed Pirandello on the stage: she would have been perfect for many of the author's extraordinary female characters.

tion, her status as "second" Emily is elevated by the presence of Wilder himself as Narrator; it is as if Wilder were personally choosing Dorothy all over again, eight years down the line, as protagonist of his play.

Dorothy as Emily Webb, with playwright Thornton Wilder and John Craven (the original George Gibbs, right) during the 1938 Broadway run of *Our Town*.]

It is easy to see why: the part fits Dorothy like a glove. She is perfect as the nice, sensitive young girl (the character is not yet sixteen when the play opens) and young woman, and her charming exchanges with the character of George especially are perfection. She is particularly touching in the scene that closes Act I, where she weaves a magical little monologue (at least in this adaptation; not in the play) about the moonlight, the stars, the solar system, the universe, and the distant sound of a train horn—counterpointed by the repetition of the boyish, naïve wonder of the more prosaic George ("*What do you know!*"). And, she is absolutely heartbreaking in Emily's beautiful final scenes, following her death, when she returns as a ghost bidding her nostalgic, philosophical farewell to George, to her family, to her town, and to the world ("*O Earth, you're too wonderful for anybody to live on.*"). Life and death, life and theater, human beings' relationship with life, visible and invisible realities—all the levels of existence intermingle in this beautiful play, and in this beautiful rendition of it.

Theatre Guild on the Air: "A Doll's House," January 19, 1947
On January 19, 1947, the prestigious *Theatre Guild on the Air* presented a one-hour adaptation of Henrik Ibsen's *A Doll's House*, starring Dorothy in the lead role of Nora Helmer and Basil Rathbone as her husband Torvald. Ibsen's seminal play, revolutionary at the time of its first performance in 1879 and still strikingly modern today, dramatizes the proto-feminist story of a young woman, Nora, who comes to certain painful realizations about her married life. She realizes that she is treated by her husband Torvald, not with love and respect but with paternalistic condescension (like a child, or a doll that is to furnish him with pleasure, in fact), and that the apparently postcard-perfect middle-class family life they enjoy is perfect in theory only. By the end of her climactic argument with Torvald in Act III, she has resolved to leave him in order to discover herself and "try to become" a human being. And she explains her reasons to him in detail.

It was, on paper, a perfect vehicle for the two featured stars, paired here for the first and only time in their careers. Once the novelty of the casting wears off, unfortunately, one is faced with its failings, and with the schematic polarity of the two performances. Whether of their own accord or following direction, the two stars take a misguided, shortcut route to reach the play's conclusion. Granted, that route was fairly conventional for radio drama: it had already been taken by Rathbone and Joan Crawford in the same play when they performed it for *Lux Radio Theatre* in 1938.

First, the production as a whole has a limitation: it is played too fast. Probably in order to make the play fit within the time limit of the program, the actors go through the script quickly, breathlessly, rushing across pages and pages of the play. Which, fundamentally, means that they have no time to stop and explore, or savor, the complex, conflictual feelings and ideas that swim both on and below the surface of the text. Because of that hurry, everything sounds simplified and colorless, reduced to the mere bones of melodrama.

Though a pretextual subplot involving the threat of a blackmail scandal is indeed melodramatic, *A Doll's House* is more than a melodrama, and the skeleton of its plot does not begin to do justice to its substance. The blackmail plot device is a catalyst designed to reveal character: to allow the characters to reveal themselves to each other (and to themselves), ideas and all. As George Bernard Shaw opined when enthusiastically presenting Ibsen's "revolution" to the English public,

> [formerly] you had in what was called a well made play an exposition in the first act, a situation in the second, an unravelling in the third. Now you have exposition, situation, and discussion; and the discussion is the test of the playwright.[412]

For Shaw, in other words, Ibsen's theater was modern because it dealt with ideas, ideals, false moralities, and conventions. It dealt with the truth about societal and interpersonal relationships (which are made of ideas, ideals, archetypes, stereotypes, and prejudices, whether the subjects are aware of this or not) and with the motivations, conscious or not, that trap the characters inside those ideas and ideals. Shaw believed that

> [in] the new plays, the drama arises through a conflict of unsettled ideals rather than through vulgar attachments, rapacities, generosities, resentments, ambitions, misunderstandings, oddities and so forth as to which no moral question is raised. The conflict is not between clear right and wrong: the villain is as conscientious as the hero, if not more so: in fact, the question which makes the play interesting (when it *is*

---

[412] Bernard Shaw, *The Quintessence of Ibsenism*, Constable and Company Ltd., 1929, 187.

interesting) is which is the villain and which the hero. Or, to put it another way, there are no villains and no heroes.[413]

No villains and no heroes. The "new" plays, then, were not melodramas where black was black and white white, but moral arguments in dramatic form, where a whole gamut of gray areas, moral, rational, and dramatic, must unfold, through story and discussion both. Those shades of gray are a priceless opportunity for the subtle actors and directors who wish to rise above the emotions of melodrama to express not only ideas and ideologies but also the rich undertones, overtones and emotional subtext of the drama itself. Shaw again:

> Up to a certain point in the last act, A Doll's House is a play that might be turned into a very ordinary French drama by the excision of a few lines, and the substitution of a sentimental happy ending for the famous last scene: indeed the very first thing the theatrical wiseacres did with it was to effect exactly this transformation, with the result that the play thus pithed had no success and attracted no notice worth mentioning. But at just that point in the last act, the heroine very unexpectedly (by the wiseacres) stops the emotional acting and says: "We must sit down and discuss all this that has been happening between us." And it was by this new technical feature: this addition of a new movement, as musicians would say, to the dramatic form, that A Doll's House conquered Europe and founded a new school of dramatic art.[414]

No happy ending is substituted at the end of this radio adaptation; but the manner of execution, together with the many cuts made to Ibsen's

---

413 Ibid., 194.

414 Ibid., 192.

original text, place this version in a zone very close to the "transformation" mentioned by Shaw.

Due to the hurry of their performances in this adaptation, Dorothy and her co-star fail to express those undertones, overtones and subtext present beneath the words. Without such subterranean elements, their vocal performances simply sing the emptiest of dramatic songs. Dorothy, the *mezzo*, sings *legato*; Rathbone, the bass-baritone, sings *staccato*.

If one were to view the two featured stars in the most superficial, clichéd way (the way Hollywood often viewed them), one would find two "types": the sweet woman on the one hand, the haughty villain on the other. These two clichés Dorothy and Rathbone fatally incarnate, unsubtly, in these performances. Dorothy telegraphs the play's theme in her early scenes by overplaying Nora as if she were twelve years old, raising the pitch of her voice half an octave and relentlessly twittering (Nora's husband calls his wife "my little bird" and "my little lark") around Rathbone's bass-baritone wolf. Rathbone plays the part of Torvald the way he had played the many villains of his film career, barking his lines with stone-cold superciliousness. This tactic of his works well enough during the first two thirds of the play; it is in the heated climax and final argumentative discussion that he seems lost. His lines come out in short, loud bursts, with pauses in between, burdening the exchange with an awkward choppiness that makes a real dramatic *decrescendo* (*A Doll's House* ends, not with a bang but with a whimper) and a smooth ideal argument difficult. Haste, lack of shading, and lack of reflection are the real sins in these performances. Given the caliber of the context and the importance of the source material, one might have to regard these sins as mortal.

This is not to say that the two stars' performances are amateurish, nor that Ibsen's text does not provide clues that could be interpreted as justifications for the vocal simplification they enact. In an early scene, for instance, Nora tells her friend Christina that she is willing to play the child for Torvald to please him, because that is how he likes her. But the actors and their director choose to take those clues literally, too literally, thereby impoverishing the drama by creating stick-figure sonic portraits of the two main characters: fleshless caricatures—or badly executed Brechtian didactic embodiments—rather than conflicted, shaded human beings.

This musical simplification, played at a fast clip, allows little musical or dramatic complexity. There is no differentiation between "fast movements" and "slow movements," only a *perpetuum mobile* chugging onward for an hour. There are no significant pauses, and no room for silence; but *A Doll's House* should have silence. Nora's full realization of what is wrong in her relationship with Torvald, and her final decision to leave him, occur when she is badgered into silence by his climactic tirade to her, while he still believes that her "financial indiscretion" will ruin both his livelihood and his reputation, before the appearance of the *deus-ex-machina* letter that announces his salvation. That important moment of Nora's, the moment in which her husband's fear of scandal forces him to revile her humanity explicitly in the interest of respectability, is not to be heard but *seen*; and it may be because of the radio's lack of visuals that stars and director felt entitled to their lowest-common-denominator *reductio*.

In this respect, the fact that this version of *A Doll's House* is performed in front of microphones for the medium of radio becomes an impediment. As would be the case with another subtle play, Terence Rattigan's *The Winslow Boy*, which Dorothy performed on the airwaves in 1954, here too the performers are hindered by the absence of visuals. Expressing those subtextual undercurrents, as well as that climactic realization of Nora's, through the voice alone is not an impossible task, but it is a very difficult one: one that would probably have required far more preparation work than was normally available for these broadcasts. Being able to use their faces and bodies in a stage production would definitely have helped the actors be subtler, and would have allowed the presence of silence, an essential ingredient of drama in general and of Ibsen and Strindberg in particular. Presumably, the reason for this adaptation's avoidance of silence is that, on the airwaves, silence comes off as mere emptiness, whereas on the stage it can be "filled" by the actors through blocking, facial expression, and the use of the *whole person* to incarnate feeling.

Even a first reading of the text of this remarkable play should reveal that there is a drastic, almost cataclysmic change of tone and pace between the climactic third-act quarrel and the closing dialogue that follows it. After that quarrel, Nora returns from her room a changed woman (her dress is not all that she has changed), and the heart-to-heart talk she initiates with her husband in the final scene of the play is a quiet, serious, rational thing: "*Sit down. It will take some time; I have much to talk over with you,*"[415] she announces to him (a line that, criminally, is cut in this adaptation). Torvald's befuddled protestations try to steer the conversation in the direction of melodrama, but Nora is adamant: there is no melodrama in what she says. She is disappointed and crushed, but lucid and clear-sighted in the extreme. Something dies in Nora during that quarrel, and something else—a new awareness—springs to life. That moment of rational discussion, that "cooling off" of the heat of drama to examine what has preceded it, is a chance for *post-mortem* introspection, for a comment on the things that generated that heat for the characters in the first place. Musically, that discussion is a slow coda after the rest of the composition has played out. On the one hand, it allows the tension to unwind; on the other, it allows all the previously gathered thematic material to be revealed and autopsied. In fact, in 1879, that final discussion must have been quite surprising, for it almost makes the play meta-theatrical from the point of view of (melo)dramatic convention.

Dorothy and Rathbone enact no such change of tone, and cannot resist the temptation to be melodramatic, or to stoke the fire of sentimental passion. In fact, Ibsen's entire transition—Nora being sent to her room, Torvald's condescending monologue about her, her return, and her announcement of their heart-to-heart talk—is eliminated in this adaptation, making that all-important change unfeasible: the final husband-wife

---

[415] Henrik Ibsen, *A Doll's House*, T. Fisher Unwin, 1889, 112.

dialogue is played as if it were a direct continuation of their quarrel. This is a misinterpretation of the text, for, in that final dialogue, Nora's passion ceases as she turns inward, towards a realization so seismic, so bitter, and so existentially shattering that her only course of action is instantaneous divorce. But Ibsen's revolution does not lie in Nora's leaving her husband, though that must have been a shock to his contemporary audience too; it lies in the fact that a woman, a wife, dares to explain to her husband exactly what is wrong with him, and with their relationship. She dares to introspect, and to be rational. Nora's is not a hostile or passionate argument; it is a rational, compassionate explanation of that realization of hers to the man whose house she has shared for eight years. The ideas spilling out of her are so sane, so reasonable, and so very insightful that, in terms of melodramatic *dynamis*, she becomes untouchable by Torvald, who ultimately can only submit to the quiet conviction of her reasoning. In Dorothy's interpretation, such rational crystallinity is missing altogether, and the subtle, complex feelings stirring within Nora after her epiphany are "sung" so superficially as to make the scene blandly sentimental, like a goodbye between two lovers after a May-December romance. Significantly, one of Nora's most despairing final lines is also cut in this adaptation (I have emphasized the cut):

> Nora: [. . .] *Torvald, in that moment it burst upon me, that I had been living here these eight years with a strange man, and had borne him three children*—Oh! I can't bear to think of it—I could tear myself to pieces![416]

Nora could tear herself to pieces, not because she realizes her marriage is not ideal, but because, after living with Torvald for eight years as his wife, she realizes with horror that the two of them are nothing but perfect strangers to each other: victims of societal custom who neither

---
416 Ibid., 120.

know nor love each other. Nora realizes that what "society" has told her about marriage, religion, honor, duty, motherhood, and love is just empty convention or, at best, moral edict, and that such convention is the hiding place for a deep contempt for women in general and for their roles as wives in particular.

I do not believe that the subtleties of *A Doll's House* were necessarily beyond the reach of either Dorothy or her British co-star; but, at 30, Dorothy probably had not reached maturity as an actress yet, and this drama was obviously under-rehearsed, or tackled with considerable ingenuousness. Likewise, there is no reason to believe that this show was the result of anything but good intentions on the part of the *Theatre Guild on the Air*, a tasteful program that always aimed high and only occasionally missed the mark.

Basil Rathbone does not mention this drama specifically in his 1962 autobiography, but he does comment on the *Theatre Guild* program in general:

> In the days of radio, of The Theatre Guild on the Air be it here said that their program was ever striving for quality, intelligence, and good taste. I have played many times for them and every time I was invited it was a worthwhile experience.[417]

Notwithstanding this high praise for the program, and for a medium that "makes us use our imaginations," Rathbone also spends some harsh words about radio in general, and about television, calling them "merciless mediums for any artist, creative or interpretive" and stating that they "have been more responsible for the growth of mass mediocrity in our culture than anything else I can think of." The reason: the incestuous mingling of art and commerce.

---

[417] Basil Rathbone, *In and Out of Character: An Autobiography*, Doubleday & Company, Inc., 1962, 176.

> No art can exist, let alone progress creatively (only mechanically), through a medium that is controlled by commercials. Both radio and television have made a great contribution to information and communication and often to specific forms of education. But as art forms they simply do not exist. They could, but they don't.[418]

Apparently, either I am dead wrong in my appraisal of those two performances in *A Doll's House*, or both the critical intelligentsia and the Hollywood powers that be did not notice any flaws in them; Dorothy was glorified for her portrayal, and she herself spoke of the radio drama glowingly. Here is Hedda Hopper asking Dorothy about it in September 1947:

> I wanted to know what [McGuire] considered the next best break after "Spiral Staircase."
> "Getting to play Nora in 'A Doll's House' for the Theater Guild on the Air," she answered without hesitation. "That gave me something solid—a sense of security at last. Then hearing it on the air gave Darryl Zanuck the idea of casting me as Kathy in 'Gentleman's Agreement,' one of the most challenging parts I've ever attempted. I don't think I'd even want to do a costume thing," then she stopped short, grinned: "There I go saying that, and the first thing you know I'll find myself in hoop skirts."[419]

David O. Selznick, too, liked the broadcast, and entertained the idea of filming *A Doll's House* with Dorothy. Production plans were made and carried out for filming in England and/or Norway; the project was shelved

---
418 Ibid., 175.

419 Hopper, "Battle" (1947), op. cit.

in May 1948 (see Part I, Chapter 6). It was a good idea, especially with a proposed screenplay by Ingmar Bergman and proposed direction by Alf Sjöberg, a sensitive, sophisticated director who won the Grand Prix at the Cannes Film Festival twice, once for *Hets* (*Torment*, 1944) and once for his exquisite *Fröken Julie* (*Miss Julie*, 1950). It is a shame Sjöberg was not in charge of this radio broadcast: he would almost certainly have paced the play differently.

The Radio Reader's Digest: "Sweet Rosie O'Grady," March 13, 1947
A sweet story from the pages of *The Reader's Digest*, *Sweet Rosie O'Grady* was made rather indifferent by Robert Sloane's middling, sentimental radio script.

Margaret Hanson is a young Irish-American woman from Boston; she is in New York looking for work, and when she goes to see writer Charles Grant for a secretarial job, she evokes far-away memories in him by wearing a pin depicting a shamrock. The writer asks to examine the back of the pin; the words engraved on it, "Sweet Rosie O'Grady," confirm his suspicions: the pin belonged to the girl's grandmother, a one-time Broadway singer and dancer, and he is the one who made it for her in his days as a jeweler.

Mr. Grant plays cupid for young Margaret by introducing her to a rich young man, Dan, who readily falls in love with the girl, and is reciprocated. Whether she can fit into Dan's aristocratic surroundings is another matter, and Margaret is quite worried about it. She meets Dan's mother, who decides to fabricate some colorful stories about Margaret's past to make her worthy of traveling in their circles.

All seems to be going well, but when old-time Broadway star Rosie O'Grady comes to New York for a nostalgic comeback, Margaret attends the show with Dan and his mother, who make light of O'Grady, snobbishly. Margaret runs out of the theater in shame to wait for her grandmother backstage, and finds Dan there. It seems that he is in love with her no matter what, and is eager to meet her grandma, too. All is well that ends well.

There are glimmers of life in several of the exchanges, especially those between Margaret and Dan, but the script as a whole is flatly written, and mawkish. More importantly, whenever any real drama develops, it is resolved—one could say deflated—instantly, making the entire unfoldment feel like nothing more than a series of tempests in so many teacups. The societal shame that Margaret seems to feel in the theater, for example, vanishes as soon as Dan tells her that he loves her. He never acknowledges his snobbishness, nor does he apologize for his harsh words about Rosie O'Grady. No matter, for Margaret ceases to care about it all at the first mention of love. Yet the script plays up the dramatic tension and gives importance to Margaret's doubts and anxiety, only to ignore them in resolving them. No issue is really addressed (as Bernard Shaw would put it, there are no discussions here), which probably means that this couple is going to have its fair share of trouble in the long run. Feh.

Dorothy stoically plays the demure, sensitive aspects of her character to the hilt, in *Enchanted Cottage* mode, but is not able to rescue the script from its hopeless sappiness.

CBS: "Lantern in the Dark," April 22, 1947
Dorothy McGuire was the star of the CBS radio drama "Lantern in the Dark" on April 22, 1947. Here is a capsule description from the *Mason City Globe-Gazette* radio listings:

> [*Lantern in the Dark* is] a special CBS documentary unit program in observance of public health nursing week. The drama is based on the life of public health nurse Elsie Scott and was written from biographical material supplied by a lifelong friend of Miss Scott. The story tells of the untiring struggle of Miss Scott to promote public health measures in San

Juan county, Washington, where she found living conditions almost primitive.[420]

The Radio Reader's Digest: "Hand on the Latch," January 15, 1948
On January 15, 1948, radio audiences heard Dorothy perform a story entitled "Hand on the Latch," dramatized by Henry Jenkins and based on a short story by Mary Connelly, as it had appeared, reworked by Anthony Abbott, in *The Reader's Digest*. The radio play was produced by *The Radio Reader's Digest* for CBS, with sponsorship from Hallmark Cards (the anthology series would be renamed *Hallmark Playhouse* later that year).

The story of this domestic thriller takes place somewhere in the Old West, around the time of the Gold Rush. John, a tax collector, lives with his wife Louise and his son Tommy in an isolated cabin, far from the nearest town. On this particular evening, he comes back to his house with a large box of cash; he hides it under the floor boards of his kitchen, explaining that he has heard the bank is on the brink of failure and he does not dare deposit the money there. As a snowstorm gathers, he leaves for town again to reach the bank first thing in the morning to withdraw the family's savings. His instructions to Louise: to latch the front door shut and not to let anyone in until he gets back.

Loud knocks on the door wake Louise and Tommy during the night. It is someone claiming to be a soldier who has been attacked by a bear and needs assistance. Still somewhat suspicious, Louise lets him in at gunpoint (the gun is not loaded, but the soldier does not know it); she tends to his wound, then allows him to sleep on the kitchen floor. Early in the morning, more aggressive knocks at the door. The soldier lends Louise his loaded gun, and Louise shoots several bullets into the intruder as she opens the door. The masked robber collapses to the ground, dead. It is none other than her husband John, come to steal the money. Louise's

---

[420] Radio listings, *Mason City (IA) Globe-Gazette*, April 22, 1947.

comment: *"A stranger. He's a stranger. [He's my] husband, yes, but I don't know him. I see now: I never really knew him at all."*

Not even Dorothy's artistry can save the contrived twaddle of this script from its repetitious, overblown writing or from the ineptitude of her co-stars (Eric Dressler and Everett Sloane, both oddly ineffectual); and the predictable story is made laughable by the *coup de grace* of its hollow, simplistic, *faux*-Pirandellian moral lesson (we never really know those closest to us), totally out of place in the context of a conventional melodramatic suspenser. Shame on writers Connelly, Abbott and Jenkins.

Theatre Guild on the Air: "Romeo and Juliet," February 8, 1948
On February 8, 1948, the *Theatre Guild on the Air* (under the sponsorship of the United States Steel Corporation) presented a broadcast of William Shakespeare's *Romeo and Juliet* from its favorite broadcasting venue, the Belasco Theatre in New York.

Popular radio commentator John Crosby (1912–1991) articulated his objections to the production in his syndicated column, "Seeing Radio in Review," a week after the broadcast. Many of those same insightful objections about the formal limitations of the broadcast he would repeat for the *Guild*'s 1951 production of *Hamlet*, also starring Dorothy. Here is Crosby:

> William Shakespeare and the United States Steel Corp., both institutions of massive respectability, clasped hands a weeks ago Sunday in a Theater Guild on the Air production of "Romeo and Juliet," which means, of course, that Shakespeare finally has arrived.
>
> Recognition was slow in coming—some 300 years—but having come finally, it will mean drastic changes in Will Shakespeare's manner of life.
>
> I understand he's already discretely withdrawn from the Mermaid Tavern, where his drinking companions were of questionable background, and applied for membership in the

Union League Club.

From a scientific point of view, the skeletonized version of «Romeo and Juliet» was interesting in a number of counts that Shakespeare never planned on.

In the leading roles were Maurice Evans as Romeo and Dorothy McGuire as Juliet, a decidedly explosive mixture of temperaments and techniques.

Mr. Evans, whose voice is more highly developed and versatile than an organ, approaches Shakespeare ritualistically—if that's the word I mean. He charges every speech with passion and meaning. Each word, each phrase is given a precise modulation that makes it seem almost inevitable, as if the whole world were holding its breath waiting for that one word, that one phrase.

Actually Evans doesn't act Shakespeare; he sings it. His farewell speech as he lay dying is a little masterpiece of orchestration, starting low and ending high in the upper registers.

There are some who suffer intensely when exposed to this style of acting and I can understand why. On the other hand, I think the Evans method is the only way to take the high school auditorium smell off such lines as «By yonder blessed moon, I swear.»

Anyone who can deliver that line without reducing me to helpless laughter is a great artist, and Mr. Evans can.

In the corner opposite this great Shakespearean organ was Miss McGuire, an actress of the naturalist school and a very good one. Together they sounded like debaters arguing opposite ideologies rather than lovers.

Miss McGuire defiantly emitted her longer speeches in large, undigested lumps as if she didn't fully understand them and was, as it were, putting them on the record.

Perhaps I'm oversensitive, but it seemed to me Miss McGuire was wholly out of sympathy with her role. I somehow got the impression she felt Juliet was a silly goose of a girl who got herself into a totally unnecessary jam which with the exercise of a little common sense easily might have been averted.

It's an opinion with which I find myself in full agreement, but I don't think anyone should undertake the part of Juliet hampered by such blasphemous ideas.

If anything was needed to fill out this weird assortment of acting techniques it was the presence of Miss Florence Reed, an actress of ferocious pretensions and almost inconceivable lung power. Well, by yonder blessed moon, she was there all right, playing the part of the Nurse.

Miss Reed believes in giving the customers their money's worth; everything becomes a lot larger than life and terribly, terribly intense. The Nurse, for example, is supposed to be old, very old; in Miss Reed's hands, she became Pleistocene.

In fact, she sounded as if she had just been disinterred for the part. Also, for reasons I can't quite put a finger on, she reminded me strongly of an ancient piano—crack voiced, out of tune but indomitable.

Nevertheless, after hearing Miss Reed declaim: «Help! Help! Juliet's de-e-e-ad!» I felt obscurely comforted for not having been present at the fall of Jericho. The blare of the trumpets on that memorable occasion could not possibly have been more shattering or more terrifying.

With those four words she made a mockery of all radio. The line would have been just as effective if they turned off the American Broadcasting Co. and opened the windows.

In spite of all these crotchety remarks, I thoroughly enjoyed the Theater Guild's «Romeo and Juliet,» though possibly not quite in the spirit Shakespeare intended.

I'd like to hear them attempt «Othello» some time with Bob Hope in the title role, Lionel Barrymore as Iago and Joan Davis as Desdemona. That should make a real acting festival.[421]

Cavalcade of America: "No Greater Love," March 3, 1948
Between 1948 and 1953, Dorothy would perform in eight radio dramas for the historical anthology program *Cavalcade of America*.

On March 3, 1948, Dorothy gave an outstanding performance in the well-written drama "No Greater Love," produced by *Cavalcade of America* (1935–1953) for NBC. Sponsored by the DuPont Company, whose motto, "Maker of better things for better living through chemistry," was stated either at the beginning or at the end of each program (or both), *Cavalcade* specialized in dramas based on real stories and focusing on the special achievements and initiatives of heroic individuals (whether industrial, patriotic or humanitarian). Many of the individuals dramatized in the series were women.

The year: 1900. Clara Mars is a courageous army nurse who wants to make a contribution to the yellow-fever crisis in Havana, Cuba, and volunteers for service on the island. After initial skepticism from the medical staff, Clara's bravery and cheerful disposition win the esteem of the entire hospital. One worker especially, Steve Dolan, member of the Sanitation Commission, becomes very attracted to her, and the two start dating. Medically, the situation is desperate. Infected patients are dying, and there is no cure for the disease, whose exact cause is yet unknown. A Cuban scientist, Carlos Finley, has a theory involving mosquitoes; but the theory needs to be tested, and Finley needs research volunteers. When Steve

---

[421] John Crosby, "Shakespeare's Romeo, U.S. Steel's Juliet," *Portsmouth (OH) Times*, February 16, 1948 (copyright 1948, *New York Tribune*); as quoted by the website Digital Deli Too (digitaldeliftp.com/DigitalDeliToo), one of the most thorough online research sources about old-time radio.

enlists, his days are numbered; Clara is by his side when he dies. Clara decides to follow Steve's example and volunteer as a test patient. She dies in the name of research, and is buried with the highest military honors.

The original play, written with skill by Virginia Radcliffe, is well dramatized, mixing humor and sentiment in appropriate doses and carrying out consistent and lively characterizations for all the characters. The relationship between Clara and Steve is especially effective, and Dorothy and her co-star Lyle Sudrow are very good. The well-written text helps carry the drama through to its conclusion, and the two actors use their natural, believable acting styles to modulate the touching story.

Theatre Guild on the Air: "Anna Christie," March 7, 1948

On March 7, 1948, Dorothy (as Anna) co-starred with Burgess Meredith (as Mat) and Oscar Homolka (as Chris) in an adaptation of Eugene O'Neill's Pulitzer Prize-winning play *Anna Christie* (1921). The radio play was broadcast from the Vanderbilt Theatre, the same venue where the stage play had opened in 1921.[422] When announcements were made of this broadcast,[423] they were accompanied by news of Dorothy's imminent trip to Sweden to begin filming on *A Doll's House* for David O. Selznick. Dorothy did travel to Europe, but the delays in the film's start date and its eventual cancellation (see Part I, Chapter 6) prompted her to transform that trip into a delayed second honeymoon with John Swope, while pregnant with her first child (see Part I, Chapter 7).

Ford Theater: "The Damask Cheek," November 5, 1948

For its sixth show, the new anthology series *Ford Theater* under producer

---

[422] The Vanderbilt Theatre was designed by architect Eugene De Rosa under the impulse of producer Lyle Andrews in 1918. From 1939 to 1952, it was used as a radio studio. It was reopened as a legitimate venue in 1953, but only lasted a year. It was demolished in 1954.

[423] See "Dorothy McGuire On Theatre Guild As 'Anna Christie,'" *Jackson (TN) Sun*, March 7, 1948.

Fletcher Markle presented an adaptation of John Van Druten and Lloyd Morris' play *The Damask Cheek* (1942). Dorothy starred.

Cavalcade of America: "Betrayal," November 29, 1948
On November 29, 1948, *Cavalcade of America* presented another of its series of historical dramas based on real events. This time, Dorothy starred as Peggy Shippen, Benedict Arnold's second wife; Alan Hewitt (sounding a bit like Basil Rathbone) played General Arnold. The play was written by Halsted Welles and directed by Jack Dollar.

Though the story concerns Arnold, its protagonist is his wife Peggy (Margaret), and not only as a mirror to the more famous historical character. The story begins in Peggy's frivolous days as a spoiled rich girl—and hopeless flirt. It is unclear whether her character is presented so negatively by the writer in order to "punish" her dramaturgically for her future association, or because of historical fact. In any event, Peggy's behavior during the first act does not bode well.

Arnold himself is introduced as a haughty brute of a man, with an elegant tongue and a violent streak. When he declares his love to Peggy two months into their frequentation, he does so with a touch of animal possessiveness, extorting his first kiss from her in spite of her protestations. Dramatically and strategically, the ploy works for us, the audience: we must perceive Arnold as seductive and repulsive, noble and ignoble simultaneously, especially in light of how things turned out in the end.

As the story progresses, and as the general's treacherous plot thickens, Arnold becomes increasingly villainous (at least in Hewitt's rendition), and the character of Peggy matures, in at least three stages: first, she is the gay socialite, then the romantic, devoted wife, and finally the mature woman willing to become a martyr for her husband's cause. This allows Dorothy to progress vocally, and use her voice to indicate the growth of her character, which she does well. Here is Peggy's final farewell to her father (she has been ordered to leave the state as an undesirable):

I am Mrs. Benedict Arnold. Father: they have heard that she loved her husband, and therefore her eyes were clouded. Together, she believed that they could do no wrong. Should the Council for Public Safety ask where she's gone, tell them that now her eyes are cleared, but that she saw the way her life must go. I will follow my husband; my duty is to him. The years ahead will be merciless, but just. And this tragedy, our tragedy, must be taken as a warning. It must never be forgotten. Oh, Father, can you forgive me? Will I ever be forgiven? I have loved all the good things too much, to have loved the better.

Despite the inevitable preachiness that seeps into the speech, the passage is quite touching in Dorothy's sensitive, thoughtful rendition.

Theatre Guild on the Air: "Summer and Smoke," April 17, 1949
On April 17, 1949, Dorothy co-starred with Tod Andrews in Robert Anderson's radio adaptation of Tennessee Williams' play *Summer and Smoke*. Andrews had created the role of John Buchanan, Jr., in the Broadway premiere the year before (October 1948).

According to John Dunning's radio encyclopedia *On the Air*:

> The April 17, 1949 show, Tennessee Williams's *Summer and Smoke*, touched off a storm of protest when it depicted a young girl turning to prostitution. "It was bad timing," [Guild officer Armina] Marshall conceded: it had been scheduled on Easter Sunday, and thereafter the fare on that day was confined to classics and comedies.[424]

In a May 1949 letter to agent Audrey Wood (after the radio broadcast

---

[424] John Dunning, *On the Air: The Encyclopedia of Old-Time Radio*, Oxford University Press, 1998, 660.

of the play), Williams, writing from Rome, Italy, expressed his views about the American tour of *Summer and Smoke*, envisaging some changes in the Broadway cast. Here is an excerpt:

> [. . .] I have always felt, very strongly, that the peculiarly dead effect created in many scenes of the play was due, unhappily, by the male lead having nothing but looks to contribute. I like the idea of McGuire, but I am sure that someone better than Todd [sic] can be found in these post-war days when so many virile young actors with real ability can be had.[425]

This radio program predates Dorothy's stage enactment of Williams' play at the La Jolla Playhouse by just over a year (see Part I, Chapter 9). I could not ascertain whether her idea for the La Jolla production came from this engagement, but it is quite likely that Dorothy, having had a taste of the character of demure Alma Winemiller on the airwaves, was eager to develop her exploration in the theater. Perhaps she had encouragement from the author himself.

Ford Theater: "Alice Adams," May 13, 1949
On May 13, 1949, Dorothy was the star of the *Ford Theater*'s adaptation of Booth Tarkington's Pulitzer Prize-winning novel *Alice Adams*.

Cavalcade of America: "Lady on a Mission," April 25, 1949
General Lafayette was one of the main movers of the French Revolution, and he was a friend to many important Americans, and to the American

---

425 Albert J. Devlin and Nancy M. Tischler, eds., *The Selected Letters of Tennessee Williams*, vol. 2, *1945–1957*, New Directions, 2004, 246–247. The 1949 Theatre Guild's post-Broadway national tour of *Summer and Smoke* ended up retaining the services of Tod Andrews, and co-starred Katharine Balfour as Alma. Interestingly, in a 1954 letter dealing with the preparations and casting for his Pulitzer Prize-winning play *Cat on a Hot Tin Roof*, Williams declared himself interested in casting Dorothy as Maggie, alongside Ben Gazzara as Brick. (Ibid., 554.) The part of Maggie eventually went to Barbara Bel Geddes.

cause. He was close to George Washington and to Thomas Jefferson, and participated heroically in the American Revolution. He was also a dual citizen. When the French Revolution degenerated into its later phase of terror, he lost the fickle favor of the revolutionary forces, and was arrested; he spent five years in prison (but was not executed). The story of "Lady on a Mission," another historical drama produced by *Cavalcade of America*, concerns his wife, Marie Adrienne Francoise Lafayette, or, better, it concerns her friends, the new American Ambassador in Paris, James Monroe, and his wife, Elizabeth, played by Dorothy.

When the story opens, Madame Lafayette has been imprisoned as an "enemy of the people" and Monroe's many requests for her release have gone unanswered. His wife Elizabeth is worried, and wants to do something about it. She gets an idea: James Monroe cannot intervene officially as an ambassador, but she, as a mere wife, can. She visits the prison, and tries to plead for Madame Lafayette's release. Fearlessly, she decides to picket the prison gates and make a show of her support for Madame Lafayette. This gesture succeeds where honest dialogue did not: Elizabeth Monroe is allowed to see the prisoner, and the news of her visit creates a stir in the public opinion; eventually Elizabeth's wish is granted; Madame Lafayette is released.

Elizabeth Monroe is depicted as an intelligent, passionate, and courageous woman, and Dorothy navigates through her story with nobility, passion and humor. The script is definitely not a masterpiece, and, in fact, is a bit too solemn for its own good, but Dorothy inhabits it well.

Suspense: "Last Confession," September 15, 1949

On September 15, 1949, Dorothy was the undisputed star of the play "Last Confession" on the series *Suspense* (June 17, 1942–September 30, 1962). Though five or six other characters speak in the play, Dorothy's character, Jessie Larkin, is definitely the protagonist, obsessively so. The play was produced and edited by series producer William Spier, and directed by Norman Macdonnell. Other characters were played by Georgia Ellis, Verna Felton, and William Johnstone.

While sitting at the breakfast table with her roommate reading the newspaper, young Jessie stumbles upon news of a murder, which has happened in the woods just outside the city limits. She begins grumbling about the crime, and about the young man who was killed. In her mind, the victim gradually merges with a recent boyfriend of hers, and Jessie becomes convinced she herself has committed the murder, even though she has no memory of the deed. When she phones the home of said former boyfriend and asks to speak to him, the man's mother informs her that her son is dead. Jessie takes this—and the fact that she has blocked out all memory of the two hours during which the crime was allegedly committed—as confirmation that she has indeed killed him; finally, she cannot help herself and goes to the police to confess. She is, however, released when (a) her roommate confesses that she has committed the crime, and (b) the mother of her former boyfriend reveals that Jessie cannot remember those two hours in her life because that is when she was attending her boyfriend's funeral (he has died of natural causes). Jessie's trauma has nothing to do with murder, but with her peculiar way of processing recent grief.

The above plot may not be a masterpiece, but the twisted psychological premise is intriguing—in *Spellbound* (1945) vein, but more believably. Also, Dorothy's delivery of what is virtually a half-hour monologue is so well paced in its crescendo, and so breathless and frenzied in its intense depiction of the young woman's torment, that she carries the entire weight of the drama on her shoulders efficiently and engagingly—without apparent effort. Especially remarkable is Dorothy's skill in making her performance appear naturally urgent, despite the far-fetched idea.

Cavalcade of America: "The Lady Becomes a Governor," October 4, 1949
Here is a capsule summary of the plot of this drama: "Dorothy McGuire

portrays Mistress Brent, who became acting governor of Maryland for a few critical days, in 'The Lady Becomes a Governor.'"[426]

Theatre Guild on the Air: "Coquette," October 16, 1949
Dorothy and Cornel Wilde played the lead roles in a broadcast of "Coquette," "a comedy drama that was one of Broadway's hit plays in the 1927–28 season."[427]

Portrait used to promote Dorothy's appearances on the *Theatre Guild on the Air*, November 1949.

Screen Directors Playhouse: "The Spiral Staircase," November 25, 1949
The central conceit of the RKO film *The Spiral Staircase* (1946), starring Dorothy and directed by Robert Siodmak, was that its protagonist, ser-

---

[426] "Better Radio Programs for the Week," *Decatur (IL) Sunday Herald and Review*, October 2, 1949.

[427] St. Louis (MO) Post-Dispatch, radio listings, October 16, 1949.

vant girl Helen, who is being stalked by a serial killer in the very home where she lives and works, is a mute. Having lost her voice due to a childhood trauma and not having spoken a word since, she makes herself understood through gestures and facial expressions, and with pen and pad.

Given such conceit, the idea of adapting the film for radio was eccentric to say the least. Adapter Milton Geiger (1907–1971) and —again— director Siodmak solve the problem by making Helen's thoughts audible. This endows the play with a curiously surreal quality, as Helen's thoughts merge and alternate with what the other characters are saying or doing: Helen's voice weaves in and out of a drama in which she is not speaking. There are pros and cons to this solution. The dreamlike, almost delirious alternation of "real" voices and an "imaginary" voice is a plus; but the device makes the drama a bit "noisy," and the unraveling of the story a bit too busy, especially in the suspenseful moments.

Dorothy is wonderful in the part, and her final moment, when (in the film) she makes a phone call and finally speaks, is in some ways more interesting than in the film. Because we have been hearing her "inner" voice all along in the radio production, Dorothy decides to make that moment special by stressing the difficulty Helen must be experiencing in speaking after years of silence; her long, breathless hesitations and the strained quality of her voice when she finally utters her "first words" out loud are quite moving.

Also touching in terms of nostalgia and interesting for its "behind-the-scenes" value is the friendly exchange that occurs between Dorothy and director Siodmak after the conclusion of the drama. Siodmak reveals himself a funny, elfin speaker, and the affection and esteem between him and Dorothy are palpable.

Hallmark Playhouse: "Christopher and Columbus," December 8, 1949
On December 8, 1949, the *Hallmark Playhouse* presented its felicitous radio condensation of Elizabeth von Arnim's novel *Christopher and*

Columbus (1919). The story concerns twins, Anna-Rose and Anna-Feliz, both played by Dorothy in top form.

Elizabeth von Arnim's delightful Edwardian oddity, which melds the comedic, the romantic, and the picaresque, is difficult to describe, as is the kooky, eccentric, Mad Hatterly-illogical, cockeyed deadpan of the twins' dialogue. This is one of those situations where you just have to be there; and being there is exactly the opportunity this radio adaptation affords the audience.

The ironic, funny novel makes its eccentric intentions immediately clear in its enthusiastic opening, through one of the longest sentences in literature, a sentence that reads like something out of modernist novels such as Samuel Beckett's *Watt* (1953):

> Their names were really Anna-Rose and Anna-Felicitas; but they decided, as they sat huddled together in a corner of the second-class deck of the American liner St. Luke, and watched the dirty water of the Mersey slipping past and the Liverpool landing-stage disappearing into mist, and felt that it was comfortless and cold, and knew they hadn't got a father or a mother, and remembered that they were aliens, and realized that in front of them lay a great deal of grey, uneasy, dreadfully wet sea, endless stretches of it, days and days of it, with waves on top of it to make them sick and submarines beneath it to kill them if they could, and knew that they hadn't the remotest idea, not the very remotest, what was before them when and if they did get across to the other side, and knew that they were refugees, castaways, derelicts, two wretched little Germans who were neither really German nor really English because they so unfortunately, so complicatedly were both,—they decided, looking very calm and determined and sitting very close together beneath the rug their English aunt had given them to put round their miserable alien legs, that what they really were,

were Christopher and Columbus, because they were setting out to discover a New World.[428]

In the novel, significant insight is gained by way of the third-person narration, which adopts much the same quirky irony used for the dialogue; through such irony, many exquisite (and searing) oblique observations are made about human beings. This narration is absent from the radio adaptation, which means that the responsibility rests solely on the shoulders of the characters and their dialogue. In other words, some of the depth of the novel is lost in the adaptation, but the verve of the characters is such that it amply compensates for the loss. One could also venture to opine that von Arnim's narration is occasionally prolix, and that its elimination gives the adaptation a snappy pace that occasionally lags in the novel, particularly in the second half.

A strange chemistry makes the two congenial nineteen-year-old twins (sixteen-year-olds in the novel) both identical and very different. As would be the case with the two Annas (Anna I and Anna II) in Bertolt Brecht/Kurt Weill's ballet/cantata *Die sieben Todsünden* (*The Seven Deadly Sins*, 1933), Anna-Rose, who is the elder by twenty minutes, something she keeps reminding her sister of, is both more practical and more optimistic, more talkative and more unflappable; but bossy. Anna-Feliz (Anna-Felicitas in the novel, Anna II in Brecht/Weill) is the dreamy, silent one. Actually, there are briefly *three* Annas in the novel: the girls' English nursemaid is also called Anna—"confusingly," von Arnim admits.[429]

There is an inherent eccentricity to the enthusiastic language of Anna-Rose's banter, as if some of the logic had been lost in translation, translation from the German of course: Anna-Rose and Anna-Feliz von Twinkler are half-German, half-English (as von Arnim puts it in the

---

[428] Elizabeth von Arnim, *Christopher and Columbus*, Macmillan and Co., Limited, 1920 (Second Edition), 1–2.

[429] Ibid., 10.

novel, they "both were very German on the outside and very English on the inside").[430] The unstoppable stream-of-consciousness wordiness of the sisters' dialogue is able to spin circles around and confuse the best of interlocutors, and to endear the twins to the best of audiences or readerships.

Orphaned sisters Anna-Rose and Anna-Feliz are sent away on a one-way ocean voyage to America by their unpleasant English uncle, who cannot stand anything even remotely German. On the ship, they befriend young Mr. Twist (Frank Lovejoy), who helps them on their adventures in the new land of opportunity. Mr. Twist also becomes enamored of Anna-Rose, while her sister Anna-Feliz takes up a romance with eligible bachelor Commander Elliott Smith of the Royal Navy. In their American peripeteia, the sisters open a luxury teahouse in California, which is closed instantly because of zoning laws (in the radio adaptation at least), and meet several other characters. Summarizing all the events in the novel, and the fewer events in the half-hour adaptation, is pointless: the story is buoyed by the wonderful, ironic wording of the dialogue. Here is one example of the radio dialogue (a condensation of an exchange occurring in Chapter XI of the novel):[431]

(Fresh off the ship that has brought them to America, the twins realize that the family friends who were supposed to meet them at the docks (and put them up at their home in Boston) are not there. Mr. Twist, who has befriended them, is concerned.)
Anna-Feliz: Remember, Anna-Rose? Uncle Arthur referred us to another friend of his, a Mr. Dellogg, who lives in a city called California.
Anna-Rose: But we needn't worry about him: Mr. and Mrs. Sack will take us to their home.
Mr. Twist: Well, why aren't they here? I'm worried about you both, you go together; you're in one lump in my mind; and on it, too.

---

430 Ibid., 2.

431 Ibid., 150–152.

Anna-Rose: Anna-Feliz and I didn't come to America to be on anybody's mind. It's our fixed determination, now that we're starting our new life, to get off any mind we find ourselves on, instantly!

Mr. Twist: I couldn't possibly permit you to go off alone without making sure you have a home!

Anna-Rose: Oh, now, Mr. Twist.

Mr. Twist: How will you get by? You don't know anybody.

Anna-Rose: Well, we're prepared to be friends with everybody, but only as co-equals, and of a reasonable soul, and human flesh subsisting.

Mr. Twist: I don't know exactly what that means, but it seems to give you a lot of satisfaction. Will you two Annas tell me what you propose to do next?

Anna-Rose: To track the Sacks to their lair, Mr. Twist. Will you call a taxi for us, please?

Mr. Twist: Call a taxi? Where do the Sacks live?

Anna-Rose: In a state called Boston, I believe.

Through no fault of their own (excepting their frank prolixity and an innocent lack of *savoir faire*) but because of a quirky form of cosmic serendipity, the twins wreak havoc in America wherever they go. After Mr. Sack of Boston proves inhospitable due to his own private life drama (his wife has just left him and he is devastated), the twins decide to pay a visit to dear Mr. Twist at his home in Clark, New York. There, they wreak havoc in the Twist family, for young Mr. Twist has neglected to inform his formidable, oppressive mother about his new acquaintances, and the sudden appearance of the twins in Mrs. Twist's dining room shocks and dismays her to no end. Mr. Twist, who is ripe for a rebellion, seizes the opportunity to tell his mother what he has thought of her for many a year.

This break-up is the insightful centerpiece of the novel, and an ideal and moral pivot for the story. In the radio adaptation, this core event is synthesized so hurriedly and succinctly as to become uninfluential. Thematically, however, it is important. The twins—Anna-Rose particularly—bring their sunny disposition and glib optimism into any environment they enter; like rays of sunshine burning a morning fog, their personalities have the effect either of wearing down the resistances of the people they encounter or of shattering the flimsy pretenses of conservative—or untruthful—worldviews.

In the novel, the Twinklers' arrival in the Twist household is the catalyst of a monumental three-hour quarrel between young Mr. Twist and his mother. This quarrel provides Mr. Twist not only with an excuse to leave home, but also with a revelation—and a Pirandellian one to boot. Here is a passage from von Arnim's book:

> [His mother] began to speak. And just as amazed as she had been at the things this strange, unknown son had been saying to her and at the manner of their delivery, so was he amazed at the things this strange, unknown mother was saying to him, and at the manner of their delivery. [. . .] Mrs. Twist had never doubted Edward. She thought she knew him inside out. [. . .] Now it appeared that she no more knew Edward than if he had been a stranger in the street.[432]

Dorothy is phenomenally good in this, perhaps the most whimsical characterization of her career. She delivers the dialogue with such quick pacing, such endearingly youthful confidence, and such forceful deadpan irony that Anna-Rose becomes both lovable and funny, touching and irritating, exciting and sweet.

Like Claudia just a few years earlier, Dorothy's Anna-Rose too is an oxymoron. She is frivolous and earnest, funny and tragic, superficial and thoughtful, innocent and wise, witty and foolish (endearing and infuriating), all at once. One can also detect, in Anna-Rose, traces of characters belonging to the Victorian tradition immediately preceding von Arnim, such as Lewis Carroll's Alice (to whom von Arnim actually refers in the

---

[432] Ibid., 213.

novel)[433] and Oscar Wilde's Gwendolen or Cecily—and had Dorothy not played Cecily Cardew in Wilde's *The Importance of Being Earnest* just four months earlier at the La Jolla Playhouse?

Just as she had done in the play that first made her a star, Dorothy is able to switch between those opposite polarities while evoking those other characters like friendly ghosts, with such airy dexterity, with such lightness of touch, that the seams between those polarities, and between those characters, are never audible. She flies through the dialogue, weightless.

Most importantly, both Annas and Mr. Twist are beautifully symbolic characters, for they embody a warm, sunny, nurturing openness and a positive attitude. They are symbols of positivity.

And surely, for those audience members who, like me, had not read von Arnim's novel before the broadcast, this dramatization enabled a well-deserved re-discovery of both writer and book.

Hotpoint Holiday Hour: "The Man Who Came to Dinner," December 25, 1949

George S. Kaufman and Moss Hart's play *The Man Who Came to Dinner* (1939) enjoyed a two-year run on Broadway, and a slew of revivals throughout the United States and the United Kingdom in the years that followed. It was filmed in 1942 under William Keighley's direction.

On Christmas Day, 1949, the *Hotpoint Holiday Hour* presented a radio adaptation for CBS featuring the Actors' Company, and the cast was certainly stellar: Jack Benny played Sheridan Whiteside, Dorothy McGuire his secretary Maggie Cutler, Gregory Peck young newspaperman Bert Jefferson, Charles Boyer Marcel Duval, Gene Kelly Hollywood funnyman Banjo, and Rosalind Russell Lorraine Sheldon the diva. John Garfield was the luxury announcer for the evening, and Henry Fonda provided the opening narration.

The play's crackling dialogue is definitely funny, though some gags

---
[433] Ibid., 41.

work better than others, and the entire cast is definitely game. Benny is right for the part of the impossibly rude wheelchair-bound eccentric, and Kelly, Boyer and Russell are for the most part hilarious, chewing the scenery left and right and spitting out the pieces with relish. Dorothy and Peck play smaller, "straight" parts—which are only mildly amusing—with gusto and finesse. Producer/director Mel Ferrer works magic with the play's pace, shaping the lovely ensemble piece into one long, judicious crescendo, which the cast sustains admirably like a well-rehearsed chamber orchestra until its frenzied farcical climax in the final five minutes. A gem.

The following year, on April 9, 1950 (Easter Sunday), the Actors' Company presented another all-star adaptation under the sponsorship of the *Hotpoint Holiday Hour*. The play this time was George S. Kaufman and Edna Ferber's *Dinner at Eight* (1932). The radio show starred Dorothy McGuire, Charles Boyer, John Garfield, Rosalind Russell, Deborah Kerr, Otto Kruger, Paul Douglas and Jan Sterling.

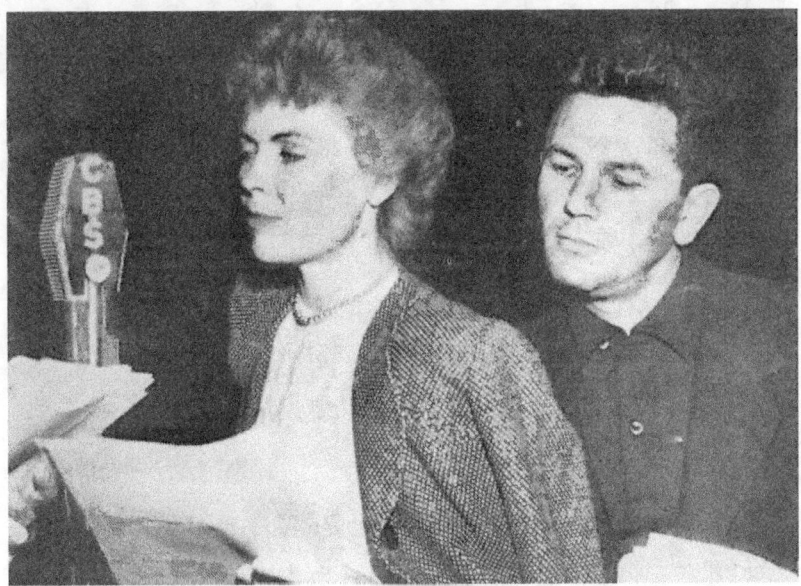

Dorothy and John Garfield, appearing as Actors' Company players for the *Hotpoint Holiday Hour*, 1950. Scan from the Actors' Company souvenir program for *Summer and Smoke*.

On May 14, 1950 (Mother's Day), the Actors' Company and the *Hotpoint Holiday Hour* would present yet another star-studded extravaganza. This time, the adapted play was Philip Barry's *The Philadelphia Story*, starring Dorothy, Jane Cowl, John Lund, John Garfield, Otto Kruger, Burt Lancaster, Margaret O'Brien, Dick Powell and Rosalind Russell. For these shows, the Actors' Company stars commanded top salaries but donated the money to a fund for the building of a new legitimate theater for the company.[434]

Cavalcade of America: "The Golden Needle," January 17, 1950
On January 17, 1950, the *Cavalcade of America* presented another true story, by dramatizing the early life of fashion designer and clothes manufacturer Nell Donnelly Reed of Parsons, Kansas. The savvy comedic script was written by Virginia Radcliffe (an assiduous writer for *Cavalcade*); Dorothy played Nell.

This well-dramatized story of the indomitable creativity and entrepreneurship of a smart, self-reliant young woman allows Dorothy to play gentle, understated comedy and to embody the virtues of her intelligent character simply and lucidly. With unfailing dramatic instinct, Dorothy neither overplays nor underplays, but finds just the right register in which to be likable, honest, and subtle.

Theatre Guild on the Air: "Autumn Crocus," February 5, 1950
The following is a plot summary for the drama starring Dorothy McGuire and Charles Boyer, which appeared in the *Chicago Tribune* in its radio listing section on the episode's airdate:

> Miss McGuire will enact the role of an American school teacher who meets a proprietor of a Swiss chalet (Boyer) un-

---

[434] Hedda Hopper, "Mauldin Production Scheduled for Summer," *Los Angeles Times*, April 25, 1950.

der romantic circumstances while on a tour of the Alps. The Hollywood actress has made numerous appearances in the guild series. Boyer, also a film veteran, recently made his first appearance on the American stage in "Red Gloves."

Screen Directors Playhouse: "Cluny Brown," November 23, 1950
Four years after he starred in Ernst Lubitsch's *Cluny Brown* (1946), Charles Boyer repeated his role as Adam Belinski in a radio adaptation of the film, produced by the *Screen Directors Playhouse* (November 23, 1950). Dorothy replaced (successfully) the film's female star, Jennifer Jones.

In some minor ways, the radio version is even an improvement on the original. The screenplay of *Cluny Brown*, adapted from Margery Sharp's eponymous novel, had benefited enormously from the contribution of a talented screenwriting team: Samuel Hoffenstein and Elizabeth "Betty" Reinhardt. Russian-born Hoffenstein especially was a delightful satirist, poet, columnist and lyricist during the years he spent in New York City, before moving to the West Coast to write for film. The poems collected in his books of verse[435] were delicately cynical and uproariously inventive, even though Hoffenstein would find himself playing second fiddle to his "successor," that other, more famous poetic descendant of Edward Lear, Ogden Nash. Here is a random example from Hoffenstein:

The apple grows so bright and high,
And ends its days in apple pie.[436]

And here is one, also random, from Nash, entitled *The Cow*:

The cow is of the bovine ilk;

---

[435] See for example: Samuel Hoffenstein, *Poems in Praise of Practically Nothing*, Boni & Liveright, 1928.

[436] Hoffenstein, op. cit., 100.

One end is moo, the other, milk.[437]

If there is a touch of Nash in Hoffenstein's poem, there is also a definite touch of Hoffenstein in Nash's, and a touch of Edward Lear in both. Hoffenstein's humor was perhaps streaked with a darker, more pessimistic vein than Nash's, but the two poets were definitely kindred specialists in the art of the frivolous rhyme.

Cluny Brown is pervaded by ironic throwaway quips that are quintessential Hoffenstein, and require a certain kind of comic delivery. In this particular version of the work, whose dialogue is transcribed virtually unchanged from the film, Boyer and his character actor colleagues somewhat surpass the original with their special deadpan emphasis and timing, making it perhaps less a Lubitsch piece than a Jack Benny piece. Delightful. As for Dorothy, equipped with a decent-enough British accent and embodying her character's considerable enthusiasm for plumbing, she plays a kooky chatterbox not dissimilar to the one she had played in her debut film, *Claudia* (1943), and rather splendidly.

Following the play, the president of the Screen Directors Guild, Joseph Mankiewicz, was on hand to present the second Quarterly Award for Directorial Achievement, which the Guild bestowed on Billy Wilder for his latest film, *Sunset Blvd.* Wilder then came on to receive the award, and he and Mankiewicz commemorated their friend and mentor, Ernst Lubitsch, who had died in 1947.

Cavalcade of America: "The Rose and the Thorns," November 28, 1950
On November 28, 1950, the DuPont Company's *Cavalcade of America* presented a strange, wistful little drama entitled "The Rose and the Thorns." Dorothy starred as Winnie, the daughter of Jefferson Davis, former president of the short-lived Confederate States.

---

[437] First published as a four-line poem in Ogden Nash, *Free Wheeling*, Simon & Schuster, 1931, 60. Thereafter reprinted in its abridged and definitive two-line form in other collections, such as *The Pocket Book of Ogden Nash*, Pocket Books, 1962, 88.

The story, taking place in the year 1885, is told in flashbacks, as Winnie sits in her room at New York's Delmonico Hotel writing a "Dear John" letter to her fiancé, Alfred Wilkinson. When the story opens, Wilkinson is a Yankee journalist visiting Mississippi to research a series of articles on "conditions in the South" for the *New York World*. Davis, who is in the process of writing a history of the Confederacy, receives his Yankee guest with indifference bordering on scorn, and instructs his daughter to entertain Wilkinson in his stead.

The journalist enjoys Winnie's company. As the story progresses, his repeated unsuccessful attempts to talk to Colonel Davis yield as a result that his frequentation of Winnie blossoms, first into a friendship, then into a romantic relationship. When Wilkinson's first article comes out, Winnie receives a copy of the New York newspaper from the town gossip; in the article, she is described as "a rose among the thorns," a young woman who is sacrificing her youth and beauty to her father's research and documents instead of receiving her admirers and blossoming into full womanhood. Winnie's pride is hurt, and, at the ball given by the gossip in her (and Wilkinson's) honor, she forces her Yankee companion to make a stand and declare his views publicly to the hostile township.

Notwithstanding this spat, or perhaps because of it, Winnie's relationship with the journalist matures into a love story. He asks her to marry him, and she finds herself torn between two worlds. She follows her fiancé to New York, and is about to be married, but her inner conflict persists. When her father sends her a letter blessing her impending wedding and regretting that she cannot be married in Biloxi, Winnie ultimately decides for her "other love," the South, and leaves her fiancé and her "dream of happiness." This she tells Wilkinson in her letter, sorrowfully, as the drama comes to a close.

A soft-hearted, nostalgic, strangely unsatisfying drama, the story is an ode to the South, but also to an antiquated sense of duty, the one that binds Winnie to her land and to her father's work. Dorothy does what she can with the sentimental, humorless material she is given, and gives a dignified, heartfelt rendition of her old-fashioned role.

Theatre Guild on the Air: "Lottie Dundas," December 10, 1950
Here is how the *Los Angeles Times* summarized the plot of this drama starring Jessica Tandy and Dorothy on the day of its airing:

> The absorbing drama of a girl who makes a bargain with death for one night's triumph on the stage.

The Big Show, December 17, 1950
NBC-Radio's short-lived *The Big Show* (November 5, 1950–April 20, 1952) was big indeed. Hosted by an unpredictable, larger-than-life Tallulah Bankhead, the hour-and-a-half variety mish-mash was a weekly container for many things: musical numbers featuring Meredith Willson's "Big Show Orchestra," comedy banter, and prestigious guests from theater, film, and radio. Above all, it was a showcase for Bankhead's over-the-top slurs.

On December 17, 1950, the comedy was provided by special guests Bob Hope, Jerry Lewis and Dean Martin; the music by Frankie Laine, Dean Martin, Louis Armstrong and Meredith Willson. The drama was provided by an unusual trio: Tallulah Bankhead, Deborah Kerr and Dorothy McGuire. Kerr and Dorothy appeared as members of the Actors' Company (of the La Jolla Playhouse), and, together with Bankhead, performed a fifteen-minute triptych of scenes from the play *The Women* (1936) by Clare Boothe Luce. Bankhead, naturally enough, played the role of Sylvia the irrepressible gossip; Kerr was Mary and Dorothy the repentant Peggy.

Dorothy is charming in her first scene, sensitive and weepy in her second, dignified in her third. Dorothy was no comedienne, but she did have a deft comedic touch, and the style of old-fashioned comedy of manners suited her quite well. Kerr is professional and committed throughout.

Bankhead never achieves the vertiginous virtuosity of Rosalind Russell (who played the character in the 1939 film) in her gossipy scenes as Sylvia, but her eccentric line readings and smoky baritone voice make for a delicious performance.

In the case of this particular evening, the fact that good things come in threes is not only true of the number of female performers or of scenes. *The Big Show* follows up its homage to *The Women* with a hilarious all-male parody of the previous scenes, performed by Bob Hope, Dean Martin, and Jerry Lewis and entitled "The Fellers," a parody which ends with Lewis's character paralleling Peggy's pregnancy announcement with his own announcement that he is "expecting a little stranger" (but it is only a situational pun). This scene is in turn topped by an "off-the-script" casual exchange between Bankhead, Kerr, and Dorothy, which is even cattier than their scenes from the play. Bankhead compliments Dorothy and Kerr, then insults them; this leads to a mounting of sarcasm from all three actresses, which climaxes with Bankhead dismissing her colleagues curtly and bellowing: "Actors' Company indeed!"

CBS: "Quiet Town," January 26, 1951
Few details were advertised for this drama starring Dorothy; according to one newspaper report, Dorothy was replacing Helen Hayes as the lead in the broadcast, which was "presented on behalf of the annual infantile paralysis fund drive."[438] A contemporary daily provided a plot summary at least:

> Thrill to the stirring performance of Dorothy McGuire in this special half-hour drama which tells the story of a polio-stricken town as it fought against 1950's rising tide of polio.[439]

---

438 *Racine (WI) Journal Times*, radio listings, January 25, 1951.

439 *Minneapolis (MN) Star Tribune*, radio listings January 26, 1951.

Theatre Guild on the Air: "Hamlet," March 4, 1951

The event that was broadcast on March 4, 1951, from the Belasco Theatre in New York was special. Produced by the *Theatre Guild on the Air* under joint sponsorship with the United States Steel Corporation and the Radio Corporation of America (RCA Victor), the play was William Shakespeare's *Hamlet*, whittled down by its star John Gielgud (Hamlet) to just under ninety minutes and co-starring Dorothy as Ophelia and Pamela Brown as Queen Gertrude. At the time, Brown and Gielgud were in New York performing a successful run (November 8, 1950–March 31, 1951) of Christopher Fry's 1948 play *The Lady's Not for Burning* at the Royale Theatre,[440] co-starring Richard Burton and Claire Bloom.

For once, the contemporary press printed more than just the customary announcements or listings, producing enthusiastic half-page spreads about the event. One such ad commented thus on Dorothy's presence in the cast:

> Scores of actresses were considered for the poignant role of Ophelia—before Dorothy McGuire was finally selected as the ideal choice.[441]

Commentators of the event were hardly unanimous in their praise of Dorothy. The issue is a complex one; radio and television commentator John Crosby discussed it in his otherwise positive syndicated review of the show, one week after the broadcast:

> Recently, Mr. Gielgud said that the soliloquies [of Hamlet] were meant to be declaimed, not whispered. He declaimed

---

[440] Today the Bernard B. Jacobs Theater, 242 W. 45th Street, New York.

[441] Half-page ad, "Hamlet," *Louisville (KY) Courier-Journal*, March 4, 1951.

them till my rafters rang like bells, frightening the bats who don't generally wake up until Jerry Lester comes on.[442]

Miss Pamela Brown, who played the Queen, and whoever played Polonius come from the same declamatory school and they, too, rang clamorously.

Miss Dorothy McGuire, who took on Ophelia, didn't. Miss McGuire, a very good actress of a more naturalist school, is, by training and possibly by instinct, a whisperer. A few years back she played Juliet on the Theater Guild's radio version of "Romeo and Juliet" opposite Maurice Evans, another declaimer, whose voice has the power and flexibility of the organ at the Music Hall. In both cases, she was overwhelmed by superior numbers.

Conceivably, a whispered "Hamlet" might be an interesting experience sometime, in which case Miss McGuire would be just the dish, but I fail to see why the Theater Guild keeps throwing us a mixture of acting styles this way.[443]

Calling Dorothy a "whisperer" was an exaggeration (Mr. Crosby never heard Nicole Kidman), but Crosby's point about acting styles was otherwise correct. John Gielgud's acting style in performing classic drama was as far from naturalism as one could get without relinquishing the emotional connection with character altogether. Gielgud was not cold, and could be as intense in expressing his characters' feelings as any

---

[442] Jerry Lester (1910–1995) was an American comedian and performer on radio, television and theater; In 1950 and 1951, Lester emceed the late-night show *Broadway Open House*, which aired from eleven p.m. to midnight.

[443] John Crosby, "John Crosby's Radio and Television," *Baltimore Sun*, March 11, 1951. For a more thorough discussion of the same issues by Crosby, see his comments on McGuire's appearance in the *Theatre Guild on the Air* adaptation of Shakespeare's *Romeo and Juliet* in February 1948.

naturalistic actor; but his approach to theater was formal. Even Laurence Olivier, compared to him, was something of a Method actor.

Pamela Brown, John Gielgud, and Dorothy recording *Hamlet* for the *Theatre Guild on the Air* in March 1951.

What is formal theater? Without getting too technical, or too philosophical, about it, it is a theater where line, gesture, sound, movement and the music of the text come first, and the truthful psychological exploration of the characters comes second, or does not come at all. A theater that harks back to ancient, stylized, or ritualistic representational manners; a theater in which some form of distancing places the sound of the verse (in Shakespeare's case) in the foreground, making it as "abstract" as a musical composition. The imitation of real life, the holding of a mirror up to nature, is seldom the objective of formal theater, a theater that can be traced back to a variety of ancient styles (Greek tragedy, medieval mystery plays) and, more recently, to a line of innovators that included Gordon Craig, Vsevolod Meyerhold, Bertolt Brecht, and the Living Theatre. Today, one of the few directors who truly understands and uses such formal approach (especially when directing opera) is Robert Wilson.

In some respects, radio was the perfect medium for such stylization, as it stripped the representation of virtually all residual "realism" (posture, movement, physical interaction between characters, "life-like" depiction), reducing the play to the minimum common denominator of sound and meter.

Barring purists such as Gielgud, classical European actors (British, French, Italian) have always been more adept at such stylizations—such declaiming, as Crosby would put it—than American actors. It is a question of schooling in the first place, and of the historical understanding of class divisions, manners, and antiquity in the second.

Dorothy was certainly no whisperer: her melodious use of the voice was one of her distinguishing qualities, especially on the radio and on the stage. She was, however, a naturalistic actress. As was customary with her, in *Hamlet* she plays the situation, truthfully and realistically, expressing it elegantly through the voice; Shakespeare's verse is a means to an end. The intonation of her voice follows the inner workings of her character and of her situation first, and the music of the verse second. The priorities are reversed; and there is nothing amiss with that, if it were not for the discrepancy in styles that follows.

Such discrepancy was, however, a minor flaw in an accomplished, fascinating rendition of Shakespeare's evergreen text; a text that is so endlessly interesting, so multi-layered and so perfect as to be, in the end, absolutely fail-safe regardless of the styles employed.

Other critics were less fastidious about those styles, and more robustly enthusiastic about the radio program. As an example, here is the review by Anton Remenih of the *Chicago Tribune*:

> Listening to drama on radio is like attending the theater wearing a blindfold. Most plays can't take this. A singular

exception was Theater Guild on the Air's superb hour and a half version of "Hamlet" last Sunday.

Radio possesses one striking advantage over the legitimate stage for plays of the caliber of "Hamlet." It gives the listener a front row seat. His ear is as close to the actor as the microphone.

John Gielgud, as Hamlet, headed a superb cast that included Dorothy McGuire, as Ophelia, and Pamela Brown, as Hamlet's mother. Gielgud took advantage of the microphone by whispering some of his lines to create effects almost impossible to obtain on the stage where the actor must speak loudly enough to be heard in the gallery.

No matter what the remainder of 1951 brings in radio drama, Gielgud's "Hamlet" will unquestionably stand as just about the top of the year. Despite TV's Comedy Hour and the tribute to Richard Rodgers, the best on the air between 7:30 and 9 p.m. last Sunday was on radio.[444]

Philip Morris Playhouse on Broadway: "The Heiress," March 15, 1951
In its debut drama for CBS, the newly-minted *Philip Morris Playhouse on Broadway* (a resurrection of the twice-defunct *Philip Morris Playhouse*, which had aired between 1939 and 1944 and then again between 1948 and 1949) presented Louis Calhern,[445] Richard Carlson, and Dorothy in the play "The Heiress."

Billboard magazine had this to say about the show and about Dorothy:

> Production leaned heavily on the emotional values, with

---

[444] Anton Remenih, "Guild 'Hamlet' Is Outstanding Radio Drama," *Chicago Tribune*, March 7, 1951.

[445] Calhern had already co-starred in a *Lux Radio Theatre* version of *The Heiress* with Olivia de Havilland and Van Heflin on September 11, 1950.

some scenes going a bit overboard. This was mainly the fault of the adaptation, which emphasized such gems as the one in which Miss McGuire lamented tearfully, "Morris, Morris, Morris, why did you do this to me?" [. . .] Miss McGuire, as the naïve Catherine, was properly restrained as the shy lass and convincingly bitter after her disillusionment.[446]

Hallmark Playhouse: "Rest and Be Thankful," April 5, 1951
A bucolic American fable of tender feelings and the search for peace, contentment and romantic fulfillment, Helen MacInnes's novel *Rest and Be Thankful* (1949) and this radio adaptation for the *Hallmark Playhouse*, probably aimed at a female audience, may appear dated today. And, like many "chick stories" then and today, it involved finding the right man to be thankful with, and for.

When the story opens, two mature women of means are driving across the United States. Their names are Sally Bly (Dorothy) and Margaret Peel (Eleanor Audley). They are consummate travelers and have already seen all the fashionable European destinations (they mention the Riviera a lot). After misreading a map, they take a mountain road in Wyoming and get lost. A storm breaks out, and their car gets stuck in the mud, seemingly in the middle of nowhere. Suddenly, a providential cowboy by the name of Jim Brent (Lamont Johnson) appears; he suggests leaving the car on the road and following him to his ranch. Sally and Margaret have glimpsed a lovely house built on a creek island; the house is vacant, and they ask Jim if they can spend the night there. He owns the house, as well as the adjoining ranch and land, and consents.

One can sense that the house has special meaning for Jim, but, like the lovely Wyoming mountain scenery around him that enchants the two women so, he is the strong, silent type, so one cannot be sure. The following day, the two women, especially Sally, are beginning to fall in love with

---

[446] Sam Chase, "Philip Morris Playhouse," *Billboard*, March 24, 1951.

the place, and Margaret asks if she can buy the house: she would like to use it as a retreat for young writers. Hesitantly, Jim consents.

Sally, the younger of the two women, becomes attracted to Jim, who gradually reveals his secret to her: it was in this house that he was briefly happy, many years ago. His wife at the time was not: she dreamed of a different life, and the couple moved to New York City. But Jim did not belong in the metropolis, and came back after divorcing his wife.

Finally, Margaret abandons the idea of a writers' retreat; she wants to continue traveling and explore the Western States, and has realized, before Sally, that the house should be a love nest for Sally and Jim. Jim declares his love for Sally in a touching letter, and the two plan to be married in the Wyoming paradise they both appreciate and love.

The script of "Rest and Be Thankful" is a curious mixture of soft-hearted clichés (the wide empty spaces of America that give serenity, the silent cowboy with a heart of gold) and surprising insights ("*Out here you've got to listen very closely to the things that aren't said, much as you listen to the words that are spoken*," says Jim to Sally). The insights are all nicely put, but the majority of the story is a bit too monotonously sentimental and predictable to be interesting. As for Dorothy, she is fine in her role but is hampered by the one-note heartfelt gushiness of both character and story. Once again, she has little to do but be nice and sensitive.

Notwithstanding the limitations of the source material that was chosen, the radio play benefits not only from the casting of Dorothy but also from the participation of two high-caliber dramatists like Jerome Lawrence and Robert E. Lee (*Inherit the Wind*, 1955; *Auntie Mame*, 1956) and of a composer named Bernard Herrmann (*Citizen Kane*, 1941; *Psycho*, 1960; *Vertigo*, 1958), who contributes a lovely score[447] that pays affectionate homage to quintessentially American composer Aaron Copland.

---

[447] See the Bernard Herrmann Society website (bernardherrmann.org), section entitled "Herrmann's Legacy Left to CBS (and the World)."

The Hedda Hopper Show, April 15, 1951

Like Tallulah Bankhead's *The Big Show*, *The Hedda Hopper Show* (October 1950–May 1951) was a radio container for a variety of show business things: drama, music, and talk. Above all, it was an occasion for Ms. Hopper to do what she did best: gossip. Different guests were showcased each week, each doing their thing, while Hopper filled the gaps with an aural version of her newspaper column, jumping from news to slurs to innuendo.

On the evening of April 15, 1951, comedians Bud Abbott and Lou Costello were the first guests, followed by actress Jane Russell and by Dorothy. Dorothy always maintained excellent relations with both Hopper and Louella Parsons, the two "Queens" of Hollywood (or queens of gossip), and she may have accepted the invitation in the interest of such relations, or as a favor to Hopper. It is unclear whether the decision to have Dorothy act the particular material that was chosen on that particular evening was Dorothy's or Hopper's; Hopper's introduction of the actress seems to suggest the latter. At any rate, the task of executing such decision turned out to be a thankless one: Dorothy was to perform some tragic scenes from *Camille*.

Launching into full tragedy mode after the loony antics of Abbott and Costello, the banter between Hopper and guest Jane Russell, Russell's singing, and the cold fact-reporting of Hopper's gossip was such a tall order as to make the job almost impossible. Dorothy gives her all to the melodramatic scenery-chewing, but the clash with the rest of the show and the fact that she is ultimately miscast in the role of Marguerite Gautier do not help at all. Her sensitive work goes to waste among the hodgepodge surrounding it.

Screen Directors Playhouse: "Wuthering Heights," August 9, 1951

Oversimplified and over-condensed, *Reader's Digest* style, this one-hour adaptation of *Wuthering Heights* may not have the sprawl or majesty of

Bronte's novel or of William Wyler's 1939 film, but it pairs—excellently—James Mason and Dorothy for the first and only time in their careers.

Both Mason and Dorothy are magnificent in this story of the conflicted, socially inappropriate, hopeless Gothic love between Cathy and Heathcliff. The defiant gruffness, animal magnetism, sensual hostility, and proud haughtiness of Heathcliff, the dark-skinned "gypsy," are stunningly conveyed by the seductive prose of James Mason, one of the best actors of the twentieth century; and Dorothy is especially splendid in expressing Catherine's obsession with her forbidden love object, and the violent consequences it brings with it. In Cathy's more unhinged scenes, Dorothy manages to shake off her normally centered persona and lose herself entirely in the moment. Her Mid-Atlantic theatrical language may never achieve the velvety perfection of Mason's pear-shaped British music, but her acting makes up for it in spades.

Also magnificent is the radio production as a whole, and the delirious soundscape it creates around the characters. The "negative," darkly romantic scenes between Cathy and Heathcliff are sheer haunting perfection, in acting and in musical/aural atmosphere.

One could, in fact, say that the atmosphere created by the combination of good voice acting, good music and good sound effects enhance the "doomed" aspect of the central relationship, endowing it with an eerie otherworldliness. Seldom have the cries of the two unhappy characters ("*Heathcliff! Heathcliff!*" and "*Cathy! Cathy!*") sounded more forlorn, more desperate, and more bodiless than in this rendition. Deprived of their physical image by the medium of radio, this Heathcliff and this Cathy are ghosts even before they die.

In its own flawed way, a minor masterpiece. It was probably in reaction to this broadcast that a month later Samuel Goldwyn—according to columnist Dorothy Kilgallen—was entertaining thoughts of a movie version for Dorothy:

> Samuel Goldwyn is planning to re-make "Wuthering

Heights" with Dorothy McGuire, but cannot find a male to equal Laurence Olivier, who starred in the original flicker version.[448]

Theatre Guild on the Air: "Look to the Mountain," January 13, 1952
Here is an announcement and capsule plot summary from the *Times* of Shreveport, Louisiana:

> Tonight "Theatre Guild on the Air" presents Dorothy McGuire and John Ireland in a radio adaptation of the best selling novel "Look to the Mountain" by LeGrand Cannon. It is the story of a young couple pioneering in 17th century New Hampshire.
> [. . .] "Look to the Mountain" was adapted for radio by Claris Ross and is directed by Homer Fickett.[449]

Theatre Guild on the Air: "The Thief," January 27, 1952
On January 27, 1952, *Theatre Guild on the Air* presented what must have been a fascinating presentation, at least judging from the unusual cast of stars assembled. Here is a summary that was printed in the *Greenville News* of South Carolina on the airing date.

> Dorothy McGuire, David Niven and Roddy McDowall will be starred in the Theater Guild on the Air presentation of "The Thief," by the French playwright Henry Bernstein, on WFBC at 8:30 tonight.
> Produced on Broadway many times since its debut in

---

[448] Dorothy Kilgallen, "Voice of Broadway," *Shamokin (PA) News-Dispatch*, September 1, 1951.

[449] Dorothy McGuire, John Ireland on 'Theatre Guild,' *Shreveport (LA) Times*, January 13, 1952.

1907, "The Thief," which was adapted for radio by S. Mark Smith, concerns the love of a young man for a beautiful woman visiting in his father's chateau.

When some funds are missing, the youth takes upon himself the guilt which rightly belongs to his inamorata.[450]

Cavalcade of America: "Thunder of Justice," February 5, 1952
It is something of a disappointment, arguably, that this radio play uses the character of Beulah Chittenden-Lyon (played by Dorothy) only as a reflection of the greatness of her historical husband, notorious Vermont congressman Matthew Lyon (played by Ian Martin) rather than vice-versa (which would have been a daring violation of convention). The script was written by William Kendall Clarke from the book *Crisis in Freedom: The Alien and Sedition Acts* (1951) by John C. Miller.

The play focuses on Matthew Lyon's fierce efforts campaigning against the above-mentioned acts, and on his imprisonment as a result of his protest against the government. The character of his wife acts as a sensitive mirror for the events, by persisting in her moral support of her spouse. The actions of Lyon's political supporters are successful, and he is re-elected to Congress while still in jail.

As usual, Dorothy's intelligent acting is a pleasure to hear, and she has a couple of good scenes to perform; unfortunately, she is not the protagonist of this story, except in billing.

Cavalcade of America: "A Medal for Miss Walker," January 6, 1953
On January 6, 1953, Dorothy played another patriotic real-life heroine on the historically minded anthology drama series *Cavalcade of America*. The title: "A Medal for Miss Walker." The setting: the American Civil War; the time: 1862. The titular character, Mary Walker, is no ordinary "Miss,"

---

[450] "Guild to Present 'The Thief' Play," *Greenville (SC) News*, January 27, 1952.

for she is a doctor, heroically practicing her profession against the odds of male prejudice and war.

The customary *Cavalcade* virtues of abnegation, heroism and devotion to an ideal are perfectly vocalized by Dorothy; what is remarkable is that they are displayed and dramatized unsentimentally. In fact, Dr. Walker is an intelligent, articulate woman who refuses to bow to stupidity, prejudice, and empty convention, and steadfastly finds a way to turn every negative situation to her advantage, or to the advantage of the advancement of professionalism and of her sex. Dr. Walker's self-reliance and delicate sense of humor make her a strong, endearing character.

In one scene, she refuses to abandon a medical camp near Chattanooga, Tennessee, during a Union retreat, and gets ready to face the advancing enemy. Found wearing a Confederate uniform she has borrowed without a regular commission, she is arrested, charged as a spy, and sentenced to death. Confederate General Braxton Bragg is displeased with the turn of events, and has no wish to shoot a woman to death; he has Walker summoned, hoping that a chat with her will allow him to be paternalistic and simply send her back home with her tail between her legs. Unfortunately for him, the woman who confronts him is not the cowering victim he was expecting; she refuses to be apologetic about anything she has done and demands to be sent to her patients and to be treated as a legitimate prisoner of war:

Dr. Walker: If my wearing a Federal uniform makes me out a spy, then I am a spy.
General Bragg: Er, no doubt there's the result of some kind of emergency: your own clothes were ripped and torn during the battle, isn't that it?
Dr. Walker: No, sir, it was not it. I wore that uniform deliberately. And I was proud to wear it.
General Bragg: But you are not entitled to wear it; you have no commission.
Dr. Walker: The only reason I don't have a commission is because of my sex! And I consider that reason invalid and immaterial.

General Bragg: Yes, yes, well, that is a call I suggest you take up with General Grant. I'll make you out a pass that'll get you through our lines–
Dr. Walker: You're sending me back?
General Bragg: I am.
Dr. Walker: As a civilian?
General Bragg: Of course.
Dr. Walker: I refuse to go.
General Bragg: What?
Dr. Walker: I demand to be treated as a legitimate prisoner of war.
General Bragg: Madam, are you out of your mind?
Dr. Walker: Not at all. Either you treat me as a prisoner of war, and permit me to go back to my patients, or you can treat me as a spy, and shoot me.
General Bragg: But that is a ridiculous alternative!
Dr. Walker: One way or the other.
General Bragg: Madam, I am busy fighting a war, I can't get involved in your attempt to wrangle a commission out of the Federal Army!
Dr. Walker: I will not go back as a civilian.
General Bragg: That is the only way I can send you back.
Dr. Walker: I refuse to go.
General Bragg: [%ç!*!@], Madam–
Dr. Walker: Invectives will get you nowhere, General.
General Bragg: Colonel! Get this woman out of here. Take her to Richmond. Take her to President Davis if necessary.

An emissary from President Jefferson Davis himself pays a visit to Dr. Walker in prison, stating that the president has reversed the decision of the court martial. Again, Dr. Walker refuses to leave the prison unless she can go to her patients. The emissary and the prison management try to trick Walker into escaping by leaving her cell door open, stating that the lock does not work. She responds by shutting the door again. The president's representative finally succumbs, and escorts Dr. Walker to Colonel Marsh, instructing him that she is to be treated as a legitimate prisoner of war. The minute she is allowed to go back to her patients, she starts barking instructions as to what needs to be done in the medical compound. After her patients recover, the Confederates consider her eligible for exchange and send her back North. In Washington, she is surprised to find she is being greeted by full military parades in her honor, and by a medal for her heroism.

Those colors of Dorothy's that Hollywood was often remiss in appreciating and eliciting were certainly brought out by this intelligent, funny script (written by Irve Tunick) and by director John (or Jack) Zoller. Dorothy's acting is nothing short of spectacular: never does she succumb to the temptation to overplay, while giving a performance that, for intelligence and forcefulness, even transcends many of her best roles in film. There are times when she is vocally transformed by the text and by her own work; her performance manages to eschew many clichés, including those she was so often forced to embody in Hollywood.

Theatre Guild on the Air: "The Scarlet Letter," January 25, 1953
Judging from the contract that Dorothy signed with Theatre Guild, Inc., on October 21, 1952, arrangements had been made well in advance for Dorothy's participation in a radio drama entitled "The Scarlet Letter," to be broadcast on January 25, 1953. These arrangements were confirmed in the contract. Here is the wording of the first three points:

> 1. We hereby engage you and you hereby agree to render your personal services to act in a radio version of the play entitled, THE SCARLET LETTER to be broadcast by us under the sponsorship of the United States Steel Corporation.
> 2. The running time of such broadcast shall be approximately one (1) hour and shall emanate from a radio theatre in New York City, on Sunday evening, January 25, 1953.
> 3. As complete compensation for your full services hereunder, we shall pay you and you agree to accept the sum of

$2500 if you are sole star and $2000 if you are co-starred. We agree to give you first co-star credit. All payments hereunder shall be made payable to your agent, Don W. Sharpe.

Lux Summer Theatre: "The Fall of Maggie Phillips," June 22, 1953

There have been naysayers dissenting as to the value of the radio play "The Fall of Maggie Phillips," produced by *Lux Radio Theatre* (or, more precisely in this case, by the *Lux Summer Theatre* or *Hollywood Radio Theatre*, an interim replacement of the above program during the summer of 1953) and aired on June 22, 1953. The play was written by Kathleen Hite (1917–1989) and directed by Frank Paris (or, according to some online sources, by Norman Macdonnell).

The website devoted to the work of writer Kathleen Hite (www.kathleenhite.com) and created by E. A. Villafranca, Jr., spends some unkind words about this particular play. For example:

> One [sic] you get beyond the opening lines [. . .] there's neither surface nor depth to this drama, and it's not helped by Dorothy McGuire's lack of voice. [The cliché-ridden episode] has less substance than a summer dress. Kathleen Hite was perfectly capable of writing pieces that conformed to formula—there are the eleven episodes of The Adventures of Philip Marlowe, if one needs examples—containing every essential element of the show, and nothing of her.[451]

The owner of that website will forgive me if I do not share the above opinion. It may be true that, in terms of plot, "The Fall of Maggie Phillips" contains its share of clichés; but the same could be said of any number of stories involving the awakening of a demure single woman to the pleasures of life, and not only on the airwaves. *Three Coins in the Fountain*

---

[451] Kathleen Hite website (www.kathleenhite.com), *Lux Summer Theatre* section.

(1954) starring Dorothy and *Summertime* (1955) starring Katharine Hepburn are just two contemporary examples in film.

What makes the difference in this instance is the handling of the raw material, i.e. the "surface," as the above reviewer puts it. And the surface, in the case of this play, is brimming with witty language and fresh takes on old themes. From the opening lines, spoken by voice-over narrator Parley Baer, one gets the feeling that the story is in good hands:

> *The fall of Maggie Phillips began in the spring. But it's doubtful anyone in Fremontville noticed its beginning.*

Already in those lines, the gentle pun of the play's title reveals a sparkling imagination on the part of the writer. The fall of Maggie Phillips is an emotional fall—or, better, a cataclysmic learning process, and an acceptance of what life can bring. Maggie's first line (*"There's got to be more...!"*) reveals that she is ready for such fall, and that all she needs is a little push to topple. But "fall" also refers, more innocuously, to the season, the fall season that is going to be full of unexpected events, such as Maggie's wedding. A small, inconsequential pun, that opening, but it softly braids the language of this conventional story into two intertwined strands through a little surprise. The script is full of such little surprises.

Maggie's opening line, for example, furnishes the play with one of its themes: the main character's dissatisfaction with her routine and her yearning for a fuller life; and Hite uses that line to punctuate the play's acts periodically, by gradually transforming its meaning. The Leitmotif *"There's got to be more"* expresses something different at the close of Act III than it does at the beginning of Act I; in that closing line, Dorothy expresses both the blossoming of her character and her sensual opening to the joys to come.

Maggie the town librarian is tired of having the usual Thursday dinner at the usual restaurant with the usual Cecil Bainbridge (who is her age, thirty-five, even though everyone refers to him as "old Bainbridge"), her boss at the library and (probably) platonic boyfriend of ten years. Desperate for a remedy, any remedy, for her "inner turmoil," she decides to enter a slogan contest for a brand of motor oil with the vague dream of winning an all-expenses-paid two-week vacation in France and Italy, and her life changes direction. In order to learn about motor oil, and at Cecil's suggestion, she consults the gruff owner of the local trucking company, a tall drink of water by the name of Heller Hawkins; against her better judgment and despite her resistance, she begins to blossom. Heller teaches Maggie all about Bulwark Oil, and much more. When she wins the contest using an idea Heller had suggested, he even teaches her some French (he spent time in France during the war). Under the gradual influence of her attraction and of Heller's frank, no-nonsense disposition, Maggie's worldview and her relation to her stifling environment begin to crumble, inexorably.

Hite unravels the story amiably and colorfully, alternating between dialogue and voice-over narration, in the easy-going, ironic style of, say, Garrison Keillor's Lake Wobegon stories on his *Prairie Home Companion*. All the characters, even Cecil Bainbridge and his aunt, Clara the town gossip, are treated with benevolent, ironic bemusement and with only a hint of condescension. Only in the final Act III dialogue between Maggie and Heller does the irony subside respectfully, to allow the final unveiling of the two protagonists' true feelings to take place.

That Maggie is ripe for her fall is clear from the start; she is wound up so tight that she reacts jumpily to anything that touches her, though she does so with intelligence and humor. When she goes to the local drugstore for a cup of coffee, Johnny the friendly owner demonstrates that he has got her number:

Johnny: Hi, Maggie.
Maggie: Hi. Black coffee, Johnny.
Johnny: Heeey! That bad, huh?
Maggie: Mmmm, it'll do, until something worse comes along.

Johnny (after a pause): I know what's the matter with you.
Maggie: Watch your language, young man!

Until the last minute, Maggie is not sure who her companion will be on the trip she has won. The audience suspects, of course, but Maggie does not know. Until the last minute, Maggie holds on to her role as a demure virgin, pretending to be shocked by Heller's frankness; until, that is, she realizes she no longer believes that role herself (until she is ready to take the fall). The audience is awarded the privilege of being a step ahead of the main character (beginning with that title, which resonates through the story!), and this makes their relationship with the character a loving one. Since Maggie does not yet "know herself," the audience can wait for her to come to a realization about herself in her own time: it can wait for her epiphany to occur, and for her transformation to be completed.

It is in Maggie and Heller's last scene together that Heller finally pierces the bubble of her resistances, which she allows to be pierced.

Maggie: You know something crazy?
Heller: Yeah. But what do you mean?
Maggie: Clara Bainbridge and half of Fremontville thought I was going to ask you to go with me! Well, isn't that silly?
Heller: No, I don't think so.
Maggie: You don't? Well, I do. I think it's about.... No, I don't. I don't think it's silly at all.
Heller: (conspiratorially) I could get away....
Maggie: You make me sick! And the awful part of it is, I'd love it if you could go with me. It'd be fun and interesting and exciting and.... Oh, I am shameless.
Heller: No, no. No, you're not. And it would be fun. And interesting and exciting. (He chuckles softly) And Fremontville'd blow right off the map. (he laughs)
Maggie: I think you're the most- the most shocking, insensitive-

Heller: No, you don't, no you don't, chief. You'd like to, but you don't think anything of the kind.
(A frog croaks in the distance.)
Heller (cont'd): Maggie. You know something?
Maggie: No. What?
Heller: A guy can do all right for himself in the trucking business. He can make a nice little pile of dough.
Maggie: Well, good for him.
Heller: He can even pay his way to Europe, and back. And take somebody along. Like, oh, say. . . . Well, let's make Fremontville happy, huh? Suppose he takes his bride along with him.
Maggie: Oh. . . . Suppose he does.
Heller: Grenoble, Dijon, Paris, Chablis. Oh, Maggie, that'll make a lot of honeymoon, for two glorious weeks. And after that. . .
Maggie: Ohh. There's got to be more. . . !

The moment that really turns the couple's relationship, and the line that really stands out in this unpretentious, intelligent dialogue, is:

Heller: No, you don't, no you don't, chief. You'd like to, but you don't think anything of the kind.

Heller has been delicate, one might say reticent, until this time, in deference to Maggie's freedom of choice. He has not argued against her attitudes, nor has he ever asked her whom she intends to take with her on her vacation. He has stood on the sidelines, respectfully, offering his help if she needed it but never forcing himself on her. With the above line, he delivers a blow that is virtually a delicate slap in the face. He exposes her lie (she lies to herself and to others), affectionately but firmly. He tells her the truth about herself, bravely and lovingly. As he does so, Maggie's cocoon cracks and she can complete her metamorphosis.

Dorothy is a perfect fit for this gentle, witty comedy.

Radio Days, 1938–1955

General Electric Theater: "Sometime Every Summertime," August 27, 1953
The curious, and curiously wistful, drama "Sometime Every Summertime," produced by the *General Electric Theater* for CBS and aired on August 27, 1953, enjoys a good reputation among some old-time radio enthusiasts.[452] Conducted entirely through melancholy, parallel voice-over narrations and flashbacks, the original play, written by Fletcher Markle, concerned itself with the fleeting, changeable nature of feelings, even feelings that appear to be sincere and intense when they are first experienced.

Through alternating narrations, the play tells the story of a memorable but "unimportant" love story between a nice young man and a nice young woman during a summer vacation in Vancouver. For two whole weeks, the love between Clem Walden and Mary Thomas, a Canadian-born Italian girl, blossoms; then, at the batting of an eyelid, it peters out and dies overnight. Both narrators/protagonists are nostalgic about the story; both are uncertain about their feelings. For both, the event of that love is unimportant but memorable, and the contrast between these two qualities creates stridently contradictory feelings in evoking that past, warts and all. Most interestingly, a dark cloud appears in Clem's narration of the couple's last meeting, when he calls at her house in the poor section of town and meets her Italian-Canadian family. This is Clem's final narration:

> *This time she was wearing a white cotton suit that had been laundered too often and was too small for her. Her hair was done up in a sort of braid wound around her head, and she wasn't the same girl at all. We went dancing, and it wasn't any good: we didn't dance the same way. Then we went to a late movie, then coffee at a drive-in, then out to her house. None of it was the same, none of it was any good. I told her I'd phone her and drove back to*

---

[452] For example E.A. Villafranca on the website devoted to Writer Kathleen Hite (www.kathleenhite.com).

my apartment the long way. I got word at the office that I was to be transferred a couple of days later, and I didn't call her. I couldn't. It's very difficult for a man to get over realizing that he's a snob. Funny: it was so important, and yet I can't even remember her name.

Dorothy is fine as sweet Mary in her tender scenes and nostalgic, puzzled narrations. Mary never learns the reasons for Clem's final coldness, and it is just as well.

Lux Radio Theatre: "Breaking the Sound Barrier," October 12, 1953
On October 12, 1953, Dorothy McGuire and Robert Newton played the characters originally played by Ann Todd and Ralph Richardson in David Lean's film *The Sound Barrier* (1952) in this radio adaptation of the film for the *Lux Radio Theatre*.

Susan Garthwaite (McGuire) is the wife of ace fighter pilot Tony Garthwaite and the daughter of monomaniacal wealthy magnate John Ridgefield (Newton), who designs airplanes. Ridgefield is trying to solve the problem of how to break the sound barrier without destroying both plane and pilot, and has already lost one flyer (his son). When young Tony becomes enthusiastic about the project and volunteers to be the next to try, his wife objects. Tony insists, and so does she. When Tony mans a plane to conduct the experiment, he loses his life. Grief-stricken, Susan moves out of her father's house and starts planning her move to London with her baby son: she is determined to spare her son the fate of the rest of the family men, that of guinea pigs for aeronautical experimentation. Ridgefield does not desist, and assigns one of his best pilots, Philip Peel, to the experiment. Philip, using a counterintuitive move, is able to succeed in breaking the speed of sound and return intact. Susan changes her mind and goes back to her father.

Already from the above plot outline one can see that Susan's role is a subservient one, and that the play's sympathies are divided. The story is really about a scientific/aeronautical challenge and about the men who meet it. Especially in the first and second of the play's three acts, there is a lot of exposition outlining the problem and hypothesizing the solutions. For Tony and for Ridgefield, who both love Susan, the woman is an obstacle and a nuisance. Thus, Dorothy's character very quickly progresses from being the loving wife and devoted daughter to being the family nag. When Susan goes back on her decision to move away from the airplane industry and from her father after the pilot's victory, her "capitulation" makes her appear weak and slavish; thus, Dorothy's character is difficult to root for throughout the story.

Robert Newton and most of the actors playing the secondary roles effect good British accents; Dorothy does her very best, successfully, but tends to revert to her "natural" Mid-Atlantic Theatrical American accent. The real problem, however, is that she cannot help but be an outsider in this male-dominated story, fighting to get in.

Lux Radio Theatre: "The Winslow Boy," January 18, 1954
On paper, the choice of Ray Milland and Dorothy as the stars of this adaptation of Terence Rattigan's 1946 play *The Winslow Boy* (which Dorothy would perform on the La Jolla Playhouse stage five months later with Vincent Price as her co-star) must have looked like perfect casting. Milland was Welsh, and his classy deadpan was an efficacious hiding place for the sarcasm or torment that always lurked somewhere in his performances; and Dorothy was often able to portray characters where intelligence and feelings were masked by irony and perfect manners.

The problems that manifest in this adaptation have to do with the nature of the play itself, which is a curious hybrid. Straddled between comedy of manners and drama, *The Winslow Boy* is a beautiful thing of stiff upper lips and reticent feelings, a discreet, understated arabesque of subtle reactions and arguments rather than actions.

As in an ancient Greek play, most of the important "events" that form the drama's plot take place offstage and are narrated by the characters onstage after the fact. The entire courtroom drama that is the apparent subject of the play is never depicted, except through the comments of the characters. Theoretically, this makes the play perfect material for a radio adaptation: the characters' voices carry the narration and the story, and we do not need to "see" the events. In the case of this play, "talky" is the whole point, and never constitutes a flaw.

On the other hand, this discretion, or reticence, on Rattigan's part makes the "events" actually happening on the stage magnificently subtle. At every stage of the story, most of what is "happening" on the stage is happening before or after an "event," as the characters are either getting ready to "do" something or cooling off after having done it. The temperature of the drama is seldom hot, but falls mostly within a middle ground that tends towards the freezing point.

The above coldness and the inherent Britishness of the play entail that, in every exchange, what is not said is just as important as what is said. The cool, rational surface of the dialogue between characters hides their feelings; subtext is an essential component of this play. But the medium of radio is not necessarily the right one for such extreme "invisibility" of feelings and thoughts; not the outer events (or words) but the inner events of this story make it necessary for us to see the actors, in order to make visible what cannot be carried by the words alone.

Thus, though the "The Winslow Boy" radio drama is conducted efficiently enough, and though it is a pleasure to hear Milland and Dorothy interact at least through their voices, much of the richness hiding below the surface of the story—richness that should make the story a truly satisfying dramatic experience—is lost in the adaptation to the medium.

Lux Radio Theatre: "A Blueprint for Murder," March 29, 1954
For once, Dorothy was cast resolutely against type in the psychological suspense drama "A Blueprint for Murder," aired on March 29, 1954. She played a murder suspect, and, as it turns out, a murderer.

When Polly, the stepdaughter of Lynn Cameron (Dorothy), ends up in the hospital with violent spasms and agonizing pain, Lynn sends for the brother of her late husband Bill. Cam (played by Dan Dailey) flies in to lend his support. When the child dies, Cam decides to prolong his visit. He begins to have feelings for Lynn, and starts visiting with some old friends of his brother's. A series of medical inconsistencies lead him (and his friends) to believe that Polly's death was not accidental, and an autopsy is ordered. Gradually, Cam begins to suspect that Lynn might have been responsible for Polly's demise. As it turns out, Lynn had motive: her husband Bill left a lot of money to his children, and if they die the money goes to Mrs. Cameron. More and more evidence is gathered, and Cam's suspicions about Lynn become obsessive.

Lynn intends to take her stepson Doug away on a European cruise, and Cam is worried that this might mean that she intends to dispose of Doug too, if his (and the police's) suspicions are correct. Cam therefore decides to also sign up for the ocean voyage. On their last night at sea, he happens to be in Lynn's stateroom as a bottle of aspirin on her dresser catches his eye. He investigates, and finds some tablets in the bottle that are different from the others. While he and Lynn are having their nightcap, he spikes her cocktail with one of those pills, and, after she downs her drink and complains of its bitterness, Cam confronts her with his accusations. In front of Mr. Connelly, the ship detective, Lynn steadfastly denies the accusations. After five minutes, nothing has happened, and Lynn is still denying, so Cam and Connelly leave. Cam returns to his stateroom, crestfallen; but Connelly soon knocks at his door to report that, immediately after the two of them had left, Lynn went into convulsions and called for help; the ship doctor pumped her stomach just in time. Lynn is convicted of murder and sentenced to life in prison.

Dorothy sinks her teeth into her unusually negative character. Her gradual shift from loving, likable friend to suspect to evil murderess is a little treasure trove of nuances. Dan Dailey has more radio time in terms of lines, but Dorothy's role is more interesting.

In her chitchat with host Irving Cummings following the drama, Dorothy commented on this unusual casting: "There's nothing an actress likes better than to play a part entirely different from her last one." This statement seems to contradict several others that Dorothy made over the years, confessing that she did not like to play negative characters. Either Dorothy had been coached to speak the above line, or she was more ambivalent in her choice of characters than she was ready to admit.

Family Theater: "Flight to Bermuda," May 5, 1954
A comedy role was the order of the day on May 5, 1954, on the show *Family Theater* (1947–1957). The host of the episode entitled "Flight to Bermuda" was Charles Boyer.

The anthology radio show *Family Theater* was produced for the Mutual Broadcasting System (also called the Mutual Network) by Family Theater Productions, an extension of Father Patrick Payton's Family Rosary Crusade (whose iconic motto was, and is, "The family that prays together stays together"). *Family Theater*'s parallel television incarnation, entitled *Family Theatre*, which had debuted in 1951, would close in 1958.

Family Theater had an inclination towards mildness, and this should not come as a surprise given its religious proclivities and family values, which were clearly expressed in its introduction, spoken on this particular evening by host Boyer: "*Family Theater*'s only purpose is to bring to everyone's attention a practice that must become an important part of our lives, if we are to win peace for ourselves, peace for our families and peace for the world. *Family Theater* urges you to pray, pray together as a family."

In this particular instance, such mildness is tempered by the odd "immoral" development of Dorothy's character, telegraph office clerk Jo (Josephine) Addison of Finchville. Jo is a young woman who dreams of a more adventurous and exotic life. She sees an opportunity when she begins processing a telegram to a Mrs. Ann McLaughlin, a local woman who has won a slogan contest and is the recipient of a two-week vacation in Bermuda. Jo steals the woman's identity and takes her place on the vacation. She meets an eligible bachelor and lets herself be wooed by him; there is talk of marriage, and things seem to be going her way, until all the lies she has told catch up with her in the form of travel agent Charles Morris of Chicago, who has flown to Bermuda to have the woman arrested. Suddenly, we (and Jo) realize that the whole story has been a daydream, and that the young man standing in front of her telegraph window waiting for her to pay attention is the perfect match for her, right here in Finchville. There's no place like home, apparently.

The radio play is pleasant enough, but the story development is heavily overwritten by writer-director John T. Kelley, and overacted by the cast. Dorothy seems more comfortable in the easy-going set-up scenes, where the comedy is delicate and witty. The second-act scenes are too breathless and shrill to be funny, and Jo's daydream actions (before we know they belong in a daydream) are so objectionable that they make her character somewhat repulsive.

Lux Radio Theatre: "Mother Didn't Tell Me," November 16, 1954
Dorothy had co-starred with William Lundigan in the romantic comedy film *Mother Didn't Tell Me* in 1950. The adaptation that the *Lux Radio Theatre* produced four years later did not do much to improve on the original; if anything, the radio version was little more than a faded carbon copy of the far-from-perfect film. Radio stalwart Frank Lovejoy co-starred in the Lundigan part.

The comedy in the film (which is discussed in Part I, Chapter 8) was amiable but slight, and its joys lay in the subtlety of the performances—or at least of some of the performances. Most of those subtleties go straight out the window in this radio version, as do a few of the most amusing lines from the film. The reason has to do with the fact that some gags needed the aural/visual combination, and do not work properly without the image. Dorothy conducts herself admirably in this, a flawed, negligible affair.

Lux Radio Theatre: "Gentleman's Agreement," March 15, 1955
Gentleman's Agreement was thoughtful and interesting—in fact, it was quite wonderful—when it appeared as a *Cosmopolitan* serial in 1946, and

as a novel in 1947, written by Laura Z. Hobson. It was just as thoughtful, interesting, and wonderful when it appeared as an Oscar-winning film in 1947, starring Gregory Peck and Dorothy and directed by Elia Kazan. Its value had not deteriorated one jot when it returned as a radio play eight years later in this *Lux Radio Theatre* dramatization, starring Ray Milland and Dorothy (in their second pairing). Gregory Peck had already starred with Anne Baxter in an earlier *Lux Radio Theatre* adaptation of the film on September 20, 1948.

The film is dealt with in Part I, Chapter 8, and there is not much to be added here. Dorothy is quite perfect as Cathy Lacey, the WASP fiancée of journalist Philip Green, who, in order to write a series of articles on anti-Semitism, chooses to carry out his research by pretending to be Jewish. This ruse allows Philip to learn "the hard way" how Jews are treated but creates many negative ripples for him and his family, and almost wrecks his relationship with Cathy.

It is nice to hear Dorothy and Milland act together—they never did on film—even though Milland is not quite so perfect for the role as Gregory Peck had been in the film. There was something stately and solemn about Peck, and his indignation and rage had a regal nobility to them that is missing in Milland, a more sanguine, sarcastic actor. A minor flaw to this pleasant narrative.

Lux Radio Theatre: "Now, Voyager," May 24, 1955
In many ways, the casting of Dorothy as the protagonist of the lost *Lux Radio Theatre* episode "Now, Voyager," based on the 1942 Warner Bros. film starring Bette Davis (in turn based on a successful 1941 novel of the same title by Olive Higgins Prouty),[453] must have made for a perfect match. The story of a bashful, neurotic woman who undergoes a metamorphosis through the effects of psychotherapy and finds love with an unhappily married man, *Now, Voyager* was the right material for Doro-

---
[453] Olive Higgins Prouty, *Now, Voyager*, Houghton Mifflin Company, 1941.

thy's melodious sensitivity and intelligence, and must have allowed her to show the two faces of her talent: demure sensitivity and girlish shyness on the one hand, intelligence, wisdom and self-reliance on the other. Versatile character actor Les Tremayne was her co-star. It must certainly have been wonderful to hear Dorothy speak that celebrated final line: *"Don't let's ask for the moon; we have the stars."*

A wistful publicity portrait of Dorothy, probably one of a series taken by RKO photographer Ernest A. Bachrach, circa 1946.

12. Tantamount, Adamant, and Others

> Homes are [Dorothy McGuire's] only extravagance—she'd love to have one in every port.
> Hedda Hopper, 1949

Dorothy's beginnings were modest, both in terms of family provenance and real-estate values. The simplicity of her lifestyle and the self-effacing, unostentatious, but eccentric elegance of her person extended to her living quarters.

Immediately after her first theatrical success, *Claudia* (1941), Dorothy was able to move out of the cheap Broadway hotel where she had been staying and into a "tastefully furnished apartment."[454] Here is a contemporary commentary on this small fifth-floor, $65-a-month walk-up:

> Dorothy's simplicity is also reflected in her apartment, a modest walk-up where Bertha, a Negro maid formerly with her mother in Omaha, keeps house for her. Dorothy loves music, and the twin prides of her small living room are a yel-

---
[454] Barron, "Girl's Persistence...," *Democrat and Chronicle*, op. cit.

low-keyed melodeon for which she paid $35 and an elderly wooden washstand in which she keeps an elderly phonograph. She loves to put on records and dance around the room, all by herself. She hates dancing in night clubs. She is an amateur painter, with a good sense of color. She likes giving tiny cocktail parties, and on these occasions calls guests' attention to her caginess in buying two screens which stand next to the two windows in her living room in the daytime and which she places on the sills at night. "Instead of Venetian blinds," she explains, looking terribly shrewd. "The windows are a special size and if you move, the blinds would be no good for the next place." She attaches great importance to her possessions, and feels insulted if anyone fails to appreciate them.[455]

A similarly modest apartment would be Dorothy's dwelling during her transfer to Hollywood, before her marriage to John Swope. Even after her exalted nuptials, however, the living quarters the couple elected as their subsequent homes were elegant but simple, more practical than palatial.

Though they would eventually choose Beverly Hills as their main place of residence in due time, for years Dorothy and John Swope shuttled regularly between New York and Los Angeles when they were not traveling to far-off lands, or when Dorothy was not filming. Both John and Dorothy had "roots" in New York, since John's family was based in and around the city and Dorothy was "Broadway-born." The Gerard Swope dynasty owned properties all through the East Coast, notably in New York City, on the Hudson River, and on Cape Cod, Massachusetts; John, Dorothy, and later their offspring would occasionally vacation at those locations. Both spouses loved the theater, and John dabbled in producing, so

---

[455] Hellman, "McGuire" (1941), op. cit., 131.

regular theatergoing trips to New York City were the norm. Dorothy and John also owned a house in Connecticut for their East Coast forays.[456]

According to reports by Dorothy herself, it was during one of their trips to New York, sometime in 1946, that the Swopes decided to buy a pied-*a-terre* in New York, in order to have easy access to what the city had to offer during their frequent trips east. This home base was described variously by Dorothy in news reports as "a tiny house," as an old carriage house facing the Hudson River, as a remodeled barn,[457] or as a Dutch stable that she and John had transformed into a home. Here is Hedda Hopper reporting:

> Dorothy McGuire calls the old Dutch stable she and her husband transformed into a home, "Tantamount"; their stone guest house is "Adamant." Wish I'd had time to see Dorothy's home when I was in New York. It faces the Hudson River.[458]

"It's on the wrong side of the tracks," Dorothy explained in an interview, "but it's so inexpensive we can just lock it up when we leave. Then we'll have it to come back to instead of a hotel."[459] After filming *Claudia and David*, Dorothy spent the greater part of a year (May 1946–April 1947) remodeling and furnishing Tantamount and Adamant. She was still busy with the New York houses when she was called to Hollywood to test for *Gentleman's Agreement*, and she flew west briefly; John stayed

---

456 Hopper, "Ideals" (1950), op. cit.

457 The barn version was reported by Hopper in her column on March 2, 1949, with an additional mention of Dorothy's nursery for her new child being a former hayloft.

458 Hedda Hopper, "Looking at Hollywood," *Los Angeles Times*, May 13, 1947.

459 Hedda Hopper, "Margaret Sullavan Career Well Mapped," *Los Angeles Times*, September 28, 1949.

behind to finish work on the property, waiting for Dorothy to join him once filming started in New York at the end of May 1947.[460]

In those years, Dorothy was evidently growing attached either to the two houses in particular or to life on the East Coast in general, for Hedda Hopper, who kept a watchful eye on the actress, reported that Dorothy did not want to leave New York and go back to Los Angeles. In fact, there was talk of her doing a Technicolor film on the coast of Maine during the summer of 1947, with Henry Fonda as her co-star (in place of *Gentleman's Agreement*, perhaps?).[461]

Those two houses, and their bucolic location on the Hudson River, were special to Dorothy and John, at least briefly. Tantamount and Adamant served as headquarters for them during Dorothy's New York filming of *Gentleman's Agreement*, and as base of operations when Dorothy and John embarked on their Italian journey in 1948, during Dorothy's first successful pregnancy. Back from that trip, it was to Tantamount that the couple brought their newborn daughter from the hospital in Ossining, New York, where the birth occurred in February 1949.

More about Tantamount and Adamant, and the connection of their curious names to Dorothy, in the book's last chapter.

According to the recollections of Topo Swope, John and Dorothy were indeed staying at Tantamount during that period, but did not own the property, which belonged to "other Swopes";[462] these Hudson River houses were not far from Gerard Swope's estate, The Croft, which in turn was near Ossining, in Westchester County.

The magnificent Croft estate was not one house, but several, with some 400 acres of land between and around them. What follows is the

---

460 Hedda Hopper, "Looking at Hollywood," *Los Angeles Times*, May 17, 1947.

461 Hopper (March 1947), op. cit.

462 Topo Swope, correspondence with the author, March 2018.

story of the intersection of that estate with the Swope family. Here is the mention that David Loth makes of it in his biography of Gerard Swope:

> In 1922 [General Electric executive Charles A. Coffin] suggested that Swope buy on Long Island, where Coffin and a good many other company executives then lived. Swope replied politely that he preferred a place away from his associates; he wanted to invite them to break in on his week end, not have them drop by casually because they were neighbors. So he elected Westchester, and left the rest to [his wife] Mary.
>
> She found a very pleasant English-style country house, The Croft, with one hundred ten acres of woods and garden, a lake big enough for boating, and trails linked with those of other estates to offer many miles of unmotorized riding for the horseman. As the years passed, they increased their property by nearly three hundred acres more, another lake and a dozen or so other houses for their children or staff or to rent, and for a time there was a substantial farming operation.[463]

The reported price Gerard Swope paid for the Yorktown, New York, estate in 1923 was $240,000.[464] The house that gave the estate its name was designed and built in 1913–1914 by its original owner, Arthur Stannard Vernay (née Avant, 1877–1960). British-born Vernay had a successful business at 1 East 45th Street in New York City, which he expanded later with two other shops in the city, one in Boston, a sales outlet in London, and a summer shop in Newport, Rhode Island. Vernay specialized in English antiques and offered restoration and interior design services; an important part of his business was offering the installation of period

---

[463] Loth (1958), op. cit., 139–140.

[464] Matt A.V. Chaban, "A Sprawling Manor for $125,000 (Some Disassembly Required)," *New York Times*, February 9, 2015.

paneled rooms, a line that employed up to forty people. Vernay invested his profits well and, by 1920, was able to cut back the hours he spent at his antiques store. He indulged his interest in collecting animal specimens for the American Museum of Natural History (AMNH) in New York and went on a number of collecting expeditions, the first of which was in 1923, when he and Colonel John C. Faunthorpe traveled to India. His last expedition was to Africa in 1946. Vernay visited Tibet (being among the first Westerners to visit Lhasa), Siam, the Malay Peninsula, and Burma. In 1930, the AMNH opened a room called the Vernay-Faunthorpe Hall of South Asiatic Mammals. After he retired, Vernay moved to the Bahamas, where he died on October 25, 1960. He was married to Marion Woodruff Kelley; they had no children. A genus of rodents, the Vernaya, was named after Vernay.[465]

Most of the interior of the 5,500-square-foot (or, according to the *New York Times*, 8,000-square-foot)[466] Tudor-style mansion was built using salvaged pieces from English buildings dating from the seventeenth, eighteenth, and nineteenth centuries, and, in the case of two fireplaces, as early as the fourteenth century. The antique details inside the house included "eight fireplaces, tongue-and-groove flooring, leaded windows, a two-story great room with a grand carved wooden staircase and newel post, and an oak-paneled bishop's room. There are also brass fixtures, stone fountains and medallions."[467] According to the *New York Times*, the house included "a pair of fireplaces from 1357, a 300-pound wrought-iron door and wooden timbers weighing half a ton that adorn the ceiling in the great

---

[465] Several sources, including the archival database of Antique Dealers of the University of Leeds, United Kingdom, and Arthur S. Vernay's business papers, The Joseph Downs Collection of Manuscripts and Printed Ephemera, Henry Francis du Pont Winterthur Museum, Winterthur, Delaware.

[466] Chaban (2015), op. cit.

[467] Bill Cary, "Historic Croft home in Teatown wins temporary reprieve," *LoHud* magazine (lohud.com), September 14, 2015.

room."[468] Upon completion, the house was featured in the December 1914 issue of *Architecture: The Professional Architectural Monthly* (1900–1936).

The Tudor-style mansion that gave Gerard Swope's estate its name, The Croft, in a recent photograph. Photo: Robert Yasinsac/www.hudsonvalleyruins.org, 2015.

In 1919, the estate was sold to Daniel Rhodes Hanna (1866–1921), a Cleveland newspaper and iron, coal, and railway magnate.[469] Hanna's father, businessman, US Senator, and friend and ally of President William McKinley Marcus "Mark" Hanna, had inherited a very profitable mining and metals conglomerate from his wife's father in the 1880s, which he renamed the M. A. Hanna Company in 1885. Daniel was a partner in this company, and owned two newspapers in Cleveland, the *Cleveland News*

468 Chaban (2015), op. cit.

469 Ibid.

and the *Sunday News-Leader*.[470] Daniel built the Leader-News Building (1912),[471] as well as the Hanna Building[472] and Theater[473] "in tribute to his theater-loving father, who had owned the Euclid Avenue Opera House [. . .]." The theater was inaugurated on March 28, 1921.[474] Both buildings were designed by prominent New York architect Charles A. Platt. As for The Croft, the four-times-married-and-divorced Hanna enlarged the property by building a stable and a carriage house.

After Gerard Swope's purchase, additions were made to the estate, including houses for his children, apartments for the staff, a paddock for horses, a green house, a vegetable garden and berry patch, an ice house, a hay barn, a cow barn and milk house, a garage, a swimming area, bathhouses and a boat house, a tea house, and other buildings.[475]

Here is the continuation of the estate's history from the website of its

---

[470] Daniel R. Hanna, Local Wiki (localwiki.org), Historic Saranac Lake. See also: Case Western Reserve University, Encyclopedia of Cleveland History.

[471] Then renamed The Leader Building. N August 18, 2014, the K&D Group, Inc., a major Cleveland real-estate owner and developer, purchased the building for $5.4 million, announcing that it intended to maintain part of the fifteen-floor property as office space, and convert the majority to housing. (See Michelle Jarboe, "Leader Building in downtown Cleveland fetches $5.4 million in sale to K&D Group," *Cleveland.com*, August 19, 2014.)

[472] The 16-story Hanna Building is now a residential tower, on the corner of East 14th Street and Euclid Avenue in downtown Cleveland's theater district. It was placed on the National Register of Historic Places in 1976 as a part of the Playhouse Square Group, the second-largest theater complex in the United States after New York City's. (See the website Cleveland Historical.)

[473] The Hanna Theater still stands; after closing in 1989, it finally reopened in 2008 after a major restoration, to serve as the home of the Great Lakes Theater Festival.

[474] For the Hanna Theater, see John Vacha, *Showtime in Cleveland: The Rise of a Regional Theater Center*, The Kent State University Press, 2001, 124–125.

[475] Lincoln Diamant, *Images of America: Teatown Lake Reservation*, Arcadia Publishing, 2002, 34. The map of the extended estate in the 1940s and '50s on page 34 was compiled from the recollections of Eileen Argenziano, a local resident who chaired many of the early Teatown fairs in the 1960s and acted as fundraiser for the organization.

current owners, the non-profit nature preserve and environmental education center named Teatown Lake Reservation, whose history is itself tied to the Swope family:

> In 1923, Gerard Swope, Sr., Chairman of General Electric, purchased "The Croft" and all its surrounding land. He and his family enjoyed riding horses, so they stabled the animals in the English Tudor outbuildings and built a network of horse trails. A few years later, he dammed Bailey Brook, which flooded a low-lying meadow, creating the 42-acre Teatown Lake.
>
> After enjoying the land almost daily for many years, Mr. Swope died in 1957, leaving the property to his children. In 1963, the heirs of Gerard Swope gave the Brooklyn Botanic Garden 194 acres to provide an outreach station in Ossining. In exchange for the donation, the Swope's [sic] directed the Botanic Garden to conserve the open space while educating the public about the resources such land could provide. Teatown began functioning with only a small staff and a few volunteers, offering nature classes and activities for both children and adults. In 1971, Teatown became formally incorporated as a separate legal entity, and 21 community members made up a board of directors. As Teatown continued to grow with the help of members and local donors, the partnership with the Brooklyn Botanic Garden became less necessary, and was eventually amicably dissolved.[476]

The Swope heirs' donation in 1963 did not, however, include the Swope family home. "The 72 acres on the east of Spring Valley Road that included the Swope family home and a farmhouse were sold to Phil

---

[476] From the History section of the Teatown Lake Reservation website (www.teatown.org).

E. Gilbert, Jr.,[477] who lived at The Croft until his death in 2008."[478] In 2012, Teatown Lake Reservation finally purchased the remainder of the original estate, including the mansion, "for $3.5 million[479] through a combination of Teatown's funds, $1.295 million in financing by the Open Space Institute and provate [sic] donors. A bridge loan from the Norcross Foundation helped pay for the balance of the purchase."[480]

In 2015, after trying to find an alternate use for The Croft mansion (apartments, office space, a conference center, a restaurant, etc.), Teatown Lake Reservation realized that keeping, restoring, or renovating the house would be quite costly, and impractical; hence, they decided to put it up for sale. With a proviso, which Chaban explained in his *New York Times* article:

> It might just be one of the greatest real estate deals in New York. For $125,000, a roughly 8,000-square-foot Tudor home overlooking lakes and forests in a nature preserve here is up for grabs, the epitome of baronial-bucolic Westchester County living.
>
> [...] The only catch for today's buyers is that they must pull a Vernay and pull the house down, carting off all or some of it to create their own Frankenstein castle. That, and endure the howls of preservationists who view the house as an integral piece of the land it sits on.[481]

---

[477] Gilbert was a Manhattan lawyer. See Chaban (2015), op. cit.

[478] Plamena Plesheva, "Teatown Acquires 59-Acre Open Space, The Croft," *Chappaqua Patch* (patch.com), June 16, 2012.

[479] According to the *New York Times*, 3 million. See Chaban (2015), op. cit.

[480] Plesheva (2012), op. cit.

[481] Chaban (2015), op. cit.

Public outcry from local preservationists and residents was virulent and deafening, "winning support from the Preservation League of New York and the Royal Oak Foundation, the American arm of the National Trust, Britain's chief conservation organization. And the state's Department of Parks, Recreation and Historic Preservation sent a letter noting it had already considered the Croft for the Register of Historic Places, though this is more a tax incentive than demolition safeguard."[482]

The result? As stated in the Teatown website, at a June 19, 2019 meeting, Teatown's Board of Trustees voted to move ahead with demolition of the Croft "in the most environmentally responsible manner."

According to Hopper, in 1947 the Swopes bought a lot of land in the Pacific Palisades coastal district in western Los Angeles, near Malibu. They planned to build a home on it, consisting of "a single huge room with bathroom and kitchen tacked onto one of the walls."[483] Dorothy still kept "a tiny apartment in the building where she [had] first lived in Hollywood as a pied-a-terre when working in the studios."[484] According to Dorothy's daughter Topo, however, after their New York period John and Dorothy lived in a modest house in Beverly Hills, whose address Topo remembers as 345 S. Crescent Drive.[485] She also remembers her family spending time in New York City.

Already in 1950, before the birth of the Swopes' second child, their Los Angeles home was becoming cramped. The ubiquitous Hopper reported the problem, her tongue firmly in her cheek:

> Dorothy McGuire will either have to add a room to

---

[482] Ibid.

[483] Hedda Hopper, "Looking at Hollywood," *Los Angeles Times*, July 5, 1947.

[484] Hedda Hopper, "Battle" (1947), op. cit.

[485] Topo Swope, correspondence with the author, March 2018.

her home or find a larger house for all the loot John Swope brought home from his world tour.[486]

The problem of finding a place for John's travel souvenirs might have been a fictitious one in 1950; by 1952, when Dorothy became pregnant with her son Mark, a new, real problem presented itself. The family definitely needed more space.

That year, Dorothy and John purchased the house that would be Dorothy's permanent home until her passing in 2001. Those who knew the couple still talk about that house, and about its tasteful beauty, with admiration.

The unostentatious mansion was situated off the beaten track of Beverly Hills, at 121 Copley Place. It was designed by architect Paul R. Williams and built by Glen O. Winget in 1928.

Paul Revere Williams (1894–1980), who would become known in Hollywood as the "architect to the stars," was born in Los Angeles, where he studied at the Los Angeles School of Art and Design and then at the University of Southern California (USC). He became a certified architect in 1921; in 1923, he became the first African-American member of the American Institute of Architects (AIA).

Practicing mostly in Southern California, Williams designed several commercial and institutional buildings that would become iconic city landmarks, such as the Beverly Hills MCA building at 360 North Crescent Drive (1938), Saks Fifth Avenue at 9600 Wilshire Boulevard (1939, in collaboration with architects John and Donald Parkinson, who in 1929 had designed the famous Bullocks Wilshire building at 3050 Wilshire Boulevard), and the Late Moderne-styled Golden State Mutual Life Insurance building at 1999 West Adams Boulevard (1949).

---

[486] Hedda Hopper, "Curtiz Will Direct Roman in 'Serenade,'" *Los Angeles Times*, June 7, 1950.

Paul Revere Williams' Golden State Life Insurance building at the intersection of Adams Boulevard and Western Avenue, Los Angeles. Wikimedia Commons, Downtowngal, 2012.

His fame as an architect, however, rests almost solely on his residential designs. Over the span of five decades, Williams designed an eclectic collection of more than 2,000 private homes,[487] many of them for celebrity clients. Among the entertainment personalities for whom Williams designed homes were Desi Arnaz and Lucille Ball, Victor Borge, Lon Chaney Sr., Bert Lahr, Grace Moore, ZaSu Pitts, Otto Preminger, Frank Sinatra, Barbara Stanwyck, Danny Thomas, and William Wyler.[488] Several of the houses he designed are now listed on the National Register of Historic Places. Closer to our topic of discussion, another Williams design,

[487] According to the American Association of Architects (AIA), who bestowed the Gold Medal on Williams in 2017, the architect designed "nearly 3,000 beautiful buildings during his five-decade career." (See their website, aia.org.)

[488] Sources: Wikipedia, and the website Paul Revere Williams, American Architect (paulrwilliamsproject.org).

the house eventually owned by Dorothy's friend Jane Wyatt Ward at 651 Siena Way in Bel Air, was placed on the Los Angeles Historic Cultural Landmark List in 2007, the year after Wyatt's death, through the admirable efforts of the Los Angeles Conservancy.[489] Jane had donated the home to the California Community Foundation prior to her death in 2006.[490]

The unobtrusive street entrance of Paul Revere Williams' house at 651 Siena Way, Bel Air, Los Angeles.

The Swopes' house on Copley Place was a three-story, five-bedroom single-family residence in the Spanish or Pueblo Revival style. Its first owner was George Schermerhorn Seward (1874–1943),[491] a prominent

---

489 See: the architectural website US Modernist (ncmodernist.com), which has an extensive, well-researched section on Williams' residential designs.

490 See the Los Angeles Conservancy website (www.laconservancy.org).

491 It would seem from the website US Modernist that Seward commissioned Williams with a second house in Beverly Hills, circa 1947.

investment banker from New York, who in 1928 took up residence in the new house while keeping offices at 626 S. Spring Street in Downtown Los Angeles.[492] The house had an open vista over the Los Angeles Country Club golf course, as well as over the famed 29-room "Playboy Mansion" designed by architect Arthur Kelly in 1927. The Swopes paid for the house in cash, which one could do in 1952–53.[493]

Unfortunately, the house was sold after Dorothy's passing, and the new owners tore the house down to build anew, even though, according to Dorothy's children, they had stated they would preserve the original house and limit themselves to internal remodeling.[494] According to Jim Fernald, actress Diane Keaton, who loved the house, had been thinking of buying it, but relented eventually (she would probably have kept the house as it was). Upon hearing of the demolition, Topo Swope was able to contact the contractors and salvage some cupboards and chests from the upper floors. The paparazzi, however, had the lion's share: Fernald went back to the house with Mark Swope shortly after Dorothy's death, and remembers photographers, journalists, and assorted "scavengers" ripping through the house and squalidly running out with sundry souvenirs.[495]

More than the building itself, those who knew the house remember its location and grounds, the exquisite workmanship and materials of its interior spaces (such as curved fireplaces and staircases made of precious exotic woods) and the Swopes' decorative taste. Here is Dorothy's daughter:

---

[492] *Who's Who in California: A Biographical Directory*, Vol. 1928–29, Justice B. Detwiler, ed., Who's Who Publishing Company, 1929.

[493] Topo Swope, conversation with the author, March 2017.

[494] At the time of writing this, several real-estate websites (such as Zillow, Inc., Redfin Corporation, and realtor.com) still listed the house as having been built in 1929; they all describe it as a 7-bedroom, 7-bathroom, 5,666-square-foot property. The US Modernist website lists the house as one of Williams' works, and mentions its destruction in 2002.

[495] Jim Fernald, conversation with the author, April 2017.

> Mother was very eccentric and had very specific taste, so the house was the result of the beautiful way she had put things together more than of any one specific object. It was both elegant and delicately eccentric. Dad took care of the garden and fruit trees; after his death mother let the place go. It wasn't as bad as Grey Gardens, but it got to be pretty run down.[496]

Family friend Jim Fernald, who rented the Swopes' downstairs poolroom between 1991 and 2001, has a less catastrophic memory of the garden's condition:

> They had this unbelievable tiered rose garden, which I think had been put in by the original owners, or at least dated from before the Swopes bought the house. I have these vivid memories of Dorothy's gardener, Mr. Martinez, who must have been 94 [in the early 1990s], sauntering down to take care of those roses.[497]

My own memories of the house being rather blurry after my limited frequentation all those years back, I have merged them with the recollections of Dorothy's family and friends for a description. Most of what follows is the result of the reminiscences of Dan Levin, Topo Swope, and especially Jim Fernald.

The ground floor, or basement, of the house was called the pool apartment, which originally was just a large space for changing into or out of bathing suits. It was a large room with a fireplace, connected to an adjoining kitchen and bathroom, plus a back room for storage.

---
496 Topo Swope, conversation with the author, March 2017.

497 Fernald (2017), op. cit.

A large staircase led to the main residence upstairs. You went through a double door, into the main hallway, where another, much larger wooden staircase with an elaborate banister connected the main floor to the three upstairs bedrooms. The hallway led to a large vestibule, which was the center of the main floor and the central exchange towards all the other rooms. On the right was the entrance to the servants' quarters. On the left was the dining room (which in the 1990s would become Dorothy's bedroom, due to her walking disability). Next to the dining room was a full bar, with a counter, a sink, glasses, and an original collection of liquors and cocktail implements from all over the world, most of them bought by John Swope over the years. Straight across were the doors to the living room and to the main terrace overlooking the swimming pool.

A detail of the large swimming pool at 121 Copley Place, set against the luxuriant vegetation that helped isolate it from its surroundings. Courtesy of Topo Swope's private collection.

The terrace was special, large enough to accommodate some fifty people. It was furnished with wicker chairs and sofas, and a stone table on a wrought-iron base with matching chairs. The weather in Los Angeles being what it is, the furniture could remain outside virtually all year round. These were the chairs and sofas where people like Marilyn Monroe, Gregory Peck, Henry Fonda, and Warren Beatty had sat over the years.

Southwestern Color: a detail of the terrace at 121 Copley Place, some of whose walls were painted a striking rust-orange. When the weather was clement, some of John's large framed black-and-whites were displayed on that orange background. Courtesy of Topo Swope's private collection.

Below the terrace, in the "back yard," was a large swimming pool: not Olympic size, but large enough, probably some forty-five feet long. Below that was a tiered rose garden, and around that fruit trees, magnolia trees and a palm tree. Below the tiered garden was an old badminton court, with great old lampposts and lights that did not work, courtesy of the original owners of the house. Through an old rusty gate, one could go out (briefly and surreptitiously) into the very exclusive Los Angeles Country Club golf course.

Bucolic path: the steps leading from the tiered rose garden, whose tail end can be glimpsed at the bottom of the photo, to the gate of the property, which separated it from the Los Angeles Country Club golf course. Courtesy of Topo Swope's private collection.

The huge living room was the crowning glory of the house. One entered the room through an arched entryway, and the room had two distinct areas: a large sitting room with "moderne" chairs and sofas, an ottoman and a coffee table, and another area with a grand piano[498] and

---

[498] The eyewitnesses are not sure about the grand piano. I seem to remember seeing one.

another sofa setup by the window overlooking the swimming pool; on the outside, the window was surrounded by a lovely Bougainvillea cascade.

A detail of the sitting room at 121 Copley Place. At first sight, Dorothy's decorating choices could seem like a hodgepodge of indecision. Gradually, an eclectic logic shone through. The odd mixture of ethnic Southwestern/Pueblo, Italianate classic, 1950s Moderne, high-end 19th-century, Old-America shabby chic, and designer modern styles could seem incongruous when set against the 1920s elegance of Paul Revere Williams' Spanish-Revival architecture. It could also reveal a friendly, casual eccentricity that was a perfect match to Dorothy and John Swope. Courtesy of Topo Swope's private collection.

As for the furniture, there was definitely a Southwestern-United States theme running through the house, as most eyewitnesses rightly point out. This theme, however, merged and alternated with an Italianate/ *faux* Renaissance motif: 19th-century American antique tables or chairs were juxtaposed with Italian-styled cupboards or cabinets; these in turn would contrast boldly with modern pieces such as a glass coffee table or a 1950s chair set. This incongruous juxtaposition of old and new, modern and antique, Southwestern-rustic and classic, endowed the house with a unique, eccentric look and with an unpretentious friendliness that were perfectly in tune with the characters of its owners.

Here is the impression that the house left on Italian journalist, critic, and historian Alvise Sapori, who conducted an interview with Dorothy for the Italian newspaper *la Repubblica* in 1986:

> In the vestibule, there are a dozen blown-up photographs, among which I notice two wonderful views, of Florence and of Piazza Navona [in Rome], which have been placed there in our honor, though [Ms. McGuire] presents them as if they had always been there. Piazza Navona towers over three splendid photo portraits: a young Marlon Brando, Bogart with cigarette and Henry Moore amongst his works. The photos are by Dorothy McGuire's late husband, famous photographer John Swope.
>
> The house is magnificent ("it's very old, it needs a lot of work," she comments, but I cannot notice any big flaws). Large white surfaces with vast windows looking out on a rose garden, which in turn slopes down towards the swimming pool against a background of hills, lawns and fantastic trees. The roses in the garden, recognizable, are bunched up in small bouquets of varying degrees of bloom. The furnishings are elegant, casual, well-traveled, with some superb pieces (for example an immense antique Moroccan carpet), a few precious art books (not many, but carefully selected), a few sculptures ("when I was in Rome I frequented Afro and Mirko[499] quite a

---

[499] Afro Basaldella (1912–1976) and his two brothers Mirko (1910–1969) and Dino (1909–1977) were three well-regarded Italian artists. Afro was a painter, Mirko a painter and

lot, at the American Academy...") and some popular arts and crafts objects of the highest caliber. But anyone thinking that this house resembles a museum would be dead wrong. "Would you help me put these cushions back over there, please? Yes, there, thank you, so they can cover up that ugly stain on the floor."[500]

Through those elegant, airy living spaces, the most amazing array of guests flowed and paused over the years of Dorothy's career and life. Business people and friends, artists and actors, directors and producers, playwrights and composers, designers and photographers, famous and less famous, young and old, sat on those chairs and sofas and absorbed the relaxed warmth of those surroundings. Most of all, they absorbed the relaxed warmth of their gracious hosts.

---

sculptor, and Dino a sculptor.

[500] Alvise Sapori, "Io vecchia star? Attrice, prego e soprattutto, mamma" ["Me an Old Star? Actress, Please, and above All, Mother"], *la Repubblica*, Rome, Italy, August 17, 1986.

13. Other Studios, 1951–1973

Callaway Went Thataway (Metro-Goldwyn-Mayer, 1951)
A disclaimer at the end of MGM's comedy *Callaway Went Thataway* reads as follows:

> This picture was made in the spirit of fun, and was meant in no way to detract from the wholesome influence, civic mindedness and the many charitable contributions of Western idols of our American youth, or to be a portrayal of any of them.

Had this film been made by a slightly more caustic team, such as, say, Billy Wilder and Charles Brackett, no such disclaimer would have been necessary, and every portrayal contained in the film would probably have been intentional, acidically so. Instead, the film was written, produced, and directed by the team of Norman Panama and Melvin Frank, a more amiable, benevolent pair (*Knock on Wood*, 1954; *The Court Jester*, 1955; *That Certain Feeling*, 1956). Thus, though the film's story aims to present a comical satire, or inside view, of the entertainment industry, its attempt at a jaded outlook on Hollywood is ironic but toothless. This being MGM, the film has an air of innocent glamour about it despite the barbs, and confirms this disposition by containing cheerful walk-ons by some of the studio's famous stars (as themselves), such as Esther Williams, Elizabeth Taylor, and Clark Gable.

Smoky Callaway (Howard Keel) is a washed-up movie cowboy. An advertising firm, Patterson & Frye, has used those old B-movies of his to plug a children's cereal on television, and suddenly Callaway's films are a big hit with America's kids. Now, if Patterson and Frye could only find the star cowboy, they would be able to produce more movies and make a fortune with tie-in merchandising. But Callaway is nowhere to be found, so Deborah Patterson (Dorothy) and Michael Frye (Fred MacMurray) hire yet another private investigator in the form of a former talent agent who used to know Callaway. The two copywriters are about to confess the truth to the cereal company's top brass in New York when a curious thing happens. In the fan mail that is pouring into their office every day, there is a letter from one Stretch Barnes (also Howard Keel), from Duck Falls, Colorado. Stretch is angry at those movies because they have made him the laughing stock of Duck Falls: he is the spitting image of the star cowboy, and does not appreciate the attention, or the fakery.

So off to Duck Falls Patterson and Frye go. They try to cajole Stretch into keeping alive the legacy of that wonderful individual, Smoky Callaway, rest his soul. Stretch will not hear of it, until he learns of his expected pay rate: $2,000 a week. The three of them head back to Los Angeles, and Stretch's training to become the reborn Callaway begins.

The screen test Stretch shoots seems to be a disaster, but—surprisingly—both the cereal executives and the Hollywood creatives love the refreshing naturalness of this "new" Callaway. The real difference between the two, which Patterson and Frye initially try to hide at all costs, is personality: the real Callaway was a mean-spirited, womanizing drunkard, while the fake one is a sweet, taciturn darling with a heart of gold. Whether the film's depiction of the real Callaway is intended as an oblique *roman-à-clef* criticism of the actor portraying him (apparently, Keel was something of an irascible, alcoholic diva)[501] is unclear.

To complicate matters, the old agent finds Callaway in a shady dive in South America, and decides to ignore Patterson and Frye's order to call off the search. He has plans of his own for the resuscitated cowboy, whom he brings back to the States. So now, just as Stretch comes back from a glorious promotional tour of the United States in the company of Deborah Patterson (he has even bought a ring for her, telling her to think about his marriage proposal and wear the ring if she decides to accept it), there are *two* Callaways in town.

The real Callaway does not like being copied, nor does he like the fact that his double, in a gesture of kindness, has created a foundation in Callaway's name and is giving away most of his princely pay to children's charities. The two Callaways have it out in a fistfight, but it is all moot: drunken Callaway is in no condition to resume his film work, at least not for free, so, instead of suing everyone around him, he resolves to go back to South America. All ends well, and Deborah decides to wear the ring.

The first half of the film contains some sparkling dialogue, which Dorothy and MacMurray deliver in perfect 1940s style. Dorothy, photographed lovingly and glamorously in Helen Rose's smart outfits, rattles off her character's sardonic repartee at a vertiginous clip, outrunning MacMurray's famously fast delivery. She does so with the dry, energetic relish of an Eve Arden or Rosalind Russell, which is a pleasure to behold. Dorothy's delightful character, however, is also the symbol of one of the film's weaknesses. Deborah Patterson is introduced as an intelligent, cynical businesswoman with a brilliant sense of humor, but her fast talk and jaded *ennui* do not last long; under the influence of Stretch's golden cowboy heart, she softens and changes, turning into... Dorothy McGuire! The standard, conventional Dorothy McGuire of the movies, that is: sensitive,

---

[501] See: Howard Keel and Joyce Spizer, *Only Make Believe: My Life in Show Business*, Barricade Books, Inc., 2005.

lovable, and with a conscience yea big. Dorothy is splendid no matter what, and her performance good all along the film's arc, but she is best in her early scenes with MacMurray, with their sparkling dialogue and relaxed disillusionment. She is, as one newspaper put it, "having the time of her life in a role sparked with amusing dialogue."[502] That sense of fun is palpable, despite a much-publicized bout of laryngitis that forced the studio to shoot portions of the film around her;[503] also palpable is the excellent chemistry she has with MacMurray. This jaded, wisecracking Dorothy is a novelty, and a revelation.

Here is Dorothy's first dialogue with MacMurray:

(As Michael Frye enters the office with a sour expression on his face, Deborah Patterson is leaning back in her chair, her feet up on a magazine rack. From the desk next to her, she picks up some darts, which she throws with violence at a poster of Smoky Callaway.)
Deborah: Hi.
Michael: Hi.
Deborah: Well?
Michael: Nothing. A big fat nothin'.
Deborah: Hmmmm.
Michael: All the way to the San Diego Poorhouse, for what? Nothin'.
Deborah: Hate to be an I-told-you-so, but I told you so.
Michael: Oh, they had a fellow named Callaway, all right. Only he was 68 years old, he doesn't drink, he hates horses, and only knows about movies as that's where you go to buy popcorn.
Deborah: Told you.
Michael: Told you, told you. You're so smart, why don't you come up with something?

---

502 "All-Star Cast Piles Up Laughs In Indiana Film," *Kokomo (IN) Tribune*, March 1, 1952.

503 Sheilah Graham, "In Hollywood," *Tampa (FL) Times*, June 5, 1951.

Deborah: I have! Let's call New York and tell them the truth: there is no Smoky Callaway.

Michael: Who says so?

Deborah: Ten thousand dollars' worth of private detectives, who scoured city, county, state and nation, and have come to the devastating conclusion that no one has seen or heard of this man the last ten years!

Michael: You call that evidence?

Deborah: Why don't we just put an ad in the paper: "Available: two charming ex-copywriters. Had brilliant idea. Gave up jobs to put cowboy pictures on television. Found pictures. Found sponsors. Couldn't find cowboy. Charming copywriters very available, have typewriter, will travel."

Michael: Tee-hee. Very funny.

Deborah Patterson (Dorothy) and Michael Frye (Fred MacMurray) in cynical mode, during their opening scene in *Callaway Went Thataway*. Production still, © 1951, Loews Inc.

Dorothy's romantic chemistry with Howard Keel, on the other hand, is a little harder to swallow, as it makes her character go completely limp: one could say that all the characteristics Dorothy establishes so charmingly for her character in the first half of the film fly out the window when Patterson begins to fall in love. This was the first time Dorothy had essayed a cynical, wisecracking character (it would also be her last), and it is a shame the film decides to switch tones in mid-stream and turn Patterson into a conventional sap.

The press was mostly kind to the film, and wrote of "performances fine on all counts."[504] *Variety* agreed with me that "[the] satire doesn't bite, being all in fun [. . .]"[505] but liked both the film as a whole and the leads' performances. Bosley Crowther of the *New York Times* was tepid and ambivalent about the film, but did not hate it. Here are his dubious reservations about MacMurray and Dorothy:

> It might be wished, too, that Fred MacMurray and Dorothy McGuire didn't so mouth their words that some of their conversation can barely be understood, for their acting as the advertising agents is amusingly arch and harassed, and it is plain that some clever dialogue has been written by Panama and Frank.[506]

Leonard Maltin sentenced wisely: "Good fun until it starts to get serious."[507]

---

[504] "Satire on Western Movies Opens at Midtown Theater," *Philadelphia Inquirer*, December 31, 1951.

[505] "Callaway Went Thataway," *Variety*, November 14, 1951.

[506] Bosley Crowther, "'Callaway Went Thataway,' a Satire on Cowboy Idols, Opens of Loew's State," *New York Times*, December 6, 1951.

[507] Maltin, *Movie Guide* (2009), op. cit.

**Studio artwork to advertise *Callaway Went Thataway*.
© 1951, Loews Inc.**

Invitation (MGM, 1952)

Admittedly, this film is in many ways a perfectly conventional product and, had it starred Joan Crawford or Bette Davis instead of Dorothy, it would have fit rather snugly in the catalogue of overblown "women's melodramas" the studios glibly churned out in the 1940s and '50s. As luck would have it, the casting of Dorothy does make a difference, as does the presence of composer Bronislau Kaper. Dorothy cannot rescue the middling material completely; she can, nonetheless, transform enough of it to make some scenes quite interesting.

The story in brief: Ellen Bowker Pierce (Dorothy) lives a quiet, content life with her loving husband, Dan Pierce (Van Johnson), in the house her well-to-do father (Louis Calhern) has bought for them; the idyll is spoiled only by her heart condition, which forces her to forgo even the slightest of exertions. A casual conversation with former friend Maud Redwick (Ruth Roman), who used to be in love with Dan and resents Ellen's marriage, plants a gnawing doubt in Helen's mind. Piece by piece, a disquieting puzzle composes itself. What exactly were Dan's motives in marrying her? When Ellen receives an invitation to attend a medical conference and dinner given by a renowned heart specialist (invitation sent by Maud), everything becomes clear: Ellen has less than a year to live, and everyone around her seems to know it. She calls her father and asks him how expensive it was to convince Dan to marry her; her father cannot deny her accusation. In the end, Ellen confronts Dan and he tells her the whole story of his "deal" with her father; he also tells her he was not expecting to fall in love with her, but he did. Ellen accepts Dan's explanation, and realizes she loves him too. The prospect of a revolutionary operation that might save her life and restore her heart's health makes the future look rosy.

I have trivialized the plot of *Invitation* because, in truth, it is rather trivial to begin with, and both the unfoldment and the denouement of the story are predictable and contrived. But the film is not all bad, and is salvaged in more ways than one by the manner in which the material is handled.

The first half of the film is more effective than the second, mainly because the gradual jelling of the ugly truth Ellen is investigating occurs without excessive expository passages; it progresses in brooding silence and solitude, holding the spectators' interest. The second half, on the other hand, is positively brimming with wordy exposition and recapitulations that make it tedious and undramatic.

The quiet gathering of evidence on Ellen's part reaches its culmination in a scene that is a little flawed masterpiece. As all the different pieces come together and the full impact of what has happened hits Ellen, the scenery-chewing scene reaches a delirious climax that is aided enormously by Dorothy's acting and by Bronislau Kaper's score. There is virtually no dialogue in the scene, and Dorothy's movements around her living room endow the moment with a stylized, balletic grace that both complements and contrasts the anguish she feels. Kaper, for his part, abandons the romantic-melodic style he has used up to this point and partially departs from conventional tonality, adopting a style reminiscent of post-romantic expressionism or early atonality—say, Alban Berg or Béla Bartók—and making the music so dissonant and disquieting that it colors the scene with a sinister, almost horrific tone. Like Dorothy, the music tries desperately to move away from sentiment and to plunge into cold, frightening despair.

The intentionality of this stylistic choice is confirmed by one of the most startling, and interesting, visual moments in the film. As Ellen traces the events of the year in reverse, she stumbles upon some telling memories of her relationship with Dan; these memories appear as brief aural and visual flashbacks that Ellen watches unfold before her. During one of these moments, Ellen is looking out one of her windows, and sees herself happily kissing Dan goodbye as he leaves for work in his car, as if the scene were happening in her driveway. Now that she knows the awful truth, that image is so repulsive to her that she violently closes the window drapes to shut out the memory. As she does so, the flashback vanishes. This simultaneous physical presence of the memory and of the person remembering is reminiscent of the flashback device used just one year earlier by Swedish director Alf Sjöberg in his film *Miss Julie* (*Fröken Julie*, 1951), in which different time levels were simultaneously present in the same image or on the same set (the past co-existing with the present).[508] A similar device was also used by Woody Allen for the flashbacks of his film *Annie Hall* (1977).

One scene doth not a good film make, and one surreal, frightening moment in Ellen Bowker Pierce's life cannot, by itself, redeem the film from its triteness. Together with Dorothy's acting, however, this peculiar centerpiece of the film (the climax of Ellen's discovery occupies the central ten minutes, from about 39 to 47 minutes in) does elevate the material somewhat, and may count as a minor filmic victory.

---

508 Sjöberg used a similar device to depict the protagonist's dreams in his *Torment* (*Hets*, 1944): the dream characters were simply present in the same room as the protagonist, without optical trickery.

Dorothy counteracts the sentimentality of the melodramatic plot with massive doses of restraint. She tends to underplay most everything in this film, never allowing her character's story to be overcome by sentiment. In the climactic scenes, she contrasts this restraint with brief bursts of hysteria that are as powerful as they are unexpected. For example: after her husband has walked out, Ellen is having a short dialogue with her father and her family doctor; suddenly, she hears the rumble of a car engine coming from outside; believing the car to be Dan's, Ellen rushes out of the house, screaming Dan's name at the top of her lungs. But it is not Dan who is leaving; it is only George, the gardener. There is a brief, innocent exchange between Ellen and George concerning the destination of the dead leaves George has raked. Here, Dorothy gives that innocent dialogue a sinister undertone of insanity by having Ellen smile, then laugh at the anticlimactic disappointment of that exchange. And, speaking of aural choices, that car engine Ellen hears is colored by director Gottfried Reinhardt and sound man Douglas Shearer with an ominous, unrealistic loudness that is pure expressionism.

Dorothy's glacial, glassy-eyed immobility as she listens to Dan confessing his side of the story in their climactic confrontation is truly chilling, as if Ellen's soul had temporarily left her and only her body were sitting on that sofa. When Dan tries to touch her lovingly, she reacts as if his hand were a snake, jerking back instantaneously with terror and repulsion. These are all comparatively small touches, that cannot alter the fundamental conventionality of the story, or of the film; but they are remarkable nonetheless.

According to Hedda Hopper, Robert Walker was supposed to be cast alongside Dorothy in *Invitation*; eerily, she reported this piece of news on August 13, 1951, only fifteen days before Walker's premature death at the age of 32, which occurred unexpectedly on August 28.[509] Therefore, it is

---

[509] Hedda Hopper, "Martin, Lewis Will Be In Broadway Musical," *Sioux Falls (SD) Argus-Leader*, August 13, 1951.

reasonable to assume that Van Johnson was a replacement. One is left to imagine how different the results would have been with Walker as co-star. Johnson, a likable but bland player, seems wrong for the part on several counts, aesthetically and dramatically. Ruth Roman is appropriately dark and poisonous as Ellen's jilted rival.

Coda: the telephone call that Ellen Bowker Pierce (Dorothy) makes to her father concludes her bitter investigation on her marriage as well as the balletic flashback scene that is the centerpiece of *Invitation* (1952). Publicity photo.

In his review, Bosley Crowther of the *New York Times* dismissed the film as inconsequential, and did so with a heavy dose of sarcasm. Here is the opening of that review:

> One of those dreadful complications to which people of great wealth are pathetically exposed—and of which the rest of us would probably live in callow ignorance if it weren't for Hollywood—is revealed and discussed and fretted over and finally brought to a completely happy end in M-G-M's "Invitation" [...].[510]

After describing the "complication" that afflicts Ellen Pierce, Crowther commented:

> You can imagine the torment and depression this causes the poor, unfortunate girl—or perhaps you can't, until you have seen it demonstrated by the emotionally elastic Miss McGuire. She goes into hurricanes of anguish, she sits for hours just staring into space and when poor Mr. Johnson tries to touch her, she leaps away as though he had the plague. But then, when at last he confesses that he did sort of marry her as a deal but subsequently came to adore her, she relaxes and all is serene. It even looks as though an operation is going to cure her completely of the heaves.[511]

The *Variety* reviewer was lukewarm but respectful. Though he complained that Bronislau Kaper's score had been permitted "to get too loud and busy in the climactic sequences," he went easy on the director and cast:

---

[510] Bosley Crowther, "The Screen in Review: 'Invitation,' With Van Johnson and Dorothy McGuire, Opens at Loew's State Theatre," *New York Times*, January 30, 1952.

[511] Ibid.

There's nothing wrong with the way the picture has been written, directed and played, but it just doesn't have the stuff that can be easily figured as appealing to the general run of filmgoers. Miss McGuire does an excellent job as the girl.[512]

Make Haste to Live (Republic Pictures, 1954)
Dorothy is impeccable in this conventional low-budget suspense melodrama, based on a novel by Mildred and Gordon Gordon, scripted by Warren Duff, and directed by William A. Seiter. In light of Dorothy's charm, it is especially unfortunate that the film never manages to rise above its tediously hesitant *noirish* genetics. The few joys it provides derive from Dorothy's acting, and from a slight moral complication that is as thickheaded as it is underdeveloped.

The new life that Crystal Benson (Dorothy McGuire) has built for herself in the small New Mexico town where she works as the editor of the local newspaper is tragically disrupted when her secret past catches up with her in the form of a mysterious stalker lurking around her home. This stalker, who suddenly makes contact with her, is her husband Steve Blackford (Stephen McNally), who has spent the last eighteen years in prison for a murder he did not commit: hers. Steve Blackford, however, is, or was, a mobster, and is guilty of at least one other murder: he killed a policeman and was not convicted of the crime. Now, he wants to re-enter his wife's life and take it over (maybe to kill her later?).

In anticipation of her demise, Crystal narrates her past into a Dictaphone, recording a message addressed to her teenage daughter Randy (Mary Murphy). This message never achieves the tone of resigned bitterness or the moral complexity of another famous *noir* confession, that of insurance salesman Walter Neff in Billy Wilder's *Double Indemnity* (1944); nor does it reach the stoic melancholy of Frank Bigelow's report of his own murder in Rudolph Maté's *D.O.A.* (1950). Crystal's message

---

[512] "Invitation," *Variety*, January 23, 1952.

is merely a temporary plot device to set in motion a series of flashbacks telling the story of her past, and to prepare the predictable denouement.

There is significant moral ambiguity to Crystal's character (the moral complication I was referring to), but this, too, is never investigated, dramatically or morally. In that distant past, Crystal let her husband go to prison for her murder, even though the charred body that was found in that long-ago fire was not hers. Knowing of her husband's criminal past and having experienced his violent, possessive disposition, she took advantage of the fact that everyone believed her dead and fled to New Mexico with a new identity. From the point of view of audience identification, this is a problem for the heroine, for, although she is imperiled, the audience knows that she is lying to everyone around her by introducing Steve as her brother and by not owning up to her past. She is lying to her daughter Randy, she is lying to her boyfriend Josh, and she is lying to her friend Lafe, the town sheriff, who loves her like a father. It is never made clear whether Randy ever listens to Crystal's recording or not.

Crystal has a chance to do away with Steve when he follows her into an archaeological site to look for some money she pretends to have hidden. She could easily push him to his death as he is standing next to her on the brim of a bottomless pit (unbeknownst to him). But, in a hysterical protestation of moral virtue, she screams that she cannot kill him, for she does not want her daughter to have *two* murderous parents. Moments later, as he chases her around the ruins, Steve slips and falls off a cliff on his own and dies, to the sound of Crystal's screams. When Josh and Lafe rescue Crystal, she tells them of her brother's end, and concludes that she is all right now. Jane Corby of the *Brooklyn Eagle* commented: "But wouldn't you know? Everything comes out all right in the end."[513]

Not quite all right, from the point of view of the spectator, for, to the bitter end, Crystal never comes clean about the truth. Presumably, now

---

[513] Jane Corby, "Dorothy McGuire Is Back On the Screen in a Thriller," *Brooklyn Eagle*, March 26, 1954.

that the status quo is restored, Crystal will continue lying, and destroy that Dictaphone recording.

Judging by the way Dorothy plays her, Crystal is an accomplished liar: Dorothy's dignified elegance and rather glacial, understated dramatics make Crystal a cold, calculating creature, who never misses a beat while hiding the truth from everyone around her. Some early scenes depicting her being stalked create some suspenseful atmospheres, but the bulk of the story is carried out rather coolly. Too coolly, in fact, despite the flashy, sinister score that Elmer Bernstein provides.

Blackford vs. Blackford: Stephen McNally and Dorothy being awkward with each other on a garden bench in *Make Haste to Live*. Production still.

It must have been obvious to both the screenwriter and the director that something was amiss in this story, for they overcompensate by going through some very elaborate, but gauche, maneuvers to swing the balance in Crystal's favor. In doing so, however, they cause the tone of the film to waver undecidedly between several extremes: *noir* thriller, suspense melodrama, family drama, family comedy, love story, murder story and psychological horror story. One scene during a garden barbecue, for example, has Steve and Crystal exchanging subtle threats, but the tender blues tunes of the party around them and the characters' dignified blocking (sitting on a garden bench) give the scene the look and feel of a tense conjugal dialogue. That scene is more *Kramer vs. Kramer* than *Cape Fear*.

It is difficult to sympathize with any of the characters in this story, particularly its protagonists. Together with a sluggish pace and an uncertain tone, that flaw makes the film ineffectual: the story is neither scary enough nor suspenseful enough (nor amusing enough: turning this into a black comedy might have improved the result).

Bosley Crowther of the *New York Times* was annoyed with the film. The following was his conclusion:

> This being the situation, the rest of the picture is spent with Miss McGuire trying to figure out dodges for getting Mr. McNally out of town. In spite of the urgency in the title, it takes her a tediously long time—much longer that it takes a mere observer of the landscape to anticipate. For off there in an old Indian pueblo, in which Miss McGuire's boy friend, John Howard, is digging around, there is shown, very early in the picture, to be a secret and bottomless well. A nice, cozy place to drop somebody. Thither the whole creation moves.
>
> Very slowly, however, and very uninterestingly. Warren Duff's screen play is hackneyed and William A. Seiter's direction is dull. No one's performance is exciting. Only Edgar Buchanan as a sheriff seems slightly real.
>
> Along about half-way through this picture you're likely to take another look at that last word of the title. It could be "leave."[514]

---

[514] Bosley Crowther, "At the Victoria," *New York Times*, March 26, 1954.

Crystal Benson (Dorothy) in the climax of *Make Haste to Live*, as her evil husband falls off a cliff. Production still.

Surprisingly, *Variety* was quite enthusiastic, stating that "McGuire scores exceptionally well";[515] however, *Variety*'s claim that Dorothy's character had "audience sympathy entirely" directly contradicted the opinion of other critics, such as Corby of the *Brooklyn Eagle*, who wrote that Crystal "doesn't merit the usual full audience sympathy with a beleaguered lady [...]."

The *Los Angeles Times*' John L. Scott also liked the film.[516]

---

515 "Make Haste to Live," *Variety*, March 31, 1954.

516 John L. Scott, "Suspense Livens Plot of 'Make Haste to Live,'" *Los Angeles Times*, April 29, 1954.

John Swope (far right) brings daughter Mary "Topo" Swope (second from left) to the set of his wife's film *Make Haste to Live*, 1954. Press photo.

Trial (MGM, 1955)

The courtroom drama *Trial*—termed a "shocking drama" by MGM's advertising—is not a thing of subtlety. This is the kind of film where a sanguine lawyer (Bernard Castle, played by Arthur Kennedy), in preparing his client (Angel Chavez, played by Rafael Campos) to take the stand, slaps him violently in the face if he gives the wrong answer, while neither his assistant (Abbe, played by Dorothy) nor his trainee (David Blake, played by Glenn Ford) raise any objection, even after the fact. This is also the kind of film where the issue of racism (a Mexican boy, Angel Chavez, is charged with murder due to circumstantial evidence in a conservative, white middle-class community) is not enough, and novelist-scriptwriter Don M. Mankiewicz throws in Communism and corruption for good measure. Full of 1950s bombast and emphasis, this is the kind of film where someone shaking a person to jog his memory does it somewhat like the passengers of *Airplane!* (1980) when they are trying to snap a fellow traveler out of her hysteria. This is also the kind of film where the score (by Daniele Amfitheatrof, in this case) forgoes the subtlety of strings and woodwinds and assaults the spectator with atonal tunes played by a loud piano and lots of percussion instruments.

Trial is the kind of film in which a fundraising rally to "Free Angel Chavez" is not organized by left-wing liberals and proletarians, but by scheming Commies and evil corporations, who do not content themselves with leftist propaganda, but insist on telling lies, lies, populist lies, in the loudest, most obnoxiously browbeating manner possible (*Elmer Gantry*-style, and then some). Oh, and they do not care if the boy is acquitted at all; in fact, they would prefer it if he were put to death, to serve as a martyr for their anti-Government cause.

Into this hornets' nest of evildoers walks young idealistic David Blake, a rational, sensitive law professor with no courtroom experience. To gain that experience and keep his job at the university, he is willing to work on the Chavez defense *pro bono*, and to play first chair in the trial. Thus, he finds himself entangled in a game he does not understand, and sinks deeper and deeper into the shady proceedings organized by Castle.

Castle's disenchanted assistant Abbe goes along with her boss's schemes, but is having second thoughts about them. Suddenly, while working with David to prepare the boy's defense, she finds herself drawn to the young lawyer's moral rectitude, as well as to the man himself. Her allegiances, however, are divided, and this causes considerable conflict between the two. Finally, she chooses David's side (the right side).

The bulk of this film might be termed a nuisance, if it were not for the pairing of Glenn Ford and Dorothy, and for the last scene.

During most of the film, David is so flustered by the mayhem around him that he seems utterly ineffectual in his actions and utterances. So halting are his speech and manner that he (and therefore Glenn Ford) seems not only naïve but unintelligent. This is a problem in terms of audience identification, and, because the device drags on too long before the character's redemption, also in terms of the story's dramatic construction and power.

At least two of the exchanges between Abbe and David (the moral core of the film) are intellectually interesting and sentimentally mature, but they are outweighed by the noise of the other characters and events around them. In the end, the character of Abbe does not stand a chance against the power of David's moral victory; this story belongs to David, and therefore to Ford.

However, the central scenes between David and Abbe give Dorothy a chance to show what she is made of. Biased and flawed in terms of the argument these scenes might be (the fact that Abbe was a Communist sympathizer seems inexplicable to David, and the only explanation Abbe is allowed to give is that when she had "drifted into" Communist groups and meetings she was a naïve college freshman who wanted to be different and meet new people), but they are written to give both actors an opportunity to bounce lines off each other and play at least one big confrontation. Bounce they do, and confront each other they do, splendidly.

Those scenes are excellently played, and—judging from the results—were excellently rehearsed. Both actors have fun with the dramatic flow of their scenes, and with their timing, with intense but subtle theatrical power. They overlap each other's dialogue, interrupt each other, change tones and colors at every turn: in short, they do some believable, urgent acting.

A word one might wish to use to describe Ford's performance, especially in the second half of the film, is subtle. For an actor without vast stage experience, Ford had an intuitive understanding of timing, of voice, and of the musical ebb and flow of a spoken part. Ford plays with all those elements, while always remembering how his character is set up. Throughout this story, his character is the thoughtful, sensitive, intelligent type, and Ford bears these qualities on his shoulders like so many crosses, in conjunction with director Mark Robson's discipline and sensitivity. It is in his last scene, however, that he shines, the scene in which David, after the conviction of his client (technically not his client anymore, since the evil Bernard Castle has taken over as counsel in mid-trial), asks to be heard and appeals to the judge for a lenient sentence.

Glenn Ford and Dorothy in *Trial* (1955). Publicity still.

One would expect, nay, fear, that such scene would deliver on the promise of all the noise that has preceded it and crank up the decibels; luckily, it is in this scene that the true gentle heart of the film reveals itself, and it is a warm, meditative heart.

Ford has heretofore tried to live up to the theatrical wolves surrounding him (particularly Kennedy, who plays the villain to the hilt, raising the volume of his voice any chance he gets) by making his silent brooding and painful emoting larger than life. In his impassioned climactic speech, where David calmly speaks to the judge and rationally goes back to the letter of the law and to his beloved books, Ford wisely quiets down his voice to a conversational volume. Thus, this last scene acts as a musical contrast to Kennedy's noise, using as its moral pivots two enlightened characters, Judge Theodore Motley, wonderfully played by Juano Hernandez, and David. These two men are desperately trying to bring the light of reason back into the sordid, calculatingly emotional world that surrounds them.

The judge's watchful, intelligent eyes positively shine with gratitude as David's rational solution, like sunshine, begins to dissipate the dark evil in the courtroom and presents the compassionate judge with an alternative. "*But where there is a harsh rule of law, the Law will always have ways of correcting its errors. The Law will always have ways of protecting itself,*" says David. Thus, by quoting a particular cavil that permits the judge to pass a lighter sentence, David gives all the power back to the judge, and appeals to his enlightenment. Castle the villain tries to provoke Judge Motley by barking contemptuous insults, but it is a futile battle: like David, the judge is a rational being, who does not yield to the temptation of emotional response. There is a deeply humanistic tone to this beautifully written finale, and that humanism is not a pose or a button-pushing ploy but a profound, heartfelt ode to love, equilibrium, and justice. That tone is somewhat reminiscent of the tone of another beautiful courtroom finale, written by the splendid team of Jerome Lawrence and Robert E. Lee: *Inherit the Wind* (the play had debuted on Broadway on April 21, 1955, some six months before the release of this film, and ran for 806 performances).

Thus, in the end, this obstreperous film redeems himself, both sonically and dramatically; so does the character of David Blake. For anyone who has had the patience to sit through all the noisy parts, that redemption is a rewarding experience. So is the last image of the film: after everyone has walked out of the courtroom, director Robson places his camera outside the open courtroom doors and lets the far-away judge sit at his bench for a moment before gathering his things and walking offscreen.

Variety was happy with the film, and even happier with the figure of the judge as played by Hernandez:

> Perhaps the most offbeat angle in "Trial," on a par with the Commie party stuff, is having the presiding judge a Negro. This role will almost certainly go into the books as the highlight of Juano Hernandez's acting career. In the careful, temperate, judicious rulings which he is constantly making, Hernandez proves himself one of the great rhetoricians among current character players. But his performance is deeper yet. It has heart, dignity, and the actor has thought through and felt through the implications to achieve an "integration" (to use actor language) seldom encountered. While the picture has many firstrate performances, [. . .] this is peculiarly Hernandez's own private coup de theatre.[517]

Variety was also positive about Ford and Dorothy, calling both players "thoroughly convincing"; about Dorothy, it lamented that her role was underwritten ("her role is somewhat mute in the writing"). The magazine concluded: "Add up the points and this is a very strong, almost a great, moving picture."

Bosley Crowther of the *New York Times* was not so enthusiastic, and did not appreciate the film's overabundance of topics (racism, Communism, justice):

> Mr. Mankiewicz has mixed these complications in an impulsive and turbulent script that moves so erratically and tries to cover so much territory that it soon becomes badly confused.[518]

Crowther called Robson's direction "frantic," which would seem to

---

517 "Trial," *Variety*, August 3, 1955.

518 Bosley Crowther, "Confused 'Trial'; Mexican Is Martyred in Music Hall Film," *New York Times*, October 14, 1955.

agree with my points about the film's noisiness, and Dorothy "amiable and earnest." His conclusion:

> We're afraid the "trial" of this picture is not so much that which goes on in the court as that which is imposed on those who have the patience to see it through.[519]

Evidently, Crowther did not feel the magic of that last scene, nor the ultimate moral valor of the picture.

Friendly Persuasion (Allied Artists Pictures, 1956)
There is real-life magic, and a near-perfect mixture of feeling, ideas, and humor, in William Wyler's splendid *Friendly Persuasion*, which confirms its status as an enduring classic many decades after its release. The film was based on Jessamyn West's novel *The Friendly Persuasion* (1945), and was filmed mostly in the environs of Los Angeles (Rowland V. Lee Ranch, Canoga Park; Chico; Republic Studios in North Hollywood). As *Variety* noted in its review, no screenplay credit appears in the film, but "the novelist, associate producer Robert Wyler and Harry Kleiner all worked with the producer-director at various times on the [Allied Artists] feature."[520] Also according to *Variety*, Wyler had worked on the project for some eight years and "brought the property over to Allied Artists from Paramount. The time and effort he has put into it results in a top show that will mean much to viewers."[521] The truth of the matter, which surfaced after the fact, is that the film was actually scripted by blacklisted (and therefore uncredited at the time) screenwriter Michael Wilson, whose credit on the film was finally restored in 1996.

---

519 Ibid.

520 "The Friendly Persuasion," *Variety*, September 26, 1956.

521 Ibid.

According to several sources, such as William Wyler biographer Gabriel Miller, Dorothy was not the director's first choice for the role of Eliza Birdwell, nor his second. Here is Miller's report:

> For the role of Eliza, Jess's religious and opinionated wife, Wyler wanted Katharine Hepburn, but she was not available. The part was subsequently turned down by both Vivien Leigh and Ingrid Bergman. Bergman wanted to work with Wyler but was still unwelcome in Hollywood because of her affair with Roberto Rossellini. Wyler then considered multiple actresses for the role, including Jane Wyman, Teresa Wright, and Maureen O'Hara, before finally choosing Dorothy McGuire.[522]

These casting vicissitudes have authorized some commentators to make *ex-post-facto* complaints about the acting that are both unverifiable and moot. Here is one such grievance:

> The eventual choice, Dorothy McGuire, is a fine actress, but her put-upon screen persona does not carry the charisma of the character in the way that Hepburn and Bergman might have done, and she therefore cedes center stage to Jess.[523]

Speaking of complaints, in his biography of Anthony Perkins, Charles Winecoff drops an uncorroborated hint about difficult relations between Dorothy and Wyler, claiming that hiring Dorothy for the film "was a choice Wyler would regret for the entire shoot"[524] and cryptically writing

---

[522] Gabriel Miller, *William Wyler: The Life and Films of Hollywood's Most Celebrated Director*, University Press of Kentucky, 2013, 339.

[523] Neil Sinyard, *A Wonderful Heart: The Films of William Wyler*, McFarland & Company, Inc., Publishers, 2013, 165.

[524] Charles Winecoff, *Split Image: The Life of Anthony Perkins*, Dutton Adult, 1996, 100.

that "The *Friendly Persuasion* set was a happy one, despite Wyler's strained relationship with Dorothy McGuire."[525] I was not able to find a source for Winecoff's claim, nor other sources siding with his version of that alleged friction.

One quote from Dorothy (from an unverified source, but quoted in a reputable biography of Wyler) may provide us with a clue as to the possible reasons for that friction. It concerns Dorothy's preparation for the role of Eliza Birdwell, and Wyler's famously oblique instructions to actors:

> [Wyler] had me spending I don't know how many hours a day on the set before production, kneading bread. He never explained why he did something, he just asked you to do it. It was funny. What director would ask you to knead bread? I guess it put me into a different period of time, with a different way of thinking.[526]

An amusing anecdote about the leads' preparatory research surfaced in the press in late 1955 via the pen of syndicated NEA correspondent Erskine Johnson.

> Gary Cooper and Dorothy McGuire, playing Quakers in "The Friendly Persuasion," visited a Quaker meeting in Pasadena, Calif.
>
> They were introduced to various members of the congregation and one very old lady asked Cooper:
>
> "Where did thee say thee was from?"

---

525 Ibid., 101.

526 Doyle, "Serenity" (2007), op. cit. Also quoted in Jan Herman, *A Talent for Trouble: The Life of Hollywood's Most Acclaimed Director, William Wyler*, G.P. Putnam's Sons, 1995, 373.

Cooper thought she meant his place of birth and answered, "Helena, Montana, ma'am."

"My goodness," exclaimed the lady in true astonishment. "Thee is indeed a cosmopolite."[527]

Like the novel, the film is a series of "scenes," or "stories" in the life of a Quaker family in Southern Indiana in the year 1862. That collection of scenes carries within it a cluster of beautifully woven thematic threads, all consistently developed and paid off; this weaving and development give both dramatic and thematic cohesion to the film as a whole. A subplot involving the arrival of Confederate rebel soldiers injects danger, and a darker color, into the story, and puts the philosophical convictions of the family to the ultimate test. It is a testament to the collective strengths of the creative team involved that those convictions, those ideas, are never inert, but grow and evolve like the characters that embody them.

William Wyler was an intelligent, sensitive director; he was also a mature director,[528] and his work (in general, and in this film in particular) manages to both fit within Hollywood convention and rise above it. (As proof of this, you can watch the final scene of his 1953 film *Roman Holiday*, with its masterly subtextual richness.) An early scene taking place during the "silent" part of a Quaker meeting[529] finds Wyler's camera slowly and methodically roaming the crowded room in an effort to observe the faces of the characters—all the characters, not just the leads—with curiosity, wonder and compassion. One might wish to compare this panoramic observation of humanity with the one carried out by Ingmar Bergman on

---

[527] Erskine Johnson (NEA), "Johnson in Hollywood: Two Stars in Quaker Roles Run into Complications," *Long Beach (CA) Independent*, November 26, 1955.

[528] As Billy Wilder put it in the *American Masters* television documentary *Directed by William Wyler* (1986), "There was a finesse in that guy which you would not expect if you just talked to him across a card table [. . .]."

[529] A practice similar to esoteric mental ascesis or to the hesychastic practice of the Orthodox Church (a moment of quietness, of silent prayer or meditation).

the faces of an opera audience listening to an overture in the opening of his *Trollflöjten* (*The Magic Flute*, 1975). In both cases, that silent observation of the countenances of human beings yields a silent revelation, a "discovery," filled with mysterious excitement, poetry, philosophy, and love. There is no judgment of any kind in Bergman's gaze, nor in Wyler's; just a willingness to observe and learn; or, to observe and love.

À la Bergman: William Wyler's camera lovingly observes the faces of the congregation at a Quaker meeting in *Friendly Persuasion*. This extraordinary face belongs to veteran actress Mary Carr (1874–1973); her character is the first to break the silence of the meeting. Carr was 82 years old when the film was released. She would live to be 99. Screen capture.

Everyone is worthy of Wyler's love, even a Confederate "villain," even a temperamental goose; his non-judgmental gaze floods over all the characters populating this story, as if the quiet observation of the geography of human (or animal) faces were the way to true knowledge. All of God's creatures roaming this earth are the recipients of Wyler's unwavering positive interest. The maturing of an all-embracing, all-encompassing love, with all the weaknesses and contradictions of its bearers, is one of the themes of the film. The opening song, crooned by Pat Boone during the credits and woven resolutely by composer Dimitri Tiomkin into the fabric of his score, announces: "Thee I love," and seldom was an opening statement more programmatic.

Friendly Persuasion is filled with details resulting from Wyler's loving gaze, details that continually pull the spectator closer to the beings populating the story. There is love, there is understanding, and there is insight in a close-up of a young woman's bare feet stretching on a man's boots in order to kiss him, or in a close-up of a father's hand tapping his son's shoulder. And whenever observing the characters' reactions, Wyler takes his time and allows those reactions to unfold and develop fully before cutting away.

Stalking: Samantha the pet goose (right) waits for the right moment to pounce on Little Jess (Richard Eyer, left, back to camera) in this early scene of *Friendly Persuasion*. Screen capture.

Samantha, the family's pet goose, is the purveyor of some of the film's funniest scenes, observed with gentle benevolence—and accomplished storytelling technique—by Wyler's camera. The character opens the film, and closes it. Little Jess (Richard Eyer), the youngest member of the Birdwell family, is convinced that the goose hates him (she is friendly towards all the other members), and hates the goose back; at every opportunity, Samantha chases him or ambushes him. His mother's advice: "*See, little Jess? Speak to her kindly; she'll not bite thee. She's a pure pet, Samantha is.*" At the end of the film, after Samantha has almost been killed by a Confederate soldier during the Rebs' looting spree, the boy loses his hostile attitude towards the animal, and Samantha loses hers towards the boy. It is a question of attitude, the film seems to be saying. Samantha is thus a symbol, or catalyst, for one of the film's central motifs: the curative power of love, and the refusal to hate.

The above-mentioned Confederate soldier, believing that he has free reign over the family's "food" during the raid, is about to wring the goose's neck; Eliza Birdwell (Dorothy) rushes out of the house and, forgetting her non-violent principles, brandishes a broom and repeatedly hits the soldier on the head with it, screaming, "*Stop it! Let her go! Let her go!*" The soldier lets Samantha go; Eliza drops the broom and covers her face in shame. Then she screams, "*Samantha's a pet! She's a pure pet!!*" Stunned, the soldier answers politely, "*I wish I'd knowed that sooner.*" He picks up his hat, and adds, "*Much obliged, ma'am.*"

Curative love: there is a new feeling, and a new relationship, between Samantha the goose and Little Jess at the end of *Friendly Persuasion*. Screen Capture.

All of God's creatures, I was saying. When Jess Birdwell (Gary Cooper) kisses his mare on the cheek after she has won a friendly race for him (Jess likes a little surrey race against his friend and neighbor Sam Jordan on First Day mornings), that kiss mirrors the purity and love of his kisses to his wife and family. And when a calf is born to one of the Birdwells' cows, the barn scene that sees Jess's son Josh (Anthony Perkins) talking to the family's faithful black farm hand (Joel Fluellen) about birth and death while the cow licks her newborn baby clean has the intimacy and atmosphere (and lighting) of the holiest of Nativity scenes.

Josh Birdwell, the elder son, only appears to be rebelling to his family's religious principles when he decides to join the fighting against the advancing Rebs; in fact, he is exploring, and discovering, himself by doubting those principles. When a Union officer, who has politely disrupted the Meeting-House gathering to urge the community to fight, questions the young men present, he asks Josh whether he is afraid to fight. "*I don't know*," answers Josh honestly. Even more telling is the answer given by Josh's friend Caleb Cope (played by the muscular John Smith):

Caleb: Oh, I've been tempted to fight. I guess the good Lord knows why. I mean, sometimes I get the sinful wish to get into a scrap. So I got to watch myself closer than most people. So I'll just stay away from the war. Because if I ever got into it, I'd be a goner.

Knowing that human beings have impulses, and that those impulses must be watched with special vigilance by the persons who feel them most, is wise advice indeed. Jess's disarming reaction to the mounting tension in the congregation is, "*I have my own doubts.*"

The pace of the film is leisurely, but not sluggish. Wyler takes his starting pitch from the silence of his setting—the silence of the bucolic countryside, the silence of the Quakers' meeting—and makes it resonate through the story, spreading it across the film's length. His silence is a harmonious, appropriate silence that informs the actions of the characters;

the humorous scenes are exceptions to this rule, their comedy enlivening the pace suddenly but delicately like tiny shots of adrenalin. The slow pace of the film is, in effect, the pace of a story that takes place before electricity, before running water, before engines, before radio, and before television: the pace of a "natural" state, or of a religious meditation. It was probably in order to search for that meditative silence that, according to columnist Dorothy Kilgallen, Dorothy moved out of her home and into a hotel during the early preparation work for the film. Perhaps this was another exercise suggested by Wyler.[530]

The central relationship in the film is the one between Eliza and Jess, and the chemistry between Cooper and Dorothy is undeniable. Dorothy reportedly idolized Cooper, and loved working with him.[531] This relationship gives voice and body to many of the film's themes, such as the one concerning the necessary adjustments and transformations one's worldview must undergo during a lifetime. The give-and-take between husband and wife is handled delicately and subtly, as is the expert "friendly persuasion" Jess exercises on his wife. Eliza is a Quaker minister, and tends to be a trifle rigid in her views. Jess knows when to yield to her, and when to be firm; yet, even when he opposes her, the love he feels for her never leaves his voice or eyes.

In one scene, Jess has purchased an upright organ from music professor Quigley (played with relish by delightful comic pro Walter Catlett) and is about to carry it into the house with the professor's help. Eliza is shocked by her husband's purchase, and issues an ultimatum:

Eliza: Jess, I forbid thee to have this instrument!
Jess: Forbid, Eliza?
Eliza: For thy own sake, Jess, I forbid.

---

[530] See Dorothy Kilgallen, "The Voice of Broadway," *Palm Springs (CA) Desert Sun*, October 6, 1955.

[531] Levin (2017), op. cit.

Jess: Eliza, when thee asks, or suggests, I'm like putty in thy hand, but when thee forbids, thee is barking up the wrong tree.

In protest, Eliza exits the house and takes up residence in the barn. Come nighttime, Jess brings a pillow and a comforter to the barn, and asks if he can join Eliza. By morning, and after an eloquent time-lapse elision from Wyler, peace has been made. Cooper is adorable as the loving, respectful, flexible Jess; the old twinkle in his eye, which he had used to great advantage in his comedic roles a decade earlier (*Ball of Fire*, anyone?), is back in this film, as is his tender, subtle emotional expressiveness.

Back from the barn: Ma and Pa Birdwell return from their night of friendly persuasion. Production still for *Friendly Persuasion*, 1956.

Staring love in the face: a Rebel bushwhacker (Richard Garland) is surprised and moved when Jess (Gary Cooper, out of shot) lowers his rifle and spares his life, telling him to "git." Screen capture from *Friendly Persuasion*.

    The role of Eliza fits Dorothy perfectly, combining as it does the traditional virginal "niceness" for which Dorothy was famous with some surprising new traits in a comedic-dramatic setting. Eliza's rigidity and severity, for example, give Dorothy a chance to play the darker, more mature side of that virginal purity, as well as feelings such as shock, outrage and wounded pride. On the other hand, she can also play the loving wife and mother and, in one particular scene, the resolute woman of "action." When facing the Confederate home invasion, Eliza decides to play hospitable and to welcome the soldiers by offering them a meal and a free run of the family's food supplies. Never was submission more forceful than in that strategic welcome: her unswerving kindness literally gives the Rebels pause. Dorothy is especially skillful in shading her performance with an entire spectrum of dramatic colors, while never exceeding the boundaries of subtlety. She is also masterful in expressing the occasional wavering, or relaxing, of her character's rigidity. A scene at the county fair she visits with her family sees Eliza momentarily responding to the dance music she so deplores by tapping the music's rhythm with her hand and foot, and wearing an expression that makes her look sixteen.

Just about everybody liked the film upon its release. Bosley Crowther of the *New York Times* certainly did, calling the film a "surprise" and adding that "what is more, [William Wyler] has got into this treatise on the old-time manners and basic beliefs of the Society of Friends a lot of homely precept and a touching display of the nobility of man."[532] Concerning the acting, Crowther added:

> While top honors go to the performances of Mr. Cooper and Miss McGuire, who are wonderfully spirited and compassionate in their finely complementary roles, a great deal of admiration must go to Anthony Perkins as Josh. He makes the older son of the Birdwells a handsome, intense and chivalrous lad. Richard Eyer is delightful and natural as the rambunctious Little Jess, while Phyllis Love is electrical as Mattie and Mark Richman is nice as her suitor, Gard. Walter Catlett, Russell Simpson and Joel Fluellen are good in lesser character roles.[533]

His conclusion: "As they put it in 'Friendly Persuasion,' thee should be pleasured by this film."[534]

Variety too was enthusiastic, adding that both Cooper and Dorothy carried their roles "off to an immense success."

One hero that went relatively unsung was Dimitri Tiomkin, who wrote an inspired score for the film. Perhaps obscured by the more popular title song, which he also set to music, Tiomkin only received a perfunctory nod from *Variety*, but his work in *Friendly Persuasion* is magnificent;

---

[532] Bosley Crowther, "'Friendly Persuasion' Persuasive Film; Story of Quakers Is at the Music Hall Civil War Indiana Is Setting for Tale," *New York Times*, November 2, 1956.

[533] Ibid.

[534] Ibid.

while he reverts to some of his trademark sinister and martial sounds in the darker moments (the Confederates), it is his accompaniment to the lighthearted scenes that is especially remarkable. His commentary to Jess Birdwell's first surrey race against Sam Jordan is a splendidly composed and orchestrated piece, where Tiomkin's gleeful melodic/Leitmotivic invention in counterpointing mood and action rivals that of Erich Wolfgang Korngold's best scores for Warner Bros.

Following the film's release, United Press Hollywood writer Aline Mosby wrote a witty little article that began with the following sentence: "My Oscar for the best supporting actor of the year goes to a beautiful blue-eyed star with a backside that outwiggles Marilyn Monroe and a temper more fiery than Anna Magnani's."[535] Here is the remainder of the article:

> This star is so temperamental that she is living outdoors in a cage where she hisses and honks like an antique taxicab in London.
>
> Samantha, a big white goose with a yellow bill, almost stole one of the year's best pictures, "Friendly Persuasion," from under the well-trained noses of Gary Cooper and Dorothy McGuire. After the critics commented on Samantha's brilliant acting job (via director William Wyler), I looked up the famous bird.
>
> The goose actress lives at Comport Animal Rentals, a firm that rents livestock to the movies and is one of the more interesting fringe businesses in movieland.
>
> Like Lassie, Samantha has a double who did many scenes in the picture. One was bought from a farm in nearby Glendora and the other from Bellflower after a long talent search.

---

[535] Aline Mosby, "Temperamental Goose Given Boost for Supporting Oscar," *San Mateo (CA) Times*, November 10, 1956.

"The part called for a mean goose who was good-looking, and that's not easy to find," explained Lionel Comport as he conducted a tour of his pens and cages in suburban San Fernando.

"Then the goose is supposed to like only Dorothy McGuire, so for the scenes in which she feeds the bird I had to find a gentle goose that looks exactly like the mean one."

Comport painstakingly taught the two Samanthas simple "tricks" that enabled them to "act." For example, one goose was taught to waddle after anybody who runs and thus appeared to be hurring [sic] home in the movie. The scenes in which the goose attacks little Richard Eyer were accomplished by teaching the bird to nibble grain hidden in the boy's pocket and trouser cuffs.

"The goose was supposed to be in just a few scenes, but after Wyler saw what the bird could do he added many more scenes," beamed Comport.[536]

The film premiered in grand style, at the Fox Wilshire Theater in Beverly Hills,[537] on October 30, 1956. The event was telecast live under the sponsorship of "Golden Land of Apple Valley." Here is an advance announcement that appeared in the *Los Angeles Times* on October 20:

> Nine filmland figures have accepted membership on the committee, headed by Chairman Samuel Goldwyn, that is planning a tribute to Producer-Director William Wyler at the invitational premiere of his "Friendly Persuasion."

---

536 Ibid.

537 Today the Saban Theatre, 8440 Wilshire Boulevard, Beverly Hills, CA.

They are Charles Brackett, Steve Broidy, Bette Davis, Sidney Franklin, Y. Frank Freeman, Greer Garson, Gregory Peck, David O. Selznick and George Stevens.

They will join other film leaders who will honor Wyler with their attendance at the premiere of the Gary Cooper-Dorothy McGuire-Marjorie Main film [...].[538]

During the telecast, Shirley Thomas and Bill Welsh interviewed "some of the 500 top Hollywood personalities attending the premiere, including William Wyler, the picture's stars, Gary Cooper, Dorothy McGuire, Anthony Perkins, and many more."[539]

Jess Birdwell (Gary Cooper) applies some friendly persuasion to his wife Eliza (Dorothy). Publicity still for *Friendly Persuasion*.

---

538 "Notables Join Group to Honor William Wyler," *Los Angeles Times*, October 20, 1956.

539 Ad, "Premiere of 'Friendly Persuasion' and an industry-wide tribute to William Wyler, director of the picture," *Los Angeles Times*, October 30, 1956.

OTHER STUDIOS, 1951–1973

Friendly Persuasion was nominated for six Academy Awards. It won the *Palme d'Or* at the 1957 Cannes Film Festival, and was named one of the "Top Ten Films" of the year by the National Board of Review Awards, who also bestowed the Best Actress Award on Dorothy. Perkins received a Golden Globe as Best Newcomer. In 1957, The Writers Guild of America brazenly gave their 9th Writers Guild of America Award for Best Written American Drama to blacklisted writer Michael Wilson, a gesture that created quite a stir.

Old Yeller (Walt Disney Productions, 1957)
The simple, well-told story of a teenage boy's friendship with a yellow stray dog in 1860s Texas, and of his transition from boyhood to young manhood, *Old Yeller*, based on Fred Gipson's novel of the same title,[540] is one of Disney's most successful early live-action films. Disney casts Tommy Kirk (sixteen at the time) more appropriately than he would three years later in *Swiss Family Robinson*. Kirk seems comfortable in the role, and acquits himself admirably, Texas drawl and all. Kevin Corcoran, who would also end up in the cast of *Swiss Family*, is as shrill and squeaky as always as the younger brother, but fits the proceedings perfectly.

Dorothy is lovely in this picture, her performance benefiting from her experience on *Friendly Persuasion* the year before: her character has more than one point in common with the one she had played in the earlier film. As would happen often in her career, particularly with Disney, she plays the mother in a children's story, but is very much involved in the plot and is not relegated to the sidelines, as she would be in *Swiss Family Robinson* (1960) and *Summer Magic* (1963).

Dorothy's eyes have seldom been bluer, or more expressive, than in this intimate Technicolor story, whose dialogue is for the most part appropriately simple and plainly laid out. The looks she shoots her freeloading neighbor Bud Searcy (a delightful Jeff York) are priceless. With great

---
540 Fred Gipson, *Old Yeller*, Harper & Row, 1956.

subtlety and even greater clarity, Dorothy articulates a performance of eloquent understatement and intelligence. Hedda Hopper, who visited the set of the film in April 1957, commented, "Dorothy McGuire plays the mother as though she had been born in the role."[541]

The human actors are, left to right: Tommy Kirk, Dorothy, and Kevin Corcoran. Production still for Walt Disney's *Old Yeller* (1957).

One of the press releases that circulated at the time of the film's release concerned Dorothy and her experiences on the set. Here is the United Press report of those experiences:

> Actress Dorothy McGuire admits she did not like some parts of her role in "Old Yeller" even a little bit. She explains that as the mother of two boys she has to pick up toads, frogs and lizards in the film.[542]

---

[541] Hedda Hopper, "Solid Acting Found on 'Old Yeller' Set," *Los Angeles Times*, April 23, 1957.

[542] "A Slimy Part," *Idaho State Journal*, April 1, 1957. The UP blurb forgot to mention snakes.

None of the actors, however, could really compete with the star of the film, Old Yeller himself. The 115-pound, gold-colored mutt answered to the name of Spike in real life and was one of the actors from the stable of Frank Weatherwax, whose kennel of trained dogs included other stars such as Lassie. Weatherwax commented to Hopper:

> Yeller fights bears, wild hogs and a wolf in this picture. He herds cows, keeps the cornpatch free of 'coons, hunts and fishes; in fact, does everything but talk.[543]

In another article, Weatherwax told the charming story of his rescue of Spike from a Van Nuys, California, animal shelter:

> He was two months old, all head and feet. He looked smart, so I decided to give the little guy a new lease on life. Spike wasn't much in the glamour department, that's for sure, but he had brains. He learned fast. I couldn't help but think some day he'd be discovered.[544]

Hopper asked Dorothy about her relationship with Spike:

> After being introduced to the much-publicized mutt who plays the title role, I asked Dorothy how she managed such a monster. She replied, "He's easier to control than Penny, my New Mexico Labrador, who weighs just three pounds."[545]

---

543 Hopper, "Solid Acting" (1957), op. cit.

544 "Disney Extends Golden Touch To Mongrel for 'Old Yeller,'" *Salt Lake Tribune*, December 15, 1957.

545 Hopper, "Solid Acting" (1957), op. cit.

Bosley Crowther of the *New York Times* was uncharacteristically warm in his review. He wrote of a "very lean and sensible screen transcription of Fred Gipson's children's book," of "a nice trim little family picture," and of "a warm, appealing little rustic tale." He also wrote of "beautifully written" scenes, as well as of "the straight-forward honesty of Robert Stevenson's direction and the aura of family love that quietly caps the entire picture." In acknowledging the players, Crowther concluded:

> Again, both boys are fine, and it's a pleasure to watch Miss McGuire exuding sweet wisdom, even in a cornfield. As for Old Yeller himself, it's just too bad he couldn't fit into one Christmas stocking somewhere.[546]

Variety was likewise pleased, though synthetic. About Dorothy, it commented: "Miss McGuire gives a lasting impression in mother role."[547]

This Earth Is Mine (Universal-International, 1959)
Either Dorothy just wanted to keep working, or she was hoping that this film would turn out better than it did, for her talent is wasted in Universal-International's *This Earth Is Mine*, a deplorable potboiler that is as handsome as it is overlong, clichéd, and inept.

The sprawling story of the Rambeau family and its California vineyards during Prohibition (1931), *This Earth Is Mine* was scripted by Casey Robinson from Alice Tisdale Hobart's novel *The Cup and the Sword* (1942).[548] It focuses particularly on the love story between John Rambeau (Rock Hudson) and his cousin Elizabeth (Jean Simmons), who comes on a casual visit to the estate only to find that a marriage has been arranged

---

[546] Bosley Crowther, "Screen: Shameful Incident of War; 'Paths of Glory' Has Premiere at Victoria," *New York Times*, December 26, 1957.

[547] "Old Yeller," *Variety*, November 20, 1957.

[548] Alice Tisdale Hobart, *The Cup and the Sword*, The Bobbs-Merrill Company, Inc., 1942.

for her. The ailing patriarch of the family, Philippe Rambeau (Claude Rains) rules with an aristocratic iron fist, while his icy daughter Martha (Dorothy) watches over him like a hawk and supervises the family affairs with a velvet glove while entertaining the ambition of taking over the winery empire. After her father's death, Martha is bitterly, almost hysterically disillusioned at the reading of the will, for Philippe has parceled out his lands to every member of the family, leaving her to rule over the house and nothing else.

Much as he had been in the early sequences of *Magnificent Obsession* (1954), Rock Hudson is the hero/villain in this piece. John Rambeau, the illegitimate son of Martha's husband and an ambitious, unscrupulous businessman, is the black sheep of the family, but redeems himself after he causes a fire on the estate and is crippled in a car accident. In his final scene, post-repentance, he and Jean Simmons, armed with rolled-up sleeves and noble intentions, work the land to rebuild the vineyard that John was responsible for destroying. The moment is drenched in solemn, sentimental rhetoric, somewhat in the style of director Mehboob Khan's socialist-realist Hindi classic *Mother India* (*Bharat Mata*, 1957);[549] without the latter film's poetic and political conviction, Technicolor pizzazz, or beautiful songs, however, such rhetoric becomes a crippling burden for *Earth*, and the result is mendacious and hollow, much like the rest of the film.

That scene cannot be credible, mainly because the tripartite thematic layering of the film—(1) the power and prestige of the dynasty, (2) romantic love as redemptive force and (3) the land as elemental communal

---

549 Mehboob Productions' Technicolor Hindi musical spectacular *Mother India* "has acquired the status of an Indian *Gone with the Wind* (1939), massively successful and seen as a national epic, although formally the film's rhythms and lyrical ruralism seem closer to Dovzhenko's later work finished by Yulia Solntseva." (Ashish Rajadhyaksha and Paul Willemen, Encyclopedia *of Indian Cinema*, British Film Institute and Oxford University Press, 1999, 350.) The film starred one of India's most versatile and revered female film stars, Nargis (1929–1981).

good—hinders rather than helps its cogency, confusing issues that might have been powerful if developed separately.

Dorothy, in a part that Barbara Stanwyck allegedly turned down,[550] has three important scenes in *This Earth Is Mine*, unfortunately outweighed and suffocated by the bulk of the Rock Hudson-dominated plot. The scene in which she defends Claude Rains from the threat of blackmail is the most impressive, with the two magnificent Hollywood pros sinking their teeth delightfully into the meat of the trite material they are given and interacting with each other with truthful intensity. Second best is Martha's scene during the reading of her father's will, which Dorothy assails with the intensity of a skilled tragedian. Would that there were more of such scenes, and of Dorothy and Rains both. No such luck.

Howard Thompson of the *New York Times* was not happy with the film. He defined it as "an ambitious family saga as handsome as it is hollow," adding that "the story holds ample family history, diversification of characters and psychological friction to cram a lively, long feature. But it hasn't happened here, with two hours to kill." As for the acting, Thompson noted that "Miss McGuire's sleek witchery is the most impressive."

It is, in fact, a pleasure to see Dorothy be so sleek, and so witch-like. Martha is a negative, power-hungry character, all calculation and aristocratic propriety, and Dorothy makes her an utterly regal—and repulsive—creature, a creature that, as *Variety* rightly put it, "verges on tragedy, but [. . .] is tripped by the sentimentality of the film's conception."[551]

Variety was scornful: "[*This Earth Is Mine*] is almost completely lacking in dramatic cohesion. It is verbose and contradictory, and its complex plot relationships begin with confusion and end in tedium."[552]

---

550 Doyle, "Serenity" (2007), op. cit. See also Eila Mell, *Casting Might-Have-Beens: A Film by Film Directory*, McFarland & Company, Inc., Publishers, 2005, 239.

551 "This Earth Is Mine," *Variety*, April 22, 1959.

552 Ibid.

Elegant witchery: Martha Fairon (Dorothy, right) tries to supervise the lives of others in *This Earth Is Mine* (1959). In this particular scene, the object of her supervision is Elizabeth Rambeau (Jean Simmons, middle). David the family chauffeur (Lawrence Ung) is a pawn in the game. Production still.

A Summer Place (Warner Bros., 1959)
Based on Sloan Wilson's bestselling novel of the same title and scripted by director Delmer Daves, *A Summer Place* is soap opera cubed; in other words, cheap melodrama with nice clothes, lots of resentment, and some adult themes. The film is rather silly in its hyperbolic Manichaeism, and some of the acting in it simple-minded. The best performances are those of Dorothy, Arthur Kennedy, and a disquieting Constance Ford.

Three couples form the geometric crisscrossing of the story's swap game. Couple one: Bart Hunter (Arthur Kennedy) and Sylvia Hunter (Dorothy); these are the impoverished owners of a summer resort inn on Pine Island, Maine. Bart is a sarcastic, disillusioned drunkard; the love has long since gone out of the marriage.

Couple two: Ken Jorgenson (Richard Egan) and Helen Jorgenson (Constance Ford); he used to be a lifeguard on the island in his youth; now he has made money, and has come back to the island to show off and rediscover his roots. These two are also unhappily married: Helen is a venomous, rancorous woman who has made herself over into a moralistic virgin through the magic power of her hatred.

Couple three: Johnny Hunter (Troy Donahue) and Molly Jorgenson (Sandra Dee), the respective offspring of the above two mismatched pairs.

When couple two arrives on the island, all romantic hell breaks loose. Sylvia and Ken remember that they used to be madly in love with each other all those many years ago, and think it would be a capital idea to give it another sporting try. They do, and the experiment is successful. The two children fall in love with each other the minute they meet, and they, too, start carrying on a clandestine relationship. Finding herself surrounded by sin, the poisonous Helen loses what cool she had left and lashes out at everyone and anyone, with spiteful relish. Divorces are negotiated and carried out. The teenagers are sent off to far-away schools, separately. Ken and Sylvia marry. The children learn to accept and respect the new couple.

For the first (and only) time, Dorothy plays a woman who is not only an adulterer, but also happy about it. The adult love affair between Sylvia and Ken is a chance for much tenderness, and much thoughtful musing on the issues of clandestineness and *carpe diem*. Dorothy is wonderful; unfortunately, she is given Richard Egan as an acting partner, a wooden, uncomplicated actor if ever there was one. Troy Donahue is helplessly inexpressive, and Sandra Dee is cute but monotonous. Arthur Kennedy acts up a storm as the embittered drunkard, and Constance Ford sinks her teeth nicely into her vicious character.

As he would two years later with the similar *Susan Slade*, director Delmer Daves packages the film slickly, with catchy tunes by Max Steiner (who also scored *Susan Slade*) and cinematography by Harry Stradling Sr.; Steiner's main theme was number 1 on the 1960 *Billboard* charts for nine weeks.

Ken Jorgenson (Richard Egan) and Sylvia Hunter (Dorothy) rekindle their ancient flame in *A Summer Place* (1959). Production still.

The film was popular with audiences, but most critics disliked it. Howard Thompson of The *New York Times* was vitriolic in his contempt; he was also morally displeased with the "frank" sexual content of the story, which did not help. His cautiously positive comments about the players notwithstanding, his review tore the movie to pieces. About Dorothy and Egan, he only stated, "Miss McGuire and Mr. Egan manage some restraint, professionally at least, without being exactly appealing." The comment that summed up his attitude: "The whole thing leaves a rancid taste."[553]

Variety showed considerable measure in its review. First, about the film as a whole, it proclaimed:

---

553 Howard Thompson, "'Summer Place' Opens," *New York Times*, October 23, 1959.

> It's one of those big, emotional, slickly-produced pictures that bite off a great deal more than they can chew and neatly dispose of their intense, highly-dramatic mélange by dropping their characters into slots clearly marked "good" and "bad."
>
> [...] What results is an uneven, superficial film that has all the trappings of soap opera imposed on what essentially is an adult, serious theme.[554]

Variety opined that Delmer Daves had "missed the mark by a mile" both as a writer and as a director. The magazine's reviewer wrote of characters that were "unreal and totally devoid of depth," of the film's "tendency to use dialog to 'preach' what should be implied" and "to be harsh where it should be sensitive." He was also contemptuous of the players, with one notable exception:

> With the single exception of Dorothy McGuire, who comes through with a radiant performance and is lovely to look at, the cast does an average job.

The Dark at the Top of the Stairs (Warner Bros., 1960)
William Inge's play *The Dark at the Top of the Stairs* (1957) was a hit when it played on Broadway. Directed by Elia Kazan, it opened at the Music Box Theatre on December 5, 1957, and closed on January 16, 1959, after 468 performances.

Inge was a sensitive playwright, who had no trouble articulating human relationships; by today's sensibility, his approach may sometimes feel a bit "soft," and his values old-fashioned. Old-fashioned is certainly how this particular film as a whole feels today. It is a good film, but the lessons in human interaction it teaches are on the stodgy side.

---

554 "A Summer Place," *Variety*, October 7, 1959.

Difficult or tormented sexual relations were Inge's specialty (e.g. in *Come Back, Little Sheba*, 1950, and *Picnic*, 1953), and here, in the last Broadway hit of his career, he examines the affection-impaired Fludd family and sets the action amidst the nostalgic Americana of a small Oklahoma town in the 1920s. The topic: the passionless marriage of Rubin and Cora Fludd (Robert Preston and Dorothy) and their relationships with their children, shy Reenie Fludd (Shirley Knight) and bullied Sonny Fludd (Robert Eyer, whose older brother Richard had played Dorothy's son in *Friendly Persuasion*).

A good illustration of how Inge's insights into human relationships may suffer from clichéd superficiality and 1950s mainstream morality is the advice Cora Fludd receives from her husband's "special friend" Mavis Pruitt (Angela Lansbury) during their confrontation. The advice can be oversimplified as follows: careful, because whenever you slam a door on your husband or withhold sexual favors from him, there is someone like me ready to please him. Which implies: it is your fault if your husband looks elsewhere for companionship. At this point, Cora almost literally runs to her husband and makes peace with him, saying she cannot live without him.

The early scenes in the film appear to be setting up a careful articulation of the discourse on love, sex, and relationships; the final confrontations, rather than paying off such articulation by delving deeper into the discourse, cheapen it and simplify it in the interest of a quick conclusion. Ultimately, nothing of real import or complexity is really said in this melodrama in disguise. On the other hand, the rules of melodrama are not obeyed either, for there is no scenery chewing, and everything is tasteful, talky and restrained. Within this hybrid middle ground, the piece does admirably, and so do the players.

Quibbles aside, this "simple, eloquent drama"[555] contains a series of quaint, thoughtful scenes, well acted by the cast. Robert Preston's inter-

---

[555] "The Dark at the Top of the Stairs," in Maltin (2009), op. cit.

pretation of salesman Rubin Fludd contains more than a few mannerisms left over from his Broadway success in *The Music Man* three years earlier. Even *Variety* noted the "similarity in manner and speech between Harold Hill of 'Music Man' and Rubin Fludd of 'Dark.'"[556] Fundamentally, whether in the bedroom, the parlor or the speakeasy, Rubin sounds like a scam artist. Dramatically, Angela Lansbury as Rubin's "special friend" and Dorothy display the most balance, and the most poignancy. Shirley Knight is heartwarming in delivering her one-note wallflower of a character.

Scam artist Rubin Fludd and disgruntled subordinate: Robert Preston and Dorothy in a production still for *The Dark at the Top of the Stairs*, 1960.

One of the most beautifully delineated and dramatically effective characters is Sammy Golden (played by Lee Kinsolving), the young Jewish military cadet who befriends and beguiles Reenie, bringing her out of her isolation. Sammy, the unloved son of a rich Hollywood star, is a

---

[556] "The Dark at the Top of the Stairs," *Variety*, September 14, 1960.

deeply unhappy outsider who insists on being flippant and sarcastic about his unhappiness, running resolutely against the sentimental grain of the rest of the story; thus, his scenes are the film's most unsentimental—and the most tragic. His death from a self-provoked car accident is a surprise both for Reenie and for the audience because it happens suddenly and unsentimentally, just as the two characters' young love is about to blossom and Reenie's shyness is beginning to melt away.

The final scene, in which Cora and Rubin "make up" and plan some hanky-panky in the bedroom, gives way to one of the most amusing moments in the story. The Fludds' plans for intimacy are potentially ruined by the arrival of their younger child Sonny and his buddy (the boy who had been bullying Sonny, Harold, has become his best friend after Sonny stood up to him by beating him up). Rubin bribes the boys into going to the movies instead of staying home to play, so he can be alone with his wife. The boys exit the house, and Rubin and Cora proceed to their bedroom. The final shot of the film focuses on the two kids as they walk away from the house, delivering this little dialogue:

Harold: Do you know why they wanted to get rid of us?
Sonny: No. Do you?
Harold: No. But it happens over at my house, regular as clockwork.

The film was well received. *Variety* liked both it and the players. About Dorothy, it noted, "Dorothy McGuire is tops [...]. With sensitivity, she is believable through all phases of her role." About Kinsolving, it wrote that he was "first-rate as the ill-fated suitor."

Trivia: Teresa Wright, who had been Dorothy's understudy for the role of Emily in Thornton Wilder's *Our Town* (1938) on Broadway, and who would become Dorothy's friend in later years, played Cora Fludd in the original Broadway production of *The Dark at the Top of the Stairs*.

Swiss Family Robinson (Walt Disney Pictures, 1960)

"Pure escapism, larger than life,"[557] film historian Leonard Maltin has written about Walt Disney's loose and overlong (126 minutes compared to the 93 of the 1940 version) remake of the 1940 film of the same title, based on the 1812 novel by Johann David Wyss entitled *Der schweizerische Robinson*.[558] The story of a nice family from Bern shipwrecked on savage New Guinea during Napoleon Bonaparte's times, this 1960 version is indeed escapist material, and is given the Walt Disney treatment in Technicolor and Panavision. The successful remake, filmed on the island of Tobago and at Pinewood Studios in England, has become something of a classic with Disney fans, but is not without problems.

First, there is verisimilitude. The shipwrecked family is supposed to be from Bern, Switzerland, circa 1812. It is composed of Father (John Mills), Mother (Dorothy) and three sons, Fritz (James MacArthur), Ernst (Tommy Kirk), and Francis (the youngest, played by Kevin Corcoran). Yet, John Mills sounds like he is from Suffolk by way of London's West End; Dorothy sounds like she is from Los Angeles by way of Mid-Atlantic Broadway; and the three sons sound like they are from ... well, from wherever the three actors playing them are from, which is modern-day New York, Santa Monica, and Downey, California, respectively. When Francis (Corcoran) squeaks loudly, "*What's goin' on?*" to his parents, he sounds like a shrill kid from the suburbs of California, circa 1960, no more, no less. Arbitrary as it is to have this Swiss family speak English in accordance with filmic convention, one would wish for a little consistency: one would like to be able to believe that these five people belong at least to the *same* family.

Verisimilitude is also a problem when it comes to the climactic

---

[557] Maltin (2009), op. cit.

[558] First published in English as *The Family Robinson Crusoe: or, Journal of a father shipwrecked, with his wife and children, on an uninhabited island*, M. J. Godwin & Co., 1814.

adventure sequences, depicting the family's battle against a band of pirates. *Variety* certainly thought so:

> The climactic scrape with a band of Oriental buccaneers is the crushing blow to any semblance of credulity that has managed to strain through. [...] In its effort to avoid gore or vivid violence, the picture is guilty of one of the most ineffectual battle sequences on record. Huge boulders and logs dispatched downhill by the Robinsons at their corsair adversaries are so obviously cardboard that the scene just about lapses into sheer slapstick for everyone but tots.[559]

The story, as told by Disney, may be all right for kids, particularly in the adventure sequences; but it may be too cloying for them in the remaining sequences, just as it is too childish in general for adults. The two adult characters, played by Dorothy and Mills, are stodgy, underdrawn, and inconsistent. After Father and his sons have built a spectacular three-tier tree house to lodge the family safely, Father presents it to his wife; at the end of the tour, he unveils the master bedroom, which is equipped with a mechanical thatched sunroof. Mother's teary response is, "*It's so wonderful; I don't deserve it.*" Illogical lines like this one come out of nowhere and go nowhere in this film, as if a fragment of character exploration (if it is even that) could replace the exploration itself.

Then there is the comedy, which is awkward to say the least. Animals especially, and their continual mistreatment by humans, are used for comic relief, and the results are clumsy and haphazard. For example, a comical race where each family member rides a different wild animal (an ostrich, a zebra, a baby elephant, and a donkey) is a largely unfunny display of playful cruelty, and might be painful to watch for any animal lover; shame on animal lover Dorothy for not rebelling. And, again for comic effect, two

---

[559] "Swiss Family Robinson," *Variety*, November 9, 1960.

Great Danes running into a makeshift tent to take refuge from a sudden downpour wreak havoc with family and tent both, but the family's hysterical reactions are overplayed and contrived.

Having been accidentally dunked in the ocean, Mother (Dorothy) is rescued by her Swiss family. Left to right: Tommy Kirk, Dorothy, John Mills and Kevin Corcoran. Production still.

The rescue of a young woman (Janet Munro) from the clutches of a band of pirates in an extended subplot involving the older Robinson boys, Fritz and Ernst, injects some tedious hormonal sibling rivalry into the film, and some even more tedious romancing scenes.

Dorothy's character, written using heavy doses of conventionality and sexism, has a couple of thoughtful moments early in the picture. Once the male adventure starts, she is virtually excluded from the proceedings; and her final announcement that she and her husband would rather stay in New Guinea than go back to western civilization is as arbitrary as it is improbable. The *New York Times* thought that Dorothy and John Mills were "fine, as usual,"[560] but that was putting it kindly. *Variety* opined that

---

560 Howard Thompson, "New Version of 'Swiss Family Robinson,'" *New York Times*, December 24, 1960.

the acting was "generally capable, but hardly memorable."[561] I beg to differ on the first half of that sentence: the kids' acting especially is as cloddish as that of any small-town amateur hour.

The *New York Times* was rapturous about the film, calling it a "grand adventure yarn,"[562] and urged parents to take their kids to see it over the Christmas holidays. They probably did.

Susan Slade (Warner Bros., 1961)

Susan Slade (1961) was Dorothy's second film with Warner Bros. It is definitely a product of its age (or, better, a belated product of the '50s): it is melodramatic, slick, and as removed from reality as human drama can be, while pretending to say something progressive about the fears of mainstream 1950s society. The film, which would make for a perfect double-feature bill with *A Summer Place*, gives lip service to non-conventionality, but plays into the squarest assumptions of middle-class morality. In glorious Technicolor.

Like the sentimental Harlequin-novel fable that it is,[563] *Susan Slade*, based on Doris Hume's book of the same title, is populated by fairy-tale "types." There is a well-meaning but glacially society-conscious mother (Dorothy); there is a handsome mountain-climbing Prince Charming (Grant Williams) who woos and conquers the vestal-virgin protagonist (Connie Stevens); and there is a handsome stable hand (he is a horse doctor, actually, and is played by Troy Donahue) who consoles Susan and stands by her in her hour of disgrace after the prince's death. In glorious Technicolor.

Grant Williams plays Prince Charming, aka Conn White, a good-looking, rich, sensitive loafer who climbs mountains compulsively and

---

561 *Variety* review (1960), op. cit.

562 Thompson (1960), op. cit.

563 *Variety* called the film a "contrived soaper-meller." October 4, 1961.

finds love at first sight when he meets Susan. Susan is not very good at kissing—she has led a very sheltered, rich life, you see—but she would like to learn. Conn easily overcomes her initial diffidence, and teaches her. He also teaches her how to copulate, though we are spared the lesson. On an ocean liner, and in glorious Technicolor.

Conn (great name, and a pun waiting to happen) is presented as a seductive but ambiguous figure.[564] Is he too good to be true? Is he after easy adventure? Is he lying when he claims he wants to do good by Susan and marry her when he comes back from his climbing expedition in Alaska? These are the questions the audience is invited to ask. Actually, the answers to those questions are no, no, and no. Conn is sincere in his affections, but he is also what you would call a free spirit: the mountain-climbing expedition he has organized comes first, with Susan a close second.

Back at the ranch (a Carmel ocean-view home that an architect has just completed for Susan's rich family), Susan waits for Conn's letters from the mountains of Alaska, but they do not come. She begins to think he has forgotten her, until she learns that he has not, and has desperately been trying to phone her, but too late. Reached by phone, Conn's father (an uncredited Everett Glass) tells Susan how much his son talked about his love for her; he also tells her that Conn has just died while climbing that far-away mountain. Susan is devastated, and pregnant. What to do? Mom has a solution: claim that she herself is with child, and take Susan away on a long Guatemalan trip before the truth begins to show so that people will not talk. In the end, after the birth of the child and the family's return to California, the truth comes out in an obligatory climactic scene.

Excluding Troy Donahue, the acting is good all around, with special marks going to Dorothy as the mother, Grant Williams as Conn, and Lloyd Nolan as the father. (It is nice to see Dorothy and Nolan reunited, sixteen years after *A Tree Grows in Brooklyn*.) The story is enjoyable, Max

---

[564] Some contemporary reviews dubbed the character "what you might call a villain." For example, Boyd Martin in "Boyd Martin's Show Talk," December 6, 1961.

Steiner's score is romantic, Lucien Ballard's Technicolor is glorious. Even the set decoration by William L. Kuehl is grand: according to contemporary reports, the photographs of Chile gracing the walls of the living room of Dorothy's character were prize-winning shots taken by John Swope.[565]

Dorothy poses with her co-star Lloyd Nolan in this publicity still for *Susan Slade*.

---

565 Leonard Lyons, "Lyons Den," *Post Standard* (Syracuse, NY), December 29, 1960.

This Warner Bros. portrait of Dorothy circulated at the time of the release of *Susan Slade*. Warner Pathe, 1961.

Unfortunately, the whole big dead pumpkin of a film sounds irreparably hollow inside.[566] The *Los Angeles Times*' Philip K. Scheuer called the film a "feeble 'family' drama."[567] Bosley Crowther of the *New York Times* detested the film. The following are the opening and closing paragraphs of his review:

---

566 *Variety*, October 4, 1961.

567 Philip K. Scheuer, "'Susan Slade' Proves Feeble 'Family' Drama," *Los Angeles Times*, November 9, 1961.

IF you want to see what the words corny and cliché-ridden mean when prudently put to a motion picture, you might muster your mental fortitude, grit your teeth, don a pair of dark glasses and take a fast look at "Susan Slade."

[...]

We stuck with it, out of morbid fascination, and can assure you it concludes with a cliché. Delmer Daves, who wrote the screen play and directed (from a novel by Doris Hume), doesn't toss one real, live, honest thing into it. It is all just one big, soft, colored blob.[568]

Summer Magic (Walt Disney Productions, 1963)
This film may suffer from a terminal case of the cutes, and what charm it has may be of the calculating kind, but some charm it has nonetheless. If you can get past the shrill talkativeness of protagonist Hayley Mills, this musical piece of Americana grows on you; aggressively, like ivy.

An unofficial, and loose, remake of *Mother Carey's Chickens* (1938), in turn based on a 1910 partially autobiographical novel by Kate Douglas Wiggin bearing the same title,[569] the film is the story of the Carey family: mother Margaret Carey and her three children, Nancy (Hayley Mills), Gilly (Eddie Hodges) and Peter (Jimmy Mathers). After her husband dies, Margaret realizes that the investments he had made have not lived up to their potential. The family is more or less indigent, and cannot afford to keep their townhouse in Boston. Eldest child Nancy, always full of ideas, has written to the postmaster of a town they had visited with their father, and discovers that a charming "yellow house" they had seen is vacant. The postmaster (Osh Popham, played by Burl Ives) is moved by

---

[568] Bosley Crowther, "Corny and Cliche-Ridden: Susan Slade' Arrives at Two Theatres Connie Steve Stars in Soap-Sudsy Drama," *New York Times*, November 11, 1961.

[569] Kate Douglas Wiggin, *Mother Carey's Chickens*, Grosset & Dunlap, 1911.

the pathetic exaggerations of Nancy's letter and takes it upon himself to rent the house to the Careys on behalf of its owner, Tom Hamilton, who is away living in China. Without telling him. So, off to Beulah, Maine, the family goes. The rest of the film is the story of the Careys' house renovation and of their settling down in their new bucolic surroundings. Nancy Carey has always imagined Tom Hamilton (Peter Brown) as an old codger, but when the owner of the house returns to Beulah unexpectedly, he is not at all what she had pictured, but a tall, dark, handsome youngster who is not pleased with Popham's initiatives. Hamilton, however, takes an immediate shine to young Nancy, and he is single... You get the picture.

Family magic: the Careys sing to the tune of their new second-hand mechanical piano before moving to Maine, in this production still for *Summer Magic.* **The song is "Flitterin'." The players are, left to right: Dorothy, Eddie Hodges, Jimmy Mathers, and Hayley Mills. © 1963, Walt Disney Pictures.**

Lamentably, the two best players in the cast, Burl Ives and Dorothy, are confined to the sidelines of benevolent supervision of the children's antics, whether feminine (dresses, crushes, jealousies) or masculine (scraps, friendships with shaggy dogs). The film belongs to the Carey children (especially Nancy) and their new friends, Popham's offspring Digby (Michael J. Pollard) and Lallie Joy (Wendy Turner). Ives, at least, gets a subplot of his own, and has a story to carry (Popham's machinations with the house rental); all Dorothy has to do is be nice and watch the children. She does it beautifully.

The songs written by the Sherman brothers (Robert B. and Richard M.) are a pleasure, as always. Ms. Mills sings three and Mr. Hodges sings two, as does Burl Ives. Even Dorothy sings one (the title song), but not with her own voice: she is dubbed by Marilyn Hooven.[570] My personal favorite: "On the Front Porch," crooned by Burl Ives with consummate artistry and relaxed charm. This song was a favorite of Robert Sherman's too, according to his autobiography.[571]

The Greatest Story Ever Told
(George Stevens Productions/United Artists, 1965)
If not the greatest, at least the biggest, for, even edited down to three hours and nineteen minutes from its original running time of four hours and twenty minutes, this prayer-card anthology film is still rather interminable.

An alternate title for this magnum opus could have been "The Gospels' Greatest Hits," for that is fundamentally what it is. The film tells the undeniably moving story of the last years of the life of Jesus Christ with heartfelt conviction—and plodding, reverential solemnity. Along the way, it crams in as many famous lines from the Gospels as it can, and as many cameos from famous Hollywood actors. The acting from these famous actors ranges from sublime (Claude Rains, Ed Wynn) to inept (John

---

570 Thomas S. Hischak and Mark A. Robinson, *The Disney Song Encyclopedia*, The Scarecrow Press, Inc., 2009, 189.

571 Robert B. Sherman, *Moose: Chapters from My Life*, AuthorHouse UK Ltd., 2013, 281.

Wayne). Oh, and along the way the film also quotes anything Christ-related, from Leonardo da Vinci's *Last Supper* fresco to the "Hallelujah" chorus from Handel's *Messiah*. More "greatest hits."

There are some nice moments in this film, and some powerful scenes. When the story shifts to high gear for the Stations of the Cross, for example, director George Stevens and composer Alfred Newman enlist the uncredited help of composer Giuseppe Verdi, whose *Messa da Requiem* (1874) adds considerable power and poignancy to the sequence (how could it not?). As far as those endless quotable lines from the Gospels are concerned, they might have been bearable if the five credited and uncredited writers who worked on this biggest of stories, together with the actors and the director, had found a way to offer us significant insight into those maxims, beyond the obvious Sunday school platitudes. They did not. Thus, despite Max von Sydow's interesting efforts as Jesus Christ, virtually all those lines sound clichéd and ponderous, like something quoted dutifully from a well-known but ill-understood book.

Dorothy, as Jesus's mother Mary, is in no more than ten shots in the entire movie, and whispers no more than three lines (beautifully and with great sensitivity). She is shot lovingly, and looks pretty and sweet in those pastel robes—and sad when Mary's son dies.

Incidentally, the Ultra Panavision 70 film is filled with beautiful visuals shot on location in Arizona, California, Illinois, Nevada, and Utah, but Jesus's death is shot unimaginatively on a soundstage at Metro-Goldwyn-Mayer Studios in Culver City, accompanied by one of the most fake-looking lightning storms ever to grace the big screen.

The worst line in the movie is spoken by the Roman Centurion who oversees the crucifixions, immediately after Jesus's death. The line is "*Truly, this man was the son of God*," and the actor delivering it in a perfect cowboy's drawl, and with no inkling as to what he is saying and why (or no ability to express it), is John Wayne. Pooh.

Bosley Crowther of the *New York Times* was deeply ambivalent about the film, praising the "supreme and solemn beauty" of "the grandeur of nature" and condemning Stevens' use of actors' cameos. He found the film "much too long," but admitted that Stevens' reverential style "should captivate the piously devout."[572]

Variety published a review that was almost as long as the film itself, and mostly positive. The magazine's reservations were few, and minor. A paragraph was devoted to the role of the Virgin Mary:

> The delicacy of the Virgin Mary role had to be faced. Who may fairly pass on camera in this secular age as the Mother of God? Sufficient to remark that Dorothy McGuire is plausible. Her large, soft, womanly eyes and pensive expression are right. Few will quibble that, as the mother of the Holy Babe and the mother of the grown man of 33, she is unmarked by age. It was obviously a deliberate decision of the screenplay of James Lee Barrett and Stevens to withhold from the Virgin all speech. Risks were minimized and she was used essentially for necessary symbolism. A reviewer may only guess that the Marianists, always a potent bloc in the Catholic Church, should be satisfied with Miss McGuire.[573]

Flight of the Doves (Columbia Pictures Corporation/Rainbow Releasing, 1971)

Having played the mother to end all mothers in her previous film, Dorothy, aged fifty-five, broke her semi-retirement to play her first grandmother in this children's story, based on a novel by Walter Macken[574] and scripted by Frank Gabrielson and by director Frank Nelson. The film was shot on location in Ireland. Little Finn Dove (Jack Wild) and his lit-

---

[572] Bosley Crowther, "'The Greatest Story Ever Told': Max von Sydow Stars in Biblical Film," New York Times, February 16, 1965.

[573] "The Greatest Story Ever Told," *Variety*, February 17, 1965.

[574] Walter Macken, *The Flight of the Doves*, The Macmillan Company, 1968.

tler sister Derval Dove (Helen Raye) are London orphans who discover that they are the heirs of a fortune left to them by their grandfather in Ireland, so they race off to the fair country and to the loving arms of their grandmother Granny O'Flaherty, "played by, of all people, Dorothy McGuire."[575] They are pursued by their wicked stepfather Tobias Cromwell (William Rushton), by the British as well as the Irish police, and by an evil uncle named Hawk Dove (Ron Moody), who is something of a master of disguises.

The fact that this is a "children's movie" based on a "children's book," and is therefore told in the simplest of tones and colors, is the least of the film's problems. So is the fact that its story is told at what could be termed a leisurely pace, and that the telling is frequently interrupted by extraneous production numbers. Its main flaw is its consistent affront to the considerable talents in its cast (Dorothy, Ron Moody, Stanley Holloway and William Rushton among them), in the form of a style so broad that it forces said talents to turn their characters into caricatures.

Dorothy plays Mary Magdalene St. Bridget O'Flaherty as a young, energetic grandmother, and as a stereotypical Irish spitfire, in a spirit reminiscent of Maureen O'Hara's in John Ford's *The Quiet Man* (1952). Granny O'Flaherty's gait is wide and strong, her spirit indomitable. When she marches into a busy courtroom and interrupts the proceedings demanding to be heard, she does so in tones so ringing and in a manner so peremptory that the crowd behind her is naturally charmed by her power, just as Judge Liffy (Holloway) is naturally flustered by it.

The vim and speed of Granny O'Flaherty (fairy tale-style, she is introduced riding a bicycle at full velocity flanked by two young men on horseback) enliven all the scenes she is in, and allow Dorothy to pull some stops that had been left muted during the previous decade. It is therefore a particular shame that her character is so underwritten, and that it is in many respects little more than an Irish cliché and a plot device.

---

575 Bernard Drew, "A Holiday 'Flight,'" *Rochester (NY) Democrat and Chronicle*, April 8, 1971.

Critics were not particularly happy with the film. Charles Champlin of the *Los Angeles Times*, while not exactly enthusiastic, thought that the film, though "not at the level of the Disney classics," was "a welcome arrival for what to do with restless Easter-vacationing small fry."[576] Bernard Drew of the Rochester *Democrat and Chronicle* thought that the film was "long on cuteness and short on thrills" and that it was "virtually a Cook's Tour of Dublin."[577] All the major critics were annoyed by the film's pace, by its lack of dramatic drive, and by its excess of cuteness. Some of them were enthusiastic about Moody, but none said much of anything about Dorothy.

Little Derval (Helen Raye) and her brother Finn (Jack Wild) are reunited with Granny O'Flaherty (Dorothy) in her cottage. *Flight of the Doves*, production still. 1970, Columbia Pictures Industries, Inc.

[576] Charles Champlin, "'Doves,' a Blend of Tradition," *Los Angeles Times*, March 29, 1971.

[577] Drew, "Flight" (1971), op. cit.

Roger Greenspun of the *New York Times* was negative, and commented:

> On the one hand the film promotes an adventure-escape story that is adequately both terrifying and funny. But on the other hand it indulges in picturesque scenery for charm's sake, suffers adult sentimentality about little children gladly and, as if unsure about its fiction, interrupts it for various pointless entertainments.
>
> The worst of these is an ecumenical St. Patrick's Day production number, like something out of a 1940's B-musical, set in a park in Dublin. A lot of local talent appears—along with Orientals, black Africans, tan Africans, continental European nationals and an Orthodox rabbi — and everybody dances a jig and shakes his arms and sings a song that goes, I swear, "You don't have to be Irish to be Irish."[578]

Jonathan Livingston Seagull (The Jonathan Company/Paramount Pictures, 1973)
It is regrettable that this film, freely adapted by director Hall Bartlett from Richard Bach's bestselling spiritual allegory of the same title (1970),[579] should turn out to be Dorothy's farewell to cinema. Virtually, anyway: more than a decade later, she would briefly lend her voice to another film as narrator, Michie Gleason's *Summer Heat* (1987). Here, she lends her voice to a seagull.

An uneven, almost soporifically slow film, *Jonathan Livingston Seagull* was made the object of several lawsuits including one from Richard Bach himself. It tells the parable of the titular seagull, a young adult bird (voice

---

[578] Roger Greenspun, "'Flight of Doves': Dublin Background for Tale of 2 Orphans," *New York Times*, April 3, 1971.

[579] Richard D. Bach, *Jonathan Livingston Seagull*, The Macmillan Company, 1970.

of James Franciscus) who is not satisfied with conforming to the conservative rules of the flock and wants to learn more about life and about seagullness. Outcast by the flock's elders, he roams the world (perhaps different worlds) and meets some enlightened teachers (and later disciples) along the way.

The Christ symbolism of the story is quite obvious, what with the gull's apparent death, resurrection, and return as a spiritual teacher, but that is the least of the film's problems. Its imagery, captured mostly through helicopter photography, is stunning, making the film look like a documentary for much of its running time. Dialogue is scarce: it takes almost fifteen minutes of wordless images for the first voice (Jonathan's) to turn up, which gives you an idea of how sluggish the pace of the storytelling is.

Even after characters start speaking, the tone of the film is far from consistent. In fact, the whole story is told in a hesitant, uncertain "voice," as if the creative team were afraid to offend its audience. This "voice" wavers between prosaic, practical monologues/dialogue and the irksome poetic enunciations of Richard Bach's metaphysical philosophy; irksome not because they have no value but because they are impoverished by their preachy *Reader's Digest* simplification. The prosaic half is uninteresting, while the philosophical half is weakly articulated, mostly composed of aphorisms or maxims. The prosaic half seems designed to annoy the New-Agers, while the esoteric half seems aimed at sabotaging the storytelling and aggravating the materialists. Add to this the dubious poetry of Neil Diamond's songs—heavily philosophical themselves, in a superficial, maudlin way—and you have a feeble result, one that deflates its own power at every turn.

Other problems mar the quality of the film. The actors who lend their voices to the characters are directed without conviction, and with no indication of style; therefore, they deliver tentative, toothless, sluggishly paced performances (only Hal Holbrook as the Flock Elder shows some authoritativeness), especially given the quality of the humorless dialogue. Philosophy aside, that dialogue is so elementary as to belong to a bland fairy tale. This story, however, is no fairy tale; it is a philosophical parable, akin to the stories of Bach's contemporary Carlos Castaneda, the "other" metaphysical novelist of the period.[580]

There is also a deep discrepancy between the style of the imagery and the style of the written parable. This intimate allegory of an individual's spiritual growth, blown up to Panavision proportions, gets lost in the vastness of the 2.35:1 screen, drowning the characters in spectacular realistic vistas for most of its length. Some close-up scenes of the protagonist during his quest fare better, and the scenes in which Jonathan suffers the consequences of his bravery are appropriately moving. Ultimately, this story works much better on the written page, where the reader is free to imagine both characters and setting and the "fakeness" of the parable is appropriate.

In view of the above, one can conclude that the biggest flaw of this film lies in the decision to visualize the story in the real world. In this respect, it does not help that seagulls, God bless 'em, are fundamentally expressionless creatures, at least from our unenlightened human point of view. So, while the actors try to endow the characters' thoughts with some feeling, the seagulls just stand there, being seagulls (visually, the birds do not "speak," i.e. they do not move their beaks during the dialogue).

Dorothy, wouldn't you know it, plays Jonathan's mother, and speaks some four lines in the entire movie.

The *New York Times* did not share my negative feelings about the film, which it called "beautiful and touching";[581] the anonymous reviewer only found some flaws in the philosophical part (too synthetic to be effective) and in the film's excessive length.

Variety was less positive:

---

580 See for example Carlos Castaneda, *Journey to Ixtlan: The Lessons of Don Juan*, Touchstone/Simon & Schuster, 1972.

581 "'Jonathan,' Rare Gull, Makes Unusual Film The Program," *New York Times*, October 25, 1973.

The pastoral allegory, filmed with live birds and locations while some well-known players essay the vocal chores, is a combination of teenybopper psychedelics, facile moralizing, Pollyanna polemic, and superb nature photography.[582]

Ultimately, *Variety* was also suspicious of the film's philosophizing, especially in its reduced aphoristic form:

> Now there's nothing wrong with uplift, except that exhortations customarily are banal, the sort of slippery, equivocal goo found on weighing machine cards, fortune cookies and dime astrology guides. That is, the end is nearly destroyed by the means. In the film, virtually every thought has a timeless value, but the conveyance is annoying, cloying and never buoying.[583]

---

[582] "Jonathan Livingston Seagull," *Variety*, October 10, 1973.

[583] Ibid.

14. Other Theater, 1945–1971

All through Dorothy's early film career, the ghost of Broadway past was never far from her memory, and the Hollywood press occasionally printed reports of some theater project or other simmering on the back burner. For the most part, reports were vague, and their columnists did not mention any specific property or co-star. Some did, such as Hedda Hopper (always ready to name names), who, on June 28, 1947, mentioned Gregory Peck's doing a "play with Dorothy McGuire at Cape Cod [that] summer."[584] Unfailingly, those reports proved to be false alarms.

In 1949, a few tidbits appeared in the press concerning Dorothy's involvement in the Broadway play *The Rat Race* for producer Leland Hayward (John Swope's college friend and Dorothy's theatrical agent) and writer Garson Kanin. That project, too, evaporated, at least for Dorothy, as Hopper reported in September 1949:

> Dorothy McGuire's en route to New York, but she won't do "The Rat Race" for Garson Kanin and Leland Hayward. Dorothy's set for a couple of air shows in the big town, and her

---
[584] Hedda Hopper, "Looking at Hollywood," *Los Angeles Times*, June 28, 1947.

husband, John Swope, will photograph two successful plays, "Mr. Roberts" and "Detective Story." Dorothy will pass her boss, Darryl Zanuck, in mid-air, so she doesn't know what picture he has lined up for her.[585]

John Swope would end up being the official photographer of *The Rat Race*. Kanin's play premiered (without Dorothy but with Betty Field) on December 22, 1949, at New York's Ethel Barrymore Theatre, and ran for a total of eighty-four performances. It closed on March 4, 1950.

At any rate, what with her radio and film career, her La Jolla Playhouse duties, her family life, and her frequent travels, Dorothy was a busy woman, and it is something of a miracle that she was even able to do as much as she did.

The earliest record of Dorothy's actual involvement in a full-length play after the beginning of her film career and before the establishment of the La Jolla Playhouse is dated 1945. Dorothy embarked on a World War II USO tour as protagonist of the play *Dear Ruth*, written by Norman Krasna. (Louella Parsons' comment: "She's leaving at a time when every studio is asking to borrow her, but she has plans.")[586] The show was produced by Joseph Hyman and Bernard Hart, designed by Frederick Fox and directed by Sterling Mace. Other actors appearing in the play were Paul Anderson, Clement Brace, Marjorie Crossland, Pat Goodwin, William Hughes, Peter Lawrence, William A. Lee, Jan Powers, and Mary Wilsey. We know from Parsons that the play opened in London;[587] of two

---

[585] Hedda Hopper, "Margaret Sullavan Career Well Mapped," *Los Angeles Times*, September 28, 1949.

[586] Louella O. Parsons (INS), "Dorothy McGuire With Two Smash Hits Behind Her, Plans USO Show In London," *Fresno (CA) Bee The Republican*, February 12, 1945.

[587] Louella O. Parsons (INS), "Dorothy McGuire With Two Smash Hits Behind her, Plans USO Show In London," Fresno (CA) Bee, February 12, 1945.

French locations where the comedy played, we can be sure: they were the *Casino Municipal* in Cannes and the *Palais de la Méditerranée* in Nice.⁵⁸⁸

The revival of Dorothy's Broadway career would have to wait until 1951. An early mention of this engagement appeared in Edwin Schallert's drama column for the *Los Angeles Times* on May 31, 1951:

> Dorothy McGuire now has a New York stage return under consideration. The play to be produced by the Theatre Guild is Jean Anouilh's "Point of Departure," as adapted from the French play by J. Black. It will be her first Broadway venture since "Claudia." She'll rest for a while at Balboa after completing her assignment in "Callaway Went Thataway" at MGM.⁵⁸⁹

Anouilh's play *Eurydice*, the very same play Dorothy's Actors' Company had produced in Los Angeles three years earlier, in this case was translated into English and adapted by Kitty Black; it was renamed *Point of Departure* for its London premiere, and *Legend of Lovers* for its Broadway premiere.⁵⁹⁰ In July 1951, it was Schallert again who mentioned the Broadway project and some potential scheduling conflicts:

> While Dorothy McGuire will star in "R.S.V.P." with Gottfried Reinhardt directing at MGM,⁵⁹¹ that doesn't mean

---

588 *Dear Ruth* playbill, 1945.

589 Edwin Schallert, "Barbara Rush to Star in 10 Plays; Dorothy McGuire Debates Stage," *Los Angeles Times*, May 31, 1951.

590 And eventually published by New York publisher Coward-McCann in 1952. According to Harold V. Cohen's syndicated column "The Drama Desk," the title was changed for its Broadway premiere "to avoid confusion with Henry Fonda's oncoming [Broadway play] 'Point of No Return.'" (See Harold V. Cohen, "The Drama Desk," *Pittsburgh [PA] Post-Gazette*, November 1, 1951.) Paul Osborn's play, starring Fonda and directed by H.C. Potter, premiered at the Alvin Theatre (now the Neil Simon Theatre) thirteen days before *Legend of Lovers* and ran for 356 performances.

591 "R.S.V.P." was an early working title of the film *Invitation*.

she will bypass "Point of Departure," by Jean Anouilh, on Broadway. She expects to join the cast in October, with Richard Burton as her vis-à-vis. Burton was in "The Lady's Not for Burning." Peter Ashmore is to direct the play. From "I Want You," the Samuel Goldwyn film, Miss McGuire goes directly to "R.S.V.P." at Metro.[592]

Scheduling problems did occur when Fidelity Pictures started negotiations to hire Dorothy for their film project entitled *Gardenia* (based on a story by Vera Caspary) immediately after the wrap-up of MGM's *Invitation*.[593] Dorothy, however, was indeed feeling the lure of Broadway, and passed on the film project.[594] Just how potent that lure was can be gleaned from Dorothy's statements during an interview for the *Brooklyn Eagle* a few days before the opening of *Legend of Lovers*. The immediate topic of discussion was her celebrated American tour with the La Jolla Playhouse production of Tennessee Williams' *Summer and Smoke* the previous year:

> And it was in one of those towns in Texas—I don't remember which—one night, just as the curtain was coming down and I was standing there taking my bows, when a feeling, a kind of depression, came over me. Do you know the feeling I mean? You don't know what's wrong but you feel a lonesomeness.
>
> The feeling got worse as I went backstage to take off my make-up. And then suddenly, as I was brushing my hair, I put

---

[592] Edwin Schallert, "Krueger to Produce Air Test Tube Story; Aspen Starts With Wise Film," *Los Angeles Times*, July 25, 1951.

[593] See Edwin Schallert, "Dorothy McGuire Rated Desirable for 'Gardenia,' *Los Angeles Times*, October 8, 1951.

[594] The film *Blue Gardenia* would be released in 1953, starring Anne Baxter and with direction by Fritz Lang.

down the brush and looked at myself and thought: I'm homesick. I want to go back to New York and do a play. I've got to go back to New York and do a play. I was just homesick for Shubert Alley and rehearsals and eight-performances-a-week before live audiences.

When the *Summer and Smoke* tour was over, I got on the train and went back to Hollywood feeling that my chances of avoiding new picture commitments and somehow getting back to Broadway were very, very thin. The company separated at the station in Los Angeles and I went home, still depressed, and as I walked into the house there lying on a table with the mail was a script of "Legend of Lovers" which [Theatre Guild producer] Lawrence Langner had airmailed to me from New York.[595]

Jean Anouilh's play *Legend of Lovers* is a modern-dress retelling of the legend of Orpheus and Eurydice with a bittersweet, pessimistic bent. In this version, Eurydice is not poisoned by a snake but dies in a bus accident; Orpheus thinks love impermanent and unreliable; his attempt to rescue Eurydice from the afterlife is unsuccessful because of his own weakness of heart and jealousy, and he must make a deal with Death and accept to die himself in order to join her. Dorothy was acquainted with the play, since her Actors' Company had produced Mel Ferrer's translation of it in a small, well-received production entitled *Eurydice* in October 1948 (see Part I, Chapter 9). That production, however, had flown so low under the radar as to go undetected except locally. Critics commenting on *Legend of Lovers* in 1951 reported that Anouilh's play was "completely new to American audiences [...],"[596] even though, in 1948, the *Los Angeles*

---

[595] "Miss McGuire Felt Homesick And Headed for Broadway," *Brooklyn Eagle*, December 23, 1951.

[596] Frank C. Porter, "'Legend of Lovers,' with Dorothy McGuire and Richard Burton, Opens in Washington," *Baltimore (MD) Evening Sun*, December 11, 1951.

Times' John L. Scott had announced that the Actors' Company's production of *Eurydice* had been the "American premiere of Jean Anouilh's play [. . .]."[597] That production had, in fact, been the play's English-language world premiere.

A portrait of Dorothy, circa 1955. Courtesy of the Omaha Community Playhouse.

---

[597] John L. Scott, "La Jolla Troupe's Projects to Turn Nation's Eyes Here," *Los Angeles Times*, October 3, 1948.

Legend of Lovers opened at the Plymouth Theatre in New York City on December 26, 1951, after some good out-of-town tryouts in Hartford and Washington, D.C. It was produced by the Theatre Guild (Theresa Helburn and Lawrence Langner, administrative directors and production supervisors) by arrangement with H.M. Tennent, Ltd. of London; the set design was by Eldon Elder, the costume design by Mildred Trebor. Peter Ashmore directed.

Dorothy (her name written larger than those of her co-stars in the *Playbill* cast list) was the lead; she was flanked by Richard Burton,[598] Hugh Griffith, Edith King, Noel Willman, and Bruce Gordon, with further support from Alexander Clark, Eric Sinclair, Ludi Claire, Clement Fowler, Roy Johnson, Chaddock Munro, and William Smithers.

Dorothy back on Broadway some ten years after her glorious star-making vehicle, *Claudia*; young Richard Burton as her co-star;[599] wonderful character actor Hugh Griffith: it was all very promising, especially since the play had been successful in London[600] and Paris.[601] Out-of-town tryouts were hopeful, too, even though Ben Atlas, who reviewed the Washington production for *Billboard* magazine, overused the adjective "competent" (not a very exciting appraisal), reserving "tender, eloquent and memorable" for Dorothy and "superb" for director Ashmore.[602] Un-

---

598 Burton (1925–1984) was already gravitating around Broadway in 1951: he had just made his debut in a successful run of Christopher Fry's play *The Lady's Not for Burning* with John Gielgud and Pamela Brown, from November 8, 1950, to March 17, 1951.

599 Initially, the Theater Guild intended to import Dirk Bogarde, star of the London production of *Point of Departure*, as Dorothy's co-star. See Ed Sullivan, "Toast of the Town," *Baltimore (MD) Evening Sun*, May 15, 1951.

600 The first officially recognized English-language version of the play, entitled *Point of Departure*, premiered in London at the Lyric Theatre, Hammersmith, on November 1, 1950, and transferred to the Duke of York's Theatre on December 26, 1950, with a cast that included Dirk Bogarde, Mai Zetterling and Stephen Murray.

601 *Eurydice* premiered at the Théâtre de l'Atelier on December 8, 1942, starring Alain Cuny as Orphée and Monelle Valentin as Eurydice.

602 Ben Atlas, "Out of Town Review: Legend of Lovers," *Billboard*, December 22, 1951.

fortunately, once the production arrived in New York City, both audiences and critics hated Anouilh's play, despite the stellar acting talent involved.

The *Los Angeles Times* first published a syndicated United Press review of the production, which was introduced by a Pirandellian reference:

> The Plymouth Theater witnessed a not unusual spectacle—a couple of good actors in need of a good play. Dorothy McGuire and Richard Burton did not find it in Jean Anouilh's "Legend of Lovers" [. . .].[603]

The anonymous UP reviewer called the play "a tedious hash of pseudopoetic drama that fails utterly to arouse compassion,"[604] and was especially grieved by the waste of Dorothy and Burton's talents:

> That [the play] fails in this respect despite the presence of Miss McGuire and Burton is further proof of the script's weakness because these two players are as capable and as beguiling as could be found anywhere at any time.[605]

A few days later, the *Los Angeles Times* published another, even more searing, review in its drama section, Radie Harris subbing for Edwin Schallert. This is how it opened:

> In Jean Anouilh's "Legend of Lovers," [. . .] this French playwright has one of his characters say, "He has choked him-

---

603 "Anouilh Play Weak Subject for Its Stars (UP)," *Los Angeles Times*, December 29, 1951. The Pirandellian reference is to his iconic play *Six Characters in Search of an Author* (*Sei personaggi in cerca d'autore*, 1921).

604 Ibid.

605 Ibid.

self with his own words." In this line, Anouilh has written his own capsule criticism. He talks about life, he talks about love, he talks about death, but too much of the talk is dull and ponderous, with only occasional sparks of vitality and humor. Again, here is an example of a French play translated into English that was both a big hit in London and Paris but is doomed to failure on Broadway.[606]

Harris, too, lamented the waste of the leads' talents, expressing disappointment that Anouilh's play should be the vehicle to bring Dorothy back to Broadway.

Most naysayers, including the usually lethal Walter Winchell, distinguished between sinners and sin, or players and play:

> Hollywood's Dorothy McGuire, an exile from Broadway for over 10 years [sic], returned to the Legit in the Theater Guild's "Legend of Lovers" (at the Plymouth) and won the nod from the critics over the play. There were no blue ribbons for Kitty Black's adaptation of Jean Anouilh's theme. Aisleman Chapman's[607] rebuff: "A cheerless hodge-podge."[608]

Society columnist Mel Heimer,[609] who could occasionally be a "waspish" commentator (his definition, not mine), out-Winchelled Winchell in his view of Dorothy, evidently failing to make the above distinction:

---

606 Radie Harris, "Dramatist 'Chokes on Own Words,'" *Los Angeles Times*, January 6, 1952.

607 John Chapman was at the time the influential theater critic of New York's *Daily News*.

608 Walter Winchell, "In New York with Walter Winchell," *Charleston Daily Mail*, January 1, 1952.

609 Biographer, historian, novelist, and society columnist Mel Heimer (1916–1971) penned a popular syndicated column, "My New York," circa 1947–1971.

Miss Dorothy McGuire, the screen performer, just laid an egg here in "Legend of Lovers," strengthening my argument that she is not yet a great actress—if she ever will be—and confusing those enthusiastic souls who already have said she is.[610]

Columnist Mel Heimer in a Central Press Association photograph, 1947.

Louis Sheaffer of the *Brooklyn Eagle* split his disappointment equally between the text and the production's lead actress. Believing that Anouilh was at his best "when talking lightly and humorously of love [. . .]" and that his ponderous philosophizing benefited no one, Sheaffer berated the

---

610 Mel Heimer, "My New York," *Cumberland (MD) News*, January 17, 1952.

play for being excessively serious, and the production for coming off as "strained, pretentious and rather phoney."[611] His main gripe, however, seems to have been about Dorothy:

> It doesn't help that Dorothy McGuire is more lugubrious and mannered than touching as Eurydice [...]. While it's true that Dorothy McGuire has a pretty thankless role in Eurydice, I still think that considerably more could have been done with the part. Her acting remains on the surface, never digs into this sad, confused girl who loves deeply but runs away at the first threat to their love.[612]

Donald Kirkley of Baltimore's *Sun*, in sizing up the play during its Washington tryouts, made a natural comparison between Anouilh's *Legend of Lovers* and Jean Cocteau's film *Orphée*:

> Neither author improved the original, and both obscured the theme with symbolism, mystical observations and modern flapdoodle regarding romantic love, which would have filled the ancient Greeks with immoderate derision. Of the two variations, Cocteau's cinematic nightmare was the more spectacular and the more interesting.[613]

Despite his sophomoric deafness to the harmonies of symbolist modernism and his ill-placed comparison, Kirkley did make a tepid argument in favor of *Legend*'s production:

---

[611] Louis Sheaffer, "Curtain Time," *Brooklyn Eagle*, December 27, 1951.

[612] Ibid.

[613] Donald Kirkley, "Theater Notes," *Baltimore (MD) Sun*, December 16, 1951.

In justice to the producers, it should be recorded that reviewers in other cities have found much to praise in the play, particularly the performances of Richard Burton, Dorothy McGuire and Hugh Griffith, and that *Variety*'s Hartford correspondent predicted that it would be a hit on Broadway.[614]

Bob Francis of *Billboard* magazine, reviewing the Broadway production ten days after opening night, was mildly appreciative, though he, too, used the adjective "pretentious," and treated the play as if it belonged to the category of realistic drama:

> Over-all, "Legend" is artistically well done. It frequently sings with a fine lyric quality, and there are short scenes of poetic beauty, which veil the essential shabbiness of its background. But Anouilh is more concerned with a philosophy than with character, with the result that it is up to the actors themselves to get any real depth into their assignments. That they accomplish as much as they do is a tribute to a fine cast.
>
> Dorothy McGuire makes the soiled little actress a pathetically touching figure, muddled and groping for happiness. But the script requires her to reiterate the same ideas over and over again, which are primarily only superficial indications of her character.
>
> [. . .] In sum, some of "Legend" is absorbing, much of it is pretentious—and very little of it is believable. Its appeal is strictly gaited to those who bow down to Anouilh's notions. It is not gay entertainment.[615]

---

614 Ibid.

615 Bob Francis, "Legend of Lovers," *Billboard*, January 5, 1952.

OTHER THEATER, 1945–1971

Legend of Lovers closed unceremoniously on January 12, 1952, after only twenty-two performances. The reasons for this Broadway debacle probably had little to do with either the casting or the production; very simply, 1951 New York may have been the wrong place and time for this text, and for this adaptation.

Jean Anouilh's mythological retellings (*Eurydice*, 1941; *Antigone*, 1942; *Médée*, 1946) are the descendants of a "modernist" French theatrical tradition that flourished in the 1920s and 1930s and whose two most celebrated authors were Jean Cocteau (*Antigone*, 1922; *Orphée*, 1926;[616] Œdipe-roi, 1928; *La Machine infernale*, 1932/1934) and Jean Giraudoux (*Amphitryon 38*, 1929; *Judith*, 1931; *La guerre de Troie n'aura pas lieu*, 1935; *Electra*, 1937; *Sodome et Gomorrhe*, 1943). A parallel theatrical revisitation of ancient drama tropes had taken place a few years earlier in Italy, through the pens of writers such as Gabriele D'Annunzio (*Francesca da Rimini*, 1901; *La nave*, 1907; *Fedra*, 1909; *Le martyre de Saint Sébastien*, 1911) and Sem Benelli (*La maschera di Bruto*, 1908; *La cena delle beffe*, 1909; *Rosmunda*, 1912; *La Gorgona*, 1912; *Orfeo e Proserpina*, 1929; *Caterina Sforza*, 1932). D'Annunzio and Benelli's versions were in many ways diametrically opposed to those authored by the French triumvirate: the Italians' search was for an evocation or "reconstruction" of ancient tropes using an archaic, archeological version of the Italian language. Where the French "modernized," the Italians tried to turn back the clock. Both the French and the Italian writers, however, had something that few, if any, American (or even British) playwrights could boast: a mysteriously "direct" connection to those ancient Greek and Roman styles, whether through "genetic" cultural/linguistic lineage or through the benefit of classical (Latin and Greek) studies, which are still the norm in several European school systems. European writers, especially romance-language writers, were, and occasionally are, still linked to those ancient texts by some sort of cultural bloodline. Which could explain, for example, why even the cheapest or

---

[616] First performed at the Théâtre des Arts in Paris in June 1926; published in 1927.

most derivative of popular mythological or pseudohistorical films made in the grade-B Italian film industry of the 1950s and '60s (e.g. *Le fatiche di Ercole*, 1958, *Perseo l'invincibile*, 1963, or *I giganti di Roma*, 1964) are arguably more sophisticated, and closer to the spirit of ancient Greek and Roman texts, than any big-budget Hollywood spectacular could ever dream to be, but only when the dialogue is left in Italian and not dubbed. Romance languages and cultures hold an intricate hereditary kinship with the ancient Roman and Greek sensibilities.

Whether in modern dress or historical costumes, the revisionist French adaptations of ancient tragedies and myths by Anouilh, Cocteau, and Giraudoux, like metamorphic offshoots or distorted mirror images of the originals, are hybrid creatures, containing equal parts of anachronistic realism, stylized abstraction, lilting lyricism, existential pessimism, cold surrealism, wry humor, *roman-a-clef* commentary, and cryptic mysticism. Their particular style is an acquired taste, and a tricky thing to pull off. It is, for one thing, inherently European, i.e. suited to a certain European theatrical stylization and to the sound of romance languages (in John Gielgud's terminology, one might say that these texts are better served by "declamation" than by naturalistic acting). It is also inextricably bound to a certain period (c. 1922–1946), except for sporadic later appearances in the canons of the above authors, such as Cocteau's film *Orphée*, 1950, which is an example of this style, and also an acquired taste. Anouilh's take on ancient tragedy may be more lyrical, philosophical, and bittersweet than Cocteau's rational/surreal reinterpretations, but, by 1951, and in English, this particular *Legend* must have sounded prolix, pretentious, and dated to the post-war, jaded ears of urbane New Yorkers.

Anouilh's play, despite some uneven writing and some prolixity, is a fascinating, complex, surreal, evocative, meta-theatrical one-of-a-kind. *Eurydice* harks back, not so much to the modernist experiments of Cocteau as to the symbolist tradition of Maurice Maeterlinck and Béla Balázs, and to Pirandello's ruminations where characters are either trapped in a story they are unable to inhabit or struggling to come to terms with the fact that interpersonal truths cannot be known. For example, *Eurydice* displays striking points of thematic similarity with Maeterlinck's *Pelléas et Mélisande* (1892) and with both Maeterlinck's and Balázs's treatments of the story of Count Bluebeard and his last wife. In Balázs's deeply existential version of the Bluebeard story, which became a one-act opera with music by Béla Bartók, *Bluebeard's Castle* (*A Kékszakállú herceg vára*, 1911), Bluebeard's new wife, Judith, forcefully insists on unlocking the seven doors of his castle, despite his pleading. Those metaphorical doors are the doors to his soul, and contain his innermost secrets and memories (as the spoken prologue to the opera announces, "*Where is the stage: within? without?*"). Judith thinks she is after Bluebeard's full disclosure in order to love him fully, when in fact her thirst for knowledge is an insecure, needy, insensitive intrusion into his private inner world ("*Give me keys to all your doorways!*"). His pleas to let the past and its memories alone and live in the present go unheeded. In the end, like the other wives that preceded her, Judith recedes behind the last door, to join the other wives in his "memory palace" and become another painful echo for the saddened Bluebeard.

In *Eurydice*, it is Orpheus who takes on the feminine, inquisitive role of Judith. Not satisfied with the bliss of his first night with Eurydice, he begins probing her with questions that are increasingly laced with suspicion, a suspicion that is exacerbated by the fact that Eurydice does not know how to reveal certain truths about her complicated past without alienating him. Like Mélisande in Maeterlinck's play, Eurydice is a delicate innocent who cannot withstand the pressures that life's realities exert on the essential mystery and poetry of human feeling.

The above is only one of the interesting themes that are woven into the play's four acts. Another is the presence of ghosts in our lives: of the people, actions, and words that have touched our lives, and of the simultaneous presence in our memory of karmic encounters big and small. Like many of Pirandello's characters, this Orpheus and this Eurydice are actors in a story, a story they themselves are creating. In their incessant act two dialogue in a hotel room, they recount the tale of their burgeoning love, commenting on the secondary characters that populate it, as if their love were a play ("We already have some characters in our story," says Eurydice).[617] From that starting point, Orpheus and Eurydice's dialogue lifts off to become a little philosophical meditation on all that is inscribed in a person's book of karma: in the script of the play of one's life. The shadows and consequences of our past are always present; the past, in a way, is always the present, and crowds our inner life inexorably. In a beautiful scene in the third act, the resuscitated Eurydice, interrogated by the mistrustful Orpheus who insists on looking into her eyes before the prescribed deadline of dawn to probe her soul (to unlock her doors), is joined on the stage by all the characters involved in her past and present story. The ghosts populating her mind and her history then interact both with her and with the other characters on stage, while Eurydice recedes sadly into the background to become dead again, to become a shadow in Orpheus's past. Orpheus must then accept to die too, in order to join Eurydice in that shadowy afterlife.

Anouilh's play is a sometimes wordy but thoughtful, atmospheric meditation on important existential themes—in the purest sense of the word existential, having little to do with the literary current. Among others: man's inability to live in the moment and know another human being fully, his difficulty in telling his life story without impoverishing it, his relationship with the actions of his past, and his relationship with life, love, and death.

Brooks Atkinson of the *New York Times* tipped his hand by confessing that it was the mixture of "esoteric" *themes*, so distant from the vibrant Broadway fare of his day, that he did not understand:

> Since Jean Anouilh has a prodigious reputation in Europe, there must be more to his dramas than meets the ear in

---

617 Jean Anouilh, *Eurydice*, in *Pièces Noires*, Calmann-Lévy, 1942, 420. The translation of the line is mine.

America. "Legend of Lovers," which the Theater Guild put on at the Plymouth Wednesday, is the fourth that has turned up in New York. But this department will have to acknowledge that it does not understand M. Anouilh, and does not have much confidence in the drama of symbols, sorcery and death. Although 50 million Frenchmen cannot be wrong, one of them can be terribly pretentious.[618]

Just how unstable the hybrid style of that cluster of French plays could be, and how fragile even when performed in French, was expressed by Cocteau in the worried prologue to his 1926 play *Orphée*, where he has the actor playing Orphée say to the audience:

> Ladies, gentlemen, this prologue is not by the author. He will undoubtedly be surprised to hear me [speak it]. The tragedy whose parts he has entrusted to us unravels with great delicacy. We therefore ask that you wait until the end before pronouncing judgment, should you not be satisfied with our work. Here is the reason for my request: we play very high up and without a safety net. The slightest uncalled-for noise runs the risk of killing my comrades and me.[619]

The enactment of this style is, in fact, a delicate balancing act, involving the earnest distillation and combination of diverse elements that, in order not to cancel each other out in the process, or result in the bathetic

---

[618] Brooks Atkinson, "Schmaltzless Schnitzler Noted in Anouilh's Play," *Cincinnati (OH) Enquirer*, December 28, 1951.

[619] Jean Cocteau, *Orphée: Tragédie en un acte et un intervalle*, Éditions Stock, 1927, 19. The original text is as follows: "Mesdames, Messieurs, ce prologue n'est pas de l'auteur. Sans doute sera-t-il surprise de m'entendre. La tragédie don't il nous a confié les rôles est d'une marche très délicate. Je vous demanderai donc d'attendre la fin pour vous exprimer si notre travail vous mécontente. Voici la cause de ma requête: nous jouons très haut et sans filet de secours. Le moindre bruit intempestif risqué de nous faire tuer, mes camarades et moi."

fall of parody, need to become "gaseous" and sublimate at a great altitude.[620]

If one accusation can legitimately be made against *Eurydice*, it is that Anouilh does not always dramatize his themes properly, but has a tendency to have his characters state them philosophically. I found that the play, while striking upon a first reading, became increasingly resonant through a second and a third: its entire beauty was not immediately apparent. The same criticism, however, applies to many playwrights, even great ones. To call Anouilh's play pretentious is both to miss the point and to express something of a teenager's impatience with lofty thought. The esoteric, mysterious truths that this play's symbols reach for are the stuff of dreams and religions, magic and psychoanalysis, poetry and philosophy. They are the ghosts that survive and linger from those old myths, haunting our daily lives in the form of cryptic archetypes, whether we acknowledge them rationally or not. Is *Eurydice* less entertaining than, say, *Come Back, Little Sheba* (1950) or *Born Yesterday* (1946)? Definitely, if the sparkle of repartee or the punch of hard-hitting drama is what one is after. Is it pretentious? Only if one can conclusively establish that it fails to express that reaching, and those archetypes, through the medium of rarified poetical exposition.

Californian spectators were probably less jaded than their New York counterparts, or more inclined towards the eccentricity of such "pretentious" style. When Anouilh's play had its (second) West Coast premiere in Los Angeles on April 29, 1960, it enjoyed the same dignified success as its 1948 Actors' Company predecessor. Under the aegis of the Stage Society, an excellent equity-waiver company in Los Angeles at the time, the revival was produced by Stephen Brown and John Harding. The two leads were Grant Williams (an earnest, melancholy player, best known

---

[620] For a fascinating analysis of Cocteau's play from an alchemical point of view, see: Charline Sacks, "Analyse alchimique d'*Orphée* de Jean Cocteau," *Chimères*, vol. 13, n.1 (1979), 85–91. See also: "Cocteau, l'alchimiste," by Christian Schmitt, on the website Espace Trévisse.

to filmgoers for having starred in Jack Arnold's beautiful metaphysical allegory *The Incredible Shrinking Man*, 1957) and Denise Alexander, with direction by Dennis Sanders.[621]

Writing for the *Los Angeles Times*, Charles Stinson was equally pleased with the production and the text of this revival:

> The Stage Society's love affair with Jean Anouilh continues as strong and happily as ever. "Legend of Lovers," his graceful and very Gallic retelling of the Orpheus and Eurydice story has just begun a run at the theater at 9014 Melrose.
>
> Producers Stephen Brown and John Harding have brought this subtle work off with the same assurance they showed last season with his "Thieves' Carnival."
>
> [...] Anouilh garlands the classical pillars of the plot with a superabundance of witty and often very surprisingly profound thoughts on love and time, the world and the ego, on the life in death and the death in life. This dramatist masquerades as an entertainer; at heart he is a relentless moralist in the Pascalian tradition.[622]

On June 22, 1966, a television adaptation of Black's translation of Anouilh's play was produced and broadcast in Australia, under the title *Point of Departure*. The TV movie, part of Australia's *Wednesday Theatre*, was directed by the French Henri Safran, and starred James Condon, Liza Goddard, Tom Oliver, and Ross Thompson.

If I may set aside the issues of commercial success and entertainment for a moment, another ingredient seems interesting when it comes to *Leg-*

---

621 See: Giancarlo Stampalia, *Grant Williams*, BearManor Media, 2018, 48–50. For my analysis of *The Incredible Shrinking Man*, see: Ibid., 95–124.

622 Charles Stinson, "Anouilh's 'Legend' Witty Morality Play," *Los Angeles Times*, May 3, 1960.

end of Lovers and Dorothy. That ingredient is the crisscrossing of karmic paths that led Dorothy (a) to co-produce the first, but unacknowledged, American premiere of Anouilh's text in 1948, and (b) to receive the script of that same play from producer Langner and to decide to perform it on the Broadway stage three years later. Whether or not Langner knew that Dorothy's Actors' Company had produced a different translation of the play in 1948, and it seems unlikely that he would not, his offer to Dorothy dovetails with her personal relationship with that text. Those paths, those events, may owe a lot to a thing called coincidence, though how one chooses to interpret that term will largely depend on one's worldview. In any event, they share one common element: Dorothy's interest in Anouilh's play, and in its "surprisingly profound thoughts on love and time, the world and the ego, on the life in death and the death in life." This, and the fact that, like Dorothy, the character of Eurydice is an actress who feels the irresistible lure of the theater, and of theatrical art as an aid to interpreting the mysteries of life, must somehow signify the intersection of that text not only with Dorothy's interest in acting, but also with her spiritual/metaphysical leanings.

Reports of a new play being prepped by producer Paul Gregory with Dorothy in mind surfaced in 1956. The play was to be called *This is Goggle*, and the stars potentially attached to the project were Dorothy, Tom Ewell and Billy Chapin. According to Gregory at the time, discussing any further details about the project would have been premature.[623] It must have been, for thereafter such details vanished altogether.

One would have to wait another two decades or so for the performance that one might call the crowning success of Dorothy's latter-day theatrical career. Meanwhile, she kept herself busy enough with her film work and with her occasional appearances at La Jolla and on television (her work for the small screen would not shift into high gear until after her last major motion picture, *The Greatest Story Ever Told*, 1965).

---

[623] Edwin Schallert, "Drama," *Los Angeles Times*, March 7, 1956.

OTHER THEATER, 1945–1971

A comparatively small but important theatrical event saw Dorothy tread the boards again in 1954. She appeared as the titular (speaking) character in the San Francisco Opera Company's American premiere of Arthur Honegger's scenic oratorio *Joan of Arc at the Stake* (*Jeanne d'Arc au bûcher*, 1935), first in San Francisco for two performances and then at Los Angeles' Shrine Auditorium for a third. The work, which Swiss composer Honegger subtitled a "dramatic oratorio," dramatizes Joan of Arc's last minutes on the stake, with flashbacks to her younger days and trial. The gloomy, difficult modern oratorio is set for large orchestra, chorus, seven solo singers and nine speaking parts.

This being Dorothy's first attempt at an oratorio, though in a speaking part, she was slightly worried about fitting in well with the musical proceedings after signing for the role, as she told Walter Ames of the *Los Angeles Times*:

> It's my first time with an opera association and I'll admit I'm a bit worried about how I'll fare. But [. . .] I like the role and I'm sure, after rehearsals, I'll get over any jitters I might have now.[624]

On this particular occasion, a prestigious conductor was on the podium: Pierre Monteux (1875–1964). Monteux's career was stellar: he conducted for Serge Diaghilev's *Ballets Russes*, world-premiering works such as Igor Stravinsky's *Petrushka* (1911) and *Le sacre du printemps* (1913), and Claude Debussy's *Jeux* (1913). He was chief conductor for the Metropolitan Opera in New York (1916–1919), the Boston Symphony Orchestra (1919–1924) and the San Francisco Symphony Orchestra (1935–1952), and guest-conducted for many major American and European orchestras. He also had an extensive recording career.

The singers involved in this production of *Joan of Arc* were Franca

---

624 Ames, "Fire" (1954), op. cit.

Duval, Charles Kullman, Rosalind Nadell, Marilyn Hall, Ralph Herbert, and others. *Joan of Arc at the Stake* was paired with a curtain raiser, Giacomo Puccini's 1918 one-act opera *Il tabarro* (another very gloomy affair), with different conductor and singers.

Dorothy as Paul Claudel/Arthur Honegger's Joan of Arc, San Francisco Opera Company, 1954. Photo: TIME Inc.

The *Los Angeles Times* gave a short description of the event:

> "Joan of Arc at the Stake" is being directed by Harry Horner, who also designed the setting and stage décor. The use of the novel Planer system of projections will enhance the unfolding of the drama and several hundred including corps de ballet and chorus will be on the stage.

The part of Joan has been freed from its rigid, static position and will have flexibility and freedom of movement in tonight's production. Lee Marvin, also of stage and screen is to play the part of Friar Dominic.[625]

The Bay Area press was enthusiastic about both the show and Dorothy's performance in it. Clifford Gessler of the *Oakland Tribune* complimented the San Francisco Opera for its groundbreaking choice of text, using adjectives like "potent," "powerful," and "fine" to qualify the production. About Dorothy, Gessler opined:

> Miss McGuire gave an intensely dramatic portrayal of the young Joan, in her simplicity, her suffering, her visionary ecstasies, and her devotion, although her voice hadn't always the strength to carry clearly in the large auditorium.[626]

INS correspondent Marie Hicks Davidson used the adjective "triumphant" for the production, and was enchanted with Dorothy's performance:

> Joan, impersonated by Dorothy McGuire of stage and screen, appeared a creature who transcended time and space. Hers was magnificent acting.[627]

Ten months earlier, film and stage director Roberto Rossellini had staged the oratorio at the San Carlo opera theater in Naples, Italy, with

---

625 "Joan of Arc at Stake' to Be Presented Tonight," *Los Angeles Times*, October 27, 1954.

626 Clifford Gessler, "'Joan of Arc at Stake' Given Potent U.S. Premiere in S.F.," *Oakland Tribune*, October 16, 1954.

627 Marie Hicks Davidson (INS), "Joan of Arc Opera Called Triumphant," *Somerset (PA) American*, October 19, 1954.

wife Ingrid Bergman as its star and Gianandrea Gavazzeni as conductor. In December 1954 (two months after Dorothy's performance), Rossellini released his film *Giovanna d'Arco al rogo*, fundamentally a filmed record of the Naples production and of Bergman's performance in it.

INS correspondent Dorothy Manners, subbing for Louella Parsons, referred to both the San Francisco production and its Italian antecedent on October 30:

> Dorothy McGuire and Lee Marvin [rate] raves in "Joan of Arc at the Stake" in the local San Francisco Opera presentation—Dorothy in the same role that got Ingrid Bergman royally roasted in Europe.[628]

An early table reading of *The Country Girl* at the Omaha Community Playhouse, 1955. From left to right: James Millhollin, director Kendrick A. Wilson, George Randol, Dorothy, Henry Fonda, and Jane Fonda. Courtesy of the Omaha Community Playhouse, Omaha, Nebraska.

---
[628] Dorothy Manners (INS), "Hollywood," *Corsicana (TX) Daily Sun*, October 30, 1954.

Other Theater, 1945–1971

In 1955, the Omaha Community Playhouse, where Dorothy had started her theatrical career, was in desperate need of a new venue. A major fundraising drive was organized, which included special benefit performances of Clifford Odets' *The Country Girl* (1950), a play about the Broadway comeback of Frank Elgin, a declining alcoholic actor, and of his tug-of-war with his long-suffering wife Georgie. A play about which the *New York Times*' Frank Rich, reviewing one of its later revivals, sentenced: "[If] Odets' play is not first-rate, it stands near the top of the second-rate."[629]

According to Francke's history of the Omaha venue, it was Dorothy who convinced Henry Fonda to participate, for he was reluctant. Henry and Dorothy jointly chose the drama that was to be performed for their Omaha comeback. Henry's daughter Jane made her theatrical debut in the play, as the press reported strenuously, and both the Fondas and the Swopes arrived in Omaha with full families in tow, children included. The production ran for five performances (June 24–June 28, 1955). The lead actors (Fonda, Dorothy, and James Millhollin) "donated salary and travel costs to the building fund [...]."[630] The cast of *The Country Girl* was as follows: James Harker (Bernie Dodd), Ken Seymour (Larry), James Millhollin (Phil Cook), James Harmon (Paul Unger), Jane Fonda (Nancy Stoddard), Henry Fonda (Frank Elgin), Dorothy (Georgie Elgin), and George Randol (Ralph). The set design was by Patton Campbell and the production was produced and directed by Kendrick A. Wilson.

A luxury crowd swarmed the playhouse to witness the event. Even Nebraska governor Victor Anderson attended, and director Bernard Szold returned to Omaha for a reunion with his two stars of *A Kiss for Cinderella* (1930).[631] Here is Francke commenting on the event:

[629] Frank Rich, "Stage: 'Country Girl' by Odets Is Revived," *New York Times*, October 19, 1984.

[630] Francke (2014), op. cit., 215.

[631] Ibid., 216.

Measured by income, attendance or publicity, the June 1955 run of *The Country Girl* ranked as the biggest event in the thirty-year history of the Omaha Community Playhouse. A profit of nearly $25,000, five near-capacity crowds in the 2,500-seat downtown Music Hall and more news clippings than generated by some entire seasons gave momentum to the campaign for a new theater. The keepers of the archives collected Country Girl matchbooks, cocktail napkins toasting "The New Playhouse" and invitations to a plethora of opening night parties and gatherings to honor the visiting stars.[632]

Another sit-down rehearsal of *The Country Girl*, with Dorothy and Henry but without his daughter Jane. Courtesy of the Omaha Community Playhouse, Omaha, Nebraska.

---

[632] Ibid., 214.

OTHER THEATER, 1945–1971

In the early months of 1958, Dorothy starred in another Broadway disappointment. The play was *Winesburg, Ohio*, Christopher Sergel's dramatization of Sherwood Anderson's short story collection of the same title (1919). Dorothy's co-stars were Leon Ames and James Whitmore. Supporting parts were played by Ian Wolfe, Crahan Denton, Arthur Hughes, Sandra Church, Ben Piazza, Claudia McNeil, Roland Wood, Lee Kinsolving (who would appear with Dorothy two years later in the film *The Dark at the Top of the Stairs*), Anthony Tuttle, Jeff Harris, and Joseph Sullivan. The sets were by Oliver Smith, the costumes by Dorothy Jeakins, and the lighting design by Jean Rosenthal (Martha Graham's favorite lighting designer).[633] *Winesburg, Ohio* was produced by Yvette Schumer, S. L. Adler, and the Saba Company, and directed by Joseph Anthony.

After a short out-of-town preview run, the play opened at the National Theatre in New York[634] on February 5, 1958. It closed on February 15, 1958, after thirteen performances. Though the New York critics mostly lambasted the adaptation rather than the production, the *New York Times* being the most pointed by writing, "*Winesburg* is not theatre,"[635] apparently the on-stage atmosphere was far from ideal. Rumor has it that Dorothy—who was a third choice after both Helen Hayes and Jessica Tandy had been rejected for her role—"did not relish the idea of portraying [the role of] a woman who was both physically and mentally disturbed. Because of her aversion to the character of Elizabeth Willard, Dorothy McGuire only half-heartedly played her role, and as the play moved from its final rehearsals to its pre-Broadway openings, the prog-

---

[633] See Martha Graham, *Blood Memory*, Doubleday, 1991, 99 and following pages.

[634] The National Theatre was designed by architect William Neil Smith and inaugurated in September 1921. It was later sold and renamed several times (as the Billy Rose Theatre, the Trafalgar Theatre, and finally the Nederlander Theatre). In its early days, it hosted, among other shows, Orson Welles' Mercury Theatre productions of *Julius Caesar* and *The Shoemakers' Holiday* (both 1938). It is located at 208 W. 41st Street, New York.

[635] "Winesburg, Ohio," *New York Times*, February 6, 1958.

nosis of *Winesburg*'s future was grim."[636] An unsubstantiated quote from co-star James Whitmore, reported by adaptor Sergel in an interview, has the actor commenting that "being on stage alone with Dorothy McGuire was like delivering a monologue."[637]

Now, Dorothy was generally a sensitive, generous actress and a kind person, and the above uncooperativeness sounds exaggerated, or may be the result of Whitmore's own subjective opinion; but something was evidently wrong with the production, which was plagued from the start by half-heartedness, and not only on Dorothy's part. Director Joseph Anthony, for one, was not happy with his leading actress, and this may have contributed to (a) his not providing Dorothy with the appropriate direction or (b) his alienating her from her co-stars and from the text. Since it is unlikely that Dorothy would choose to participate in a production for motives other than wholehearted interest (she certainly did not need the money), it is also unlikely that she did not realize what she was getting herself into. She probably read the text before accepting, and therefore knew the nature of the character she was to play. It is possible, however, that Dorothy's irrepressible desire to return to Broadway made her accept the part in haste, and that, once she had studied the text more carefully, her deep-rooted preference for nice, lovable characters prompted her to try and negotiate changes that were not to Anthony's liking, which in turn might have created a conflict.

In 1971, seventeen years after the premiere San Francisco production, Dorothy again appeared in the oratorio *Joan of Arc at the Stake*, this time with Roger Wagner's Los Angeles Master Chorale. The semi-staged production was presented at the Music Center's "new" Dorothy Chandler Pavilion on April 24, 1971, and closed the chorale's seventh season. The spoken part of Friar Dominic was played by actor Clifford David; the pro-

---

[636] Frank Stoddert Johns, "Sherwood Anderson, Christopher Sergel, and *Winesburg, Ohio*," Master's Thesis, University of Richmond, 1973, 17.

[637] Ibid.

duction was directed by Michael Montel and the chorale and the Sinfonia Orchestra were conducted by Roger Wagner. Among the singers were tenor R. G. Webb and bass-baritone Douglas Lawrence.

Daniel Cariaga, music critic of the Long Beach *Independent*, provided some witty insights into the work, and some details of the production:

> "Joan of Arc at the Stake" is an attractive and piquant sound-mural which reasserts both human faith and its possibilities, and human folly and its consequences.
>
> In the mind, it is a puzzle to be unraveled. Symbolism, allegory and satire inhabit its text (by Paul Claudel): to appreciate it fully, the receiver really ought to be 1) a Frenchman, 2) a Roman Catholic and 3) very intelligent. Or at least two of the three.
>
> Still, its superficial beauties are many: there are levels of pleasure here, and each can delight.
>
> [...] Michael Mantel [sic] supervised a minimal staging, with the actors utilizing a four-step dais occupying approximately one-third the right-stage area.
>
> The solo singers sat in darkness, stepped into a lit area for their portions; the Chorale, wearing black, hooded cloaks, were unobtrusive except when they sang, which is as it should be.
>
> [...] Dorothy McGuire was a Joan of modest poignance and wonderful projection (she really didn't need that bothersome microphone).[638]

Music critic Martin Bernheimer of the *Los Angeles Times* was pleased, but reported some problems in the mechanics of the production:

---

[638] Daniel Cariaga, "Chorale closes out successful year," *Long Beach (CA) Independent*, April 27, 1971.

A joint portrait of Henry Fonda and Dorothy, one that was used to publicize their return to the Omaha Community Playhouse in 1955. Courtesy of the Omaha Community Playhouse.

[The] over-amplification system proved more hindrance than help for the radiant Dorothy McGuire, whose noble utterances in the title role often sounded as if they were reaching us via a bad telephone connection.

[. . .] Miss McGuire, who also enacted the role here in 1954 with the San Francisco Opera under Pierre Monteux, dominated the proceedings, quite legitimately, with her artful and urgent juxtaposition of mellow resignation and girlish rapture.

"Joan of Arc at the Stake" is, perhaps, a period piece. It does not wear its 35 years with any striking grace, and, with rehearing, Honegger's musical inspiration may seem a bit flimsy for the poignant mysticism of Paul Claudel's drama. (The text, incidentally, was presented Saturday in an excellent, uncredited translation which I suspect belongs to Dennis Arundell.)

But the work is an undeniably impressive demonstration of virtuoso craftsmanship, and its straightforward dynamic impact cannot be minimized.[639]

---

[639] Martin Bernheimer, "'Joan' Ends Chorale Season," *Los Angeles Times*, April 26, 1971.

15. *Iguana*

Hannah is one of Tennessee Williams' most fascinating characters—the gentle hustler, wise-innocent, fragile but strong as Hercules, tender but iron-willed. Dorothy McGuire played her with matchless understanding.

Raymond Massey[640]

By July 1975, preparations were well under way for a regal Los Angeles revival of Tennessee Williams' 1961 play *The Night of the Iguana*, to be presented at the Music Center's Ahmanson Theater by managing director Robert Fryer. The *Los Angeles Times* shivered with anticipation, and announced a start date, December 19, and two cast members: Richard Chamberlain as defrocked minister T. Lawrence Shannon and Dorothy McGuire as Hannah Jelkes, his "savior."[641] *Times* staff writer Sylvie Drake noted that, while the role of Rev. Shannon was definitely a "stretch" for Chamberlain, the role of Hannah was "made to order" for Dorothy and

---

[640] Raymond Massey, *A Hundred Different Lives: An Autobiography*, Robson Books, 1979, 411.

[641] In the original 1961 Broadway production, the two parts had been played by Margaret Leighton and Patrick O'Neal. Richard Burton and Deborah Kerr played the roles in John Huston's 1964 film version.

"should fit perfectly."[642] As it turns out, it did, and then some. Over the next months, two more players were announced, and a cast that was already golden became platinum. The two players were Raymond Massey (Chamberlain's co-star in television's *Dr. Kildare*, 1961–1966) and Eleanor Parker.

The Night of the Iguana opened on December 19, 1975, for its six-week run at the Ahmanson Theater, and closed as scheduled on January 31, 1976. The production was directed by Joseph Hardy. The other members of the Los Angeles cast were: Ricardo Landeros (Pancho), José Martin (Pedro), Ben Van Vacter (Wolfgang), Jennifer Savidge (Hilda), Michael Ross Verona (Herr Fahrenkopf), Norma Connolly (Frau Fahrenkopf), Matt Bennett (Hank), Allyn Ann McLerie (Miss Judith Fellowes), Susan Lanier (Charlotte Goodall), and Benjamin Stewart (Jake Latta).

On November 26, 1976, the production (with some cast substitutions) started preview performances for a limited engagement in New York's Circle in the Square, where it closed on February 20, 1977. Sylvia Miles replaced Parker as Maxine the hotel owner, while William Roerick (who had been in the original Broadway production of Thornton Wilder's *Our Town*)[643] replaced Massey as Nonno.[644] Undoubtedly, the new players carried less star power than their illustrious predecessors; which only gave more potency to the two leads. In New York, the play ran for a total of 23 previews and 77 performances. The new supporting players were William Paulson (Pancho), Gary Tacon (Pedro), John Rose (Herr Fahrenkopf),

---

642 Sylvie Drake, "Chamberlain, McGuire in 'Iguana,'" *Los Angeles Times*, July 10, 1975.

643 In *Our Town*, he had played the "Assistant Stage Manager" and the "Baseball Player."

644 Several reasons probably contributed to Parker not appearing in the New York run of the play; one of them, the fact that, immediately after *Iguana* in Los Angeles, she starred in the previews of the musical *Pal Joey* at the Circle in the Square theater in May–June 1976. Due to "artistic differences" with Circle in the Square principals, Parker and other cast members left the production before its June 27 opening. See: Doug McClelland, *Eleanor Parker: Woman of a Thousand Faces*, Rowman & Littlefield, 2003, 22.

Amelia Laurenson (Frau Fahrenkopf), Barbara Caruso (Miss Judith Fellowes), and Allison Argo (Charlotte Goodall).

The Ahmanson Theater in Los Angeles was, and is, a large (about 2,000 seats), cavernous venue with rather dull acoustics. Over the years, drama critics would complain about this inadequacy, especially when reviewing intimate, dialogue-based plays. A few mentioned this limitation during the run of *The Night of the Iguana*, such as Richard Stiles of the *Pasadena Star-News*.[645] Rex Reed also disliked the venue, and made the following comments on it in his first review of *Iguana* in January 1976:

> The Ahmanson Theater in the Los Angeles Music Center does not look like a theater, smell like a theater or feel like a theater. It always makes me feel sorry for Los Angeles and homesick for New York and London. One does not expect to be transported into a world of make-believe in an atmosphere of air-conditioned, antiseptic, architectural apathy. Even the programs look like Technicolor time-wasters on TWA.[646]

Hence, it could be argued that in some way the production's transfer to New York's Circle in the Square Theater was beneficial, despite the cast changes. The latter theater was (and still is, with a few added seats, even though its use as a Broadway venue seems to have ceased) an intimate 650-seat in-the-round venue where the audience was "immersed" in the play's action by being placed around it.

In Los Angeles as in New York, the show was a triumph. The audiences loved it; the critics (with few exceptions) loved it. And, with the exception of *New York* magazine's Alan Rich[647] and Richard Stiles of the

---

[645] Richard Stiles, "'Iguana' at Ahmanson—Unsettling, Uneven Enigma," *Pasadena Star-News*, December 21, 1975.

[646] Rex Reed, "'Iguana': way off Broadway, but right on target," *New York Daily News*, January 25, 1976.

[647] Rich sentenced: "Dorothy McGuire, as the wavering New England spinster, is some-

Pasadena Star-News,[648] they loved Dorothy. Not even the notices she had received for her 1941 debut in *Claudia*, based as they had been on the freshness of novelty and the sweet promise of a future, had articulated so much thoughtful praise on the actress. An example of this praise: critic Ray Loynd of the Los Angeles *Herald-Examiner* declared: "Dorothy McGuire has the toughest role... and she is unassailably glowing."[649] These notices of 1975 and 1976 were the recognition of Dorothy's maturity, and of her subtlety; they were a nod to the richness of the evolution of her instrument, a richness that was more easily visible on stage than on the silver screen. Dorothy had delivered on that early promise, and exceeded it. She won the Los Angeles Drama Critics' Circle Award, and was nominated for a Drama Desk Award; also, it is as a direct result of her performance in Williams' play—as well as of all her other achievements—that she was chosen as [*Los Angeles*] *Times* Woman of the Year for 1976. No wonder.

As usual, Dorothy was reticent about how she prepared for her stage role, or how she put herself in its shoes. She gave one brief indication in an interview with Charles Champlin:

> Just before rehearsals began, [my husband] John and I went on a trip. London, Paris, Majorka, Ibiza, Madrid. I started looking at people through the eyes of Hannah. I started sketching them in cafes, so I could do it with authority on stage. When she talks of the inward and outward look of the

what better, but not truly good." See Alan Rich, "Broadway at Mid-Season: a Land of Ghosts and Ghouls," *New York* magazine, January 10, 1977.

[648] Stiles grumbled about everything and everybody in the Los Angeles production, except Raymond Massey. Here he is grumbling about Dorothy: "Dorothy McGuire, another great film actress, is cold enough for the spinterish [sic] New England itinerant painter Hannah Jelkes. [...] [Both McGuire and Eleanor Parker] seem insecure, missing the microphones, groping for the reality of their characters. Things may improve later in the run of "Iguana" [...]." See Stiles, "Enigma" (1975), op. cit.

[649] Ray Loynd, "Stalking Iguanas in Williams' Country," *Los Angeles Herald-Examiner*, December 22, 1975.

character, I knew what she meant. So many things Tennessee says about life in the play are sharp and true.[650]

From left to right: Raymond Massey, Richard Chamberlain, Eleanor Parker, and Dorothy in Joseph Hardy's production of *The Night of the Iguana* at the Ahmanson Theater, Los Angeles, 1975. Photographer undetermined. Victoria University, E.J. Pratt Library, Special Collections.

I did not see the Los Angeles production in 1975; however, I saw the show three times during its 1976–1977 New York run, and am happy to join the critics in their praise.

It may be foolish to try to analyze a good performance (rather than to enjoy it without judgment), but, theater being the disappearing act that it is, especially in the absence of a filmed record, one must try. That is what

---

650 Champlin, "Sensitivity" (1976), op. cit.

Los Angeles Times drama critic Dan Sullivan did, twice, in the two reviews he wrote of the show (he saw the production twice during its West Coast run). His first review was splashy with quotable enthusiasm, as in his statement that "it's impossible to speak too highly of Miss McGuire's and Chamberlain's acting here (or anywhere else, but especially here). On one level she is an angel, he a mortal in mortal trouble. On another level they are two tough minds locked in witty debate."[651]

A month or so later, Sullivan's second review took its time making subtler considerations about the leads' acting, and about the delicate balance they struck with each other's parts.

> [. . .] Chamberlain and Miss McGuire do give this "Night" a cool luster that it wouldn't have with other actors. It was an unexpected pairing, but an astute one, based on somebody's realization [. . .] that Hannah and Shannon can both be thought of as moonchildren, hence susceptible to the kind of fine crystal ring that both Miss McGuire and Chamberlain have as actors.
>
> The scene everyone remembers in "Night of the Iguana" is the one where Hannah, the virgin, talks Shannon, the seducer of teen-agers, down from his worst freakout yet. In the film the image was that of a nurse (Deborah Kerr) taming a wild man (Richard Burton). Not so at the Ahmanson. Miss McGuire suggests a bright, loving sister telling her bright invalid brother some truths about himself in a language they both grew up speaking—among them the truth that he's getting too much satisfaction out of his fit to deserve an excess of sympathy from her. From Miss Kerr, those lines sounded like a therapeutic ploy. Miss McGuire obviously means them and

---

[651] Dan Sullivan, "Talking Shannon Down in 'Iguana,'" *Los Angeles Times*, December 22, 1975.

Chamberlain plays the part so as to convince us that she's absolutely right.[652]

But, first things first. A number of factors played their part in making Dorothy's acting in the production as successful as it was.

Autographed Playbill for *The Night of the Iguana*, New York, Circle in the Square, December 4, 1976.

(1) Fame and recognition. More than thirty years had passed since Dorothy's last successful Broadway appearance (*Claudia*, 1941–43), and more than twenty since her last major theater performance (*Summer and Smoke*, 1950). Between those performances and *The Night of the Iguana*, Dorothy had aged (in the good sense, as when one speaks of certain good

---

[652] Dan Sullivan, "'Night of the Iguana'—a Revival Revisited," *Los Angeles Times*, January 25, 1976.

wines), and a maturation had taken place. She had also become a household name, and a famous film star. Her return to the stage was a welcome surprise for many, as was the depth her acting had gained in those intervening years.

(2) Presence. This hard-to-define artistic quality (call it charisma, if you will), which cannot be perceived or felt anywhere as potently as in live performing, endows those players who possess it with a special magnetic power, with a "glow" that transcends the things they say or do. Those players simply *are*, in a very special and powerful manner. Dorothy certainly *was*.

(3) Color, or liveliness. Certain theater players have a special way of making their characters seem alive: the result of their acting is greater than the mere sum of the parts. Those players have a way of veering their performance in different directions, subtly, and shifting colors and tones—without overacting, and without flashy artifice—so that at every turn a different facet, or aspect, of their character comes to life and is revealed to the audience. That quality Dorothy demonstrated even in her film performances (it is always a surprise that someone who could be so balanced and subtle could also be so varied); on stage, that special colorfulness of hers, enclosed in an apparently crystal-clear equilibrium, positively exploded, like invisible fireworks.

Sullivan commented on this special balancing act on Dorothy's part in his second review:

> A colleague was saying the other day that she's never seen Hannah played badly. It is a lovely part, otherworldly, yet wonderfully human, but it could be botched by an actress of less discrimination and grace than Miss McGuire. A smug Hannah, a self-righteous one, an unhealthily repressed one—these aren't hard to imagine. Miss McGuire has the balances of the part just right without making us aware that there's any problem striking them. Shyness and toughness, delicacy and

frankness, chastity and a full commitment to life don't seem opposites or even separate qualities here. They are all part of a light-footed girl from Nantucket who knows what is for her in this world and what is not—and knows what is for you, too, if you'll listen to her (which she doesn't insist on).

What keeps the blessedness from being oppressive or cute is our awareness of Hannah's vulnerability—like so many of Williams' people she, too, has had to depend on the kindness of strangers. (And return it: Miss McGuire tells a haunting story of an encounter on a boat with a women's underwear salesman, and you can hear the silence in the theater deepen as she goes on with it, a tribute both to author and actress.)[653]

(4) Lightness. In movement and in speech, Dorothy was a nimble, energetic performer. In *Claudia*, this energy took the form of physical speed and inexhaustible patter; in later years, the physical speed slackened, but the agility of her speech remained unaltered, though always subtle and balanced. Dorothy's subtlety and equilibrium never turned into inertness, or dullness. Energy and agility notwithstanding, she was always, as Sullivan put it, light-footed, i.e. weightless. Even in her most tragic scenes, Dorothy's acting was never ponderous. And it was with feather-like lightness that she could change colors and expressions in her speech.

(5) Irony and humor, and this is connected to the fourth point. Even when she essayed characters that required her to be dead serious, Dorothy was able to let some humor surface, in the form of a delicate irony. One need only watch her performance in *A Tree Grows in Brooklyn*, which is essentially serious, if not sad, to realize that her seriousness, or sadness, is often enlivened by a complementary aspect. This, too, Dorothy embodied with light-footed subtlety. Sullivan noticed this:

---

653 Ibid.

Finally, there's the humor, much less overt than in Chamberlain's bitchy Shannon, indeed so sly that one can't be absolutely sure this Hannah has a sense of humor at all (though you know Miss McGuire does). One of the biggest, nicest laughs in the show [. . .] comes before the underwear salesman story. Shannon has been chaffing Hannah on her lack of romantic experiences. She answers that not only has she had one, she's had two "and I'm not exaggerating!" It's not itsy-poo, it's not false-naïve, it's. . . you'd have to hear Miss McGuire read it to know what it is.[654]

(6) Clarity and simplicity. On stage and on screen, Dorothy's acting was seemingly free of artifice. Feelings were isolated and expressed with precision, lucidity, and measure. Instinctive Dorothy may have been, but there was always an intelligence at work in her acting, which allowed her to enunciate the substance of the characters she played with a simplicity that could be called natural, and to articulate feeling after feeling with effortless transparency. This same simplicity allowed feelings to come to the surface free of obstacles or filters, which meant that their natural complexity was not censored or edited. On the stage especially, this lack of censorship meant that those feelings were not simplified or schematized, but could manifest in all their vibrant contradiction; which would explain Sullivan's awed perplexity at some of Dorothy's line readings. Those readings, clear and simple though they were, could straddle more than one feeling at once.

Dorothy's combination of artlessness, emotional penetration, and subtlety had been noticed early in her career, by an Omaha critic reviewing her 1930 performance in *A Kiss for Cinderella* (see Part I, Chapter 4). That critic had stated that Dorothy, precociously, combined "a perception of emotions far beyond [her] years" and an "artless innocence [. . .]." Matu-

---
[654] Ibid.

rity did not dissipate that combination in Dorothy; rather, it strengthened and amplified it.

(7) Delicacy. The stage was truly Dorothy's element not because she could be broader there, but because she could be subtler. This may seem paradoxical—normally, film acting is logically considered subtler than stage acting—but it is true. In Dorothy's hands, the empty theatrical space became a rarified bubble where the softest of modulations lived and breathed a microscopic (as in "under a microscope"), vibrant life and fluttered with a thousand harmonic, melodic, and spiritual metamorphoses. Notwithstanding the occasional audibility problems, particularly in vast venues such as the Los Angeles Ahmanson Theatre, Dorothy's performances were a magical invitation for the audience to concentrate and pay attention—to watch and listen immersively. They were a fluid stream of close-ups, even at a distance. In his review of *Iguana*, Rex Reed, then syndicated film and theater critic with the *New York Daily News* (more about him later), writes of a "haunting" and "delicate" performance, and of an audience so attentive that one "could hear every sigh."[655] Similarly, Sullivan tells us about the silence in the theater deepening as Dorothy speaks. It is singularly appropriate that Reed should use that first adjective, "haunting," to describe Dorothy's performance: for it suggests something otherworldly, something ghostly or spiritual, that will just not leave you alone. For Reed and for many who experienced that production of *Iguana*, the effects of Dorothy's performance lingered and resonated long, long after the performance had physically vanished. They still linger and resonate for me, more than forty years later.

Dan Sullivan's conclusion about Dorothy, a veritable valentine, was:

> The sum of it is an immaculate performance by an actress

---

[655] Rex Reed, "The 'Iguana'—What a Night!," *Manchester (VT) Journal*, January 24, 1976.

we're going to want to see in the older classics as well as the modern ones.[656]

Social note: a lavish cast party was organized after the Los Angeles opening night at the Beverly Wilshire Hotel's Don Hernando's Restaurant (in honor of the play's Mexican locale). Among those in attendance besides the cast: the Messrs. and Mmes. Charles Chamberlain, Edgar Ward (Jane Wyatt), Walter Mirisch, Armand Deutsch, Norman Lloyd, Maurice Jarre, Henry Fonda, as well as Mrs. Howard Ahmanson and Mark and Topo Swope.[657]

Critics were equally enthusiastic about Dorothy during the production's New York run. Some adaptation was necessary, since Circle in the Square, as the name suggests, was a smaller "in-the-round" venue, with the audience enveloping the central stage by at least three quarters.[658] Not all critics were equally enthusiastic about Joseph Hardy's direction, nor about Chamberlain's performance, but the praise for Dorothy was almost unanimous.

Tim Holley of the *Bridgeport Post* of Connecticut called Dorothy "simply superb in her uptight, chatty but always confident performance." He added:

> There's something extra special about Dorothy McGuire that I have always loved. It's her warmth and the host of other very human qualities she always exuded so strongly and yet poignantly in the myriad of movies she made.

---

[656] Sullivan, "Revisited" (1976), op. cit.

[657] See: Camilla Snyder, "Party Time for 'Iguana,'" *Los Angeles Times*, December 20, 1975.

[658] Part of the Paramount Plaza complex, the Circle in the Square Theatre is located at the northern end of New York's Broadway theater district, at 235 W. 50th Street (between Broadway and 8th Avenue but closer to 8th Avenue). The venue was designed by Alan Sayles and built in 1970. It opened in 1972.

> But now, after seeing her brilliantly quintessential performance in Tennessee Williams' "The Night of the Iguana" at the uptown Circle in the Square theater, I realize she is one of the best and maybe forgotten actresses around.
>
> [...] Without a doubt it is the best piece of acting in this production which has been somewhat slowly staged by Joseph Hardy.[659]

John Simon of *New York* magazine (more positive than his colleague Alan Rich), in a 1988 discussion about another revival of Williams' play, reminisced about the 1976 production: "Even the 1976 Circle in the Square revival provided at least one lovely performance, Dorothy McGuire's Hannah."[660] And Clive Barnes of the *New York Times* spoke highly of both the cast and the director, calling the production "a great evening in the theater."[661] About Dorothy, he wrote: "Dorothy McGuire, tight, gentle, confident and yet inwardly nervous, makes a fine foil to [Chamberlain] as the spinster [...]."[662] He was quite complimentary about Hardy, too:

> Joseph Hardy, the director, we have long known, is an expert at drawing new things out of old plays. He approaches revivals not as resuscitations, but as renewals, and this enables him to bring the kind of freshness [...] that he provides in this "Night of the Iguana."[663]

---

[659] Tim Holley, "Dorothy McGuire Is Splendid In 'The Night of the Iguana,'" *Bridgeport (CT) Post*, December 23, 1976.

[660] John Simon, "Sublimations," *New York* magazine, July 18, 1988.

[661] Clive Barnes, "'Iguana,' Effectively Revised," *New York Times*, December 17, 1976.

[662] Ibid.

[663] Ibid.

Rex Reed loved the Los Angeles production, and had some glowing comments about director Hardy:

> Neither the original Broadway production nor the raucous John Huston film version ever managed to communicate just why the characters in this run-down Mexican resort were so hopeless, so helpless or so deserving of the compassion and sympathy that might make their suffering meaningful. Joseph Hardy has discovered so many layers of colors and textures in the play's central vision, and the play has been so richly rewarded with performances of the highest caliber, the result is a stunning new awareness of Tennessee Williams and the ghosts that haunt him.[664]

Reed was even more enthusiastic about Dorothy (whom he would also interview for a profile during the play's New York run):

> I have left the luminous Dorothy McGuire for last because I feel so inadequate in describing her or the devastating effect her soaring performance had on my nervous system. I have always admired and appreciated her work in films with such wide-eyed schoolboy devotion that it is possible I am not rationally qualified to reach any sensible assessment of her work here, but all I can tell you is she gives a performance so haunting and so delicate you could hear every sigh in the vast expanse of the Ahmanson [theater] when she was on stage.
>
> [This production] revived my faith in the theater, and it happened, like most good things in life, unexpectedly, with the swiftness of a miracle.

---

[664] Reed, "'Iguana'" (1976), op. cit.

Another photo of the four leading actors in *The Night of the Iguana*, Ahmanson Theater, Los Angeles, 1975. Photographer undetermined. Victoria University, E.J. Pratt Library, Special Collections.

Almost a year after his first review, Reed too, like Sullivan had done in Los Angeles, saw the show again, and wrote another assessment of it during its New York run. This time, tellingly, he entitled the review "All Hail, Dorothy McGuire!" Not only had his adoration of Dorothy not abated during that interval; if anything, it had expanded to cosmic proportions. Here is the opening of his New York review:

> Dorothy McGuire! All attempts to describe her beauty and power and artistry in the magnificent, miraculous new production of Tennessee Williams' *The Night of the Iguana* at the Circle in the Square seem like schoolboy jottings in a dog-eared Big Chief tablet, compared to the actuality of the magic she conjures onstage. Suffice it to say she is back in New York after a long, lamented and sadly empty absence from the

Broadway stage, and her re-entry is the theatrical event of the season.⁶⁶⁵

But that first round of praise is only the first salvo preparing what comes at the end of the review. After a positive discussion of the play, the production, and the contribution of the rest of the cast, Reed not only canonizes Dorothy as an untouchable icon in the annals of theatrical quality, but also insightfully sizes up the state of the art of her talent at that stage of her career.

> Luminous Dorothy McGuire is so haunting and delicate that she leaves the audience transfixed. From her entrance, breathless from the steep climb to the hotel veranda from the steamy road below, I began to tremble. As lovely, fragile and tender as one of her faded pastel watercolors, she projects a portrait of a New England old maid with hidden feelings of observation and understanding so full of pride and kindness that no sympathy, however deeply felt, could ever match her capacity for suffering.
> In her scenes with Chamberlain, there is a mercurial tension that raises the play to heights of power I have seldom seen equalled [sic] in a theater. Her silent scream, when the grandfather dies, distorts her perfect mouth into the mask of tragedy itself, yet everything she does demands attention.⁶⁶⁶

The "silent scream" of Dorothy's that Reed refers to, occurring just before the curtain closes on the play (a blackout in Circle in the Square, where there was no curtain), when her character discovers that Nonno has died while she was not looking, was indeed an arresting final image, and a

---
665 Rex Reed, "All Hail, Dorothy McGuire!," *New York Daily News*, December 17, 1976.

666 Ibid.

curiously deliberate theatrical gesture. That stylized moment, where Hannah's body and face freeze "into the mask of tragedy itself," looked like a moment of formal theater, more specifically of the Japanese Noh style, and inserted a visual/physical caesura into the naturalistic proceedings. I never asked Dorothy about that choice, but it is possible that there was indeed a Japanese inspiration at work, and that she had discovered Noh during her most recent trip to Asia with John Swope.

Back to Reed's review. Even the above paragraphs are Reed at half-speed. In the last two paragraphs, the critic gives way to the mystic, in what is almost literally an apotheosis of Dorothy McGuire:

> The audience is hypnotized. She moves like a poem, her voice fills the stage like music, she has the dignified beauty of a butterfly trapped in a Mason jar. There is no more radiant actress alive today, and this production of *The Night of the Iguana* provides her with a rare chance to use every dramatic facility at her disposal to demonstrate her unique artistry.
>
> How the movies have wasted her. She's been away too long. Seeing her now, at the top of her form, is a heart-piercing experience I shall not soon forget. She is like the coming of spring in a winter of discontent. Nothing we've seen of Tennessee Williams' work in recent years is in the same league with this vital, memorable production or Dorothy McGuire's inspired performance in it.[667]

My own experience of that production, and of Dorothy's performance in it, was strikingly similar to Reed's, so I can attest to the fact that his statements, purple though they may have been, were no exaggeration.

It is interesting to note that at least two drama critics of the time, Dan Sullivan and Rex Reed, were so impressed by Dorothy's performance

---

667 Ibid.

in *The Night of the Iguana* as to become befuddled, and this after years of experiencing Dorothy's excellence on screen and stage. This phenomenon should tell us something about the production, and about Dorothy's performance. Sullivan tried to counteract his bewilderment by analyzing what he had witnessed in great detail (in his second review); Reed was more transparent in admitting his reaction, which resembled nothing so much as a Stendhal syndrome.

In those years before *Iguana*, Dorothy had given many noteworthy, sometimes splendid, performances; but it was on the stage, and especially in that tardy production of the Tennessee Williams play, that something very special occurred, as if the finer points of that previous excellence had been distilled into a mystery, a mystery that could not be easily verbalized. It was on the stage that Dorothy was full of surprises. Sullivan and Reed, each in his own way, were responding to something that ultimately defied definition. Even Sullivan, after his analysis, admitted that Dorothy's performance as Hannah was so shaded as not to permit cut-and-dry certainties. The power of that performance, the kind of power that leaves a spectator or critic enchanted and speechless, is what one sometimes calls "magic." Reed, who did not try to analyze Dorothy's performance but only to remember it, was ultimately admitting that a great performance such as hers had to remain *inexplicable*.

When interviewed, Dorothy seldom, if ever, spoke about acting, or about technique. When she did, she sounded more like an oracle than like a trained actress. Here she is doing just that after her Los Angeles performances of *Iguana*:

> It's something I've noticed. Certain plays and parts nourish you. They put you in a direction and guide you, so that doing them is not just play-acting. It's a life experience. Some people can talk about acting, about technique and approaches. For me acting is mysterious, hard to pin down. But some of

the material I've been given has shaped me; that's all I can say. It's curious and gratifying.[668]

Dorothy with Raymond Massey in Tennessee Williams' *The Night of the Iguana*, Los Angeles, 1975. Photographer Undetermined. Victoria University, E.J. Pratt Library, Special Collections.

---

668 Champlin, "Sensitivity" (1976), op. cit.

16. Theater after *Iguana*, 1976–1987

Just before moving to New York for the Circle in the Square run of *The Night of the Iguana,* Dorothy found time to star in another Tennessee Williams play as a generous gesture towards the drama school of the University of Southern California, and perhaps to architect William L. Pereira, who had been a friend of the Actors' Company and had just designed USC's new Bing Theater. The play was *Sweet Bird of Youth* (1959) and the role Dorothy played was that of Alexandra Del Lago,[669] the aging star who takes up company with a young opportunistic gigolo. All the supporting players were cast from among USC Drama students; the production was directed by Alex Segal. The play enjoyed a five-day run as the inaugural production of the Bing Theater,[670] from October 19, to October 23, 1976.

[669] Dorothy had probably learned, or perhaps performed, the role before, for in a 1976 personal card she mentioned that she was "'learning lines' actually recovering 'Alexandra del Lago' in 'Sweet Bird of Youth.'" It is unclear what exactly she meant by "recovering": more evidence of how mysterious Dorothy could sometimes be when talking about acting. It is, however, my belief that the extra study, rehearsal, and performance time she put into *Sweet Bird* reinforced her role in *Iguana* for the New York run of the play, and added yet another gear to her New York performances.

[670] USC's Bing Theatre was designed by William L. Pereira & Associates and inaugurated in 1976.

In 1979, Dorothy co-starred with Anne Baxter in another limited-run play at the Ahmanson Theater in Los Angeles, this one not quite so successful as *The Night of the Iguana*. The play: *Cause Célèbre* by British playwright Terence Rattigan, in its US premiere. The play concerns a murder trial in which a woman (Baxter) is charged with murdering her impotent husband with the help of her teenage lover. Dorothy played the forewoman of the jury, who had her own personal problems and subplot. Supporting players included Jack Gwillim, Val Bettin, Kate Fitzmaurice, and Patricia Fraser. George Keathley directed.

On August 5, 1979, Ahmanson managing director Robert Fryer explained one of the reasons at least for his casting choice:

> We're going to do Terence Rattigan's last play, 'Cause Celebre,' a great success but never done here. We did get the rights and will open the [1979–80] season at the Ahmanson with Dorothy McGuire, a wonderful actress. Dorothy just lost her husband [on May 11]. I told her, "Dorothy, you have to go back to work." This all happened within the last four days.
>
> George Keathley is going to direct. I've known George for a long time and have admired his work. It's important for Keathley to have his work seen on the coast. He is one of the most important directors and I hope he likes it out here.[671]

Cause Célèbre opened on October 12, 1979, and ran for fifty-one performances, as scheduled. Dan Sullivan of the *Los Angeles Times*, always a staunch supporter of Dorothy's work, was not particularly pleased with Rattigan's text; to show his chagrin, he wrote his sarcastic review of the production in the form of a courtroom dialogue between himself (a witness) and a nameless British judge. Here are two excerpts:

---

[671] Maggie Daly, "Mayor, family will see Shaun," *Chicago Tribune*, August 5, 1979.

Q—You have, I believe, been a drama critic for some years?

A—Nearly 20, my Lord.

Q—In that time, you would, of course, have witnessed many curious examples of playwriting?

A—Yes.

Q—In one word, how would you describe the proceedings at the Ahmanson Theatre on Thursday evening?

A—Tosh.

Q—You would call the American premiere of Terence Rattigan's "Cause Celebre" tosh? Even with Anne Baxter?

A—Even with Dorothy McGuire, my Lord.

Q—How do plays afflicted with tosh behave, in a general way?

A—Well, it depends on the country. Your British tosh is high-minded. Like, Mr. Rattigan is not just writing about a sexy murder trial here. He has a message. You can tell from the other play.

Q—"Cause Celebre" is two plays?

A—Two in one, my Lord. There's the part about whether Miss Baxter and her teen-age lover murdered her impotent husband ...

Q—The juicy part.

A—Correct. And there's the part about whether Miss McGuire is going to lose her teen-age son to his randy father, who takes him to nightclubs.

Q—The earnest part. I assume the two plays intersect at some point along the line?

A—Oh, regularly, my Lord. Miss McGuire is the forewoman of Miss Baxter's jury.

[...]

Q—And Miss McGuire?

A—Well, given the role...

Q—A valiant effort?

A—You almost sympathize with her.[672]

---

[672] Dan Sullivan, "'Cause Celebre' at Ahmanson," *Los Angeles Times*, October 13, 1979.

On Saturday, January 10, 1981, Dorothy joined an ailing Henry Fonda for another benefit event at the Omaha Community Playhouse (like the one to which she had contributed in 1955). Proceeds from "An Evening with Mr. Fonda" (500 tickets at $50 apiece) went towards the playhouse's half-a-million-dollar drive to improve its facilities. John Springer, Fonda's publicist, was responsible for packaging the event. Aside from Dorothy, Fonda's son Peter and wife Shirlee also participated.[673] During the evening, Fonda called Dorothy to the stage "to learn that a theater chair now bore her name."[674] Between this event and a 1982 full-buffet benefit screening of the film *On Golden Pond* (1981), Jane Fonda present, the expansion plans for the playhouse were underway. When the new performing space and expanded facilities were inaugurated in 1986 as a result of the Henry Fonda Theater project, the series of four shows that was to go up on the new stage ended up being called the Fonda-McGuire Series, at Henry's request. Dorothy also contributed $5,000 to the October 1982 fundraiser for the proposed new Fonda Theatre Center, in memory of Fonda.[675]

Two more shows were in store for Dorothy at the Ahmanson Theater of Los Angeles in the 1980s. The first one: a revival of Lillian Hellman's *Another Part of the Forest* (1946), an unofficial prequel to her *The Little Foxes* (1939).

In an interview she gave the *Los Angeles Times* a few days before the play's opening, Dorothy announced:

> The audience is in for a surprise. We had the big luxury of having Lillian Hellman at rehearsals. *She's riveting, talks like a*

---

[673] See: Barbara Saltzman, "Fonda Returns to Theatrical Roots," *Los Angeles Times*, January 3, 1981.

[674] Francke (2014), op. cit., 360.

[675] Ibid., 367.

writer, and told us the story in a visual way. The first thing she said was, "Remember—this is a black comedy."

I have the most marvelous idea. I think we should take it to London and play in repertory with [Elizabeth Taylor's revival of] "The Little Foxes." A la "Nicholas Nickleby." Five hours of the Hubbard family! How marvelous![676]

Perhaps because of Hellman's advice to the cast, director George Schaefer emphasized the comedic aspect of *Forest*; but, according to *Los Angeles Times* drama critic Dan Sullivan, such comedy was "more cheerful than it [was] black."

"Ain't we rascals?" That's the gist of the smiles as the Hubbards recompose themselves for the next power struggle at the end of the play. Rather than being taken aback by their viciousness, the audience is encouraged to take it as lightly as the Hubbards do. That makes the play funnier than expected, but also removes the tension that comes with the working out of really dark deeds on the stage.[677]

Another Part of the Forest opened at the Ahmanson Theater on February 12, 1982, and ran through March 27, 1982. In the cast: Tovah Feldshuh as Regina, David Dukes as Ben, Dorothy as Lavinia, Richard Dysart as Marcus,[678] Edward Edwards as Oscar, and Barbara Whinnery as Birdie; other players were Virginia Capers, Patricia McCormack, Barry Cutler, Jack Fletcher, Wiley Harker, Dino Shorte, and Laurence Guittard. The sets were designed by Douglas W. Schmidt, the costumes by Noel

---

[676] Rosenfield, "Fate," 1982, op. cit.

[677] Dan Sullivan, "Hellman's 'Forest' at Ahmanson," *Los Angeles Times*, February 13, 1982.

[678] For some reason, Sullivan referred to actor Richard Dysart as "Martin Dysart" in his review (possibly confusing him with Dr. Martin Dysart of *Equus*?).

Taylor, and the lighting by Martin Aronstein. The music was composed by Conrad Susa. The production was directed by George Schaefer.

According to cast member Feldshuh, Lillian Hellman's presence at the Ahmanson rehearsals was perfunctory:

> Hellman observed the first rehearsal, which was the first read-through, but I don't remember her coming back much. I was thrilled to meet the playwright, but she was in a wheelchair, carrying a bag of fluid, and, like Mike Wallace,[679] she was not out to please anybody. Which is not saying that she was mean. I personally respond very well to that kind of individual. To me she said, "Hello, Miss Feldshuh; I hope you're as good as Patricia Neal."[680] I responded, "I hope so too, Miss Hellman."[681]

About her experience with Dorothy, Tovah Feldshuh is extremely positive.

> My experience with Dorothy was superb, both humanly and professionally. She was open and friendly, reliable, and a gracious conversationalist. In terms of acting, she was able to connect her truth to her instrument, beautifully and effortlessly, and she stuck with that truth; she also had a beautiful voice,

---

[679] Journalist and game show host Myron Leon "Mike" Wallace (1918–2012) had a long career in American radio and television; from 1968 to 2006, he was the host of the award-winning television program *60 Minutes*.

[680] *Another Part of the Forest* first opened at the Fulton Theatre on Broadway on November 20, 1946, and ran for 182 performances. The production starred Mildred Dunnock as Lavinia Hubbard and Patricia Neal as Regina.

[681] Feldshuh (2017), op. cit.

though I was often worried about her audibility, especially in the large Ahmanson auditorium.[682]

Dan Sullivan, who liked the show well enough, wrote about Dorothy:

> What was Regina's mother like? Hellman draws her as a gentle, pretty woman, driven to distraction by the sharks around her. Dorothy McGuire adds a faded patrician vivacity that's both touching and comical. She doesn't, however, suggest a woman brought up in the piney woods, as the script would have it. She's a porcelain figurine that [her husband] bought years ago for show, like his Greek mansion.[683]

Between Friday, December 17, and Sunday, December 19, of the same year, Dorothy put in an appearance as special guest narrator in three performances of a Christmas concert with Roger Wagner's Los Angeles Master Chorale, accompanied by "brass, bells, organ and percussion."[684] The title of the concert, held at the Music Center's Dorothy Chandler Pavilion, was "A Carolful Christmas." Christopher Pasles of the *Los Angeles Times* gave the Friday performance a cautious nod in his review, mentioning Dorothy's participation with special joy: "Fortunately, Wagner's 'Christmas Story' this year got in actress Dorothy McGuire an uncommonly warm, credible and enthusiastic narrator."[685]

The revival of Robert Anderson's *I Never Sang for My Father* (1968), which eventually landed at the Ahmanson Theater in Los Angeles in

---

[682] Ibid.

[683] Sullivan, "Forest," 1982, op. cit.

[684] *Los Angeles Times*, music listings, December 5, 1982.

[685] Christopher Pasles, "Chorale Greets Holiday with Glorious Sound," *Los Angeles Times*, December 20, 1982.

1987, took off as a Berkshire Theatre Festival production promoted by director Josephine R. Abady. The production turned into a larger project than originally envisaged, and enjoyed a nationwide tour to twelve cities (Chicago, Detroit, Toronto, Dallas, Louisville, Atlanta, Providence, Washington, DC, Ames, Iowa, Denver, and Los Angeles). It was co-produced by Jay H. Fuchs, the Kennedy Center/ANTA in Washington, D.C., and PACE Theatrical Group, in association with Sports Entertainment Group Inc. There was even talk of the production reaching Broadway. The play, a musing about relationships between fathers and sons, or parents and sons, is built as a series of flashbacks outlining the rapport among three main characters: Gene Garrison, the son (Daniel J. Travanti), from whose point of view the story is told, Tom Garrison, the father (Harold Gould), and Margaret Garrison, the mother (Dorothy). Completing the cast were Margo Skinner, William Cain, Scott Kanoff, Sonja Lanzener, Edward Penn, Jeni Royer, and Richard Thomsen.

The idea of casting Dorothy in the role of Margaret Garrison had originated with the playwright's wife, Teresa Wright (Dorothy's understudy in the Broadway production of *Our Town*). This is Dorothy herself telling the anecdote in an interview:

> Teresa called me and said, "You've got to do this." And I said, "But what about you?" And she said she had another commitment. So that made way for Dorothy. It was very generous of her.[686]

The play is fundamentally plotless; it is a series of scenes, or vignettes, focusing on the son's puzzlement at not being able to pinpoint his exact feelings towards his difficult, irascible, egocentric father. His feelings towards his mother are simpler, as is the mother's character. A sweet lady,

---

[686] Roger Fristoe, "Touring Gives Dorothy McGuire chance to feel country's heartbeat," *Louisville (KY) Courier-Journal*, September 27, 1987.

she finds herself sandwiched between the two quarrelsome men, when not eclipsed by them entirely; she tries her best to keep peace between them.

The above description is an over-simplification, but it gives the gist of the piece. Most scenes in the play are everyday dialogues between two of the main characters, when not all three. These dialogues are captured with Polaroid simplicity and candor by Anderson.

As far as Dorothy and her character are concerned, this play (at least in Abady's conception) seemed to limit Margaret Garrison's range from "nice" to "very nice," with stops on "sad" and "worried" along the way. In other words, the production and its director played into the very Dorothy McGuire stereotype that the actress's best performances were able to transform; rather than allowing Dorothy to explore and articulate several avenues for the character, they built safe fences around her and kept her cushioned from any rough edges. I am only speculating that this state of things was the result of the director's concept, though it is also possible that it was Dorothy's own preference. As possible corroboration for the latter hypothesis, one need only look as far as Dorothy's latter-day television appearances (in the mid- to late eighties), where her roles often seemed designed to obscure her old snap.

Daniel J. Travanti, who played the part of Gene Garrison, Dorothy's son, reminisces about the production with mixed feelings:

> It was a total pleasure to work with both Dorothy and Harold [Gould], a charming fellow, in that production. That experience was mostly delightful from the human point of view. Artistically, we did all right, but I thought that the production as a whole was just off-kilter in some way. It didn't quite have the right tone. For one thing, *Father* is a difficult play. I called it "a beautiful play" when reporters came and asked me about it; but when I went to do it, I thought, "Where is the real pep here?" I couldn't find it. For another thing, I didn't think Harold was mean enough as the father. They had

tried to get Hal Holbrook to do it, but he wasn't interested, I believe. In one scene, my character had to say something to the effect that he had hated his father for something he had said; and it was one of the hardest lines I had ever had to say: there was just not enough coming from Harold to justify it. Dorothy, on the other hand, was playing all sweetness and light and darling, and that's all. But we were stuck, so to speak.

I never thought of leaving, but the production was definitely not what I had thought it would be, or could be. It was a little bland. Robert Anderson was like that too, as a person. I would have been miserable if I hadn't accepted to be in the production, but it was a disappointment once I did. I loved Josie, our director, but things somehow did not come together as they should have. I later went and looked at the 1970 version with Gene Hackman and Melvyn Douglas, and I thought about our version, "not as good as the film." Some people were moved by our production, some weren't. Some critics liked it, some hated it. It was all right, but not great. Robert Anderson, who was present quite a bit during the tour, seemed noncommittal about it; he was there, but I couldn't tell if he liked the production or not.[687]

Lou Cedrone of Baltimore's *Evening Sun*, reviewing the play when it played the Kennedy Center, opined about Dorothy's performance: "She is, though, hesitant with her lines, but then so are the others, particularly in the first act, something the director should correct."[688] The director, however, did not correct that flaw; in fact, she might have been the cause of it.

To compound this general weakness of the production, at least in Los

---

[687] Daniel J. Travanti, conversation with the author, March 2018.

[688] Lou Cedrone, "'Father' doesn't quite sing at the Kennedy," *Baltimore Evening Sun*, September 8, 1987.

Angeles, where I saw it, another problem had to do specifically with the venue in which this intimate play was performed. Darryl H. Miller of the *San Bernardino Sun* was quite vociferous about it:

> [...] So why does the current production of this play at the Ahmanson Theatre fall apart before it progresses much beyond the opening speech?
>
> Certainly not because of the acting. Daniel J. Travanti, Harold Gould and Dorothy McGuire, the show's triumvirate of stars, contribute performances that are, for the most part, exemplary.
>
> The problem is that their performances get swallowed up in The Great Void of the Ahmanson's vast stage and auditorium. In fact, the whole play gets sucked right into this black hole.
>
> [...] The Ahmanson clearly was a poor choice of venue for this production, which originally was presented at the Berkshire (Mass.) Theatre Festival and now is touring the country before a possible New York run.
>
> Even in a more suitable environment, though, this production likely would have problems. Josephine R. Abady's lethargic direction of the play fails to set the blood rushing.
>
> [...] McGuire offers a warm performance as the mother. She seems to combine all of the most lovable qualities of mothers the world over into one woman.[689]

Travanti concurs that the choice of venues throughout the play's tour, and specifically in Los Angeles, was wrong for both production and play:

---

[689] Darryl H. Miller, "Ahmanson's size detracts from intimate nature of 'Father,'" *San Bernardino (CA) Sun*, December 13, 1987.

Not only the Ahmanson, but almost all of the theaters we played in during the tour were huge. I hated that. The producers had promised me that we wouldn't do the Ahmanson, and I kept after them on that issue; I asked, "Can you guarantee this?" Anyway, when we got to LA, there we were in that huge barn of a theater. The producers said that they had tried to get another, reasonably sized theater for us, but it had not been available. Theater is small: it's a small medium. It's as big as the human being. All plays should be done in small spaces, so that everybody can see and hear you. Most people in an Ahmanson audience can't see the actors' eyes![690]

The venue, however, was not the only problem where Dorothy's performance was concerned. The last fact mentioned by Miller in his review of the show may have been an even bigger flaw. Combining "all of the most lovable qualities of mothers the world over into one woman" did not yield a woman, nor a character, but a type, or cliché. Of course, for any fan of Dorothy's, seeing her even in this play was a great pleasure; it certainly was for me. But one cannot honestly list this performance as one of her best, nor as one of her most memorable.

Dan Sullivan of the *Los Angeles Times* was relatively positive about both the show and the acting ("the touring revival at the Ahmanson is decently enough acted so that you can put yourself in the situation"),[691] with some reservations. Here is one about Dorothy's performance:

> [...] Dorothy McGuire confined herself to the top half of the mother's role—the sweet, helpful, frail, worried-about-your-father part. A line like "You haven't a mean bone in your

---

[690] Travanti (2018), op. cit.

[691] Dan Sullivan, "Fathers and Sons—Still a Timeless Battle," *Los Angeles Times*, December 7, 1987.

body" emerges as an innocent compliment to Travanti, without the slight hint of contempt that a touchy son might pick up, or might think that he picked up.[692]

Oddly enough, when the play was filmed as an *American Playhouse* drama with the same cast and broadcast on June 15, 1988, things seemed to improve, probably because of Jack O'Brien's direction. O'Brien was, among other things, the artistic director of the Old Globe in San Diego from 1981 to 2007.

---

692 Ibid.

17. Television, 1938–1990

Though Dorothy would work in television with regularity during the last decade and a half of her career (after 1975), there were early experiments in the 1930s, and some effective appearances in live television dramas in the 1950s.

Like radio, television was another vehicle for Dorothy's acting, and a way to keep busy and maintain her craft. By definition, however, television's product tended to be a middling one, and few of her forays in the medium are capable of purveying the quality and depth of her film and theater performances. Always a professional, even in those later decades Dorothy acted her heart out in inferior properties that mostly relegated her to nice-mother or, worse, nice-grandmother roles.

Curiously, Dorothy's first involvement in television predates not only her film career but also her Broadway triumph in 1941. In fact, it even predates the official debut of standard television broadcasting itself.

Excitement was high among journalists in New York City in May–June 1938, as Radio City Music Hall became the headquarters of a series of experiments in live dramatic television transmissions. Earlier experiments by RCA had not yielded the expected results, but these new attempts by RCA and NBC were deemed successful, and coincided with the commercialization of a whole line of television receivers, on sale at three New York department stores, at prices ranging from $150 to $650, and with the building of a new television studio for future regular broadcasting at Radio City. Larry Wolters of the *Chicago Tribune* commented on the events.

> [. . .] There is a lot of television activity in New York this spring (as there has been for almost two years in London). Radio City has got around to a lot of exploration in the programming end of this new visual art. In the last fortnight real television history has been made.[693]

Several plays were televised during those weeks, some short, some long, including the Broadway hit *Susan and God* (1937–1938). The original cast appeared in the full-length broadcast of the current play, together with its author Rachel Crothers and its producer John Golden. Pictures were carried on 65.5 cycles and the associated sound on 49.75 megacycles.

Some shorter plays were also broadcast. One of these was *The Mysterious Mummy Case*, starring radio star/writer/director Tom Terriss (1872–1964) and Dorothy. The twenty-five-minute play was broadcast live on May 18, 1938, and required nine players, three studios, five sets, slides, and several special effects. More than twenty switches of action from one studio to another were carried out. The play was directed by Tom Hutchinson.

That early experiment aside, Dorothy's "modern" television debut took place on March 26, 1951, when she co-starred with John Forsythe in the live television adaptation of the film *Dark Victory* (1939) for the drama

---

[693] Larry Wolters, "Radio City Plans Public Showing of Television," *Chicago Tribune*, June 12, 1938.

series *Robert Montgomery Presents* (1950–1957). Though Dorothy would later espouse the cause of television, especially live television, her initial reactions to the experience were a bit frazzled (but always positive):

> It was a terrifying, awful, exhilarating, wonderful experience. During the week's rehearsal for our hour-long show I nearly died of fright. I felt like a rank beginner. Everything, it seems, had to be learned over again.
>
> I was strictly on my own. There were none of the hundred and one aides and assists we've learned to accept from the big movie studios. If I muffed a line, I muffed it.
>
> Television already has left its stamp on the production of pictures. Producers and studio tops today, more than ever, demand good, workmanlike jobs. Actors must report each morning with their lines learned. When they are not in movies, they must turn to TV, radio, the stage, recordings—any excuse at all to keep acting.[694]

Dorothy's experience in theater, in other words, came in handy for her tackling of the new live medium.

Three more years went by—during which Dorothy starred in one Broadway play, one La Jolla Playhouse play, five films, and fourteen radio dramas—before her next foray into live television. This took place on July 20, 1954. The show: the *United States Steel Hour*; the play: "A Garden in the Sea," an adaptation of Henry James' novella *The Aspern Papers* (1888). Dorothy's co-star was Mildred Natwick, who had played with her in *The Enchanted Cottage* (1945).

Cecil Smith, drama critic for the *Los Angeles Times*, doubled as television reviewer in this case, and was quite enthusiastic (almost embarrassingly so):

---

694 "Hollywood" (UP), *Canonsburg (PA) Daily Notes*, August 4, 1951.

> I think [TV drama is] as effective a way of theatrically spinning a tale as man has ever invented, from Sophocles to De Mille. It is not movies, it is not theater, it is not radio—nor is it a combination of the three. It is a separate and distinct and new dramatic art form.
>
> I'm writing this the day after watching the Theatre Guild production of ["A Garden in the Sea"]. I can remember no play, movie, opera or ballet that moved me more.
>
> This is the story of the seclusion of a woman, brilliantly played by Mildred Natwick. Once the inspiration of a great poet, she has carried into her dark house in Venice his letters and papers, and she clings to them because they are her youth, her past. With her is a niece, Dorothy McGuire, whose own youth is lost to this dark seclusion of her aunt's. And into this darkness there comes a young writer, Donald Murphy, seeking the poet's letters for a biography he's writing.
>
> It was beautifully done. Those who saw it last Tuesday were lucky.[695]

Dorothy told a curious anecdote related to "Garden in the Sea" just a month after it aired. Here is *Los Angeles Times* columnist Walter Ames reporting it:

> As an example of how intimate live TV can be, when the ash blond actress returned to her hotel after [performing in] "Garden in the Sun," [sic] she found a note pinned to her pillow. It read: "You were very good," and it was signed "night maid." Dorothy still has the note, one of her prized remembrances from New York.[696]

---

[695] Cecil Smith, "TV Drama Called One of Greatest Ways to Tell Tale," *Los Angeles Times*, July 25, 1954.

[696] Ames, "Fire" (1954), op. cit.

Dorothy was actively courted by television, and received substantial offers, even to have a weekly situation comedy built around her. She turned those offers down, even though she liked most of the material she read (including the script of the new sitcom). As Dorothy explained, "I'd have to do 39 shows, and I simply couldn't face it. I want to be free."[697]

Dorothy's enthusiasm for the challenge posed by live television was apparent in the interview she gave Ames before tackling her next television assignment, the 1954 season opening of *Lux Video Theatre* (1950–1959) in the form of an adaptation of *To Each His Own* (1946). This was Dorothy's first television drama produced in Hollywood rather than New York.

> Before I went East to do the hour shows, many of my friends warned me I'd be sorry for tackling an hour-long drama on TV. They said it was too nerve-racking to enjoy. It was a bit hectic, I'll grant, but it was also very exciting.
>
> In fact, I feel an actor or actress should be prepared to try anything these days. He or she should insist on good scripts and roles in which they feel right. Then their performance has no reason to fail. If I found the right part, I wouldn't even be afraid to tackle a two-hour live TV show.[698]

Dorothy's arguments in favor of television—indeed all her arguments about the acting media—seldom hinged on fame, money, or career; they were all about craft, and about the acting itself. If she could not have live theater, then she could at least have something that approximated it. As in live theater, she learned her lines with impeccable discipline, something

---

697 TV Key, "Dorothy McGuire Doesn't Want Her Own TV Show," *Waco (TX) News-Tribune*, August 7, 1954.

698 Ames, "Fire" (1954), op. cit.

that created occasional conflicts with co-stars. Here is Dorothy telling of one such conflict with a male lead (probably referring to John Forsythe, her co-star in "Dark Victory"):

> He was busy with two other shows while we were in rehearsals and he thought I was trying to show him up. Everything straightened itself out before the show, however, and we're great friends now.[699]

Even the intrusion of live commercials was seen by Dorothy exclusively from the point of view of craft and performance at the time, and a whimsical, refreshing point of view it was:

> Please don't be too harsh on what you might consider extra long commercials during live shows. Remember they're the only breathing spells performers get during the show. And if one has to make radical costume changes [the short commercial sentences] can be the shortest sentences in the world. I'm all for longer sponsors' talks.[700]

In "To Each His Own," Dorothy was supported by Gene Barry, Mary Anderson, Leonard Carey, Edward Ashley, Herb Butterfield, Ronald Brogan, Nancy Kulp, Ottola Nesmith, Joan Eland, and others. The show was adapted by S.H. Barnett (based on the original screenplay by Charles Brackett and Jacques Théry) and directed by Buzz Kulik.

Variety was tepid about the show, but was prepared to gush (several times in its review) about Dorothy:

---

699 Ibid.

700 Ibid.

That "To Each His Own" lacked the dramatic quality of the original could be attributed to the newness of the approach in strange surroundings and a supporting cast for the star, Dorothy McGuire, that didn't catch the spark of her sensitive performance. [...] Aside from Miss McGuire's compelling poignancy—that overshadowed all around her—the acting and direction were below network par for a live show from Hollywood. [. . .] [It] was too bad the casting wasn't equal to the demands. This is no reflection on Miss McGuire, who invested the role with a credible performance.[701]

Fred Remington of the *Pittsburgh Press* was more positive about the show as a whole, and positively glowing about Dorothy:

> The mechanics of newspaper production being what they are, this is the first good chance I've had to see if you felt as I did about Thursday's "Lux Video Theater."
>
> This, as you'll recall, had Dorothy McGuire in "To Each His Own," the movie role which won an Oscar for Olivia DeHavilland in 1946.
>
> I did not see the movie, but it is difficult to imagine how anyone could have done much better than Dorothy McGuire. Her charm and artistry are such that, in my opinion, she can't go far wrong in any role. She seemed, I thought, rather youthful appearing to have a son a lieutenant in the Air Force, though come to think of it, the Air Force has some very young lieutenants.
>
> [The play itself was, as I say, darn good, but ...] I will never

---

[701] "To Each His Own," *Variety*, August 30, 1954.

be sold on the star of a gripping dramatic show suddenly sliding out of her role to do a commercial as Miss McGuire did.[702]

This July 1954 National Broadcasting Company press photograph depicts Dorothy hugging her script for *Lux Video Theatre*'s production of "To Each His Own." The rocks on which Dorothy is sitting are those of La Jolla, California.

The next live televised play Dorothy tackled was none other than Philip Barry's *The Philadelphia Story*, which had premiered on Broadway fifteen years earlier and had been made into an unsurpassable film in 1940. In both cases, it had starred Katharine Hepburn.

---

[702] Fred Remington, "Dorothy McGuire Delightful on Lux Show," *Pittsburgh Press*, August 30, 1954.

The cast of the one-hour television adaptation, written by Philip Barry Jr., the late playwright's son, was as follows: Dorothy (Tracy Lord), John Payne (C.K. Dexter Haven), Mary Astor (Margaret Lord), Richard Carlson (Mike Connor), Herbert Marshall (Seth Lord), Dick Foran (George Kittredge), Neva Patterson (Liz Imbrie), and Charles Winninger (Uncle Willie). The show was directed by Sidney Lumet.

Casting seems to have been the main problem. Comparing this adaptation to the 1940 film: Richard Carlson in place of young James Stewart, John Payne in place of Cary Grant, Neva Patterson in place of Ruth Hussey? And especially, Sidney Lumet in place of George Cukor? It just could not be.

Variety was quite ornery about the show, and not shy in expressing its scorn.

> [*The Philadelphia Story*] has been around thru numerous stage revivals and on the screen since Katharine Hepburn created its central character. For her it was a natural. Last night, in the reflection of her artistry Dorothy McGuire was forced to go to extremes to manage only a carbon of the original.
>
> Role called up every nervous emotion of Miss McGuire to give a convincing ring to the rich and rapacious female who had no patience for any kind of human weakness. With Miss McGuire it could be said that she overacted; perhaps her forte is not light comedy.
>
> [Despite all the supporting players,] the fluffed lines and slow cues stunted the play's casual pace. It was perhaps because of Miss McGuire's overwhelming dominance that the others had little chance to distinguish themselves.
>
> There were only a few scattered laughs. [. . .] Apparently the adapter, Philip Barry Jr., [. . .] was too family-proud to

change or update it. More humor would have given it more life.[703]

Director Sidney Lumet was not known for his comedic expertise, and something was definitely wrong with the whole machine. The cast, however, must take the most blame, if blame there must be. If this was an attempt to cast "against type," it failed, for Dorothy was not believable as a rapacious, supercilious spoiled socialite (and overplayed to compensate for the inadequacy), John Payne was not believable as a suave, rich ironist, and Richard Carlson was definitely not believable as a charming, romantic, idealistic journalist. Despite the valiant efforts of everyone involved, this naively acted version of *The Philadelphia Story* ends up a shadow of the great text.

Probably, the issue was as film critic Carlos Clarens stated in his book about director George Cukor, who directed the film adaptation:

> Barry wrote the play for the greater glory of [Katharine] Hepburn, and without her, Tracy doesn't play, at least not sympathetically. The play is beyond revival [. . .].[704]

Both of Dorothy's performances on the drama series *Climax!* (1954–1958) were panned without pity by *Variety*. The episodes were: "The Gioconda Smile," aired on November 11, 1954, and "Pale Horse, Pale Rider," on March 22, 1956. In the first case, her role as a jilted lover and murderess was a meaty one, but *Variety* complained, "[McGuire has the] unfortunate tendency to overact, diminishing role's impact. In one key sequence, when she learns she's been jilted, her histrionics were particularly unconvincing. Less hysteria and more depth was needed for a difficult but meaningful

---

[703] "The Philadelphia Story," *Variety*, December 9, 1954.

[704] Clarens (1976), op. cit., 62.

part."[705] Nonetheless, Dorothy was nominated for a Primetime Emmy Award for her performance.

Much the same complaint was made by the magazine about Dorothy's performance in "Pale Horse, Pale Rider," a story about World War I and the flu epidemic. *Variety* accused Dorothy of portraying her character "in an overmannered and overwrought style"; about the episode, it sentenced, "Chalk this one up as a noble experiment that flopped."[706]

After the second *Climax!* episode, sixteen years would pass before Dorothy essayed television again. In 1972, she returned to the medium with a TV movie entitled *She Waits*, an intimate ghost story co-starring Patty Duke, David McCallum, and Lew Ayres.

The story of a house haunted by the ghost of a wronged wife who may or may not have been killed by her husband two years back, *She Waits* never quite succeeds in its ambition to be a scary, atmospheric chiller, but manages instead to be a rather sluggish rehash of many old ghost clichés and explanations, its tone somewhat reminiscent of a *Rebecca* (1940) without Mrs. Danvers.

When Mark Wilson (David McCallum) brings his new wife Laura (Patty Duke) to the old house where he was unhappily married with his first wife Elaine, he does not dream that the anguished warnings his mother Sarah (Dorothy) issues to anyone who will listen—namely, that Elaine is still in the house and seeks revenge for her wrongful death—are actually true. Sarah begs Mark to get Laura out of the house for her own safety, but no one heeds her advice. Sure enough, demure, impressionable Laura soon falls under the spell, or possession, of Elaine's spirit, and, in a climactic scene involving Mark and his business associate David (James Callahan), Laura/Elaine finally remembers what happened on that fateful night: it was David (her lover at the time) and not her husband Mark who

---

705 "The Gioconda Smile," *Variety*, November 12, 1954.

706 "Pale Horse, Pale Rider," *Variety*, March 26, 1956.

killed her. After confessing the accidental murder, panic-stricken David rushes down the stairs to leave the house, and falls to his death.

The by-the-numbers script is no help at all, nor is director Delbert Mann's (who had directed Dorothy in *The Dark at the Top of the Stairs* twelve years earlier) plodding pace. The dialogue is unimaginatively written, and it is a miracle that Dorothy manages to instill it with life in her scenes.

As the agitated oracle who predicts doom, Dorothy is the spookiest thing in the film, much spookier than the ghost's presence. In one of her exchanges with Duke (after Laura's first "experience" of Elaine's presence), Dorothy's reading of the line "*She was here!*" is truly spine-tingling. Dorothy—though bedridden for much of the proceedings—is effective in all the colors of the acting spectrum, covering the range from loving mother to insane doomsayer.

In an interview she gave after the filming of *She Waits*, Dorothy commented on her character work on television:

> We went on location to a huge old house in Fremont Park. The bed that was mine in the picture is enormous and ornate and made of mahogany with sliding panels and bats carved on it. From the looks of it, I'd guess it may have come from the Hearst collection.
>
> Lying on it, I tried to develop the character I was playing by wondering why a woman would have a bed like that.
>
> In television, you don't have time to develop all the facets of a character, you know. You really have to do your homework for television, because everything moves so quickly. But it was easy working with our director, Delbert Mann. He is so sympathetic; has such infinite understanding.[707]

---

[707] "Dorothy McGuire critical of work," *New Castle (PA) News*, April 3, 1972.

Though Dorothy had certainly played mothers in her film career, this was the first of what would be a long string of elderly mother figures on television. "Typecasting" is too kind a word to describe the unimaginative use to which this actress was subjected on the small screen.

Dorothy made some twenty-nine guest appearances, large and small, on non-live television from 1972 to the last year of her career, 1990. For some of these appearances, she received nominations for prestigious awards[708] and became a household name for a whole new generation of viewers, a generation that might not have known her from her movie roles (the miniseries *Rich Man, Poor Man*, 1976, is an example). For the most part, and with the exception of two filmed plays, those series, TV movies, soaps, and miniseries were mediocre vehicles for her acting talent and power, even though there was occasionally some bite to the characters she played—the mother in *Rich Man, Poor Man* being an example. Those guest appearances mostly represented a reduction of her persona to a sentimental cliché; those benevolent old lady roles were—you will excuse the extremity of the opinion—fodder between meatier scenes involving the real protagonists. Regardless of this waste, Dorothy was undeniably lovely, and her performances accomplished and sometimes brilliant.

Dorothy never addressed this particular issue in interviews; occasionally, however, she did comment on the failings of the material that was proposed to her. Here are some comments she made in 1972:

> So many of the parts offered now are offensive. They are not only deprecating to women, they aren't terribly realistic. [...] I have a happy private life. I love to work. I love the people I work with, but, if the right offers don't come, it's not a big thing.[709]

---

[708] After "The Gioconda Smile," Dorothy was also nominated for Primetime Emmy Awards for *Rich Man, Poor Man*, 1976, and *Amos*, 1985.

[709] "Critical," *New Castle News* (1972), op. cit.

Dorothy as Lavinia Hubbard in the Hollywood Television Theatre production of Lillian Hellman's *Another Part of the Forest*, which was telecast nationally by PBS on October 2, 1972.

The two televised plays in which Dorothy co-starred, spaced sixteen years apart and bookending as many years of theatrical activity, were *Another Part of the Forest* (1972), which Dorothy would then perform on the stage in Los Angeles ten years later, and *I Never Sang for My Father* (1988), which followed her successful US tour with the play's revival in 1987. While the first televised drama can be seen as a dry run for her 1982 live stage performance in Lillian Hellman's play, the second was a footnote to her 1987 stage performance, a footnote which, according to some critics, cemented and improved on her original stage work.

Don Shirley of the *Los Angeles Times* happily noted such improvement in the performances:

> Harold Gould makes his lines sing in "I Never Sang for My Father" [. . .]. As garrulous old Tom Garrison, filling up his declining years with self-important blather, bushy-browed

Gould is alternately exasperating and amusing, but always fascinating. [...]

For preserving this performance, and improving two others, we should be grateful for this installment of "American Playhouse," directed at KCET by Jack O'Brien of San Diego's Old Globe Theatre.

Dorothy McGuire has retained the sweetness inherent in Tom's wife. But when she argues with her husband in a restaurant, her voice has a sharper edge than it had during the play's run at the Ahmanson Theatre last winter. The prodigal daughter (Margo Skinner, still lively and vital) may have learned how to argue from her mother as well as her dad.

Dorothy with co-star Daniel J. Travanti in the American Playhouse television production of *I Never Sang for My Father*, 1988.

At the Ahmanson, Daniel J. Travanti's put-upon son, Gene, faded too far into the woodwork in the first part of the play and then pushed too hard near the end. At one point in tonight's show, his voice sounds as artificially intense as it did at the Ahmanson, but generally Travanti's performance is much more carefully modulated here. And it's easier to appreciate his baleful sidelong glances at his father when they're in close-ups.[710]

In other words, as far as Dorothy's performance is concerned, the clichéd niceness of her Ahmanson performance was tempered by complementary colors that created a fuller character with a sharper edge.

These television plays were an opportunity for Dorothy to return to her first love, the theater, but not only: they were also a chance to work with good scripts and inhabit well-written characters, trying to evoke the type of acting that only good texts, and well-rehearsed stage work, can yield.

For, the problem with Dorothy's later television material—the problem with most television of that period—was conventionality. With middling scripts, middling direction and sometimes mediocre acting colleagues, there was only so much even an actress like Dorothy could do. She could act competently, even touchingly, but she could scarcely elevate the quality of the material by herself. As a result, her own contribution to that material was diminished by her surroundings.

Or, Dorothy was involved in sprawling projects where her characters got "lost" in a sea of alternating subplots, and her appearances were merely a series of recurrent cameos, with little depth, development, or growth. For all its resounding success and indubitable quality, for example, the

---

[710] Don Shirley, "Television Reviews: Improved Performances in 'I Never Sang for My Father,'" *Los Angeles Times*, June 15, 1988.

miniseries *Rich Man, Poor Man* (1976) offered a mere weekly dollop of Dorothy's character at the intersection of the stories of her character's two sons (Nick Nolte and Peter Strauss), and somewhat clichéd to boot. As lovely as it was to see Dorothy essay a rather conflictual (but underdeveloped) character week after week, it was also a melancholy thing to see her on the sidelines—with other past glories such as her radio co-star Ray Milland, with whom she had a few interesting scenes. Dorothy was nominated for a Primetime Emmy Award for her performance in the miniseries.

From left to right: Dorothy, Barry Sullivan, and Tiffany Bolling in television's *Another Part of the Forest*, October 1972.

Even the best of these television properties, those in which her character was allowed to develop somewhat, did not belong to her. For example, *Amos*, a 1985 TV movie about an evil nurse who works in a retirement home and secretly kills her patients, is obviously dominated by protagonist Kirk Douglas as the patient who investigates the Angel of Death's poisonous evildoings and sacrifices his life to expose them, and by Elizabeth Montgomery as the villainess. Dorothy has some nice scenes with Douglas, and one with Montgomery, but *Amos* is not her movie. Dorothy was nominated for another Primetime Emmy Award for this performance.

It is also possible that Dorothy's own preference for playing "nice" characters had increased as the years passed. Dorothy had occasionally been adventurous in allowing herself to be cast against type, but, already in 1955, in commenting on her role in the film *Three Coins in the Fountain* (1954) with NEA correspondent Erskine Johnson, she had remarked:

> I didn't like playing the part. I prefer playing characters who are liked and loved by the audience.[711]

Yet, arguably, her character in *Three Coins* had been sympathetic enough, with only a few sharp angles to make her human. Dorothy was evidently hypersensitive when it came to her characters, and may have been an enabler in the process of typecasting; ultimately, she was at least partially responsible for typecasting herself. In her 1977 interview with Rex Reed, she quipped to explain the slackening of her career:

> I just didn't want to play monsters, and after a long list of rather distinguished roles, I just wasn't getting the kinds of scripts that interested me. I had my husband and my family and a very rewarding life at home, and I didn't feel the need

---

[711] Erskine Johnson, "Hollywood Today!," *Eureka (CA) Times Standard*, May 18, 1955.

to work when the work wasn't interesting or fulfilling, so I just waited.[712]

With age, this "softness" probably grew, making her choices (or the choices of those who hired her) even more conservative.

In film as in theater, in the presence of rich, well-balanced, well-written scripts (say, the play *The Night of the Iguana* or the film *A Tree Grows in Brooklyn*), that "niceness" provided a foundation on which Dorothy could build organically and show her characters' contrasting facets. In good properties, Dorothy's performances were never one-note performances. On the other hand, without such scripts, and without adequate co-stars to play against, that "niceness" might remain relatively inert and not germinate properly. The latter scenario presented itself often in television.

Sometimes it did not. The teleplay of the touching TV movie *The Runaways* (1975) may not be the most original ever written, and the film's leisurely pace and sentimental heart may make it predictable and thin, but Dorothy gives an excellent performance in it as widowed kennel owner Angela Lakey. The story concerns orphan boy Johnny Miles (Josh Albee) and runaway leopard Yarra. Both these lonely creatures run away from an unhappy life, and find each other on the road. Mrs. Lakey is the woman who gives Johnny a part-time job at the kennel, and discovers that he has a magic touch with animals. Joe Ringer (Van Williams) is the man who supplies the meat for the kennel, and befriends the boy as a surrogate father figure. The growth of Johnny's relationships with Mrs. Lakey and Joe is delineated cleanly and efficiently. Acting-wise, Williams is serviceable but superficial, and Albee tries awfully hard and almost succeeds; it is Dorothy who, consummate thespian that she is, paints her character deftly with the few brush strokes she is allowed, and makes Mrs. Lakey into a real person.

In 1978, Dorothy guest-starred in the television miniseries *Little*

---

[712] Reed, "Spirit" (1977), op. cit.

Women, playing the important part of Marmee March. *Downton Abbey* this period miniseries was not, and, as the *Los Angeles Times* noted, its studio "ambience [was] more reminiscent of Knott's Berry Farm than 19th-century Concord, Mass."[713] Notwithstanding the limitations of its production values and direction, however, the miniseries contains good performances by just about everybody in the cast, from the young actresses playing the four "little women" (Susan Dey as Jo, Meredith Baxter Birney as Meg, Ann Dusenberry as Amy, Eve Plumb as Beth) to the old Hollywood glories who play the character parts: Dorothy as Marmee, Greer Garson as Aunt Kathryn, and Robert Young as Grandpa Lawrence. William Shatner puts in an appearance as one of the beaus, Professor Bhaer.

Dorothy ranges from very good to almost sublime in the screen time she is given, and the entire package is pleasant and slick, Old Hollywood-style. Elmer Bernstein provided the catchy music and famed designer Edith Head the costumes.

Dorothy also made a few television appearances as herself; in most cases, the events were live public celebrations, and her presence merely leant moral support to the featured honorees. In 1973, she warmly kissed Vincent Price, the guest of honor of *This Is Your Life*, while he mentioned *The Winslow Boy*, the play in which they had co-starred at the La Jolla Playhouse in 1954. In 1978, she was a guest (together with husband John) in the special documentary *The American Film Institute Salute to Henry Fonda*.[714] In 1989, she was present at a similar salute to Gregory Peck. In 1986, she was one of the nominees at the 38th Annual Primetime Emmy Awards. Dorothy also appeared in two documentaries, one about David

---

[713] Marylouise Oates, "'Little Women' in a Slick, Shiny Glow," *Los Angeles Times*, October 2, 1978.

[714] Directed by Marty Pasetta and written by Hal Kanter, the TV special sported an array of prestigious guests, from Jane Alexander to Richard Burton, from Lucille Ball to Bette Davis, from Lillian Gish to Fred MacMurray, from Jack Lemmon to Gregory Peck, from James Stewart to Lloyd Nolan. And of course Dorothy. The two-hour show aired on CBS on March 15, 1978.

O. Selznick (*Hollywood: The Selznick Years*, 1969)[715] and one about Samuel Goldwyn (*American Masters: Goldwyn: the Man and His Movies*, 2001). Her most substantial appearance as herself was in the Disney documentary *The Best Doggoned Dog in the World* (1957), the bulk of which she hosted and/or narrated together with Walt Disney to plug the film *Old Yeller* before its release.

The most delightful of these live guest appearances was Dorothy's stint as "mystery guest" on *What's My Line?* (1954), where she affected a Deep South accent to fool the panel of blindfolded showbiz experts (Dorothy Kilgallen, Steve Allen, Arlene Francis and Bennett Cerf) who were supposed to guess her identity. She fooled them so well that only Cerf recognized her—though the ignorance that the other panelists professed might have been a ruse. Bennett Cerf, of course, was one of the founders of Random House and had published John Swope's book *Camera Over Hollywood* in 1939. Here is part of her exchange with Cerf from that show:

Cerf: This is a very familiar voice to me. Uh... I have a vague idea I know you personally. Do I know you personally? Besides seeing you on screen and on stage?
McGuire: Well, Sugar, not nearly enough. Not nearly enough.
Cerf: Have you got a husband?
McGuire: I ha-a-ave.
Cerf: Would this husband be a scoundrel who promised to take pictures of my children for about four years and finally turned up at the end of that time to do it?
McGuire: Now, Bennett!

---

715 The one-hour documentary was produced, scripted and directed by Marshall Flaum, and aired by NBC on March 21, 1969. The host/narrator was Henry Fonda. Among the guests: Ingrid Bergman, Joseph Cotten, George Cukor, Joan Fontaine, Janet Gaynor, Katharine Hepburn, Alfred Hitchcock, and Dorothy.

Cerf: I do know who it is and I'm going to pass, because I know this girl and love her very dearly.

One did not need to see publisher Bennett Cerf smile to glimpse the amiable irony that always lurked in his facial expressions. The founder of Random House was a born humorist even when he did not try to be one. Press photo, 1955.

Even on television, when the material was good, it was good, and when a teleplay was shrewdly written and expertly acted, the results could partially redeem the stalest of conventions. That is what happened with *Between the Darkness and the Dawn* (1985), written by N. Richard Nash and Dennis Turner and directed by Peter (Dan) Levin. Not that there is no conventionality in the movie; there is, and plenty of it, but it is handled intelligently. A sentimental disease-of-the-week story this TV movie might well be, but it is wrapped up in a luxury package through balanced writing, good direction and the casting of two wonderful actresses, Elizabeth Montgomery and Dorothy. Montgomery, as Abigail Foster, the seventeen-year-old high school cheerleader who is suddenly stricken with a rare form of encephalitis and falls into a semi-vegetative state, and Dorothy, as the mother who devotes her life to taking care of her, give riveting performances. When Abigail suddenly wakes up after twenty years (initially thinking she is still seventeen), she has to learn how to live all over again and adjust to her new world; Montgomery is mesmerizing in expressing her character's confusion, shock, and ultimate joyful determination to live and make something of her new self. The movie closes with Abigail happily graduating from high school, twenty years too late. One may quibble about this or that flaw in script or story, but for 1985 television, this drama counts as a minor gem.

The *New York Times*' John J. O'Connor evidently did not appreciate having his buttons pushed, and detested the movie, writing an unforgiving review that qualified the movie as "a candidate for worst television movie of the year" and as "television of the blatantly exploitative variety."[716] He also detested Montgomery's performance. For O'Connor, obviously, the answer to the question whether convention could be rescued by manner of execution was a resounding "no." Here is director Levin commenting:

> The critics rarely liked my TV movies; at any rate, they were insulting to most TV directors. Dorothy and Elizabeth were both dreams to work with.[717]

I had been tempted to overlook Dorothy's many guest appearances, or even starring appearances—as a series of old ladies, more or less nice, more or less feisty, or more or less infirm—in the soap operas (*The Young and the*

---

[716] John J. O'Connor, "'Between the Darkness and the Dawn' on NBC," *New York Times*, December 23, 1985.

[717] Dan "Peter" Levin, correspondence with the author, March 2017.

Restless, 1985), TV movies (*The Incredible Journey of Dr. Meg Laurel*, 1979; *Ghost Dancing*, 1983), and series of the late 1970s and 1980s (*Love Boat*, 1982 and 1984; *Fantasy Island*, 1983; *Hotel*, 1985; *Glitter*, 1985; *American Geisha*, 1986; *St. Elsewhere*, 1986; *Highway to Heaven*, 1986 and 1988). But I felt obliged to comment at least on a few of these.

Noble intentions, and more than a little dose of political polemic, animated the authors of *Ghost Dancing* (1983), a TV movie that aired on ABC on May 30, 1983, causing a long-running controversy to flare up again in the valleys of California. Specifically, they animated Phil Penningroth, the author of the teleplay, which won the ABC Theatre Award. The controversy to which the script refers concerns the effects of the diverting of water streams from the Owens Valley, located 250 miles northeast of Los Angeles, to the City of Angels by the city's Department of Water and Power (Polanski's *Chinatown*, anyone?).

The story Penningroth tells is that of Sarah Bowman, a tough old Valley farmer who, impoverished by the shortage of water, plans to dynamite the Owens Valley-L.A. aqueduct, in order to be arrested and try to help focus public attention on the plight of the Valley residents.

The real controversy that the TV movie caused, however, was not limited to the environmental issue on hand. On April 3, 1983, the *Los Angeles Times* published a long article[718] reporting the complex series of alleged political pressures that ABC, Titus Productions, and producer Robert "Buzz" Berger received from the Department of Water and Power (at the time the nation's largest public utility with a $2 billion budget), pressures that prevented Penningroth's script from being filmed as he had written it.

The DWP forbade filming from taking place on its property in the Owens Valley, forcing the production company to excise all references to the California locations, and therefore to historical events, from their script. A series of denials and excuses ensued, from both the power authority and the film's producers. Filming was carried out in St. George,

---

[718] Michael London, "Watered-Down Drama," *Los Angeles Times*, April 3, 1983.

Utah, in a valley meant to stand in for any desert valley where the events of the film *might* have taken place.[719] Owens Valley protests surged, and the residents' opposition to the Los Angeles DWP was rekindled (the aqueduct had last been bombed by protesters in 1979).

Due to the changes made to Penningroth's script, the film lost some of its potency, and the results, despite a "fine cinematic quality [. . . and] good performances,"[720] were deemed tepid by most reviewers. Howard Rosenberg of the *Los Angeles Times*, for example, wrote, "The story takes a frustrating middle position, finding merit in each side of the dispute."[721] Those reviewers treated Dorothy, and her performance, with respect if not admiration, but at least one of them considered her miscast in the role. Most negative criticism not targeting the "watering down" of the story was aimed at the film's pace and dramatic drive, which were considered slothful.[722]

Here is one of the best appraisals of Dorothy's performance:

> [. . .] Sarah is played beautifully by Dorothy McGuire, an actress whose presence has been unfailingly elegant since the days, a few decades ago, when she co-starred with Robert Young in "The Enchanted Cottage." An enormously attractive woman, McGuire gives a performance of powerful dignity.[723]

---

719 Bill Carter, "'Ghost Dancing' shows TV can act nobly," *Baltimore (MD) Sun*, May 29, 1983.

720 Howard Rosenberg, "The Tube Tonight: Watered-Down 'Ghost Dancing,'" *Los Angeles Times*, May 30, 1983.

721 Ibid.

722 Ibid.

723 John O'Connor (*New York Times* News Service), "'Peanuts' special explores war and peace," *San Bernardino (CA) County Sun*, May 30, 1983.

Dorothy never got involved in the controversy per se, but her participation in the film, after a four-year absence from both film and television, must be seen as eloquent. Always an environmentalist, Dorothy took the fate of the Earth, and of California, to heart, in all its facets. "She's a woman of principle," Dorothy said about her character in an interview;[724] she might as well have been saying it about herself. Despite Dorothy's discretion (she seldom preached), it is not difficult to see that she, too, was animated by noble intentions in accepting the part of Sarah Bowman. Dorothy's co-stars in *Ghost Dancing* were Bruce Davison, Bill Erwin, Richard Farnsworth, Bo Hopkins, and Victoria Racimo. The film was directed by David Greene, who had directed Dorothy in the miniseries *Rich Man, Poor Man* in 1976.

In 1986 and then again in 1988, Dorothy played Jonathan Smith's (Michael Landon) widowed wife in three episodes of the series *Highway to Heaven* (1984–1989). Smith, of course, is not really Smith but a wingless angel who used to be Arthur Thompson in his earthly life. In the first episode ("Keep Smiling," 1986), his weekly assignment (from God) is to help his beloved widow through a difficult moment in her life: she has just lost her only surviving close friend, and her out-of-town children never visit her. The three episodes ("Keep Smiling," 1986; "We Have Forever," Part I, 1988; and "We Have Forever," Part II, 1988) in which Dorothy plays the character of Jane Thompson are sentimental, button-pushing hogwash in many ways; but Dorothy's performances in them are phenomenal.

In those episodes (as in *Between the Darkness and the Dawn*) we can see the flip side of that "negative" argument I was making about Dorothy's television work. For, despite the shameless sentimental conventionality of the material she is given, Dorothy is neither lazy nor jaded about her acting. That acting contains not only all her past acting expertise, but also

---

[724] Jerry Buck, "Film 'Ghost Dancing' Literally All Wet," *Cincinnati (OH) Enquirer*, May 30, 1983.

a lifetime of human experience. It is impossible to describe the power of some of her line readings, where she is literally transformed by the deep truthfulness of her rendering of a human being; her voice especially undergoes a series of metamorphoses that are as interesting as they are apparently effortless. In "We Have Forever, Part I," Dorothy enacts her own character's death, and the combination of her acting and the background music (Claude Debussy's "Clair de lune," which was Jane and Arthur's "song" while they were husband and wife) yields a very moving result indeed. Dorothy's whole life flows naturally into those lines, and that confluence of natural talent and humanity is a wonder to watch.

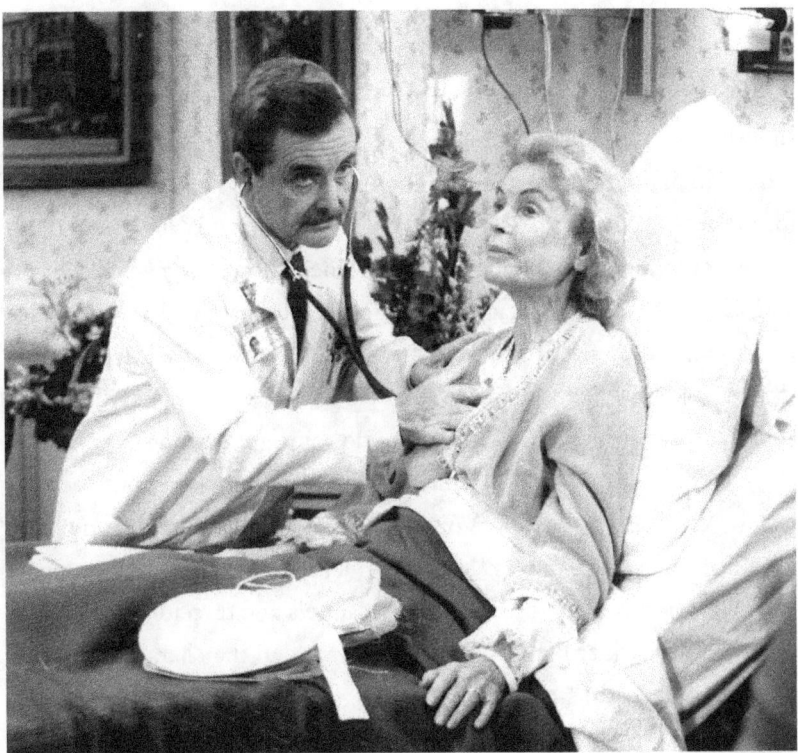

Dr. Craig (William Daniels) examines the matriarch of a famous New England political family (Dorothy) who checks into St. Eligius Hospital, in the *St. Elsewhere* episode "Family Ties," January 1986. NBC Photo, ©1985.

Even in the smallest of roles, as for example that of VIP hospital patient Augusta Endicott, the dying matriarch of the influential Endicott family of politicians (*St. Elsewhere*, three episodes, 1986), Dorothy's talent and experience endow her performances with authoritativeness. It is with extreme subtlety that Dorothy paints the characterization of Mrs. Endicott, making her the epitome of softness. Her voice a warm whisper, her speech slow and slightly slurred (the character likes to drink), Augusta Endicott is, in Dorothy's hands, a delicate, slightly faded watercolor portrait of frailty and melancholy. This is seen to best advantage in the moving scenes Dorothy plays with Norman Lloyd (Dr. Daniel Auschlander). Even spread thin within the choral maze of the series' subplots, Dorothy stands out.

Dorothy's last television appearance was also her last appearance in show business. She played a mother, once again. The project, luckily, was a well-written one, and starred two good actresses who gave excellent performances. Another disease-of-the-week movie, *The Last Best Year* (1990) is the story of inoperable-cancer patient Jane Murray (Bernadette Peters) and of Wendy Haller (Mary Tyler Moore), the psychiatrist who helps her through those last months of her life. Dorothy plays Tyler Moore's mother, and has only two scenes, but the caliber of the material is high, and those two scenes allow Dorothy to do some good acting.

The TV movie is, as O'Connor of the *New York Times* put it in his review, "exquisitely crafted."[725] A sign of this is the fact that it is not easy to tell who the protagonist is between Tyler Moore and Peters: the compassionate curiosity of writer David W. Rintels and director John Erman extends to the inner life of both characters; of all the characters, in fact. Thus, even Dorothy's character, Ann, is given a chance to reveal herself tellingly in the two brief scenes that she is assigned. While it is true that the film suffers from an excess of sentimentality (disease stories usually

---

[725] John J. O'Connor, "The New Woman Finds Her Place on The Small Screen," *New York Times*, November 4, 1990.

feel obliged to express themselves sentimentally, even melodramatically, or cannot resist the temptation), it is also true that its exploration of human relationships is sincere, and fruitful. A small but worthy parting gift from Dorothy.

18. Olympian Jamborees

In 1977, Rex Reed interviewed Dorothy for a profile of her, and a rather good one at that. At one point during the interview, Reed and Dorothy broached the subject of socializing, or, as it is called in Hollywood, parties.

Reed opined: "[Even at the peak of her film career, McGuire's] name seldom appeared in columns. You never read stories about her going to flashy parties, or jumping into swimming pools." And Dorothy confirmed:

> I was never glamorous or beautiful, and I considered myself a theater actress. There were never any scandals or drinking champagne out of slippers, or nude orgies. I suppose we drank our share of champagne, but I don't remember any slippers. If there were Hollywood orgies, they must have waited until John and I went home.
>
> [Even today], we don't go to parties or premieres. We have an old circle of friends you don't read about in the headlines.[726]

---

[726] Reed, "Lack of Competitive Spirit," 1977, op. cit.

Those statements (both by Reed and by Dorothy), though partly true at least in spirit, must be taken with a grain of salt. It is true, for example, that Dorothy was never involved in any scandals, and that the parties she (or she and John) went to were seldom "flashy," in the sense of "wild." But the image that is suggested by those statements, of a demure, modest woman who stayed home with her husband and only frequented a small circle of intimate friends, is false.

Dorothy, with or without John Swope, was far from averse to parties, and one must not imagine that the expression "old circle of friends" had the same meaning, or conjured the same image, as it might for the average mortal. The Swopes' circle of friends included captains of industry, studio moguls, producers, movie stars, directors, actors, artists, prominent socialites, bankers, and writers. The word "party" did not carry exactly the same connotations for Dorothy as it commonly does for people in general, or even for many Hollywood players in particular.

A Hollywood party is normally not like any other party. It is often a place where business is done between the lines, or where the have-nots can grovel, or beg for crumbs, before the haves. Or, it is a place where the rich and beautiful can be seen by the rich and beautiful, or admired by the poor and hopeful. Either way, this kind of party is a place where certain needs (desperate or otherwise) find expression and masquerade as sociality, or as fun. To this kind of party, one often goes either to prove something or to achieve something.

Dorothy certainly went to parties, both in the period when her film career was in full swing and afterwards; but she did not go to the parties described above, nor for the reasons described above. She also went to premieres, and to events honoring famous people in the film industry (for example, Olivia de Havilland, 1986).[727] Most often, these famous people were people she knew or had worked with. She participated in charities,

---

[727] "Cinema Awards Foundation to honor Olivia de Havilland," *Palm Springs (CA) Desert Sun*, January 10, 1986.

fundraisers, and inaugurations of theaters and museums, and attended award ceremonies (not necessarily the Academy Awards), tributes, and commemorations. She both gave parties at home and went to parties at other people's homes (mostly dinner parties, but not only).

Mirror selfie: the author (right) with Dorothy and John Swope in the vestibule of their house at 121 Copley Place, Yuletide 1977. When this photograph was taken by John (as he wrote on its verso when he sent it to me, "This is not good example of my work but thought it might amuse you") with one of his Rolleiflex cameras, the three of us were about to go to Samuel Goldwyn Jr.'s Christmas party.

What I am trying to say is, the Swopes enjoyed a rich social life, and were very much part of the social texture of their adopted city, or at least of its upper strata. They enjoyed a good party, and keeping in touch with friends and acquaintances; but they never did this because they were after something, or because they needed to prove something.

As far as Reed's contention that Dorothy's name "seldom appeared in columns," it is simply not true, not literally at least. Those columns were filled with her name throughout her career, quite often in conjunction with parties, premieres, and social and charitable events. There were no scandals, there was no "dirt," but Dorothy was not an invisible woman.

A few days after I arrived in Los Angeles for my first personal visit to the Swopes in December 1977, our friendship still in the budding stage, Dorothy and John took me to a party, and not just any party: they took me to Samuel Goldwyn Jr.'s Christmas party. That party, a quiet, informal, relaxed, sophisticated affair at Goldwyn's home, was filled to the gills with celebrities, and what celebrities. The first person to whom I was introduced was Samuel Goldwyn Jr. himself; the second, actor Charlton Heston; the third, screenwriter Ernest Lehman; the fourth, director William Wyler (who had directed Dorothy in *Friendly Persuasion*); and so on, until my head spun.

Two days later, Dorothy herself gave a party at her house, and although technically the caliber of young artists, writers, actors, and directors present was a notch or two below that of the first event, we were still traveling in some fairly exalted, and enlightened, creative circles. On Christmas Eve, Dorothy and John then took me to a dinner at the house of Ed and Hannah Carter, two prominent Los Angeles patrons and benefactors.[728] We had pineapple glazed ham, and it was delicious.

I mentioned the above events not in order to drop names, but to prove

---

[728] Edward W. Carter (1911–1996) was a prominent Los Angeles businessman. Aside from serving as executive in several successful department stores, he served on the Boards of the Los Angeles Area Chamber of Commerce, the California Retailers Association, the Los Angeles branch of the Federal Reserve Bank of San Francisco, the Northrop Aircraft Corp., and others. He was also a philanthropist, and was among the co-founders of the Los Angeles County Museum of Art (LACMA) and the Los Angeles Music Center.

a point. Dorothy not only entertained and socialized, but did so with the utmost comfort and ease: unostentatiously, and with real charm and conviviality. She may have avoided the spotlight of empty glamour and fame, but those celebrities, those dazzling "big names" she socialized with, were her "old circle of friends"; to an outsider, the association of this state of things with glamour and fame was unavoidable. Those parties that Dorothy threw, or took me to, during my first visit also prove another point. Far from being mere luxury "tourist attractions" that she exhibited for my benefit, those gatherings were Dorothy's "natural" milieu, a world of which Dorothy, effortlessly and sincerely, enjoyed being a part, and this despite her lack of interest for the trappings of fame, gossip, and career. In this respect at least, when her daughter Topo complains that Dorothy "was such a movie star," one must admit that she may have a point.

Jane Wyatt Ward (1910–2006) is a good example of Dorothy's circle of friends, and here another personal anecdote will serve as illustration.

Jane, the descendant of a wealthy Dutch-Scottish family from New York, came from a grand background. Her mother was Euphemia van Rensselaer Waddington Wyatt, her father Christopher Billopp Wyatt. As a young girl, Jane attended the exclusive Chapin School, then Barnard College at Columbia University, and was on the New York City Social Register. Her decision to choose acting as a career was frowned upon in high society, and her name was taken off the Social Register when she left college to tread the boards. It was reinstated when, in 1936, she married investment broker Edgar Bethune Ward, whom she met while they were both guests of Franklin D. Roosevelt's at Hyde Park, New York.

I had first met Jane, one of Dorothy's closest friends, during my 1977 visit to the Swopes, but had had limited social interaction with her. We met again while I was studying playwriting and screenwriting at USC and she happened to be on an industry jury (accompanied by her friend Dorothy) that was to judge a play competition in 1989; my first full-length play was competing. The jury included a producer from the Los Angeles Theatre Center (LATC) and *Los Angeles Times* theater critic Robert Koehler.

My play won first prize; the following day, Jane sent me a glowing letter praising my work both as writer and as director,[729] and she and I started socializing again.

Jane lived in a beautiful house on Siena Way, in the hilly haven of Bel Air (the house, built in 1936, was designed by "Architect to the Stars" Paul Revere Williams, the same who had designed Dorothy's house on Copley Place in Beverly Hills). She had two pianos in her home that nobody used at the time, and I had no piano at all. During a party at which both she and Dorothy were present, Jane suggested that, if I felt like playing, I could do so at her place. I took her at her word, and made arrangements to meet. On the day of the appointment, I sauntered up Siena Way, piano scores under my arm (I did not drive at the time), until I reached her house. As I walked to her front entrance at the appointed time, I noticed a handwritten note taped to the door: "Giancarlo: I went to the market. The door is unlocked. Make yourself at home. The pianos are downstairs." I took the note off the door and entered. Nobody else was in the house. I went downstairs to their game/music room and started playing on the well-maintained concert grand that was the centerpiece of the room. Half an hour later Jane walked in, illuminating the space around her with her sunny disposition. If nothing else, this anecdote proves how well Bel Air must have been patrolled.

It proves something else as well. When one thinks of the rich and famous, one often thinks of a class of ostentatious, egotistic, or diffident people. Jane may have been one of Los Angeles' rich and famous, but, like Dorothy, she was also one of the most disarmingly modest, friendly, warm people I have met. In both these women, fame and wealth were balanced by massive doses of inconspicuous elegance and self-effacing open-

---

[729] The text of that letter was: "Dear Giancarlo, You were so crowded with well-wishers the other night that I didn't have a chance to congratulate you properly. 'Gentleman's Gentleman' was a delight. Not only did it deserve the writing prize but also the casting prize, the acting prize, the costume prize and the directing prize! Many, many more congratulations and best wishes for your writing career. Jane."

ness, as well as by a fine artistic/human sensitivity. In theatrical terms, the "characters" that both these women played in life had few of the classic characteristics of the wealthy, and none of the classic flaws of the famous.

The Swopes were Los Angeles royalty, and only a certain tenor of party would do for a king and queen. Sometimes, this tenor could be deceptively simple. It was probably on the occasion of the Swopes' purchase of their house on Copley Place, and of their preparations for the birth of their son Mark, that the couple gave the party mentioned by Hedda Hopper in her column in December 1952, with a tone between melancholy and facetious:

> The party given by Dorothy McGuire and John Swope was a real joy. They regret having to give up their little house where they've been so happy for one large enough for the addition to the family. John has two beautiful photographs blown up to four feet square and set right into the plaster of their living room. They're better than many paintings I've seen around and about.[730]

For once, Hopper did not specify any details of the party or the names of any of the guests, which seems to denote a certain affection for the hosts, and a certain respect.

Early news of the Swopes' party-going activities appeared in Hopper's column during Yuletide 1947; here is her colorful report, which is less interesting for the facts reported, or the names dropped, than for the undertone of flippant irony and political sarcasm running through the text:

> Clare and Henry Luce's party was as bright as his magazines. The place was so star-studded you could hardly tell

---

[730] Hedda Hopper, "Gen. LeMay Briefs Stewart for Air Film," *Los Angeles Times*, December 27, 1952.

"right" from "left."⁷³¹ Charlie Chaplin nearly fell through a window when he saw his bitterest enemy. Bob and Betty Montgomery greeted the Doug Fairbankses. It was Mary Lou Fairbanks' first appearance since the birth of her third daughter. The Ray Millands were with Mrs. Bob Hope. Mrs. Milland wore pale blue paradise that matched her hair. Ginger Rogers was hatless and glamorous. Merle Oberon, in a Paris creation, danced with Adrian, while Adrian's wife, Janet Gaynor, in a new Adrian brocade, danced with Reggie Gardiner. The Gary Coopers and Jimmy Cagneys proved they hadn't forgotten their dancing steps. Marlene Dietrich chattered in French with Louis Jourdan. Elsie and Charles Mendl, who was being congratulated on his 76th birthday, were with Ethel Barrymore, Charles Brackett and George Cukor. The Nunnally Johnsons were being congratulated on "The Senator Was Indiscreet."

Everybody was there, including the Merian Coopers, Rouben Mamoulians, Vic Flemings, Darryl Zanucks, Greer Garson, in bright red brocade, Jimmy Stewart, Dorothy McGuire and John Swope, and Ann Warner's beautiful daughter Joy Ann, with husband Bill Orr. Clare floated through the hotel-like rooms in blue chiffon, while Henry met many of his guests for the first time.⁷³²

Of the premieres of her own films, the splashiest Dorothy attended were those for *Friendly Persuasion*, which included a special tribute honoring director William Wyler (see Part I, Chapter 13), and for *The Greatest*

---

731 This was the period of McCarthy's House Un-American Activities Committee hearings; Hedda Hopper, an enthusiastic pro-HUAC spokesperson, was always ready to plant veiled (or not so veiled) hints about Communist suspects.

732 Hedda Hopper, "Looking at Hollywood," *Los Angeles Times*, December 18, 1947.

Story Ever Told; the latter took some considerable planning by an ad-hoc committee whose honorary chairman was Democratic governor of California Pat Brown. The committee, which included Arthur Hanish as co-chairman and Dorothy, met several times in advance. The event took place at Pacific's Cinerama Theater[733] on February 17, 1965, under the auspices of the United Nations Association of the United States of America and the Eleanor Roosevelt Foundation.

Naples, April 26, 1953: Clare Boothe Luce (foreground, right), new US Ambassador to Italy, is all smiles for newsreel cameramen after disembarking from the *Andrea Doria* to take up her new post in Rome. With her is her husband, publisher Henry Luce (foreground, left). Photo: United Press/Alberto Blasetti.

[733] Pacific Theaters' arresting Cinerama Dome movie theater is located at 6360 Sunset Boulevard near Vine Street in Hollywood, California. Created by Welton Becket & Associates based on the geodesic dome design developed by architect R. Buckminster Fuller, the theater was designed to show single-lens Cinerama films on its 86-foot-wide screen. The Dome opened to the public on November 7, 1963. Plans for demolition in the late 1990s were luckily thwarted by preservationists, Cinerama enthusiasts, and LA's planning department; the Dome was declared a Los Angeles Historic-Cultural Monument in 1998. In 2002, the Dome was extensively refurbished and refreshed, reopening as part of ArcLight Hollywood in March 2002.

Patrons of the event included President Lyndon B. Johnson and Mrs. Johnson, Vice-President and Mrs. Hubert H. Humphrey, Speaker and Mrs. John W. McCormack, Chief Justice and Mrs. Earl Warren, Secretary of State and Mrs. Dean Rusk, Senator and Mrs. George Murphy, Honorable and Mrs. James Roosevelt, Mayor and Mrs. Sam Yorty and Honorable and Mrs. Warren Dorn. Many members of the film's gargantuan creative team attended, including Dorothy, Max von Sydow, and director George Stevens.[734]

Dorothy and John attending "Hollywood's greatest star preview of the season," i.e. Warner Brothers' Silver Anniversary of sound film, introducing Warners' film *Captain Horatio Hornblower*, R.N., starring Swope family friend Gregory Peck. The preview of the film was "the highlight of Warner's anniversary week, honoring a quarter century of talking pictures." Warner Bros. photo and press release, 1951.

---

734 See: "Expect VIP's for 'Greatest Story' Debut Tomorrow," *Van Nuys (CA) Valley News*, February 16, 1965; see also: *Los Angeles Times*, Arts Section, January 15, 1965.

In this photo, Dorothy, attending a party celebrating the end of the shooting of Bette Davis's *Hush ... Hush, Sweet Charlotte*, seems to be wondering if what Davis is displaying is a smile or not. UPI photo, March 1965.

Premieres of films starring her closest friends and collaborators, of course, Dorothy often attended, usually with John—for example, Gregory Peck's *Captain Horatio Hornblower, R.N.* (1951). However, she did not disdain attending premieres of other films as well, possibly in the interest of keeping good relations with studios new and old, and colleagues new and old. One such event was the gala premiere of RKO's *Bundle of Joy* (1956), starring Eddie Fisher and Debbie Reynolds. Some sixty stars attended the event at the Egyptian Theater in Hollywood, including Ann Blyth, Charles Coburn, Robert Cummings, Paul Henreid, Danny Kaye, Deborah Kerr, Jerry Lewis, Ray Milland, Ann Miller, Agnes Moorehead, and Shelley Winters.[735]

---

[735] "Notables to See Comedy," *Los Angeles Times*, December 6, 1956.

Among the other star-studded film premieres or special screenings Dorothy attended were those of *Prince Valiant* (Chinese Theater, April 1954, and everybody was there, from John Wayne and Tony Curtis to Gene Tierney and Ronald Reagan, from William Holden and Jane Russell to Ethel Merman and Clifton Webb, from Susan Hayward and Tyrone Power to Richard Widmark and Elizabeth Taylor),[736] *Hush... Hush, Sweet Charlotte* (1964) and *Raise the Titanic* (July 1980).

Here is a little report about the *Titanic* event (one of the first Dorothy attended after the death of her husband) by the *Los Angeles Times* society column:

> A carved ice sculpture of the Titanic rising out of the Atlantic was the first thing you saw at the party accompanying the press screening of "Raise the Titanic" earlier this week. Greeting the crowd in the Goldwyn Theater of the Academy of Motion Picture Arts and Sciences were Marble Arch chief Martin Starger, producer William Frye and director James Jameson. Among the guests: James and Gloria Stewart, Irene Dunne with her nephew Allen, the Ray Millands, Lady Sarah Churchill, Dorothy McGuire with Frank McCarthy.[737]

Another star-studded screening that Dorothy attended was the Directors Guild advance screening of George Cukor's *Travels with My Aunt*, starring Maggie Smith, which took place in November 1972, coincidentally on the night of the opening of Bonwit Teller's Beverly Hills branch on the corner of Rodeo Drive and Wilshire Boulevard. The film would be released in New York on December 17. The astonishing turnout included

---

[736] "Gala Event Due Tonight," Los Angeles Times, April 2, 1954.

[737] "On View," *Los Angeles Times*, July 24, 1980.

Lucille Ball ("in a brunette wig, a tryout for her role as 'Mame'"),[738] Bill Bixby, Red Buttons, Samantha Eggar, Fox's Jere Henshaw, Tom Mankiewicz, MGM's studio chief Dan Melnick and TV chief Harris Katleman, Suzanne Pleshette and husband Tom Gallagher, Barbara Rush, Stella Stevens, Jill St. John, Dorothy and John Swope, Liv Ullmann, King Vidor, Jon Voight, and Mae West ("the top star of the evening, as usual").[739] The *Los Angeles Times* concluded, given the scheduling conflict with the razzle-dazzle of the department store opening:

> Proving that movie people are still intrigued by movies. I hear the film was such a success that no one sneaked past the producers at the end, as is the custom. In fact, the guests stayed on so late that director George Cukor finally had to start dimming the lights—as a hint.[740]

Often, studio-organized parties were designed to honor a particular player. In the case of the party held by RKO Radio Pictures in November 1956, the honoree was Henry Fonda. Here is syndicated columnist Mike Connolly reporting on the event:

> RKO Production Chief Bill Dozier, an Omaha boy, threw a party for his old Omaha boyfriend, Hank Fonda, in the Beverly Hills Hotel's Rodeo Room, to signal the start of "Stage Struck," in which Hank is starring for Bill. When I arrived, Omaha's Nate Cutler, a photog, was taking a picture of Omaha's Fonda and another Omaha-born star, Dorothy McGuire, for an Omaha newspaper.

---

[738] "Top Turnout for 'Travels,'" *Los Angeles Times*, November 27, 1972.

[739] Ibid.

[740] Ibid.

The Baroness Afdera Francheti [sic] of Rome[741] flew out from New York for the party. She is Fonda's new heart and I am convinced they'll get married. She's about 25 (to Hank's 50) and, although half her fiancé's age, she's fast on her feet conversationally same as the foreign-born wives of Gregory Peck and Kirk Douglas—matter of fact, she even looks like Veronique[742] and Anne[743]—and is sleek and chic. Besides which she is very rich.[744]

These honors were not always dependent on film studios. Occasionally private institutions in Los Angeles would take it upon themselves to pay homage to a celebrity; if this celebrity fell within Dorothy's "old circle of friends," she would sometimes participate in the event.

One such event found Dorothy honoring her friend and colleague Gregory Peck in the context of a USC fraternity. This particular fraternity was Delta Kappa Alpha, the "cinema fraternity of USC." On the occasion of ΔKA's twenty-eighth anniversary, three film and television personalities

---

[741] Her last name was Franchetti, and her family was from Veneto rather than from Rome. Born in July 1931 in the town of Preganziol near Treviso and named after an Ethiopian volcano (her father Raimondo, 1889–1935, was a well-known explorer who loved Africa, and named Afdera's siblings Simba, Lorian and Raimondo Nanuk), the baroness became Henry Fonda's fourth wife in 1957; the couple divorced in 1961. Afdera enjoyed her status as socialite in New York society for many years; she also worked for *Vogue* magazine. At the time of writing this, she lived in London. The exoticism of names such as Afdera and Simba is not attributable only to Mr. Franchetti's career as an explorer. African and patriotic names were common during Italy's Fascist regime, and during Mussolini's dreams of an African expansion, which would lead to the Second Italo-Ethiopian War of 1935–1936. Here are some rather improbable names for female babies in that period: Addisabeba, Libia, Italia, and Benita.

[742] Peck married Veronique Passani (1932–2012) in 1956, and remained married to her until his death.

[743] Anne Buydens (born 1919) married Douglas in 1954.

[744] Mike Connolly, "Ketty Is Sexy, In 'Love to Love,'" *Palm Springs Desert Sun*, November 29, 1956.

were honored on January 30, 1966: Lucille Ball, Gregory Peck and Hal Wallis. Plaques were presented to the three personalities, and additional "Film Pioneer Awards" were given to early screenwriter Frances Marion and to Hollywood veteran Sol Lesser. Wallis could not attend, and his plaque was picked up by actress Shirley Booth. Bob Crane served as master of ceremonies. "A panel consisting of Miss Booth, writer Edward Anhalt and associate producer Paul Nathan was interviewed by the cinema faculty's Arthur Knight."[745]

Baroness Afdera Franchetti (left), soon to be the fourth Mrs. Henry Fonda, chats with Dorothy at a party taking place at the Beverly Hills Hotel in Beverly Hills, November 1956. This candid photograph was taken for King Features Syndicate by famed celebrity photographer Nat Dallinger (1911–2006).

---

[745] "USC Fraternity Cites 3 Film-TV Personalities," *Los Angeles Times*, February 1, 1966.

The two honorees in attendance were to answer questions fired at them by a panel. Lucille Ball was questioned by George Cukor, Henny Backus, Gale Gordon, and her husband, Gary Morton. Gregory Peck was interrogated by Dorothy, Jane Wyatt, and director King Vidor, who was also teaching at USC at the time.[746]

Another special tribute to a Hollywood personality took place at USC in April 1975, when representatives of Hollywood's film industry poured into the large ballroom of the alumni organization's Town and Gown building, to celebrate (posthumously) the great David Oliver Selznick. The tribute was sponsored by Friends of the USC Libraries. Director George Stevens commented during the event, "You might call this the Alumni of the Selznick University."[747]

As Joyce Haber of the *Los Angeles Times* put it, "The mind boggled, contemplating the 'students' [of such University]. They represented the entertainment, intellectual and financial worlds. One could have been attending a postgraduate seminar at Hollywood's MIT."

Just about everyone who could have been there, was there. A list would take up pages, but we can mention at least the categories: directors, producers, talent agents, publicists, former studio executives, USC administrators and film scholars, film students, and of course actors, Gregory Peck and Dorothy among them. Selznick's son, producer Daniel Selznick, was also present. Memories were shared by many, and film tests and clips were screened. Some of Selznick's famous memoranda were read, as well as excerpts from a twenty-five-foot-long telegram that Selznick publicist Paul McNamara had received once from his boss the day before a scheduled meeting between the two, announcing the imminent arrival of several memoranda.[748]

---

746 Ibid.

747 This quote and next: Joyce Haber, "Tribute to an Irreverent Titan," *Los Angeles Times*, April 8, 1975.

748 Joyce Haber, "Tribute to an Irreverent Titan," *Los Angeles Times*, April 8, 1975.

The University of Southern California was a regular haunt for Dorothy, and for events concerning the drama world of Los Angeles. On March 29, 1981, for example, Dorothy was among the presenters of the 12th Los Angeles Drama Critics Circle Awards at USC's Town and Gown building. Together with Dorothy, among others, were Gordon Davidson, Betty Garrett, John Guare, Charlton Heston, Edward James Olmos, and Gretchen Wyler.[749]

June 1951: John Swope squires Dorothy to yet another formal Hollywood reception. Press photo.

---

[749] "Stage Notes," *Los Angeles Times*, March 26, 1981.

Occasionally, a private party designed to honor a particular theatrical icon would find Dorothy on the guest list. One such party was given in honor of Helen Hayes and her son, James MacArthur. The event took place at Romanoff's restaurant (1941–1962) in Beverly Hills in June 1956.[750] Hayes, who was about to fly to London for the filming of her scenes in *Anastasia* (1956), was feted by the likes of Joan Crawford, Ann Rutherford, Donna Reed, and Dorothy.

Of course, any event celebrating Dorothy's close friends and collaborators found the actress present. Anything honoring Henry Fonda and Gregory Peck, for example, she was likely to attend, or actively participate in. One such event was the American Film Institute's 6th Life Achievement Award dinner honoring Fonda (1978). Four tiers (and 1,300-plus seats) of the International Ballroom of the Beverly Hilton Hotel were filled with guests and participants. Tickets were $350 per couple. The event, which was organized for airing on CBS, became a formal "special" on the actor. James Stewart, Dorothy, Bette Davis, Margaret Sullavan, Fred MacMurray and Kirk Douglas were among the friends.[751]

More celebrations for Fonda took place on Sunday, February 10, 1985, at a gala fund-raising event to celebrate the posthumous naming of a concert venue at 6126 Hollywood Boulevard. The former Music Box Theater (built in 1926), later renamed Guild Theatre, Fox Theatre, and Pix Theatre, had closed in 1977. The renovated venue re-opened in 1985 as the Fonda Theatre. Colleagues, friends, and fans of Mr. Fonda were on hand to pay tribute to Fonda the stage actor. James Stewart reminisced about his experiences with Fonda, as did Dorothy, John Forsythe, Gene Kelly, John Houseman, and David Rintels. The *Los Angeles Times* provided a brief description of the event:

---

[750] Of Michael Romanoff, Rosalind Russell wrote: ". . . Mike Romanoff, that famous pseudo prince [. . .] was a real prince in everything but blood lines, a dreamy man [. . .]. See: Rosalind Russell and Chris Chase, *Life Is A Banquet*, Random House, 1977.

[751] Paul Rosenfield, "Glamor, Glitter for Henry Fonda," *Los Angeles Times*, March 3, 1978.

Backed by the Rush Robinson Orchestra, Sunday's program was a hodgepodge of the sentimental and entertaining: from a touching welcome by Shirley [sic] Fonda (with stepchildren Peter and Jane, and grandchildren Vanessa and Troy in tow), to the glitzy song-and-dance of Debbie Reynolds, to impressions by George Kirby, crowd-pleasing numbers by Joe Williams and Linda Hopkins, a short reading from "Mr. Roberts," a buoyant sing-around-the-piano interlude by a dozen stars and a taped replay of Fonda's Kennedy Center Honors tribute in 1979.[752]

The reborn Fonda Theatre opened on February 26 with a production of the play *Twelve Angry Men* (1954) by Reginald Rose, in the film adaptation of which Fonda had starred in 1957. Among the cast members were Jack Klugman (also in the film), Ken Kercheval, Howard Hesseman, and John Randolph. The production was directed by Robert Lewis.

On March 9, 1989, the American Film Institute organized a gala tribute to Gregory Peck, and bestowed on him its 17th Life Achievement Award. The event took place at the Beverly Hilton Hotel in Beverly Hills, California, and was televised by NBC. Audrey Hepburn acted as host. An impressive roster of stars, directors, producers, and studio and television network heads were among the 1,300 in the audience, seated at tables. Friends and colleagues stood up in turn to pay tribute to Peck with their testimony; film clips covering Peck's vast career in pictures were screened; and George Stevens, Jr. presented AFI's Life Achievement Award. Dorothy's testimony was among the warmest and most generous, as *Los Angeles Times*' staff writer Paul Rosenfield recounted two days after the event:

---

[752] Janice Arkatov, "A Theater for Henry Fonda," *Los Angeles Times*, February 12, 1985.

The most expansive praise came from the women with whom he shared the screen.

"From the moment Greg arrived in Hollywood, he was an event," said Dorothy McGuire, who co-founded the La Jolla Playhouse with Peck. "Greg came here under the banner of David [O. Selznick]—and we already had the Duke [John Wayne], Coop [Gary Cooper], Jimmy [Stewart, who was at McGuire's table]. But the serape, the mantle—whatever stardom is—was immediately extended to Greg."[753]

Occasionally, John Swope attended parties and celebrations on his own, if Dorothy was busy elsewhere. In August 1972, we find John at a poolside party honoring director Lewis Milestone and his wife, Kendall, on the occasion of their thirty-seventh wedding anniversary. A motley crowd of happy campers included denizens of Old and New Hollywood both, as well as members of the theatrical, artistic, and academic communities. Among the Old Hollywood guests, Sam Jaffe and his wife, Bettye Ackerman, Anita Loos, and Jane Wyatt and her husband, Edgar Ward.[754]

The party that Dorothy attended on June 23, 1982, was not given to honor any particular celebrity, but an entire film studio. A huge firmament of veteran stars and studio executives gathered at UCLA to celebrate the donation of RKO Pictures' archives, 1928–1959, to the university. The historic occasion was televised.

Half ceremony and half party, the celebration boasted an impressive turnout. Aside from UCLA deans and librarians waxing enthusiastic about their research library (ranked fourth in the nation at the time, after

---

[753] Paul Rosenfield, "Gregory Peck Accepts AFI Life Award," *Los Angeles Times*, March 11, 1989.

[754] Joyce Haber, "Sinatra Reunion Transferred to Hawaii," *Los Angeles Times*, August 2, 1972.

Harvard, Yale, and UC Berkeley), a large contingent of RKO stars of all sizes and temperaments participated in the festivities, from Fred Astaire to Ginger Rogers, from Jane Greer and Guy Madison to Fay Wray, from Dorothy McGuire to Joel McCrea, from Jane Wyatt to Ralph Bellamy. The paperwork that was donated, reputed to be among the best-organized studio files in existence at the time, included original literary materials, scripts, contracts, correspondence, memos on casting and financing, personnel records, on-set shooting diaries, musical scores, press books, still photographs, and distribution records. The RKO archives filled 200 four-drawer filing cabinets, 100 trans-file drawers, and various other files, making the grand total an estimated 4,000 linear feet of documents. The material was compiled by Vernon Harbin, a 50-year RKO veteran.[755]

Dorothy at an undetermined event, circa 1982.

---

[755] See: Dave Smith, "RKO Pictures: Ah, Yes, They Remember It Well," *Los Angeles Times*, June 25, 1982.

Parties with international royalty were also on the Swopes' calendar occasionally. In November 1965, the whole of Los Angeles was fibrillating with anticipation at Princess Margaret of England and husband Lord Snowdon's three-day visit to the city. The princess visited several of L.A.'s landmarks including the newly-inaugurated Los Angeles County Museum of Art (LACMA), a Beverly Hills elementary school, and a department store. But Hollywood was the main theme of the visit. After a tour of movie studios and a visit to the set of Alfred Hitchcock's *Torn Curtain*, the couple attended a luncheon at Universal Studios. The city tour culminated in a gala "Imperial Ball" at the Hollywood Palladium in aid of the World Adoption International Fund.

On the princess's first evening in town (November 7), however, a small (only some ninety guests) dinner party was organized by the prime mover of the Countess of Snowdon's United States tour, Ms. Sharman Douglas.[756] The dinner party took place at the Bistro restaurant in Beverly Hills.[757] Here is a 1965 UPI syndicated article describing the antics at this "intimate" affair:

> Princess Margaret and husband Lord Snowdon [are] short on sleep after dancing until the wee hours at a party attended by Hollywood's own royalty [...].
>
> The princess, glittering in a cream silk evening dress, and Snowdon met Hollywood's movie elite last night at a dinner party at Beverly Hills at the Bistro restaurant. Hostess was Sharman Douglas, a close friend of the princess since childhood.

---

[756] Sharman Douglas was the daughter of Lewis Douglas, former US Ambassador to Britain.

[757] Kurt Niklas' The Bistro restaurant (established in 1963) was located at 246 N. Canon Drive in Beverly Hills.

The press release for this Associated Press wirephoto, November 8, 1965, recited: "Princess Margaret, wearing a creamy silk evening gown embroidered with gold and silver flowers, arrives last night for a party in her honor at the Bistro Restaurant in Beverly Hills, Calif., where she met scores of movie stars. At left is her husband, Lord Snowdon."

The royal couple did not leave the night spot until shortly before 3 a.m. PST.

Among the motion picture celebrities at the popular French restaurant were Gregory Peck, Fred Astaire, Natalie Wood, Dorothy McGuire, Jimmy Stewart, Frank Sinatra and Mia Farrow.

Princess Margaret danced with television's Dr. Kildare, Richard Chamberlain, and with an old and dear friend, comedian Danny Kaye.

Elizabeth Taylor and husband Richard Burton also attended. They arrived with Rosalind Russell in a 1932 English taxi.

The 90-odd guests, invited by Miss Douglas, were entertained by several of their number, including singer Judy Garland and a small ensemble.

One departing guest said, "it was a swinging party." Several others said the princess and her husband were "delightful ... charming."[758]

British aristocracy of a different echelon was at the center of the event that took place, again at the Bistro Restaurant of Beverly Hills, on Tuesday, August 24, 1976. The guest of honor was British socialite Margaret Campbell, Duchess of Argyll (1912–1993).

As Jody Jacobs of the *Los Angeles Times*' society column put it, "Around midnight, Tuesday, the Bistro's upstairs was rocking—literally. Bernie Richards was pounding out a combination of old favorites [. . .] on the piano. And the beautifully dressed guests were keeping a frenetic pace on the tiny parquet dance floor."[759]

---

[758] "Princess Maintains Dizzy Pace in L.A.," *San Mateo (CA) Times*, November 8, 1965.

[759] Jody Jacobs, "First-Nighters Begin the Evening Early," *Los Angeles Times*, August 29, 1976.

Host Gordon Greene Guiberson organized this as well as a previous fete for the visiting Duchess, who on this particular night was dressed in pale chiffon and jeweled satin pumps. Between the music and the dining, much dancing was done by some 120 guests, among whom were Gordon and Ann Getty, Mr. and Mrs. William Hamm, radio and film producer Carlton Alsop, and philanthropists Jules and Doris Stein; also present were Daphne and John Ireland, Rupert Allan, Jane Wyatt Ward, Dorothy McGuire, John Swope, and many prominent Angelinos, Santa Barbarans, San Franciscans, La Jollans, Pasadenans, Parisians, and Palm Beachites (Jacobs' terms, not mine).

Most of all, Dorothy, with or without her husband, was heavily involved in the promotion of Los Angeles' artistic, musical and theatrical advancement.

When the Music Center was created, Dorothy was one of the prominent citizens of Los Angeles who helped organize the many celebratory events surrounding its inauguration. In April 1967, she participated in the preparations for the inaugural week of the two new venues within the complex: the Ahmanson Theater and the Mark Taper Forum.

A grand-scale party was envisaged for the opening of the Mark Taper Forum, and a committee of celebrity "hostesses" was created for the event, composed of members or wives of members of the Performing Arts Council and the Music Center Group, and guest celebrities. Co-chairpersons of such committee were two old friends: Mrs. Gregory Peck and Mrs. John Swope.

A press luncheon/meeting of the committee and its chairpersons to announce the event took place at the Pavilion Restaurant of the Music Center; Christy Fox of the *Los Angeles Times* reported on April 7, 1967:

> There were more than a few discreet whispers and an unusual bit of head turning as the women were seated at a longish table headed by Olive (Mrs. George) Behrendt.

In a restaurant where opera stars, ballet dancers and world-renowned musicians are an almost everyday sight, this movie celebrity group was having an electric effect on others present. But a funny thing, the women themselves did not even realize it.

Veronique (Mrs. Gregory) Peck was so busy explaining to me about the hostesses for the dedication party of the Mark Taper Forum and Mrs. John Swope (actress Dorothy McGuire) was animatedly explaining who was going to be doing what, that they were hardly conscious of where they were.

Suddenly, handsome dark-haired Zubin Mehta, musical director of the Philharmonic Orchestra, walked by, recognized some of the women and stopped for a few moments chat. Then everyone in the rest of the room seemed to have heads on pivots!

[...] In the Behrendt party were Joanne Woodward (Mrs. Paul Newman), Jean (Mrs. Robert) Sully, Harriet (Mrs. Armand) Deutsch, Adri (Mrs. Robert) Butler, Mrs. Alan Lerner, Mrs. Gill Maass, Hope Lange (Mrs. Alan Pakula), Jane Wyatt (Mrs. Edgar Ward), Audrey (Mrs. Billy) Wilder, Dinah Shore, Jarma (Mrs. B.E. Bensinger ...

And among those to be added to this group for the glamour hostesses on Sunday [April 9] Evening's Mark Taper Forum opening are Cyd Charisse (Mrs. Tony Martin), Capucine, Betty (Mrs. Alfred) Bloomingdale, Mrs. Glenn Ford, Mrs. Samuel Goldwyn Jr., Vera Miles, Edie (Mrs. Lew) Wasserman, Jean Simmons, Natalie Wood, Ingrid (Mrs. Jerry) Ohrbach [sic], Anouk Aimee and, perhaps, the Redgrave sisters, Lynn and Vanessa, if they are in town.[760]

---

[760] Christy Fox, "Mehta Makes Heads Pivot at Pavilion Luncheon Fete," *Los Angeles Times*, April 7, 1967.

The circular Mark Taper Forum, 135 N. Grand Avenue, Los Angeles, seen here from the Ahmanson Theater in a 1971 post-inauguration press photograph, is, as the press release stated, "the smallest of the Music Center's venues, seating 750 patrons in a semi-circular arrangement. The theater was designed for intimate drama, recitals, chamber music, lectures and civic-cultural events. Surrounded by a shallow blue pool, with three walkways crossing the pool, the Forum features an abstract precast concrete mural on the upper level which suggests the form and movement of theatre." The venue was designed by Welton Becket and Associates. Photo and release: Music Center Operating Company.

At the dedication party itself, the cream of Los Angeles and Hollywood society was present. This is not the place for a complete list of attendees, but two names connected to Dorothy should be mentioned: Gene Kelly (of the former Actors' Company/La Jolla Playhouse) and Lloyd Nolan (Dorothy's co-star in *A Tree Grows in Brooklyn* and *Susan Slade*).

In fact, any important event concerning the theatrical life of Los Angeles in general or the Music Center in particular often found Dorothy participating, if nothing else as a guest. She was just that at the enormous party thrown by Mrs. Norman Chandler at the Mark Taper Forum, on Sunday, October 1, 1972, to honor Gordon Davidson (1933–2016), founding artistic director of Los Angeles' Center Theatre Group. Seven hundred friends, colleagues, and fans of Davidson's work and influence (Davidson was only thirty-nine when this party was given) attended the event. Adjectives such as "extremely talented" and many other laudatory superlatives were thrown around by speakers and well-wishers at the party. One noun, or name, was used for Davidson, and the person using it was Dorothy. Mary Lou Loper of the *Los Angeles Times* reported it:

> But it was Mrs. John Swope (Dorothy McGuire), appearing Saturday night on KCET's "Another Part of the Forest," who told Davidson toward the end of the party, "You are Mr. Charisma."[761]

In 1981, it was the gala premiere for the American Ballet Theater's Los Angeles season opening on January 26 that attracted a stellar cast of organizers, sponsors, patrons, and guests. The ballet was the Minkus/Petipa classic *La Bayadère* (1877), and the gala benefit supper dance that followed was attended by a Gotha of dance, theater and show business from both Coasts. Aside from American Ballet Theater artistes, organizers, and sponsors (Mikhail Baryshnikov among them), Music Center management and friends and former First Lady Betty Ford, some of the show business people attending were Gary Collins, the Kirk Douglases, 20th Century-Fox's Sherry Lansing, Marsha Mason, Dorothy, the Gavin McLeods, Dudley Moore with Susan Anton, Herbert Ross, and Gore Vidal.

---

[761] Mary Lou Loper, "Gordon Davidson in the Taper Spotlight," *Los Angeles Times*, October 3, 1972.

Music Center fundraisers usually found Dorothy involved, as organizer, speaker, or guest. For example, she was sometimes present at the annual Celebration Luncheon of the Music Center's Club 100, held at different locations over time to present Distinguished Artist Awards to 10 distinguished people. In 1983, the event was held at the gardens of Sally and Ben Kurtzman, and Dorothy was one of the 10 being honored.[762]

In October 1982, Dorothy was an enthusiastic guest and honorary co-chairman at the fundraising extravaganza organized by the Music Center's Center Theatre Group to honor William Ahmanson, president of the Ahmanson Foundation, and Robert Fryer, artistic director of the Ahmanson Theater. The event included the West Coast premiere of the film *The Right Stuff* at the Academy of Motion Picture Arts and Sciences' Samuel Goldwyn Theatre and an "all-American dessert and champagne feast." Tickets for the astronautically-themed gala evening were priced at $125 each, tax-deductible of course.

Anything theatrical, I was saying. Play premieres were also within the scope of the Swopes' social involvement in the life of Los Angeles.

One such event was the opening of a revival of Patrick Hamilton's *Angel Street* at the Los Angeles Biltmore Theatre on December 1, 1947. The play co-starred Gregory Peck and Laraine Day, and was co-produced by the La Jolla Actors' Company (see Part I, Chapter 9). Several members of the company attended, such as Dorothy, Joseph Cotten, and Mel Ferrer, as well as Mr. and Mrs. Freddie Brisson (Rosalind Russell), Walter Wanger and Joan Bennett, writers Stephen Ames and Harry Kurnitz, James Roosevelt, Charles Coburn, and Sylvia Kaye.

Another premiere and party, several years later, was the Los Angeles opening of Lanford Wilson's play *The Hot l Baltimore* at the Mark Taper Forum on August 2, 1973. A champagne reception was organized at the Biltmore Hotel in Downtown Los Angeles after the premiere. One of the "cute" ideas that the Biltmore's manager Bill Warholy had for the party

---

[762] Tia Gindick, "On View," *Los Angeles Times*, June 24, 1983.

was ordering a huge ice sculpture of the missing "e" in the play's title and placing it on a pedestal in the middle of the hotel's lobby. Another was providing replicas of the hotel's original room keys to first-nighters as they signed the register.

Some of the celebrities attending, just to drop some names: artist Don Bachardy, author Christopher Isherwood, Center Theatre Group artistic director Gordon Davidson, poet and playwright Jack Larson, actor Roscoe Lee Brown, and director François Truffaut. And here is what some of the female guests were wearing: Jacqueline Bisset, a tiered taupe jersey; Janet Dubois, a black dress and black horsehair hat; Elsa Lanchester, a coral robe; Margo Albert, a Japanese brocade robe; Mrs. Armand Deutsch, an aqua and white Adolfo knit; Mrs. Armand Oppenheim, a white cherry strewn navy blazer and white pants; and Dorothy, a peasant smock and pants.[763]

Then there were the visual arts. In November 1971, the UCLA Art Council honored Dr. Nelson Ikon Wu, Chinese and American scholar and professor of Asian art, by giving a party to celebrate Wu as the recipient of that year's Art Council lectureship. A Gotha of Los Angeles businessmen, socialites, academics, artists, and patrons of the arts was present at the party, which was organized by Jane Wyatt Ward on behalf of the council. The event took place at the Bistro restaurant in Beverly Hills. Among the film people attending, director William Wyler and Dorothy. John Swope introduced the guest of honor, who then gave a short speech.[764]

Gallery openings were also on the Swopes' list, even when John's photography was not involved. In 1972, for example, we find the Swopes attending a special invitational champagne preview of the latest exhibit organized by the Egg and the Eye, a crafts gallery-restaurant; young Is-

---

[763] See: Jody Jacobs (Times Society Editor), "First-Nighters Crack Case of Missing 'E,'" *Los Angeles Times*, August 6, 1973.

[764] Jody Jacobs, "Art Council Fete for Dr. Wu," *Los Angeles Times*, November 17, 1971. As usual, Ms. Jacobs used a lot of ink to write about what everyone was wearing.

raeli Consul General Yeheskel Carmel served as host/master of ceremonies. The Israeli-themed exhibit was meant to honor the twenty-fourth anniversary of the State of Israel. Many important city players were in attendance, together with academics and artists, and John and Dorothy Swope.[765]

Dorothy never won an Academy Award, and was only nominated once (for *Gentleman's Agreement*, 1947). Occasionally, however, she was chosen for other awards. One such honor was bestowed on her on December 14, 1984, when the American Cinema Awards Foundation honored four Hollywood stars with its second annual American Cinema Award for Distinguished Achievement in Film. The awards had been established by the foundation to recognize "those individuals who have been responsible for creating a body of work that has left an indelible impression in the minds of the public."[766] The previous year, Dorothy had been among the 200-some Hollywood guests at the awards ceremony.[767]

The 1984 ceremony and party took place in the Grand Ballroom of the Beverly Wilshire Hotel; Tristan Rogers served as host. The four honorees were Dorothy, Robert Mitchum, Robert Preston (her former co-star in *The Dark at the Top of the Stairs*), and Jane Wyman. Interior designer Robert Sherr designed the party *décor* "around a pink, red, gold and silver theme (masses of balloons, curls of pink motion picture film, and plenty of red, pink and white flowers donated by Conroy's)."[768]

Both during her marriage to John and after it, Dorothy was also known to attend parties at the homes of prominent citizens of Los Angeles who were not directly involved in the arts. Such was the case with the

[765] Sharon Fay Koch, "Israeli Consul at Preview of Exhibit," *Los Angeles Times*, April 13, 1972.

[766] "Four to Receive Cinema Awards," *Los Angeles Times*, December 13, 1984.

[767] American Cinema Awards Foundation ad, *Palm Springs (CA) Desert Sun*, January 21, 1984.

[768] *Los Angeles Times* society listings, December 13, 1984.

two parties taking place during the spring of 1981. The hosts were Gerald and Virginia Oppenheimer, Los Angeles benefactors (Gerald's parents were Jules and Doris Stein, who, together or separately, had contributed extraordinarily to medical, artistic, and charity causes in Los Angeles, even creating foundations of their own). Here is the *Los Angeles Times'* social column recounting those parties:

> Gerald Oppenheimer has a new toy, a computer he puts to work on serious affairs during the day, and to more frivolous affairs in the evening when he and Virginia are entertaining.
>
> For two recent parties Gerry was doing his guests' biorhythm charts. But since that requires a true birthdate, some of the guests, and Virginia, balked. "You know," commented the hostess, "it's the men who really object to telling their age. When Vladimir Horowitz was here he waited until everyone had left the room before he whispered the date into Gerry's ear.
>
> Still, the baby computer was kept busy every night as guests like Mrs. Clark Gable, Martha and Jimmy Kilroe, [. . .] Frances Bergen, Val Arnold, Rupert Allan, Mary and Brad Jones, the Anthony Duquettes, Mrs. Jules Stein (Gerry's mother), Mervin and Kitty Kilroe, Elsie and Frank Pollock, Virginia and Si Ramo, Pascal and James Regan, Dorothy McGuire, Frank McCarthy and many more lined up to find out what the future of their mental and physical status was.[769]

And then, of course, there were assorted benefit events. Dorothy was often involved in charitable efforts. As early as May 29, 1956, for example, we find her taking part, as one of a star-studded group of actors (Charles Boyer, Rory Calhoun, Charles Coburn, Joan Crawford, Tony

---

769 "More Parties," *Los Angeles Times*, April 5, 1981.

Curtis, Henry Fonda, Kathryn Grayson, Charlton Heston, Judy Holliday, Danny Kaye, Burt Lancaster, Angela Lansbury, Jerry Lewis, Shirley MacLaine, Fred MacMurray, Guy Madison, Dean Martin, Ann Miller, Debbie Reynolds, Jane Russell, James Stewart, Ed Sullivan, Robert Wagner, and many more), in a large benefit variety show to raise funds for the Boys Club of L.A. The event was advertised in the *Los Angeles Times* as "Wonder World Premiere" ("Lights! Glamour! Excitement! Bleachers! . . . Stars. . . Stars. . . Stars . . . and More Stars . . . in person!") and took place at the Fox Wilshire Theatre.

On May 24, 1984, Dorothy participated in the charity Shooting Star Ball at the Palm Springs Racquet Club. The event, benefiting the American Cinema Awards Foundation, was a busy evening of ethnic buffets, casino gambling, star memorabilia auctions, and a concert by former MGM singing star Kathryn Grayson. Joseph Cotten and wife Patricia Medina (who was the chairwoman of the event) sat at a table with Dorothy. Other guests included Marsha Hunt, Virginia Mayo, and Martha Scott.[770]

Dorothy loved animals, and contributed to several charities, such as the "Fund for Animals" and "Actors and Others for Animals." An example: October 1975 finds John and Dorothy co-chairmen of the benefit art exhibition entitled "Stars on Canvas." Hollywood art dealer Gregg Juarez contributed his gallery. The exhibition, sporting paintings by the likes of Claudette Colbert, Peter Falk, Henry Fonda, George Gershwin, Edith Head, Katharine Hepburn, Charlton Heston, Alfred Hitchcock, Rosalind Russell, Claire Trevor, and even Winston Churchill, ran from October 22 to November 20; its proceeds went to the Fund for Animals. Co-chairmen with the Swopes were the Grant Tinkers (Mary Tyler Moore) and the Steve Allens (Jayne Meadows). An invitational benefit preview took place on October 21 from 6 to 9 p.m. (with tax-deductible donations at $25 each).[771] Reporter/writer/critic Cleveland Amory, founder and presi-

---

770 See Allene Arthur, "Gang Gets Together, Puts on Show in Barn," *Desert Sun* (Palm Springs, CA), May 25, 1984.

771 Joyce Haber, "VIPs' Art Goes Out to Animals," *Los Angeles Times*, September 29, 1975.

dent of the Fund for Animals, announced that the highlight of the benefit event was to be Gloria Swanson. Not only was Swanson's sculpture of her own head one of the major exhibits on display, the actress, in her capacity as sculptor, would also be present to sculpt the head of the highest bidder.

Another example: on January 18, 1978, the day after the opening of Josh Logan's show *A Musical Evening* at Studio One's Backlot, Josh and Nedda Logan entertained pals old and new at a party in order to raise money for Actors and Others for Animals. James Stewart, friend of both the Logans and the Swopes, acted as unofficial master of ceremonies. Among the guests: Lucie Arnaz with Walter Willison, George and Joan Axelrod, Freddie Brisson (two years after wife Rosalind Russell's passing) with Gloria Romanoff, Armand and Harriet Deutsch, Richard Harris and his wife Ann Terkel, Merle (Oberon) and Rob Wolders, Gloria Stewart, Dorothy and John Swope, Betty White with Allen Ludden, and Audrey and Billy Wilder.[772]

Whether for the Fund for Animals, Actors and Others for Animals, the Boys Club of Los Angeles, or the Times Camp Fund, Dorothy (or the Swopes, while John was still alive) was always ready to contribute, with time, work, and money. For instance, she and Jennifer Jones volunteered their time at the UCLA Medical Center in 1966–1967, and Dorothy made yearly contributions to the Times Camp Fund until 2000, the year before her passing.

Environmental causes also held a special place in her heart. Whether as simple guest, for example at the 1974 Expo in Spokane, Washington, the city hosting the first World Environment Day celebrations, or as contributor, Dorothy was ready to take an interest in the planet she lived on. On the occasion of the Los Angeles bicentennial, which coincided with the opening of Lane Bryant's 200th store in the Sherman Oaks Galleria, the company donated 200 trees, to be planted throughout the San Fer-

---

[772] See Jody Jacobs, "A Showcase House Tour," *Los Angeles Times*, January 20, 1978.

nando Valley. In addition, more than 1,000 pine tree seedlings were given away to those present at the ceremonies. The dedication of the first tree was made by Dorothy. This happened in 1980.[773]

At the Spokane, Washington, Expo, Dorothy talks with Elizabeth Sales, a hostess at the Philippines Pavilion. Press photo, June 27, 1974.

After John Swope's death, Dorothy's social activities abated somewhat, but by no means completely. Even in the last decade of her life, Dorothy enjoyed being out of the house, and certain established habits persisted. She still enjoyed going to the movies, particularly to screenings at the Academy of Motion Picture Arts and Sciences, where she could be among old friends, colleagues and acquaintances.[774] She enjoyed the oc-

[773] "Trees mark Lane Bryant's 200th Store," *Los Angeles Times*, November 27, 1980.

[774] During my first visit to the Swopes in 1977, Dorothy took me to see an Academy screening of Disney's *Candleshoe*, starring Helen Hayes and David Niven. She tended to like

casional party, too, and regular dinners away from home. She still grocery-shopped at Gelson's,[775] and—at least until her ability to walk deteriorated to cane, walker and then wheelchair status in her last years—walked rather than drove as much as she could.

In her last decade, once the razzle-dazzle of fame and Hollywood had waned, those established habits assumed the status of unassailable rituals. Sunday night was *60 Minutes* night; family and friends, including her dog Swopie, would gather around the television with her, to the accompaniment of pizza and beers (but she preferred white wine in the evenings). Friday night was dinner night, most often at one of Dorothy's favorite restaurants, such as El Coyote,[776] a "hole-in-the-wall" Mexican diner Jim Fernald had discovered on Beverly Boulevard. As Fernald puts it:

> The restaurant was one of these historic places from a different Los Angeles time. There was always a long line of people waiting to get in. It was cheap and it was old. The owner either knew Dorothy from the old days or knew who she was, anyway, and no matter who Dorothy was with, her party would always be able to go to the table directly, without standing in line at all. Dorothy, who was using a cane in those years, would wave her cane to the people standing in line. Whether those people recognized her or not, I think they accepted the fact that she was a VIP. Dorothy ate little. We were always

---

"nice" movies, and she admired Ms. Hayes greatly.

[775] During that first week of mine with the Swopes, Dorothy took me to Gelson's too. "The supermarket of the stars," she remarked to me with a big grin and a touch of irony, but with undeniable joy: she herself could be quite childlike in her enthusiasm for Hollywood, and was never a cynic.

[776] El Coyote Mexican Café opened on March 5, 1931. Before moving to its permanent location at 7312 Beverly Boulevard, the restaurant was situated on First Street and La Brea. Source: the restaurant's website.

pushing her to eat more. She would give half her dinner to her dog. She did like her white wine, however.⁷⁷⁷

El Coyote Mexican Café, side view. From the blog of Oak boutique, New York City.

One day a week was reserved for answering fan mail, of which there were stacks and stacks. As Fernald puts it, "It was like Christmas every day: that mailbox was always full."⁷⁷⁸

Even in a wheelchair, and to the very end, Dorothy was "sharp as a tack" mentally (as friend Dwight Holing puts it), and the life of the party. Always proud and enthusiastic about her son's photographic work, she never missed his exhibitions, and, wheelchair or not, navigated the artistic crowds like a pro. As Holing explains:

---

777 Fernald (2017), op. cit.

778 Ibid.

Gallery openings tend to attract a younger group of people, and she just always seemed to blossom under those conditions.[779]

Dorothy's ability to be kind and sociable had not diminished. She was plagued with some physical handicaps in her last years, but she was spared the indignity of mental and social deterioration.

---

[779] Holing (2017), op. cit.

Part II: *Coagula*[780]

---

[780] Present imperative of the transitive Latin verb *'coagulare'* (coagulàre): to coagulate, to clot, to make solid, to collect and put together, to reunite, to synthesize.

Southern belle: Dorothy, armed with a fan and a Southern accent, charms a blindfolded panel of showbiz experts with cryptic answers to their questions in *What's My Line?*, 1954. Screen capture.]

1. Mysteries and Un-definitions

Bennett Cerf: I have an idea I know you personally. Do I know you personally, besides seeing you on screen and on stage?
Dorothy (affecting a Southern accent): Well, Sugar, not nearly enough. Not nearly enough.
Swope family friend and publisher Bennett Cerf, blindfolded, interrogating Dorothy, mystery guest on the television program *What's My Line?* (July 25, 1954)

When examining a person like Dorothy McGuire, or indeed when examining any person at all, famous or not, one sometimes forgets that contrast does not mean conflict. For there is undoubtedly contrast between the different personality traits one may discover in a person when one tries to go even slightly beyond the superficial layers of one's initial understanding of such person.

In life as in films, a typecasting takes place in judging people, whereby one tries to pin one or more adjectives (or, worse, nouns) on them that synthetically describe their nature, or their main characteristics. This determination, however, often occurs too quickly, before a real examination has been carried out; in scientific terms, before sufficient data have been examined and weighed. So eager are we to arrive at a "definition" of a person quickly, that we often forget that a definition should be a synthesis of something that has come before. One should arrive at a definition (a concept) after carrying out another process altogether, for a definition is a reduction to essentials; and a reduction implies starting with something larger and reducing that to a smaller size by eliminating all accidentals. Sometimes, such examination is skipped: our first impression of, or prejudice about, a person is elevated to the status of definition.

In the interest of speed, economy, and, let's face it, laziness, one treats people as if they were simple entities, in order to arrive at a quick "definition" of them. We speak of "a nice person" or of "a jerk" with the same nonchalant ease with which we define a comfortable chair, a shiny piece of fabric, or a color. Most often, this glib casualness results, not in a definition of people, but merely in a description of our superficial impression of, or reaction to, people. Similarly, the fact that "a nice sunset" is nice has little to do with our intrinsic understanding of a sunset; it is, rather, the acknowledgment of our feeling about our experience of a sunset.

This simplification leads, in most cases, to the perpetuation of a cliché (one cliché for each person). The press and the public at large seize on that cliché and only elaborate on it in order to confirm or deny facts related to it. Even biographies often do this, with the best of intentions, only exploring the details and confirmations of that initial cliché, or occasionally coming to life when a "dirty secret" is discovered and needs to be corroborated. This is doubly true in the Age of the Internet, where judgments are made employing something that *New Yorker* writer Naomi Fry has called "the quick meanness of the Internet that tends to flatten a person's story to a caricature, even if it is motivated by all the right reasons in the world."[781]

Some people might be "simpler" than others, or might appear simpler than others; but that simplicity is deceptive, and only holds true until we discover something that contradicts our simple understanding of them

---

[781] Naomi Fry, "The Great Sadness of Ben Affleck," *New Yorker*, March 24, 2018.

and confuses us. As an extreme example, and this is a common occurrence in the news, the young man next door is "a nice man" and "a polite neighbor" only until he slaughters his entire family with a kitchen knife. Then, he becomes a mystery—too late, for he ought to have been a mystery to us from the start.[782]

The more one knows a person, the more difficult it should be to define them, for such knowledge should lead to complexity and contrast rather than to simplification.

We began this discussion of Dorothy by stating that she was a nice person, and that many of the people who met her thought of her as a nice person. With some justification, for she was indeed nice. As a starting point, that is acceptable, though generic; as a conclusion or determination, it is a meager, simplistic finding indeed. There was much more to her person (as there is to any person, whether "nice" or "nasty") than that universally recognized niceness, and it is in an effort to do justice to her complexity, and not to find fault with her, that I have looked for contrasting aspects of Dorothy.

In terms of her screen persona, one does not have to look very far, or very deep, to find characteristics that are in contrast (but not in conflict) with that niceness; one has only to go back to Dorothy's debut as a film actress to find a different image of her. In *Claudia* (1943), Dorothy's character gave her a chance to expose certain raw nerves that would gradually disappear (apparently) from her later portrayals. The Claudia-ness of Dorothy was as much part of her as the "niceness" that would characterize her in later years. And it does not take any great leap of intuition to posit that, psychologically, in *Claudia* Dorothy was expressing parts of herself.

In fact, the character of Claudia being the "admirable amalgamation" that it is, it could be said to contain, one way or another, the germs of all the future characters that Dorothy would essay. Though one might have

---

[782] He becomes a mystery, that is, in the best of cases. Otherwise, he becomes a serial killer or a devious, disturbed individual in our eyes, and nothing else. That definition too is incomplete, and a cliché.

to look harder, and deeper, for some of these traits than others, *in potentia* Claudia contained the sharp, confident intelligence of Cathy Lacey (*Gentleman's Agreement*, 1947), the irony of Ann Winslow (*Mister 880*, 1950), the sophistication of Miss Frances (*Three Coins in the Fountain*, 1954), the cynical wittiness of Deborah Patterson (*Callaway Went Thataway*, 1951), the bravery of Mary Walker (*Cavalcade of America*, "A Medal for Miss Walker," 1953), the free-spirited humor and sentiment of Pat Ruscombe (*Till the End of Time*, 1946), the ruthless calculation of Lynn Cameron (*Lux Radio Theatre*, "A Blueprint for Murder," 1954), and the Pollyanna optimism of Anna-Rose Twinkler (*Hallmark Playhouse*, "Christopher and Columbus," 1949). All these were aspects that Dorothy could find in herself.

Those colors, those aspects that occasionally contradicted Dorothy's warm "niceness," would be gradually obscured over the years. In the public's perception, perhaps to a certain extent in Dorothy's own perception as well, those colors were extinguished little by little, leaving only her niceness. Significantly, her last major film appearance was as the Virgin Mary (*The Greatest Story Ever Told*, 1965), a speechless, symbolic role in which all realism (all humanity) had been drained from the character until what remained was a stylized religious icon. An abstract paragon of niceness.

Personally as well as professionally, niceness was Dorothy's dominant trait. As Tovah Feldshuh, Dorothy's co-star in *Another Part of the Forest* (1982), put it:

> I remember the round pools of her big angelic eyes. Dorothy had these big "tool" eyes, these blue eyes that were *tools of goodness*. She was ethereal, she was thin, she was graceful, she was gracious, she was soft-spoken, she was refined and she was kind. She was generous and big-hearted, very kind to strangers, and very kind to younger actors. So of course she would be compared to an angel: we're already in angel-land with her.[783]

---

[783] Feldshuh (2017), op. cit.

Dorothy was generous in all kinds of contexts, both private and theatrical. Hellman commented in his profile of Dorothy:

> This sort of generosity persists in Dorothy, who is too impersonal for the usual theatrical jealousies. For example, when Phyllis Thaxter, now the Chicago Claudia, was trying out for this role, Dorothy cheerfully allowed her to take her part in a Broadway performance of *Claudia*—even though according to the Golden-McGuire contract she would not have had to do this.[784]

Still, even in later years there was a place within Dorothy where those contrasting colors existed and could be retrieved, regardless of the fact that she had stopped tapping it. That place existed in Dorothy the person as well as in Dorothy the actress.

"*You make up your mind too quickly about people, Mr. Green,*" says Dorothy's character, Cathy Lacey, to Gregory Peck's Philip Green in the film *Gentleman's Agreement* (1947). In that film, the statement referred to the film's topic, prejudice. In general terms, that statement could be—should be—extended to our entire lives, and to our relationships with people. It should be extended without limit, to the last, to the bitter end. We may spend a lifetime with a person and still feel that we are on the outside looking in (we may spend a lifetime with ourselves and still feel like outsiders to ourselves); this we should remember before drawing any conclusions, before reaching any definitions of people. As the transformed Tracy Lord says in Philip Barry's *The Philadelphia Story*, "*The time to make up your mind about people, is never.*"[785]

---

[784] Hellman, "McGuire" (1941), op. cit., 125.

[785] Philip Barry, *The Philadelphia Story*, Samuel French, 1969, 77 (Act II, Scene II).

2. *Turangalîla* I: A Streak of Bravery[786]

When I look back at my early meetings with Dorothy during our acquaintance, I can recall my surprise at discovering that her personality was not confined to those "nice" colors that she undoubtedly possessed and displayed. Indeed, I can recall my surprise at discovering that she even *had* a distinctive personality: that she was a sprightly, ironic, perceptive, outspoken, down-to-earth woman with an elfin, hard-to-define quirkiness to her. I was surprised, in other words, to discover that her personality did not correspond exactly to those naïve, helpless, saintly goody-two-shoes characters she had so often played in her career.

One day, Dorothy told me an anecdote in her living room, and I wish I could remember to whom it referred, whether to Selznick or Zanuck. The gist of the story I remember clearly, however: it involved a studio mogul attempting to "bribe" Dorothy by delivering a luxury car at her

---

[786] The word *turangalîla* is a composite of two Sanskrit words: *turanga*, meaning the passage of time, movement, rhythm, speed; and *lila*, a complex idea that cannot be translated exactly, but denotes the joyful creative activity of the divine (the "play," or song, of the creative force), the interplay whereby the transcendent becomes immanent: the joyful act of the *Logos* (the Word, or "Verbum") as it creates the forms of the world, or ideas through matter. The composite word was created by composer Olivier Messiaen (1908–1992) as a title for his *Turangalîla-Symphonie* (1949).

doorstep; it also involved Dorothy driving the car back to the studio upon discovering it, marching into the mogul's office and dropping the car keys onto his desk, with the words "No, thank you" (she acted that part out for me). The reasons for the mogul's gesture escape me, but the image the story left with me was that of a woman endowed not only with a healthy ambition but also with a *steely integrity*—an adamantine rectitude: another trait one does not readily associate with Dorothy.

The same determination and willfulness that made Dorothy march instead of walk into a studio head's office was responsible for her endurance as a star, and for her persistence in searching for Broadway fame during her lean years in New York (1937–1940). An episode that occurred during those disheartening years stands out, and tells the story of her magnificent resourcefulness and initiative. Here is Dorothy herself recounting it in 1976:

> I marched into Spaulding Brothers sporting goods store on Fifth Avenue[787] and insisted on seeing the president. I don't know where I found the courage but I was ushered in and I said firmly, "What you need is a Spaulding Girl who'll wander about the store displaying different getups in the different departments." I wasn't a model type but I must've arrested his attention.
>
> I got the job—at $25 an hour, which astonished us both, me for asking it, him for paying it.
>
> There was a huge clock outside the store and I can't tell you how slowly the day passed. My hours were 10 to 4 and the clock hands seemed not to move at all. I abandoned the job very quickly. If you must be an actress, nothing else satisfies you.[788]

---

[787] Spalding & Bros., 520 Fifth Avenue, New York.

[788] Champlin, "Sensitivity" (1976), op. cit.

The above episode shows how strong Dorothy could be, and how grand and theatrical. *Chutzpah* was another element in her psychological makeup, one that probably did not vanish once fame was achieved but was only shaded more carefully and used when needed.

When we think of a "nice," positive person—the way many have thought of Dorothy—we often think of a soft-willed person rather than of a person of action, as if the two qualities, of willfulness and niceness, were somehow in contradiction with each other. The adjective "willful" often suggests a stubborn persistence in doing what one wishes, especially in rebellion to authority. In other words, it suggests selfishness. Those two qualities, however, can co-exist, and be of service to each other. After all, "willful" has a positive aspect, whose synonyms might be "purposeful," "deliberate," "self-willed," "steadfast" and "adamant," all words that can be associated with a positive, ethical way of behaving. Being willful in this positive sense means having initiative, or achieving mastery of one's will impulses; it means exercising one's will, and being ready to take action where action is needed. It is in this sense that philosopher, esotericist and founder of Anthroposophy Rudolf Steiner meant the word when he designed the five "fundamental" or "supplementary" daily exercises that he prescribed to the pupils of his esoteric school in Dornach, Switzerland. The exercise having to do with the will, or with "control of our actions," was the second. [789]

These strong character traits, of irony, intelligence and strength of will, Dorothy was able to use to create some of her harder, less positive characters. In film, two roles come to mind: the cynical Deborah Patterson in *Callaway Went Thataway* (1951) and the haughty Emily Pennypacker in *The Remarkable Mrs. Pennypacker* (1959).

In real life, those traits often allowed Dorothy to take charge in situations that found others around her stymied. An incident that occurred

---

[789] See: Rudolf Steiner, *Six Steps in Self-Development: The 'Supplementary Exercises,'* Selected and compiled by Ates Baydur, Rudolf Steiner Press, 2010, 17–26.

on the evening of the press performance of *The Night of the Iguana* at New York's Circle in the Square theater in 1976 made the rounds of American newspapers, adding yet more glory to Dorothy's person. Here is a report from the *Asbury Park Press* of New Jersey:

> [That night] Dorothy McGuire [. . .] proved to the audience that she was a real star—before the play even began. The performance was delayed, and a woman in the crowd began to shout ["I want to see Dorothy McGuire! I came to see Dorothy McGuire!"].[790] Ushers began to hover anxiously, not knowing quite what to do. Security people closed in, causing the woman to protest loudly that she "loved Dorothy McGuire" and wasn't about to leave the theater until she had seen her.
>
> After the first act had been delayed more than a half hour (with the audience becoming increasingly restless and the management clearly undecided on what to do), suddenly Dorothy McGuire walked onstage and headed straight up the stairs—towards her vociferous (and as it turned out, very inebriated) fan. She gripped the woman's hand and propelled her toward center stage. She asked the woman's name and proceeded to introduce her: "Ladies and gentlemen," she said, "this is . . . a fellow human being."
>
> That gesture completely wowed the audience, because it was so much in character for Ms. McGuire's onstage self, Hannah Jelkes. Hannah, a New England spinster, has one of the play's most touching lines: "Nothing human disgusts me unless it is violent or unkind."[791]

---

[790] Exact wording of the woman's shouts from a 1982 interview with Dorothy McGuire; see Rosenfeld, "Fate" (1982), op. cit.

[791] Lillian Africano, "Big Stars Shine for Holidays," *Asbury Park (CT) Press*, December 30, 1976.

It must be noted that, though the gesture of taking the offensive drunk audience member by the hand and leading her center stage was definitely theatrical, and muscular, Dorothy was able to turn that negative event upside down to expose its positive side, and to effect a compassionate, welcoming reaction to it, by introducing the woman to the audience as "a fellow human being" (according to the *Detroit Free Press*, Dorothy also gave the woman "a hug and a kiss").[792] Even in the face of an emergency, Dorothy could not have been any nicer. But strong-willed, and demonstrating plenty of initiative in action. "I'm not thrown," Dorothy would state about her personality in 1982.[793]

In perusing the press devoted to Dorothy during the latter half of her career, and in listening to the testimony of those who knew her, one usually encounters adjectives such as "nice," "graceful," "warm," and "genteel." Occasionally, there are surprises. In 1967, in an article that was not about Dorothy but about her husband John, one meets the adjective "vivacious." And in his 1941 profile of Dorothy, Geoffrey T. Hellman (1907–1977), a regular writer for the *New Yorker* from 1929 until the year before his death, described a quality of her personality using a curious combination of words:

> This sort of whimsical quaintness, which is without affectation, has inspired McGuire intimates to devise such nicknames for her as "McGoo" and "Frou."[794]

Those adjectives and nouns are something of a jolt because they appear to contradict the narrow definitions that were given of Dorothy through most of her career, especially when describing her roles on screen;

---

[792] "Actress Saves Day as Kook, Crowd Erupt," *Detroit Free Press*, December 29, 1976.

[793] Rosenfield, "Fate" (1982), op. cit.

[794] Hellman, "McGuire" (1941), op. cit., 126.

in fact, there is no contradiction. Adjectives like "elfin" and "pixieish" had been used to describe the actress when she had first appeared in *Claudia* (1943), and to refer both to the role and to Dorothy herself. Here is Hedda Hopper in 1947:

> Writers frequently employ the word "elfin" when writing about Dorothy. But it doesn't cover the sense of her capricious charm. She has an instinctive dislike for trodden ways, conventional gestures, hackneyed conversation, and mobilized fashions.[795]

Those adjectives and nouns expressed two things, primarily: an undefinable, almost magical quality of Dorothy's, and a puzzlement in those who studied her. Just as the character of Claudia was mercurial and multi-faceted, so Dorothy was effervescent and somewhat unpredictable, evanescent and atypical. The best definitions of her were those that did not define. In fact, some of that puzzlement might have been due to the apparent contradiction those observers found in a person who was so strong-willed (who knew what she wanted) and yet so irreducibly nice. Gradually, those lively appellatives ceased to appear in the press, giving way to easier, treaclier definitions.

Raymond Massey, who co-starred with Dorothy in *The Night of the Iguana* in 1975–1976, unwittingly came closest to an important insight about his co-star and her contrasting traits when he wrote, about the character she was portraying, that she was "wise-innocent, fragile but strong as Hercules, tender but iron-willed [. . .]."[796] It was in those oxymoronic juxtapositions that a mysterious core of *Dorothy's* own personality lay. Just as Hannah Jelkes, her character in *Iguana*, was puzzling and interesting because she was simultaneously wise and innocent, fragile and strong, and

---

795 Hopper, "Independence" (1947), op. cit.

796 Massey (1979), op. cit., 411.

tender and iron-willed, Dorothy was remarkable for having reconciled those apparently opposite traits harmoniously as a person. And it is probably this deep communion between character and actress, between art and life, that acted as a fountainhead of insight for what was arguably Dorothy's most spectacularly complex theater performance ever (see Part I, Chapter 15).

Equally searing was drama critic Dan Sullivan's appraisal of a special balance he saw in Dorothy (again in *The Night of the Iguana*). That balance incarnates a concept similar to the one expressed by Massey, and is worth repeating. Whenever I read the following, I do not think of Hannah Jelkes; I think of the Dorothy I knew:

> Miss McGuire has the balances of the part just right without making us aware that there's any problem striking them. Shyness and toughness, delicacy and frankness, chastity and a full commitment to life don't seem opposites or even separate qualities here. They are all part of a light-footed girl from [Omaha] who knows what is for her in this world and what is not—and knows what is for you, too, if you'll listen to her (which she doesn't insist on).[797]

Just as the furnishings in Dorothy's house at 121 Copley Place could, at first glance, seem eclectic and disconnected from each other but ultimately formed a unitary composite picture that made sense, especially if you knew Dorothy, so Dorothy was strangely able to balance contrasting traits of her personality that, in someone else, might have been hopelessly contradictory.

While speaking about the inner life of humans, or more specifically about the contrasting, confused feelings present in the breasts of humans, Italian novelist, editorialist, music critic, and lecturer Alessandro Baric-

---

[797] Sullivan (1976), op. cit.

co—during his extraordinary 2016 "Mantova Lectures"—referred to the sign that was posted outside the lions' cages in ancient Roman gladiator arenas, a sign that announced "*Hic Sunt Leones*" (Here there are lions). In Baricco's colorful metaphor, if one were to be truthful about one's inner life, one would have to acknowledge that the correct answer to the routine question "How are you?" should be "*Hic sunt leones.*" Our inner universe is not an ordered one, but a wild, hungry one. Somehow, Dorothy had tamed many, if not all, of those lions.

In her private life, Dorothy could be more playful, and more capricious, or vivacious, in her characterization than she was ever allowed to be on the screen. Dorothy was a cheerful, sunny woman; she was also a strong, determined woman, with a propensity for joy and irony (a trait that her son Mark inherited from her), and a phenomenal sense of initiative (action).

That Dorothy was a strong woman with a sense of initiative and a streak of bravery in her, despite her enormous niceness, is apparent—if one wishes to look for symbols—from her handwriting. That handwriting, more akin to an ancient hieroglyphic than to a clean mode of communication, was an irregular, enthusiastic scrawl that contained and expressed a boundless vitality bordering on nervousness. I do not think, however, that nervousness was one of Dorothy's traits; rather, her handwriting expressed a strength of character and an explosive life force that was only intermittently present in her fictional roles. The sample below, from a postcard Dorothy wrote to me in 1977, should give the reader an idea.

When I first met Dorothy, I was a naïve and immature eighteen-year-old, so it is understandable that I would not know much about human beings. Still, it was probably excessively juvenile of me to be so surprised that Dorothy as a live person was different from Dorothy McGuire the film star. One "new" trait I discovered in her was intelligence. In this respect, Dorothy was indeed vivacious, and her vivaciousness was a surprise to me, as it must have been to the journalist who met her and used that adjective in 1967. Too few of her film roles after *Claudia* allowed this characteristic to emerge in its full glory, with the result that the film-going public was deprived of one essential piece of the puzzle. Given the roles that Dorothy was famous for, the concept that the public was able to have of the actress based on her film performances was an incomplete one.

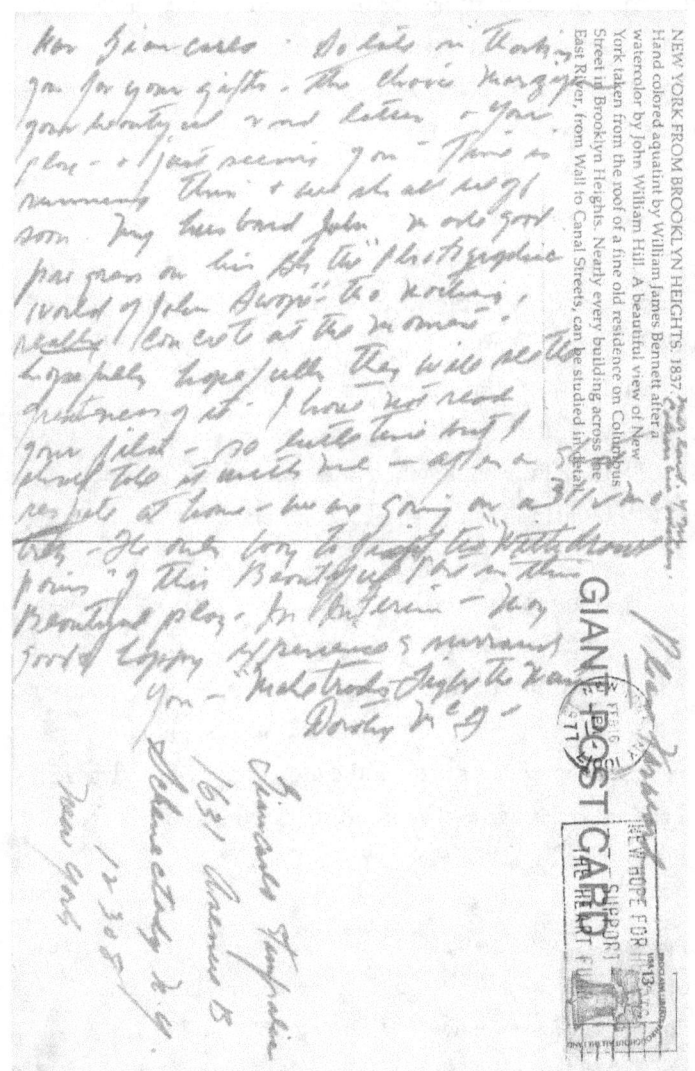

Verso **of one of the first postcards Dorothy sent me, in February 1977.**

Dorothy was full of initiative. She was warm, delicate, and generous, but forcefully so, and always ready to put those feelings to the test through action. I experienced this first-hand. In the early phases of our acquaintance, Dorothy was always interested in what I was doing. One of my budding passions was writing, for theater and cinema; mine was an awkward, untutored passion, but strong and sincere. When I sent her my very first attempt at a screenplay—I shudder to think how awful it was—with a female protagonist somehow tailored around her, Dorothy did not just send me kind words or compliments; she immediately sprang into action. She sent me a telegram telling me that she had forwarded my work to a young television director she knew, asking him to have a look and send me comments and suggestions. He did. I was never capable of "exploiting" my friendship with Dorothy, but that is not the point. Had I wanted to do so, she would have been willing to let me. Her sense of friendship was no passive feeling, and no pose.

That Dorothy was intelligent, curious, active, and outspoken was first noticed by Hellman in his 1941 profile of her:

> It is impossible to think of [the character of Claudia] as having the remotest interest in politics, philosophy or world affairs. Dorothy, on the other hand, discusses these subjects with the enthusiasm of an intellectual sophomore, reads weighty books about them at the drop of a friend's suggestion, believes violently in all-out aid to Britain, and is a frequent attender of Fight for Freedom meetings.[798]

Speaking of intelligence, Dorothy had other talents besides acting. She dabbled in painting (though she claimed that her husband was much better at it than she ever was),[799] photography, and writing. As early as

---

[798] Hellman, "McGuire" (1941), op. cit., 122.

[799] "Dorothy McGuire Escaped From Claudia Long Enough to Do Two Pictures," *Oakland Tribune*, November 26, 1944.

1944, she sold an article to *Mademoiselle* magazine;[800] in the late 1940s, she sold at least two short stories, entitled *Peripaty* and *Blood*, to *Mademoiselle* and *Promenade* magazines. A third story, entitled *The Irritant*, was being considered for publication in 1950.[801]

In 1945, Dorothy was even planning to take on a writing assignment as a correspondent from the War Office. Syndicated filmland columnist Sheilah Graham reported as follows:

> Dorothy McGuire and husband, John Swope, are planning to go abroad as a news-photographer team, Dotty to do the writing, Johnny to use his camera on the war front. The War Office is usually opposed to husband-and-wife teams—it still has not forgotten the Humphrey Bogart-Mayo Methot uproar on the African front last year. But I have a hunch Dorothy soon will be off to the wars with her husband. This means, of course, that Movie Boss David Selznick will have to wait a long time before Dorothy works again in a picture.[802]

I could not ascertain whether anything came of this project. Probably not, since John was reassigned to Edward Steichen's Navy photographic unit, and Dorothy started planning a USO tour as an actress soon after the above article was published.

---

800 Ibid.

801 "Dorothy McGuire's Stories Published," *Rochester Democrat and Chronicle*, September 30, 1950.

802 Sheilah Graham, "In Hollywood Today," *Indianapolis (IN) Star*, January 30, 1945.

3. *Turangalîla* II: Apollonian

Despite her protestations to the contrary, it is undeniable that Dorothy was a film star (and theater star), and that she partook gladly of a world of glamour and fame. This important proviso is one that her daughter repeats to this day, and often.[803] Her being a film and theater actress, with all the subtle traps that the condition hides, might be one of the reasons why her daughter perceived Dorothy as a distant parent, and was rebellious towards her—but the dynamics of a family, any family, are mysterious, complex things, and mother-daughter relationships are arduous, volatile entities. In any event, being a hard-working film star and theater/radio actress must have exercised some influence on Dorothy's choices and decisions, even though it was counterbalanced by her cultivation of certain virtues such as unselfishness, self-control, discretion, compassion, and a remarkable equilibrium.

Though she cared little about the mechanics of career (see next chapter), Dorothy wanted to be an actress; she wanted to keep acting. She was ambitious during her early fame-seeking theatrical days, and continued to be ambitious after arriving in Hollywood. "I set out to be an actress and

---

[803] Topo Swope (March 2017), op. cit.

never stopped believing it. I meant to be a hit in a hit. I still do," she told Paul Rosenfield as late as 1982.[804] That ambition might have been partially motivated by economic considerations in the early stages of her career; it certainly was not after marrying John Swope in 1943. Dorothy could easily have retired to a private life of leisure, but did not, for she found a deep fulfillment in acting, and in being a star. Fame, visibility and especially the practice and development of her craft were values, or priorities, in Dorothy's life. It is only natural that those values, those priorities, would touch her life as a human being, occasionally creating a slight interference. But only a slight one.

Given what one knows of Hollywood, and of the stories of its famous denizens, it is something of a miracle that Dorothy turned out the way she did, with fewer rough edges than most of her peers. Though some chinks are to be expected even in an armor as golden as Dorothy's, there were no tales of alcoholism, of addiction, of depression, of scandals, or of momentous conflicts where she was concerned. There were no divorces in her private life, and few suspensions in her professional life. As Charles Champlin put it in his 1976 profile of McGuire:

> In a profession known to be mercilessly disruptive of domestic tranquility and personal happiness, she has reconciled her public and private selves with grace and dignity [...].[805]

The general equilibrium that Dorothy was obviously able to find for herself was probably the result of soul-searching, initially stemming from a reaction to her own family of origin (a restless mother, an affectionate but melancholy—and suicidal—father). Dorothy mentioned this soul-searching in a 1976 interview, saying that the shock resulting from her father's suicide had led her to a better understanding of herself, "of him,

---

804 Rosenfield, "Fate" (1982), op. cit.

805 Champlin, "Sensitivity" (1976), op. cit.

of the emotional struggles in us all."[806] This statement would seem to indicate that she made a conscious decision not to repeat history, and not to accept her blood inheritance blindly. She did what she could to achieve the balance that her parents lacked.

Dorothy did indeed achieve a remarkable personal equilibrium. She was a positive, equanimous person, with nary an invidious thought in her. She did not run hot and cold emotionally, but achieved a balance in her inner world, an inner composure. As she put it in an interview, "[…] until you have inner peace you can't extend warmth to other people."[807] This equilibrium, which we might also call forbearance, was aided and abetted by her marriage to John Swope, a levelheaded, cheerful, affectionate man who had few rough edges himself, and exercised a stabilizing influence on her life. John helped Dorothy with her balance, through love, humor, and lack of vanity. When I think of Dorothy and John during my brief acquaintance with them as a couple, I think of two loving people who had achieved an uncommon complementarity in their relationship.

John, on the other hand, had passions of his own. Again, not for economic reasons, and regardless of results and success, his love for photography—which he often practiced on his travels with his wife—was potent enough to absorb his time almost completely, and to create some problems in his own parenting skills. His daughter, for example, had a better, and closer, relationship with him than with her mother; notwithstanding this, she says:

> When he wasn't away on one of his trips, he was locked in his darkroom. If I were to write a book about my relationship with father, I would probably entitle it "The Dark Side of the Darkroom Door."[808]

---

806 Ibid.

807 Lydia Lane, "Dorothy McGuire Contends a Calm Outlook Enhances Beauty," Los Angeles Times, October 24, 1954.

808 Topo Swope (March 2017), op. cit.

It is evident that both the complicated mother-daughter relationship and the father-daughter relationship in the Swope family were not as smooth or as successful as Topo Swope would have wished. As far as the former is concerned, something in that relationship, it is impossible to determine exactly what, and in exactly what proportion, impeded the full expression of an instinct that Dorothy certainly possessed otherwise. Actor Daniel J. Travanti, who worked with Dorothy in the play *I Never Sang for My Father* in 1987, recalls having the feeling that something about that relationship was amiss, and on Dorothy's mind:

> Dorothy was a smiling, glowing woman—both as the character she was playing and as herself. Always. I had been smitten with her from her films: I remembered this glowing creature on the screen, and there she was, just as radiant in person. I definitely got the impression that there was no turmoil there. But she did talk a little about her daughter. I forget what it was exactly, and Dorothy was not one to tell tales, or to express any particular tension, but she did mention that relationship. It was a clue that all was not sweetness and light with Dorothy; if it had all been sweetness and light, that problem, if there was indeed a problem, could not have occurred. It would be highly unlikely that it *could* be all sweetness and light. Nobody lives in total tranquility with other people, especially not in close quarters.[809]

Be that as it may, according to many who knew her, myself included, Dorothy was indeed tranquil with most people, and maternal and welcoming. She could be maternal with friends, old and new, and with acquaintances; she was definitely maternal towards me during our ac-

---

[809] Daniel J. Travanti, conversation with the author, March 2018.

quaintance. At a small party in 1989, Dorothy told the other guests the (unsolicited) story of our first meeting and of my first visit to Los Angeles thirteen years earlier. What was extraordinary about her story was that, when she recalled how she and John had picked me up at the airport, she added, "We never picked *anybody* up at the airport; but we picked *him* up." Whether that fact was literally true or not (Dan Levin recalls being picked up at the airport by the Swopes as a young man, so it was probably not), Dorothy's comment, I think, expressed her puzzlement at the extent of her feelings towards me, disproportionate to the degree of our relationship at that point. What Dorothy was expressing was surprise at her maternal feeling for me.

I was not the only one who evoked such feelings in her. Director Dan Levin, who started his career in show business as an apprentice at the La Jolla Playhouse in 1952, remembers with great affection how warmly, openly, and generously both Dorothy and John took him under their wings during the years of his La Jolla tenure, including him and the other apprentices in their after-show dinners with the featured stars. That same warmth and that same generosity withstood the test of time: even during her last decades, Dorothy would, for example, take special trips to Levin's house to deliver thoughtful, occasionally exquisite unsolicited gifts. To this day, Levin recounts these stories with special feeling, and with a broken voice.[810]

Actor Dennis Hopper (1936–2010) was also "discovered" by the Swopes while an apprentice at the playhouse in the early 1950s; John and Dorothy took him under their wings and sent him off to the Hal Roach Studios with a glowing letter of introduction, which earned him parts in

---

[810] Levin (2017), op. cit.

the television shows *Cavalcade of America*[811] and *Medic*.[812] This led to his being offered a contract with Warner Bros. (the day after the airing of the *Medic* episode), and the rest is history.[813]

Film historian Dan Van Neste, who began a correspondence with Dorothy in the early 1990s, provides corroborating evidence confirming that she was capable of the warmest, most maternal of feelings towards acquaintances old and new:

> It started with a fan letter from me; she wrote me back, a very nice letter. Then one day, out of the blue, the mail truck pulled up in front of my house, and there was a package from Dorothy. She had sent me a small metal globe, a lovely desk-sized representation of the Earth with a pedestal. There was no letter accompanying the gift, no explanation; but it occurred to me later that the date coincided with World Environment Day, which is in June, around the date of her birthday. Such a delightful thought on her part. From that moment on, our correspondence grew, and I would talk to her briefly on the telephone once or twice a year, usually to wish her a happy birthday. Never did Dorothy fail to say something nice to me, whether it was about my writing, about life, or about my person. In our superficial interactions, she was thoughtful and very humble, loving and nurturing. The warmth that she could put into even the smallest of notes or postcards was astonishing, and truly uncommon. She was a classy person, and a

---

[811] The episode in question, entitled "A Medal for Miss Walker," was a television adaptation of an amusing Civil War radio comedy-drama Dorothy herself had performed for the "other" *Cavalcade of America* the previous year. Here, Maura Murphy took on the part of Dr. Mary Walker. The television version aired on December 14, 1954.

[812] The *Medic* episode, entitled "Boy in the Storm," aired on January 3, 1955.

[813] See: Tom Vallance, "Dennis Hopper: Hollywood actor, director and oft-married hell-raiser who rose to fame with 'Easy Rider,'" *London Independent*, May 30, 2010.

person with great integrity. In short, she was everything I had imagined she would be, and much more.[814]

Daniel J. Travanti, who toured the United States with Dorothy in *I Never Sang for My Father* (where she played his mother) in 1987, also recalls an unsolicited present from her:

> One day she gave me a present: a bottle of lilac water, which she said had been her husband's favorite. I've had that long-necked bottle of cologne forever.[815]

Back to Dorothy's equilibrium. The virtue of equanimity entails the person's capacity to remain "equal," i.e. even-tempered and stable, in relation to his or her feelings, reactions, and emotions. Inwardly equal, that is. It entails, in other words, the discovery of a "zone" of the person's inner world that can be made free of the ups and downs of inner turmoil: a barycenter that is not swayed by inner or outer pressures. One finds a discreet hint that Dorothy possessed such quality in the thoughtful profile that Geoffrey T. Hellman penned for *LIFE* magazine in 1941. In fact, Hellman detected an element of Dorothy's personality that no other journalist seems to have noticed when he stated that she had "an odd detachment from life" and when, in comparing her with her breakthrough character, Claudia, he added:

> [. . .] Claudia is a distinctly cuddly type, whereas Dorothy, although possessed of a languorous charm that has won her a circle of almost worshipful beaux, has an impersonal,

---

[814] Dan Van Neste, conversation with the author, March 2018.

[815] Travanti (2018), op. cit.

inaccessible quality which tends to preclude intimacy, and has caused her friends to compare her to Garbo.[816]

Although some of the traits described by Hellman would be tempered in later years (she was never inaccessible, for instance), they offer a curious glimpse into a personality attribute that could occasionally be mistaken for coldness. Dorothy's impersonal detachment—her equanimity—might sometimes give the impression that she was not passionate, when in fact she was a warm, expansive, generous, and cordial person; but the passions that she displayed were displayed because she chose to display them. Equanimity enables the elimination of unwanted, excessive, or dominating passions; what remains is a luminous area—the heart, if you will—where the passions that are under the person's control can be channeled, cultivated and brought into the world, voluntarily.

Twice in his profile Hellman mentioned the word "impersonal," so it was not an accident; paired with his definition of Dorothy's "odd detachment from life," that word could indeed suggest that Dorothy was a cold person. Yet she was not a cold person. Nor was she uninvolved with others, or ungenerous. So what exactly was Hellman suggesting, and what exactly were this detachment and this impersonality?

Don Bachardy, artist and former significant other of writer Christopher Isherwood for over thirty years, plays devil's advocate and suggests a negative interpretation of that detachment and of that impersonality where his relationship with Dorothy is concerned. Though he admits that Dorothy was always very nice to him, he also adds that

> we saw each other on social occasions, parties, openings and such, but to the best of my recollection we were never in each other's homes. I know for certain I wasn't invited to her house; and Christopher's relationship with her and her

---

[816] Hellman, "McGuire" (1941), op. cit., 122.

husband was really the result of *my* friendship with her. There was always a polite distance between us as friends. It might have been, faintly or not so faintly, a consequence of the fact that we—Christopher and I—were known homosexuals. We couldn't possibly *not* be known as homosexuals, and, in the '50s and '60s, that was not recommended socially. I don't think that fact went down easily with either Dorothy or her husband. I myself was surprised, upon hearing this suggestion coming out of my own mouth a moment ago; but it comes from somewhere, most likely from my knowledge of Dorothy and her husband. She wasn't impolite with me, ever, but there was a certain block to our becoming closer friends. Christopher and I were never invited to the Swopes' house: I think they would have been afraid to have a homosexual couple in their home. It simply didn't fit their standards. Now that I think of it, I had a similar feeling about Jane Wyatt, who was one of Dorothy's close friends; she gave me quite a chilly acknowledgment when we met. Like Ms. Wyatt, I think Dorothy and John had some kind of idea of their social importance in this town, and [being straight, or at least not openly gay] was one of the requirements to become closer friends. The Swopes were part of a social elite, and they behaved as such, with an ever-so-faint air of *grandeur*. That feeling of mine about Dorothy was there, but clearly not in my conscious dealings with her; those dealings were polite and gracious.

In fact, Dorothy was always extremely nice to me, even charming. I remember that during our first portrait sitting (I believe she sat for me three times over the years), I did three different drawings of her; and she was very patient with me. When she saw that third drawing I had done of her, it suddenly was what she was hoping for, and she picked up the drawing and danced around the room with it, singing to it!⁸¹⁷ I thought that was very charming. There was often something whimsical about her; that's why I liked her, despite that slight hint of frost in her.⁸¹⁸

Portrait of the portraitist as a young man: Don Bachardy as he was around the time of his first meeting with Dorothy, circa 1955. Frame capture from the documentary film *Chris and Don: A Love Story* (2007), by Tina Mascara and Guido Santi.

When I mentioned Dorothy and John's status as Los Angeles royalty in discussing their life in society (see Part I, Chapter 18), I had not yet heard Bachardy's confirmation of this view of the Swopes, nor his hint about their grand behavior. Bachardy, however, colors that view with the insinuation of snobbery, which goes against the grain of everything I

---

817 The song was "I Believe in You" from the musical *How to Succeed in Business Without Really Trying*, 1961. (Don Bachardy, conversation with the author, August 2018.)

818 Bachardy (2018), op. cit.

Portrait of Dorothy by Don Bachardy, created during an April 1962 sitting. Courtesy of Don Bachardy.

have experienced or discovered about Dorothy. Aristocratic the Swopes may have been, but I never saw much *grandeur* on Dorothy's part, nor on John's. I have scoured my memory—and other sources—for indications that Bachardy's characterization of the Swopes as snobs might have a basis in fact, but was not able to find credible clues to that effect. In spite of their exalted social status, Dorothy and John (and their close friend Jane Wyatt) were open to all kinds of people, and disarmingly willing to develop friendships in the most improbable of quarters. I certainly did not fit any aristocratic "standards" when I first met the Swopes, despite the fact that my intellectual/theatrical aspirations and mixed European/American provenance might have been charming conversation starters. Yet, after just three meetings and a brief correspondence, these aristocrats were willing, not only to continue our acquaintanceship, but also to invite me into their *sanctum sanctorum*, with open arms, and to "present" me in society by introducing me to their circle of friends.[819]

As for Bachardy's startling suggestion that Dorothy was a homophobe, I certainly never experienced *that*, even though, during my early visit with her in Los Angeles, I displayed some extremely conspicuous mannerisms that she would have had no trouble decoding in terms of sexual orientation; in the spirit of full disclosure, I am ready to admit that those mannerisms were "copied" from the speaking style of British author and *raconteur* Quentin Crisp, whose one-man show I had just seen. Even more tellingly, a full-length period play I wrote and directed a decade later, which won a competition judged by a jury that included Jane Wyatt (accompanied in an unofficial capacity by her friend Dorothy), was enthusiastically, almost militantly, endowed with explicit gay themes, and with a happily resolved gay love story. Neither my personal behavior nor the pro-gay dramatic manifesto I had written, virtually a literary coming

---

[819] Among the people to whom Dorothy had wanted to introduce me privately (not at a party) was James Stewart; as we were driving by his house one evening, she pointed it out to me, and told me of her intention. Unfortunately, Mr. Stewart was suffering from the flu that week, and the visit never happened.

out, altered Dorothy's warmth towards me, nor Jane's. I do not dispute that Bachardy's feeling may be true, nor that it may have been triggered by something equally true; but his position as public figure (and longtime companion of a public figure) and as outspoken gay person in the 1950s and '60s placed him in a particularly vulnerable spot in that particular period of history. Because of that position and because of that outspokenness, he probably experienced, or had a hypersensitive radar for, discrimination the way I never did while coming of age in the 1970s.

First portrait of Dorothy from Don Bachardy's January 1974 sitting with her. Courtesy of Don Bachardy.

Second portrait of Dorothy originating from Don Bachardy's January 1974 sitting. Courtesy of Don Bachardy.

In any event, when Bachardy states that there were "blocks" to his becoming "closer friends" with Dorothy, he is opening a Pandora's Box of possible factors that simply cannot be explained away by homophobia, even assuming that homophobia was an issue, subliminal or not. There are usually multiple reasons, karmic and otherwise, why friendships do not develop beyond the initial stage; and those reasons are often reciprocal. However, even if the facts as hypothesized by Bachardy are true, it seems to me that Dorothy's discretion in choosing not to fuel inevitable press gossip in pre-Stonewall Hollywood, a discretion that involved not inviting a famous gay couple to her home, does not quite qualify her as homophobic, especially given her private frequentation of both Isherwood and Bachardy.

Leaving the issue of homophobia aside, Bachardy too, like other commentators (see Hellman above), interprets Dorothy's grace and impersonal detachment as frostiness. In the city of passions and drama, it is more than logical that this should be so. Many in Hollywood might not have been able to conceive the difference between impersonality or detachment on the one hand and coldness or *grandeur* on the other. They might also not have been able to imagine a middle zone between the two extremes of personality and absence of personality, or of passion and passionlessness. Equanimity occupies that middle zone.

In medio stat virtus; *est modus in rebus*:[820] these two Latin maxims—the one derived from medieval scholastic philosophers, the other from Horace's first *Satire*—owe a debt to Aristotle's thought; both are Aristotelian in spirit.[821] They suggest a place, or inner position, in which the subject can eschew extremes, whether physical, intellectual, emotional, or spiritual. They also suggest that this inner place, or position, is not reached accidentally, but through "mediation" or inner processing. Horace puts the accent on the *way* ("*modus*") or manner in which one thinks and acts, and thus in the discerning and choosing one does to negotiate those extremes. Buddhism has a kindred concept, usually referred to as the Way of the Middle. Horace also mentions something called *aurea mediocritas*, which could be translated as "golden moderation," "golden way of the middle," or "golden mean" (not as "golden mediocrity"). Horace's principle is an invitation to equilibrium, measure, and freedom from excess, which must be gained through choice and/or abstention.[822]

---

[820] The first maxim can be translated as "Virtue stands in the middle" or "Virtue lies in moderation"; the second, as "There is a way in things," or, as the Merriam-Webster Dictionary suggests, "Everything in proportion."

[821] See: Horace, *Satires, Epistles, Ars Poetica*, Harvard University Press, 2005.

[822] Horace's principle of "golden moderation" appears in Book II of his *Odes* (Ode X,

Philosopher and spiritual scientist Rudolf Steiner defined the equanimous state as a fortitude, and an inner composure.[823] The exercise Steiner prescribes to the pupils of his esoteric school, the third of five "fundamental" or supplementary daily exercises, is designed to help develop this quality. One finds similar exercises in many ancient (and less ancient) schools for the betterment of the human being, both western and eastern, for example in Pythagoras and in Buddhism.[824] The exercise does not consist in negating, opposing, or repressing the contradictory feelings that course through our inner being, but in dominating them by knowing them and being independent of them: in letting them be, so to speak, and extinguishing one's reactions to, or participation in, them. Steiner makes it clear that practicing this "impersonality" of feeling runs no danger of rendering the person cold:

> Whoever does not wish to [practice this exercise] because he thinks it will deprive him of spontaneity or artistic sensitivity will be unable to embark on esoteric schooling. Composure means mastering the greatest joy and the profoundest pain. In fact we only become fully receptive to the joys and sufferings in the world when we no longer lose ourselves in pain and pleasure, no longer immerse ourselves in them egotistically. [...] This certainly does not need to engender dullness or lack of feeling. On the contrary, it develops in us a still more refined

---

verses 5–8): *Auream quisquis mediocritatem/Diligit, tutus caret obsoleti/Sordibus tecti, caret invidenda/Sobrius aula*. ("Whoever cherishes the golden mean, safely does without the squalor of the decrepit hovel, and, soberly, does without the Palace that people envy." The literal translation is mine.) The verb "*caret*" is particularly thorny to translate, for it could also mean "shuns," "stays away from," or "is free from."

823 Steiner, *Six Steps*, (2010), op. cit., 29–30.

824 In both Pythagoras' *Golden Verses* and in the teachings of Buddha, one finds this kind of exercise on passions and feelings as part of a process of Purification through self-knowledge and self-control.

and sharpened sensitivity. [It] actually makes us more sensitive and receptive; but we ourselves must be master, rather than being mastered by the feelings.[825]

Dorothy was not cold, but she was usually impersonal—not dominated by her ego—and balanced. Her sensitivity was sharp, subtle, and refined, attuned to the joys and sufferings of the world around her. Her composure did not impede her warmth and her generosity, but allowed them to unfold unfettered by the mood swings of natural, spontaneous feeling, negative or positive.

When film and theater critic Rex Reed described Dorothy as having "a voice like creamy melted cocoa," he was describing, not so much the instrument (which was a versatile one capable of contrasting colors) as the effect that the instrument's sound could inspire in listeners. In life as in films, that voice carried with it "kindness, warmth and understanding" like few other voices. It radiated "a gentle, unselfish femininity" that transcended acting and stardom and contained something authentic, something deeply human. As Charles Champlin of the *Los Angeles Times* stated in his post-obituary homage to Dorothy:

> Her voice, I came to feel later, was what Shakespeare had in mind for Lear's daughter Cordelia: "soft, gentle and low, an excellent thing in women."[826]

Reed rightly stated that Dorothy "illuminated the dark corners of the screen around her" in her film performances; in life, she illuminated the dark corners of the rooms around her. The source of that illumination was not her acting, but her person.

---

[825] Steiner, *Six Steps* (2010), op. cit., 31.

[826] Charles Champlin, "Moving Work from Memorable Actress: Appreciation," *Los Angeles Times*, November 9, 2001.

Despite occasional unsubstantiated rumors to the contrary, on-set belligerence was a rare occurrence with Dorothy, except as an expression of professionalism. Here is the only example I could find, as reported by the vigilant Hedda Hopper:

> Dorothy McGuire believes in realism on the screen and fights for accuracy. The other day for a sequence in "Claudia and David," she was supposed to have rushed 80 miles by motor to reach her sick husband. Just before she started the scene, a hairdresser wanted to pretty up Claudia's tresses. Dorothy put her foot down hard and firm. "I won't look like a woman who's just come out of a beauty parlor," she said. "I've come through wind and storm to reach the bedside of my husband, and I'm going to look as if I had." She did. And more power to her! I suppose now she'll be getting the reputation of being hard to handle.[827]

But Dorothy never got such reputation, and these stand-offs were rare.

Direct conflict Dorothy usually avoided, both in her professional and in her private lives: in her dealings with other human beings, she was mostly free of the aversion that is a staple of natural living. As she put it in an interview: "I'm not a struggler [...]."[828] It would be erroneous, however, to see this as a form of passivity or, worse, cowardice, and as a mere desire to keep the peace. In her interactions, Dorothy normally *elected* to resolve conflict without resorting to opposition. As anyone who has attempted to eliminate the word "no" from his or her vocabulary knows, this entails some artfulness in transforming situations, and some degree of self-knowledge. The fact that Dorothy completed the above statement

---

[827] Hedda Hopper, "Looking at Hollywood," *Los Angeles Times*, April 10, 1946.

[828] Rosenfield, "Fate" (1982), op. cit.

with a second part, "And I'm not thrown,"[829] confirms that, humanly, she was on her toes in most situations, and was ready to take inventive action.

Apollonian equilibrium: a serene portrait of Dorothy, circa 1955.

---

829 Ibid.

4. The Conundrums of Commerce

Dorothy had her share of suffering, and her share of grief. Her experience of sorrow started early, with her father's suicide in 1932. In 1977–78 came the news of her husband John's terminal illness;[830] in 1978, twenty-five-year-old Mark Swope's brief bout of testicular cancer gave the family quite a fright, though the outcome in that case was positive.

---

830 Dorothy and John's daughter Topo was not aware that anything was wrong until her father missed her 30th birthday party in February 1979, but in hindsight thinks he already knew about his prostate cancer, and may have been undergoing radiation therapy for it, (though I presume she did not investigate this fact). The illness seemed to disappear for several weeks thereafter, until John insisted on being hospitalized on the evening of May 10, 1979, surrounded by his family. "In hindsight, I know it was for goodbyes," Topo writes, "but we just thought we were there to tuck him in for the night! And then he was gone the next day. I am sure he willed himself to die, and to die in hospital, rather than at home. He didn't want to die in their bed, and he never wanted to be a burden to Mom, or to anyone else. We were all in shock for a very long time. Yes, it was somewhat sudden. And the cancer had spread to his bones. Very painful, but he never complained." (Topo Swope, correspondence with the author, June 2018.) It is very likely that, if John knew about his illness ahead of time, so did Dorothy, and that the fact that his ailment was something of a surprise to their children rather late in the game suggests the delicacy with which John and Dorothy prepared for John's passing. It also suggests that John and Dorothy faced the illness with relative serenity: if John did not want "to be a burden" to anyone, neither did Dorothy. This state of things suggests remarkable self-control on both their parts.

In all the above instances, Dorothy was able to take a positive, unselfish position in dealing with those events. Humanly speaking, her reaction to tragedy was one of love, compassion and personal growth. It has been argued (see Feldshuh on page 25) that this steadfast movement of Dorothy's towards the positive (her choice to be "nice") limited her acting instrument to some extent, and influenced her choice of roles. In other words, one may argue that digging deep inside herself to find "negative" colors in order to play "negative" characters (the characters she seldom played, or often refused to play) ran the danger of connecting her once more to the pain she had rejected, and of contradicting the virtues she practiced as a human being. As Feldshuh put it when I discussed the issue with her, Dorothy's "choice to be the 'good kid' influenced her whole life, and limited her whole life."[831] That choice and that suffering, according to this view, enriched Dorothy humanly but may have hampered her from an artistic point of view.

This opinion may be partially true. While it is undeniable that, especially in the latter half of her career, Dorothy preferred to play characters that were "lovable" and could serve as human models of behavior, it is also true that Dorothy processed the negative events in her life sensitively, thoroughly and positively, leaving little or no damaging residue. In fact, despite her way of choosing projects and roles, her personal investigation helped her explore her characters more deeply from a human standpoint, and led to a new artistic growth: to a new distillation, particularly on the stage (see Part I, Chapter 15). In film and television, her choices limited her range only insofar as they limited her capacity to compensate for the lack of depth of inferior scripts and directors. The greatness of her acting, for greatness there often was, manifested subtly, without flash; aided by the extensive rehearsal time and silent, temple-like concentration of the theater, it could blossom properly. One could put it this way: in the theater, she came off as actress and star both—in the best sense of the word

---

[831] Feldshuh (2017), op. cit.

"star": she could conquer and dominate the theatrical space with her presence and her positive humanity. In film, in the absence of great material, she only came off as a working actress, with occasional touches of sublime sensitivity, but not necessarily as a star. This self-limitation, the "low-temperature," slow sizzle of her performances, and her unglamorous, homey beauty, could account for her failure to rise to the top echelon of A-list stardom in Hollywood, a failure that left Hedda Hopper melancholy with regret on several occasions, for example in 1946:

> Dorothy really deserves an award for "A Tree Grows in Brooklyn," but I doubt her getting it."[832]

and then again in 1947:

> Dorothy McGuire has never given anything but Academy Award performances, but she has yet to get an Oscar.[833]

Speaking of awards, Neil Doyle, in his *Classic Images* article about Dorothy entitled "Quiet Serenity," offers a practical, perhaps cynical reason for the Academy's snobbish attitude towards her:

> Surprisingly, her Best Actress nomination for 1947's *Gentleman's Agreement*, would be as close as she would get to an Oscar. Her superb performances in *A Tree Grows in Brooklyn*, *The Enchanted Cottage* and *The Spiral Staircase* would be overlooked by the Academy. She was handicapped in this respect, because although Fox would buy 50% of her contract from

---

832 Hopper, "Hollywood" (1946), op. cit.

833 Hedda Hopper, "Looking at Hollywood," *Los Angeles Times*, March 13, 1947.

Selznick, she did not have a lot of major studio backing in the Oscar races.[834]

Dorothy's transition from stage to screen was the hot topic of a batch of articles that were written soon after her arrival in Tinseltown. In these articles, various technical worries were voiced by Dorothy; truth be told, they were minor, almost uninfluential complaints. Here are a couple, reported by NEA correspondent Erskine Johnson in 1943:

> Dorothy McGuire's work before the camera is a joy to the studio, but not to herself. Not that she's finding much difference between stage acting and screen acting, but it's just that it's all new to her.
> Dorothy says: "I talk fast—at least I think I'm talking fast—and then on the screen it comes out slow."
> [...] "Honestly," she says, "I'm still so scared of the camera my teeth chatter every time a scene starts."[835]

Though on the one hand these dutiful reports were part of an understandable strategy to market Dorothy as young, fresh talent (as Claudia), on the other hand they do point to a disarming character trait that Dorothy would retain and express for several years thereafter: a humble insecurity. Dorothy was never one to boast, nor one to feign total confidence or self-importance. This humility may be another reason why Dorothy's persona never ascended to the status of the forbidding star, despite gaining the love and respect of audiences and critics, and being awarded a star on the Hollywood Walk of Fame on February 8, 1960.[836]

[834] Doyle, "Serenity" (2007), op. cit.

[835] Erskine Johnson, "Screen Chats," *Shamokin (PA) News-Dispatch*, June 29, 1943.

[836] Her star is located at 6933 Hollywood Boulevard, at the corner with N. Orange Drive near Highland Avenue.

The Conundrums of Commerce

The combination of reasons why Hollywood careers are what they are is often a mysterious one, having little to do with an actor's talent. Careers are complex creatures, made of equal parts of ambition, deals and negotiations, logistics, financing, audience reactions, studio executives' fears or moods, scheduling, and, ultimately, fate and blind luck. One has only to look at the "botched" deals during Dorothy's Selznick years (from 1943 to 1949) to have an idea of how flimsy the thread is that ties together one project to the next, or the timeline of an entire career. "I always like to remind young people about fate; fate made my career," Dorothy mused in a 1982 interview.[837]

For a similar combination of reasons, but mostly because of fate, some great actors are "forgotten," or neglected, by audiences and scholars after their careers are over, while others are elevated to the stature of mythological figures, sometimes disproportionately to their talents. Just as Dorothy's "niceness" may have hurt her career to some extent while her career was in progress, it may have hurt future generations' perceptions of her as well, which may suggest that monsters and misfits fare better in the eyes of audiences than balanced human beings. In other words, human equilibrium and enlightenment might not always be valued commodities when it comes to Hollywood careers and to the way those careers are judged by posterity.

Dorothy's friend Jane Wyatt was as puzzled as I am by this issue when it came to Dorothy's career. She commented on it, saying:

> Dorothy wasn't interested in being a star; she wanted to be a pure actress. She really was an actress through and through, and everybody adored her.[838]

---

[837] Rosenfield, "Fate" (1982), op. cit. Curiously, in one 1955 interview, Dorothy used the plural, "fates," thus envisaging the fates as actual entities (see Phyllis Battelle [INS], "Assignment America," *Daily Courier,* Connellsville, PA, October 30, 1956).

[838] Quoted in Dennis McLellan, "Dorothy McGuire, 85; Favorite Leading Lady," *Los Angeles Times,* September 15, 2001.

The issue of film stardom, or of the conflict between acting and career, became a thorn in Dorothy's side soon after her arrival in Hollywood. In a 1944 United Press interview honoring her as the new star of *Claudia*, Dorothy twisted the knife in her own wound and lamented the exaggerations of the film industry:

> "You're young and you've been in a Broadway play or two or three with fairly long runs, and you're beginning to feel as if you're learning something about acting," [McGuire] said with that sort of a worried smile, across a lunch table in the Café de Paris at Twentieth Century-Fox.
>
> "Then Hollywood signs you. And suddenly there is a tremendous whoop-de-do. Simply because you have been on Broadway, you are ballyhooed as a Broadway 'star.'
>
> "You don't know what they mean by star, and you don't know what they expect. But it terrifies you. You feel as if you've just started learning your trade, really, as a stage actress.
>
> "And suddenly here you are, learning to act in an entirely new medium. They start ballyhooing you as a star, as if you are a sensational person. You don't crave to be sensational. All you crave is to be believable in front of that camera.
>
> "So you sort of shrink into yourself and try to concentrate on your work. You hope you'll learn fast how to be a movie actress."[839]

The truth is, Dorothy cared very little about her career per se. She cared about acting, and about tackling the roles she chose, but not about the machine one sometimes calls "career." She was a free spirit who never quite fit in, who never quite played the "Hollywood game" with great con-

---

[839] "Movies Scare Dorothy McGuire" (UP), *Rochester (NY) Democrat and Chronicle*, November 21, 1944.

viction. In a 1976 interview, Dorothy talked about the three "big things," or priorities, in her life:

> The acting and the roles have been one of the big things in my life. The other is John [Swope], who is miraculous. Another is the traveling we do, which keeps us alive and stimulated.[840]

Interestingly, she did not mention her children. In any case, Dorothy's attention was divided between her private and her professional life, between human and artistic development. Dorothy also tended to shy away from publicity per se, especially during the latter half of her career, as Ron Miller reports in the introduction to his 1983 interview with the actress:

> Dorothy McGuire's disdain for publicity always brings a smile to my face because I remember how severely I was warned about that subject when she agreed to do an interview with me in 1983 in connection to the ABC TV movie *Ghost Dancing*. The publicist insisted, "Don't ask her about anything except the new movie. She hates talking about the past. If you try asking her about the 'good old days,' she may get up and walk out on you!"[841]

That publicist, however, had been exaggerating. Dorothy, Miller reports, ultimately did not rebel to being asked about those gone days, and "turned out to be a friendly and relaxed lunch companion, still a handsome woman with genuine class."[842] Dorothy, in fact, liked to reminisce

---

[840] Champlin, "Sensitivity" (1976), op. cit.

[841] Ron Miller, interview with Dorothy McGuire, in James Bawden and Ron Miller, *Conversations with Classic Film Stars: Interviews from Hollywood's Golden Era*, University of Kentucky Press, 2016, 221.

[842] Ibid., 223.

about her past, but on her own terms and with self-effacing understatement. What she was wary of, probably, was the journalists' tendency to ask about success rather than about craft, about commerce ("career") rather than about art, about quantity rather than about quality.

In its obituary of Dorothy, the London *Telegraph*, like most newspapers, could not resist assessing her development as an actress through the concepts of success and commerce, i.e. through the slippery—and quantitative—idea of stardom:

> Here was an actress who might have gone on to bigger things. But it never developed that way—whether through want of encouragement or personal drive. Star quality demands commitment as well as talent. In the final reckoning, Dorothy McGuire—fine actress, handsome woman, attractive personality—just did not want to be a big star badly enough.[843]

This superficial assessment may hold true if one views Dorothy quantitatively, and from the outside; Dorothy, however, had her own personal reasons (many of them) to choose the career path she did. One could say that she did not care *at all* if she became a big star or not. The concept of stardom, *qua* stardom, was alien to her.

The issue of money in cinema is of course important for the people spending it or earning it, be they studio heads, agents, producers, or audience members. It may even be important for the actors participating in the films (though it was never very important to Dorothy). Half a century or more later, however, we, the audiences of the twenty-first century, have the privilege of ignoring that issue when watching or studying the films of the past. We can separate art from commerce, quality from quantity, and craft from success. We can consider those films, and that craft, from a distance, and through the impersonality of History.

---

[843] *London Telegraph*, obituary of Dorothy McGuire, September 18, 2001.

THE CONUNDRUMS OF COMMERCE

In my senior year at Columbia University, I wrote a paper for one of my cinema courses, using semiotics to analyze certain narrative codes in a current film that had fascinated me, *Perceval le Gallois* (1978) by French Director Éric Rohmer. The film certainly had its flaws, as did my academic ardor, but my professor's reaction to my effort was curious nonetheless. He began his final comments on my paper with the sentence: "Interesting analysis, but there is something perverse in using semiotic codes to analyze the box-office failure of a film." The professor had misinterpreted my intention: I was not analyzing the box-office failure of the film, but analyzing the film while disregarding its performance at the box office. Success, or the lack of it, had colored my professor's reading of film and paper, just as it tends to color people's assessments of books, films, and actors. Is a writer who publishes sixty books more successful than one who publishes three? Certainly, at least from the point of view of income. Is he greater, or as great? That is a different issue.

Dorothy defined her career as "erratic,"[844] and found it hard to comment on it even after the fact. Here she is, responding to a query about the topic from Rex Reed in 1977:

> If I seem vague and evasive about my career, it's because I didn't think about it that heavily. [...] I was always the good woman. I don't know to this day what shapes a career out in Hollywood. It's still rather mysterious.
>
> It has, I think, a lot to do with how you look, what's available, and how you take off at the box office. Or sometimes they don't know how to use you, so you find yourself lost. I was never a classic beauty. I had no image, so I found myself in a lot of things accidentally [...]
>
> I did [insist on making] one picture called "Till the End of Time" in which I played an older woman who seduced Guy

---

844 Rosenfield, "Fate" (1982), op. cit.

Madison and everyone was shocked, and the film was a failure. [...] I went right back into playing nice girls and faithful wives, which today wouldn't be considered very appealing. Movies have changed and women are looked at quite differently.

Looking back I wasn't all that aware of what was happening. [My career in films began when] David Selznick saw me on Broadway in "Claudia" and brought me to Hollywood to do the film version in 1943. By that time I was married and not very ambitious. It never occurred to me that I should direct my career in any direction. I just wanted to act.[845]

Given what Dorothy says in that interview, one could conclude that playing the roles she played was only partially her choice. It was part of an overall strategy—initiated by the studios and by her representatives—that somehow guaranteed the continuance of her career; the powers that be believed that what "worked" for Dorothy was to continue playing "nice." Dorothy, in all fairness, did not so much choose her roles as accept them when they were offered to her; with the exception of the La Jolla Playhouse, this was true of her stage career too. The most one can accuse her of is not fighting such state of things very aggressively. Tovah Feldshuh, for instance, suggests that Dorothy should have hired some good acting teachers once she was established in Hollywood, thus continuing to grow as an actress—and digging herself out of the typecasting rut.[846] Dorothy's learning, however, occurred on a different battlefield: it happened, *not technically but humanly*; she learned by living, by discovering and rediscovering herself as a person, by loving and traveling rather than by concentrating on the technical aspect.

The things that Dorothy said about her film work, when she was

---

[845] Reed, "Competitive Spirit" (1977), op. cit.

[846] Feldshuh (2017), op. cit.

not forced to comment on the mechanics of her career, could sometimes sound cryptic and elusive, always with a touch of mystery that hinted at some hidden depth. She did not talk about acting as a craft or technique, and seldom elaborated about her manner of investigating character. She did not talk about methods or exercises, only about human beings. After putting herself in someone else's shoes, she drew conclusions within herself about the human entity she was observing from within herself. Just as she preferred not to talk about career, she did not like to talk about acting. In her acting as in her living, she did not elaborate about her insights dialectically, but occasionally dropped a hint that left the field open to interpretations. For example, in a letter to Dan Van Neste, in response to his enthusiastic appraisal of her performance in *The Spiral Staircase*, she stated that it had been "a wonderful exploration."[847]

If any credence is to be given to Feldshuh's opinion, it may find partial corroboration in the fact that Dorothy—who was not a Method actress—was inclined to choose characters whose inner make-up overlapped with her own to some extent, in order to gain sufficient access to the appropriate feelings. She rarely tackled anything excessively Dionysian, for that would probably have required a technical approach that was not familiar to her, and would have contradicted her own nature. Playing in an area close to "home," or only slightly peripheral to it, was her strategy.

Occasionally, Dorothy did express concern about typecasting, and about the "regimentation" that came with it. Here she is doing just that in a 1947 interview with Hedda Hopper:

> I've had ideas, Hedda, and I've fought for [roles]. Sometimes I've been right, other times I've missed. The thing I fought hardest for was the role of the young war widow in "Till the End of Time." It was really my least successful part.

---

[847] Van Neste (2018), op. cit.

> Mostly my battle has been against being typed. I wanted to get away from the ingénue flutter of Claudia [...].[848]

In his sensationalist Hollywood memoir *Black Sunset*, talent agent Clancy Sigal (1926–2017) tells an anecdote about Dorothy. Here is his set-up, circa 1955:

> Latest incident: Mary [Baker of the Jaffe Agency,[849] where Sigal was an agent] calls me in to cool off the unhappy actress Dorothy McGuire who is fed up playing nice girls. No more *Claudia* and *The Enchanted Cottage*, which is how we make our money.
>
> McGuire played a sexy, promiscuous war widow in *Till the End of Time*, but the studio bosses are so uncomfortable with their nice virgin as a whore that they've made her Waspy-clean again in *Gentleman's Agreement* and *Three Coins in the Fountain*, causing the frustrated actress to listen too closely to the siren calls of rival agencies promising they'll get her grittier, more Academy Award-winning jobs.[850]

Most of Sigal's anecdote, in typical Sigalist hyperbole, is devoted to a mental fantasy of his about Dorothy as object of carnal desire, like the character she had played in *Till the End of Time*, and not to the issue of Dorothy's typecasting at all. In conclusion, Sigal seems disappointed not to be able to unearth a "dirty" side of Dorothy, and doubly disappointed

---

848 Hopper, "Independence" (1947), op. cit.

849 By 1949, the agency had been sold by Sam Jaffe to Phil Gersh; the agency would later be renamed The Gersh Agency. Among Gersh's clients were actors Mary Astor, Humphrey Bogart, Richard Burton, James Mason, Zero Mostel, and David Niven, writer Ernest Lehman, and directors Robert Wise and Mark Robson.

850 Clancy Sigal, *Black Sunset: Hollywood Sex, Lies, Glamour, Betrayal and Raging Egos*, Soft Skull Press, 2016, 263–264.

that she is as "warm and sincere" as her reputation suggests. Upon leaving the restaurant after their lunch date, Dorothy, realizing his dismay, comforts Sigal perceptively: "I am so sorry I am who I am." As for the subject of their discussion, Sigal only reports:

> In the end, Dorothy [...] stays with the Jaffe office and, accepting her career karma, submits to our casting her with Gary Cooper as a Quaker wife in *Friendly Persuasion*; she suffers so well.[851]

Irony and exaggeration aside, Sigal seems to be indicating that Dorothy was indeed feeling *some* tension with regard to the issue of typecasting, and some boredom with the types of roles she was assigned. In any event, Dorothy did not view this as a tragedy. Since she considered herself an actress first and a star second, if she had to play nice roles, she would gladly play nice roles, and endow them with as much honesty and precision as she could.

Dorothy may even have welcomed typecasting occasionally, if it meant working and if the roles she was offered had sufficient texture and depth. Here she is commenting on her mother roles in 1961:

> I've been fortunate enough to play mothers with dimensions. They haven't been just symbols of motherhood.
>
> I don't know why people always ask me about these roles. It's almost like I'm being put on the defensive.
>
> People say "When are you going to quit playing mothers?" They ask about it almost as though mothers should be kept in a closet and not make a picture. [...] But "mother," who was some sort of a vague symbol before, is now a human being. I think it's a good thing. Mother can mean much more than

---
[851] Ibid., 266–267.

just having children. Nowadays families don't just have mothers and children and let it go at that. Real life mothers get into family problems more than ever before. That involvement should be reflected on the screen. I see no reason not to present honesty and life on the screen if it's in good taste.

Some actresses feel that [playing mothers] takes away from their romantic appeal. I should think that by now that idea would have been exploded.[852]

Dorothy might have made "bad choices" of her own during her career (her friend Jane Wyatt thought so, stating that "When she was [not under a studio], she often chose the *wrong* part for herself."),[853] but, in hindsight, one can also safely say that, mostly, it was the *studios'* choices of roles for Dorothy that were limited. The same could be said, however, of many a Hollywood career, and of many a Hollywood star. Both Dorothy and those responsible for casting her usually chose characters that were closest to her real-life personality, and probably did not overtax their imagination by envisaging anything different. For example, casting Dorothy as Marmee March in the television miniseries *Little Women* (1978) was a perfectly logical choice, perfectly in tune with her track record and reputation; but having her play the formidable Aunt Kathryn would certainly have been an interesting experiment.

It is also reasonable to surmise that a lot depended on the directors Dorothy was assigned. In film as in theater, certain directors were able to keep her inspired (or perhaps slightly off balance) and elicit unusual, deeply personal performances from her. Edmund Goulding (*Claudia*, 1943; *Mister 880*, 1950), Elia Kazan (*A Tree Grows in Brooklyn*, 1945;

---

[852] Joe Finnigan (UPI), "Actress Feels Mother Roles Now Meatier," *San Bernardino (CA) Sun*, January 18, 1961.

[853] Jane Wyatt, quoted in Leo Verswijver, *"Movies Were Always Magical": Interviews with 19 Actors, Directors, and Producers from the Hollywood of the 1930s through the 1950s*, McFarland and Company, Inc., Publishers, 2003, 219.

Gentleman's Agreement, 1947), Robert Siodmak (*The Spiral Staircase*, 1946), William Wyler (*Friendly Persuasion*, 1956) and, to a certain extent, Melvin Frank and Norman Panama (*Callaway Went Thataway*, 1951) did just that in film. On stage, Joseph Hardy (*The Night of the Iguana*, 1975–77), whom drama critic Clive Barnes of the *New York Times* considered "an expert at drawing new things out of old plays," was able to draw new things out of an "old" player who, at least in theory, was set in her ways by 1975.

It was probably to this particular director-actor relationship that Peggy Ann Garner was referring when, after the fact and with more than a touch of hostility towards Dorothy, she said about her director and co-star in *A Tree Grows in Brooklyn*:

> Kazan had a marvellous quality. He even knew how to handle Dorothy McGuire, and there was a certain way you had to handle that lady.[854]

Jane Corby of the *Brooklyn Eagle* cryptically referred to the discrepancy between the "standard" McGuire and the off-balance (or inspired) McGuire in her review of *Make Haste to Live* (1954):

> Dorothy McGuire [...] is as compelling an actress as ever, poised, and when she lets herself go, revealing snatches of the whimsical quality that marked her performances in the "Claudia" pictures.

Dorothy claimed "vagueness" about her career, but one has only to look at the sheer number of her engagements at any given point during

---

[854] Vallance, "McGuire" (2001), op. cit. I was unable to find the exact source for Garner's quote, which appears to be an isolated negative assessment of Dorothy in the work place. Garner biographer Sandra Grabman states she did not run across frictions between Dorothy and Garner in her research. (Sandra Grabman, correspondence with the author, March 2018.)

that career to see that she was a very busy actress indeed. In the 1950s, for example, between her acting commitments for film, radio, theater, and television, she even found time to be a co-executive producer at the La Jolla Playhouse. Dorothy may not have "directed" her career in any particular direction, as she claimed, but she definitely directed it forward.

A publicity portrait of Dorothy by 20th Century-Fox, circa 1950.

Above all, particularly after the expiration of her studio contracts, Dorothy wished to retain her status as a freelancer. Content with her private life and with her traveling, she wanted to be able to choose her projects independently. Her refusal to appear in a regular weekly sitcom that was offered to her in 1954 hinged upon her desire to "be free";[855] this would be her position for the bulk of her career.

Dorothy knew how much her career—any career—depended largely on fate, or on blind luck. For this reason—and because of her balanced personality—she never assigned blame to herself or to others for any of her missed opportunities. A shrug was the most she conceded on such occasions. Director Dan Levin remembers one instance where, as a young actor, he became upset about not getting a part he coveted (in a television show in which Dorothy was to star), and Dorothy scolded him quite sternly, saying, "Stop that. This isn't the last part you're not going to get."[856]

If the issue of career concerns anyone at this late date, it concerns the viewers, reviewers, and biographers who examine an actor's work with the benefit of hindsight. For, these after-the-fact appraisers often tend to consider the actor's body of work as a single entity, in which the responsibility of any substandard film or badly chosen role falls by default on the actor, because each film, each role, is examined through the way it fits within the actor's career. This is especially true of biographies in which the chronological flow of the narration prevents a precise analysis and discrimination of those films and performances on their own merit, and in which the brevity of the biographer's exegesis is subservient to the examination of those performances and films *as parts of a whole*. An inevitable judgment seeps into the biographer's examinations, which normally yields a classifications of those films and performances as, for example, "best," "worst," or "passable" with regard to their placement in the actor's body of work.

This is natural enough, especially since the issues of career and success stretch out to touch the biographer's work itself: from the point of view of marketing and sales, the biography of an actor with an "important" or stellar career is a surer bet than the biography of a minor or less successful

---

[855] "Her Own TV Show" (1954), op. cit.

[856] Levin (2017), op. cit.

player. The ideas of money and success, in other words, contaminate the appraiser, and hence the appraised after the fact.

It seems to me that the sane position to be taken is the one where the concept of career is allowed to vanish or fade: both humanly and artistically, each performance should stand as an isolated event. It is not the biographer's place to consider a career as a whole, just as it is not his or her place to consider a life as a whole, except in passing and using a fair amount of conjecture.

An elegant portrait of Dorothy, circa 1946.

5. *Turangalîla* III: In the Eye of the Beholder

If you want to be beautiful, start from the inside and work out.
Dorothy McGuire

Dionysius the Areopagite and St. Thomas place Beauty in the attributes of lucidity and proportion; Winkelmann endows it with the quality of serenity.
Niccolò Tommaseo

Beauty is, as Plotinus states: the victory that form achieves over matter.
Torquato Tasso

Throughout her career as a radio star (circa 1945–1955) and beyond, Dorothy McGuire was a celebrated spokesperson for Lux soap, sponsor of the *Lux Radio Theatre*. She certainly was a celebrated "face" for the product, a face that appeared in numerous newspaper ads, with or without a mention of the specific radio play that might be associated with the sponsor on a given day. Those same ads often mentioned the film in which Dorothy was currently appearing. "Be Lux Lovely," those ads intimated, adding, "says Dorothy McGuire." Other words of wisdom were quoted as coming from the film star, promoting a particular Lux soap and giving beauty tips to women throughout the nation. Here is one such ad, for Lux Toilet Soap:

"My Lux Soap Facials make skin softer... really lovelier!"
This glamorous star knows a lovely-skin care that works!

"I cream Lux active lather well in," says Dorothy McGuire. "Rinse with warm water, then cold. I pat with a soft towel to dry. Right away, my skin looks and feels soft."

Wonderful how this Lux care brings quick new beauty! Try it—you, too, will be Lux-lovely!⁸⁵⁷

Below, by way of signature: "Dorothy McGuire starring in the Samuel Goldwyn production 'I Want You.'" Below this, in bold type: "9 out of 10 Screen Stars use Lux Toilet Soap."⁸⁵⁸

Dorothy as the face of Lux Toilet Soap: newspaper ad, December 1951. Scan from newspaper.

857 In the *Odessa (TX) American*, December 13, 1951. Occasionally, Dorothy would lend her face to the promotion of other beauty products, such as "Overglo by Westmore" liquid-cream foundation make-up. In this respect, she was more than willing to play the "career game."

858 On rare occasions, Dorothy was also willing to lend her image to the advertising of other products not related to beauty. Three examples: in 1941, after her successful Broadway debut as Claudia, she publicized Chesterfield cigarettes in a full-page newspaper ad with film actor Robert Allen. In 1952, she acted as spokesperson for Rheingold Extra Dry Lager Beer. (During the height of Rheingold Beer's popularity between the 1940s and the 1960s, many popular figures from the worlds of sports, music, theater, film, and television acted as figureheads on the beer's print ads.) In 1956, an ad coinciding with the release of her film *Friendly Persuasion* had Dorothy standing up for Stieff's sterling silver cutlery set named "Silver Surf."

Radio or no radio, over the years Dorothy was the willing accomplice of various columnists and articles, especially for the *Los Angeles Times*, and lent her expertise as an "advisor" on beauty by dispensing advice to American women, or, at least, by recounting her beauty practices and principles. Much of this advice is interesting because it is not about outer beauty at all.

One of the earliest examples was a 1942 article by Sylvia Blythe of the *Los Angeles Times*, who gave her readership advice on how to be beautiful by being natural, through the example of Broadway star Dorothy McGuire:

> [...] [As] a vitamin-fed, pink-scrubbed, sweater-and-skirt girl, Miss McGuire has captivated Broadway, which usually pays its homage to sophisticated glitter.
>
> What is her formula for naturalness? A well-thought-out simplicity from top to toe, which gives the real you a chance to come through, she says.[859]

Though Blythe then goes into technical explanations of what this naturalness entails from a beautician's point of view, mentioning hair styling, make-up, eyebrow adjustment, skin care, and clothes, it is her premise and her conclusion that count. Here is the latter:

> All of this gives you an idea of the surface aspect of naturalness. You increase the effect a hundredfold when you have the kind of unaffected charm that a girl has when she finds much of her fun out-of-doors. When you look at Dorothy McGuire, you know instinctively that she has known the bite of cold winds on her cheeks; that she and the sun are friends;

---

[859] Sylvia Blythe, "Be Natural!," Los Angeles Times, January 18, 1942

that she could take you on at tennis, or hop on a bicycle and race you for miles.[860]

Already in Blythe's article an important hint was planted, one that would be developed further in the years of Dorothy's Hollywood career: that the appearance of beauty has a lot to do with overall health, and with the special glow of personal equilibrium.

A like-themed, but much more interesting, syndicated article appeared in October 1951 in the *Chicago Tribune*, signed by Arlene Dahl, who was not a regular columnist but, as the byline of the article specified in parentheses, a "Noted Hollywood Beauty." The title of the article: "Actress Dorothy McGuire Tells Her Rules of Beauty."

Some of Dorothy's "golden rules of beauty" actually sound quite reasonable, and not really about beauty at all, as in the following statement:

> If you want to be beautiful, start from the inside and work out. Painting a face doesn't do any more good than painting the outside of a house if the inside is falling to pieces from abuse and neglect.
>
> I am not beautiful, but during my screen career I've tried to project beauty into the women I portrayed. To do this realistically, I had to master the tricks which suggest beauty.[861]

Starting "from the inside" and working outward is enlightened advice, which has little to do with conventional beauty. It indicates two things at least: that Dorothy was aware of the existence of an "inside"—of an inner world—and that she was aware that such inner world could be operated

---

860 Ibid.

861 Arlene Dahl, "Actress Dorothy McGuire Tells Her Rules of Beauty," *Chicago Tribune*, October 15, 1951.

upon: it could be improved and transformed through active intervention. Dahl then elaborates on some of Dorothy's qualities, writing:

> Dorothy's tricks are the things that make a woman memorable.
>
> Graceful gestures are important, and they can be learned by every woman who wants to be beautiful. Dorothy never makes a quick or awkward movement; everything she does is controlled, yet natural.
>
> A lovely voice is also high on the list of a beauty's qualities. Dorothy's is so much a part of her that it could hardly be classified as a "trick." It is low, but not masculine, equally clear across a stage or hushed to a low whisper [...].[862]

Dorothy then goes on to list some of her limitations:

> I've learned thru mistakes. When I first came to Hollywood I relaxed into an easy atmosphere of sloppy slacks and disheveled hair. I'll admit that I enjoyed the wonderful freedom of not paying any attention to my appearance, but I was brought up short by overhearing some mighty uncomplimentary things about myself.
>
> I'm not very tall, and I'm not blessed with bountiful curves. I prefer low heels, and this means that my posture has to be perfect at all times, to give the illusion of willowy height. My clothes have to fit in the right places to suggest curves. All of this takes time and effort, but it is well worth while because of the self-confidence I feel.

---

[862] Ibid.

And personality is the warmth and friendliness you feel for other people. At least, that's my definition, and I don't want to know any other kind of people.[863]

Dahl's comment on that last statement by Dorothy was:

The woman who cultivates a generous, outgoing personality by translating kind thoughts into deeds will find that beauty is an inevitable by-product.[864]

It is interesting to note that, beauty aside, this article seems to be more a psychological profile of Dorothy, and most of the advice given in it more about the inner person than about the body. The same could be said about all the beauty talk involving Dorothy between 1951 and 1960.

If the above article concerned the person's psychological outlook, the article that appeared in the *Los Angeles Times* on October 24, 1954, under the byline of beauty expert Lydia Lane[865] concerned psychological and physical health. The title: "Dorothy McGuire Contends a Calm Outlook Enhances Beauty."

Lane takes as pretext a "plug" for Dorothy's role as Joan of Arc, a speaking part she was about to present in Arthur Honegger's oratorio *Joan of Arc at the Stake* (*Jeanne d'Arc au bûcher*, 1938) with the San Francisco Opera Company at the Shrine Auditorium in Los Angeles. Dorothy expresses satisfaction and happiness at her latest enterprise, and Lane asks

---

[863] Ibid.

[864] Ibid.

[865] Syndicated columnist Lydia Lane (1904–1994) wrote for the *Los Angeles Times* and for the *Los Angeles Mirror* from 1938 to 1980; her column, entitled "Beauty," was syndicated by the *Los Angeles Times* to 387 newspapers. (Source: *Los Angeles Times* obituary, March 29, 1994.)

her about her secret for feeling and looking so good. Dorothy turns philosophical (emphasis mine):

> I've learned through failure. When we get slapped down it's an opportunity to examine ourselves and find out the causes of our failure.
>
> It takes time and deep introspection to uncover weaknesses, but you end up knowing yourself, and until you have *inner peace* you can't extend warmth to other people.
>
> Things can be told to you dozens of times, but they make no impression until you experience them.[866]

The topic then turned to eating habits, and Lane complimented Dorothy on her menu of cheese soufflé, milk and fruit salad. Dorothy commented:

> I used to be very erratic about eating. I was always dieting because I liked myself terribly thin. These bad habits undermined my health so slowly that I was not aware of it until I became terribly ill.
>
> When you are not properly nourished it affects not only your energy, your appearance but the quality of your thinking.[867]

And in another article, she confessed:

---

[866] Lane, "Calm" (1954), op. cit.

[867] Ibid.

> Food is not as important to me as I know it should be [...]. I'm conscious of the value of a well balanced diet, but that's as far as I go with it.[868]

Again, it appears that, for Dorothy, any discourse about external appearance inevitably turned into a musing about deeper issues, thus revealing a sensitive and investigative nature. Given her radiant disposition and warmth, this is not surprising. Her passing analysis of the connection between physical nourishment and the quality of thinking is particularly insightful; and her prescription for inner peace quoted elsewhere—in discussing the frivolous topic of beauty—sounds positively Pythagorean, or Augustinian.

Dorothy's frugal undereating was probably a reaction to her early "erratic" dietary habits, during her Broadway days in the early 1940s. A photograph illustrating Geoffrey T. Hellman's 1941 pre-Hollywood profile of Dorothy shows her enthusiastically wolfing down buttered rolls; the caption states: "Dorothy breakfasts on tea and rolls, admits she loves to eat."[869] Her swing in the opposite nutritional direction was probably an adaptation to the Hollywood environment and to its spoken and unspoken aesthetic rules. Dorothy's daughter confirms this environmental pressure. Never a *gourmande*, in Hollywood Dorothy became Spartan about eating. She frequented a nutritionist, and referred him to her friends. She recommended him to Henry Fonda, who began a regimen comprised of "vitamins, niacin, lecithin, yeast, and other assorted natural products."[870] Fonda also enthusiastically passed these dietary recommendations on to his daughter Jane.

---

[868] Lydia Lane, "All People Have Beauty," *Miami (FL) News*, July 29, 1951.

[869] Hellman, "McGuire" (1941), op. cit., 126.

[870] Teichmann (1981), op. cit., 310.

The problem of Dorothy's Hollywood eating habits would be exacerbated in her last years, ultimately undermining her health dramatically. Dorothy was never a food enthusiast, and was always very careful about her figure. As Hopper put it in one of her profiles of Dorothy, "Her taste in food is simple—she shares this happily with her husband, which makes it very nice for both of them."[871] In her mature years, this disinterest for food would apparently become a revulsion, and the ghost of anorexia haunted her dangerously. Dorothy might have been described as "slim" or "svelte" during the first phases of her Hollywood tenure; in later years, journalists began using adjectives that implied (never stated) a certain degree of alarm, such as "wafer-thin."[872] It is Topo Swope's belief that, by the time Dorothy began experiencing heart trouble during the last decade of her life, her undernourishment had become a serious health hazard. If there was one way in which Hollywood hurt Dorothy as a person (in which she hurt herself as a person in response to her thoughts about Hollywood), this was it.

> When she was in the hospital, they fed her by IV, and her body just rejected the solution, because it was so used to being deprived of nourishment. She was definitely anorexic. She had always wanted to be thin—those were the dictates of Hollywood—and she was also critical of people who were not sufficiently slim, such as myself (and I was not fat by any means). In later years, she developed a real hatred of food, an active dislike of food. She would move the food around in her plate and not eat it.
>
> For example, during the last seven years of her life, she would have her caregiver, a wonderful woman by the name of Mary Hart, cut a banana in seven tiny pieces for her, and she

---

[871] Hopper, "Battle" (1947), op. cit.

[872] For example in Rosenfield, "Fate" (1982), op. cit.

would have one piece of that in the morning with her coffee. She really did not like food at all. I would sometimes joke that if I had wanted to kill my mom, all I would have had to do was take her to Costco, where there is an overabundance of food stuff.[873]

Tovah Feldshuh, who co-starred with Dorothy on the stage in Lillian Hellman's *Another Part of the Forest* in 1982, remembers those eating habits of Dorothy's, as well as her advice about eating:

> I am athletic and have a nice figure, but I have always been a voracious eater. Dorothy was always very thin and lithe. She and I would go to lunch together, and I would be eating half a moose, and she would be eating a grapefruit and a yogurt. And I remember her saying to me: "As you get older, your appestat goes way down and you don't want to eat too much." She was very much in control that way; she was in no way addicted to food.[874]

Food was one of Dorothy's *bêtes noires*, and exposed one of the few areas in which her customary positivity occasionally gave way to negative criticism of others, according to Topo Swope. If Topo's recollections are true, one may infer that in that area Dorothy's personality succumbed to Hollywood's cultural worldview, and became vulnerable to its negative influence.

Back to Lane's article. In closing, Lane probed Dorothy about perfumes, and Dorothy responded:

---

[873] Topo Swope (March 2017), op. cit.

[874] Feldshuh (2017), op. cit.

> I feel that perfume has great power to evoke memories and that we should take advantage of this.
>
> I have three favorites, and while I may try something new, I always come back to them with enjoyment. One is especially good for winter. Another I prefer in warm weather, and the third I can wear any time.[875]

Here, Dorothy's comment correlating perfumes with memory is eccentric, and once again focuses on the person's inner world.

In another syndicated article by Lane published in 1951, Dorothy's views on beauty as an inner issue became even more explicit:

> Being conscious of beauty is not vanity, I know now. It has a deeper, more constructive side [...]. Being conscious of beauty is a note of friendliness—a way of saying you want to be pleasing.
>
> [...] All people have beauty, and all people have charm. But this may not be discernable to anyone. Sometimes we fail to realize that there are many kinds of beauty—it has a larger periphery than the physical.[876]

After stating that Hollywood taught her to have discipline, a discipline she did not have while she was young, Dorothy extends the discourse to that "larger periphery" of beauty, and muses about one particular problem she had to overcome. Here is Lane asking:

> "What is the biggest thing you've had to overcome?"
>
> "Shyness," Miss McGuire said without a moment's hesitation. "It's a dreadful and a painful thing. It prevents people

---

[875] Lane, "Calm" (1954), op. cit.

[876] Lane, "All People" (1951), op. cit.

from reaching out and knowing each other. It's a handicap—you have to fight through psychic scars collected during the struggle to grow up."

That handicap of shyness was heart-rending for Dorothy because it prevented people "from reaching out and knowing each other," and she so wanted to reach out to people, and people to reach out to her. Dorothy was always after an authentic connection with others, beyond the limitations of the conventional roles assigned by circumstances. She was willing to let relationships be transformed by the fates, and kept herself open to the signs of those transformations. On the evening of December 4, 1976, I was a mere fan (and a badly dressed one, at that) asking for her autograph on the threshold of her dressing room door at the Circle in the Square theater in New York after her insightful performance in *The Night of the Iguana*. But Dorothy was a vigilant listener, a seeker of truth, and a willing participant in the workings of fate. More than that: she was an active player in, or accomplice to, those workings. The conventional roles that she and I had in the backstage area of that theater—fan and star—only acted as starting points, or catalysts; they were changing the minute we met, partially through my enthusiasm but mostly through Dorothy's amazing, *active* openness. If this was her way of counteracting her natural shyness, it worked, for it succeeded in shattering more than the conventions of reciprocal roles, and with the unstoppable momentum of a runaway train.

Dorothy's claim that she was "not beautiful" might have been an exaggeration, and an expression of self-effacement. It did, however, point to a problem that plagued both the film industry in particular and public perception in general when it came to her as a star. In its brief biography of the actress, the Internet Movie Database describes Dorothy as follows: "A quiet, passive beauty, she had a soothing quality to her open-faced looks and voice."

In terms of stardom, Hollywood did not quite know what to do with Dorothy's "passive" beauty, a beauty that was not potent or glamorous enough to qualify her either as an object of sin or as an object of desire (as a *femme fatale* or as a glamour girl). Dorothy could not be pigeonholed as a new Garbo, a new Bacall, or a new Bergman. She was not a foreigner, either, so she could not be exotic. Hollywood thus resigned itself to using her not as a beauty but as an actress; but she was too nice to be a new Bette Davis, too "normal" to be a new Katharine Hepburn, and too level-headed to be a new Jean Arthur. She was seen neither as a *farceuse* nor as a drama queen, but always as something in the middle. (Dorothy also started her Hollywood career as a Selznick star, which did not help: David O. Selznick was not known for his decisiveness in handling his players—all of her work under Selznick was done as a "loan-out.")

A sleek portrait of Dorothy, circa 1955.

Thus, her beauty and talent notwithstanding, as far as Hollywood's perception and management were concerned, Dorothy soon became trapped in a queer middle ground between beauty and non-beauty, between personality and non-personality. It was as if Hollywood could not quite make up its mind what it saw when it looked at Dorothy McGuire.

Defense exhibit A: though Dorothy played opposite several good-looking leading men during her film career, in hindsight one can clearly see that Hollywood did not consider her a glamorous beauty. For every Guy Madison or Burt Lancaster that played opposite her, there was a Kent Smith or James Dunn; for every Howard Keel or Dana Andrews, a Clifton Webb or Lloyd Nolan. The latter groups of homely or superannuated character actors constituted a majority. In Hollywood's view, Dorothy McGuire could not attract the real lookers.

Already in 1943, as Dorothy was being groomed for stardom in her "jump" from Broadway to Hollywood, newspapers all over America recognized the "problem":

> They've given up trying to turn Dorothy McGuire into a glamour girl.
>
> "They" are the executives of the 20th Century-Fox studio, and Dorothy is the girl who is making her screen debut as a star in the film version of "Claudia" after 722 performances on Broadway.
>
> They've given up trying to turn Dorothy McGuire into a glamour girl because, you see, it just can't be done. Her blond hair won't stay put. When she sits down, she usually straddles the chair. She has eyebrows almost as bushy as Lionel Barrymore's. She prefers slacks and loose-fitting sweaters and floppy-soled shoes and unpainted fingernails. She doesn't slink—she walks with the stride of a marine. And she's the healthiest looking individual in Hollywood.
>
> But "they" aren't worried. Dorothy McGuire, who looks

a little like Ingrid Bergman and talks a little like Katharine Hepburn, is an actress.

"One helluva actress," Eddie Goulding, her director, says.

"The greatest actress I've seen in years," William Perlberg, her producer, says.

"A born actress," her boss, David O. Selznick, says.

[...] There's also the problem of her upper lip. It's thin and it just about disappears when she smiles.

"They fix it up every day in the make-up department," she says. "They thought it was awful."[877]

In 1942, just as Dorothy was starting to be known for her stellar Broadway role as Claudia, another columnist reported:

> Simple and sophisticated, Dorothy has no theatrical mannerisms. She usually wears flat heels, seldom gets around doing anything about her stringy hair until just before curtain time, wears no nail polish, and pays little attention to clothes.
>
> [Says McGuire,] "Mother is always dogging me about my hair, but what can I do? Everything's against me in the clothes line. I wear flat heels, so I can't wear a bird in my hair and look like an actress. Nobody could wear a bird in their hair if they had hair like mine."[878]

Hair was not the only thing Dorothy disliked about her own figure. She was also unhappy with her feet, as Hellman's 1941 profile pointed out:

> [Dorothy's feet] are surprisingly large, and Dorothy recalls

---

[877] "Hollywood," *Arizona Republic* (1943), op. cit.

[878] Irwin, "Cinderella" (1942), op. cit.

her unrealistic sense of outrage when a pair of rather roomy slippers were brought out for her to put on. The dimensions of her lower extremities are still a source of wonder and dismay to her, and only the other day she was noticeably vexed when a young man with size 9 ½ feet, trading on a long friendship, kicked off his shoes in her living room and easily and ostentatiously slipped into a pair of pumps she had left under a chair. As a general thing, however, Dorothy is far from vain. Even the size of her feet has not induced her to wear high heels, which would tend to minimize this; low-heeled shoes are more comfortable, and for this reason she usually wears them.[879]

In 1945, after the release of her first two films, in which she had starred as unadorned, childish Claudia (1943) and as unglamorous, despondent Katie Nolan (1945), Dorothy was reported as being worried about the issue of beauty:

> Dorothy McGuire has reason to debunk the popular interchange of the words "Hollywood" and "Glamour." She had held the view of most people that in Hollywood she would go through a certain metamorphosis and come out labeled "glamorous." She is still waiting.
> "The two roles [of Claudia and Katie] have been completely different—which has made them both wonderful from an acting standpoint," says Dorothy, "but there comes a time when every girl wonders what it would be like to be 'glamorous,' and, she adds with a frank smile, "I'm beginning to wonder."[880]

---

[879] Hellman, "McGuire" (1941), op. cit., 125.

[880] "State Picture Based On Popular Novel," *Dunkirk (NY) Observer*, April 14, 1945.

Turangalila III: In the Eye of the Beholder

The fact that Dorothy participated to some extent in this dirge about her looks seems to indicate that, as her Hollywood days began, she did indeed contribute (reluctantly) to glamorizing herself to some extent, or to give some credence to the implicit conventions that Hollywood imposed.

As late as 1951, an Associated Press syndicated tidbit discussed this very issue of glamorization on the occasion of the release of Samuel Goldwyn's *I Want You* starring Dorothy:

> Dorothy McGuire, the genteel lady of Broadway and Hollywood, once told a reporter:
>
> "I feel sorry for publicity men assigned to me. They try their hardest to find something glamorous, even interesting about me. Gradually they give up." That didn't stop the press agent on Sam Goldwyn's "I Want You." Look what he came up with this week about Miss McGuire, the movie's star.
>
> "She's the girl men might have married but didn't. Women see in her what they might have been. On the screen she suffers and smiles through it. (She's best in the ten hankie picture, i.e. a super tearjerker.)
>
> "No beauty, she transcends beauty. She's bourbon, without the hangover. She rarely raises her voice but her films smack you with the intensity of a half-track."[881]

This self-flagellation about Dorothy's lack of beauty occupied the press obsessively during the first ten years of her career. Some of the statements attributed to Dorothy seem improbable, or might have been spoken by her to please the career machine, if they were spoken at all. For example this one, reported by Jimmie Fidler in 1945:

---

[881] "Accolade for Miss McGuire," *Middletown (OH) Sunday News Journal*, September 30, 1951.

> [. . .] It's a very exceptional beauty who can stomach unglamorous roles for any length of time, no matter how much professional prestige may be had by doing so.
>
> Consider, for instance, Dorothy McGuire, who, by playing four great acting parts that were completely lacking in glamour, seemed on the way to being a second Bette Davis. Was she satisfied by the critics' raves? Not at all! Last month her natural feminine pride got the best of her, and she ultimatumed studio bosses. Either they could find a role in which she could be charming and beautiful, or else.[882]

Which does not sound like Dorothy at all, even though it might be true. The following portrayal, in an extended profile by Hedda Hopper, sounds more credible:

> [Dorothy's] great plea with movie men is: "Let me look myself. Don't try to make me resemble some movie beauty; I want to keep my individuality for whatever it's worth." She keeps hairdressers and wardrobe women at a respectful distance, admits frankly she's careless about dress and doesn't intend to do anything about it because it isn't native to her to be punctilious where modes are concerned. She thinks movies can depersonalize an actress quickly if the actress doesn't fight against it.[883]

Beauty, at any rate, was an implicit given even when it came to "non-beautiful" leading ladies such as Dorothy; both her entire career as a film star and her consultancies in the above articles by Lane and Dahl are

---

[882] Jimmie Fidler, "Movie Actresses Most Want Meaty Character Roles," *Pottstown (PA) Mercury*, October 5, 1945.

[883] Hopper, "Independence" (1947), op. cit.

ultimately tacit proof of precisely what Dorothy so graciously negated in words. For instance: even today, the transformation of Dorothy's character in the film *The Enchanted Cottage* (1945) is startling to the audience not because she becomes beautiful after her magical metamorphosis, but because she is introduced as an ugly duckling to begin with. Dorothy's audience presumes that she is beautiful rather than homely, and is reassured by her "reverting" to her movie-star beauty.

That implicit, unacknowledged beauty (and Dorothy's sometime experience as a model) was certainly showcased in America's newspapers when, on several occasions, reminders were printed of her participation in this or that film consisting entirely of photographs of her wearing the beautiful costumes or gowns from said films. An example was the elaborate two-piece gown made of white satin and Alencon lace that she wore for her character's wedding in the film *Invitation* (1952). This gown appeared in several newspapers nationwide, with a caption describing not the movie but the gown.

Both in her film career and in her private life, Dorothy was known for the simple, unpretentious elegance of her choice in clothing. "[Her] favorite costume is a skirt and sweater, the latter habitually several sizes too large for her," reported Hellman in his 1941 profile of Dorothy. And Robbin Coons, in his 1943 profile, stated:

> She bought her first pair of 3-inch heels to wear for fashion photos at the studio. She doesn't own a single gown designed for "glamour." She owns simple dresses and neat little suits, some slacks and cardigans. She has never had a permanent, but wears her ash blonde hair brushed back from her face, just as nature grew it. Nature was good to her.[884]

Occasionally, this simplicity and elegance displayed a touch of ec-

---

[884] Coons, "Name" (1943), op. cit.

centricity. Here is Hedda Hopper hinting at such eccentricity in a 1950 profile of Dorothy:

> When I meet Dorothy McGuire nowadays I recall that scene in a recent novel in which an agent gets a younger player all minked and marcelled up for an audition. His cynical partner looks her over, snorts with disgust and says, "Muss up her hair and give her a hat that looks as if a horse stepped on it, like Dorothy McGuire wears, if you want a producer to take her seriously."[885]

Dorothy loved hats, though sometimes more as curios than as accessories. Even in her early Broadway days, this had been noticed:

> She loves elaborate little hats, done up with flowers and veils, but this is almost an esthetic rather than a sartorial passion, since these objects do not go with the rest of her get-up, and she often buys them simply to look at them. "You must come up and see my new hat," she frequently says to friends, crinkling up her eyes ecstatically, "because I can't ever *wear* it."[886]

Eccentric perhaps, but elegant and svelte Dorothy certainly was. In fact, in her early pre-fame days, she supported herself with modeling jobs (at $25 an hour). According to her daughter, Dorothy also designed and made several of her dresses. In her early days as a Broadway star, she surprised many by purchasing fabrics from the Fortuny company, all based on

---

[885] Hedda Hopper, "New Dorothy McGuire Comes Down to Earth," *Sioux Falls (SD) Argus-Leader*, January 22, 1950.

[886] Hellman, "McGuire" (1941), op. cit., 125.

designs by celebrated Venetian designer Mariano Fortuny.[887] This sophisticated material she used to design some dresses.[888]

That Dorothy's special beauty, both as a reality and as a construct, had to do with her unique mixture of aesthetics and personality was gently posited by Hellman in his 1941 profile. Hellman, who was an expert profiler by 1941, having written many insightful human portraits for the *New Yorker* in the preceding decade, could skillfully hide his clues between the lines without being too explicit. Here he is discussing Dorothy's attitude towards men:

> Dorothy enjoys the company of men, especially men whom she considers brainy, but there is nothing flirtatious about her. She has an odd detachment from life that makes her both surprised and a little frightened when, as often happens, a man falls in love with her. Under these circumstances, the man generally comes to look on her as a particularly enchanting sister.[889]

The Hollywood film industry was probably too primitive and unsophisticated to conceive of a sense of beauty that went beyond mere aesthetics, or mere cultural convention. It never understood that advice such as Dorothy's to the readers of Arlene Dahl's column in 1951 was really an invitation to look deeper within themselves, and to envisage a broader cultural, or personal, idea of what beauty could mean. Hollywood and the cosmetic industry, in other words, were not inclined to widen the scope

---

[887] Spanish-born set designer, lighting engineer, painter, photographer, and textile designer Mariano Fortuny (1871–1949) lived and worked in Venice, Italy, most of his adult life. The Venetian palazzo (San Marco 3958) where he worked is now called Palazzo Fortuny and houses the Fortuny Museum.

[888] Topo Swope (February 2017), op. cit.

[889] Hellman, "McGuire" (1941), op. cit., 130–131.

of their aesthetic thinking beyond their concept of beauty to encompass, for example, the concept of the sublime, in the manner of, say, Johann Joachim Winckelmann,[890] Edmund Burke,[891] Samuel Taylor Coleridge,[892] or Niccolò Tommaseo.[893] Dorothy—in her own view as well as in the film industry's—may not have been classifiable as beautiful by Hollywood convention; she may, however, have been beautiful in many other ways, and by many other parameters. She may even have been sublime.

For, a human being is not a statue. A mind entangled in desire may be content with the simple parameters (whether societal, artistic, or sexual) that tell it that a human being's body and face are beautiful. But a human being is a complex entity, endowed, at a minimum, with movement, and, at a maximum, with the effects of thought, feeling and will. A human being is a thing of metamorphosis, poetry, affects, morality, and ideas in motion. Philosopher Niccolò Tommaseo stated that "the sublime is in the breadth of the idea, unified by feeling."[894] When he wrote this, he was thinking of beauty applied to the arts, but the concept could just as easily be applied to a person: it is in the manner in which the individual realizes the *idea* of the human being through living form that his or her beauty lies, and breathes. In the fullness of the incarnation of a potential. In that beauty which transcends "beauty" because it has little to do with the physical body per se.

---

[890] Giuseppe Pucci, "Winckelmann e il sublime," *teCLa: Rivista di temi di critica e letteratura artistica*, n. 4, December 2011, pp. 54–67.

[891] Edmund Burke, *A Philosophical Enquiry into the Origin of Our Ideas of the Sublime and Beautiful*, Routledge and Kegan Paul, 1958.

[892] Raimonda Modiano, "Coleridge and the Sublime: A Response to Thomas Weiskel's The Romantic Sublime," in *The Wordsworth Circle*, vol. 9, n. 1 (Winter 1978), pp. 110–120.

[893] Niccolò Tommaseo, *Bellezza e civiltà, o delle arti del bello sensibile: studii*, Felice Le Monnier, 1857.

[894] Ibid., 56.

6. *Turangalîla* IV: Positivity

In general, people of all persuasions got along with Dorothy McGuire, just as she got along with them. Mentions of on-set or on-stage tensions between Dorothy and her colleagues were so rare and unsubstantiated as to be non-existent.[895] In a *Los Angeles Times* article on the occasion of the premiere of the revival of *Another Part of the Forest* (1982), Jim Hansen, associate artistic director of the Center Theater Group of Los Angeles, had this to say about Dorothy in the workplace:

> I've worked with Dorothy during three plays at the Ahmanson. She's completely without frills. And there's nobody who can't get along with her. How many actresses can you say that about?[896]

---

[895] One such mention was dropped by Ed Sullivan during the La Jolla Playhouse tour of *Summer and Smoke* in November 1950: "'Summer and Smoke' folded because of friction between Dorothy McGuire and John Ireland. . . ." (Ed Sullivan, "Little Old New York," *Oil City [PA] Derrick*, November 29, 1950.)

[896] Rosenfield, "Fate" (1982), op. cit.

Dorothy's habit of keeping her dressing room door open in the theater (except when undressing), mentioned by columnist Bob Thomas in his 1945 article about her, persisted through the years, and can be seen as an expression of her big-hearted openness to the world. That gesture of staying open for the world so that anyone "with or without business"[897] could readily talk to her is a metaphor of her welcoming, unguarded, unpretentious attitude. That gesture, to mention only two examples, allowed me to feel welcome upon my approaching her when she was performing in *The Night of the Iguana*, just as it had allowed John Swope to meet his future wife when she was performing in *Claudia*. In each of those examples, that openness changed the courses of two lives (or, better, three).[898]

In a microcosm so often populated by gorgons, harpies, and other insecure monsters (Hollywood), Dorothy refused to speak ill of others, whether in the press or in person, not because she was able to bite her tongue in restraint, but because she genuinely thought it was not the right thing to do. This same rectitude she expected of those around her. Director Dan Levin remembers being scolded quite harshly by Dorothy after watching a film in her company and telling her that she would have acted the lead role better than the actress who had been cast in the role.[899]

There can be little doubt that the quality she displayed when refusing to speak negative thoughts can be called positivity. This quality she cultivated throughout her life, in various forms (she probably refused to think those thoughts as well); this quality has been "simplified" by public opinion and whittled down to the definition of "niceness."

Positivity is not so much a natural character trait as a deliberate, vol-

---

[897] Thomas, "Roles" (1945), op. cit.

[898] According to John Swope historian Carolyn Peter, John met Dorothy at Leland Hayward's home sometime around 1940, before Dorothy's starring role in *Claudia*, which directly contradicts the reports given by the press at the time and by Dorothy herself in later years. (See Peter, *Japan* [2006], op. cit., 35.) No matter: Dorothy did, in fact, leave her doors open, even if this was not literally true where her meeting John was concerned.

[899] Levin (2017), op. cit.

untary, and programmatic stance, one that does more than just contrast the damaging influence of natural negative thoughts. Put in practice with constancy, positivity is a constructive tool, and not only where thoughts are concerned; it is a reality-penetrating force and a creator of equilibrium. So important is this force for the development of the person (and for the adjustment of personality) that Austrian esotericist and philosopher Rudolf Steiner listed it as a "fundamental" daily exercise in the spiritual teachings/discipline of his Anthroposophy.

Certain aspects of the definition of "positive" are often misconstrued in everyday usage. Here is what is pertinent to this particular inner quality in the definitions one finds in dictionaries.

The *Merriam-Webster Dictionary* gives the following among its definitions of "positive":

1)   Independent of changing circumstances; unconditioned.

2)   Not fictitious; real.

3)   Indicating, relating to, or characterized by affirmation, addition, inclusion or presence rather than negation, withholding or absence.

4)   Something of which an affirmation can be made: reality.

The *Oxford English Dictionary* offers the following definitions:

1)   Having no relation to or comparison with other things; free from qualifications, conditions, or reservations; unconditional.

2)   Having relation only to matters of fact; dealing only with matters of fact and experience; practical, realistic; not speculative or theoretical; dealing with facts, apart from any theory; actual, real; sensible, concrete. Opposite of negative.

And Niccolò Tommaseo, in his extraordinary *Dizionario della lingua italiana*, adds:

1) From its Latin origin "Pōněre": since "pōněre" was used to mean to Affirm, to lay down, thus Positive comes to mean Real: that which affirms.

2) Of the idea or of the word inasmuch as it clearly sees and affirms the reality of an object.

3) Positive doctrine or Positive reasoning: that lays down what needs to be laid down as true, wherever it might recognize it both in the real world and in the ideal; that does not presume haphazardly or oppose arbitrarily.[900]

"Wherever it might recognize it": that which is true, or real, i.e. the conceptual reality of the object, must be recognized where it appears, i.e. in the object itself. Looking at an object positively does not mean ignoring what is not good about it, as one sometimes means when one uses the word. There is often confusion between "positive" and "optimistic"—as in the expression "think positive." The word's everyday meaning often contains an element of blind faith that is technically absent from its etymological/philosophical meaning, the latter pointing to a scientific,

---

[900] Niccolò Tommaseo, *Dizionario della lingua italiana* ["Dictionary of the Italian Language"], Società L'unione Tipografico-Editrice, Turin, 1879. A word about this dictionary of the Italian language. More than just a dictionary, and more than just an Italian counterpart to the *Oxford English Dictionary*, this gigantic, profound seven-volume masterpiece (in its original oversized-tome, double-column format, the volume for letters R-S is 1,336 pages long) conceived by Dalmatian-born Italian writer and philosopher Niccolò Tommaseo (1802–1874) examines each word and element of the Italian language linguistically, literarily, historically, philosophically and conceptually, digging deep into its origins and into its ideal nature, citing myriad examples of its use, both in print and in everyday life, with sources.

Each word, each concept, is dissected and unraveled, by correlating it with its conceptual kin and making both microscopic and macroscopic distinctions about everything related to it. Not just a tool for understanding and re-discovering a language, this is a masterly guide for exploring ideas and the connections between ideas. Hugely influential for over a century, the dictionary has now been largely, and undeservedly, forgotten, possibly because of its deep-rooted Neo-Platonic and Christian bent. Much the same fate has befallen Tommaseo's *Nuovo dizionario dei sinonimi della lingua italiana* ("New Dictionary of the Synonyms of the Italian Language," second edition, Giuseppe Reina, 1851), which, despite its title, is too philosophical and too complex to be viewed as a simple thesaurus.

or gnoseological, intent. Even the myriad "self-help" books authored by many writers throughout the twentieth century often invoked this attitude—starting with Napoleon Hill's seminal *Think and Grow Rich* (1937), Emmett Fox's *Power through Constructive Thinking* (1940) and W. Clement Stone's *The Other Side of the Mind* (1964). Mostly, these books referenced optimism rather than true positivity.

Looking at an object or phenomenon positively, in the purest sense, means looking at it without prejudice and persisting in this "constructive" gaze in order to be able to "see" the entire reality of that object or phenomenon, of its parts and of the synthesis of its parts, in order to form a full concept of it; it means embracing its reality without deciding the outcome beforehand. A negative prejudice or judgment (the thoughts or opinions we often entertain about an object) can paralyze our capacity to see what is in front of our very noses, for the simple reason that, once that negative impression or thought has penetrated us, we stop "looking." The positive observation of an object entails an impersonal eye, not weighed down by ego, opinion or feeling, if it is to gain a firm grasp of that object and its concept. If such observation persists, the object can then begin to reveal things about itself that we would never recognize from a fleeting or prejudiced glance.

One can see that the activity of positivity hinges upon two things: (1) the absence (or elimination) of classic obstacles to a full knowledge of reality such as prejudice, changeable opinion, and ego, and (2) the impulse to know: the impulse to open our "doors" to the world.

One finds descriptions of this attitude, and activity, in most exponents of the millenary philosophical Tradition of self-knowledge, from Plato to Aristotle, from Buddhism to Vedanta, from the Doctors of the Roman Catholic Church to Rudolf Steiner (more about that Tradition later). Of the five fundamental or supplementary exercises that Steiner prescribed as an aid to the meditation and concentration discipline comprising an occult education, "positivity," which he also called "the greatest open-mindedness," is the fourth. It consists in searching for all that is good, beautiful, useful, true, etc. in all things and beings. According to Steiner,

> [The] 'sense of affirmation' is a particularly important quality. This can be developed by seeking out good, fine or useful characteristics in all things, rather than focusing primarily on what is reprehensible, ugly or contradictory. [. . .] In everything, even the most distasteful, an earnest seeker can find something worth acknowledging.[901]

Steiner emphasized the usefulness of this exercise for the seeker, in a three-step development that ultimately involved an extreme inner "openness" to one's surroundings, "[growing] beyond [one's self] and "learning to regard a part of [one's] environment as belonging to [one's self]":[902]

> All affirmation enlivens, all negation exhausts and kills. This is not only because an ethical power is involved in turning to the positive aspect of something, but also because affirmation enlivens us and renders the soul's faculties free and secure.
>
> In an age such as ours, nervousness also predominates. Being nervous and highly critical belong together. The virtues I propose are there to release higher powers for human beings. Such virtues, which aim to infuse all lower impulses with a rhythmic quality, endow the soul with powers that enable it to turn towards higher development.[903]

---

[901] Rudolf Steiner, *Stages of Higher Knowledge*, G.P. Putnam's Sons, 1930; as quoted in Steiner, *Six Steps* (2010), op. cit., 39–40.

[902] Rudolf Steiner, "General Requirements," (*Gesamtausgabe* 267, pp. 58 f.), as quoted in Steiner, *Six Steps* (2010), op. cit., 46.

[903] Rudolf Steiner, Lecture in Berlin, April 19, 1906, as quoted in Steiner, *Six Steps* (2010), op. cit., 41.

A photo portrait of Austrian philosopher and esotericist Rudolf Steiner (1861–1925), founder of Anthroposophy.

In other words:

> This exercise is somewhat related to what we can call the withholding of criticism. It does not mean calling black white and white black. But there is a difference between judging things in a way that issues merely from one's own personality, reacting accordingly in sympathy and antipathy, or the stance which enters lovingly into the other being or phenomenon and continually asks: 'Why is the other like this,' or 'Why does he act as he does?' Such a stance inevitably leads to greater efforts to aid what is imperfect rather than simply criticize and find fault with it.[904]

---

[904] From the collected works of Rudolf Steiner, GA 267: *Seelenübungen, Band I*; as quoted in

Dorothy might not have been familiar with Steiner's instructions—though she was conversant with similar instructions from other spiritual disciplines, such as Buddhist thought, which she studied—but, particularly in the latter half of her life, she made it a point to practice the above virtue, and was surprisingly adamant about it. Temptations to do otherwise usually met with iron-fisted rejection. Such was the case with Dorothy's reaction to *Chicago Tribune* writer Marilyn Beck in 1975. Here is Dorothy's reaction to one of Beck's questions, and Beck's reaction to that:

> "Don't ask me about the unpleasant side of the business. We both know that Hollywood can be rough and tough and that the experiences of some actresses have been sad. But to think about that would be negative."
>
> Her refusal to touch upon negative thoughts also became her explanation for declining to discuss pictures she's made which she didn't enjoy.[905]

Despite Beck's prodding, Dorothy refused to comment on "the unpleasant side of the business," and to give any details about negative experiences in film. Much the same puzzlement was felt by Italian journalist and theater historian Alvise Sapori in his 1986 interview with Dorothy:

> [Before starting the interview, Dorothy McGuire] has declared that she does not care where the camera and lights are positioned, that we can ask whatever we want, that she does not like to be surprised but does not want to know in advance what we will ask her, [...] but that she will not indulge in gossip.
>
> While she listens to the questions, she has the expression of an enchanting middle-class lady in a dentist's waiting room. No. She does not want to talk about politics, "those are unpleasant things I don't wish to remember." [Our questions about stars and

---

Steiner, *Six Steps* (2010), op. cit., 45.

[905] Beck, "Name" (1975), op. cit.

directors she has worked with produce only vague, reticent anecdotes.]

On less personal topics, perhaps she will be less elusive. Nothing doing. We get a beautiful quote from Laurence Olivier, reported as if it were a piece by Shakespeare on the art of the actor, which ends with "I don't think there is a more beautiful job than teaching the human art of knowing oneself." Can we tell her that she was sexy in "Till the End of Time"? "Of course you can tell me. Thank you." And she turns back to the art of the actor . . . "This is the mystery of the actor. There is something intangible standing between character and actress. And the film camera is a magical instrument that can take you anywhere, and this is true for those in front of the camera as well as for those seeing the end result, the film." She responds to several questions with curt refusals ("I am too old to play this game," "You always ask the same questions," "No, thank you, I don't wish to answer."). Or else, she defuses the tension by telling an anecdote, such as a delightful one about the shooting of *Swiss Family Robinson*, during which, upon mentioning a snake wrangler, she says, "I have often asked myself if snakes are better than human beings," and then she tells an incongruous story about parasols which during the first days protected only the actresses and then, gradually, were extended to the ostriches who were stupefied by the heat.

In short, once again, it is a constant; we are faced with a perfectly organized defense. It is as if there were layers upon layers in this woman, all smiling, with a few leaves of refusal to separate them, and all peripheral. You do not seem to make many concessions, as a person, Miss McGuire. "I'm an actress, I worry, I prepare, one often has to shoot in conditions of hardship, in a tabernacle or baseball field, without a dressing room, and so one has to be very controlled." Would you like to tell us something else, Miss McGuire? "No. This is already a lot. Any more, would be too much."[906]

---

[906] Sapori, "Actress" (1986), op. cit. The translation is mine.

Both Beck and Sapori were obviously surprised at Dorothy's adamant evasions. Perhaps even peeved, but certainly surprised. Beck made a curious observation when describing the actress:

> There was a look of self-containment about her. More than that, there was a feeling—that grew ever stronger during our two-hour lunch—that an invisible gossamer veil shielded her from offending images, from intrusions of an imperfect world.[907]

The image that Beck evoked, of something invisible, of something silky and incorporeal hovering about Dorothy, was pertinent; her definition of that something as a veil or shield, however, was not. Positivity does not impede one's gaze towards reality; it strengthens it and develops it. Positivity is not a protection from the knowledge of reality; it is a force that allows a fuller knowledge to unfold unimpeded and unveiled, and allows us to perforate and shatter the ego-based membrane that does, indeed, shield us from the reality we do not like—usually through opposition. Beck seemed to view Dorothy's dismissal of the negative as some sort of blindness, or isolation: as a defense against the world. Positivity, on the contrary, opens up avenues of knowledge that would shut when approached through the natural tools of prejudice and negative criticism: it allows us to penetrate the reality of the world. Concentrating on the positive does not mean refusing to see the negative, only setting it aside as a pernicious influence during our investigation of reality.

Sapori was even more put off, viewing Dorothy's refusals as "a perfectly organized defense"; he saw Dorothy as an antagonist, even though she dropped more than one salient hint as to how she wished the conversation to be conducted, for example by referring to self-knowledge (through acting) and self-control. Sapori, however, did not take the bait, nor steer away

---

[907] Beck, "Name" (1975), op. cit.

from the conventional questions about Hollywood and stardom. "You always ask the same questions," admonished Dorothy, but even her curious observation about snakes being superior to human beings did not elicit a thoughtful response from Sapori, even though that observation certainly merited some investigation.

A parenthesis about Dorothy and her statement about snakes. Dorothy loved dogs especially, and owned several in succession over the years, but, according to family friend Jim Fernald, her love extended to all species, Buddhist style. Here is an anecdote from him:

> Dorothy loved *all* animals. My wife and I realized just how much as we were moving into the pool apartment at 121 Copley Place. The place was infested by rats, and Dorothy refused to do anything about it. She thought those rodents were sacred, I guess; or at least cute. She had affection for them, and I think she might even have been feeding them. We finally put our foot down and told her we would not be moving in unless she did something about the infestation. Reluctantly, she did.[908]

The Fernalds' concern with the rat infestation at 121 Copley Place was understandable enough given their roles as tenants, and their view of Dorothy's affection for the vermin as an unacceptable eccentricity reasonable. Viewed from a slightly broader perspective, however, Dorothy's respect for "objectionable" forms of life reverberates with the precepts of several Eastern philosophies, revealing a rather unique, enlightened (if unpopular) worldview.

Back to our Italian journalist. Sapori could not take a hint even when Dorothy corrected him at the beginning of the interview. When he asked, "Can we talk about Dorothy McGuire the star?," she stated unequivo-

---

[908] Fernald (2017), op. cit.

cally, "Let me make something clear: I am an actress." She might as well have said "I am a human being," but Sapori took this, too, as a refusal, rather than as a subtle distinction between art and commerce, or as a musing about the acting craft as human investigation, and immediately changed the subject. In all fairness, he did notice some positive qualities: "Everything about her is discreet. There is a hint of detachment, but her graciousness and finesse are absolute, and unassailable."[909] Yet, ultimately, Sapori mistook equilibrium, positivity, and detachment for coldness and antagonism.

Dorothy had always been something of a free spirit, but, for decades, she had graciously played the Hollywood press game without grumbling, by finding ways to spin interviews in inventively centrifugal directions without completely ceasing to play the part that was expected of her. In the 1970s and '80s, whether because of a touch of disillusionment with humanity's "games" or because of a new capacity to distinguish between what was essential and what was not from a human standpoint, Dorothy set new rules for that game. Her entire tactical approach in those late interviews pointed to a desire to talk positively about something significant, and to allude to topics that had a broad, universal scope. Her hopeful suggestions, however, fell upon deaf ears. At least, Beck seemed to realize that something special and evanescent was at work in the woman she was trying to appraise. That "invisible gossamer" something that Beck perceived in Dorothy was the undefinable quality of an uncommonly spiritual being who was brave enough to meet the world positively and meaningfully, and did not suffer foolishness, falsity, or shallowness. Dorothy's new capacity to concentrate on human essentials, and her adamantine positivity, revealed a moral choice on her part. Yet Dorothy was apparently neither overtly religious, nor esoterically inclined; as family friend Jim Fernald puts it, "She had not found God."[910] One could argue that God (in the

---

[909] Sapori, "Actress" (1986), op. cit.

[910] Fernald (2017), op. cit.

broadest sense of the word) had found *her*, or, if she had indeed found Him, she had not alerted anyone to the fact. At any rate, something she had searched for, and found.

Dorothy's daughter Topo states that she and her brother "were not raised in any religion," and that there was "no religion in the family." However, she also states that her father "was Pantheistic, but probably a bit more agnostic."[911] Which does not mean that Dorothy and John Swope were not spiritual, only that they did not belong to any one orthodox organized church, nor subscribe to any one dogma. Pantheism is a relatively modern term, introduced explicitly in Western thought by Dutch philosopher Baruch Spinoza, but it describes a concept that was conceived by many philosophers in the past (Italian philosopher and playwright Giordano Bruno was burnt at the stake for it on February 17, 1600), and touched upon importantly by various ancient, especially Asian, religions, such as Hinduism, Taoism, and Vedanta. In the West, during the nineteenth century, many writers and artists embraced the concept of Pantheism, or of the interconnectedness of all things, and of reality as a non-dualistic manifestation of a non-anthropomorphic, infinite, and immanent God. Among them, Samuel Coleridge, Ralph Waldo Emerson, Henry David Thoreau, and Walt Whitman. Philosophers from the Hellenistic Stoics to Johann Gottlieb Fichte and Georg Wilhelm Friedrich Hegel embraced variations of the idea in some form.

The idea that God is both singular and plural (or a plurality in a unity) is a seminal one; in our Judeo-Christian world, it dates as far back as the Sepher of Moses, commonly known as Book of Genesis. An exegetical tradition pointedly alerts us to the fact that, grammatically, ancient Hebrew expresses the Supreme Being as both a singular and a plural entity, often with a plural verb attached to it.[912] Thus, if one looks at both ancient

---

[911] Topo Swope, correspondence with the author, June 2018.

[912] Most interestingly, in Antoine Fabre d'Olivet, *La langue Hébraique restituée et le veritable sens des mots hébreux rétabli et prouvé par leur analyse radicale*. Barrois et Eberhart, 1815, Part II, 24–33.

and modern polytheistic religions without prejudice, one can see a Pantheistic spirit in them: the many deities are not arbitrary idols, but plural expressions or ramifications of a single emanating force, each symbolizing a different aspect of the forces at work in the human being, in the cosmos, and in time. Even being agnostic does not mean being a materialist, necessarily; it means being willing (perhaps eager) to know, but only through proof, experience, or certainty. It means wanting to know and experience rather than to believe.

Back to Dorothy's positivity. In a world (the entertainment world) dominated by fakery, flattery, and the glorification of ego, and especially in the second half of her life, the private Dorothy was sincere, direct, and constructive; she was balanced and focused in her thinking.[913] She did not suffer lies, harsh judgment or prejudice[914] in others or in herself, and was always ready to give of herself to others and to partake of their experience.

In those responses Dorothy gave to Beck and Sapori, we can clearly see that certain elements of her character that might at first glance seem contradictory were, in fact, complementary. Equanimity and positivity co-existed with strength of will and readiness for action; artistic ambition co-existed with adamantine human aspiration; detachment co-existed with warmth and graciousness. As for her relationship with the film industry, throughout her life, but especially in her later years, Dorothy was able to pull away (detach herself) from the turmoil of career concerns and observe Hollywood from a sidereal distance, where petty details dissolved, permitting an unobstructed view of a larger picture. This is probably the reason why Sapori's attempts to prod Dorothy for details about star colleagues

---

[913] Regulating one's course of thinking, mastery of thought processes, objectivity and focus in one's thinking were the objectives of the first (of five) supplementary exercise that Rudolf Steiner advocated in order to achieve certain positive qualities and regulate his students' inner turmoil. See Steiner, *Six Steps* (2010), op. cit., 5–16.

[914] Open-mindedness, lack of prejudice, and freedom from ego-dictated judgment were the objectives of the fifth (of five) supplementary exercises that Rudolf Steiner gave to his students in his esoteric teachings. See Steiner, *Six Steps* (2010), op. cit., 49–57.

during his interview (Gary Cooper, Sandra Dee, Greta Garbo, Hedy Lamarr) met with cordial reticence. Probably feeling that Sapori was after gossip or empty anecdotes about glamour and fame, Dorothy was unwilling to comply ("I don't know, I'm not good at quoting people").[915] Only when asked about Gregory Peck did she respond positively, dropping the adjective "magical," which neither satisfied the interviewer nor prompted him to help her elaborate.

Unable to envisage that larger picture, or even to inquire what it might have been, Sapori portrayed Dorothy's reticence as a vagueness, almost as a confusion; which it might have been, since he systematically thwarted every attempt she made to spin the discourse in a universal direction. In this sense, too, Dorothy was a positive person: when faced with negativity or superficiality, she always tried to avoid direct opposition; rather than contradicting a negative person or an idle curiosity, she retreated into silence.

Though it would be too optimistic, especially with the unfair advantage of hindsight, to wish that journalists such as Beck and Sapori had helped Dorothy develop some of the statements she made during their interviews, we are authorized to intervene now, decades after the fact. Let us then try to interpret some of those statements constructively. One strand stands out in Sapori's interview, rife with possibilities: "Let me make something clear: I am an actress. [...] I don't think there is a more beautiful job than teaching the human art of knowing oneself. [...] This is the mystery of the actor." Dorothy took a clear position when she declared herself an actress, and when she relayed that quote from Laurence Olivier. For Dorothy, acting was more than a craft or a career; it was something of a Delphic mission. She never stated exactly what she did to carry out that mission, but her definition of acting as "teaching the art of knowing oneself" spoke volumes. That particular aspect of being an actress, which dovetailed with Dorothy's view of the mysterious craft of the actor as

---

[915] Sapori, "Actress" (1986), op. cit.

a "life experience," revealed her emphasis on the investigative nature of art, and on its role as aid in being human. The actor was not at the service of the art, but vice versa. More mysterious was Dorothy's mention of "something intangible standing between character and actress." Here, her wonder and puzzlement at something supersensible separating the actress from the entity she was to incarnate clearly pointed to a metaphysical, or spiritual, realm existing just outside (or within) the reach of the artist: existing at some kind of human intersection with the "intangible."

It may be that Dorothy needed the help of Laurence Olivier, or of other artists or writers, to be able to verbalize that realization about acting; it is evident, however, that Olivier et al. ignited something important that was latent, or already developed, in Dorothy: a revelation about the subservience of art to self-knowledge. Had she been offered further help, or at least a friendly ear, Dorothy might have been able to articulate an argument about art and self-discovery similar to the one made years earlier by artist Wassily Kandinsky in his remarkable book *On the Spiritual in Art* (1911).[916]

As for Dorothy's positivity, very early in my acquaintance with her, I discovered that her warmth and generosity were neither simple natural feelings nor societal poses; they were expressions of a powerful impulse to reach out authentically to other human beings. Dorothy's interest in, or attention to, her fellow humans was a loving, penetrating weapon. A gentle irony, and the willingness to offer friendly, benevolent advice, for example, were two qualities of that impulse that have stuck in my memory. Dorothy was not merely nice: she was willing to intervene in someone else's life. In my particular case, she was willing to point out a behavioral flaw of mine with affection, instead of pretending not to see it; to my face, but without even the faintest trace of reproach.

---

[916] The first English edition of Kandinsky's German original was published in 1914 by Constable in London and entitled *The Art of Spiritual Harmony*. The second edition (the so-called New York Edition) was published in 1946 by the Solomon R. Guggenheim Foundation and entitled *On the Spiritual in Art*.

Turangalila IV: Positivity

Immature for my age, in 1977 I had not "found" my personality yet, and, to counteract my shyness, I had built a character for myself based on some flamboyant, rather British-sounding theatrical mannerisms. Those affectations, which were not really part of my true nature but revealed an awkward attempt to "defend" myself from the dangers of social interactions, Dorothy noticed, cheerfully pointing out that I had developed them to perfection, and that perhaps I should try out some other "character" for myself. That kind of intervention, usually reserved for family members or confidants, Dorothy took on with the loving impetus of a best friend, even though we had only known each other (superficially) for just over a year. What is even more remarkable is that she was able to do it *positively*: not by concentrating on that flaw as a negative, but simply by acknowledging it as something that had probably run its course—almost in the manner of a compliment—and pointing to its possible evolution, or alternative. Dorothy was not chiding me for behaving in a certain way, but rather suggesting that it might be time to experiment with something different. That delicate, positive criticism, which was not actually posed in the form of criticism, rang absolutely true to me, and I soon shed those excessive mannerisms.

Positive Dorothy certainly was. As Tovah Feldshuh puts it: "I loved being around her. Who didn't? She made you feel good. She was a great listener and a great giver, and she was always interested in your life story. In her own way, she was a bit of a saint."[917] Family friend Dwight Holing confirms this particular unselfish trait of Dorothy's:

> Dorothy was always interested in and curious about what other people were doing, especially young people; always interested in hearing about their lives. This I noticed from my very first meetings with her, during the period her son Mark and I were roommates in school, and kept noticing over the

---
[917] Feldshuh (2017), op. cit.

years: she was always more interested in what you were doing than in revealing what she was up to. There never seemed to be anything standoffish about her.[918]

So does Dan Levin:

> Immediately after my period as apprentice at the La Jolla Playhouse, I was doing a play in New York. Not only did Dorothy and John come to see it, they also came backstage to say hello and compliment me. It was such a generous gesture on their part, and a thrill for me.[919]

Hollywood columnist Bob Thomas had also noticed this trait, and had humorously turned it into a mock complaint, in his 1945 profile of Dorothy:

> However pleasant [this nice, generous personality] may be to her fellow workers, it is not too favorable to an interviewer. Dorothy, unlike most actresses, does not have the knack of being able to talk glibly about herself. She is the kind that asks the interviewer as many questions as he asks her.[920]

Being interested in others more than in herself, being welcoming towards acquaintances old and new, was a special gift of Dorothy's, one that made friendships spring up left and right. This gift was no affectation, either, and was so potent that it allowed Dorothy to win the hearts of many.

---

[918] Holing, conversation (2017), op. cit.

[919] Levin (2017), op. cit.

[920] Thomas, "Roles" (1945), op. cit.

Turangalila IV: Positivity

During Dorothy's last decade, a "negative" trait surfaced, but a natural, understandable one. As Jim Fernald explains:

> During her last years she needed help, and the family went through a number of caregivers; or, rather, Dorothy went through them (about ten) one after the other, for she was really mean to them. It was as if an evil twin, an "evil Dorothy," had suddenly been born. Finally, we found Mary Hart, a wonderful woman whom Dorothy adored, and whom she ultimately could not do without. "Nice Dorothy" was restored.[921]

The exact nature or cause of Dorothy's uncommon, accomplished humanity continues to be something of a riddle to me even after knowing her personally, and after studying her years after the fact. Even with the benefit of hindsight, many of her qualities appear to me inexplicable. It is to solve this riddle that I have looked for clues that might point to a personal study on her part, or to a voluntary moral stance rather than to a mere natural character trait. I claim no definitiveness in my findings, but those clues are abundant. They appear in the form of spiritual readings (Buddhism), in the form of moral statements and decisions, and in the form of sterling examples of positive behavior. They appear in the form of love for the environment and for animals of all kinds (rats and snakes too!), in the form of her attitude towards the press, and in the impression that the press received from her. They appear in the form of a conception of the acting craft that borders on the esoteric. They appear in the form of her openness and generosity towards people, and in the affection and admiration she elicited from them. They appear in the form of stable relationships. They appear in her letters and in her interviews. Exactly what, and how much, she studied to achieve such behavior, such stability, and such stance is not known, but clues pointing to an answer exist.

---

[921] Fernald (2017), op. cit.

In 1953, during the first year of her management of the La Jolla Playhouse with John Swope, Dorothy starred in John Van Druten's theatrical adaptation of Christopher Isherwood's *Berlin Stories* (1945),[922] *I Am a Camera* (which had premiered on Broadway in 1951), at the playhouse. It is uncertain how much contact she had with Van Druten, but she must have had some, for the playhouse put on not one but three plays by him between 1951 and 1958 (*The Voice of the Turtle* in 1951, *I Am a Camera* in 1953, and *Bell, Book and Candle* in 1958). In 1948, Dorothy had also starred in a *Ford Theater* radio adaptation of Van Druten's play *The Damask Cheek* (1942).[923] It is certain, at any rate, that she had extensive contact with British writer Christopher Isherwood (1904–1986), who was friends with Van Druten and would become a friend of Dorothy's.

By the 1950s, Isherwood had settled in Hollywood (and later in Santa Monica) definitively; both he and Van Druten had converted to Vedantism, Isherwood through the introduction of writers Aldous Huxley and Gerald Heard, also Vedantists. Through Huxley (author of the book *The Perennial Philosophy*, 1945), Isherwood had met philosopher, scholar, monk of the Ramakrishna Order and religious teacher Swami Prabhavananda (1893–1976), who had created the Vedanta Society of Southern California in 1930 after working at the Vedanta Society of San Francisco and founding the Vedanta Society of Portland in 1925. The Vedanta Society of Southern California would grow to become the largest in the West. Prabhavananda would lead the society until his death in 1976. Swami Sarvadevananda is the current head of the society.

The term Vedanta refers to an Indian philosophical current based on a series of ancient Sanskrit texts, the *Vedas*, believed to have been written between circa 2000 b.c. and 500 b.c. "Veda" can be translated as "knowl-

---

[922] Christopher Isherwood, *Berlin Stories*, New Directions, 1945.

[923] The episode, directed by Fletcher Markle, aired on November 5, 1948, on CBS. See *Five Directors: The Golden Years of Radio*, edited by Ira Skutch, The Scarecrow Press/Directors Guild of America, 1998, 103.

edge" or "Wisdom."[924] The presence of the Divine in all beings and in the world, karma and reincarnation, the possibility of attaining the equilibrium and insight necessary to develop and liberate Man's divine nature, and the essential unity of the world and of all its religions, are some of the themes of Vedanta. But, like many philosophies outlining a path to spiritual knowledge, Eastern and Western, Vedanta too is also a tool for self-knowledge.

Writer Christopher Isherwood (left) and artist Don Bachardy as they were in the mid-1950s. Frame capture from Tina Mascara and Guido Santi's documentary film *Chris and Don: A Love Story* (2007).

---

[924] Among the Western words that retain a kinship with the Sanskrit original, we can count the Latin "video" and the Italian "vedo," present indicatives respectively of the verbs *"videre"* and *"vedere"* (to see).

Isherwood did not only practice Vedantism and its meditations, and become a disciple of Prabhavananda's, whom he met with regularity every Wednesday for many years; he also became one of Vedanta's most enthusiastic endorsers and divulgators. He collaborated with Prabhavananda on several books outlining the Vedanta philosophy (*Vedanta for Modern Man*, 1951)[925] and on a new translation of the *Bhagavad Gita* (*The Song of God: Bhagavad-Gita*, 1944);[926] he also penned a biography of Prabhavananda's guru and teacher (*Ramakrishna and His Disciples*, 1965),[927] and wrote for the Vedanta Society's journal, *Vedanta for the Western World*.

How close was Dorothy to Isherwood, and to his overriding interest in Vedanta? Not very, if one is to believe the opinion of Isherwood's significant other, artist Don Bachardy, who was also acquainted with Dorothy (see page 620). The exact tenor of Dorothy's frequentation of Isherwood we do not know, but frequent each other they did. In April 1955, Isherwood was hard at work (January–September 1955) on a screenplay entitled *The Early Life of Buddha* for MGM, which was to be produced with sponsorship from the Indian and Japanese governments. The film was never made.[928] During that same month, Dorothy was shooting *Trial* at MGM. On the 21st, Isherwood noted in his diary:

> [...] Worked on Buddha, talked to Dorothy McGuire on the set of Trial [...].[929]

---

[925] Christopher Isherwood, ed., *Vedanta for Modern Man*, Harper & Brothers, 1951.

[926] Swami Prabhavananda and Christopher Isherwood, translators, *The Song of God: Bhagavad-Gita*, Marcel Rodd Co., 1944.

[927] Christopher Isherwood, *Ramakrishna and His Disciples*, Simon & Schuster, 1965.

[928] David Garrett Izzo, *Christopher Isherwood Encyclopedia*, McFarland & Co., Inc, 2010, 46.

[929] Katherine Bucknell, ed., *Christopher Isherwood Diaries: 1939–1960*, vol. 1, Harper Collins, 1997, 492.

The following month, Dorothy was invited to a birthday party given by Isherwood for Bachardy.[930] Both Bachardy and Isherwood met the Swopes often, though always at social occasions involving other people. Dorothy also sat for Bachardy a number of times for portrait work.[931] Several of Dorothy's friends also gravitated around the Vedantists. Ardent Catholic convert Clare Boothe Luce[932] and her husband Henry Luce were friends with British historian, science writer and philosopher Gerald Heard (1889–1971), who was a friend of Isherwood's, an early disciple of Swami Prabhavananda's, and the earliest supporter of the Vedanta Society of Southern California. Dorothy certainly frequented the Luces socially (Clare was also friendly with John Swope's uncle Herbert Bayard, and Henry was the publisher of *LIFE* magazine, which published John's photographic work for years).

Dorothy may not have spoken about her interest in metaphysical matters, or her belief in them; but believe in them she did, and there are indications of this everywhere, both in her attitude and in her statements, oral and written, particularly during the last three decades of her life. Words and phrases like "soul," "spirit," "lighting the way," and "heart" (metaphorical heart, i.e. the "interior"),[933] were not alien to her, and she was not afraid to use them.

The hard data of Dorothy's frequentation of this or that disciple, or of her study of this or that current of metaphysical thought, is not the issue; the fact that she was able to embody the virtues that are set as goals by most of those currents, consistently and steadfastly, is. For, such embodiment does not happen overnight. Disciples and gurus, teachers and

[930] Ibid., 497–499.

[931] Bachardy (2018), op. cit.

[932] See: Sylvia Jukes Morris, "In Search of Clare Boothe Luce," *New York Times*, January 31, 1988.

[933] This from a short letter Dorothy sent to film historian Dan Van Neste: "It is indeed the *interior*—the heart—that counts."

students, of all the past and present schools of spiritual self-investigation have strived to achieve an ideal of perfection in being human (of learning what it is to be human to the full extent) through decades of trial and error, through lifetimes of hard practice. Whatever form of investigation Dorothy practiced, it worked remarkably well.

7. *Turangalîla* V: Tapping the World Source

It is symbolically appropriate that Dorothy should manage her first successful pregnancy while taking a European tour with her husband John Swope, driving around Italy in a tiny Italian coupe—the car that would suggest the nickname of Topo for her first child. The announcement of Dorothy's pregnancy was made to the Hollywood press from Naples, Italy, and her child was born in New York rather than in California.

Dorothy was a frequent traveler, but seldom of the tourist type. The evidence, however, suggests that she did not travel much before meeting John, nor after his death: John wore the traveling pants in the Swope household.

John started traveling to far-away locations early in life. In 1930, shortly after graduating from Harvard University, he took a ten-month trip around the world with a friend, stopping in Japan for almost a month. Thanks to his father Gerard's connections, he was able to stay at the home of Mr. Kunihiko Iwadare, founder of the Nippon Electric Company and friend of John's father. Thus, John, armed with a diary, a film camera, and above all a curious mind, was able to go beyond the classic tourist's view of the country by visiting many private homes and experiencing the people of Japan first hand.[934] The germ of a globetrotting passion was planted, and would germinate and develop for the rest of John's life.

Photography was John Swope's art of choice, which acted as an agent of curiosity and discovery for him: it pushed John to want to look, see, and experience. For John, the objective of photography was the search for the "Ah" instant, for the intersection of something special occurring "outside" and the inner instrument of the photographer's gaze. The camera was simply a mechanical device that mediated between those two ends of the phenomenon, and allowed the capturing of that intersection. John was constantly trying to put himself in situations where that phenomenon, and that mediation, could happen. He was constantly seeking new occurrences of those intersections, and new locations where they could manifest. More than the end results of that capturing (the photographs), it was the possibility of those intersections that he was seeking.

For John, this search could light on people, art, landscapes, workplaces, historical events, or the theatrical process. For Dorothy's kindred, but not photographic, search, the targets were almost invariably people. For both Swopes, an unpretentious, positive curiosity, and a happy desire to meet the people and things of the world (of many worlds), drove their travels big and small, whether in California and America or in other continents. Their manner of travel was without frills. More than that: it was often poverty-row simple.

Occasionally, in the early years of Dorothy's career, some glimmer of rich-person eccentricity colored their movements. Until the birth of their daughter, the Swopes kept a private plane on hand, and often took short flights, if nothing else to avoid traffic. John would sometimes fly his wife to work, for example during her first La Jolla Playhouse season. Here is a syndicated tidbit from Sheilah Graham:

> Though the idea has been often discussed and used for

---

934 See Peter, *Japan* (2006), op. cit., 14–15.

phoney [sic] publicity purposes, Dorothy McGuire is the first screen actress to actually commute to and from work by airplane.

Miss McGuire is starring in Darryl F. Zanuck's "Gentleman's Agreement," and, at the same time, is both a director and star in productions at the La Jolla playhouse on the seacoast some 120 miles south of Hollywood. Dorothy's husband, John Swope, an expert pilot, has a converted AT-6 military training plane and flew her to town from La Jolla every morning of last week and back at night. Fox studio is only about five miles from the Los Angeles municipal airport, and the weather this summer has been ideal for the purpose.[935]

As I have suggested elsewhere, John Swope was a strong, positive influence in his wife's life ("a wonderful man, who's very strong—and who has helped me avoid the troubles that happen to so many in my business," Dorothy defined him in a 1975 interview),[936] and his style of travel was no exception. Private plane rides aside, the Swopes traveled light and fast, with minimum baggage and often under less than glamorous conditions. Dorothy referred to this, the lesson she had learned from her husband, in her 1977 interview with Rex Reed:

> My favorite quotes for myself are that I can now travel light and fast and make tracks and light the way.[937]

John, a flexible, world-curious photographer, had practiced this commando style of traveling during and after World War II, often taking

---

[935] Sheilah Graham, "Movies Have Loose Control Over Life," *Bluefield (WV) Daily Telegraph*, August 9, 1947.

[936] Beck, "Name" (1975), op. cit.

[937] Reed, "Competitive Spirit" (1977), op. cit.

Dorothy with him on trips that were less than characteristic for her; their motorcycle honeymoon in the Arizona wilderness in 1943 is an example. As Carolyn Peter, the curator of the Swope exhibit *A Letter from Japan* (2006), explains:

> [John Swope] took numerous extended trips to different parts of the world, most often with Dorothy and usually with the same two purposes: to devote much of his time to photographing the people in the places they visited for his ongoing artistic series exploring the universal human experience, and to help Dorothy decompress after her intensive filming schedules.
>
> [...] Throughout his life Swope continued to take photographs at home, on his travels, and even in the midst of producing plays for the La Jolla Playhouse in San Diego. He was always ready to photograph and kept a camera close at hand. His longtime friend Norman Lloyd recalled that "John saw the camera as an extension of himself."[938]

John's traveling, and consequently Dorothy's, was not designed for the accumulation of sightseeing landmarks. It was, rather, a way of experiencing the realities of the world and of looking at those realities with a sharp, curious, positive eye. For Dorothy, this unadorned, guerrilla-styled wandering became a new way of seeing the world and its people—as if her husband's camera and his way of moving in the world had become extensions of her, too. She hinted at this in an interview she gave in Louisville, Kentucky, during her 1987 tour with the play *I Never Sang for My Father*. Driving through Louisville one late afternoon, Dorothy was impressed by the beauty of the light, and commented:

---

[938] Peter, *Japan* (2006), op. cit., 30–31.

> My husband (the late John Swope) was a photographer, so it was part of his psyche to be sensitive to light. I guess I inherited a little bit of that.[939]

Daniel J. Travanti, who was on that tour with Dorothy, was puzzled by her willingness to subject herself to the exhausting regime of such frill-less roaming:

> I wondered why Dorothy had done that tour at that point in her life. It was grueling. Every actor, especially at the beginning of his career, thinks he'd like to go on tour; but tours are lonely, even when you have all that company. You're away for a long time, away from home, away from your animals, away from your loved ones. It's fun for a few weeks out of six or seven months.[940]

In the case of that tour, Dorothy's fearlessness had certainly something to do with the impulse to act, and to be involved in the magic of theater, even at a considerable price. Frugal and unpretentious, Dorothy, aged seventy-one, could be as enthusiastic and energetic as an eager beginner; having been trained by her theatrical past and by her husband's simple style of travel, she could withstand a lot.

Before cellular phones and Internet connections, this style of traveling often meant that John and Dorothy were not reachable while roughing it around the world. Here is a curious report of one such disappearance from Hedda Hopper:

> Clifton Webb's "Mr. Pennypacker" has been postponed again. An announcement was made that Dorothy McGuire would play opposite him, but the truth is she doesn't know

---

[939] Fristoe, "Touring" (1987), op. cit.

[940] Travanti (2018), op. cit.

anything about it. In fact, they can't find her. Dorothy and John Swope are motoring throughout Spain with the A. Blake Brophys of UP. Dorothy always avoids big hotels, loves quaint out-of-the-way inns or farm houses, picturesque places away from the crowd. And John, a magnificent photographer, likes the same thing. So now UP has sent wires to all their contacts throughout Spain to find one missing actress, and even if found, she may not want to come home for the picture.[941]

Dorothy might have inherited a new way of looking at things from her husband, but it was her own open, unprejudiced gaze, her open-door policy towards the world, that predisposed her to the skill. Reinforced by her husband's propensity, her own openness in viewing things and people also became an acting tool. She explained this in her 1982 interview with the *Los Angeles Times*' Paul Rosenfield:

> It was the globetrotting, with Swope, that gave McGuire her actor's eyes. "I got nourished. I never took travel for granted. We lived simply; we didn't need a second house or a yacht, but we needed to roam. If I ticked off all the places we went while John was photographing the world—sometimes on assignment, sometimes on holiday—you'd see the advantages I had. I've seen the most sophisticated life, and the most primitive tribal life, side by side. It helped me totally as an actress."[942]

In another interview, Dorothy went even further in her appreciation of her travels: "I've always been rather shy and not very adventurous. But travel freed me."[943]

---

[941] Hedda Hopper, "Dorothy McGuire Sought for Film," *Los Angeles Times*, May 31, 1958.

[942] Rosenfield, "Fate" (1982), op. cit.

[943] Reed, "Competitive Spirit" (1977), op. cit.

Turangalila V: Tapping the World Source

Dorothy's ease and warmth with people from all walks of life may have been an instinctive aspect of her personality, but it certainly benefited from her being exposed to the people of the world in her travels—not as a film star, but as a curious, interested woman. It helped, in this respect, that, although she was a famous actress, she never became an icon or a myth: it helped that she could go unnoticed in many corners of the world. Her exposure to people and places developed that openness towards which she was already inclined; it also developed her propensity for simple, no-frills living: for example, for decades Dorothy walked rather than drove, and kept a simple economy car—a gift from John—even though she could have afforded to drive Bentleys and Rolls Royces.

Camping, too, fell within the Swopes' traveling style, sometimes in the wilderness next door (for example the Pacific Northwest), though possibly where there were no cacti around (see Part I, Chapter 7). This occasionally elicited the bewilderment of columnists. Here is Christy Fox reporting a curious sighting for the *Los Angeles Times*:

> If you just happened to be fishing up in the Rogue River area lately and saw some familiar faces—yes, you were right. Camping under the stars and broiling their catch like seasoned chefs were the Edgar B. Wards (Jane Wyatt) and the John Swopes (Dorothy McGuire). Who says camping isn't glamorous?[944]

Of course, visiting far-away lands afforded the most unexpected discoveries for unglamorous travelers such as John and Dorothy. "[Traveling gives you the opportunity to] go to new places, meet new people, feel the heartbeat. It's a way of seeing what [a] country's all about,"[945] stated Doro-

---

[944] Christy Fox, "Fellows of Art Museum to Take Wing to Windy City," *Los Angeles Times*, October 11, 1968.

[945] Fristoe, "Touring" (1987), op. cit.

thy during that same 1987 tour. It is fitting that a woman of such heart should want to "feel the heartbeat."

In an interview she gave in 1975, Dorothy hinted at some unnamed discoveries made while traveling, with a touch of mystery that, once again, puzzled syndicated columnist Marilyn Beck:

> "These last four years," [McGuire] volunteered, "have been spent world tracking with my husband, exploring the South Pacific, India, the Orient—and filling in the puzzle." Pieces of the puzzle of life that she's acquired in her travels are treasures not to be shared.[946]

Why those treasures, those discoveries, were "not to be shared," we do not know. The fact that "pieces of the puzzle of life" were acquired, however, seems to hint at the results of a personal investigation of Dorothy's that had nothing to do with tourism, results that could not be easily verbalized. Dorothy's positive observation of life and of human beings could not be verbalized dialectically, not (probably) because Dorothy was not capable of verbalizing it, but (probably) because verbalizing it would have meant simplifying it—and simplifying it would have meant impoverishing its mystery and diminishing its depth. It would have meant giving "dead," misconstruable form to something living, private, and delicate.

When, in her preparation for her role of Hannah in *The Night of the Iguana* (1975), Dorothy used a European trip she took with John to look at people "through Hannah's eyes," she was doing more than just character preparation; she was putting herself in someone else's shoes, and trying to look at human beings without her own ego. Since for Dorothy acting was never merely acting in the technical sense but something "mysterious, hard to pin down" and "a life experience," it makes sense that the "exercis-

---

[946] Beck, "Name" (1975), op. cit.

es" she did to prepare for that life experience would not be technical, but life-based—and that these exercises were not to be shared except vaguely.

John Swope's positive gaze (with or without his camera), always willing to embrace the world and be surprised by it, was the example that helped Dorothy develop a gift she herself possessed. Running enthusiastically to meet the world, the Swopes made tracks and lit the way as they went.

"Make tracks, light the way" was a favorite quote of Dorothy's during the 1970s, an obviously metaphorical quote she used often in her correspondence (see the postcard pictured on page 609), in the form of an exhortation: an encouragement to travel light-footedly through life and illuminate the road along the way.

Dorothy was often outspoken about her ideas, at least in private: always ready to defend principles such as liberty, unselfishness, compassion, and love, whether in political form or not.[947] However, especially in later years, Dorothy was not one to preach or lecture about those beliefs. She taught by example and by good deed rather than through words. Those quotes in her correspondence were the exception to the rule—and a luminous exception too. If one looks at the end portion of that postcard on page 609 ("In interim—may good and happy experiences surround you—make tracks and light the way."), one can clearly see that those final exhortations were more than just a "nice" formal close, and no mere lip service to moral principles. Those wishes, those pieces of advice that she dispensed forcefully (not half-heartedly), Dorothy also incarnated through the example of the way she lived with others.

In all likelihood, it was on that latest trip to the Orient with John that Dorothy bought a book that would become a staple of her library and that she would cherish and study often: the Japanese-published 1975 edition of *The Teaching of Buddha*, edited by Bukkyō Dendō Kyōkai, i.e. the Tokyo Society for the Promotion of Buddhism.

---

[947] Holing (2017), op. cit.

That book was not just one of Dorothy's favorite readings; it represented an aspiration, and—synecdochically—a worldview. Just as Dorothy was not a member of any political organization but was definitely outspoken about her progressive, humanitarian political views, so she was not officially affiliated with any religious group. Her reading about Buddha or Vedanta was neither a sign of religious fanaticism nor mere intellectual curiosity. Not her reading this or that teaching counted, but her being able to embody, from the bottom of her heart, some of the essential content that formed its core. One paragraph from that book will suffice, and it is hard not to feel that the disposition described by such paragraph might as well be referring to the one Dorothy herself displayed and practiced with remarkable consistency through most of her life:

> Through meditation, Buddha preserves a calm and peaceful spirit, radiant with mercy, compassion, happiness and even equanimity. He deals equitably with all people, cleansing their minds of defilement and bestowing happiness in a perfect singleness of spirit.[948]

The fact that Dorothy was searching—we do not know how much, how often or in which phases of her life, but definitely in the 1970s—for those teachings constitutes sufficient confirmation that her positivity, her unselfish openness towards others, and her detached equilibrium were more than just natural states, and more than just felicitous accidents.

That book can also be seen as a symbolic representation of the character of the Swopes' traveling. The couple did not travel to tick names off their list of destinations; their openness, curiosity, and desire for cultural understanding far outweighed their fascination with the exotic. Reading about the teachings of an ancient initiate may have fallen under the heading of spiritual learning for Dorothy, but it may also have signified cul-

---

948 *Teaching of Buddha* (1975), op. cit., 32–33.

tural curiosity, and her desire to investigate the cultures she visited with a deeper, more inquisitive eye. When she traveled, Dorothy brought home much more than slideshows or souvenirs.

8. *Turangalîla* VI: Shinings

> The fates looked down on me and said, "this girl will never get anywhere without plenty of help."
> Dorothy McGuire, 1955

According to statements she made over the years, Dorothy believed both in the power of fate (or luck,[949] or destiny)[950] and in the mystery of coincidences.[951] Here are three coincidences that involved Dorothy herself.

One.

During an interview promoting her role in the TV movie *She Waits* (1972), and in keeping with the movie's supernatural theme, Dorothy recounted an anecdote about a strange coincidence that had lured her back to film work in 1971 after a six-year "retirement":

---

[949] Reed, "Competitive Spirit" (1977), op. cit.

[950] Rosenfield, "Fate" (1982), op. cit.

[951] "Stars of Ghost Tale Inclined To Believe," *Kittanning (PA) Simpson's Leader-Times*, January 22, 1972.

Ralph Nelson called me from Ireland and asked me to do [the film] Flight of the Doves. My character's name was Granny Mary O'Flaherty—and that was my own grandmother's maiden name. The day he called was the date of Grandmother O'Flaherty's birthday.[952]

Two.

Even a sunny, self-effacing person like Dorothy suffered from some vanity, and in one particular case, this delicate pride of hers turned out to be a lifesaver. The following story, which contains both a gentle tragic irony and an amazing coincidence, is told by family friend Jim Fernald, who occupied the ground-floor apartment of Dorothy's house on Copley Place with his wife during the actress's last decade:

> During the ten or so years of our stay at 121 Copley Place, my wife and I became quite attached to Dorothy, and the feeling was mutual. Soon after our first child was born in 2001, it became clear to my wife and me that our living arrangements were too cramped for our enlarged family, so we began to make plans to move. We arranged for an apartment in Boston, where I also scheduled some job interviews.
>
> When it came time to tell Dorothy, we braced ourselves for drama, and were not disappointed. With the help of her son Mark, we told her the news, but she was so stunned by it she did not want to believe it. When she did, she was very unhappy about it. At any rate, we moved out after the painful goodbyes, and drove across the country with all our things stuffed into two cars. When we arrived in Boston, it was late August; Dorothy became ill with heart problems and had to be hospitalized. Mark kept me abreast of the developments by

---

[952] Ibid.

phone. Of course, my first thought was to visit her, and I made plans to fly west.

When Dorothy got worse instead of better, I resolved to cancel a job interview I had scheduled and fly to Los Angeles. Dorothy, however, did not want me to go: she did not want me to see her in that condition; so I canceled my flight and proceeded to my early-morning interview, which in any case was disrupted by the news of the two planes crashing into the New York Twin Towers. I did not get the job, but that is not important: had I flown out that day, I would have been on one of those planes, the morning flight from Boston to Los Angeles. Dorothy saved my life. She died two days later.[953]

Three.

This coincidence involves me personally. On January 1, 1978, shortly after my return to New York from my first Los Angeles visit with the Swopes, Dorothy sent me flowers for my twentieth birthday. I must have mentioned the January 1 date during one of our conversations, and she must have paid attention and made a note of it. The card that accompanied the flowers contained a message scribbled in Dorothy's unmistakably passionate handwriting: "In 2001 you will be 43 years old—Happy Birthday—Happy New Year. Swopes."

Dorothy died at St. John's Hospital in Santa Monica, California, on September 13, 2001. She was eighty-five. The cause of death was heart failure. As per her wishes, her ashes were scattered over the Pacific Ocean, some three nautical miles off the coast of Marina Del Rey.

Both Dorothy's wording on that 1978 birthday card and her choosing the year of her own death to express wishes, not for an immediate future but for a far-away future, were indeed peculiar, and contained a coincidence that, in hindsight, smacks of divination in a most disquieting way.

---

[953] Fernald (2017), op. cit.

There was often an element of wizardry in what Dorothy did in life, and in the way she expressed her warmth, understanding and generosity. Her welcoming openness and interpersonal style were not only special; they were often an elfin, puzzling miracle.

"It is only a coincidence," people are wont to exclaim skeptically when confronted with events that somehow cross-reference each other in unexplained ways. Well, yes; but why "only"?

Dorothy's birthday card to the author, January 1, 1978.

9. *Turangalîla* VII: Adamant

Sometime in 1946, Dorothy and John Swope took up residence in two houses located in the New York area, on the Hudson River (see Part I, Chapter 12). These two houses, according to what Dorothy told Hedda Hopper in a 1947 interview, they bought and named Tantamount and Adamant. According to Topo Swope, Dorothy and John did indeed stay at Tantamount and Adamant for a few years, but the dwellings belonged to other members of the Swope family. The proximity of Gerard Swope's Croft estate to Tantamount and Adamant seems to corroborate Topo's version of the facts. If that version is true, one must concede that that story and that interview may have been embellished somewhat, either by Hopper or by Dorothy. In general, however, Hopper's items about Dorothy were respectful and affectionate, and contained little, if any, fabrication on Hopper's part. Given the length of the Swopes' stay at the houses (over two years), I am inclined to believe that Dorothy only omitted ownership details from that interview to be able to talk about the houses and their names without involving John's family; but talk about them she did, which is revealing in itself.

If the version that Dorothy told the public through Hopper was something of a fable, I will accept that fable at face value, and buy into the myth that Dorothy decided to leave behind, the myth of her title to those houses with such unusual names. If we are to believe Topo's version of the story, those names, which Dorothy "appropriated" as hers as if she herself had chosen them, cannot be considered relevant when it comes to equity values in Dorothy's life; they can, however, be considered relevant in other ways, for they intersected Dorothy's life in other personal areas with their symbolic meanings. I will therefore take the symbolic route, and acknowledge a connection of those names with Dorothy's character and values that has little or nothing to do with the actual houses, but speaks to ideas that were very relevant to Dorothy, and are very relevant to our assessment of Dorothy after the fact.

"Tantamount," meaning "essentially equal to something," "equivalent in value, significance, or effect," or "equivalent in force to," retains its element of mystery, for we have no evidence of why it was assigned to the main house, or what it meant to the assigners. If I were to venture a theory, I would point out that the name suggests a state of equality and equilibrium: a state in which forces are equal to each other and cancel each other out; a state of equanimity, perhaps.

"Adamant," though cryptic, is much more transparently congruous with Dorothy's person and convictions. While it is true that the word could be a mere poetic synonym for "stone," and that the guest house was made of stone, "Adamant" reverberates nonetheless with deeper, or higher, connotations, and is an oddly deliberate choice for the name of a house. At the very least, that word and that choice merit an investigation.

If one looks up the word "adamant" used as an adjective, one finds meanings such as: unshakeable, immovable, unwavering, determined, steadfast, resolved; this usage is fairly common in everyday English. As a noun, "adamant" describes a legendary rock of old to which many extraordinary properties were attributed, such as impenetrable hardness and magnetism.[954] Various hypotheses have been made as to the rock's geo-

---

[954] There is also an unincorporated community, or village, named Adamant in the town of Calais, Vermont. Originally named Sodom, the village changed its name after an official

logical identity; among them, haematite, platinum, diamond, magnetite, lodestone, iron, and steel. Its geological reality, however, seems less important than its metaphorical or philosophical implications, of which there have been many over the centuries.

Plato, who associated gold with adamant both in his *Timaeus* and in his *Statesman*, states that the dark metal adamant "is the 'offshoot' or 'scion of Gold,'"[955] and that it is a byproduct of the refining of the precious metal (the "alchemical" overtones of this last statement are unmistakable).[956] By implication, then, the adamant is more precious, or more evolved, than that most precious of metals. In Book X of his *Republic*, the closing tale of a man named Er and of his voyage to the regions of the Afterlife after his near-death experience describes (among other things, such as the process of reincarnation) a cosmological Spindle of Necessity, attached to a mysterious body of light that holds the Universe together. Such Spindle is made of one main element: adamant.[957] Other mythical references to the

---

petition was granted; the name was chosen for the granite quarries that had flourished in the area in the 1880s, and for the hardness of their stone. The village is known for its Adamant Co-operative, which serves as general store and post office, and for the Adamant Music School, founded in 1942 by free-spirited artists Edwine Behre, Alice Mary Kimbal and Harry Godfrey.

955 Timaeus 59b, Statesman 303e. See: Clinton DeBevoise Corcoran, *Topography and Deep Structure in Plato: The Construction of Place in the Dialogues*, SUNY Press, 2016, 86. The original Greek definition in *Timaeus* is χρυσοῦ ὄζος, a branch or offshoot of gold.

956 See the Afterword.

957 See for example: Griet Schils, "Plato's Myth of Er: the Light and the Spindle," in *L'antiquité classique*, Année 1993, vol. 62, n. 1, 101–114. For a translation of Plato's text, see: *The Republic of Plato*, translated by Allan Bloom, Basic Books (A Division of HarperCollins Publishers), 1968. The tale of Er is on pages 297–303. English poet John Milton made direct reference to Plato's Spindle in his masque *Arcades* (1633): "[. . .] And turn the Adamantine spindle round, / On which the fate of gods and men is wound." Charles W. Eliot, ed., *The Complete Poems of John Milton*, P.F. Collier & Son, 1909, 44–45 (vv. 66–67).

mineral can be found in Hesiod's *Theogony*[958] and *Shield of Herakles*,[959] and in Apollodorus's (known as "pseudo-Apollodorus") *The Library*, where the sickle that Zeus uses to wound the monster Typhon is described as ἀδαμαντίνη (adamantine).[960]

Medieval and Renaissance writers harkened back to this Greek past when they referred to the metal. As Rebecca Totaro explains:

> [In] its original Greek context adamant took its name from the word αμαστος *adamastos*, meaning untamable. As this word suggests, it was a term conveying far more than just the hardness we associate with it. It also conveys a complex and yet irreducible kind of resilience.
>
> [...] Adamant is pressed into a wide range of services by [Edmund] Spenser and [John] Milton, and among the characters who know its power are none other than the goddess of Justice, God, and Satan. These are uses of adamant highlighting not the rigidity or hardness *per se* but resolution, the ability to stand "against," to have staying power. [...]
>
> The early modern range of meanings for the word "adamant" is a vestige of a pre-scientific era that had not entirely lost its enchantment with heroes and things, love and places; moreover, employed in full by early modern writers like Spenser and Milton, this range of meanings helps us to gain access to the early modern condition of ecosystemic embeddedness that we have largely lost. It is a sense of ourselves

---

[958] Sections 161–185, 233. The sickle used by Kronos to castrate his father Ouranos was made of adamant.

[959] Section 137. Herakles' helmet was made of adamant.

[960] Apollodorus, *The Library*, translated by Sir James George Frazer, William Heinemann, 1921, I–vi, 47–51.

as meteorophysiological—as wind, water, earth, and fire, with potential, motion, metamorphosis, and power.[961]

From Plato on, mentions of the name of this stone unfailingly betray its esoteric, or metaphorical, nature: the stone may be an actual stone, but it is always cited in contexts where something special—something metaphysical, supernatural, or cosmological—occurs. Just like the word "gold," the word "adamant" too tends to become a symbol.

The poetic, literary, and moral extensions of the above associations make the word "adamant" perfect to describe certain hard-to-achieve virtues, such as absolute immovability in the face of temptations or entreaties, or, on the negative side, obstinateness in not accepting the truth. Whatever the contrast that is opposed, however, the adamant person is immovable because of a commitment to a personal integrity of some sort. One finds the word adamant mentioned in Greek and English versions of the Bible (Ezekiel 3:8 and 3:9, Zechariah 7:12), and its literary uses cannot be counted, in anything from Virgil to Giovanni Boccaccio, from Torquato Tasso to John Donne, from Aeschylus to William Shakespeare, from Jonathan Swift to John Milton, from Baldassarre Castiglione to Gilbert and Sullivan.[962] Because of its impenetrable hardness, the adamant stone also acquires a connotation of durability, or, indeed, of eternity. In book 7, stanza 32 of his epic poem *La teseida*,[963] Giovanni Boccaccio refers

---

[961] Rebecca Totaro, *Meteorology and Physiology in Early Modern Culture: Earthquakes, Human Identity, and Textual Representation*, Taylor Francis Ltd., 2017, 83–89, 141–142.

[962] On a more modern note, the fantastic alloy with which Wolverine's artificial skeleton and claws are made in Marvel Comics' mythology is called "Adamantium," and, in the very mythical sci-fi film *Forbidden Planet* (1956), the material used by the extinct Krell civilization who lived on the titular planet is said to have included a metal called "adamantine steel."

[963] *La theseida*, or *La teseida*, sometimes also referred to as *Teseide* or by its full title, *Teseida delle nozze di Emilia*, is an epic poem written by Giovanni Boccaccio in "*lingua volgare*" (early Italian as opposed to Latin) between circa 1339 and 1341. The poem's twelve books deal nominally with the career and rule of the titular hero Theseus, but give prominence to the "romantic" subplot of the rivalry of Palemone and Arcita for the love of Emilia.

to the adamant as "*etterno adamante*" (eternal adamant). So does Geoffrey Chaucer ("of adamant eterne") in *The Knight's Tale* of his *Canterbury Tales*, which was largely based on Boccaccio's poem.⁹⁶⁴

Saint Cyril, Archbishop of Alexandria (376–444 A.D.) and Doctor of the Roman Catholic Church, wrote voluminous commentaries on sacred texts; in one of these, he describes Jesus Christ as an Adamant:

> Wherefore God the Father in the holy Prophets called Christ an adamant too, saying, *Behold, I am setting an adamant in the midst of My people Israel.* The adamant signifies to us as in a figure, that the Divine and Ineffable Nature of the Word can never yield to those who oppose it.⁹⁶⁵

In the European literary tradition, the word has also been used in place of "diamond" (cf. Dante, *Divine Comedy*, *Paradise* II, 33),⁹⁶⁶ because of the diamond's (Latin and Greek *adamas*) properties, such as its hardness, purity, and ability to refract light. The relation of the adamant stone to light was already explicit in Plato's myth, where the Spindle of Necessity was attached to the shaft of light that sustains the world.

The connection of the symbolic adamant to the diamond adds two important characteristics to its mythical occurrences: its crystalline nature, and its capacity to be a refractor of light. Crystals, with their ordered, geometric constituents and their borderline-organic growth patterns,

See Giovanni Boccaccio, *Teseida, delle nozze d'Emilia*, Gius. Laterza & figli, 1941.

964 See: *Sources and Analogues of the Canterbury Tales*, vol. 2, edited by Robert M. Correale and Mary Hamel, D.S. Brewer, 2005, 109.

965 Saint Cyril, *Commentary on the Gospel According to Saint John*, vol. 1, translated and edited by P.E. Pusey, James Parker, 1874, 505.

966 The original Italian text is: "*Parev'a me che nube ne coprisse / lucida; spessa, solida e pulita, / quasi adamante che lo sol ferisse.*" In Longfellow's translation: "It seemed to me a cloud encompassed us, / Luminous, dense, consolidate and bright / As adamant on which the sun is striking."

have fascinated humans for millennia, and have been considered symbols of something higher, and purer: of a cosmic force able to manipulate and shape inorganic matter with ordered criteria. When used as a symbol or metaphor, the adamant, or diamond, is also a physical vehicle for light—a symbolic rather than physical light, representing the *Logos* (the Light of the Word, representing cosmic Thought).

If, literarily, passions are often associated with fire and heat, the states or thoughts that oppose such passions are often associated with ice. Thus it is that Italian poet Francesco Petrarca (1304–1374), in describing the "frozen thoughts" with which he surrounds his heart in order to avoid feeling the heat of Love's "assault," writes that such thoughts have created an "adamantine enamel," an impenetrable crust that prevents the unraveling of the unwanted passion.[967] Passions are a thing of disorder and unbalance; only the coldness of "frozen" thought (which in the case of Petrarca was a refusal to fall in love) can counteract them. In Petrarca's conceit, the adamantine coldness of those thoughts acts as a defensive weapon, thwarting the flowering of the poet's love. Viewed positively, however, such coldness acts as a temperature regulator, as an equalizer: it extinguishes the heated dominance of passion and balances it with purity, measure, and equilibrium (and, in the case of a poet, creativity, i.e. sublimation).

Used positively, for example as an exercise of personal betterment, the "coldness" of adamantine thought, though certainly a weapon against the damage of feelings, does not merely permit a subtraction of feeling, but also a healthy impersonality that is able to restore strength to thinking by shifting its hierarchical standing in the inner make-up of the person. No longer a subservient instrument of feeling and of ego, thinking acquires a

---

[967] Francesco Petrarca, *Canzone* IV, from his *Rime*, Giuseppe Bettinelli, 1781, 63. The Italian text is: *"E d'intorno al mio cor pensieri gelati / Fatto avean quasi adamantino smalto, / Ch'allentar non lassava il duro affetto."* Literally translated: "And around my heart frozen thoughts / Had created an almost adamantine enamel, / Which did not allow the thawing of the hardened feeling." (Translation mine.)

crystalline independence, an impersonal fullness. This fullness, in the view of a long Tradition of illustrious metaphysicians, theologians and esotericists, reveals the role of thinking as junction between the material and the spiritual, the fallen and the enlightened, the human and the divine.

It is in the above sense, connected to the purity, order, and transparency of a crystalline thinking, that the words "adamant" and "adamantine" often manifest in texts dealing with spiritual investigation and human moral progress. If one looks at translations of texts of Eastern philosophy, for example of Buddhism (especially Vajrayana Buddhism, sometimes called the "Adamantine Vehicle")[968], one often encounters words like "adamantine" to qualify certain enlightened states, particularly states of inner freedom (from the ego, from the troublesome crowding of thoughts and feelings) and "emptiness." Tsong kha pa, in his commentary on the Perfection-of-Wisdom Sutras, writes of "adamantine thought ... a sublime thought ... an unshakeable thought ... [...]" and of the disciple "standing in the adamantine stabilization."[969] One finds the same words, or something like them, in any number of similar texts, such as *The Large Sutra on Perfect Wisdom*,[970] and in a long, rich tradition of Western thinkers who either incorporated those Eastern thoughts and discoveries into a new version of the philosophy of spiritual enlightenment, or arrived at similar conclusions through a kindred spiritual search (Aristotle, the Fathers of the Roman Catholic Church, Christian theologians, Theosophists, Anthroposophists).

Nicholas Roerich (1874–1947),[971] Russian archaeologist, poet, art

---

[968] The term "Vajra" denotes both the thunderbolt and the diamond; its reference both to the hardness of something crystalline and incorruptible and to the celestial flash of Light is clearly symbolic.

[969] Tsong kha pa, *Golden Garland of Eloquence* translated by Gareth Sparham, Fremont, 2015, 403–404.

[970] *The Large Sutra on Perfect Wisdom: With the Divisions of the Abhisamayalankara*, translated and edited by Edward Conze, University of California Press, 1975.

[971] For more information about the artist, visit the Nicholas Roerich Museum at 319 W.

Turangalila VII: Adamant

historian, painter, Nobel Peace Prize nominee and Theosophist who, after working as set and costume designer for Serge Diaghilev's *Ballets Russes*,[972] emigrated to the United States and started his own Theosophy-oriented art school, Agni Yoga Society, and museum, entitled one of his writings *Adamant*. In his impassioned peroration for the awakening of man's spiritual life and for the roles of art and beauty in such awakening, he referred to the awakened spirit as a newly found strength and as an "impenetrable veil"; he then quoted a passage from the ancient *Bhagavad Gita* that assimilated such strength to the hardness of the adamant stone:

> "The weapon divideth it not, the fire burneth it not, the water corrupteth it not, the wind drieth it not away; for it is indivisible, inconsumable, incorruptible and is not to be dried away; it is eternal, universal, permanent, immovable.... Some regard the indwelling spirit as a wonder, whilst some speak and others hear of it with astonishment; but no one realizes it, although he may have heard it described." (*Bhagavad Gita*, Ch. II.)[973]

One of Roerich's public speeches, reproduced in his anthology *Realm of Light* (1931) and addressed to the members of the Origen Roerich Association, is entitled "Adamantius." This is what he says about the word in reference to Origen (also called Origen Adamantius, c. 185–254), an

---

107th Street, New York, or the museum's website: www.roerich.com.

[972] For Diaghilev, Roerich suggested, and designed the sets and costumes for, Igor Stravinsky/Vaslav Nijinsky's ballet about primitive Russia *Le Sacre du printemps* (*The Rite of Spring*, 1913).

[973] Nicholas Roerich, *Adamant* [1923], Nicholas Roerich Museum, 2017. Some titles of his other books: *Altai-Himalaya* (1925), *Flame in Chalice* (1930), *Shambhala* (1930), and *Realm of Light* (1931). For information about Origen, see: Richard Finn, "Origen and His Ascetic Legacy," in: *Asceticism in the Graeco-Roman World*, Cambridge University Press, 2009, 100–130.

early Christian theologian who has often been considered a Father of the Catholic Church by later generations, but was condemned during his lifetime for partially contradicting Christian orthodoxy: "Adamant, the hardest diamond, unbreakable, even cutting that which is itself hard. Origen, Adamantius! Does not this express the Teacher's entire devotion to Truth? A devotion which could not be shaken by privations, nor by temptations nor by customs?"[974]

This photo portrait of Nicholas Roerich was taken in Shanghai, China, in May 1934. Courtesy of the Nicholas Roerich Museum archives, New York.

---

974 Nicholas Roerich, *Realm of Light*, Roerich Museum Press, 1931, 214.

Spiritually, something that is adamantine is, yes, hard and "unshakeable," but not rigid or inflexible. Rather, any state of spiritual enlightenment is associated with a weightless peacefulness, a positive, impersonal emptiness or transparency—where the heavier, or more solid, elements of the person's inner turmoil have been melted or sublimated to make space for something more voluntary—that allows the pure force of the *Logos* (the Light of the Word) to touch the inner make-up of the subject unfettered by inner or outer obstacles. Something that is adamantine is pure, resplendent, ordered, and incorruptible.

Massimo Scaligero, one of the most enlightened "descendants" and propagators of Rudolf Steiner's Anthroposophic philosophy, referred to such positive, unshakeable purity when discussing the basic (but all-important) exercise of inner concentration,[975] aimed at achieving the perception of the supersensible concept of the object of concentration:

> The experience of the concept is actually an initiatory operation: we have already seen how the concept is not a synthesis of representations [mental images], but a supersensible, adamantine *quid* that makes use of that synthesis to emerge within the soul, as a sign of the world whence it originates. The experience of the concept allows the investigator to mine

---

[975] Thus recites the text describing the exercise, to be performed with one's eyes closed: "Concentration. The researcher concentrates on an object and considers its shape, substance, color, use, etc., the series of mental images [representations] exhausting its physical structure, until what is left is the thought content. This operation must not engage the researcher's conscious attention for less than five minutes. At the end of it, the object must stand before his consciousness as a symbol, or a sign, or a synthesis, undialectically containing all the processed thought content." (see Massimo Scaligero, *Tecniche della concentrazione interiore*, Edizioni Mediterranee, 1975, 14. The translation is mine.) The original Italian text is as follows: "*Concentrazione. Il discepolo si concentra su un oggetto, del quale considera la forma, la sostanza, il colore, l'uso, ecc., la serie delle rappresentazioni che ne esauriscono la struttura fisica, sino a che al suo luogo rimanga il contenuto di pensiero. Questa operazione non deve impegnare l'attenzione cosciente del discepolo meno di cinque minuti: al termine di essa, l'oggetto deve essere dinanzi alla coscienza di lui come un simbolo, o un segno, o una sintesi, avente in sé indialetticamente tutto il contenuto di pensiero elaborato.*"

a pure thought, capable of identity with the deep forces of feeling and willing. The experimenter deals with something more than dialectical thought: with the *Thought-Force* that produces such thought in relation to a datum. The datum is removed from its immediacy by the thought capable of autonomous movement: such thought can itself be contemplated as a datum, so that the I may feel its independence from it.[976]

A photograph of Italian philosopher and esotericist Massimo Scaligero (1906–1980).

---

[976] Massimo Scaligero, *Kundalini d'occidente: il centro umano della potenza*, Edizioni mediterranee, 1980, 32. The translation is mine. The original text is as follows: "*L'esperienza del concetto è in realtà un'operazione iniziatica: si è già veduto come il concetto non sia una sintesi di rappresentazioni, ma un* quid *sovrasensibile, adamantino, che si serve di tale sintesi, per affiorare nell'anima, come segno del mondo da cui ha origine. L'esperienza del concetto dà modo all'indagatore di enucleare un puro pensiero, capace d'identità con le forze profonde del sentire e del volere. Egli ha a che fare con qualcosa di più che il pensiero dialettico: con la* Forza-pensiero *che lo produce in relazione a un dato. Il dato viene tolto alla sua immediatezza dal pensiero capace di automovimento: questo pensiero può essere esso stesso contemplato come un dato, così che l'Io senta la propria indipendenza rispetto ad esso.*"

Turangalila VII: Adamant

Whether Dorothy was aware of the rich connotations associated with the word "adamant" cannot be verified at this time, but it is not difficult to see that many of those connotations describe elements of her personality, or virtues that she put in practice on a daily basis, and with adamantine constancy. Dorothy knew what it meant to be adamant, and those "esoteric" meanings of the word are far from irrelevant where she is concerned. For, in this religious or literary tradition, anything adamantine is associated with the practice of a certain moral firmness or rectitude (put in practice with adamantine conviction), and with certain moral virtues, namely courage, magnanimity, devotion, patience, courtesy, a feeling for the truth, inner equilibrium, perseverance, unselfishness, contentment and compassion.[977] These same virtues one finds in a wide variety of "schools" for the human being's betterment, from Pythagoras to Buddhism, from Aristotle to the Roman Catholic Church. For example, in Catholic doctrine, the four Cardinal Virtues are prudence, justice, fortitude and temperance (self-control); in Plato, the main virtues are wisdom, courage, temperance or moderation, and justice or rectitude; and in the Japanese Bushido the eight virtues to be embodied by the Samurai are rectitude, courage, compassion, respect, integrity, honor, loyalty, and temperance.[978] These virtues Dorothy strove to incarnate.

In fact, it must be clear to any careful observer that Dorothy put in practice such virtues above and beyond the call of personality. She may have been aided by her intrinsic nature in embodying some of them occasionally,[979] but nature by itself is far from sufficient to guarantee con-

---

[977] The above are some of the twelve monthly virtues that philosopher and Anthroposophist Rudolf Steiner suggested his students study, meditate and practice, one for each month of the year. See: Rudolf Steiner, *Guidance in Esoteric Training: From the Esoteric School*, Rudolf Steiner Press, 1999.

[978] See Inazo Nitobe, *Bushido: The Soul of Japan*, G.P. Putman's Sons, 1905.

[979] Tovah Feldshuh, for example, puts two and two together stereotypically but logically when she concludes that one of the reasons for Dorothy's niceness was that she hailed from the Heartland of America. (Feldshuh, 2017, op. cit.)

sistency, especially when faced with the dangers of adverse nurture. What was truly surprising about Dorothy was not that she was positive, equanimous, unselfish, courageous, magnanimous, patient, courteous, temperate, determined, content, and compassionate, but that she was those things consistently and steadfastly (voluntarily), and in an environment like Hollywood. How much study and research she put into this endeavor we do not exactly know, but her statements, her interests and her results indicate that study and research she did. The positive trace she adamantly *determined* to leave in others is proof of that.

Afterword: What's in a Name III

"No no, my friend, be quiet! You don't seriously think that I don't know what you like and what you don't like? I know your tastes well, my dear, and the way you think."
I don't know how many times my wife Dida had said this to me. And, idiot that I am, I had never noticed.
No wonder she knew that Gengè[980] of hers more than I knew him myself! She had constructed him herself! And he was no puppet, either. If anything, *I* was the puppet.
Luigi Pirandello, *Uno, nessuno e centomila*[981]

Hovering over every biography, like a restless *daimon* or a sword of Damocles, is the impossibility of knowing any person fully, or the incompleteness associated with enumerating the facts of a person's life.

The fact that human beings know little of each other, and of them-

---

[980] The nickname that the protagonist's wife uses for him.

[981] Pirandello, *Uno* (1926), op. cit., 57. The translation is mine. Here is the original Italian text:
'No, no, bello mio, statti zitto! Vuoi che non sappia quel che ti piace e quel che non ti piace? Conosco bene i tuoi gusti, io, e come tu la pensi'. Quante volte non m'aveva detto così Dida mia moglie? E io, imbecille, non ci avevo fatto mai caso. Ma sfido ch'ella conosceva quel suo Gengè più che non lo conoscessi io! Se l'era costruito lei! E non era mica un fantoccio. Se mai, il fantoccio ero io.

selves, has occupied the conscious thought of countless philosophers and artists through the centuries, but it would be wrong to view such investigation as a mere intellectual pursuit. Anyone who has earnestly wished to know a fellow human must have encountered that subtle invisible membrane that separates one person from another existentially, leaving each of them an outsider looking in. This membrane Dorothy tried to perforate every chance she got, with friends, acquaintances, and loved ones.

A portrait of author Luigi Pirandello, with typewriter. Circa 1928.

Nobel Prize-winning Italian playwright and novelist Luigi Pirandello (1867–1936) authored some of the most searing—and revolutionary to this day—musings on the subject, under the guise of fiction or drama. Pirandello was no spiritualist, and no metaphysician,[982] yet his inquiries into the lives of his characters, and his meditations on the relationships between people, reached beyond the realms of drama and psychology, into an odd existential no man's land where the deeper dilemmas of a person's

---

[982] Pirandello, however, was an avid reader of Theosophist/esoteric literature, and occasionally a participant in séances and other spiritualist experiments.

life and interactions lurked. Before Beckett, before Sartre, before Brecht, and before Pinter, Pirandello articulated human doubt, or doubt about humans and about the lies they tell themselves and each other, like few other writers had before him, and few would after him.

The roles that people play in the lives of other people are the first obstacles barring the way to true reciprocal knowledge. Thus, a hypothetical woman—let's call her Dorothy—is, ineluctably, "mother" to her children, "wife" to her husband, "friend" to her friends, "daughter" to her parents, "actress" or "film star" to her public, etc. Those spouses, those parents, those children, may not label her as such: they may even just call her Dorothy, and not "wife," "daughter," or "mother" at all. That name, nonetheless, encapsulates a concept of Dorothy as mother to her children, as wife to her husband, as friend to her friends and as actress to her public, a concept that is as incomplete as it is subjective in each of those cases, and carries with it an avalanche of subjective ideas and judgments. That concept encapsulates the opinions, feelings, and subjective perceptions of those children, spouses, friends, and spectators.

The protagonist of Pirandello's novel *Uno, nessuno e centomila* realizes how tangled the web of subjective thought, perception, and judgment is, a web that obscures one person's inner being from another's:

> Listen: if for you I am endowed with no other reality than the one you give me, and I am willing to concede and admit that it is no less real than the one I might give myself; that, on the contrary, it is for you the only real one (and God only knows what that reality is that you attribute to me!); would you now want to complain about the one I will give to you with all the good will of imagining you as closely as possible to your way?
>
> I do not presume that you are as I imagine you. I have already affirmed that you are not even that "one" that you imagine yourself to be, but many at once, according to all your pos-

sibilities of being, to events, to relations and to circumstances. So, what wrong am I doing you? Rather, you are doing wrong to me, by believing that I do not, cannot, have any reality beyond the one you attribute to me; a reality that is only yours, believe me: an idea of yours, the one you have conceived of me, a possibility of being the way you feel it, the way you decide, the way you believe possible within you; for, of what I can be for myself, it is not only impossible for you to know anything, it is also impossible for me.[983]

Surrounded by people who claim to know him, understand him, and love him, that protagonist tries to dismantle the views that his family and friends hold of him (views that he does not recognize as concepts of himself) by acting differently from his usual manner and experimenting with his inner nature. In a process that resembles nothing so much as the old Delphic precept "Know thyself" (or the disciplines of Pythagoras and of Dorotheus of Gaza), this particular human being starts shedding the superficial "facts" of his life—those that others hold true for him, and those that he himself has held true for himself. He tries, in other words, to dismantle everything that is tacitly contained in the names by which others have called him, in the name by which he has called himself.

Given this premise, Pirandello's novel is surprisingly lithe and hu-

---

[983] Pirandello, *Uno* (1926), 90. The translation is mine. Here is the original Italian text:

Ma scusate: se per voi io non ho altra realtà fuori di quella che voi mi date, e sono pronto a riconoscere e ad ammettere ch'essa non è meno vera di quella che potrei darmi io; che essa anzi per voi è la sola vera (e Dio sa che cos'è codesta realtà che voi mi date!); vorreste lamentarvi adesso di quella che vi darò io, con tutta la buona volontà di rappresentarvi quanto più mi sarà possibile a modo vostro?

Non presumo che siate come vi rappresento io. Ho affermato già che non siete neppure quell'uno che vi rappresentate a voi stesso, ma tanti a un tempo, secondo tutte le vostre possibilità d'essere, e i casi, le relazioni e le circostanze. E dunque, che torto vi fo io? Me lo fate voi il torto, credendo ch'io non abbia o non possa avere altra realtà fuori di codesta che mi date voi; la quale è vostra soltanto, credete: una vostra idea, quella che vi siete fatta di me, una possibilità d'essere come voi la sentite, come a voi pare, come la riconoscete in voi possibile; giacché di ciò che possa essere io per me, non solo non potete saper nulla voi, ma nulla neppure io stesso.

morous (it starts with a dispute about a nose), most of its chapters not much longer than two or three pages. For its protagonist, however, who is also the first-person narrator, the issue of identity, and of the chasm that separates people and prevents them from knowing each other, evolves into a crucial, momentous argument, and into a life-changing realization. That issue is very Kantian: at every turn, our protagonist is confronted by the fact that there is a part of a person's being that can be known and understood (*phenomenon*), and another that can never be experienced: the thing-in-itself, or the being-in-itself (*noumenon*). Eventually, the novel's protagonist realizes that the battle is a futile one, and that his solitude is real and deep. Finally, he finds solace only in a definitive retreat from humanity, in a solitary, meditative process of self-knowledge that is fuller, and more fulfilling, than anything he has known in the company of others:

> No name. No memory today of yesterday's name; of today's name, tomorrow. If the name is the thing; if a name is within us the concept of every thing placed outside ourselves; and without name we do not have the concept, and the thing remains within us as if blind, indistinct and undefined; well then, this that I have brought among men, may each of them etch, like a funerary epitaph, on the forehead of that image with which I appeared to him, and leave it in peace and not mention it any more. For a name is nothing but this, a funerary epitaph. It befits the dead. It befits those who have concluded. I am alive and do not conclude. Life does not conclude; life knows nothing of names.[984]

---

[984] Ibid, 226–227. The translation is mine. Here is the original:

Nessun nome. Nessun ricordo oggi del nome di jeri; del nome d'oggi, domani. Se il nome è la cosa; se un nome è in noi il concetto d'ogni cosa posta fuori di noi; e senza nome non si ha il concetto, e la cosa resta in noi come cieca, non distinta e non definita; ebbene, questo che portai tra gli uomini ciascuno lo incida, epigrafe funeraria, sulla fronte di quella immagine con cui gli apparvi, e la lasci in pace e non ne parli più. Non è altro che questo, epigrafe funeraria, un nome. Conviene ai morti. A chi ha concluso. Io sono vivo e non concludo. La vita non conclude. E non sa di nomi, la vita.

If a name is something that allows the vibrant reality, the continuous transformation of a living entity, with its fluidity and its maddening complexity, to be crystallized within a definition, a construct, or a judgment, then a name is an enemy. It gives dead form to a human entity for other human entities, entitling them to stop knowing—giving them the illusion of knowing.

In his unofficial "preface" to his seminal meta-theatrical play *Sei personaggi in cerca d'autore* (*Six Characters in Search of an Author*, 1921), entitled "How and Why I Wrote the 'Six Characters'" and first published in the journal *Comoedia* in January 1925, Pirandello made the following statement in discussing the birth of his characters:

> The immanent conflict between vital movement and form is an inexorable condition not only of the spiritual order but also of the natural one. The life that has been set, or locked, into our bodily form in order to be, gradually kills its form. The lament of this locked-in nature is the irreparable, continuous aging of our body.[985]

A name, a concept, an image, a judgment, freeze and lock the living flow of a person's life and of his/her inner complexity: they squeeze it into the dead form of a tacit, synthetic, hopelessly incomplete definition, as if that definition were a concept of the person. We do this all the time with those around us, with the best of intentions: to know, to understand, to define.

In discussing Dorothy's name, Robbin Coons thought that "it [was]

---

[985] Luigi Pirandello, "Come e perché ho scritto i 'Sei personaggi,'" *Comoedia*, January 1925. The translation is mine. Here is the original:
Il conflitto immanente tra il movimento vitale e la forma è condizione inesorabile non solo dell'ordine spirituale, ma anche di quello naturale. La vita che s'è fissata, per essere, nella nostra forma corporale, a poco a poco uccide la sua forma. Il pianto di questa natura fissata è l'irreparabile, continuo invecchiare del nostro corpo.

the little lady herself who [made] 'Dorothy McGuire' an unusual, distinctive, wonderful name": in Coons' vision, there was still some life left in that name, provided by the person herself. Thirty years later, Rex Reed, his affection notwithstanding, saw that same name crystallized, as a dead symbol of something that was well known. The act of repeating the name, for Reed, was "an act of reassurance"; there was "something solid and comfortable" in the name's sound. The name contained a comfortable concept of the person.

In Pirandello's vision, there can be no "reassurance" in a name, nor an easy concept or definition of a person. If we are to gain even an imperfect insight into people, the gaze itself with which we look at them must become a "virgin" gaze, a way of looking without judging, even without thinking: an unprejudiced, selfless act of pure positive perception. Here is the novel's protagonist musing on this act:

> Oh my God, and will they not feel deprived suddenly of their pretty self-assurance when they see themselves looked at by these eyes of mine that *do not know what they are seeing*?
>
> Stopping a while to look at someone who is performing the most obvious everyday action; looking at him in such a way as to evoke in him the doubt that it is not clear to us what he might be doing, and that it might not be clear to him as well: this is enough to cause his certainty to vacillate and be overshadowed. Nothing troubles and disconcerts more than two vacuous eyes that show that they do not see us, or that they do not see what we see.
>
> —Why are you looking at me like that?—
>
> And no one thinks that we should all look thus, each with his eyes full of the horror of his helpless solitude.[986]

---

[986] Pirandello, *Uno* (1926), op. cit., 151. The translation is mine. Here is the original:
Oh Dio mio, e non sentiranno ora venir meno a un tratto la loro bella sicurezza, vedendosi guardati da questi miei occhi che non sanno quello che vedono?
Fermarsi per un poco a guardare uno che stia facendo anche la cosa più ovvia e consueta della vita;

That sense of solitude, of incompleteness, is one of the symptoms of the psychological malaise that plagues many a human being today, and has plagued many a human being through the centuries. It has been felt by individuals the world over, and not only where human relationships are concerned. For many of these individuals, this "negative" feeling has been accompanied by a yearning for meaning, for the missing *noumenon* of existence, and for a deeper fulfillment than the one usually afforded by natural human experience: like a perennial unanswered question.

Answers to this deeply personal question have come in many forms (e.g. religion, psychology, psychoanalysis, etc.), but, through the millennia, a subtle thread has connected the manifestations of one particular type of self-investigation. This thread we could call alchemical.

Over the centuries, alchemy has been seen with suspicion both by the practitioners of science, philosophy and religion and by public opinion in general. In the modern era, it has been viewed as charlatanry or, worse, as something evil and demonic—which is understandable, if one only focuses on its material (exoteric) side. The idea of a "science" obsessed with transforming base metals into gold is curious indeed, and may logically appear to be a vain, even demented pursuit.

Consistently, however, there has always been another side to alchemy, a side that one can call esoteric. In this respect, the other alchemy—with its metallic endeavors—was merely a front, or metaphorical code, for a different kind of research, one that had little or nothing to do with metals in the material sense.[987]

---

guardarlo in modo da fargli sorgere il dubbio che a noi non sia chiaro coò che egli stia facendo e che possa anche non esser chiaro a lui stesso: basta questo perché quella sicurezza s'aombri e vacilli. Nulla turba e sconcerta più di due occhi vani che dimostrino di non vederci, o di non vedere ciò che noi vediamo.
"Perché guardi così?"
E nessuno pensa che tutti dovremmo guardare sempre così, ciascuno con gli occhi pieni dell'orrore della propria solitudine senza scampo.

[987] See: Stanton J. Linden, *The Alchemy Reader: From Hermes Trismegistus to Isaac Newton*, Cambridge University Press, 2003. See also: René Guenon, *Symbols of Sacred Science* [1962], Sophia Perennis, 2004.

The special knowledge that was sought through these esoteric pursuits—themselves viewed with suspicion, whether alchemical, hermetic, magical, spiritualist, or lacking in specific labels—was secret (hidden, or reserved for few), for various reasons. These reasons had to do with a range of factors, such as (a) the fear of persecution from state rulers, religious authorities, or the public in general, (b) the fact that these metaphysical practices required a commitment to a discipline by "students" possessing a sincere yearning for such knowledge, and (c) the fact that the "Great Work" required extensive preparation and careful individual instruction, and was not suited for everyone. Such secrecy qualified these pursuits as "occult," a word that, viewed from the outside, gave a sinister ring to something that was not sinister in the least.

A wide range of practices and texts, ancient and modern, eastern and western, qualify as alchemical in this restricted sense. Their objective: a full knowledge of the human being as spiritual entity (and of the laws that govern it) and his betterment or transformation. This long Tradition—that Aldous Huxley called The Perennial Philosophy—has included initiators and supporters in the form of a heterogeneous collection of figures from all cultures (eastern and western) and periods (ancient and modern). It has included sages and prophets (Zarathustra, Siddhartha Gautama, the followers of Buddha and Mohammed, Hermes Trismegistus, Pythagoras[988]), philosophers (Taoist philosophers, Sufist philosophers, Plato, Aristotle, Zeno of Citium, Plotinus, Giordano Bruno). theologians (Origen Adamantius, Dorotheus of Gaza, Augustine of Hippo, Bernard of Clairvaux, Thomas Aquinas, Antonio Rosmini[989]), artists and musicians

---

[988] For a translation of Fabre d'Olivet's (1767–1825) take on Pythagoras' verses, see: Antoine Fabre d'Olivet, *The Golden Verses of Pythagoras* [1813], Solar Press, 1995.

[989] As an example of Antonio Rosmini's (1797–1855) work, see the posthumous *Teosofia*, Bompiani, 2011. Probably his most remarkable publication was his *Nuovo saggio sull'origine delle idee* ["New Essay on the Origin of Ideas"], published by Tipografia Pogliani in 1838.

(Nicholas Roerich, Wassily Kandinsky, Paul Klee, Alexander Scriabin, Bruno Walter), writers (Andrei Bely, Clifford Bax, Saul Bellow, Richard Matheson), legitimate scientists (Sir Isaac Newton), and occult researchers, Freemasons or "spiritual scientists" (Christian Rosenkreuz, Antoine Fabre d'Olivet,[990] Helena Blavatsky,[991] Howard W. Percival,[992] Rudolf Steiner,[993] Massimo Scaligero[994]). There have been "alchemists" in ancient Egypt, in ancient India, in ancient Persia, in ancient China, and in ancient Greece, as well is in our modern eastern and western worlds.

The knowledge pursued by this esoteric Tradition was in some ways "occult," but one should not think of the word "occult" as something malevolent, nor imagine its practitioners lurking in shadowy basements in the name of some devilish quest. These researchers were engaged in an earnest, methodical pursuit of Knowledge, an impassioned inquiry that actually made them quite impatient with "pseudo-occultism and mysticism."[995]

Without the "help" of that long tradition of practices and texts, the Delphic diktat, "know thyself," might seem like an ominous threat, or a tall, impossible order—or a cliché, for the phrase is used incessantly by dramatists, self-help gurus and charlatans of all kinds. That tradition has told us how to follow that order.

---

[990] Fabre d'Olivet's most fascinating work is his comparative exegesis of the first book of Genesis, whose full title is: *La langue Hébraique restituée et le veritable sens des mots hébreux rétabli et prouvé par leur analyse radicale*, Barrois et Eberhart, 1815.

[991] Helena Blavatsky, *The Secret Doctrine* [1888], 3 vols., Theosophical Publishing House, 1978.

[992] Howard W. Percival, *Thinking and Destiny*, 2 vols., Word Publishing Inc., 1961.

[993] Steiner's seminal book is *The Philosophy of Freedom* [1918], Rudolf Steiner Press, 1964.

[994] For translations of Massimo Scaligero, see: Massimo Scaligero, *A Practical Manual of Meditation*, Steiner Books, Inc., 2016. See also: Massimo Scaligero, *Techniques de concentration interieure*, Anthroposophiques Romandes, 2011.

[995] Nicholas Roerich, *Realm of Light*, Roerich Museum Press, 1931, 43.

In this line of esoteric inquiry, the philosopher's stone is not a stone at all, and gold is not mineral gold. The alchemist separates/discerns and unites, melts and solidifies ("*solve et coagula*"), not chemicals or metals but their spiritual equivalents—the supersensible forces and elements that are active within the human being and in the cosmos. The distillation, fermentation, and transformation that the alchemist enacts are not physical. The *athanor* is not a literal furnace but a metaphor for the "forum" where the individual's spiritual search is ignited within the individual's inner world through the "spark" of the *Logos*. And so forth.

The full process of self-knowledge is fundamentally an alchemical one, in which the constituent elements that make up the individual must be known, distinguished, and separated. It was at this inner process that Pythagoras hinted when he wrote, in his *Golden Verses*, that a disciple should know the things that affect his soul "by distinguishing them well";[996] or, in another translation: "Make a just distinction of [things], and examine all things well."[997]

As for the human being's happiness, or fulfillment, Pythagoras promised, "You shall see that the evils that consume men are the fruits of their own choices; and that these unhappy individuals seek far from themselves the good of which they carry the source within themselves. Few know how to be happy."[998]

Self-knowledge, in this Tradition, is neither anatomical nor chemical, neither intellectual nor psychological, neither mineral nor mystical; it is *gnosis* (esoteric knowledge of spiritual truth), or, better, gnoseology (the investigation of the process of knowing), involving both visible and

---

[996] The translation I am using as a basis is Antoine Fabre d'Olivet's, from his book *Les vers dorés de Pythagore, expliqués, et traduits pour la première fois en vers eumolpiques français*, Treuttel et Würtz, 1813.

[997] Florence M. Firth, *The Golden Verses of Pythagoras and Other Pythagorean Fragments*, Theosophical Publishing House, 1904.

[998] My translation of Fabre d'Olivet's version.

invisible (to the physical eye) elements. This *gnosis* or gnoseology is to be carried out with the same experiential rigor we associate today with the physical and natural sciences, and entails a second step: the transformation of the base elements one may discover and separate into something higher, purer and nobler—into something more perfect and precious, similar to gold. In turn, in this tradition, gold is the mineral trace, or symbol, of the sun, which in turn is the symbol of the Light emerging from and illuminating the Darkness, which in turn is the symbol of the *Logos*—the supersensible Word—illuminating the darkness of "fallen" thought. This kind of knowledge also requires regularity and discipline, and an adamantine determination, for nature and spontaneity have a tendency to claim their dominion over the human being, and to contrast such investigation.

In discussing Dorothy's performance in *Friendly Persuasion*, the *New York Times*' Richard Severo wrote that the role of Eliza Birdwell "showcased Miss McGuire's ability to project simplicity, warmth and forbearance";[999] the same could be said of many of her other roles, and of Dorothy in her private life. In life as in film and on stage, she could project those qualities because she possessed them.

Against all odds, Dorothy McGuire was able to incarnate many of the virtues that normally constitute the aim of years of self-investigation for practicing spiritual researchers in this Tradition. (Insightfully, and despite the veiled irony, Tovah Feldshuh uses two words to describe Dorothy: "angelic" and "saint.")[1000] Dorothy's spiritual quest was neither fashionable pose nor mystical passion, neither intellectual curiosity nor religious devoutness, but a silent, very personal inquiry, carried out unobtrusively and with happy abnegation; of this inquiry she never spoke explicitly, so much so that friends and family alike profess absolute ignorance of it, or state

---

[999] Richard Severo, "Dorothy McGuire, Steadfast Heroine of Film, Dies at 83," *New York Times*, September 15, 2001.

[1000] And Raymond Massey, in his autobiography (op. cit., 416), calls Dorothy "such an angel."

that Dorothy had "not found God." She may not have found God, but she certainly found the workings of some kind of unpretentious, authentic wisdom in herself. She put in practice her scrutiny by giving the example, by embodying without fuss or fanfare a code of conduct the equivalent of which can be found, not only in the world's "alchemical" Tradition we have mentioned, but also in many of the "moral schools" for the human being's healing.

And here one thing must be made clear: just as Dorothy did not preach or flaunt, so this Tradition of self-knowledge is not a thing for a boastful elite, but is open to anyone with a desire to learn. It is not meant to be an intellectual toy for bored would-be philosophers or New Age dreamers, nor an impossible pursuit for rarified initiates. It is, rather, an instrument of knowledge (Rudolf Steiner called it a "spiritual science," "*Spirituelle Wissenschaft*") available to anyone—from any walk of life—who is alert enough to recognize and follow the "coincidental" encounters that can lead to the discovery of the wonders of this kind of human investigation.

If there is a solution to the dilemma presented in this book's introductory caveat, it is the "new perception" that stems and develops from such investigation.[1001] Knowledge of oneself, and of the other—a deeper, more positive knowledge of the processes of the human entity than any materialist could dream of—is indeed possible. This life-changing, sense-giving knowledge lies within easy reach of every human being, if one only desires it.

[1001] Both Origen Adamantius and Saint Augustine wrote of the "senses of the heart," and Augustine (centuries before Rudolf Steiner) hinted at the acquisition, or development, of new organs of perception in the "inner man." See the interesting discussion "From the Limbs of the Heart to the Soul's Organs," by Jean-Louis Chrétien, in *Carnal Hermeneutics*, edited by Richard Kearney and Brian Treanor, Fordham University Press, 2015, 92–114.

Selected Bibliography

Books

Alighieri, Dante. *The Divine Comedy.* Ticknor and Fields, 1867.
Anderson, Robert. *I Never Sang for My Father: A Play in Two Acts.* Dramatists Play Service, 1968.
Anderson, Sherwood. *Winesburg, Ohio: A Group of Tales of Ohio Small Town Life.* The Modern Library, 1919.
Anouilh, Jean. *Legend of Lovers.* Coward-McCann, 1952.
Apollodorus. *The Library,* translated by Sir James George Frazer. William Heinemann, 1921.
Armstrong, Charlotte. *Mischief.* Coward-McCann, 1950.
Bach, Richard. *Jonathan Livingston Seagull: A Story.* Macmillan, 1970.
Bard, Mary. *The Doctor Wears Three Faces.* J.B. Lippincott, 1949.
Barry, Philip. *The Philadelphia Story: A Comedy in Three Acts.* Samuel French, 1969.
Bawden, James and Miller, Ron. *Conversations with Classic Film Stars: Interviews from Hollywood's Golden Era.* University of Kentucky Press, 2016.

Beckett, Samuel. *Watt*. The Olympia Press, 1953.

Blavatsky, Helena. *The Secret Doctrine* [1888], 3 vols. Theosophical Publishing House, 1978.

Boccaccio, Giovanni. *Teseida, delle nozze d'Emilia*. Gius. Laterza & figli, 1941.

Boothe, Clare. *The Women: A Play*. Random House, 1937.

Bordman, Gerald. *American Theatre: A Chronicle of Comedy and Drama, 1930–1969*. Oxford University Press, 1996.

Bosworth, Patricia. *Montgomery Clift: A Biography*. Harcourt Brace Jovanovich, 1978.

Bowers, Ronald. *The Selznick Players*. A.S. Barnes and Company, 1976.

Bront‧, Emily. *Wuthering Heights*. Harper & Brothers, 1848.

Buford, Kate. *Burt Lancaster: An American Life*. Alfred A. Knopf, 2000.

Burke, Edmund. *A Philosophical Enquiry into the Origin of Our Ideas of the Sublime and Beautiful*. Routledge & Kegan Paul, 1958.

Busch, Niven. *Till the End of Time*. Grosset & Dunlap, 1944.

Castaneda, Carlos. *Journey to Ixtlan: The Lessons of Don Juan*. Touchstone/Simon & Schuster, 1972.

Cerf Wagner, Phyllis and Erskine, Albert, eds. *At Random: The Reminiscences of Bennett Cerf*. Random House, 1977.

Chansky, Dorothy. *Composing Ourselves: The Little Theatre Movement and the American Audience*. Southern Illinois University Press, 2004.

Clarens, Carlos. *George Cukor*. Secker and Warburg/the British Film Institute, 1976.

Conze, Edward, ed. and transl. *The Large Sutra on Perfect Wisdom: With the Divisions of the Abhisamayalankara*. University of California Press, 1975.

Correale, Robert M. and Hamel, Mary, eds. *Sources and Analogues of the Canterbury Tales*, vol. 2. D.S. Brewer, 2005.

Coward, Noel. *Tonight at 8.30*. Doubleday, Doran and Company, Inc., 1936.

De Havilland, Olivia. *Every Frenchman Has One*. Random House, 1962.

Devlin, Albert J. and Tischler, Nancy M., eds. *The Selected Letters of Tennessee Williams, vol. 2, 1945–1957*. New Directions, 2004.

Diamant, Lincoln. *Images of America: Teatown Lake Reservation*. Arcadia Publishing, 2002.

Dunning, John. *On the Air: The Encyclopedia of Old-Time Radio*. Oxford University Press, 1998.

Eiselein, Gregory and Phillips, Anne K., eds. *The Louisa May Alcott Encyclopedia*. Greenwood Publishing Group, 2001.

Eliot, Charles W., ed. *The Complete Poems of John Milton*. P.F. Collier & Son, 1909.

Fabre d'Olivet, Antoine. *Les vers dorés de Pythagore, expliqués et tradiuts pour la première fois en vers eumolpiques français*. Treuttel et Würtz, 1813.

——— *La langue Hébraique restituée et le veritable sens des mots hébreux rétabli et prouvé par leur analyse radicale*. Barrois et Eberhart, 1815.

———*The Golden Verses of Pythagoras*. Solar Press, 1995.

Finn, Richard. *Asceticism in the Graeco-Roman World*. Cambridge University Press, 2009.

Firth, Florence M., ed. *The Golden Verses of Pythagoras and Other Pythagorean Fragments*. Theosophical Publishing House, 1904.

Fishgall, Gary. *Gregory Peck: A Biography*. Scribner, 2002.

Francke, Warren. *The Omaha Community Playhouse Story: A Theatre's Historic Triumph*. Omaha Community Playhouse, 2014.

Franken, Rose. *Claudia*. Samuel French, 1941.

Garrett Izzo, David. *Christopher Isherwood Encyclopedia*. McFarland & Co., Inc., 2010.

Gipson, Fred. *Old Yeller*. Harper & Row, 1956.

Grabman, Sandra. *Plain Beautiful: The Life of Peggy Ann Garner*. BearManor Media, 2005.

Graham, Martha. *Blood Memory*. Doubleday, 1991.

Granger, Farley and Calhoun, Robert. *Include Me Out: My Life from Goldwyn to Broadway*. St. Martin's Press, 2007.

Greco, J. *The File on Robert Siodmak in Hollywood, 1941–1951*. Dissertation.com, 1999.

Guenon, René. *Symbols of Sacred Science* [1962]. Sophia Perennis, 2004.

Hadden, Alexander H. *Not Me! The World War II Memoir of a Reluctant Rifleman*. Merriam Press, 2007.

Hall, Holworthy and Middlemass, Robert. *The Valiant*. Longmans, Green & Co., 1924., Lillian

Hellman, Lillian. *Another Part of the Forest: A Play in Three Acts*. Viking Press, 1947.

Herman, Jan. *A Talent for Trouble: The Life of Hollywood's Most Acclaimed Director, William Wyler*. G.P. Putnam's Sons, 1995.

Hesiod. *The Works and Days; Theogony; The Shield of Herakles*, Translated by Richmond Lattimore. University of Michigan Press, 1959.

Hobart, Alice Tisdale. *The Cup and the Sword*. Bobbs-Merrill Company, 1942.

Hobson, Laura Z. *Gentleman's Agreement*. Simon & Schuster, 1946.

Hoffenstein, Samuel. *Poems in Praise of Practically Nothing*. Boni & Liveright, 1928.

Horace. *Satires, Epistles, Ars Poetica*. Harvard University Press, 2005.

Hume, Doris. *The Sin of Susan Slade*. Dell Publishing Co., Inc., 1961.

Huxley, Aldous. *The Perennial Philosophy*. Harper & Brothers, 1945.

Ibsen, Henrik. *A Doll's House*. D. Appleton & Co., 1889.

Inge, William. *The Dark at the Top of the Stairs*. Random House, 1958.

Isherwood, Christopher and Prabhavananda, Swami. *The Song of God: Bhagavad Gita*. Marcel Rodd Co., 1944.

———*Vedanta for Modern Man*. Harper & Brothers, 1951.

Isherwood, Christopher. *The Berlin Stories*. New Directions, 1945.

———*Ramakrishna and His Disciples*. Simon & Schuster, 1965.

Ivory, James. *Autobiography of a Princess: Also Being the Adventures of an American Film Director in the Land of the Maharajas*. Harper & Row, 1975.

Selected Bibliography

Kadloubovsky, E. and Palmer, G. E. H. *Early Fathers from the Philokalia*. Faber and Faber, 1981.

Kahn, E. J. *The World of Swope: A Biography of Herbert Bayard Swope*. Simon & Schuster, 1965.

Kandinsky, Wassily. *The Art of Spiritual Harmony*. Constable and Company, Ltd., 1914.

———*On the Spiritual in Art*. Solomon R. Guggenheim Foundation, 1946.

Kanin, Garson. *The Rat Race*. Dramatists Play Service, 1950.

Kaufman, George S. and Ferber, Edna. *Dinner at Eight*. Doubleday, Doran & Co., 1932.

Kaufman, George S. and Hart, Moss. *The Man Who Came to Dinner*. Random House, 1938.

Kearney, Richard and Treanor, Brian. *Carnal Hermeneutics*. Fordham University Press, 2015.

Keel, Howard and Spizer, Joyce. *Only Make Believe: My Life in Show Business*. Barricade Books, Inc., 2005.

Krasna, Norman. *Dear Ruth: Comedy in Two Acts*. Dramatists Play Service, 1945.

Kyōkai, Bukkyō Dendō. *The Teaching of Buddha*. Kosaido Printing, Tokyo, 1975.

Linden, Stanton J. *The Alchemy Reader: From Hermes Trismegistus to Isaac Newton*. Cambridge University Press, 2003.

Loth, David. *Swope of G.E.: The Story of Gerard Swope and General Electric in American Business*. Simon & Schuster, 1958.

MacInnes, Helen. *Rest and Be Thankful*. Little, Brown and Co., 1944.

Macken, Walter. *The Flight of the Doves*. The Macmillan Company, 1968.

Mankiewicz, Don M. *Trial*. André Deutsch, 1955.

Massey, Raymond. *A Hundred Different Lives: An Autobiography*. Robson Books, 1979.

McClelland, Doug. *Eleanor Parker: Woman of a Thousand Faces*. Rowman & Littlefield, 2003.

Mell, Eila. *Casting Might-Have-Beens: A Film by Film Directory*. McFarland & Company, Inc., Publishers, 2005.

Miller, Gabriel. *William Wyler: The Life and Films of Hollywood's Most Celebrated Director*. University Press of Kentucky, 2013.

Miller, John C. *Crisis in Freedom: The Alien and Sedition Acts*. Little, Brown, 1951.

Molyneaux, Gerard. *Gregory Peck: A Bio-Bibliography*. Greenwood Publishing Group, 1995.

Nitobe, Inazo. *Bushido: The Soul of Japan*. G.P. Putnam's Sons, 1905.

O'Brien, Liam. *The Remarkable Mr. Pennypacker: A Comedy in Three Acts*. Samuel French, 1954.

Paris, Barry. *Audrey Hepburn*. Berkley Books, 1996.

Pathak, Dr. R. S. *Profiles in Literary Courage: Studies in English Literature*. Academic Foundation, 1992.

Peter, Carolyn. *A Letter from Japan: The Photographs of John Swope*. Grunwald Center for the Graphic Arts/Hammer Museum/Steidl, 2006.

Petrarca, Francesco. *Rime*. Giuseppe Bettinelli, 1781.

Pinero, Sir Arthur Wing. *The Enchanted Cottage: A Fable in Three Acts*. William Heinemann, 1922.

Pirandello, Luigi. *Sei personaggi in cerca d'autore: Commedia da fare* (second edition). R. Bemporad & Figlio, 1923.

———*Uno, nessuno e centomila*. Bemporad, 1926.

———*One, None and a Hundred Thousand*. E.P. Dutton, 1933.

Plato. *Plato in Twelve Volumes*, translated by Harold N. Fowler. Harvard University Press, 1921.

Prouty, Olive Higgins. *Now, Voyager*. Houghton Mifflin Company, 1941.

Rajadhyaksha, Ashish and Willemen, Paul. *Encyclopedia of Indian Cinema* (New Revised Edition). British Film Institute/Oxford University Press, 1999.

Rathbone, Basil. *In and Out of Character: An Autobiography*. Doubleday & Company, Inc., 1962.

Rattigan, Terence. *The Winslow Boy*. Dramatists Play Service, Inc., 1946.

———*Cause Célèbre: A Play in Two Acts*. Hamish Hamilton, 1978.

Raw, Laurence. *Adapting Henry James to the Screen: Gender, Fiction, and Film*. Scarecrow Press, Inc., 2006.

Reed, Mark. *Petticoat Fever: A Non-Tropical Farce in Three Acts*. Samuel French, 1935.

Roerich, Nicholas. *Realm of Light.*. Roerich Museum Press, 1931.

———*Adamant*. Nicholas Roerich Museum, 2017.

Rosmini, Antonio. *Nuovo saggio sull'origine delle idee*. Tipografia Pogliani, 1838.

———*The Origin of Ideas*. Kegan Paul, Trench and Co., 1883.

———*Teosofia*. Bompiani, 2011.

Russell, Rosalind and Chase, Chris. *Life Is A Banquet*. Random House, 1977.

Scaligero, Massimo. *Tecniche della concentrazione interiore*. Edizioni Mediterranee, 1975.

———*Kundalini d'occidente: il centro umano della potenza*. Edizioni mediterranee, 1980.

———*Techniques de concentration interieure*. Anthroposophiques Romandes, 2011.

———*A Practical Manual of Meditation*. Steiner Books, 2016.

Schrecker, Ellen. *The Age of McCarthyism: A Brief History with Documents*. Palgrave, 2002.

Secondari, John H. *Coins in the Fountain*. J.B. Lippincott Company, 1952.

Sergel, Christopher. *Winesburg, Ohio*. The Dramatic Publishing Company, 1960.

Shaw, Bernard. *The Quintessence of Ibsenism*. Constable and Company Ltd., 1929.

Sherman, Robert B. *Moose: Chapters from My Life*. AuthorHouse UK Ltd., 2013.

Sidonius, Dorotheus. *Dorothei Sidonii carmen astrologicum*. B.G. Taubner, 1976.

Sigal, Clancy. *Black Sunset: Hollywood Sex, Lies, Glamour, Betrayal and Raging Egos*. Soft Skull Press, 2016.

Sinyard, Neil. *A Wonderful Heart: The Films of William Wyler*. McFarland & Company, Inc., Publishers, 2013.

Smith, Betty. *A Tree Grows in Brooklyn*. Harper & Brothers, 1943.

Stampalia, Giancarlo. *Grant Williams*. BearManor Media, 2018.

Stanislavski, Constantin. *An Actor Prepares*. Theatre Arts, 1936.

Steinbeck, John and Swope, John. *Bombs Away*. Viking, 1943.

Steiner, Rudolf. *The Philosophy of Freedom*. Rudolf Steiner Press, 1964.

———*Guidance in Esoteric Training: From the Esoteric School*. Rudolf Steiner Press, 1996.

———*Six Steps in Self-Development: The 'Supplementary Exercises.'* Rudolf Steiner Press, 2010.

Sweeney, Kevin. *Henry Fonda: A Bio-Bibliography*. Greenwood Press, 1992.

Swope, John. *Camera Over Hollywood*. Random House, 1939.

Teague, Frances. *Shakespeare and the American Popular Stage*. Cambridge University Press, 2006.

Teichmann, Howard. *Fonda: My Life, As Told to Howard Teichmann*. New American Library, 1981.

Tommaseo, Niccolò. *Pensieri morali*. Antonio ed Angelo Cappelli Tipografi Editori, 1845.

———*Bellezza e civiltà, o delle arti del bello sensibile: studii*. Felice Le Monnier, 1857.

———and Bellini, Bernardo. *Dizionario della lingua italiana*. Società L'unione Tipografico-Editrice, Torino, 1879.

Totaro, Rebecca. *Meteorology and Physiology in Early Modern Culture: Earthquakes, Human Identity, and Textual Representation*. Taylor Francis Ltd., 2017.

Tsong Kha Pa. *Golden Garland of Eloquence*, translated by Gareth Sparham. Fremont, 2015,

Vacha, John. *Showtime in Cleveland: The Rise of a Regional Theater Center*. The Kent State University Press, 2001.

Van Druten, John. *I Am a Camera*. Random House, 1951.

Verswijver, Leo. *"Movies Were Always Magical": Interviews with 19 Actors, Directors, and Producers from the Hollywood of the 1930s through the 1950s*. McFarland and Company, Inc., Publishers, 2003.

Von Arnim, Elizabeth. *Christopher and Columbus*. Macmillan, 1919.

Watters, James and Horst. *Return Engagement: Faces to Remember – Then and Now*. Clarkson N. Potter, Inc., 1984.

Wertheim, Albert. *Staging the War: American Drama and World War II*. Indiana University Press, 2003.

West, Jessamyn. *The Friendly Persuasion*. Harcourt, Brace and Company, 1945.

West, Nathanael. *The Day of the Locust*. Random House, 1939.

White, Ethel Lina. *Some Must Watch*. Ward, Lock & Co., 1933.

Wiggin, Kate Douglas. *Mother Carey's Chickens*. Grosset & Dunlap, 1911.

Wilde, Oscar. *The Importance of Being Earnest*. Samuel French, 1893.

Wilder, Thornton. *Our Town: A Play in Three Acts*. Coward-McCann, 1938.

Williams, Tennessee. *Summer and Smoke*. New Directions, 1948.

——— *Sweet Bird of Youth*. New Directions, 1959.

——— *The Night of the Iguana*. New Directions, 1961.

Wilson, Sloan. *A Summer Place*. Simon & Schuster, 1958.

Winecoff, Charles. *Split Image: The Life of Anthony Perkins*. Dutton Adult, 1996.

Wyss, Johann David. *The Family Robinson Crusoe*. M.J. Godwin and Co., 1814.

Articles about Dorothy McGuire

Ames, Walter. "Miss McGuire Full of TV Fire." *Los Angeles Times*, August 22, 1954.

Anderson, Nancy. "Dorothy McGuire Hated First Role." *Green Bay (WI) Post-Gazette*, March 26, 1972.

Beck, Marilyn. "Dorothy McGuire ... A name from the past reappears for a TV special." *Chicago Tribune TV Week*, March 30–April 5, 1975.

Champlin, Charles. "An Endearing Sensitivity." *Los Angeles Times*, April 29, 1976.

Clymer, Adam. "John Swope, Noted Photographer." *New York Times*, May 15, 1979.

Cohen, Harold V. "Nixon Gets Smash Hit in 'Claudia.'" *Pittsburgh (PA) Post- Gazette*, March 10, 1942.

Coons, Robbin. "Dorothy McGuire to Keep Her Name." *Lancing (MI) State Journal*, June 1, 1943.

Dahl, Arlene. "Actress Dorothy McGuire Tells Her Rules of Beauty." *Chicago Tribune*, October 15, 1951.

"Dorothy McGuire Is Scared." *Brooklyn Eagle*, August 23, 1943.

"Dorothy McGuire's Hobby Now Family Photography." *Brooklyn Eagle*, February 24, 1952.

Fristoe, Roger. "Touring Gives Dorothy McGuire chance to feel country's heartbeat." *Louisville (KY) Courier-Journal*, September 27, 1987.

Hellman, Geoffrey T. "Dorothy McGuire: Actress Fits Her Part So Well It Is Hard to Tell Where McGuire Ends and "Claudia" Begins." *LIFE*, November 17, 1941.

Hopper, Hedda. "Battle Won by Dorothy McGuire." *Los Angeles Times*, September 21, 1947.

———"Independence Pays for Dorothy McGuire." *Pittsburgh (PA) Press*, September 21, 1947.

———"New Dorothy McGuire Comes Down to Earth." *Sioux Falls (SD) Argus-Leader*, January 22, 1950.

——— "Dorothy McGuire Retains Ideals While Maturing in Film Parts." *Los Angeles Times*, February 5, 1950.

Irwin, Virginia. "Cinderella Girl of the Stage." *St. Louis (MO) Post-Dispatch*, December 21, 1942.

"La Jolla Plans New Theater." *Los Angeles Times*, January 27, 1954.

Lane, Lydia. "Dorothy McGuire Contends a Calm Outlook Enhances Beauty." *Los Angeles Times*, October 24, 1954.

"Miss McGuire Felt Homesick and Headed for Broadway." *Brooklyn Eagle*, December 23, 1951.

Mizota, Sharon. "Mark Swope Spies Drama Along the Sidewalk." *Los Angeles Times*, December 18, 2012.

Ollman, Leah. "Mark Swope at Craig Krull Gallery." *Los Angeles Times*, February 5, 2010.

Reed, Rex. "The 'Iguana'—What a Night!" *Manchester (VT) Journal*, January 24, 1976.

———"Lack of Competitive spirit helped her survive." *Long Beach (CA) Independent Press-Telegram*, January 16, 1977.

Rosenfield, Paul. "Fate Takes a Hand Again for McGuire." *Los Angeles Times*, February 7, 1982.

Sapori, Alvise. "Io vecchia star? Attrice, prego e soprattutto, mamma." *la Repubblica*, August 17, 1986.

Savoy, Maggie. "John Swope: a Light, Shadow Artist." *Los Angeles Times*, September 25, 1967.

Schallert, Edwin. "La Jolla Film Festival Plans Expand." *Los Angeles Times*, June 19, 1954.

Seldis, Henry. "Lipchitz Hewn by the Camera Eye." *Los Angeles Times*, October 1, 1967.

Smith, Betty. "Author's Word for 'Brooklyn': 'Good.'" *Minneapolis (MN) Star Tribune*, March 18, 1945.

Smith, Cecil. "TV Drama Called One of Greatest Ways to Tell Tale." *Los Angeles Times*, July 25, 1954.

"Stars of Ghost Tale Inclined to Believe." *Kittaning (PA) Simpson's Leader-Times*, January 22, 1972.

Sullivan, Dan. "Talking Shannon Down in 'Iguana.'" *Los Angeles Times*, December 22, 1975.

———"'Night of the Iguana'—a Revival Revisited." *Los Angeles Times*, January 25, 1976.

The Actors' Company. Souvenir Program for *Summer and Smoke*, 1950.

Thomas, Bob. "Roles of Dorothy McGuire in Movies Now Questioned." *St. Cloud (MN) Times*, October 27, 1945.

Von Blon, Katherine. "Plan Links Theater With Picture Houses." *Los Angeles Times*, September 17, 1950.

About the Author

An American despite his very Italian name, Giancarlo Stampalia grew up bilingual in Italy and received his B.A. from Columbia University in the City of New York, then studied screenwriting and playwriting at the University of Southern California (USC), devoting several years to playwriting and directing, and briefly working as dramaturg at the Celebration Theatre in Los Angeles. For his play *Devil's Advocate*, he received a nomination as Best Playwright from the L.A. Weekly Annual Theater Awards in Los Angeles. In 1997 his book *Strehler dirige* ("Strehler Conducts"), about the work of seminal Italian theater director Giorgio Strehler, was published by Marsilio Editori in Venice, Italy. His biography of actor Grant Williams (best known to filmgoers for the beautiful allegory *The Incredible Shrinking Man*, 1957) was published stateside by BearManor Media in 2017 and nominated for the Richard Wall Memorial Award by the Theatre Library Association in New York. Stampalia has been a collaborator of several film festivals over the years, such as the International Science Fiction Festival in Trieste and the Pordenone Silent Film Festival. He has taught English, theater, creative writing, screenwriting, and film history. He is currently working on a book about American actor Richard Harrison and his work in Italian genre films in the 1960s and '70s. He lives in Trieste, Italy.

Index

Numbers in **bold** indicate photographs

Abady, Josephine R. 518, 519, 520, 521
Abbott, Anthony 312, 313
Abbott, Keene 32, 33
Act of Violence 76
Aeschylus 717
Ahmanson, William 583
Albee, Josh 543
Alice Adams 320
Alighieri, Dante ix, 718
All Out Arline 72
American Film Institute Salute to Gregory Peck, The 544, 573-574
American Film Institute Salute to Henry Fonda, The 544, 572
American Masters: Goldwyn: the Man and His Movies 545
Ames, Leon 219, 245, 246, 485
Ames, Walter 3, 479, 528
Amfitheatrof, Daniele 407
Amos 542
Anderson, Nancy 54
Anderson, Robert 319, 517, 520
Anderson, Sherwood 485
Andrews, Dana 158, 177, 278, 282, **283**, 664
Andrews, Tod 319, 320
Angel Street 209, 211-215, **215**, 219, 583

Anna and the King of Siam 75
"Anna Christie" 317
Another Part of the Forest 25, 514-517, **538**, 538, **541**, 582, 598, 660, 673
Anouilh, Jean 177, 221, 236, 237, 461, 462, 463, 464, 466-467, 468, 469, 470, 471, 472, 474-475, 476, 477, 478
Apollodorus 716
Aquinas, Thomas 735
Armstrong Theater of Today 288
Armstrong, Louis 44, 45, **46**, 336
Arnim, Elizabeth von 324, 326, 329
Arthur, Jean 6, 168, 663
Arundell, Dennis 489
Astor, Mary 76, 152, **152**, 533, 644
Atkinson, Brooks 3, 46-47, 132, 474-475
Augustine of Hippo 735, 739
Autobiography of a Princess 95
"Autumn Crocus" 332-333
Bach, Richard 454, 455
Bachardy, Don 584, 620-627, **622**, **623**, **625**, **626**, **693**, 694, 695
Bachelor Born 38-39
Bachrach, Ernest A. **14**, **248**, **275**, **365**
Bailey, Robert 288
Balázs, Béla 472-473
Ball, Lucille 379, 544, 567, 569, 570
Bankhead, Tallulah 176, 216, 336-337, 345
Baricco, Alessandro 607-608
Barnes, Clive 503, 647
Barrie, Elaine 43
Barrie, James M. 29, 32, 60
Barry, Philip 53, 130, 133, 237, 332, 532, 533, 599
Barrymore, Ethel 59, 66, 255, 263-264, **265**, 562
Barrymore, John 6, 42, 43, 44, 59
Bartók, Béla 397, 473
Basaldella, Afro 387
Basaldella, Dino 388
Basaldella, Mirko 387
Bax, Clifford 736
Baxter, Anne 71, 177, 364, 462, 512, 513
Beck, Marilyn 3, 680, 682, 684, 686, 687, 704
Beckett, Samuel 298, 325, 729
Bellow, Saul 736
Bely, Andrei 736
Benelli, Sem 471
Benny, Jack 210, 285, 330, 331, 334
Berg, Alban 397
Berger, Robert "Buzz" 548
Bergman, Ingmar 78, 310, 415-416

INDEX

Bergman, Ingrid 11, 68, 74, 413, 482, 545, 663, 665
Bernard of Clairvaux 735
Bernheimer, Martin 487-489
Bernstein, Elmer 260, 403, 544
Best Doggoned Dog in the World, The 545
"Betrayal" 318-319
Between the Darkness and the Dawn 546-547, 550
Big Show, The 336-337, 345
Big Sister, The 40, 287
Binyon, Claude 91-92, 166, 168, 171, 172, 173
Black, Kitty 221, 461, 467
Blavatsky, Helena 736
Blondell, Joan 6, 142, 144, 147
Blood 611
Blue Bird, The 29
Blue Gardenia, The 177, 256, 462
Bluebeard's Castle 473
"Blueprint for Murder, A" 360-362, 598
Blythe, Sylvia 653-654
Boccaccio, Giovanni 717, 718
Bogarde, Dirk 465
Bogart, Humphrey 158, 285, 289-293, **290**, 387, 611, 644
Bolling, Tiffany **541**
Bombs Away 92-93
Boone, Pat 417
Boyer, Charles 210, 235, 285, 330, 331, 332, 333, 334, 362, 586
Brando, Dorothy "Dodie" 27
Brando, Marlon 21, 27, 103, 387
Brazzi, Rossano 191
"Breaking the Sound Barrier" 358-359
Brecht, Bertolt 305, 326, 340, 729
Bride by Mistake 72-73
Bright Scarf, The 175
Brown, Pamela 58, 338, 339, **340**, 342, 465
Brown, Stephen 476, 477
Bruno, Giordano 685, 735
Buchanan, Edgar 404
Buddhism 627, 628, 677, 691, 705–706, 720, 725, 735
Bundle of Joy 565
Burkley, Jr., Harry V. 23
Burton, Richard 338, 462, 463, 465, 466, 470, 491, 496, 544, 578, 644
Calhern, Louis 342, 395
Callaway Went Thataway 8, 389-394, **393**, **395**, 461, 598, 603, 647
Camera Over Hollywood 90-92, 99-100, 545
Candleshoe 589
Captain Horatio Hornblower, R.N. 239, **564**, 565
Cardosi, Andrea 258

Cariaga, Daniel 487
Carlson, Richard 237, 342, 533, 534
Carmody, Jay 59
Carolful Christmas, A 517
Carr, Mary **416**
Carroll, Lewis 329
Carter, Ed and Hannah 558
Casella, Alberto 32
Castaneda, Carlos 456
Castiglione, Baldassarre 717
Cat on a Hot Tin Roof 320
Catlett, Walter 420, 423
Cause Célèbre 512-513
Cavalcade of America 298, 316-317, 318-319, 320-321, 322-323, 332, 334-336, 348-351, 598, 618
Cedrone, Lou 520
Cerf, Bennett 35, 88-89, 90, 158, 286, 545-546, **546**, 595
Chamberlain, Richard 5, 491, 492, **495**, 496-497, 500, 502, 503, **505**, 506, 578
Champlin, Charles 3, 11, 41, 92, 453, 494-495, 614, 629
Chapman, John 467
Charell, Erik 44, 45
Chaucer, Geoffrey 718
Chodorov, Edward 50, 219, 220, 245
Chris and Don: A Love Story **622, 693**
"Christopher and Columbus" 324-330, 598
Clair, René 125, 182-183
Clarens, Carlos 259, 534
Claudel, Paul 480, 487, 489
Claudia (1943) 3-4, 8, 54, 69-70, 71-72, 129-141, **132, 133, 134, 136, 138, 140**, 148, 149, 150, 151, 152, 153, 170, 172, 173, 181, 261, 268, 329, 334, 499, 597, 598, 606, 608, 610, 619, 636, 638, 644, 646, 647, 664, 666
Claudia (play) 3-4, 14, 50, 51-61, **57**, 65-66, 67-68, 84, 129, 130, 131, 135, 137, 142, 230, 237, 268, 288, 367, 461, 465, 494, 497, 599, 642, 652, 665, 647
Claudia and David 110, 133, 134-135, 149-154, **150, 152, 154**, 167, 369, 630
Climax! 534, 535
"Cluny Brown" 285, 333-334
Coburn, Charles 198, 201, 203, 565, 583, 586
Cocteau, Jean 469, 471, 472, 475, 476
Cohen, Harold 44, 50, 51, 59, 61, 268-269, 277, 461
Coleman, Nancy 53
Coleridge, Samuel Taylor 672, 685
Columbia University 5, 35, 121, 559, 641
Comport, Lionel 425
Cone, Theresa Loeb 202, 204, 214
Connelly, John H. 94
Connolly, Mike 567-568
Cook, Donald 56, **57**

Coons, Robbin 12, 13, 669, 732-733
Cooper, Gary 107, 414-415, 419, 420, 421, **421**, 423, 424, 426, **426**, 562, 574, 645, 687
Copland, Aaron 44, 344
"Coquette" 323
Corby, Jane 402, 405, 647
Corcoran, Kevin 427, **428**, 440, **442**
Corrigan, Alan 47-48
Cotten, Joseph 74, 76, 205, 212, 216, 244, 285, 293, 294, 545, 583, 587
Country Girl, The **482**, 483-484, **484**
Cowan, Lester 176
Coward, Noël 217, 218, 227
Craig, Gordon 340
Cranach the Elder, Lucas 16
Craven, John **300**
Crawford, Joan 8, 301, 395, 572, 586
Crisp, Quentin 624
Crosby, John 313-316, 338-339, 341
Crowther, Bosley 3, 148, 151, 164, 165-166, 170, 171-172, 184, 186, 195, 196, 203, 251-252, 281, 394, 399-400, 404, 411-412, 423, 430, 446-447, 450-451
Cukor, George 259, 533, 534, 545, 562, 566-567, 570
Cummings, Irving 361-362
Curtiz, Michael 177
D'Annunzio, Gabriele 471
Da Ponte, Lorenzo 200
Dahl, Arlene 654, 655, 656, 668, 671
Dailey, Dan 361
"Damask Cheek, The" 317-318, 692
Dandridge Sisters 45, **46**
Daniels, William **551**
Dark at the Top of the Stairs, The 8, 436-439, **438**, 485, 536, 585
Dark Medallion, The 76
"Dark Victory" 181, 526-527, 530
Dassin, Jules 49, 174
Daves, Delmer 433, 434, 436, 447
David, Clifford 486
David, George L. 148-149
Davidson, Gordon 571, 582, 584
Davidson, Marie Hicks 481
Davis, Bette 8, 364, 395, 426, 544, **565**, 572, 663, 668
Day, Doris 6, 198
Day, Laraine 72, 73, 209, 211, 213, 214, 215, 219, 583
Dazzling Hour, The 240, 241
De Havilland, Olivia 76, 176, 216, 240, 241, 342, 531, 556
De Vol, Frank 198
Dear Ruth 219, 460
Death Takes a Holiday 32-33

Debussy, Claude 479, 551
Dee, Sandra 434, 687
del Piombo, Sebastiano 16
della Robbia, Andrea 16
Diamond, Neil 455
Dietrich, Marlene 6, 297, 562
Dinelli, Mel 257
Dinner at Eight 210, 331
Disney, Walt 44, 112, 427, 440, 441, 447, 453, 545, 589
Dmytryk, Edward 270, 271
Doll's House, A 77-80, 173, 200, 217, 285, 301-310, 317
Don't Bother to Knock 174-175
Donahue, Troy 434, 443, 444
Donaldson, Ted 143, **146**
Donne, John 717
Dorotheus of Gaza 18, 730, 735
Douglas, Kirk 542, 568, 572, 582
Douglas, Melvyn 6, 520
Douglas, Sharman 576, 578
Doyle, Neil 635-636
Drake, Sylvie 491-492
Dressler, Eric 313
Drew, Bernard 453
Duff, Warren 401, 404
Duke, Patty 535, 536
Dunn, James 142, 143, 147, 288, 664
Dunne, Irene 6, 75, 566
Dunning, John 319
Dunnock, Mildred 278, 280, 516
Early Life of Buddha, The 694
Egan, Richard 238, 434, **435**, 435
Elfman, Danny 260
Ely, Ron 201, 203
Emerson, Ralph Waldo 685
Enchanted Cottage, The 8, 27, 249-254, **253**, 289, 311, 527, 549, 635, 644, 669
Erickson, Leif 169
Erman, John 552
Eurydice 221-223, 461, 463-464, 465, 471, 472-473, 476
Evans, Maurice 68, 285, 297, 314, 339
Eve of St. Mark, The 71
Evening with Mr. Fonda, An 514
Ewell, Tom 478
Eyer, Richard **417**, 417, 423, 425, 437
Eyer, Robert 437
Fabre d'Olivet, Antoine 735–736, 737
"Fall of Maggie Phillips, The" 352-358
"Family Ties" **551**

Fanchon and Marco (producers) 210, 236
Fantasy Island 548
Feldshuh, Tovah 25, 515, 516-517, 598, 634, 642, 643, 660, 689-690, 725, 738
Fernald, Jim 127, 381, 382, 590-591, 683, 684, 691, 710-711
Ferrer, José 158, 176, 216, 237
Ferrer, Mel 101, 156, 205, 206, 208, 209, 210, 211, 212, 216, 217, 221, 222, 224, 225, 226, 228, 233, 235, 237, 238, 239, 241, 242, 243, 246, 247, 331, 463, 583
FIAT 500 "Topolino" 111–112
Fichte, Johann Gottlieb 685
Fickett, Homer 297-298, 347
Fishgall, Gary 206-207
Flight of the Doves 451-454, **453**, 710
"Flight to Bermuda" 362-363
Foley, Greg 30
Fonda, Henry 4, 23, 27, 29-30, **31**, 32, 60, 62, 64, 76, 83, 90, 94, 108-110, 119, 210, 236, 330, 370, 384, 461, **482**, 483, **484**, **488**, 502, 514, 544, 545, 567-568, **569**, 572-573, 587, 658
Fonda, Jane 62, **482**, 483, 514, 573, 658
Fontaine, Joan 131, 545
Ford Theater 317-318, 320, 692
Ford, Constance 433, 434
Ford, Glenn 406, 407, **409**
Forsythe, John 526, 530, 572
Fortuny, Mariano 670-671
Fox, Christy 579-580, 703
Franchetti, Baroness Afdera 568, **569**
Francis, Bob 470
Francis, Robert 29, 41
Francke, Warren 29, 30, 483-484
Frank, Melvin 389, 394, 647
Franken, Rose 51, 52-55, 56, 58, 66, 67, 69, 129, 130, 131, 133, 135, 136, 137, 152, 201, 230, 237
French, A.H. **86**
Freshman, Jerry 50, 51
Friendly Persuasion 9, 107, 412-427, **416**, **417**, **418**, **421**, **422**, **426**, 437, 558, 562, 645, 647, 652, 738
Fryer, Robert 491, 512, 583
Garbo, Greta 6, 620, 663, 687
"Garden in the Sea, A" 527, 528
Gardiner, Reginald 137, **138**, 219, 244, 245, 246, 562
Garfield, John **155**, 157, 158, 159, 164, **165**, 175, 176, 210, 211, 224-225, 230, 236, 330, 332
Garland, Richard **422**
Garner, Peggy Ann 142, 143, **146**, 147, 647
Gavazzeni, Gianandrea 482
Geiger, Milton 324
Gelson's 590

General Electric Theater 357-358
Gentleman's Agreement 8, 76, 77, 80, 154-166, **155**, **156**, **157**, **159**, **162**, **163**, **165**, **166**, 172, 285, 309, 363-364, 369, 370, 585, 598, 599, 635, 644, 647, 699
Gersh Agency 644
Gersh, Phil 644
Gessler, Clifford 481
Ghost and Mrs. Muir, The 75
Ghost Dancing 548-550, 639
Gielgud, John 285, 338-340, **340**, 341, 342, 465, 472
Gilbert and Sullivan 717
"Gioconda Smile, The" 534-535
Giovanna d'Arco al rogo 482
Giraudoux, Jean 471, 472
Glitter 548
Golden, John 51, 52, 54, 58, 526
"Golden Needle, The" 332
Goldwyn Jr., Samuel 108, 558, 580
Goldwyn, Samuel 222, 277, 281, 346-347, 425, 462, 545, 652, 667
Gould, Harold 518, 519, 521, 538-539
Goulding, Edmund 131, 133, 135, 139, 140, 168, 181, 182, 183, 186, 187, 646, 665
Grabman, Sandra 647
Graham, Sheilah 3, 230, 611, 698-699
Granger, Farley 278, 281, 282
Grant, Cary 94, 135, 136, 168, 533
Greatest Story Ever Told, The 8, 449-451, 478, 598
Greenspun, Roger 454
Gregory, Paul 478
Griffith, Hugh 465, 470
Guiberson, Gordon Greene 579
Gwenn, Edmund 178, 180, **180**, 183, 184
Haber, Joyce 570
Hallmark Playhouse 312, 324-330, 343-344, 598
Halton, Charles **146**
"Hamlet" 285, 313, 338-342, **340**
"Hand on the Latch" 312-313
Hanna, Daniel Rhodes 373-374
Hansen, Jim 673
Harbin, Vernon 575
Harding, John 476, 477
Hardy, Joseph 492, 502, 503, 504, 647
Harmon, Frank 206
Harris, Jed 37-38, 40
Harris, Julie 6, 239-240
Harris, Radie 466-467
Harrison, Rex 75, 76
Havoc, June 158, 160, 169, **171**
Hayes, Helen 283, 296, 337, 485, 572, 589

Hayward, Brooke 108
Hayward, Leland 83, 84, 90, 94, 459, 674
He Ran All the Way 175
Heard, Gerald 692, 695
Hedda Hopper Show, The 345
Hegel, George Wilhelm Friedrich 685
Heimer, Mel 467-468, **468**
"Heiress, The" 342-343
Hellman, Geoffrey T. 3, 37-38, 53, 57-58, 599, 605, 610, 619-620, 627, 658, 665-666, 669, 671
Hellman, Lillian 25, 79, 514-515, 517, 538, 660
Heming, Violet 60, 64
Hepburn, Katharine 6, 191, 294, 353, 413, 532, 533, 534, 545, 587, 663, 665
Hernandez, Juano 45, 410-411
Herrmann, Bernard 260, 344
Hewitt, Alan 318
Hidden Fear 177
Higgins Prouty, Olive 364
Highway to Heaven 548, 550-551
Hirschfeld, Al 45-46
Hite, Kathleen 352-353, 354
Hobson, Laura Z. 164, 364
Hodges, Eddie 447, **448**, 449
Hoffenstein, Samuel 333-334
Holbrook, Hal 455, 520
Holing, Dwight 99, 122, 126-127, 591-592, 689-690
Holley, Tim 502
Hollywood Fights Back 158
Hollywood: The Selznick Years 545
Holm, Celeste 155, 163, **165**
Homolka, Oscar 317
Honegger, Arthur 479–482, 489
Hooven, Marilyn 449
Hopper, Dennis 617-618
Hopper, Hedda 1-3, **2**, 4, 71, 75, 77-78, 80, 81, 85, 110-111, 112, 113, 149, 153-154, 160, 172-173, 175, 176, 208, 227, 232, 234, 283, 309, 345, 367, 369, 370, 377-378, 398, 428, 429, 459-460, 561-562, 606, 630, 635, 643-644, 659, 668, 670, 701-702, 713
Horace (Latin poet) 627
Horner, Harry 108, 480
Horwin, Jerry 6, 43
Hot Rock, The 119-120
Hotel 548
Hotpoint Holiday Hour 330-332, **331**
Howe, Graham 99
Hudson, Rock 198, 430, 431, 432
Hush . . . Hush, Sweet Charlotte **565**, 566

Hussey, Ruth 216, 219, 533
Huston, John 158, 174, 491, 504
Hutchinson, Tom 526
I Am a Camera 239-240, 241, 692
I Never Sang for My Father 264, 517-523, 538-540, **539**, 616, 619, 700
I Want You 277-283, **283**, 462, 652, 667
Ibsen, Henrik 77, 78, 79, 200, 217, 301, 302, 303, 304, 305, 306, 307
"I'll Be Seeing You" 285, 293-294
Importance of Being Earnest, The 225-226, **225**, 227, 330
Incredible Journey of Dr. Meg Laurel, The 548
Inge, William 237, 245, 436, 437
Invitation 105, 106, 177, 395-401, **395**, **399**, 461, 462, 669
Ireland, John 216, 227, 230, **231**, 231, 232, 233, 347, 579, 673
Irritant, The 611
Irwin, Virginia 33-34, 36, 56-57
Isherwood, Christopher 240, 584, 620-621, 627, 692, **693**, 694-695
Ives, Burl 447, 448, 449
Ivory, James 95, 123
Jacobs, Jody 578, 579, 584
Jaffe Agency 644–645
James, Henry 74, 527
Joan of Arc at the Stake 479-482, 486-489, 656-657
Johnson, Al 224
Johnson, Bertha French 224
Johnson, Erskine 3, 175, 414-415, 542, 636
Johnson, Van 106, 395, 399, 400
Jonathan Livingston Seagull 454-457
Jones, Jennifer 67, 75, 76, 108, 205, 211, 213, 216, 219, 333, 588
Jourdan, Louis 189, **190**, 191, **192**, 216, 219, 562
Joyce Jordan, M.D. 51, 288
Kandinsky, Wassily 688, 736
Kanin, Garson 237, 459, 460
Kant, Immanuel xviii, 731
Kaper, Bronislau 395, 396, 400
Kazan, Elia 8, 141-142, 155, 156, 364, 436, 646, 647
Keathley, George 512
Keaton, Diane 381
Keel, Howard 390, 391, 394, **395**, 664
"Keep Smiling" 550
Kennedy, Arthur 406, 409, 410, 433, 434
Kerr, Deborah 6, 210, 236, 331, 336, 337, 491, 496, 565
Keys of the Kingdom, The 67-68
Kilgallen, Dorothy 286, 346, 420, 545
Kind Lady 50, 219-220
Kinsolving, Lee 438, 439, 485
Kirk, Tommy 427, **428**, 440, **442**
Kirkley, Donald 469-470

Kiss for Cinderella, A 29-30, **31**, 32, 33-34, 35, 42, 60, 483, 500
Kleiner, Harry 412
Knight, Shirley 437, 438
Koehler, Robert 559
Kohn, Herbert 276-277
Korngold, Erich Wolfgang 424
Krasna, Norman 73, 219, 237, 246, 460
Krasner, Milton 194, 196
Krull, Craig 95-96, 99, 124, 126
"Lady Becomes a Governor, The" 322-323
Lady Esther Screen Guild Theater, The 289-293, **290**
"Lady on a Mission" 320-321
Lancaster, Burt 158, 178, 179, **180, 182**, 183, 184, **185**, 186, **186**, 211, 332, 587, 688
Landon, Michael 550
Lane, Lydia 3, 656-657, 660-662, 668
Langner, Lawrence 463, 465, 478
Lansbury, Angela 437, 438, 587
"Lantern in the Dark" 311-312
Last Best Year 552-553
"Last Confession" 321-322
Latenser, Sr., John 26
Lawrence, Jerome 200, 344, 410
Lee, Robert E. 200, 344, 410
Lee, Robert Tyler 217, 232
Legend of Lovers 177, 236, 461-471, 475, 477
Leigh, Vivien 413
Les belles de nuit 183
Levin, Dan "Peter" 63-64, 201, 239, 382, 546, 547, 617, 649, 674, 690
Levin, Henry 201, 203
Lewis, Sinclair 177
Lewton, Val 255
Liberty Jones 53-55, 130
Little Princess, A 29
Little Women 75, 646
Lloyd, Norman 49, 216, 239, 244, 246, 502, 552, 700
Logan, Joshua 89, 92, 588
"Look to the Mountain" 347
Loper, Mary Lou 582
Loth, David 371
"Lottie Dundas" 336
Love Boat 548
Lovejoy, Frank 169, 327, 363
Loy, Myrna 6, 158, 226
Loynd, Ray 494
Luce, Clare Boothe 336, 561-562, **563**, 695
Luce, Henry 561-562, **563**, 695
Lumet, Sidney 533, 534

Lundigan, William **167**, 167-168, 171-172, 173, 174, 363
Lux Radio Theatre 169, 244, 289, 293-294, 301, 342, 352, 358-359, 360-362, 363-365, 598, 651
Lux Summer Theatre 289, 352-356
Lux Video Theatre 529, **532**
Lyons, Leonard 52, 158
MacArthur, James 440, 572
MacMurray, Fred 390, 391, 392, **393**, 394, **395**, 544, 572, 587
MacPherson, Virginia 3, 262-263
Madison, Guy 216, 219, 270, **272**, 273, 274-275, **274**, 275, 277, 575, 587, 642, 664
Maeterlinck, Maurice 29, 472-473
Main Street to Broadway 175-176
Make Haste to Live 401-405, **403**, **405**, **406**, 647
Maltin, Leonard 254, 394, 440
Man Who Came to Dinner, The 210, 285, 286, 330-331
Mankiewicz, Don M. 406-407
Mann, Delbert 536
Manners, Dorothy 74, 482
March, Fredric 32, 177
Markle, Fletcher 318, 357, 692
Marshall, Herbert 250, **253**, 254, 533
Marvin, Lee 245, 481, 482
Mason, James 80, 216, 245, 285, 346, 644
Massey, Raymond 216, 237, 491, 492, 494, **495**, **505**, **509**, 606, 607
Mathers, Jimmy 447, **448**
Matheson, Richard 736
Mathews, Tom 232
Mayerhold, Vsevolod 340
McAnuff, Des 247
McDonald, Alan and John 28, **28**
McDowall, Roddy 216, 347
McGuire, Isabelle Flaherty Trapp 21, 22, 23, 24, 35, 37, 43, 60, 84, 367, 614-615, 633
McGuire, Thomas Johnson 23, 24, 25, 37, 42, 614-615
McNally, Stephen 401, **403**, 404
McNamara, Maggie 188, **190**, 191, 195
McNamara, Paul 570
"Medal for Miss Walker, A" 348-351, 598, 618
Medicine Show 48-50
Mehta, Zubin 580
Meredith, Burgess 296, 297, 317
Merkel, Una 230, 231, 232, 233, 237, 245
Messiaen, Olivier 260, 601
Middlemass, Robert 289, 290
Miles, Sylvia 5, 492
Milland, Ray 244, 285, 297, 359, 360, 364, 541, 562, 565, 566
Miller, Darryl H. 521
Miller, Gabriel 413

Miller, Ron 639
Millhollin, James **482**, 483
Mills, Hayley 447, **448**, 449
Mills, John 440, 441, **442**, 442
Milton, John 717
"Miracle in the Rain" 288
Miss Julie 245, 310, 397
Mister 880 8, 177-187, **178**, **179**, **180**, **182**, **185**, **186**, 598, 646
Mister Antonio 33
Mitchum, Robert 76, 232, 270, **272**, 274, 585
Mizota, Sharon 125
Mockridge, Cyril 166-167
Monroe, Marilyn 6, 175, 384, 424
Monteux, Pierre 479, 488
Montgomery, Elizabeth 269, 542, 547
Moody, Ron 452, 453
Moore, Mary Tyler 552, 587
Mosby, Aline 424-425
Mother Didn't Tell Me 81, 92, 166-173, **167**, **171**, 363
Mother India 431
Munro, Janet 442
Musical Evening at Studio One's Backlot, A 588
Musuraca, Nicholas **255**, 256-257
My Dear Children 6, 42-44, 59
Mysterious Mummy Case, The 526
Nash, Ogden 333-334
Natwick, Mildred 38, 216, 225, 226, 227, 250, 254, 527, 528
Negulesco, Jean 80, 187, 195-196, 264
Neilson, James 216, 225, 226, 227, 232
Nelson, Ralph 710
Newman, Alfred 450
Newton, Robert 358, 359
Newton, Sir Isaac 734, 736
Night of the Iguana, The 5, 13-14, 491-509, **495**, **497**, **505**, **509**, 511, 512, 543, 604, 606-607, 647, 662, 674, 704
Niven, David 216, 237, 285, 296, 347, 589, 644
"No Greater Love" 316-317
Nolan, Lloyd 142, 144, **144**, **147**, 147, 444, **445**, 544, 581, 664
Notorious 251
"Now, Voyager" 364-365
O'Brien, Jack 523, 539
O'Brien, Liam 197
O'Connor, John J. 547, 552
O'Donnell, Bob 235
O'Hara, Maureen 413, 452
Odets, Clifford 483
Old Yeller 9, 427-430, **428**, 545

Olivier, Laurence 340, 347, 681, 687, 688
Ollman, Leah 124
On Golden Pond 514
On the Air 319
On the Spiritual in Art 688
Oppenheimer, Gerald and Virginia 586
Origen 721–722, 735
Orphée 469, 471, 472, 475
Our Town 29, 39, 40-42, 43, 59, 61, 237, 278, 285, 295, 298-301, **300**, 439, 492, 518
"Pale Horse, Pale Rider" 534-535
Panama, Norman 389, 394, 647
Parker, Eleanor 492, 494, **495, 505**
Parsons, Louella 1, 3, 70, 72, 79, 80, 135, 174, 220, 249, 345, 460, 482
Pasles, Christopher 517
Patterson, Neva 533
Payne, John 177, 533, 534
Peck, Gregory 68, 74, 76, 101, 108, 155, **155, 156**, 156, **157**, 158, **159**, 159, **162, 163**, **165, 166**, 176, 205, 206, 208, 209, 210, 211, 213, 214, 215, **215**, 217, 219, 220, 221, 224, 227, 229, 233, 234, 235, 238, 239, 241, 242, 243, 246, 247, 330, 331, 364, 384, 426, 459, 544, 565, 568, 569, 570, 572, 573, 574, 578, 579, 580, 583, 599, 687
Penningroth, Phil 548-549
Perceval le Gallois 641
Percival, Howard W. 736
Pereira, William 209-210, 235, 511
Peripaty 611
Perkins, Anthony 413, 419, 423, 426, 427
Perlberg, William 64, 71, 131, 665
Peter, Carolyn 91-92, 100, 674, 700
Peters, Bernadette 552
Peters, Jean 188, 191, 192, 195
Petrarca, Francesco 719
Petticoat Fever 226-227
Philadelphia Story, The 210, 294, 332, 532-534, 599
Philip Morris Playhouse on Broadway 342-343
Pinter, Harold 729
Pirandello, Luigi 199, 298, 299, 472, 473, 727, **728**, 728-732, 733
Plato 677, 715, 717, 725, 735
Plymouth Adventure, The 177
Point of Departure 477
Pollock, Arthur 48-49
Prabhavananda, Swami 692, 694, 695
Preston, Robert 437-438, **438**, 585
Price, Vincent 216, 238, 244, 246, 359, 544
Prince Valiant 566
Princess Margaret and Lord Snowdon 576-578, **577**
Prowler, The 174

Pryor, Thomas M. 265
Pythagoras 18, 628, 658, 725, 730, 737
"Quiet Town" 337
Radcliffe, Virginia 317, 332
Radio Reader's Digest, The 310-311, 312-313
Rains, Claude 251, 431, 432, 449
Raise the Titanic 566
Randol, George **482**, 483
Rat Race, The 459-460
Rathbone, Basil 217, 285, 301, 304, 306, 308, 318
Rattigan, Terence 244, 305, 359, 360, 512, 513
Raye, Helen 452, **453**
Reed, Florence 297, 315
Reed, Rex 3, 13-14, 62, 63, 104, 493, 501, 504, 505, 506, 507-508, 542-543, 555, 556, 558, 629, 641-642, 699, 733
Reinhardt, Elizabeth "Betty" 333
Remarkable Mr. Pennypacker, The 8, 196-204, **204**
Remenih, Anton 341-342
Remington, Fred 531-532
"Rest and Be Thankful" 343-344
Revere, Anne 155, **156**, 156, 158, 227
Reward Unlimited 73, **73**
Rich Man, Poor Man 537, 541, 550
Rich, Alan 493, 503
Rich, Frank 483
Rintels, David W. 552, 572
Robert Montgomery Presents 527
Robinson, Casey 430
Robson, Mark 280, 281, 409, 410, 411-412, 644
Roerich, Nicholas 720-721, **722**, 736
Roerick, William 492
Roger Wagner's Los Angeles Master Chorale 486, 487, 517
Roman Holiday 195, 239, 415
Roman, Ruth 395, 399
Romanoff, Michael 572
"Romeo and Juliet" 285, 291, 297, 313-316, 339
"Rose and the Thorns, The" 334-336
Rosenberg, Howard 549
Rosenfield, Paul 3, 65, 573-574, 614, 702
Rosenkreuz, Christian 736
Rosmini, Antonio 735
Rossellini, Roberto 413, 481, 482
Rózsa, Miklós 260
Runaways, The 543
Rushton, William 452
Russell, Rosalind 6, 210, 211, 230, 236, 330, 331, 332, 337, 391, 572, 578, 583, 587, 588

Ryskind, Morrie 133, 140
Sales, Elizabeth **589**
Sapori, Alvise 387-388, 680-681, 682-684, 686-687
Say, Darling 28
Scaligero, Massimo 723-724, **724**, 736
"Scarlet Letter, The" 351-352
Schaefer, George 515, 516
Schallert, Edwin 3, 67-68, 69-70, 71-72, 77, 78-79, 139-140, 172, 175-176, 177, 210, 222-223, 233-234, 238-240, 242-243, 252-254, 461-462
Scott, John L. 405, 464
Scott, Martha 40, 41, 61, 219, 299, 587
Screen Directors Playhouse 323-324, 333-334, 345-347
Seiter, William A. 401, 404
Selznick, David O. 58, 64, 67, 68, 69, 70-71, 72, 73, 74-75, 76, 77, 78, 79-81, 110, 129, 135, 155, 173, 205-206, 249, 309, 317, 426, 545, 570, 574, 601, 611, 636, 637, 642, 663, 665
Sergel, Christopher 485, 486
Severo, Richard 738
Seward, George Schermerhorn 380-381
Shaw, George Bernard 200, 227, 241, 245, 302-303, 304, 311
Shaw, Irwin 280, 281
Shay, Kay **276**
She Waits 535-536, 709
Sheaffer, Louis 78, 79-80, 468-469
Sherman, Robert B. and Richard M. 449
Sherr, Robert 585
Sherwood, Robert E. 176, 219, 237
Shirley, Don 538-540
Show-Off, The 38
Siddhartha Gautama 735
Sidney, Sylvia 6, 35, 216, 219, 220
Sigal, Clancy 644-645
Simmons, Jean 6, 430, 431, **433**, 580
Simon, John 503
Siodmak, Robert 254, 256, 257, 260, 262-263, 265, 323, 324, 647
Sjöberg, Alf 78, 79, 310, 397
Skinner, Margo 518, 539
Sloane, Everett 313
Sloane, Robert 310
Smith, Betty 141, 142-143
Smith, Cecil 527-528
Smith, Kent 219, 240, 258, 263, **266**, 664
Snake Pit, The 75-76
Soanes, Wood 3, 11, 59-61, 211-214, 219, 268
"Sometime Every Summertime" 357-358
South Pacific 101
Spellbound 74, 260, 322

INDEX

Spiegel, Sam 174
Spink, Al 59-60
Spinoza, Baruch 685
Spiral Staircase, The 7, 8, 71, 74, 249, 254-269, **255**, **261**, **265**, **266**, **267**, 309, 323-324, 635, 643, 647
Spoon Handle 76
Springer, John 514
St. Elsewhere 548, **551**, 552
St. John, Jill 201, 203, 567
Stadio dei Marmi 189
Stanislavski, Constantin 62
Stanwyck, Barbara 379, 432
Starr, Frances 56, 83, **84**
Steichen, Edward 95, 611
Stein, Edwin C. 68
Stein, Jules and Doris 579, 586
Steinbeck, John 92-93
Steiner, Max 434
Steiner, Rudolf 603, 628, 675, 677-678, **679**, 680, 686, 723, 725, 736, 739
Stevens, George 426, 449, 450, 451, 564, 570
Stevenson, Robert 430
Stewart, James 4, 83, **84**, 90, 94, 108, 533, 544, 562, 566, 572, 574, 578, 587, 588, 624
Stickney, Dorothy 201
Stiles, Richard 493, 494
Stinson, Charles 477
Stockwell, Dean **162**
Stop-over 40
Strasberg, Lee 62
Streep, Meryl 268
Sudrow, Lyle 317
Sullavan, Margaret 30, 83, 90, 94, 131, 572
Sullivan, Barry 219, 237, 246, **541**
Sullivan, Dan 3, 496-497, 498-500, 501-502, 505, 507, 508, 512-513, 515, 517, 522-523, 607
Sullivan, Ed 587, 673
Sullivan, William 207
Summer and Smoke 175, 211, 228, **228**, 230-234, **231**, 246, 319-320, 462-463, 497, 673
Summer Heat 454
Summer Magic 427, 447-449, **448**
Summer Place, A 9, 433-436, **435**, 443
Summertime 191, 353
Susan Slade 434, 443-447, **445**, **446**, 581
Suspense 321-322
Swanson, Gloria 6, 588
Sweeney, Kevin 29, 30
Sweet Bird of Youth 511

"Sweet Rosie O'Grady" 310-311
Swift, Jonathan 717
Swingin' the Dream 44-48, **46**
Swiss Family Robinson 8, 427, 440-443, **442**, 681
Swope, Gerard **86**, 87-88, 89, 94, 368, 370, 371, **373**, 374, 375, 697, 713
Swope, Henrietta **87**, 88, 107, 108
Swope, Herbert Bayard 35, 88-89, 94, 695
Swope, John 4, 5, 28, 35, 61, 62, 83-127, **84**, **115**, **120**, 154, 224, 238, 241, 242, 243, 244, 317, 368-370, 371, 377, 378, 380, 381, 382, 383, **384**, 387, **406**, 445, 459, 460, 483, 494, 507, 544, 545, 555, 556, **557**, 557-558, 559, 561, 562, **564**, 565, 567, **571**, 574, 576, 579, 580, 582, 583, 584-585, 587, 588, 589, 590, 605, 611, 614, 615, 616, 617, 621, 622, 624, 633, 639, 674, 685, 690, 692, 695, 697-698, 699-702, 703, 704, 705, 706, 711, 713
Swope, Jr., Gerard 88, 107
Swope, Mark 22, 99, 107, 108, **115**, **120**, 120, 121-127, **122**, **123**, 239, 378, 381, 502, 561, 608, 633, 689, 710, 729
Swope, Mary 127
Swope, Topo 22, 23, 78, 85, 103, 106, 107, 108, **113**, 113-121, **114**, **115**, **116**, **117**, **120**, **122**, 370, 377, 381-382, **406**, 502, 559, 613, 615, 616, 633, 658, 659, 660, 670, 685, 697, 698, 713, 714, 729
Szold, Bernard 30, 32, 33, **33**, 216, 483
Tandy, Jessica 296, 336, 485
Tarkington, Booth 33, 320
Tasso, Torquato 717
Taylor, Don 239, 240, 241, 244, 245, 246
Teaching of Buddha, The 705-706
Teichmann, Howard 108
Temple, Shirley 11
Terriss, Tom 526
Thaxter, Phyllis 58, 76, 599
Theatre Guild on the Air 41, 217, 295-310, 313-316, 317, 319-320, 323, **323**, 332-333, 336, 338-342, **340**, 347-348, 351-352
Theremin, Léon 260
"Thief, The" 285, 347-348
This Earth Is Mine 430-432, **433**
This is Goggle 478
This Is My Best 288
This Is Your Life 544
Thomas, Bob 3, 7, 229-230, 262, 674, 690
Thompson, Howard 432, 435
Thoreau, Henry David 685
Three Came Home 80
Three Coins in the Fountain 8, 115, 187-196, **188**, **190**, **192**, **194**, 352, 542, 598, 644
"Thunder of Justice" 348
Tierney, Gene 7, 75, 177, 566
Till the End of Time 8, 71, 160, 270-277, **271**, **272**, **274**, **275**, **276**, 598, 641, 643, 644, 681

Time of Your Life, The 44, 50, 51
Tindall, Loren **271**
Tiomkin, Dimitri 260, 417, 423-424
"To Each His Own" 529-532, **532**
Tommaseo, Niccolò 651, 672, 675-676
Tonight at 8:30 217-219
Totaro, Rebecca 716-717
Tracy, Spencer 68, 177, 534
Trapp, Andrew J. 22
Trapp, Mary A. Lavelle 22-23
Traube, Shepard 211-214, 219
Travanti, Daniel J. 264, 518, 519-520, 521-522, 523, **539**, 540, 616, 619, 701
Travels with My Aunt 566-567
Tree Grows in Brooklyn, A 8, 141-149, **144**, **146**, **147**, 199, 268, 444, 499, 543, 581, 635, 646, 647
Tremayne, Les 365
Trial 45, 406-412, **409**, 694
Trilby 80
Turner, Marjorie 105-106
Turney, Catherine 6, 43
United States Steel Hour 527
University of Southern California (USC) 118, 378, 511, 559, 568–570, 571
University Players 29, 30, 89
"Valiant, The" 285, 289-293, **290**
Van Druten, John 211, 237, 239, 246, 318, 692
Van Neste, Dan 249, 618-619, 643, 695
Verdi, Giuseppe 450
Vidor, King 175, 239, 567, 570
Villafranca, E.A. 352
Virgil 717
Von Blon, Katherine 3, 220, 235-236
Von Sydow, Max 450, 564
Walker, Robert 216, 219, 398-399
Ward, Edgar 108, 502, 559, 574, 703
Watts, Jr., Richard 65-66
Wayne, John 450, 566, 574
"We Have Forever" 550-551
Weatherwax, Frank 429
Webb, Clifton 192, 193, **194**, 194, 197-198, 201, 202, 203, **204**, 566, 664, 701
What's My Line? 35, 286, 545-546, **594**, 595
Whitman, Walt 685
Whitmore, James 245, 485, 486
Wild Party, The 123
Wild, Jack 451, **453**
Wilde, Cornel 323
Wilde, Oscar 64, 225, 226, 330
Wilder, Billy 334, 389, 401, 415, 580, 588

Wilder, Thornton 29, 39, 40, 41, 42, 237, 285, 298-300, **300**, 439, 492
Williams, Grant 443-444, 476-477
Williams, Paul R. 378-380, **379**, **380**, 381, **386**, 560
Williams, Tennessee 5, 13, 211, 219, 228, **228**, 230, 232, 319, 320, 462, 491, 494-495, 499, 503, 504, 505, 507, 508, 511
Williams, Van 543
Wilson, Kendrick A. **482**, 483
Wilson, Michael 412, 427
Wilson, Robert 341
Winchell, Walter 1, 59, 70, 467
Winecoff, Charles 413-414
Winesburg, Ohio 485-486
Wings of the Dove, The 74
Winslow Boy, The 244, 285, 305, 359-360, 544
Winters, Shelley 175, 565
Wolters, Larry 526
Women, The 336-337
Wood, Audrey 319-320
Wright, Teresa 40, 216, 237, 245, 413, 439, 518
Wu, Dr. Nelson Ikon 584
"Wuthering Heights" 285, 345-347
Wyatt, Jane 108, 157, 158, 216, 225, 226, 380, 502, 559-561, 570, 574, 575, 579, 580, 584, 621, 624-625, 637, 646, 703
Wyler, Robert 412
Wyler, William 107, 108, 195, 346, 379, 412, 413-414, 415-417, **416**, 419, 420, 421, 423, 424, 425, 426, 558, 562, 584, 647
Wyman, Jane 80, 413, 585
Wynn, Ed 449
York, Jeff 427
Young and the Restless, The 548
Young, Loretta 131
Young, Robert **132**, 132, **133**, 135, 136, **136**, 139, **152**, **154**, 154, 250, 251, 252, **253**, 254, 289, 544, 549
Zanuck, Darryl 8, 70, 77, 80, 129, 155, 160, 173, 174, 175, 309, 460, 562, 601, 699

www.ingramcontent.com/pod-product-compliance
Lightning Source LLC
Chambersburg PA
CBHW052006290426
44112CB00014B/2152